MAR 2 5 2008

D1526594

Andrew Johnson
A Biographical Companion

Andrew Johnson
A Biographical Companion

Glenna R. Schroeder-Lein and Richard Zuczek

A B C   C L I O

Santa Barbara, California   Denver, Colorado   Oxford, England

Library of Congress Cataloging-in-Publication Data

Schroeder-Lein, Glenna R., 1951–
    Andrew Johnson : a biographical companion / Glenna R. Schroeder-Lein
and Richard Zuczek.
        p. cm. — (ABC-CLIO biographical companions)
Includes bibliographical references and index.
    ISBN 1-57607-030-1 (hardcover) — ISBN 1-57607-586-9 (e-book)
    1. Johnson, Andrew, 1808–1875. 2. Presidents—United
States—Biography. 3. Johnson, Andrew, 1808–1875—Encyclopedias.
4. United States—Politics and government—1865–1869—Encyclopedias.
I. Zuczek, Richard, 1955– II. Title. III. ABC-CLIO biographical companion.
    E677.S33 2001
    973.8'1'092—dc21   2001001777

05 04 03 02 01   10 9 8 7 6 5 4 3 2 1

ABC-CLIO, Inc.
130 Cremona Drive, P.O. Box 1911
Santa Barbara, California 93116-1911

This book is printed on acid-free paper ∞.

Manufactured in the United States of America

To
Lonnie K. Lein,
persevering husband,
and
Marion O. Smith,
extraordinary researcher

ABC-CLIO BIOGRAPHICAL COMPANIONS

Benjamin Franklin, Jennifer L. Durham
Thomas Jefferson, David S. Brown
Susan B. Anthony, Judith E. Harper
Napoleon, David Nicholls
Joseph Stalin, Helen Rappaport
Adolf Hitler, David Nicholls
Andrew Johnson, Glenna R. Schroeder-Lein and Richard Zuczek

ABC-CLIO Biographical Companions are encyclopedic guides to the lives of men and women who have had a significant impact on the social, political, and cultural development of the Western world. Each volume presents complete biographical information in an easily accessible format. An introduction and a chronology provide an overview, while the A-to-Z entries amplify a myriad of topics related to the person. Ample illustrations give the reader an acute sense of the individual's life and times.

CONTENTS

Andrew Johnson: A Biographical Companion

PREFACE AND ACKNOWLEDGMENTS

*B*ecause this book is a companion to the study of Andrew Johnson rather than to that of the Civil War or Reconstruction, we have not included some important topics that were unrelated to Johnson. In other cases, broad topics were narrowed and treated mainly as they relate to Johnson, for example, the entries on Andrew Jackson and Abraham Lincoln.

Birth and death dates are generally given only by years, where known, except for Johnson family members and persons whose exact date of death is relevant to the Johnson era, for example, Mary Surratt and Thaddeus Stevens. If a date is given as fl. (flourishing), this means that it was the latest date that we were able to find for the person, but we were unable to find an exact death date. A date given as ca. (circa) means that the person was born or died in approximately that year based on ages or other information given in one or several sources, but we do not know the exact date. Genealogical information on Johnson family members beyond that found in published biographies was located in the project files of *The Papers of Andrew Johnson*, at the University of Tennessee, Knoxville. Since the completion of the project, these files are housed in the university library's Special Collections department.

All quotations of Johnson materials are taken from appropriate volumes of *The Papers of Andrew Johnson*, even if they are also available in other sources.

References are generally to what is most relevant and readily available to the interested reader. We have not listed everything that we used nor are the references an exhaustive list of what is available. U.S. representatives' and senators' careers are summa-rized in the *Biographical Directory of the United States Congress*, and notable historical figures are usually included in the *Dictionary of American Biography*. Both works are good starting places and we have used them when relevant, but have not included them in the references section of individual articles. We have usually suggested monographs rather than journal articles because the large volume of relevant articles available on many topics would make a short but meaningful list all but impossible. However, in some cases journal articles are all that is available. For other topics, we have cited newspaper clippings and census records when significant information appears in no secondary sources, as in the case of Johnson's slaves. The person doing in-depth research on a topic will often find clues about further sources to pursue in the footnotes to relevant documents in the sixteen volumes of *The Papers of Andrew Johnson*.

When we began this project in 1997, we naively supposed that it would not be difficult to finish it in the two years allotted. After all, at that time Glenna had worked for *The Papers of Andrew Johnson* for seven years, and Richard for three. The process turned out to be far more time-consuming and research-intensive than either of us had ever imagined. Important national affairs also changed perspectives on Johnson, as the impeachment of President Bill Clinton made Johnson the first, rather than the only, president to suffer impeachment. In addition, Richard's having two small sons and his moving to a faculty position at the U.S. Coast Guard Academy left Glenna ultimately doing the majority of the work, and needing three years to do it.

We wish to thank the people who have

helped us in important ways to prepare this companion. Paul H. Bergeron, editor of *The Papers of Andrew Johnson*, turned down this project and gave us the opportunity to do it. Some days we are not sure whether to say "Thanks a lot!" with enthusiasm or sarcasm. We are grateful, however, that he gave us free rein to use all of the materials collected for the Johnson Papers so that we had access to many things not yet published or previously used only for annotation purposes. The entries are more complete because of easy access to this material.

Marion O. Smith, chief ferret of the Johnson Papers for more than twenty-five years, did much of the original research necessary to annotate the published documents, beginning with volume five. His work was as vital to us as it has been to other Johnson students. Marion even turned up useful information for this companion, such as some railroad statistics. The dedication helps to express our thanks.

Patricia J. Anthony, long-time administrative assistant for the Johnson Papers, listened to many expressions of frustration and even put some of these entries on the computer.

Jim Small and Elaine Clark, historian rangers at the Andrew Johnson National Historic Site in Greeneville, Tennessee, furnished us with some useful family material from their collection.

Glenna's friends Kathy Burke, Bob Conrad, and Gayle and Jeff Fokens provided Glenna with particular encouragement.

Alicia Merritt, our editor at ABC-CLIO, was supportive, even when we missed the original deadline.

Lonnie K. Lein put up with years of having the Johnson companion as his companion, too. Information for various articles went with us on cross-country trips, and work on the companion at times restricted what he wanted to do. His patience makes the dedication of this book well deserved.

INTRODUCTION

*O*ne of the most controversial figures in U.S. political history, Andrew Johnson remains a paradox to this day. Here was a man who never attended school a day in his life, yet fought for public education; here was a Southern slaveholder who opposed secession and enforced emancipation; here was a man born into poverty who came to be president of the United States and who, after holding nearly every elective position attainable, is regarded as a political failure. Johnson was the only senator from a Confederate state to remain in Congress during the Civil War, the only president to receive no formal schooling, the only president reelected to the Senate after his presidency, and the first president to be impeached. Yet polls consistently place him among the most unpopular and unsuccessful of all U.S. presidents.

This volume is not intended to create sympathy for, or resuscitate the reputation of, Andrew Johnson. The authors do, however, attempt to place his ideas and actions within historical context to help explain his attitudes and decisions. More important, this work examines Johnson's place in the history of the United States because, regardless of how Americans feel about the man, Johnson's successful political career spanned five pivotal decades. His issues were the nation's issues: the increasing democracy of politics, the beginning of industrialization and the market revolution, the question of slavery, growing sectional tensions, secession and the Civil War, and finally Reconstruction. His personal contradictions reflected those of his country: a democratic nation conceived in liberty, yet existing half slave and half free; an economy of yeoman farmers and independent artisans being swept into industrialization and a market system; a country fond of tradition but caught up in social, economic, and political revolutions.

The challenges and changes of the nineteenth century appeared to pose more opportunities than obstacles for Andrew Johnson. Born into poverty in 1808 in Raleigh, North Carolina, Johnson knew hard times and at an early age demonstrated independence, self-determination, and the ability to overcome hardship and opposition. His father, Jacob Johnson, a constable, porter, and town bell-ringer, had died in 1812. Andrew's mother, Mary McDonough Johnson, supported him and his older brother, William, by working as a seamstress. The situation barely improved when she remarried; her new husband, Turner Daughtry, was no better off financially.

With the family desperate, schooling was out of the question. Immediate and practical considerations won out; the boys needed to learn a trade and earn money. When Andrew was nine years old, his mother apprenticed him to James Selby, a local tailor, for whom William was already working. Andrew was pledged to Selby until he was twenty-one and in return learned a valuable craft. It appears that he also learned the rudiments of reading and writing because the masters had an obligation to help educate the apprentices. Local men would come to the shop and read to them as they worked. At least one man presented a book to young Andrew because he was so fond of it.

For reasons that are still unclear, Andrew and his brother broke their contracts and fled Raleigh. Andrew made his way to Laurens, South Carolina, where he worked for a brief time, but soon returned to Raleigh. When he found it impossible to patch up relations with Selby, he headed west, across the mountains to Tennessee.

Young and restless, needing to find work and yearning for adventure, Andrew passed through East Tennessee, made his way into northern Alabama, traveled back up through Middle Tennessee, and headed back home to Raleigh. His exploration had convinced him that his future lay in one of the many small towns of East Tennessee, where an uncle lived; there his skills would be welcome and his past ignored. In Raleigh he persuaded his mother and stepfather to make the trek back to Tennessee with him in 1826. After some drifting, in the spring of 1827 the family settled in Greeneville, possibly because some citizens there welcomed a new tailor, and possibly because there Andrew saw the woman who would become his wife. Apparently the attraction was mutual; legend has it that, when the family first passed through Greeneville in September 1826, Eliza McCardle, Andrew's future wife, told a group of friends, "There goes my beau, girls, mark it." They were married within the year. Andrew was eighteen; Eliza, sixteen.

In Greeneville the couple built a family and Johnson built a career. They had five children: Martha (b.1828); Charles (b.1830); Mary (b.1832); Robert (b.1834); and Andrew Jr. (b.1852), whom everyone called Frank. Under the tutelage of his better-educated wife, who had attended school, Johnson also worked on improving his education. He practiced his reading and writing and hired people to read to him while he worked. His surviving account books and ledgers indicate that his business prospered as well. The well-to-do bought entire suits and paid in cash; the less wealthy had repairs done and paid by barter.

It did not take long for Johnson to begin moving in the social and political circles of his adopted town. He stepped into the current discussions on local and national issues, and his shop became a gathering place for those eager to voice their opinions—or hear Johnson's. He was popular in local debating clubs, in part because of his commanding physical presence and unpretentious common-sense style, but also because he seemed to embody the Jacksonian Democracy of the 1820s and 1830s. Here was a living example of the new Democratic Party, a self-made man and independent entrepreneur who succeeded by his own hard work. Johnson's humble roots, honest egalitarianism, strict view of the Constitution, and distrust of government and the wealthy gained him enough admirers to win election as alderman in 1829 and mayor of Greeneville in 1834.

Johnson's name and contacts spread beyond Greeneville, and so too did his ambition. The principles he advocated were popular with many farmers and artisans of East Tennessee, and Johnson developed a reputation for being a fierce and entertaining stump speaker. He won election to the state legislature in 1835, 1839, and 1841. But sometimes Johnson's stubborn attachment to principle worked against him; he lost in 1837 because he opposed government aid to a railroad, which many of his constituents supported. Government funding of internal improvements was a hallmark of the Whig Party, and Johnson opposed the idea on both constitutional and moral grounds. His inflexibility would eventually be his undoing.

In the state legislature Johnson espoused the cause of the working class and the common laborer. He despised privilege and those who used others to get ahead, and he distrusted equally the wealthy planters of the South and the powerful bankers of the North. But the simple life he advocated, that of the independent farmer and the local artisan, was under siege as Northern interests, promoted by the Whig Party, pushed for government intervention and economic conversion to a primitive factory system. Johnson fought for those things he believed in: he supported the disbursing of public lands to landless families; pushed for public schools for those who could not afford private education; and opposed high tariffs, which the Whigs claimed would help manufacturing. Hoping to bring politics closer to the average citizen and reduce government meddling, Johnson advocated a direct election for Tennessee's U.S. senators, rather than having the legislature make the choice. Believing he was protecting taxpayers from big government, he opposed legislative reimbursement for travel, criticized pay raises, and tried to reduce the number of clerks and other officials on the state's payroll.

All of this reflected Johnson's philosophy of government. He believed that it was the government's obligation to protect the rights of citizens and ensure that all citizens—within the current nineteenth-century definition of the same—had an equal opportunity to succeed. The government's authority to do so was spelled out clearly in the U.S. Constitution. Conversely, because the Constitution was a written guardian of citizens' rights, to tamper with it set a dangerous precedent. As a result, throughout his career Johnson favored a strict interpretation of the Constitution, which allotted power to the federal government only when it was expressly stated. Johnson consistently opposed the expansion of governmental powers into areas traditionally controlled by the states. This translated into opposition to Whig programs that allowed the federal government to dredge harbors, build bridges and canals, and finance railroads. Such activities spent federal tax dollars to benefit only a small region and a few individuals and sapped energy from free enterprise and local entrepreneurs; this struck at the ideals of American self-reliance and independence.

Having made his mark at the state level, Johnson found his local following powerful enough to elevate him to the national arena. He was elected to Congress in 1842 and served five consecutive terms in the U.S. House of Representatives until he was gerrymandered out of office by a Whig-controlled Tennessee legislature in 1852. In Congress, as in Tennessee, his devotion to his own narrowly defined principles earned him admirers and critics. Johnson continued to oppose most Whig programs, such as increased tariffs and federally funded construction plans, but also found himself at odds with the Democratic president, Tennessean James K. Polk, over patronage. In addition, the Tennessee representative criticized military academies, the electoral college, and even the Smithsonian Institution. Johnson was equally obstinate in pushing for measures he desired, such as his pet project, the Homestead Bill.

Tennessee's Whigs spoiled Johnson's congressional run in 1852, but he had the last laugh: ever the fighter, Johnson turned around and ran for governor in 1853. He was elected to the first of two terms and held the gubernatorial chair from 1853 until 1857. As governor, he won several victories, including the initiation of the first Tennessee state tax to finance public schools and libraries and the creation of a state fair so farmers and artisans could exhibit products and exchange information.

In 1857 Johnson was the beneficiary of a practice he had tried to end: the election of U.S. senators by the state legislature. When Democrats reclaimed the state government, they promptly returned Johnson to Washington, D.C., this time as senator. But national politics had changed since his stint in the U.S. House of Representatives, and the stakes were far higher. With the acquisition of vast western territories after the Mexican-American War, one issue dominated the discourse: the expansion of slavery into the new lands. The Democratic Party had always been strong in the South, as its focus on strict constitutionalism dovetailed with regional economic, political, and social interests. As the debate over the expansion of slavery took center stage, Southerners came to dominate the party, eager to protect slavery in the West. By the mid-1850s a new party, the Republicans, had displaced the Whigs as the voice of Northerners and Midwesterners. The Republican Party sought to block the extension of slavery so that whites would not need to compete with slave labor in the West.

As Americans chose sides in the growing sectional crisis, Andrew Johnson found himself balancing his ideals. Johnson was a lifelong Democrat and a slaveholder. He owned few slaves and, according to their own remarks later, never mistreated or sold a slave. But despite his views on slavery and his belief that the federal government could not interfere with the institution—after all, it was protected by the Constitution—another issue overrode the question of slavery. Like Andrew Jackson, father of the Democratic Party, Johnson believed that the United States was an indivisible union and states had not the power to come and go at will. As talk of secession grew and Southerners threatened to exit the Union if their rights were not acknowledged, Johnson found little difficulty making his choice. He believed, as many in the North did, that a small clique of planters were bent on undermining the nation and that secession was simply an unconstitutional rejection of the democratic system. So, on the subject of secession, the man who once feared Republicans as dangerous proabolition fanatics found that he had more in common with them than with his own party.

Ambitious, yet eager to avoid endangering the Union, Johnson envisioned himself as a compromise candidate for the 1860 presidential election. This idea met with little enthusiasm, but the election of Abraham Lincoln had the ironic effect of placing Johnson in the national spotlight nonetheless. In early December, amid growing threats of secession, Johnson took the floor of the Senate and delivered a moving and scathing attack on the theory of secession, calling it "levying war against the United States" and "treason." Heralded across the North as a "patriot," he could do nothing to stop South Carolina from seceding in December, and the other states of the Deep South followed; in February 1861 the Confederate States of America was formed. Although Johnson hoped to protect the Union—he had supported the Crittenden Compromise in an effort to avert war—he would not compromise on secession and lashed out from the Senate again in February against Southern disunionists.

As with other states of the Upper South, Tennessee did not seriously consider secession until after President Lincoln's call for volunteers in April 1861. Even then, the Unionist sentiment was strong, especially in East Tennessee, and such men as Andrew Johnson, Horace Maynard, and former Whig and Johnson rival William G. "Parson" Brownlow worked feverishly to keep Tennessee in the Union. Their efforts failed, and in early June 1861 Tennessee seceded, the last state to leave the Union.

Although other members of Congress from his state abandoned Washington, Johnson refused to leave, claiming that Tennessee was still in the Union. Johnson was the only senator from a seceded state to remain in Congress. This slaveholder's unswerving devotion to the Union—especially considering the action of his state and his party—made him a hero among Republicans and Northern War Democrats. When federal forces secured West and Middle Tennessee in 1862, Johnson was the obvious choice for military governor of the state. Operating from Nashville, Johnson attempted to rekindle latent Unionism and reinstate a civil government, but his efforts were met with numerous obstacles, including Confederate forces, squabbles over authority with federal military commanders, and divisions within the Unionist population. A personal tragedy made his stay even more depressing; in 1863, just outside Nashville, his oldest son Charles, a physician with the Union army, died in a fall from his horse.

Republicans liked what they saw in Johnson because he dealt severely with Confederates and their sympathizers and even supported emancipation when it became clear that slavery was doomed. But admirers overlooked his motivations. Johnson embraced harsh actions only as *wartime* measures and never swayed from his belief in *individual,* rather than state, disloyalty and his overriding conviction that military authorities were subordinate to civil ones.

Johnson's stance on secession and his no-nonsense approach as military governor earned him the position as Lincoln's running mate in 1864 on the Union Party ticket. Republicans hoped that Johnson would broaden the party's appeal among War Democrats and border-state voters. Many Republicans were also unhappy with Lincoln's lenient plans for postwar Reconstruction and hoped that Johnson would be able to sway the president toward a more severe policy. The Lincoln-Johnson partnership soundly defeated former general George B. McClellan, and the "rail-splitter and tailor" set out to finish the war and restore the Union.

Destiny had other plans, and from the outset the omens boded ill. At his inauguration the new vice president appeared obnoxious and intoxicated—he had been given several drinks to calm his nerves and stomach. Making matters worse were rumors that he had views very like those of the president and might not move to punish the South after the war. Everyone would learn soon enough because a month after his second inauguration Abraham Lincoln was assassinated, and on April 15 Johnson took the oath of office as the seventeenth president of the United States.

Some Republicans saw the hand of God at work. Lincoln was a brilliant war leader and politician, but too conciliatory for many Republicans. His second inaugural address spoke of "malice towards none" and "charity for all," which seemed too good for those responsible for such bloodshed. At first some Republicans were gratified because Johnson showed no sympathy as he directed the arrest and trial of the assassination conspirators.

But presidential assassins were exceptions to Johnson's policy, and the new president took a far more conciliatory view toward average Southerners who had been in the war. Johnson had been military governor during wartime, when the normal relationships among the population, the Constitution, and military-civil authorities were disrupted. But the war had ended, and Johnson saw nothing in the Constitution about secession or the subjugation of entire populations. So he reasoned that states had never really left the Union and therefore they could not be punished; only individuals were guilty of treason, and they must be dealt with.

Because the Constitution assigned pardoning power to the executive, Johnson assumed that Restoration—he avoided the term "Reconstruction"—was an executive prerogative. Without waiting for Congress to reconvene, Johnson began the Restoration process. He appointed provisional governors to oversee the former Confederate states and demanded the abolition of slavery, the repudiation of secession, and the writing of new state constitutions. He also issued a general amnesty that restored political and civil rights to most former Confederates, and those not covered could apply directly to Johnson for pardon. His cabinet, meaning Lincoln's cabinet, agreed with this approach.

By late summer 1865 everything appeared to be moving smoothly. Johnson's family, including Eliza and five grandchildren, finally arrived at the White House. Johnson's daughter Martha took up station as hostess because Eliza still suffered from tuberculosis that she had contracted earlier. The Southern states were electing new governments and new federal representatives, and Johnson was bombarded by correspondence that backed his approach.

When Congress reassembled in the autumn of 1865, it was clear that Republicans' goals differed from those of the president. Many wanted protection for freed blacks, the establishment of a Southern Republican Party, and real evidence of Southern penitence. Among the evidence of Southern defiance was the passage of Black Codes, which placed the freedpeople under severe legal and economic restrictions; the election of former Confederates to Congress; and indifference toward the widespread violence against blacks and Unionists. The Republican-dominated Congress expressed its displeasure with these developments by refusing to seat the Southern congressmen and creating the Joint Committee on Reconstruction, which offered Congress's alternative to Johnson's program.

At first, congressional Republicans hoped that a moderate approach would convince this Democratic president to change his mind. In the spring of 1866, Congress offered two moderate bills, the Freedmen's Bureau Bill and the Civil Rights Bill, designed to assist the freedpeople in their transition to citizenship. Johnson vetoed both bills—the first of twenty-nine vetoes—and sent back arrogant responses that chastised Congress for treading on executive powers and the Constitution. Many Republicans had hoped that compromise was possible and that Johnson would display his wartime vigor regarding the rebellion and sympathy regarding the blacks. Now they learned what those who knew Johnson had long understood, that is, he never compromised on principle. Johnson had succeeded in driving moderates into the fold of the more radical Republicans, men who were bent on a political and social revolution.

Johnson could never come to see the Constitution as a living, dynamic creature that adapted to the changing needs of the nation. His support for emancipation had been a war measure, and he had no intention of granting black suffrage, or, worse yet, allowing the federal government to impose it. He appeared callous in the face of Southern violence—in particular the New Orleans riot in July 1866. Johnson, hoping to promote his policy of conciliation and rapid Restoration, formed a new party, the National Union Party, for the fall 1866 congressional elections. His ill-fated Swing-around-the-Circle campaign tour, an effort to publicize his party, failed miserably as Johnson engaged in impromptu harangues and hostile arguments with hecklers.

The 1866 elections seemed to repudiate the president's course. Republicans took control of the U.S. House and Senate with a two-thirds majority in each, making those bodies veto-proof and free to implement their own Reconstruction program. But Johnson would not try to meet Congress halfway or concede defeat. He tinkered with the idea of replacing Radical secretary of war Edwin M. Stanton and condemned Congress in his December annual message. The president's closed-mindedness, which contributed to his increasing isolation from Northern public opinion, was reinforced by his incoming correspondence. As researchers with *The Papers of Andrew Johnson* have discovered, those opposed to Johnson's course quickly learned how stubborn he was and stopped sending their complaints. On the other hand, his supporters never ceased writing, so Johnson received a skewed sample of the public's opinion toward his policy. This lack of critical correspondence convinced Johnson that the American people were with him. During the secession crisis, Johnson had believed that a few arrogant planters had deluded the Southerners; he was now convinced that another minority, Radical Republicans, were bent on a similarly unconstitutional revolution.

In the spring of 1867 Congress embarked on its own plan of Reconstruction. In March the first two Military Reconstruction Acts became law, placing the former Confederate states (except Tennessee, which had already been readmitted to the Union) in a sort of political limbo until new state constitutions and governments were created, based on a new citizenry—under these acts adult black males began voting in the South. Republicans in Congress, determined to prevent the president from removing Republican officeholders and in particular Secretary of War Stanton, also passed the Tenure of Office Act. Johnson swiftly vetoed each measure, but Congress easily overrode his opposition.

With one executive weapon nullified, Johnson sought other means of thwarting the Republican revolution. He encouraged opposition to the laws among Southerners, nurtured opposition in the North, and removed military commanders for interfering with civilian jurisdiction. Oddly enough, although the executive and legislative branches grappled over the authority of the federal government, neither contested its right to expand U.S. borders; in April of 1867 Congress approved the purchase of Alaska for 7.2 million dollars, even though the treaty was brokered by Secretary of State William Seward, one of Johnson's closest supporters.

But isolated incidents of cooperation did not indicate reconciliation, and Johnson continued in his attempt to reassert executive privilege. In August 1867, hoping to force a Supreme Court ruling on Congress's policy, Johnson challenged the Tenure of Office Act by suspending Secretary Stanton. The president's cabinet largely agreed that the act did not apply in this case. For two years the president and the secretary had been at odds, yet Johnson had vacillated on Stanton's future despite Stanton's duplicitous actions and complicity with Radical generals and members of Congress. At the same time, state elections in the North resulted in a significant Democratic resurgence, and Democrats wrested control of several legislatures and governorships from Republicans. Johnson was convinced that his actions were both constitutional and popular and felt vindicated in December when the House of Representatives rejected the Judiciary Committee's impeachment resolution. Unfortunately for Johnson, the Senate voted in January 1868 to not concur with his suspension of Stanton. When Johnson formally removed him, the House added its disapproval and voted on February 24, 1868, for impeachment on the grounds that Johnson had violated the Tenure of Office Act.

The president's trial before the Senate lasted from March 30 until late May. His defense counsel, composed of Reverdy Johnson, Benjamin R. Curtis, William Groesbeck, William Evarts, and T.A.R. Nelson, ably dismantled the Radicals' charges, while Republican senators grew increasingly restive over the dangerous precedent they might set: the conviction and removal of a president. On May 16, senators voted on the eleventh article of impeachment and found Johnson not guilty by a vote of 35 to 19, one vote shy of the two-thirds required for conviction. Ten days later two more articles met exactly the same fate. Sensing failure, Republicans closed the Senate as a court of impeachment, and Secretary Stanton vacated his office. (In fact, under President Grant the Tenure of Office Act was modified to allow the executive more latitude and in 1887 was largely repealed. In 1926 the Supreme Court declared it unconstitutional.)

Letters and telegrams offering congratulations and praise poured in from across the country, and the president was serenaded and visited by droves of well-wishers. Johnson never doubted his acquittal and attributed it to the righteousness of his course. In truth, the ability of his defense team, the waning of his term, and the de facto success of Congress's Reconstruction policy spelled defeat for impeachment. Complicating matters further was Benjamin Wade, who as Speaker of the House was next in line for the executive chair should Johnson be removed. (There was currently no vice president.) An obnoxious Radical, Wade was too much for even other Republicans to bear, and his promotion might interfere with the Republican heir apparent, Ulysses S. Grant.

Johnson had won the battle, but Congress was still far ahead in the war. For a brief time Johnson had hopes of being vindicated by winning the 1868 Democratic presidential nomination and, as usual, supporters encouraged and exaggerated his chances. In fact, Johnson was second as balloting opened at the Democratic National Convention in July, and he continued with a strong showing until political machinations cut out the early leaders. Once the nomination was lost, Johnson could only wait for further developments as his administration drew to a close. The letters predicting his future glories and place in history as "defender of the Constitution" offered little consolation. To the end, Johnson defended and flaunted his policy, closing his term with an annual message that savaged Congress, a Christmas amnesty that defied Congress and the Fourteenth Amendment, and a string of pardons that included such notables as Dr. Samuel Mudd and other Lincoln assassination conspirators.

Although much of the country said good riddance to an obstinate relic who only seemed capable of looking backward, others viewed him as a martyr. Cities across the South invited the ex-president to speak after he had departed Washington. But despite his sporadic popularity, Johnson was still a defeated man, and the spring of 1869 saw other calamities as well. A painful illness struck him in March. Some newspapers even reported that he had died. In April another son, Robert, died.

Ever the fighter, Johnson quickly overcame the personal and professional setbacks and dove back into public life. He spoke across Tennessee, and threw his hat into the ring for a U.S. Senate seat in 1869. Beaten but stubborn as ever, he ran for a seat in the U.S. House in 1872, only to lose again. Johnson remained an enemy to most Republicans, while Democrats clearly remem-bered his defection during the Civil War. Troubles continued as he suffered financial losses in the Panic of 1873 and contracted cholera that same year. Extant writings by Johnson indicate that he sincerely believed he was going to die.

Not until January 1875 did Johnson achieve what he believed to be "vindication," when the Tennessee state legislature elected him to the U.S. Senate. Johnson was the only former president to earn this distinction. Years had not mellowed the man or his temperament, and in a special March 1875 session he attacked President Grant for his support of the "unconstitutional" Reconstruction government in Louisiana. However, Johnson's return to the national arena was short-lived. In July, while visiting his daughter Mary and her family in Carter County, Tennessee, he suffered a stroke; he died two days later, on July 31, 1875.

Andrew Johnson had lived an interesting and productive life, with more than its share of accomplishments, controversies, and failures. Just as his life mirrored the passions and struggles of an era, so too his death was appropriate, perhaps even welcomed, because the world that Johnson knew, the society and nation whose growth and development he witnessed, had passed away as well; gone was the apprentice, the artisan-tailor, the slaveholder, the Constitution of Jefferson and Jackson. Johnson's tragic flaw was his inability to understand that change did not mean destruction and that the nation and Constitution that he had defended were not eliminated, but improved; they had evolved, not disappeared, and become stronger and more meaningful in the process.

References: Benedict, Michael Les, *The Impeachment and Trial of Andrew Johnson* (1973); Castel, Albert, *The Presidency of Andrew Johnson* (1979); Graf, LeRoy P., Haskins, Ralph W., and Bergeron, Paul H., eds., *The Papers of Andrew Johnson* 16 vols. (1967–2000); McCaslin, Richard B., *Andrew Johnson: A Bibliography* (1992); McKitrick, Eric, *Andrew Johnson and Reconstruction* (1960); Trefousse, Hans L., *Andrew Johnson: A Biography* (1989).

Alabama Claims

On May 15, 1862, the CSS *Alabama* left Liverpool, England, to begin a devastating tour as a Confederate commerce raider. U.S. Minister Charles Francis Adams had pleaded with British officials to detain the ship, but bureaucratic delays blocked his path, and the ship managed to leave the harbor under the guise of a trial run. Ships such as the CSS *Alabama,* the CSS *Florida,* and the CSS *Shenandoah* wreaked havoc with Union shipping and nearly destroyed the U.S. merchant marine. More than 200 ships were lost and some 100,000 tons of cargo were destroyed, driving up insurance costs, forcing shipowners to convert to foreign registries, and crippling businesses dependent upon imports and exports. Despite Great Britain's own neutrality laws and a decided pro-Union sentiment after the Emancipation Proclamation of January 1, 1863, shipbuilding for the Confederacy was a lucrative, and not very secretive, business. Not until midway through 1863, when U.S. secretary of state William H. Seward presented the British government with a detailed demand for redress, did construction fall off.

The CSS *Alabama* was devastating to Union shipping but the Confederate raider's career was short-lived. Under the command of Raphael Semmes, the CSS *Alabama* destroyed or captured some sixty-nine ships before being sunk by the USS *Kearsarge* in June 1864 off Cherbourg, France. After the war, the United States sought compensation for U.S. financial losses caused by Confederate raiders built or outfitted in Great Britain. Losses from the CSS *Alabama* were estimated at nearly $7 million. "*Alabama* Claims" became the umbrella term that encompassed all private claims for redress.

In January 1869, after years of negotiations, private petitions, public meetings, and halfhearted compromises, Secretary of State Seward and U.S. minister Reverdy Johnson concluded with England the Johnson-Clarendon Convention. Supported by President Johnson, who desperately wanted an end to the ongoing issue, the convention established a commission to examine all U.S.-British claims arising since 1853; no mention was made of the CSS *Alabama* or other Confederate raiders. The agreement contained no apology, and the value of the claims reflected only direct shipping losses, not indirect or resulting costs. This last item U.S. Senate powerhouse Charles Sumner believed vital to any resolution; Sumner claimed that this "collateral damage" exceeded $2 billion and demanded as compensation the cession of Canada to the United States. In April 1869, not long after Andrew Johnson left office, the Senate rejected the convention, due in part to animosity toward President Johnson and Minister Reverdy Johnson (an Anglophile who many believed betrayed U.S. interests) and in part to the convention's narrow definitions and conciliatory attitude.

Negotiations began anew under President Ulysses S. Grant and his secretary of state, Hamilton Fish, resulting in the Treaty of Washington, ratified May 21, 1871. The treaty itself and the ensuing decisions differed little from Johnson's convention.

An international tribunal was created, consisting of representatives from Italy, Switzerland, Brazil, and the two contending parties, and presided over by Otto von Bismarck of Germany. The tribunal awarded the United States $15.5 million (which Great Britain paid in 1873), reprimanded England for its violation of neutrality laws, and established new maritime neutrality laws. The outcome was not a total U.S. victory because payment was far below Sumner's demands, the tribunal refused to rule on the issue of indirect losses, and specific costs of individual raiders were never addressed.

See also: Foreign Affairs; Johnson, Reverdy; Seward, William Henry; Sumner, Charles.

References: Balch, Thomas W., *The Alabama Arbitration* (1900); Donald, David Herbert, *Charles Sumner and the Rights of Man* (1970); Graf, LeRoy P., Haskins, Ralph W., and Bergeron, Paul H., eds., *The Papers of Andrew Johnson* vol. 15 (1967–2000); Taylor, John M., *William Henry Seward: Lincoln's Right Hand* (1991).

Alaska, Purchase of

Alaska, which was purchased by the United States during Andrew Johnson's administration, had been under the control of the Russian American Company (Russian fur traders) for many years. By the 1860s the company was in decline and had refused to renew its contract with the Russian government, which had no interest in exerting actual control over the territory because its resources were already spread thin elsewhere. Furthermore, the Russians

were concerned about incursions of the British Hudson's Bay Company into the area. The Russians had already fought the British in the Crimean War and feared further struggles in Alaska. Russia had good relations with the United States and preferred to see the latter take over the territory. Some unofficial discussions were held as early as 1859 but nothing resulted from them because of the American Civil War.

By 1867 the Russians were anxious to sell the territory. For three weeks in March, Secretary of State William H. Seward and Russian minister to the United States Baron Edward de Stoeckl negotiated a treaty, which was signed by the two on March 30. The Senate considered the treaty in a special session and ratified it on April 9. The Russians ratified it by May 15, and the two parties exchanged ratifications on June 20. On July 6 Andrew Johnson submitted the treaty to Congress with the request for an appropriation of $7.2 million to pay for the purchase. The House of Representatives, responsible for financial legislation, did nothing about it until after Johnson's impeachment trial the next year. Meanwhile, Johnson sent his friend General Lovell H. Rousseau to Sitka, Alaska, in company with the Russian commissioner Captain Alexy Pestchouroff, to accept the transfer of the territory to the United States. This took place in a brief ceremony on October 18, 1867.

By June 30, 1868, when the House began to consider the appropriation for the purchase of Alaska, there were two well-established opinions in and out of Congress. Those who knew something about Alaska, either through experience or study, believed that the United States had gotten an enormous bargain. The area possessed great wealth in fisheries, furs, lumber, and probably minerals, and it would provide the United States with industrial and trade advantages. Opponents of the purchase, abetted by the press, viewed Alaska as a wasteland, an uninhabitable desolate area covered with ice and snow, and its purchase as a waste of U.S. money. The press attached numerous nicknames to the area: "Seward's Folly," "Icebergia," "Polaria," "Seward's Icebox," and "Walrussia." However, the United States had already taken possession of the territory eight months earlier. The appropriations bill passed on July 14, 1868.

Initially Alaska was placed under a military government. A number of entrepreneurs and would-be territorial officeholders wrote Johnson urging that a civil territorial government be established for Alaska as soon as possible. However, the Congress passed only two pieces of legislation: one establishing customs regulations and the other pertaining to seal fisheries. Alaska languished under a badly managed military government until 1884 and did not become a state until 1959.

See also: Foreign Affairs; Rousseau, Lovell Harrison; Seward, William Henry; Territorial Affairs.
References: Bancroft, Hubert Howe, *History of Alaska, 1730–1885* (1886); Graf, LeRoy P., Haskins, Ralph W., and Bergeron, Paul H., eds., *The Papers of Andrew Johnson* vols. 12–15 (1967–2000); Gruening, Ernest, *The State of Alaska* (1954, 1968).

Alta Vela

Alta Vela is a small, bell-shaped island, three-quarters of a mile long and a half mile wide, in the Caribbean about twenty miles southwest of Santo Domingo (now the Dominican Republic). The island had no value except as a source of guano (dried bird droppings), which was much in demand as a fertilizer during the nineteenth century. In the spring of 1860 two different groups of American guano explorers landed on and claimed Alta Vela under provisions of the Guano Islands Act of 1856, passed by the United States Congress, which was supposed to protect the rights of American citizens who discovered and occupied unclaimed guano islands.

Captain S. R. Kimball, who was employed by Abraham D. Patterson (ca. 1821– fl.1893) and Prudencio de Murguiondo (ca. 1831–1910), Baltimore commission merchants and guano importers, actually set up on the island a mining operation that functioned from March 24 to October 24, 1860, and shipped nearly 1,075 tons of guano to Baltimore at an average profit of $8.32 per ton. However, on October 23, 1860, a warship from Santo Domingo arrived at Alta Vela and its captain ordered the miners to leave within twenty-four hours. When the manager protested that they would be unable to do this because they had no transportation, soldiers from the ship came ashore, destroyed the camp, confiscated some equipment, and arrested the miners at gunpoint, taking them to Santo Domingo, where they were imprisoned for three weeks before they were released and returned to Baltimore.

Patterson and Murguiondo immediately protested to the U.S. state department, requesting assistance in recovering the island and regaining more than $22,000 compensation for their property. Jeremiah S. Black, secretary of state in James Buchanan's outgoing administration, was interested in the case but could do little before he left office. Once out, however, he became the attorney for Patterson and Murguiondo and, over time, pestered both the Lincoln and Johnson administrations with the claims of his clients.

Although William H. Seward, as senator, had designed the Guano Islands Act, as secretary of state he had little interest in enforcing it. Naturally his first concern was matters relating to the Civil War, and each year during the war he informed Black that pursuing Patterson and Murguiondo's claim at that time would be inopportune. Yet after the war's conclusion, Seward still delayed until finally in 1867 Black took the matter directly to Andrew Johnson, urging him to take action to protect the rights of U.S. citizens and put Patterson and Murguiondo in possession of their island.

Seward did send the Patterson and Murguiondo matter to the Bureau of Claims, whose examiner, E. Peshine Smith, reported that Alta Vela, because of its proximity to Haiti and Santo Domingo, undoubtedly belonged to one or the other. Therefore it would not be appropriate for the United States to support the claims of Patterson and Murguiondo.

Matters became more complex because Seward was trying to lease Samana Bay from Santo Domingo for a naval station and pressing claims to Alta Vela at this time would doubtless ruin the negotiations. Also about this time, the New York firm of Webster and Company (also known as the Alta Vela Guano Company) leased Alta Vela from Santo Domingo and was mining guano there. Black was irate and accused Seward of ignoring the just claims of Patterson and Murguiondo in order to benefit his own friends (although there is no evidence that Seward had any connection with the New York company).

Meanwhile, Johnson had been seeking advice on other matters from Black, who was somewhat of an elder statesman. Johnson also hired Black to be part of his defense team during the impeachment crisis. But Black used this relationship with the president to try to pressure Johnson to do something for his Alta Vela clients. When Johnson still made no move, Black resigned from Johnson's defense team explicitly because of Johnson's "determination to determine nothing for the relief of the owners of Alta Vela."

Black continued to write to Johnson about the Alta Vela issue both during and after the impeachment crisis. Black became increasingly critical of Seward, who he believed had "committed a foul wrong upon my clients." He claimed that Santo Domingo had no title to the island but that Seward had made one up for that country and thus betrayed his own fellow citizens. In a blistering letter written in July 1868, Black called Seward a "drivelling charletan [sic]"

and other choice epithets and criticized Johnson for keeping Seward as secretary of state since "all the troubles of your unfortunate administration have sprung directly or indirectly from his crooked policy."

Although Black apparently ceased to write to Johnson after this, his son Chauncey Black protested that Seward had failed to forward all the important Alta Vela documents to Congress for consideration and urged Johnson to take action. But Johnson never did. After Johnson left office, even Black's appeal to Ulysses S. Grant's administration in 1869 brought no results, probably because Grant was interested in annexing Santo Domingo to the United States.

See also: Black, Jeremiah Sullivan; Foreign Affairs; Seward, William Henry.
References: Graf, LeRoy P., Haskins, Ralph W., and Bergeron, Paul H., eds., *The Papers of Andrew Johnson* vols. 12–15 (1967–2000); Skaggs, Jimmy M., *The Great Guano Rush: Entrepreneurs and American Overseas Expansion* (1994).

Amnesty Proclamations

Andrew Johnson differed from many of his Republican wartime allies on how to reconstruct the former Confederate states. Among the issues at the heart of their differences were the degree of leniency to be used and the question of who, the executive or the legislature, should direct Reconstruction. Nowhere were these points of contention more obvious than in the matter of presidential amnesties.

As with most aspects of Reconstruction, there was no easy answer to the question of how to treat Southerners who had participated in or aided the rebellion. Most Northerners agreed that eventually former rebels would be reintegrated into U.S. society and politics, with all the rights and privileges of loyal citizens. But disagreement existed over what sort of balance should be struck between conciliation and punishment. Surely those responsible for four years of bloody war must be made to pay, either figuratively or literally, for the damage they had done.

During the war years, Congress deferred to President Abraham Lincoln as commander in chief and allowed the president great latitude in granting amnesties and pardons. An amnesty was a blanket forgiveness for some crime or transgression, applicable to a large group of people. A pardon had the same effect, but was directed toward a single individual. Both Congress and the president believed that offering amnesty to those in rebellion might coax some into abandoning their cause and pledging loyalty to the Union. To aid in this, Congress passed the Second Confiscation Act on July 17, 1862. The act defined treason and its penalties and authorized the president "to extend to any persons who may have participated in the existing rebellion in any state or part thereof, pardon and amnesty" if they professed loyalty to the Union.

President Lincoln, relying on this act and the pardon power afforded by the U.S. Constitution, issued his Proclamation of Amnesty and Reconstruction on December 8, 1863. This offered full pardon to anyone taking an oath to support the Constitution and abide by all acts and proclamations concerning slavery. Six classes of people were excluded from this general process and had to apply directly to Lincoln for a pardon. These included high ranking civil and military officials and anyone who resigned from the U.S. military or Congress to join the Confederacy.

Andrew Johnson, who had been military governor of Tennessee since April 1862, endorsed his superior's policy and even foreshadowed his own. Headquartered in Nashville, Johnson agreed that "the erring and misguided will be welcomed upon their return" to the Union and, although the government must "punish intelligent and conscious treason in high places, no merely retaliatory or vindictive policy will be adopted." In a speech at the state capitol in 1864 he told Tennesseans "Go over there; there is an altar for you. There is President Lincoln's altar if you want pardon or amnesty. . . . we cannot put all in prison; we can't suspend all upon the gallows. No, this is not a war of extermination, but a war for the restoration of Government; and while restoring the Government, if we reclaim honest men we have only done our duty." Lincoln apparently lived up to his 1865 inaugural address, which spoke of "malice toward none" and "charity for all": No voluntary application for an individual pardon was denied.

Oddly enough, Governor Johnson later advised Lincoln that his amnesty was too lenient and that Tennessee Confederates were abusing it. In another preview of his later policy, Johnson suggested that his state be excepted from the general amnesty and that all Tennesseans desiring pardon be required to apply individually to the president.

After becoming president in April 1865 Andrew Johnson implemented an amnesty policy that was built on Lincoln's but took into account the new situation. Since the war had ended, there was no reason to offer a carrot-and-stick approach to speed the war's end or to be fearful that pardoned persons would continue in rebellion. Therefore, Johnson believed that amnesties could be broader and more generous; after all, just before his assassination Lincoln spoke of the need for conciliation and harmony. Like Lincoln, Johnson believed that the pardoning power was an executive privilege. That the war was over—and with it the executive's special war powers—meant little to Johnson, for he based his authority on Article II, Section 2, of the Constitution, which stipulated that the president "shall have power to grant reprieves and pardons for offenses against the United States. . ." Finally, the new president followed in his predecessor's footsteps by exempting several classes from his general amnesties and forcing these, as did Lincoln, to apply directly to the executive for clemency.

Nonetheless, contemporary Republicans and later historians have charged President Johnson with being hypocritical and deceptive. Much has been made of his stern remarks, such as those in a speech to an Indiana delegation in late April 1865, when he made the famous statement "treason must be made odious, and traitors must be punished and impoverished." When it became clear that Johnson was far more forgiving, the North howled in rage. In fact there was nothing deceptive about this; in the same speech cited above, Johnson also offered "leniency, conciliation, and amnesty to the thousands whom they [the Southern leaders] have misled and deceived." As a military governor and as president, Johnson made no attempt to hide his readiness to extend clemency. That clemency came in the form of four amnesty proclamations and thousands of individual pardons.

Just after becoming president in April of 1865, Johnson asked Attorney General James Speed for an opinion regarding the president's authority to issue an amnesty proclamation. Speed insisted that the U.S. Constitution authorized a president to issue such a proclamation, and he also encouraged Johnson to issue one because Lincoln's proclamation was a war measure and its effects ceased with the ending of hostilities. Johnson turned the matter over to his cabinet, who assisted in drafting the First Amnesty Proclamation.

Issued May 29, 1865, Johnson's proclamation offered blanket forgiveness to hundreds of thousands who participated in or aided the Confederacy. All the petitioner had to do was take an oath of future allegiance to the Union before a civil or military officer of the United States or of a loyal state government. That oath was then witnessed, a copy provided to the petitioner, and the original was forwarded to the State Department. The petitioner was then returned to full citizenship, with all rights and privileges, including the ability to participate in politics.

However, fourteen classes of people were excluded from the blanket amnesty. In addition to the six categories that had been exempted by Lincoln, Johnson added such exclusions as individuals under indictment, graduates of U.S. military academies, and those who had possessed property worth $20,000 or more in 1861. Johnson has been criticized for this last exception, and both contemporary Republicans and modern historians claim that the president was merely striking out at his old enemies, the planters. Although there may be some truth in this, Johnson, like Lincoln, was a believer in the "slave power" conspiracy and was convinced that the wealthy, intelligent Southern elite was ultimately responsible for starting the war. As Johnson told a group of Richmond merchants, "you know perfectly well that it was the wealthy men of the South who dragooned the people into secession." Because slaves were included as property in 1861, some estimates claim that this exclusion affected 150,000 people.

Anyone falling into one of the exempted categories had to apply for an individual pardon, and without it one could not participate in politics, hold office, acquire or transfer property, or get patents and copyrights. Many feared confiscation of their property, and some even had difficulty getting married because of the proscription. Those in business found that they could not obtain credit or loans.

But the application process was not an easy one. First, petitioners had to take the oath of allegiance and forward this and a petition for clemency to the provisional governor of the state. The governor then collected "memorials" (which amounted to character references) for the applicant and forwarded these to the U.S. attorney general's office. Applications were then classified and sent to the president, who either signed them or rejected them. If the pardon was granted, a copy was sent back to the applicant, with the original kept on file at the State Department. The procedure was fraught with bureaucratic snags and was incredibly time-consuming for governors, the attorney general, and the president. Provisional governors complained to President Johnson about the amount of time they spent reviewing petitions, and Johnson had to appoint a pardon clerk, Matthew F. Pleasants, to handle the correspondence coming into the attorney general's office. Even cabinet members and department heads criticized Johnson for spending too much time evaluating pardons. In all, Johnson eventually granted individual pardons to some 13,500 applicants.

The complexity of the system also opened doors for entrepreneurs who styled themselves "pardon brokers" or "pardon attorneys." For a fee, these men, and a few women, took responsibility for seeing a petition safely through the complicated process, making sure it got the right consideration from the right people. Some brokers, the notorious Lucy L. Cobb for instance, managed to circumvent the usual channels and see President Johnson in person. Provisional governors even employed their own agents to make sure that friends' applications received the proper attention.

While many Republicans in 1865 criticized Johnson for his leniency, Southerners complained of his harshness toward certain leaders. For instance, Johnson denied pardons to several leading Confederates who applied in 1865, including Robert E. Lee, James Longstreet, Edmund Kirby Smith, Raphael Semmes, and Howell Cobb. (Most of these men were included in an amnesty issued in July 1868.) Many civil leaders had to wait as well; Johnson did not even begin reviewing their applications until 1866. The most famous delay involved former Confederate president Jefferson Davis, who had been arrested and indicted for treason in 1865. Not until December of 1868 was Davis included in an amnesty; he never received an individual pardon because he refused to ask for one, saying that "if it were to do over again I would again do just as I did in 1861."

Yet the denials and delays did not sway many Republicans from the conviction that Johnson was being far too lenient with former Confederates. The rate of individual pardons increased in 1866, as did the animosity between Congress and President Johnson. When the fall elections brought triumph for Republicans and disaster for Johnson's National Union Party movement, it was clear that the Northern electorate did not approve of the president's policy either. Sensing this, the lame-duck Congress that assembled at the end of 1866 began to whittle away at the president's program, starting with his amnesty policy. Hoping to prevent another blanket amnesty, Congress repealed in January 1867 the section of the Second Confiscation Act, which allowed the president to grant mass pardons, but because Johnson claimed that his authority derived from the Constitution and not Congress, this did not deter him. At the same time, Representative James M. Ashley introduced a proposition to begin an impeachment investigation of the president, charging, among other things, that Johnson "has corruptly used the pardoning power."

Although Congress could not stop Johnson from granting pardons or amnesties, it could nullify their effect—in fact, the effect of his Reconstruction program altogether. In March 1867 Congress began reshaping the South with the Military Reconstruction Acts, which eliminated from political activity anyone who would be "excluded from the privilege of holding office under the proposed amendment." This referred to the pending Fourteenth Amendment, which would bar from holding office anyone who had taken an earlier oath to the United States but then supported the Confederacy. According to the pending amendment, only Congress could remove this office-holding disability. Thus, the army, which was responsible for administering the Reconstruction Acts, used a *future* disability as a guideline for implementing an immediate one: the exclusion of many former

Confederates from any political activity whatsoever. Thousands of men who had received pardons under Johnson now found themselves banned from participating in politics and holding office. Confusion followed across the South, and protests flooded into the White House as many who had received pardons learned that they were again disfranchised.

Johnson's control of Reconstruction was swiftly slipping away, despite the fact that both the Supreme Court (in *Ex parte Garland*) and Attorney General Henry Stanbery denied the power of Congress to interfere with presidential pardons. With the Military Reconstruction Acts eliminating so many former Confederates from political roles while enfranchising black males, Johnson sought a means to counter the change. The president calculated that if he reduced the number of excepted classes from his first amnesty, and those persons *were not* ineligible under the proposed Fourteenth Amendment, those persons should regain their political rights.

On September 7, 1867, Johnson issued his Second Amnesty Proclamation. The message, largely written by Secretary of State William Seward, reduced the excepted classes to those who held high rank in the Confederacy, mistreated prisoners, or were under indictment. Some 300 individuals were still excluded from clemency, including many leading generals and civil officials, but wealthy former planters were now readmitted to their rights. Because many of these men did not fall under the Fourteenth Amendment's proscription, they were allowed to participate in the new Southern state governments. But their numbers could not offset the new voting block created by Unionists and blacks.

Johnson's Third Amnesty Proclamation extended clemency to those high-ranking officials who had been excluded from his earlier proclamations. Issued on July 4, 1868, just as the National Democratic Convention met in New York City, this was not the "universal" amnesty for which many had hoped, as persons under indictment were still excluded. Also, as with prior amnesties, the effect was partly negated by Congress and by the Fourteenth Amendment, which had been ratified that same month. Most of those pardoned under this amnesty were barred from holding office until they received clemency from Congress.

The impact of Johnson's Third Amnesty fell short in another way as well: it did not win for Johnson the Democratic nomination for president. Absurd as it may sound, many correspondents and political insiders suggested that a universal amnesty could earn Johnson a place on the ticket. But the main reason for granting a universal amnesty would be to pardon Jefferson Davis, who was still under indictment for treason but whom Johnson detested. With the election of Ulysses S. Grant in November 1868, Johnson and his Reconstruction policy became lame ducks. With nothing left to lose, on Christmas Day in 1868 Johnson issued his last amnesty, which, coupled with his last annual message, was the final slap in the face to the Republican Party.

Johnson's Fourth Amnesty Proclamation granted a complete amnesty to anyone charged with treason, meaning in particular Jefferson Davis. Davis, former Confederate vice president Alexander Stephens, and a handful of other leading Confederates were returned to full citizenship with one exception: they could not hold office.

Republicans had made much of Johnson's leniency and his method of forcing individuals to petition him directly for pardons. But congressional Republicans soon found themselves in the same predicament as thousands petitioned Congress for removal of the Fourteenth Amendment's office-holding disability. Over the next few years Congress granted thousands of individual pardons, each of which required a congressional vote. Overwhelmed by the task, in 1872 Congress passed its own Amnesty Act, which removed the office-holding disability from all except the highest ranking officers and a few Confederate congressmen. For more than two decades Congress continued to grant individual pardons for these remaining persons. Finally, a universal amnesty passed in 1898 that removed the Civil War disabilities from anyone still suffering from earlier proscriptions.

See also: Ashley, James Mitchell; Cabinet Members; Congressional Reconstruction; Constitution, Johnson's Attitude toward; Davis, Jefferson; Democratic Convention; Democratic Party; Fourteenth Amendment; Governors, Provisional; Impeachment; Military Governor of Tennessee, Johnson as; Military Reconstruction Acts; National Union Convention and Party; Pardons (Individual); Presidential Reconstruction; Republican Party; Speed, James.

References: Dorris, Jonathan Truman, *Pardon and Amnesty under Lincoln and Johnson: The Restoration of the Confederates to Their Rights and Privileges, 1861–1898* (1953); Graf, LeRoy P., Haskins, Ralph W., and Bergeron, Paul H., eds., *The Papers of Andrew Johnson* vols. 5–8, 12, 14 (1967–2000); Harris, William C., *With Charity for All: Lincoln and the Restoration of the Union* (1997); Sefton, James E., *Andrew Johnson and the Uses of Constitutional Power* (1980); Trefousse, Hans L., *Andrew Johnson: A Biography* (1989). For the full text of the First Amnesty Proclamation, and excerpts of the others, see Appendix II.

Annual Messages

As president of the United States, Andrew Johnson delivered four annual messages, one each December when Congress reassembled. The annual message was the equivalent of the modern-day State of the Union address presented in late January. Both are responses to Article II, Section 3, of the U.S. Constitution, which states that the president "shall from time to time give to the Congress Information of the State of the Union." During Johnson's time the annual message was not given as a speech but as a written document delivered to the Congress and read by a clerk. It is known that historian George Bancroft wrote much of Johnson's first (1865) message and that Secretary of State William H. Seward assisted with the second (1866).

Each message was composed of two parts. In the first section Johnson gave his opinions on such issues as Reconstruction laws or whatever happened to be of concern to him at the time. These subjects varied somewhat from year to year and are discussed below.

In the second part Johnson summarized or commented upon the reports of his cabinet members. The Department of the Interior had the most varied responsibilities. The report of its land office always gave Johnson a chance to comment on the success of his pet project, the Homestead Act, and to list how many acres of land had been distributed under its provisions. The Interior Department also oversaw the construction of the transcontinental railroad, and managed the Patent Office, Pension Bureau, and Indian Affairs Office.

Johnson usually gave only brief attention to the reports of the War and Navy Departments and was mainly concerned that both military agencies continue to decrease in personnel and budget. Similarly, his comments about the postmaster general's report were short. Johnson devoted more space to the State Department, depending on what had been happening in foreign affairs. At times he might simply list the countries with which the United States had a good relationship. He also mentioned treaties, such as that with the King of Denmark by which the United States was trying to acquire two of the Virgin Islands. In his fourth message (1868), Johnson went into a long description of a problem with Brazil and Paraguay.

Johnson usually spent a lot of time in both sections on matters related to the Treasury Department and federal government finances. He was always in favor of reducing the debt by paying it off as quickly as possible. He also wanted to reduce interest payments to wealthy bondholders, who he believed had an unfair advantage over the rest of the citizens because bondholders were paid in gold and everyone else was paid in depreciated currency.

In his December 4, 1865, message Johnson, who had been president for less than eight months, determined "to state with frankness the principles which guide my conduct." He emphasized the idea that the Constitution could be amended but that states could not nullify its provisions or secede from the union created under it. In addition he detailed what would be wrong with having military governments in the former Confederate states and explained why he had appointed provisional governors, who were to call elections and restore the states to normal government as soon as possible. To aid this process he had exercised the pardoning power but refused to proclaim suffrage for the freedmen because he believed that this would be an unconstitutional infringement of the rights of the states to determine their own suffrage qualifications.

A year later, on December 3, 1866, Johnson was particularly concerned that Congress had failed to seat the loyal, elected senators and representatives from ten of the seceded states (all except Tennessee). The states were being unconstitutionally, without their consent, deprived of their right to congressional representation, and Johnson wanted to see their representatives be admitted to their seats.

By the time of the third message, December 3, 1867, relations between Johnson and Congress had deteriorated badly. Congress had continued to refuse to seat the representatives of the Confederate states, a situation that Johnson characterized as "the continued disorganization of the Union." He complained that "at this time there is no Union as our fathers understood the term" and threatened that if the Constitution were not obeyed the Union would be destroyed. He gave several reasons why the Reconstruction Acts were unconstitutional and should be repealed, particularly

complaining about the Tenure of Office Act, which prohibited him from carrying out his duties by preventing him from removing unscrupulous Treasury Department officials from office.

When Johnson issued his fourth message on December 9, 1868, he had survived the congressional attempt to impeach him, had failed to be nominated for president by the Democratic Party, and had had most of his plans stymied by Congress. But he was not going to leave office without giving his opinion of Congress. He claimed that "most, if not all, of our domestic troubles are directly traceable to violations of the organic law and excessive legislation," specifically the Reconstruction Acts, which "have substantially failed and proved pernicious in their results." He believed that the situation was now worse than when Congressional Reconstruction began. He also urged that the people be able to vote on several potential constitutional amendments that he proposed: the direct election of senators, the president, and the vice president; the designation of a line of succession after the vice president; and the establishment of term limits for federal judges. He pronounced that "in Congress are vested all legislative powers, and upon them devolves the responsibility as well for framing unwise and excessive laws as for neglecting to devise and adopt measure[s] absolutely demanded by the wants of the country." In other words, Johnson blamed Congress for all the problems of Reconstruction.

After each of the messages, Johnson received complimentary letters from his supporters, but, as usual, opponents did not write to him with their criticisms.

See also: Black Suffrage; Cabinet Members; Congressional Reconstruction; Constitution, Johnson's Attitude toward; Constitutional Amendments, Proposed; Democratic Convention; Finances, Johnson's Attitude toward Governmental; Foreign Affairs; Governors, Provisional; Homestead Act; Impeachment; Military Reconstruction Acts; Pardons (Individual); Presidential Reconstruction;

Railroads; Reconstruction; Seward, William Henry; Tenure of Office Act.

References: Graf, LeRoy P., Haskins, Ralph W., and Bergeron, Paul H., eds., *The Papers of Andrew Johnson* vols. 9, 11, 13, 15 (1967–2000); Handlin, Lilian, *George Bancroft: The Intellectual as Democrat* (1984).

Apprenticeship

The practice of apprenticeship was imported to the United States from England during the colonial period. In North Carolina in the early 1800s the master legally was supposed to provide food, clothing, and lodging for his apprentices and teach the youths to read and write, in addition to instructing them in a trade. The apprentice owed his master complete obedience until the end of his apprenticeship, which was usually when he reached the age of twenty-one, no matter when he began his term.

Andrew Johnson's older brother, William, was first apprenticed to Colonel Thomas Henderson, editor of the *Raleigh Star,* and then to James J. Selby, a Raleigh tailor, that is, a maker of men's clothing. Andrew himself may have chosen apprenticeship to Selby as well because of the practice of hiring someone to read to the tailors while they were working. Andrew, eager to learn, apparently hung around the shop even before he began to work there.

Two possible dates are recorded for the beginning of Andrew's apprenticeship. The first, November 8, 1818, was on an agreement with Selby made by Johnson's mother and stepfather when Andrew was just short of ten years old. In 1869 this paper was in the possession of Selby's son who lived in Mississippi. The second date, three and a half years later, on February 18, 1822, was on apprenticeship papers officially recorded by the court in Wake County, North Carolina. No one knows which date is correct or whether they may have indicated both an informal and an official apprenticeship.

Andrew Johnson did not comment on the issue in any document that survives. The main argument in favor of the later date is that it was officially recorded by the court. The arguments in favor of the earlier date are based on a variety of circumstantial evidence. The biographies published during Johnson's lifetime virtually all said that he was apprenticed when he was ten years old and no attempt to contradict this statement has been found. Another factor suggesting an earlier apprenticeship date is the collection of stories from people who knew Johnson in his youth. They recall a "harum-scarum" boy who frequently ripped his clothes climbing over fences, earning him punishment from Mrs. Selby. Finally, there is the question whether Johnson would have been able to develop the fairly sophisticated tailoring skills he needed in little more than two years of apprenticeship had he started at the later date.

Regardless of when Johnson began his apprenticeship, he ended it long before his twenty-first birthday in 1829. In June 1824 Andrew and William Johnson, with several friends, pelted the home of a neighboring widow, Mrs. Wells, with stones or chunks of wood. Whether they did not like the woman and wished to annoy her or whether they hoped to impress her two daughters, the teens soon found that the widow threatened to sue them. So, on June 15 they fled Raleigh. Selby advertised in the *Raleigh Star* and offered a $10 reward for the return of both William and Andrew or Andrew alone, presumably because he had more than five years of apprenticeship left to serve. Selby seems not to have pursued the brothers otherwise since they remained at large. However, because North Carolina law mandated the return of runaway apprentices and forbade other tradespeople from employing such fugitives, the brothers soon moved out of state, from Carthage, North Carolina, to Laurens, South Carolina.

Sometime around 1825 or 1826 Selby moved to the countryside, twenty miles from Raleigh. Once or twice during this period Andrew returned briefly to Raleigh, but could not get a job there because of his broken apprenticeship contract. In fact, Johnson visited Selby and tried to make an arrangement whereby he could pay off his unexpired time. But Selby was in no mood to be lenient and demanded a large sum of money as security. Not having that amount available, Johnson decided to leave North Carolina and move to Tennessee. As a result, by the time his apprenticeship should have expired, Johnson was already married and had a tailoring business of his own.

See also: Education, of Johnson; Johnson (Daughtry), Mary McDonough "Polly"; Johnson, William P.

References: Graf, LeRoy P., Haskins, Ralph W., and Bergeron, Paul H., eds., *The Papers of Andrew Johnson* vols. 1, 15 (1967–2000); Trefousse, Hans L., *Andrew Johnson: A Biography* (1989).

Army Appropriations Act (1867)

With the passage of the First Military Reconstruction Act on March 2, 1867, Congress tied the fate of its Reconstruction program to the U.S. Army, which was responsible for implementing Congressional Reconstruction. To prevent President Johnson from either interfering with the army or using it to disrupt the congressional program, Congress immediately followed the Reconstruction Act with the Army Appropriations Act and the Tenure of Office Act.

While the Tenure of Office Act was designed to protect federal officeholders in general and Secretary of War Edwin M. Stanton in particular, the Army Appropriations Act was designed to protect General of the Army Ulysses S. Grant. It was generally believed that Grant, a professional soldier of moderate views, supported Congress as the representative of the people and would ensure that the army executed congressional directives.

The first section of the act was fairly ordinary, containing the fiscal appropriations for the army. It was this section that guaranteed the act's passage because Johnson could not veto the act without eliminating funding for national defense. In fact this was the only Congressional Reconstruction measure he did not veto. Instead he sent to Congress a formal "protest" that criticized the Republicans' usurpation of executive privileges.

Johnson's protest was directed at sections two and six. Section two was a rider called the Command of the Army Act, which Congress protected from a veto by attaching it to the appropriations bill. The Command of the Army Act required the general of the army to have his headquarters in Washington, D.C., so that he could be near to Congress itself. The previous general of the army, Winfield Scott, had relocated to New York City to avoid political intrigue. The section also stated that the general of the army, at this time Ulysses S. Grant, could not be suspended, removed, or even transferred without Senate approval. (Earlier Johnson had tried to send Grant to Mexico on a diplomatic mission.) Most important, all orders to the army had to pass through the general of the army, and anyone obeying orders that did not follow this path faced fine and imprisonment. In this way, congressional Republicans hoped to prevent Johnson from issuing orders directly to sympathetic or conservative generals in the South. So while the act protected the Republican program, it also protected Grant's position, making the two more interdependent and further tying their destinies together.

Section six of the appropriations measure disbanded all militias in the South. These groups, at the time made up of white conservatives and former Confederate soldiers, were tied to the harassment and terrorism of blacks and Unionists in the South. Johnson also criticized this section in his protest, claiming that it interfered with the right of a state to organize for its own defense. With the passage of the act on March 2, 1867, no state could form a militia, white or black, until Congress readmitted the state to the Union.

See also: Congressional Reconstruction; Constitution, Johnson's Attitude toward; Grant, Ulysses Simpson; Military Districts; Military Reconstruction Acts; Reconstruction; Republican Party; Stanton, Edwin McMasters; Tenure of Office Act.

References: Graf, LeRoy P., Haskins, Ralph W., and Bergeron, Paul H., eds., *The Papers of Andrew Johnson* vol. 12 (1967–2000); Sefton, James E., *The United States Army and Reconstruction, 1865–1877* (1967); Simpson, Brooks D., *"Let Us Have Peace": Ulysses S. Grant and the Politics of War and Reconstruction, 1861–1868* (1991).

Ashley, James Mitchell (1824–1896)

James Mitchell Ashley, whom some contemporaries called "the great impeacher," had much in common with Andrew Johnson, the president that he sought to destroy. Born near Pittsburgh, Pennsylvania, this eldest son of a Campbellite minister (a spin-off sect from Presbyterianism) moved at an early age with his family to Portsmouth, Ohio. Like Johnson, Ashley traveled a good deal during his youth, which he spent accompanying his preacher father around Ohio and into western Virginia and Kentucky. Also like Johnson, Ashley had no formal schooling; his mother taught him at home to read and write. At sixteen Ashley left home, purportedly because of his father's strict regulations and discipline. Just as his future adversary had done, young Ashley set out to make his way in the world.

Ashley drifted through several states and many occupations, including working on an Ohio steamboat and clerking. His journeys through Kentucky, Tennessee, and into Virginia galvanized a sentiment he developed while traveling with his father: an intense hatred for slavery. His experiences in the South and observations concerning blacks convinced him that the system was evil, inhumane, and inconsistent with American principles. He was even asked to leave Virginia because of his outspoken criticisms of the slave system.

By the early 1840s he had returned to Ohio and a slightly more stable, but not less ambitious, existence. He operated a newspaper for a short time, studied law, was admitted to the bar in 1849 (although he never practiced), and married Emma J. Smith in 1851. About that time he moved to Toledo, where he entered the wholesale drug business, and through connections there, politics. Like Andrew Johnson, Ashley had been a Jacksonian Democrat, but his opposition to slavery moved him into the Free Soil and then Republican ranks. He helped create the Republican Party in the Toledo area and served as a delegate to the 1856 Republican National Convention.

Seeing politics as a way of shaping national policy concerning slavery, Ashley ran for Congress as a Republican in 1858. He won election to the House of Representatives and carried the district in the next four consecutive elections (1860, 1862, 1864, 1866). In Congress he became the chairman of the Committee on Territories, and during the Civil War he sponsored the first Reconstruction measure. This proposal, which Ashley presented in March 1862, classified Southern states as "territories" and suggested that those states be treated in ways similar to other territories trying to gain admittance to the Union. Although the proposal was tabled at the time, Congress used many of the same guidelines in the Reconstruction policy it pursued in 1867.

The abolition of slavery, however, remained Ashley's primary goal. He supported Lincoln's Ten Percent Plan, but wanted black suffrage added to it. He helped draft the bills that abolished slavery in Washington, D.C., and the territories and was the first to introduce (December 1863) a measure advocating the abolition of slavery nationally. The resolution was defeated early on, but his tenacity and ability to cut political deals, plus the support of Abraham Lincoln, revived it. In January 1865 it passed as the Thirteenth Amendment, which was ratified in December 1865.

When Andrew Johnson became president, Representative Ashley, like many Republicans, believed that Johnson could be the right man to reconstruct the Union. Johnson's stern treatment of Confederates in Tennessee, as well as his enforcement of emancipation while military governor, convinced Ashley that Johnson deserved a chance. By the fall of 1865, however, Ashley had moved into what became the Radical Republican camp, believing as he did that Johnson was an obstructionist and even floating rumors that the new president was somehow involved in the murder of Lincoln.

Ashley established himself as a leading Radical in January 1867 when he introduced the first resolution for the impeachment of Johnson. Ashley charged Johnson with illegal use of his pardon privilege, interference in elections, and usurpation of power. Ashley's resolution initiated the Judiciary Committee's investigations into Johnson. The committee examined the president's relationship with pardon brokers, former Confederates, and even his role in the execution of the assassination conspirators. The committee found insufficient evidence to move forward on impeachment.

When the Fortieth Congress convened (the same day that the Thirty-Ninth adjourned), Ashley reintroduced his impeachment resolution. Again the Judiciary Committee undertook investigations, but Ashley's reputation began to sour when

he offered a convicted perjurer named Charles Dunham (alias Sanford Conover) a pardon if Dunham would testify against Johnson before the committee. Ashley hurt his cause further when he appeared before the committee in November 1867, defending his theory that all presidents who died in office were the victims of foul play.

When the House finally brought impeachment charges in early 1868 it was due largely to Johnson's political high-handedness, not Ashley's allegations. With the defeat of impeachment in May 1868, Ashley's political career lost steam, and he failed to win reelection in the fall of the year. He left Congress in March 1869, the same day that Johnson stepped down from the presidency.

Ashley remained politically active for a time, serving briefly (1869–1870) as governor of Montana Territory under President Grant and working feverishly for Horace Greeley in the 1872 Liberal Republican campaign. Ashley became involved in railroad ventures later in life and helped build a line from northern Ohio into Michigan. He was president of the Toledo, Ann Arbor, and Northern Michigan Railroad from 1877 to 1893 and died in Alma, Michigan, in 1896.

See also: Black Suffrage; Butler, Benjamin Franklin; Congressional Reconstruction; District of Columbia Franchise; House Judiciary Committee; Impeachment; Lincoln Assassination Conspirators; Military Reconstruction Acts; Pardons (Individual); Patronage; Reconstruction; Republican Party; Territorial Affairs; Thirteenth Amendment.

References: Horowitz, Robert F., *The Great Impeacher: A Political Biography of James M. Ashley* (1979); Trefousse, Hans L., *Andrew Johnson: A Biography* (1989).

Assassination Conspirators

See Lincoln Assassination Conspirators

Bartlett, Margaret Johnson Patterson (1903–1992)

The last living great-grandchild of Andrew Johnson, Margaret Johnson Patterson Bartlett was the granddaughter of Martha Johnson Patterson and David T. Patterson and the only child of Andrew Johnson Patterson and his wife Martha Ellen (Mattie) Barkley Patterson. Margaret was born and raised in the Johnson "Homestead" (the house Andrew Johnson bought in 1851) and lived there much of her adult life as well. A 1924 graduate of Tusculum College in Greeneville, Tennessee, she taught home economics at Greeneville High School and later in Johnson City, Tennessee, before she became a National Park Service employee. On June 14, 1949, at the "Homestead," she married Dr. William Thaw Bartlett (d. 1954), a widowed Presbyterian minister from Maryville, Tennessee. The couple had no children.

Growing up in what had been Johnson's last home, Margaret heard many stories about the family from her father. Andrew Patterson tried to gain recognition for Johnson and his accomplishments, but aside from selling Johnson's old tailor shop to the state of Tennessee in 1921 for $5,000, he was unable to achieve his purpose before his death in 1932. However, Margaret and her mother took up the Johnson cause, which became her life goal and achievement.

In 1933 the two women began working toward the goal of uniting all the Johnson sites in Greeneville—the cemetery where Johnson was buried, his tailor shop, and his home—as a national monument under the Park Service. Over the next two years Margaret made five trips to Washington, D.C., to further her goal. In August 1935 Congress passed an act granting monument status when all three of the sites were the property of the federal government. Because only the cemetery—which became a national cemetery in 1906—was federal property, she made more trips to Washington over the next seven years to persuade members of Congress to appropriate money to purchase the home and tailor shop. In 1936 Margaret even had tea with Franklin and Eleanor Roosevelt, and the president promised to sign the bill if Congress passed it. Finally, in 1941 the state of Tennessee gave the tailor shop to the federal government, and the next year Congress appropriated $44,000 to buy the home from the family.

The Andrew Johnson National Monument was established by presidential proclamation on April 27, 1942 (it was renamed the Andrew Johnson National Historic Site in 1963). Margaret promptly began working for the National Park Service as a hostess and guide for the home, a job she held until she retired in October 1976 (she officially retired September 30, 1973, but kept working for three more years). Margaret loved giving tours and telling stories about her family, especially trying to capture the imaginations of visiting children. She lived in the house until restoration began in 1956.

Beginning in the 1880s the home had been given Victorian additions, porch sections had been enclosed and turned into bathrooms, and some rooms had been made into apartments. The purpose of the restoration project, which lasted until 1958, was to return the home to its appearance when Johnson lived there after his presidency (1869–1875). It was much easier to restore it to this period both because a photograph of the exterior at the time of Johnson's death existed and because Margaret donated much family furniture and other personal items purchased by the Johnsons after the war. Most of their belongings from the antebellum period had been stolen during the Civil War.

In 1968 Margaret built a replica of the Johnson home for herself several blocks from the original site, but she was not able to live in it for very long due to ill health. In her later years she suffered from severe arthritis and then a series of strokes. She lived in a nursing home from April 1983 until her death. Her affairs were administered by her first cousin on her mother's side, Ralph M. Phinney, who continued to use money from her estate to support various Johnson-promoting projects including statues in Greeneville and Nashville and the publication of Johnson materials in *The Papers of Andrew Johnson*.

Margaret participated in various civic activities such as organizing the Girl Scouts in Greene County, organizing rural food canning projects during World War II, and being active in the Daughters of the American Revolution and Christ United Methodist Church. But her life centered around the goal of establishing a memorial to her great-grandfather, and that such a site now exists is proof of her success.

Margaret Johnson Patterson Bartlett died on August 1, 1992—117 years and one day after President Johnson. She lay in state in the parlor of the Johnson home, where her funeral service was held on August 4, followed by burial in the Johnson family plot on the top of Monument Hill in the national cemetery. She was the last family member who will be interred there.

See also: Grandchildren; Greeneville, Tennessee; Patterson, David Trotter; Patterson, Martha Johnson.

References: *Greeneville (Tennessee) Sun,* Aug. 3–5, 1992.

Bell, John (1797–1869)

Born near Nashville, Tennessee, to Samuel and Margaret Edmiston Bell, John Bell grew up among five sisters and three brothers. He eventually became a successful mine owner, lawyer, politician, and leader of the Whig Party in Tennessee, yet he died believing himself a failure.

As a young man, Bell seemed destined for greatness. He graduated from Cumberland College (which evolved into the University of Nashville and eventually part of Peabody College and Vanderbilt University) at the age of seventeen, was admitted to the bar at twenty, and by twenty-one had been elected to the state senate. He declined to run for a second term and chose to concentrate on his law practice and family instead; he had married Sally Dickinson in 1818, and they would eventually have five children.

In 1826, convinced that fellow Tennessean Andrew Jackson had been swindled out of the presidency two years earlier, Bell reentered politics as a Jacksonian Democrat. He was elected to the U.S. House of Representatives for the first of seven terms. When Jackson entered the White House in

1829, Bell followed Jacksonian policy, including opposing internal improvements and arguing for the removal of the Cherokee Indians.

But in the 1830s Bell's life took on new directions. In 1832 his wife died, and three years later he married a wealthy Nashville widow, Jane Erwin Yeatman. Differences had also been developing with President Jackson. Still considering himself a Democrat, Bell, chairman of the House Judiciary Committee, unsuccessfully opposed the force bill (which authorized Jackson to use federal troops to enforce federal laws) and supported Congress's claim that a national bank was constitutional. Bell finally broke with Jackson over the election of 1836, when he supported, and some claim even directed, the presidential candidacy of Tennessean Hugh Lawson White against Jackson's heir apparent Martin Van Buren. Although White lost the election, he carried Tennessee; almost accidentally, John Bell had become not only a member of the Whig Party, but its leader in that state.

Bell was now at war with the Democratic Party, and with it, its newest standard bearer from East Tennessee, Andrew Johnson. In the presidential election of 1840, Bell himself led the William Henry Harrison campaign into East Tennessee in an effort to counter the influence of Johnson. Harrison, a Whig, was elected president, and Bell, who left Congress in 1841, became secretary of war. After Harrison's sudden death most of the cabinet, Bell included, resigned rather than work under President John Tyler. Bell was a Southerner and a slaveholder, but he was also a Unionist who found Tyler's pro-Southern bias dangerous for the Union.

Bell returned to Tennessee and his law practice for a few years, but reentered political life with his election in 1847 to the Senate, where he remained until 1859. Again Johnson and Bell crossed paths. As senator, Bell had the power of patronage, and Johnson demanded that East Ten-

nesseans, even Democrats, get their share. Later, in 1855, when Johnson ran for his second term as governor of Tennessee, Bell was again an obstacle, supporting Meredith Gentry of the Know-Nothing Party against Johnson. Unlike most Southern Whigs, Bell had gravitated toward the American (Know-Nothing) Party after the Kansas-Nebraska Act in 1854 destroyed the Whig Party; most Southern Whigs joined the Democratic Party. Bell feared that Democrats had become too proslavery and prosecession, and so he sought refuge in what he considered the only national party.

Nonetheless, Johnson was reelected governor of Tennessee, and two years later, eyeing a seat in the U.S. Senate, he went on the attack against Bell and the Know-Nothings. Because the Tennessee legislature elected the state's senators, Johnson campaigned vigorously for Democratic legislators and was brutal in his attacks upon Know-Nothings and Bell. Democrats seized control of the state assembly, and Johnson was elected senator in 1857.

Now Johnson and Bell were paired against each other on the same stage. Similarities did exist: the two one-time Jacksonians were both Unionists, and each regarded Southern secessionists and Northern abolitionists with equal disdain. They even agreed on issues such as land grants and public education. But their personal and professional backgrounds and previous encounters ensured that hostility would prevail. Perhaps the most notorious encounter occurred on the floor of the Senate in February 1858, when a bitter shouting match erupted over Bell's refusal to vote for Kansas's proslavery Lecompton Constitution (the Tennessee General Assembly passed a resolution calling on its senators to support it). Over two consecutive days the rival senators tossed insults and challenges at each other, until Johnson finally closed the embarrassing scene with a self-serving memorial to his own plebeian roots and self-made status.

When Bell retired from the Senate in 1859, that body lost one of its last nationally minded statesmen. At a time when sectional politics and regional interests were tearing the nation apart, Bell remained fairminded and moderate. National parties—the Whigs and Know-Nothings—had already evaporated as a result of sectional tensions, so Bell was left without a political affiliation. A slave owner, he years before had opposed the Gag Rule (which prevented the discussion of antislavery petitions in Congress), accepted the idea that Congress could prohibit slavery in the territories acquired from Mexico, and predicted (accurately) that the Kansas-Nebraska Act would divide the country over the slavery issue.

It was this issue that dominated the election of 1860 and threatened to destroy the Union. A cadre of former Whigs, Northern and Southern, who sought to avoid disunion also sought a compromise, Unionist candidate who could deflect the sectional animosities that were building to a climax. The obvious choice was Tennessean John Bell, a nationally recognized politician who lived the life of a Southerner but acted politically as a Northerner. At the same time, some were attempting, unsuccessfully, to nominate Johnson as the Democratic candidate. In the four-way contest of 1860, Bell was the candidate on the Constitutional Union ticket, with Edward Everett as his running mate. But decades of compromising had failed, and it was time for a final decision on the nature of slavery and the nature of the Union. Bell secured the electoral votes of only three states: Virginia, Kentucky, and his native Tennessee.

With the election of Abraham Lincoln, Southern states began seceding in the winter of 1860 and the spring of 1861. For the first time, Johnson and Bell were fighting on the same side. Each opposed secession and the fanatic planters and abolitionists whom the Tennesseans believed were causing it. Both men campaigned across the state, trying to keep their state in the Union. This cooperation, and its temporary success, evaporated after President Lincoln called for volunteers to suppress the "rebellion." John Bell, like thousands of other Tennesseans, had a change of heart and joined his state in seceding from the Union; his sons, stepsons, and sons-in-law all joined the Confederate army.

Bell's wartime life was characterized by depression and illness as he watched his country wrestle with forces that he had tried to contain. He left Tennessee in 1862 to avoid the Union advance and lived in Alabama and Georgia for the rest of the war. He returned to Tennessee after the war, but his political career, mining interests, and health were shattered. He died at his house in Stewart County, on the site of one of his once-successful rolling mills.

See also: Blacks (Slave and Free), Johnson's Attitude toward; Democratic Party; Harris, Isham Green; Jackson, Andrew; Lincoln, Abraham; Maynard, Horace; Polk, James Knox; Secession Referendums (Tennessee, 1861); Senator, Johnson as; Whig Party.

References: Abernathy, Thomas Perkins, "Origins of the Whig Party in Tennessee," *Mississippi Valley Historical Review* 12 (1925–1926), 502–522; Crabb, Alfred Leland, *Nashville: Personality of a City* (1960); Crofts, Daniel W., *Reluctant Confederates: Upper South Unionists in the Secession Crisis* (1989); Parks, Joseph H., *John Bell of Tennessee* (1950).

Bennett, James Gordon, Jr. (1841–1918)

Bennett, James Gordon, Sr. (1795–1872)

Born in Scotland and educated at a Catholic seminary, James Gordon Bennett, Sr., proved too ambitious and restless for life as a member of the clergy. Instead he abandoned the church, expanded his learning, and, on a chance offer from a friend, emigrated to Nova Scotia in 1819. After teaching there briefly, he moved to Maine, then Boston, and by 1822 had reached New York. Working as a clerk in a newspaper office, he caught the eye of the owner of the *Charleston Courier,* A. S. Willington, who offered him a position in South Carolina. Bennett spent 1823 working at the *Courier,* where he developed an affection for the South, a dislike of blacks, and an appreciation for slavery.

Late in 1823 Bennett returned to New York, where he filled a wide range of journalistic positions with several different newspapers. His break came in 1826, when his reports as Washington correspondent for the *New York Enquirer* earned him national attention. In 1829 Bennett convinced James Watson Webb, owner of the *New York Courier* to purchase the *Enquirer.* Bennett was largely responsible for operating the new organ, which benefited his reputation and allowed him to perfect his management style.

A Democrat, Bennett left the *Enquirer* in 1832 when Webb began showing Whig tendencies. In 1835, in a New York cellar, Bennett and two printers issued the first edition of the *New York Herald,* an inexpensive paper that purported to be worldly, open-minded, and politically evenhanded. Soon the paper gained attention for its superb reporting, its dearth of minor details (no sports, no weather, no headlines), and its aggressive and even caustic treatment of politics. Circulation grew, attracting lucrative advertising contracts, which enabled the owner to station excellent reporters out West, across the South, and even in Europe.

But Bennett's criticism of members of the business community, politicians, and journalists alike brought retaliation. He was sued and attacked in the street, and during his honeymoon—he married Irish immigrant Henrietta Agnes Crean in 1840— some rivals tried to lock him out of his shop. The attention only increased the *Herald*'s popularity, so that by 1841 Bennett had

reporters sitting in Congress, had moved to a new building with facilities capable of producing 60,000 papers a day, and had subscribers as far away as New Orleans.

Politically, Bennett and the *Herald* were usually linked with the Democratic Party but, although Bennett openly supported James K. Polk, he later backed Whig Zachary Taylor. Bennett, known for his extreme opinions, opposed extremism in politics. He was a staunch Unionist and criticized secessionists and abolitionists alike. He believed that slavery benefited both blacks and whites, yet claimed it was treason to leave the Union to defend the system. In the election of 1860 the *Herald* backed Stephen Douglas, but with the coming of war the astute Bennett quickly shifted support to the new Lincoln administration.

Bennett's relationship with Abraham Lincoln changed with the issues of war. Bennett opposed any move toward emancipation and adhered to a strict reading of the war's goals: preservation of the Union and suppression of rebellion. In fact Bennett openly broke with Lincoln before the 1864 election, and only an offer to the publisher to be minister to France mended the breach. Bennett declined the offer, which was made to avoid completely alienating what had become one of the most widely read papers in the country. Bennett had his own army following the armies, and their reporting was unsurpassed.

Not surprisingly, Bennett heartily supported Andrew Johnson when he became president, calling him "Joshua" to Lincoln's "Moses." For Bennett, Johnson was ideal for implementing a postwar restoration process: he was an ardent Unionist, a Southerner and former slaveholder, and a Democrat. It soon became clear that Johnson desired a speedy restoration of the former Confederate states to Congress; limited, if any, rights for former slaves; and no radical changes to either the South or the Constitution—all ideas Bennett strongly advocated. Bennett contacted Johnson early in his administration to offer advice on domestic and foreign affairs, and it was clear that the two thought similarly and could each benefit from the other's position. Indeed, in an October 1865 letter to Bennett, President Johnson confided that "there is no man in America, who can exercise more power in fixing the Government upon a firm and enduring foundation than you can."

From there a partnership of sorts developed. Immediately after the war Bennett had briefly favored black suffrage, but recanted when he learned that Johnson opposed it. Bennett agreed with Johnson's veto of the 1866 Freedmen's Bureau Bill and the Civil Rights Bill and repeatedly defended the president in print. The *New York Herald* was the largest-circulation paper to openly back Johnson in his growing conflict with Congress. Bennett offered advice to President Johnson on how to stem the revolutionary tide in Congress, including using the federal patronage to destroy opponents and reward party allies. Bennett also argued for a new moderate party, one that could bring together conservative Republicans, War Democrats, and moderate Democrats from the South. In late 1866 this gave rise to the National Union Party, an attempt to elect Johnson supporters to Congress. The *Herald* enthusiastically backed the campaign, and its reporters produced glowing accounts of Johnson's Swing-around-the-Circle.

But early state elections showed that the Northern electorate preferred Congress's policies to Johnson's. Again sensing the swing of public opinion, Bennett shifted course and turned his back on Johnson, although the publisher never lost his dislike for blacks or Radical Republicans. Through 1867 Bennett and his paper lambasted both the Congress and the president, one for bringing about a revolution and the other for allowing it. Yet by the end of the year Bennett and his paper were again defending the president because Bennett believed impeachment to be a grave danger to the system of checks and balances necessary in a republic. Privately, in fact, Bennett shared with Johnson his belief that the removal of Secretary of War Edwin M. Stanton was completely legal. The *Herald* predicted Johnson's acquittal and happily mocked Republicans when the Senate failed to convict. Still, Bennett had no illusions about Johnson's political status and never saw him as a plausible candidate in 1868.

Even before Johnson left the White House, however, James Gordon Bennett, Sr., had already stepped down as publisher. With him went his superb editorial manager, Frederic Hudson. In 1867 Bennett's son, James Gordon Bennett, Jr., began assuming the day-to-day management of the *New York Herald* and by 1869 was fully directing it. James Sr., who *was* the *Herald* according to one contemporary, did not survive long outside his paper; he suffered an epileptic seizure in May 1872 and died on June 1. He was spared the pain of seeing his son, an energetic but ill-disciplined playboy, slowly destroy the empire that he had created.

Ambitious but inexperienced, James Jr. had lived most of his life in France with his sister, Jeanette, and his mother. The only living Bennett children (another son, Cosmo, had died at the age of five and a daughter had died in infancy), they had been taken to France at an early age to avoid the hostile environment that surrounded their father. James Jr. lived in Paris until he enlisted in the U.S. Navy during the Civil War. Not until 1866 did the younger Bennett even begin working at the *Herald,* and he was unprepared to fill his father's shoes.

The younger Bennett's love for the extravagant, the dramatic, and the expensive was well-known, and for a time it brought publicity for the *Herald* (it was James Jr. who hired Henry Stanley to find David Livingstone, for example, and he who built the Herald Building in New York, for which Herald Square is named). His associations with politicos were limited and largely unwanted; politicians saw him as erratic and unreliable, and he saw them as corrupt, lazy do-nothings. There is no evidence of any relationship between Andrew Johnson and James Jr., and even after the elder Bennett left the *Herald,* Johnson continued to correspond with him, rather than with his son.

In the end, James Jr.'s private and professional adventures, endless philanthropy, and lavish tastes drove the paper into debt, and a somewhat scandalous personal life forced him to move to France in the late 1870s. Absentee leadership, poor staff decisions, risky business gambles, and a declining reputation for news gathering left the *Herald* unable to compete with the rise of cheaper papers such as Joseph Pulitzer's *New York World* and William Randolph Hearst's *New York Sun.* James Gordon Bennett, Jr., died of heart disease in France on May 11, 1918. The *New York Herald* was sold off in 1920, the last independent edition appearing in January of that year. It was owned briefly by the *Sun* and then was finally absorbed by the *New York Tribune.*

See also: Black Suffrage; Blacks (Slave and Free), Johnson's Attitude toward; Civil Rights Act; Conservatives; Democratic Party; Election of 1866; Fourteenth Amendment; Freedmen's Bureau Bills (and Vetoes); Impeachment; Jackson, Andrew; Lincoln, Abraham; National Union Convention and Party; Patronage; Polk, James Knox; Swing-around-the-Circle; Vetoes; Whig Party.

References: Carlson, Oliver, *The Man Who Made News: James Gordon Bennett* (1942); Crouthamel, James L., *Bennett's* New York Herald *and the Rise of the Popular Press* (1989); Graf, LeRoy P., Haskins, Ralph W., and Bergeron, Paul H., eds., *The Papers of Andrew Johnson* vols. 9, 12, 13 (1967–2000); Hudson, Frederic, *Journalism in the United States from 1690 to 1872* (1873); Seitz, Don C., *The James Gordon Bennetts, Father and Son, Proprietors of the* New York Herald (1928).

Bingham, John Armor (1815–1900)

A native of Pennsylvania, John Armor Bingham was born in 1815 to a family of moderate means. His father, a carpenter, at first expected his son John to pursue an artisan's life and apprenticed him to a printer. When young Bingham showed unexpected intellectual potential, his family focused on school instead, which led to college and eventually the study of law.

Bingham moved to Cadiz, Ohio, in the late 1830s, passed the bar, and established a law practice. There he married a cousin, Amanda Bingham, and they eventually had three children. Bingham developed an interest in politics and, as an antislavery Whig, supported the William Henry Harrison ticket in 1840. Bingham's superb speaking skills earned him the attention of party notables, and he found his professional practice flourishing; by 1846 he had earned an appointment as district attorney.

By the 1850s Bingham, like most "conscience" Whigs, had evolved into a Republican. In 1854 Bingham won election as a Republican to the U.S. House of Representatives and, with a one-term exception, served consecutively until 1873 (he was defeated in the 1862 election). In 1864 President Lincoln appointed him judge advocate, and later that year, solicitor of claims.

Bingham attracted national attention in 1865 as the government's judge advocate at the trial of the Lincoln assassination conspirators. Bingham was a man of moderate views who refused to stretch constitutional limits, and some feared that he would oppose the military trial. But Bingham had won a treason case earlier in the war, and those who expected him to take a severe stand against the Confederacy and its supporters were not disappointed. He defended President Andrew Johnson's use of military proceedings, was relentless in his attack on the defendants, and played to popular opinion by associating the conspirators with the likes of Jefferson Davis.

Bingham's congressional career exhibited the same dynamic speaking ability but little of its radical fervor. During Reconstruction his presence in the House of Representatives served as a counterbalance to men like Thaddeus Stevens and Benjamin F. Butler, Radical Republicans who sought to punish the South and extend black rights as far as possible. Bingham was a member of the Joint Committee on Reconstruction, but opposed the 1866 Civil Rights Act for many of the same reasons that Andrew Johnson did. The following year, Bingham succeeded in weakening the First Military Reconstruction Act, so that Johnson's civil governments retained control of civil operations (except voting registration and legal cases involving blacks); only if officials defied congressional legislation could the army intervene.

Bingham is best remembered for his roles in the formation of the Fourteenth and Fifteenth Amendments. One of the principal authors of the Fourteenth Amendment, Bingham was personally responsible for the crucial due process and equal protection clauses, which comprised the very heart of the amendment and the federal government's power to enforce it. As for the Fifteenth Amendment, Bingham was one of the key figures to oppose, and help defeat, the office-holding clause, which intended that "the right to vote and hold office shall not be" discriminated against on racial grounds.

Although he would serve in Congress until 1873, Bingham's last hurrah came as one of the House's impeachment managers. His selection gave the group much-needed legitimacy because the radicalism of other members, such as Stevens, Butler, and John A. Logan, projected a prejudiced image. In fact, Bingham voted against impeachment in the fall of 1867 and initially opposed it in the winter of 1868 as well. Only after the Senate formally objected to the removal of Edwin M. Stanton and Johnson refused to reinstate him did Bingham vote to impeach. Bingham agreed that Johnson had defied Congress and possibly broken the law—issues that Bingham brought across forcefully in the closing

speech at Johnson's trial—but did not believe that Johnson deserved impeachment. Always wary of harming the delicate balance established by the U.S. Constitution, Bingham was not convinced that removing a president was an appropriate response to Johnson's obstructionism.

Like many Republicans who passed from Congress under Ulysses S. Grant's administration, John Bingham did not have his political career ended by defeat in the fall of 1872. In 1873 President Grant appointed Bingham minister to Japan, a post he held until 1885. Afterward he returned to Ohio and died at his home in Cadiz in 1900.

See also: Civil Rights Act; Congressional Reconstruction; Fifteenth Amendment; Fourteenth Amendment; Impeachment; Impeachment Managers; Joint Committee on Reconstruction; Lincoln Assassination Conspirators; Military Reconstruction Acts; Republican Party; Whig Party.

References: Anderson, Eric, and Moss, Alfred A., Jr., eds., *The Facts of Reconstruction: Essays in Honor of John Hope Franklin* (1991); Beauregard, Erving E., *Bingham of the Hills: Politician and Diplomat Extraordinary* (1989); Benedict, Michael Les, *A Compromise of Principle: Congressional Republicans and Reconstruction, 1863–1869* (1974); Roseboom, Eugene, *The Civil War Era, 1850–1873,* vol. 4 of Wittke, Carl, ed., *A History of the State of Ohio* 8 vols. (1941–1944).

Black Codes

Certainly one of the most significant achievements of the Civil War was the destruction of U.S. slavery. But the abolition of slavery resulted from wartime necessities, not preconceived plans, so the victorious North had no prepared response for dealing with millions of Southern blacks. In 1865 Congress created the Bureau of Refugees, Freedmen, and Abandoned Lands, a division of the War Department, to help blacks adjust to freedom by supervising labor and educational issues. With the exception of this understaffed and underfunded agency, the federal government made no attempt to assist in the social and economic revolution that it had created.

The lack of federal involvement, generated perhaps by the traditional view of a state's responsibility for its citizenry, opened the door for the former Confederate states to define the freedpeople's status. Borrowing from existing regulations developed by Federal army units during the war, and relying heavily on antebellum rules restricting slave activity, Southern states, in the summer and fall of 1865, created a series of Black Codes to regulate the lives and work of the freedpeople.

These statutes varied from state to state, but usually involved two topics: the granting of new rights and the imposition of restrictions. Many codes legalized black marriages and legitimized black families and allowed the freedpeople to sue and be sued, to testify in cases involving other blacks, and to receive an education. Most codes also made a point to define "negro" by some percentage of blood, often using one-eighth black blood as the distinction.

Controversy over the codes developed as a result of their restrictions. Intermarriage with whites was forbidden, as was the ownership of firearms (except perhaps for a small fowling piece). Some codes limited the distance blacks could travel or the amount of property they could own. Most important, all codes addressed the issue of labor. With their economy in shambles and their labor force in chaos, Southern states sought a way to restart agricultural production. Because many whites believed that blacks would not work unless compelled to do so, Black Codes were especially explicit in their discussion of labor. Most codes forbade blacks from performing any work other than farming; a license could be purchased for other occupations, but this required money and the authorization of a white official. Some states required blacks to work for former owners, stated specific work hours, and even forbade speaking while laboring. Any freedman not em-ployed fell victim to a state's vagrancy laws, under which the offender could end up being loaned out for work, assigned to public jobs, or in jail. Some codes were so severe that blacks who had been free during the antebellum period actually *lost* rights that they had previously enjoyed.

While many white Southerners, Andrew Johnson included, saw these codes as a natural reaction to the disruption of emancipation, Northerners saw them as an attempt to salvage the slave system. The codes, along with violence against Unionists and blacks and the election of former Confederates to Congress in late 1865, convinced many in Congress and across the North that former Confederates were neither chastened nor contrite.

As a result, Congress refused to seat Southern representatives in December 1865 and created the Joint Committee of Fifteen on Reconstruction. This began Congress's reaction to Johnson's lenient Reconstruction program and led directly to the passage of the Civil Rights Act and the Fourteenth Amendment, designed to outlaw the Black Codes and protect the rights and status of black Americans in the South.

See also: Blacks (Slave and Free), Johnson's Attitude toward; Civil Rights Act; Congressional Reconstruction; Conservatives; Fourteenth Amendment; Freedmen's Bureau Bills (and Vetoes); Governors, Provisional; Joint Committee on Reconstruction; Presidential Reconstruction; Readmission of Southern States; Thirteenth Amendment.

References: Carter, Dan. T., *When the War Was Over: The Failure of Self-Reconstruction in the South, 1865–1867* (1985); Foner, Eric, *Reconstruction: America's Unfinished Revolution, 1863–1877* (1988); McKitrick, Eric L., *Andrew Johnson and Reconstruction* (1960); Nieman, Donald G., *To Set the Law in Motion: The Freedmen's Bureau and the Legal Rights of Blacks, 1865–68* (1979); Wilson, Theodore B., *The Black Codes of the South* (1965).

Black, Jeremiah Sullivan
(1810–1883)

Born near Stony Creek, Pennsylvania, Jeremiah Sullivan Black, who was apparently a homely youth and subject to much harassment, developed the art of verbal self-defense when quite young and eagerly took on controversies. Restless and inquisitive, Black did a lot of studying on his own, in addition to attending several schools, before his father sent him to Somerset, Pennsylvania, to read law with Chauncey Forward when Jeremiah was seventeen. Forward had a tremendous impact on Black's life.

Black was admitted to the bar on December 3, 1830, and initially took charge of Forward's practice while the latter went to Congress. Black soon had a practice of his own and was appointed deputy attorney general for the county. He quickly became a noted lawyer and became, in fact, rather fixated on the law. He had no use for business and merely making money, and his interest in politics focused on the legal aspects of political issues.

In 1836 Black married Forward's oldest daughter, Mary, just before her seventeenth birthday. Between 1837 and 1852 they had five children. In May 1843, after a period of intense soul-searching provoked by the deaths in quick succession of his father and father-in-law, Black became an ardent member of the Campbellite denomination, also known as the Disciples of Christ.

From 1842 to 1851 Black served as president judge of the court of common pleas for Pennsylvania's sixteenth judicial district. This was followed by six years (1851–1857) on the Pennsylvania Supreme Court, the first three years as chief justice. When Pennsylvania Democrat James Buchanan, whom Black had actively supported politically for twenty years, was elected president, he chose Black to be his attorney general.

In this cabinet post he had to deal with the important issue of California land titles. After the United States acquired California in 1848 as part of the Treaty of Guadalupe Hidalgo, Congress decided that prior residents had to prove their Spanish and Mexican land titles. This was easier said than done, as the Hispanic records were widely scattered. Black sent Edwin M. Stanton to California to consolidate the archives and investigate various title disputes. Among other things, Stanton discovered widespread fraud, which resulted in the reversal of some land title confirmations.

Crucial to the future of the United States as a whole, however, was Black's other problem: how to enforce laws that were locally unpopular in either the South or the North. These issues included the slave trade, filibustering expeditions, and the return of fugitive slaves. From Black's perspective the law was the law and ought to be obeyed, but many other people did not share this view and observed the issues from a moral perspective. As a result, Black met little success enforcing such laws and these disputes became a part of the tensions that eventually contributed to the coming of the Civil War.

Black served Buchanan in political as well as legal ways. When Illinois Senator Stephen A. Douglas challenged Buchanan's administration and his own party by publishing an article on popular sovereignty in *Harper's Magazine* in September 1859, Buchanan chose Black to defend the administration's viewpoint, leading to an extensive pamphlet war between Douglas and Black. Black also considered the controversial Lecompton Constitution, passed by proslavery Kansans who hoped for statehood, to be legal.

As the Southern states threatened to secede after the election of Lincoln in the fall of 1860, Black stated that, although secession was illegal, the president could not "coerce" or force a seceding state back into the Union, but it was Buchanan's responsibility to enforce the laws and protect federal property. He urged Buchanan to more strongly garrison the Southern forts as a precaution, but Buchanan would not do so. Allegedly as a result of this unwillingness to act, Lewis Cass resigned as Buchanan's secretary of state and Black was appointed to the post on December 17, 1860.

Three days later South Carolina seceded from the Union. Black urged reinforcing Southern forts and mobilizing troops to protect Washington, D.C., as other states soon followed South Carolina out. But Buchanan took little action, finally sending the *Star of the West* on an unsuccessful mission to resupply Major Robert Anderson and his troops at Fort Sumter, but mainly relying on the outcome of a peace convention, which also failed. In February 1861, Buchanan, about to leave office, nominated Black to a seat on the Supreme Court, but the Senate refused to confirm the nomination.

When Black vacated his cabinet post on March 4, 1861, as Abraham Lincoln took office, Black was in poor health, had lost his savings as the result of bad investments by a relative who was handling his funds, had no office and, as a member of a defeated party, had no prospect of one, and was generally discouraged. However, the situation soon improved. In December 1861 Black was named Supreme Court reporter and, as such, assembled two volumes of accounts of Supreme Court cases. His law practice also grew dramatically. His familiarity with the California land claims brought him substantial fees for work on such cases. Although he supported the war effort, he opposed the Lincoln administration's "unconstitutional" lack of concern for civil rights. At the conclusion of the war, he served on the defense teams of noted Confederates Jefferson Davis and Clement C. Clay, but neither case ever came to trial.

More importantly, during the Reconstruction era, Black headed the team of defense lawyers in two key Supreme Court cases. *Ex parte Milligan* concerned the question of whether a civilian could be tried and convicted by a military commission in a state (Indiana), which was not a battleground and where the civil courts were in operation (the Court ruled that a civilian could not be so tried). *Ex parte McCardle* was a similar case involving the military commission trial of a Vicksburg, Mississippi, newspaper editor for printing "libelous and incendiary articles." A major difference in the cases was that Mississippi was subject to a certain amount of military oversight under the Reconstruction laws, and seeing a threat to its legislation, Congress removed jurisdiction in the case from the Supreme Court. Black's arguments in these two cases are often considered to be the greatest of his career.

Meanwhile, Black also became an advisor to President Andrew Johnson on a variety of matters. Black recommended several persons for office, but his more important advice came on legal matters such as how to remove the commissioner of internal revenue without violating the Tenure of Office Act. He also played a major role in writing Johnson's vetoes of the First and Second Military Reconstruction Acts as well as Johnson's Third Annual Message. Some people recognized Black's style and summoned him to testify before the House Judiciary Committee on his role in writing or at least providing ideas for the first veto message, as the committee looked for a reason to impeach Johnson.

While Black was briefly secretary of state at the end of Buchanan's presidency, he had encountered the case of Abraham D. Patterson and Prudencio de Murguiondo and their claim to the guano island of Alta Vela in the Caribbean near Santo Domingo. Once out of office, Black became attorney for the men in their attempt to regain their property. He wrote numerous letters to Johnson explaining the situation, lambasting Secretary of State William H. Seward for neglecting to do anything about the claim and urging Johnson to take action for his clients. Johnson's failure to do so caused

Black to resign as one of Johnson's defense attorneys for his impeachment trial. Some advisors had urged Johnson not to employ Black anyway as a result of his lack of discretion in what he might say when in the heat of controversy.

In May of 1869 Black had his right arm seriously crushed in a railroad accident. He refused to have an amputation. Although the arm did heal, he was never able to use it again, but he learned to write with his left hand and was always thereafter attended by a valet to take care of things that he could not manage one-armed. He continued to practice law and write legal briefs and controversial articles.

Black was a rather colorful character, inclined to be absent-minded about ordinary affairs of life while totally engrossed in his current project. He dressed carelessly and was notoriously eccentric. In later years when his bushy eyebrows turned white, he continued to wear an ill-fitting reddish-brown wig. He also perpetually fidgeted with his silver tobacco box (he chewed tobacco). Black died at his home, "Brockie," near York, Pennsylvania, on August 19, 1883, of acute urinary complications caused by an enlarged prostate gland.

See also: Alta Vela; Annual Messages; Impeachment; *McCardle, Ex parte;* Military Reconstruction Acts; *Milligan, Ex parte;* Seward, William Henry; Stanton, Edwin McMasters; Vetoes.

References: Brigance, William Norwood, *Jeremiah Sullivan Black: A Defender of the Constitution and the Ten Commandments* (1934); Graf, LeRoy P., Haskins, Ralph W., and Bergeron, Paul H., eds., *The Papers of Andrew Johnson* vols. 3, 8, 12–15 (1967–2000); Skaggs, Jimmy M., *The Great Guano Rush: Entrepreneurs and American Overseas Expansion* (1994); Trefousse, Hans L., *Andrew Johnson: A Biography* (1989).

Black Suffrage

In an era marked by phenomenal changes, perhaps no development was as astounding as extension of voting privileges to black men. In the ten years from 1860 to 1870 the idea of blacks voting went from being an abolitionist's dream, opposed by both Southerners and Northerners, to being part of the U.S. Constitution.

It was not unknown for black Americans to vote in the United States; five New England states allowed black suffrage before the Civil War. Still, only a handful of abolitionists advocated black suffrage on a national level, and their calls fell on racist ears. White Americans could not conceive of what they believed to be an inferior race participating in, and even controlling, the political system. Even many who supported emancipation could not bear to elevate blacks to an equal level with whites.

Just as the war convinced many people of the need for emancipation, the looming crisis of Reconstruction forced many to consider extending voting rights to blacks. By late 1863, when the tide had turned in the Union's favor, men such as Charles Sumner, Thaddeus Stevens, and Salmon P. Chase were privately espousing black suffrage, believing it was not only morally right but also practical. It seemed unlikely that any real change would occur in the South unless the electorate was significantly modified.

The Republican Party's leader, President Abraham Lincoln, largely avoided the controversial subject. His Ten Percent Plan for Reconstruction made no provision for black voting. In Louisiana, which underwent Lincoln's Reconstruction program, the president suggested that the state constitution extend suffrage to educated blacks and black Union army veterans, but the 1864 constitution restricted the vote to those eligible to vote in 1860. By now many Republicans were looking for at least impartial suffrage in the South (voting with equally restrictive qualifications for all races), although few espoused universal suffrage (total adult male voting with no restrictions). Largely for this reason Congress, dominated by Republicans, refused to accept the state's 1864 electoral vote and the Senate refused to seat its senators.

Yet although the Republicans were ready to slap down former Confederates who would not embrace some form of black suffrage, they themselves were still wary of its dangers. For instance, Congress's Reconstruction agenda embodied in the Wade-Davis Bill restricted voting to whites, and an attempt by Charles Sumner and others to strike out the word white failed. In early 1865 several Republicans floated another Reconstruction measure, one which would enfranchise Southern black males, but it never passed Congress. Events across the North that same year drove the point home: constitutional amendments granting black males the right to vote failed in Minnesota, Wisconsin, and Connecticut, states with tiny black populations.

The more radical Republicans, those favoring black suffrage, noticed an encouraging sign. The failure of these amendments was not by as large a margin as many had predicted. Other events were also transpiring to sway public and political opinion. With the advent of the Thirteenth Amendment, concern grew over representation in Congress. Formerly slaves were counted as three-fifths of a person for the apportioning of congressional seats; with slavery abolished, blacks would be counted as whole people, so the South stood to gain seats in Congress despite losing the war. Also, after the death of Abraham Lincoln in April 1865, Radicals such as Sumner felt encouraged as the new president, Andrew Johnson, seemed more intent on punishing the South and eliminating the old leadership. In meetings with Sumner and Benjamin Wade, President Johnson spoke of his desire that Southern states enfranchise some blacks, although he wanted it to occur by state, and not federal, instigation.

Many Republicans felt betrayed by Johnson's May 29, 1865, proclamation for the restoration of North Carolina. The president's directive did not provide for black suffrage, but instead kept voting in the hands of the same prewar electorate.

Conservative Republicans and Democrats wrote to Johnson to voice their approval, agreeing with the executive's argument that only states could alter suffrage. In fact, in August Johnson even wrote to William L. Sharkey, the man appointed provisional governor of Mississippi by Johnson, suggesting that the state grant voting rights to blacks who could read the Constitution and write their names or owned real estate worth more than $250. Johnson believed that this would "completely disarm the adversary and set an example the other States will follow." Such provisions would place the South on the "same basis with Free States . . . the Radicals, who are wild upon negro franchise, will be completely foiled. . . ." As a result, Johnson posited, the Southern states would be readmitted.

Johnson expanded on his views in an October interview. He remained convinced that the initiative had to come from the Southern states themselves, for "our only safety lies in allowing each State to control the right of voting by its own laws." If the federal government stepped in to expand suffrage, it could also restrict it, which might lead to despotism. Speaking of Tennessee, Johnson admitted that he would like to enfranchise blacks gradually, beginning with Union veterans, the educated, and property owners. But the granting of universal suffrage immediately would "breed a war of races." He reiterated these ideas in his First Annual Message in December, even claiming that blacks would get the vote faster and be better treated by "those on whom they [Southern blacks] have heretofore most closely depended."

The naiveté of this remark was already clear by the time Johnson delivered the address. Under Johnson's Reconstruction program, not a single state offered to enfranchise blacks. Even worse, blacks were discriminated against in the courts and the workplace, and state laws, called Black Codes, reduced the freedpeople to a status of near slavery. Violence against blacks in the South was rampant, and neither the army nor the Freedmen's Bureau could protect them. Former Confederates were voting and holding office, whereas former slaves and black Union soldiers were not even second-class citizens.

Because neither the president nor Southern leaders seemed to be looking out for the rights of blacks, Congress stepped up to the task. Immediately upon convening in December 1865, some Radicals in Congress began moving toward enfranchising Southern blacks; everyone understood that Northerners were not yet ready to accept black suffrage, but might support it as a penalty imposed upon the South. No blanket measure to enfranchise Southern blacks emerged, but a compromise did: the Fourteenth Amendment, which acted as a carrot-and-stick to entice Southern states into granting blacks the right to vote. More Republicans were moving into the Radical ranks, and interest in expanding the franchise was growing.

Because of Johnson's obstinacy and the former Confederates' hostility, Republicans were coming to see the ballot as the key to protecting Southern blacks, or rather, a means of allowing them to protect themselves. Johnson, wedded to state's rights and a narrow definition of the Constitution, could not abide by this. Despite warnings that rejection of the Fourteenth Amendment might force Congress to impose suffrage, Johnson advised the former Confederate states to reject the amendment, and all but Tennessee did.

Republican victories in the 1866 fall elections demonstrated that the Northern electorate was not satisfied with the president's Reconstruction policy. By January 1867 Republicans in Congress had won several peripheral victories over Johnson vetoes, including enfranchising blacks in the District of Columbia and requiring universal suffrage for the admission of Nebraska and Colorado.

By the spring of 1867 a Republican consensus had emerged on the need to impose black suffrage on the South itself. The failure of compromise, the refusal of Southern states to make even limited gestures toward enfranchising blacks, and the continued violence against freedpeople in the South drove some Republicans to seek a more drastic method of protecting blacks. Other members of Congress believed that by their heroic efforts in the war black males had earned the right to participate in the government that they helped preserve. Certainly some Republicans were motivated by party self-interest and the desire to create a Southern wing composed of Southern Unionists and former slaves.

Regardless of the reasons, Republicans were convinced that a fundamental shift in power in the South was necessary, possible, and just. The Military Reconstruction Acts of March 1867 imposed black suffrage on the former Confederate states, and the U.S. Army and U.S. Congress made sure that new Southern constitutions opened voting to both races permanently. But blacks voting the Republican ticket in formerly rebel states was not the same as blacks voting in the North; state elections in the fall in California, New York, New Jersey, and Ohio resulted in Democratic victories when Republicans endorsed black suffrage for their own states. Still, Radical Republicans fully understood the double standard that they had set. President Johnson, taking advantage of Northern anxiety, addressed the issue directly in his 1867 Annual Message, warning that granting voting rights to people "utterly ignorant of public affairs" was "worse than madness" during this time of confusion.

But the Republican Party was now committed to black suffrage, although its leaders were still wise enough to downplay the issue when necessary. In the election of 1868, for example, the Republican platform carefully avoided discussing extending black voting into the North. Oddly enough, the ever-ambitious Salmon P. Chase considered running as a Democrat if he could convince the party to embrace universal suffrage. The election over, Republicans now controlled both the executive branch, in the person of Ulysses S. Grant, and the legislative. But a threat was coming from the judiciary, for the Supreme Court was hearing *Ex parte McCardle,* a case that could overturn the Military Reconstruction Acts.

Congress solved the problem in two ways. First, it removed the case from the court's jurisdiction by a fancy bit of legislative maneuvering. Then, Republicans decided to end their hypocrisy and remove the threat posed by any future court at the same time. The solution was a constitutional amendment eliminating racial discrimination in voting, which required approval by the state legislatures, but not the public. The Fifteenth Amendment, which prohibited racial discrimination at the polls, was ratified in 1870. The amendment applied to all states within the Union; four Southern states were still in limbo (Texas, Virginia, Mississippi, and Georgia) but were soon restored after accepting the Fifteenth Amendment and agreeing to never change their constitutions to deprive any newly enfranchised group of the ballot.

Unfortunately the issue of black suffrage did not end with the passage of the Fifteenth Amendment. Even before its ratification, white paramilitary groups had arisen in the South to deprive blacks of their right to vote. Organizations such as the Ku Klux Klan and the Knights of the White Camelia used violence, intimidation, and blackmail to keep blacks away from the polls. In 1870 and 1871 Congress passed three Enforcement Acts designed to punish voting interference, and the army and Department of Justice attempted to arrest and incarcerate violators. By the late 1870s the former Confederate states had been "redeemed," that is, returned to native white political control, and the next few decades saw a steady erosion of black voting rights. Fraud and violence declined, for with state judiciaries and legislatures in white hands, lawmakers turned to loopholes in the Fifteenth Amendment to legally disfranchise most blacks through literacy tests, property requirements, and poll taxes. Not until the 1950s and 1960s brought a new era of federal activism would the promise of black suffrage again become a reality.

See also: Annual Messages; Bingham, John Armor; Blacks (Slave and Free), Johnson's Attitude toward; Chase, Salmon Portland; Colorado (Admission to Statehood); Congressional Reconstruction; Constitution, Johnson's Attitude toward; Democratic Party; District of Columbia Franchise; Douglass, Frederick; Elections of 1867; Election of 1868; Fifteenth Amendment; Fourteenth Amendment; Grant, Ulysses Simpson; *McCardle, Ex parte;* Military Reconstruction Acts; Nebraska (Admission to Statehood); Presidential Reconstruction; Readmission of Southern States; Republican Party; Stevens, Thaddeus; Sumner, Charles.

References: Donald, David Herbert, *Charles Sumner and the Rights of Man* (1970); Foner, Eric, *Reconstruction: America's Unfinished Revolution, 1863–1877* (1988); Graf, LeRoy P., Haskins, Ralph W., and Bergeron, Paul H., eds., *The Papers of Andrew Johnson* vols. 8, 9, 13 (1967–2000); Trefousse, Hans L., *The Radical Republicans: Lincoln's Vanguard for Racial Justice* (1969).

Black Troops in the South

With the surrender of the Confederate armies in the spring of 1865, the U.S. government immediately began mustering out Union regiments. Soldiers were still needed in the South, largely to keep the peace and assist the Freedmen's Bureau. But terms of enlistment were due to expire, and many Americans, including President Andrew Johnson, opposed keeping an expensive force in the field.

President Johnson and the War Department faced a dilemma because most of the enlistments due to expire were for white troops, whereas black soldiers, recruited later in the war, still had their terms to serve. This, in combination with pressure from Northerners who wanted to see their loved ones return, meant that demobilization largely affected white soldiers. At the war's end, blacks comprised eleven percent of the army, but by the fall of 1865 they made up nearly forty percent. A few white regiments did remain in the South, but others that remained active were sent out West, where their experience was needed. As a result, black soldiers, units from the U.S. Colored Troops (USCT), made up the bulk of the troops occupying the South, and the percentage grew through the fall of 1865 and in the spring of 1866.

There were advantages to using black soldiers in the South. Some Republicans hoped that the USCT would exercise a positive influence over freedpeople, showing the need for work and discipline. Officials and abolitionists believed that the army helped those soldiers who were former slaves because they were paid, fed, clothed, and housed at government expense (many units, however, were made up of free blacks from the North, who wanted to return home). Because the Freedmen's Bureau was designed to help former slaves adjust to freedom, it also made sense to have black soldiers assisting that agency. Black soldiers also built schools and churches, enforced the law (always under the guidance of white officers), and even labored at battlefields reinterring the dead.

Many conservatives and Southerners believed that black troops were part of a deliberate policy to humiliate the defeated Confederates. Although there is no evidence of such a plot, the policy of keeping the USCT in the South heightened tensions, caused problems with the freedpeople, and resulted in violence.

Many white Southerners, already suffering the loss of their slaves and their would-be nation, now faced black soldiers who refused to act like inferiors. Whites claimed that black troops intimidated white women,

attacked former Confederates, and encouraged former slaves to refuse to work. Some Southern officials asked President Johnson for permission to create local militia units, claiming that black soldiers were committing "depredations." Blacks were involved in many skirmishes and brawls, but evidence indicates that most incidents were started by whites. Even some of the worst riots, those in Memphis and New Orleans in 1866, were partly the result of tensions between local whites and black soldiers.

In every Southern state, black soldiers outnumbered white soldiers, and the percentage grew as the months wore on. In Mississippi, for instance, eleven of twelve infantry regiments were black in December 1865, and of the 14,000 soldiers in South Carolina, nearly 12,000 were black. Twelve of thirteen regiments in Tennessee were black, and less than a third of the 20,000 soldiers stationed in Texas and Louisiana were white. Other states had similar proportions.

It was no surprise that in 1865 and 1866 Southern officials and private citizens bombarded President Johnson with requests calling for the removal of USCT units. In June of 1865 North Carolina governor William Holden told Johnson that blacks were insulting and assaulting whites and that their presence hindered "reconciliation." Holden asked Johnson that, if troops had to be stationed in towns, only white soldiers be used. Governor William L. Sharkey of Mississippi wrote to Johnson in August of 1865 to ask if white militia units could replace the USCT, but Johnson replied that arming former Confederates would only increase tensions. Letters complaining of black "outrages" poured into Johnson's office from the mayor of New Orleans; the commissioners of New Bern, North Carolina; municipal officials from Wilmington, North Carolina; the governor of South Carolina; and even Johnson's recent ally, William G. Brownlow of East Tennessee. Most of the communications were the same, claiming that blacks were troublesome, ill-disciplined, and had a bad influence on local freedpeople. In many cases white army officers wrote to Johnson defending their men, explaining that altercations were begun by local whites or that soldiers charged with harassing citizens were in fact executing orders and performing duties. Most information was exaggerated or fabricated, such as the report that Johnson's Greeneville home was being used as a "brothel" by black troops or the account of black soldiers attacking a train (they stopped the train to seize confiscated cotton). Still, even petitioners who admitted the need for U.S. Army protection requested that white troops be used instead.

White troops were not available, so even Andrew Johnson, no supporter of black soldiers, was forced to deny many requests. On August 25, 1865, Johnson himself explained to Governor Sharkey that the government "does not intend to irritate or humiliate the People of the South" and will remove USCT units "at the earliest period it is practicable to do so." An October 1865 plea from Kentucky was met with the same response, but it was April 1866 before all black units in the state were removed. Because Johnson knew that the presence of black troops would cause tension among the defeated whites, he allowed the War Department to shift black units away from large towns into garrison forts and posts, so that constant contact could be avoided. Soldiers still performed patrols and duties as needed, but resided away from other blacks and whites. In some states black troops were not even allowed to purchase their arms upon discharge, a courtesy extended to whites; again, the War Department sought to avoid possible conflict. By late winter 1866 General Ulysses S. Grant ordered the removal of most black units from the interior of the Southern states to the borders or western frontier, but as late as the fall some USCT regiments were still on occupation duty in South Carolina and Texas.

Despite contemporary sentiment and generations of historian's biased accounts, there was no deliberate attempt to punish the South by using black troops. It may have been a poorly conceived policy, but it served as a temporary expedient when nothing else was possible. That President Johnson, a racist Southerner who opposed enlisting blacks, upheld the policy speaks to its necessity. In a speech to the 1st Regiment, USCT, in October 1865, Johnson revealed his prejudices when he warned soldiers to avoid "licentiousness" and stressed the importance of "controlling your passions." He reiterated that after their discharge black men needed to avoid laziness, be industrious, and lead virtuous lives. But the president also thanked the troops, admitting that they had "served with patience and indurance [sic] in the cause of your country;" there is every indication that they did the same in the first two years of Reconstruction.

See also: Blacks (Slave and Free), Johnson's Attitude toward ; Brownlow, William Gannaway "Parson"; Governors, Provisional; Grant, Ulysses Simpson; Greeneville, Tennessee; Memphis Riot; New Orleans Riot; Presidential Reconstruction.

References: Berlin, Ira, Reidy, Joseph P., and Rowland, Leslie S., eds., *Freedom's Soldiers: The Black Military Experience in the Civil War* (1998); Glatthaar, Joseph T., *Forged in Battle: The Civil War Alliance of Black Soldiers and White Officers* (1990); Graf, LeRoy P., Haskins, Ralph W., and Bergeron, Paul H., eds., *The Papers of Andrew Johnson* vols. 8–10 (1967–2000); Pollard, Edward A., *The Lost Cause: A New Southern History of the War of the Confederates* (1866); Sefton, James E., *The United States Army and Reconstruction, 1865–1877* (1967); Trudeau, Noah Andre, *Like Men of War: Black Troops in the Civil War, 1862–1865* (1998); Zalimas, Robert J., Jr., "Black Union Soldiers in the Postwar South, 1865–1866" (M.A. Thesis: Arizona State University, 1993).

Blacks (Slave and Free), Johnson's Attitude toward

As a nineteenth century Southerner and slaveholder, Andrew Johnson had many of the prejudices and attitudes typical of his social group. His distrust of, and sometimes indifference toward, blacks as a race was exacerbated by his belief in self-reliance and a limited government. Yet by their own admission his slaves were well treated, and he had good personal and professional relationships with blacks close to him.

Born poor and forced into an apprenticeship that he eventually abandoned, Johnson might logically have sympathized with slaves. But in January 1844, in one of his first speeches in Congress, Johnson used the Constitution to defend slavery (arguing that slaves were private property) and later warned that abolition of slavery would lead to race war. Even early in the Civil War, whether he was speaking against secession or in favor of the ill-fated "unamendable amendment," Johnson supported slavery and denied the right of the federal government to interfere with it. The outbreak of war forced Johnson to choose between slavery and Union, and he chose the Union. While Johnson was military governor of Tennessee, his attitudes evolved further, and he came to believe that slavery threatened the existence of the Union. By 1863 he turned against slavery and slaveholders with a vengeance and worked to destroy both. In October of 1864 Johnson proclaimed freedom to all slaves in Tennessee.

Although Johnson's perception of slavery as an institution changed, his attitude toward blacks did not. He delayed using blacks as soldiers—even though Abraham Lincoln implored him to use them—and allowed them to be impressed for labor by military and city officials. Johnson even suggested that freedpeople should work for their previous masters. He opposed giving freed blacks confiscated land and building them schools, and he proposed laws prohibiting vagrancy and large black assemblies. Johnson also opposed concentrating black housing. He wanted blacks to live scattered among whites, for he believed that they were good "imitators" and that "the influence of the whites upon them is beneficial." In a Nashville speech on January 21, 1864, Johnson admitted that, although he would "not argue that the Negro race is the equal to the Anglo-Saxon—not at all," he believed that as a people they could become productive and self-sustaining. Beyond that, Johnson offered no assistance to former slaves, a preview of his stance as president: blacks would get no special help, no government protection, no land, and no voting or office-holding rights. The war changed Johnson's view of slavery, but his racism, constitutional conservatism, and devotion to whites-only democracy remained intact.

These traits received national attention and had a national impact once Johnson arrived in Washington. Allegedly the black abolitionist Frederick Douglass, when he spotted Johnson at Lincoln's 1865 inauguration, remarked: "Whatever Andrew Johnson may be, he certainly is no friend of our race." Once Johnson became president some leading Republicans, including Charles Sumner, thought that Johnson might support black rights, and even black suffrage. Soon it became clear that Johnson could not conceive of blacks on an equal footing with whites. His creation of provisional governments run by former Confederates and his indifference toward Black Codes demonstrated this. Speaking to black soldiers in October 1865, President Johnson warned them against "licentiousness" and impressed upon them that "liberty" meant work and obedience to civil and moral law. Johnson was merely reflecting the racist views of millions of white Americans, that blacks would not work without coercion, that they could not understand the laws of marriage, and that, now free, they would slip into barbarity.

Some whites, including abolitionists and early Radical Republicans, believed differently. They sensed an equality that others did not and would argue for civil rights and even black suffrage. But, North and South, the belief in white supremacy was pervasive, and historians forget that many Northern states defeated attempts to enfranchise blacks. Yet even Northerners who had no interest in black rights felt ashamed and angered by the Black Codes and the stories of antiblack violence in the South. But Johnson would claim that the future status of the freedpeople was not an issue of racism, but an issue of constitutionality. The destruction of slavery was necessary to defeat the Confederacy and preserve the Union. If the preservation of the Union was paramount, why now try to disrupt it further by altering time-honored procedures? Blacks were the "mudsill," the lowest echelon in society, and, free or not, should remain so. For instance, Johnson's lenient pardon policy toward former Confederates also allowed them to reclaim their confiscated property, thus forcing freedpeople to be laborers, not landholders. The vast majority of Southern land remained in white hands, and, without capital to buy land, freedpeople returned to their traditional role of farm laborer. As for rights and privileges, these had always been the jurisdiction of the states, so the federal government should not intervene. If blacks were to be admitted to the system of white democracy, the individual states must do it.

One particular incident demonstrated both Johnson's racism and his narrow constitutional views. On February 7, 1866, a delegation of leading blacks, among them Frederick Douglass, met with Johnson to discuss the possibility of black suffrage. Johnson was irritated through the whole session, angered that black men dared question his approach. Although Johnson said he was "a friend of the colored man," he admitted that he would not support black suffrage, al-

though he also hinted that states could extend the franchise if they desired. Afterward, according to the *New York World*, Johnson said, "Those D——d sons of b——es thought they had me in a trap! I know that d——d Douglass; he's just like any nigger, and he would sooner cut a white man's throat as not." Although much has been made of this quote, its source is dubious at best, and even if true, it depicts an outburst made in the heat of frustration and anger.

Johnson's racism, mixed with his unwillingness to extend any federal assistance to freedpeople, resulted in several vetoes, in particular those of the two Freedmen's Bureau Bills, the Civil Rights Bill, and the District of Columbia franchise bill. A similar sentiment was partly responsible for his opposition to the Fourteenth Amendment and, to a lesser degree, the Military Reconstruction Acts. Tales of atrocities against blacks, and even the Memphis and New Orleans riots, could not shake the president from his policy. Johnson's resistance to granting freedpeople even minimal civil rights drove moderate and Radical Republicans together and doomed Johnson.

Yet in his personal life, his racism and distrust gave way to a trust and affability that seemed out of character. Johnson admitted that he bought slaves, but claimed never to have sold one (a statement challenged by at least one historian). Yet his slaves described their relationship with him as one of benevolent paternalism; apparently Johnson made sure that they never wanted for material goods, and he showed the children of his slaves affection and humor. When freedom came, all the Johnson slaves chose to stay with the Johnson family, and some even accompanied Johnson to Washington. Johnson had other black servants while president, such as steward James L. Thomas, to whom Johnson entrusted large sums of money to handle grocery and supply accounts for the White House. After Johnson left the presidency, Thomas wrote expressing his gratitude for Johnson's kindness, claimed he had "never been treated better by any person," and hoped he might serve Johnson in the future.

Ironically, the last extant Johnson letter, dated July 26, 1875, deals with family and former slaves rather than politics. Johnson alerted his daughter Mary that he was coming to visit. The aged patriarch was bringing former-slave-turned-servant William, who wanted to see "Liz and the children," other former Johnson slaves. Johnson made it clear in the letter that he could not disappoint William.

See also: Black Codes; Black Suffrage; Black Troops in the South; Civil Rights Act; Congressional Reconstruction; Conservatives; Constitution, Johnson's Attitude toward; District of Columbia Franchise; Douglass, Frederick; Fourteenth Amendment; Freedmen's Bureau Bills (and Vetoes); Memphis Riot; Military Governor of Tennessee, Johnson as; Military Reconstruction Acts; "Moses of the Colored Men" Speech; New Orleans Riot; Presidential Reconstruction; Republican Party; Slaves, Owned by Johnson.

References: Bowen, David Warren, *Andrew Johnson and the Negro* (1989); Castel, Albert E., *The Presidency of Andrew Johnson* (1979); Graf, LeRoy P., Haskins, Ralph W., and Bergeron, Paul H., eds., *The Papers of Andrew Johnson* vols. 1, 3, 4, 6, 16 (1967–2000); Trefousse, Hans L., *Andrew Johnson: A Biography* (1989); Trefousse, Hans L., *Impeachment of a President: Andrew Johnson, the Blacks, and Reconstruction* (1975).

Blair, Francis Preston, Jr. (1821–1875)

Blair, Francis Preston, Sr. (1791–1876)

Blair, Montgomery (1813–1883)

*T*he prominent political Blair family served as advisors to three presidents, and its experiences and contributions exemplified the chaotic and fluid nature of nineteenth century U.S. politics.

Francis Preston Blair, Sr. (1791–1876), the patriarch of the family, was born in Abingdon, Virginia, but moved to Kentucky while still a youth. He graduated from Transylvania University in Lexington, read law, and passed the bar in 1817. In 1812, while in school, he met and married Violet Gist, with whom he had at least five children: Montgomery (1813–1883), Juliet (b. 1816), Elizabeth (b. 1818), James (b. 1819), and Francis Jr. (1821–1875).

Unpopular as a lawyer (perhaps due to a speech defect), Francis Sr. soon found his niche as a banker and journalist during the financial Panic of 1817. His involvement with the Relief Party served as a segue into politics, where he first supported Kentuckian Henry Clay before shifting to Democrat Andrew Jackson in the mid-1820s. In fact, Jackson believed that Blair's editorials and pamphlets were so influential in the 1828 campaign that the new president asked Blair to move to Washington, D.C., to start an administration newspaper. Blair complied, and in 1830 the *Washington Globe* appeared, which served as the administration's voice for both of Jackson's terms and that of Martin Van Buren. Although the *Globe* was no longer an administration paper after 1840, Blair continued to edit it until forced out by President James K. Polk in 1845.

Blair also served as a member of Jackson's "kitchen cabinet," a pun that referred to the unofficial coterie of advisors upon which Jackson often relied. Blair helped establish the *Congressional Globe* (now the *Congressional Record*), a written record of the proceedings and debates in Congress. While in Washington, Blair built an estate in Maryland named "Silver Spring," the origin of the current suburb.

As with the nation as a whole, by the late 1840s Blair became preoccupied with the expansion of slavery and drifted away from the Democratic Party as a result. Nominally a Whig but courted by leading Democrats in the early 1850s, Blair led many Westerners in a bolt toward the new Republican Party after the Kansas-Nebraska Act of 1854. Blair presided over the party's first national convention (1856) and, after some hesitancy, threw his strength behind the party's 1860 presidential nominee, Abraham Lincoln. As Blair was experienced and influential, especially among the border states, Lincoln often relied on him for advice; the ill-fated Hampton Roads peace talks of 1865 originated, in part, with Francis P. Blair, Sr.

Francis Sr. was not the only Blair dispensing advice to President Lincoln. The family's connections and regional importance made it politically valuable, thus it was no surprise when Lincoln appointed Blair's eldest son Montgomery postmaster general in 1861. Montgomery (1813–1883), a native Kentuckian, had graduated from West Point in 1835 and served briefly in the Seminole War before resigning. He studied law at Transylvania University and moved to St. Louis, Missouri, in 1837 to open a law practice. As a Democrat he held a variety of local offices, including judge and mayor, but made no attempt to hide his Free Soil ideals. While living in St. Louis, Blair lost his first wife Carolina Bruckner (d.1844) and married Mary Elizabeth Woodbury in 1847. They moved to Washington, D.C., in 1853, where Blair became the first U.S. Solicitor in the Court of Claims (1855–1857).

One of Montgomery Blair's last appearances before the Supreme Court came as defense counsel in the unsuccessful Dred Scott case. As with his father, his views on slavery led him into the Republican camp, and the Blairs became a dominant force in the Republican Party. Lincoln's selection of him as postmaster general was politically shrewd: Blair being a Democrat-turned-Republican with connections to three of the so-called border states (slave states that remained in the Union), the advantages of tying the family to the administration were obvious. Recognizing the importance of mail services during war, Montgomery Blair demanded efficiency and creativity; money orders, free rural delivery, prepaid postage, and the introduction of mail sorting on trains can all be traced to Blair. Just as politics earned Blair his appointment, political needs cut short his tenure; pressed by Radicals to include less conservative persons in his cabinet, Lincoln asked for and received Blair's resignation in 1864.

Despite his position and seniority, Montgomery Blair lived in the shadow of his younger sibling, Francis Jr. (1821–1875), usually called Frank. Seemingly destined for great things, Frank Blair had intelligence, flair, a handsome appearance, and a love of adventure, characteristics scattered among other family members. His parents doted upon him as their favorite child and spared no expense in advancing his career.

Born in Kentucky, Frank spent his early youth with his father in Washington, D.C. He attended Princeton and then followed the family tradition by studying law at Transylvania University. Admitted to the bar in Lexington in 1842, he left a year later for St. Louis, where his older brother already had a law practice. Blair fought in the Mexican-American War (he enlisted as a private), married Appoline Alexander in 1847 (with whom he had at least eight children), and was appointed attorney general for the New Mexico Territory. With now-entrenched views on the extension of slavery, he returned to his wife and law practice in St. Louis. He became the most outspoken Free Soiler in Missouri, and by the early 1850s was advocating an emancipation-colonization program. His popularity took him to the state legislature (1852–1856). Along with his father and brother, Blair helped create the Missouri Republican Party and represented that state in the U.S. House of Representatives during 1857–1859, June 1860, 1861–1862, and March 1863–June 1864 (the irregularities are due to contested elections).

During the secession crisis, the Blairs

played a crucial role keeping Missouri in the Union, and Francis Jr., the most charismatic and energetic of the Blair men, led the crusade opposing secession. He served in the Union army; he resigned from Congress in 1862, raised and paid for his own regiment, and in between congressional terms participated in the Vicksburg, Chattanooga, Atlanta, and Carolina campaigns.

At war's end, the Blairs were leading Republicans and Lincoln confidants. But victory brought to the fore the differences between the Blair family and other Republicans. The Blairs sought to preserve the Union and prevent the expansion of slavery, but had no intention of punishing Southerners, enfranchising freedmen, or offering equal rights to blacks. With the emergence of the Radical Republicans in Congress, the goals of the Blairs and at least some Republicans began to diverge.

Another change that came in 1865 was the accession to the presidency of Andrew Johnson. The Blairs and Johnson were well acquainted. Francis Jr. had been in Congress when Johnson was in the Senate. When Johnson was military governor of Tennessee, he had interacted with both Postmaster Montgomery Blair and General Francis P. Blair, Jr. In fact, after the inebriated Vice President Johnson spoke before the Senate on March 4, 1865, he fled Washington for the more sympathetic environs of "Silver Spring," where he recuperated and hid from the press. A month later, when Johnson took the executive oath of office at the Kirkwood House hotel, Francis Sr. and Montgomery were witnesses.

The Blairs and Johnson were kindred spirits, conservatives caught up in a revolution. Like Johnson, the Blairs believed a swift, conciliatory policy of Reconstruction was best, one that altered as little as possible the prewar relationship between the states and the federal government. Neither the Blairs nor Johnson wanted the federal government to become a welfare agent or to assume the responsibility for suffrage requirements, items traditionally left to the states. Moreover, Johnson and the Blairs agreed that sectional harmony could best be attained via a new national party, one comprised of Democrats and conservative Republicans. As a result, the Blairs soon became confidants of yet another president, offering advice on everything from patronage matters to legislation. In the summer of 1865 the Blairs took an active role in promoting Johnson's Presidential Reconstruction program. Francis Jr. toured the North and Midwest, speaking on behalf of Johnson's conciliatory policy. His brother Montgomery wrote numerous letters to conservative Republicans and leading Democrats, trying to get them to unite in support of Johnson's approach.

The Blairs believed that patronage was the key to creating a new constituency, so they actively promoted the interests of influential party members. The Blairs wrote scores of letters on behalf of office-seekers, and, knowing that the family had the president's ear, many applicants referred to Montgomery or Francis Jr. in their own petitions. Many patronage requests went directly to Montgomery or Francis Jr., asking that the petition be forwarded to the president. Although Johnson received letters accusing him of being under the control of the Blair family, this does not appear to be the case, as the president did not pursue many military and political patronage requests.

The Blairs offered other suggestions as well. Francis Sr. urged repeatedly that Johnson change his cabinet and called for the removal of Secretary of State William H. Seward and Secretary of War Edwin M. Stanton. Interestingly, other correspondents presented similar ideas, and several suggested Francis Jr. as a replacement for Secretary Stanton. Montgomery was the most consistent in his pleas for a general amnesty, the release of Jefferson Davis, and executive intervention to restrain military commanders during Congressional Reconstruction.

In March 1867, perhaps to reward the loyal family, Johnson nominated Francis Jr. as minister to Austria. Although the Senate rejected the nomination, Francis Sr. and Montgomery had advised the younger Francis to decline the position, as his help was required in rebuilding the Democratic Party. Ironically, Francis Jr. did serious damage to the party a year later, after his nomination as vice president in the 1868 campaign. The Democratic nominee for president, Horatio Seymour, had little chance against Republican Ulysses S. Grant, but a letter from Francis Jr. to James O. Broadhead squelched any hope whatsoever. In the June 25, 1868, letter Francis Jr. called the Military Reconstruction Acts unconstitutional and advocated the overthrow of the Republican governments in the South.

The unsuccessful vice presidential bid marked the peak of the Blair's national presence. With Johnson's departure from office in 1869, the Blairs ceased to be Washington insiders, although the Missouri legislature did send Francis Jr. to the Senate from 1871 to 1873 to fill a vacancy. Francis Jr. never fulfilled his family's dream, the presidency, and passed away earliest of the trio. He was paralyzed by a severe stroke in 1873 and never fully recovered; he died in an accident two years later, in July 1875. Francis Sr. passed away in October 1876. Montgomery ran unsuccessfully for Congress several times and served during the disputed election of 1876 as counsel to Democratic presidential contender Samuel J. Tilden. Montgomery's health declined in the early 1880s, and he died on July 27, 1883, from a spinal inflammation.

See also: Blacks (Slave and Free), Johnson's Attitude toward; Cabinet Members; Congressional Reconstruction; Conservatives; Constitution, Johnson's Attitude toward; Davis, Jefferson; Democratic Convention; Democratic Party; Drunkenness; Election of 1868; Grant, Ulysses Simpson; Military Governor of Tennessee, Johnson as; Military Reconstruction Acts; Patronage; Presidential Reconstruction; Republican Party; Senator, Johnson as; Seward, William Henry; Seymour, Horatio; Stanton, Edwin McMasters; Vice President, Johnson as.

References: Graf, LeRoy P., Haskins, Ralph W., and Bergeron, Paul H., eds., *The Papers of Andrew Johnson* vols. 11–15 (1967–2000); Moroney, Rita Lloyd, *Montgomery Blair, Postmaster General* (1963); Parrish, William E., *Frank Blair, Lincoln's Conservative* (1998); Smith, Elbert B., *Francis Preston Blair* (1980); Smith, William E., *The Francis Preston Blair Family in Politics* (1933).

Browning, Orville Hickman (1806–1881)

Orville Hickman Browning, born near Cynthiana, Kentucky, and the son of a prosperous farmer, attended Augusta College, a Methodist school in Augusta, Kentucky (1825–1829), but did not finish his degree because of family financial problems. He read law with his uncle, William Brown, in Cynthiana and was admitted to the bar early in 1831, after which he promptly moved to the small town of Quincy, Illinois. He traveled the local legal circuit and in 1837 formed a law partnership with Nehemiah Bushnell that lasted until the latter's death in 1873.

In 1836 Browning married Eliza Caldwell (ca. 1808–1885) of Kentucky. The happy marriage lasted forty-five years but the couple had no children. On June 13, 1853, they took a motherless five-year-old girl, Emma Lord (1848–1885), into their home and always treated her as a daughter, although they never officially adopted her.

Also in 1836 Browning began his political career as a Whig by being elected to a four-year term in the Illinois state senate, where he strongly opposed various internal improvement bills as detrimental to the state's economy. In 1842 he was elected to the state house of representatives for a two-year term. After an arduous campaign in 1843, Browning lost the election for a congressional seat to Stephen A. Douglas. Although Browning remained influential in

Whig politics while not in office, his chief occupation was the practice of law. He often argued cases before the state and federal courts, sometimes in conjunction with Abraham Lincoln.

A staunch, practical Presbyterian with strict moral standards, Browning favored temperance legislation but had no objection to dancing. He opposed the institution of slavery for moral reasons and therefore opposed the extension of slavery into the territories. After being twice (1850 and 1852) defeated for Congress by Democrat William A. Richardson, Browning, a vocal opponent of the Kansas-Nebraska Act, helped to organize the Republican Party in Illinois in 1856. Browning favored Edward Bates of Missouri for the Republican presidential nomination in 1860, but when the Illinois delegates to the nominating convention (of which he was one) were pledged to support Lincoln, Browning worked hard for the latter's nomination.

After Lincoln was elected, Browning wrote the incoming president various letters of advice and also critiqued a preliminary draft of the inaugural address at Lincoln's request. Browning did not, however, receive a cabinet post, a much-desired appointment to the Supreme Court, or, in fact, any appointment at all from Lincoln. However, on June 12, 1861, Illinois governor Richard Yates gave Browning an interim appointment to the U.S. Senate to replace the recently deceased Stephen A. Douglas. Here Browning voted as a conservative rather than as a Radical Republican on numerous war measures until January 30, 1863, when he was replaced by the man elected by the state legislature, William A. Richardson. In the fall of 1863, after spending some time in Quincy, Browning returned to Washington, D.C., joining a firm to practice law before the Supreme Court and serve as a legal agent or lobbyist for persons needing to deal with various government departments.

After Lincoln's assassination Browning paid a number of social and business visits to Andrew Johnson. The two men soon discovered that they held similar attitudes on many aspects of Reconstruction politics, such as a conciliatory policy toward the South. Browning became Johnson's strong supporter. For example, he wrote Johnson a note thanking him for his Freedmen's Bureau Bill veto because Browning believed that the bill would have subverted the Constitution and substituted "a military despotism for constitutional government." Browning was part of the inner circle of those who planned and called for the meeting of the National Union Convention in Philadelphia during the summer of 1866. When James Harlan, William Dennison, and James Speed, three cabinet members who objected to the call, resigned, Johnson nominated Browning in July to replace Harlan as secretary of the interior. Browning and the new postmaster general, Alexander W. Randall, attended the convention and kept Johnson posted on the meeting. When Johnson made his Swing-around-the-Circle tour soon after, Browning, among others, urged him to make no impromptu speeches, but Johnson damaged his cause by ignoring this advice.

As secretary of the interior, Browning was responsible for various patronage positions in Indian offices and land agencies. In general, anything related to land cessions, public lands, the transcontinental railroad, pensions, patents, and Indian affairs came under the jurisdiction of this office. After Indians massacred Brevet Colonel William J. Fetterman and his eighty-one men in December 1866 near Fort Phil Kearny, Dakota Territory, conflict worsened between the Interior Department, which favored negotiation with the Indians, and the military, which believed in the use of force and that the whole department of Indian affairs should be under War Department control. No transfer of power was made at this time, however.

On March 31, 1868, during the impeachment crisis, when Attorney General

Henry Stanbery resigned his position to serve as one of Johnson's lawyers, Browning took on the additional responsibility of serving as attorney general ad interim. William M. Evarts became the new attorney general on July 20.

Just after Johnson left office in March 1869, some citizens of Baltimore gave him a large reception and a dinner attended by several hundred persons. Browning was one of only two of Johnson's former cabinet members who joined the festivities. By early April 1869 Browning was back home in Quincy and was soon involved in his legal practice and business affairs. During 1869–1870 he served as a member of the Illinois state constitutional convention. After this Browning did not run for or hold any more political offices, but he never lost his interest in politics, although he seemed to be rather disillusioned by them. During this late period of his life Browning frequently served as a lawyer for the Chicago, Burlington, and Quincy Railroad. He died after a short illness. Unfortunately, his considerable estate was quickly lost through the dishonest schemes of his son-in-law, Orrin Skinner, leaving Browning's wife and daughter impoverished and running a boardinghouse for the few remaining years of their lives.

See also: Cabinet Members; Conservatives; Freedmen's Bureau Bills (and Vetoes); Impeachment; Indians; Lincoln, Abraham; National Union Convention and Party; Presidential Reconstruction; Randall, Alexander Williams; Stanbery, Henry.

References: Baxter, Maurice G., *Orville H. Browning: Lincoln's Friend and Critic* (1957); Graf, LeRoy P., Haskins, Ralph W., and Bergeron, Paul H., eds., *The Papers of Andrew Johnson* vols. 10–14 (1967–2000); Randall, James G., ed., *The Diary of Orville Hickman Browning* (1925–1933); Trefousse, Hans L., *Andrew Johnson: A Biography* (1989).

Brownlow, William Gannaway "Parson" (1805–1877)

Born in Virginia, William Gannaway Brownlow was orphaned at a young age and raised by various uncles in eastern Tennessee. He worked on a farm, was briefly apprenticed to a carpenter, and, although he had little formal schooling, learned to read and write.

In 1825 he attended a Methodist camp meeting in Washington County, Tennessee, and apparently found his calling. He had earlier removed to Abingdon, Virginia, but now returned to Tennessee, studied briefly for a life of preaching, and in late 1826 was admitted as a circuit rider for the Holston Conference of the Methodist Church. His rugged background prepared him well for the rigors of preaching in Southern Appalachia, and before long the name—and aggressive religious rhetoric—of "Parson" Brownlow was familiar throughout East Tennessee and western North Carolina. Within a few years of his appointment he had written several books criticizing other denominations and had been convicted of libel in North Carolina.

The religious conflict that raged in the so-called Southern Highlands, among Methodists, Baptists, and Presbyterians, was not the only fray the Parson entered. In the early 1830s Brownlow began directing his ire and vehemence toward political issues, and his particular target was the Democratic Party. He earned regional attention for his stinging denunciations of Democrat John C. Calhoun and his theory of nullification, which Brownlow, an uncompromising Unionist, saw as leading to a division of the United States. Interestingly, he had no problem with what would become the most divisive issue of all, slavery, and even believed it could be a positive good for blacks and whites alike. As a new party, the Whigs, developed to counter Andrew Jackson and the Democrats, Brownlow found himself more involved in political topics and less active in the church.

In the mid–1830s it became clear that Brownlow's life was headed in a different direction. In 1836 he moved to Elizabethton, Tennessee, and married Eliza O'Brien, with whom he had seven children. About this time he also began his first newspaper, the *Tennessee Whig,* which viciously attacked Democrats and Presbyterians alike with the religious fervor that had become Brownlow's trademark. A year later he moved his family and paper to Jonesboro, where he fought in the press and on the street with local politicians, editors, and clergy.

In the 1840s "Parson" Brownlow shifted from commenting on politics to participating in them. His first campaign pitted the preacher-journalist against another East Tennessean, Andrew Johnson, who had already made a name for himself in the state legislature. In 1845 Brownlow ran opposite the Democratic Johnson for Congress. As he had since 1840, Brownlow mercilessly attacked Johnson's politics and his religion, calling him a bastard, a traitor, and a pagan (Johnson was not formally affiliated with any church). But Johnson was already a veteran politician, and he handily defeated the Parson. The defeat did not blunt Brownlow's assault, and he would continue to lambaste Johnson through his paper, even as Johnson grew more prominent and more powerful.

In 1849 Brownlow moved to Knoxville, where he renamed his paper *Brownlow's Knoxville Whig and Independent Journal,* more commonly called the *Knoxville Whig.* No longer a practicing preacher, the Parson used his paper to promote Whig ideas and attack extremists, secessionists, and abolitionists alike, who threatened the Union. Nor did Brownlow's assault on Johnson weaken; when Johnson was elected governor of Tennessee in 1853 and again in 1855, Brownlow published prayers in the *Whig* asking God's forgiveness for Tennesseans who voted for him. As a Unionist, Brownlow supported the Constitutional Union candidate, former Whig and Tennessean John Bell, in the election of 1860.

Abraham Lincoln won the election, and the secession of South Carolina brought a temporary truce between Johnson and Brownlow. Both ardent Unionists, the former rivals found themselves campaigning across East Tennessee against the state's secession referendums, risking life and limb in what turned out to be a fruitless effort. Their cool cooperation continued through the war, at first with Johnson in the U.S. Senate defying the Confederacy while Brownlow continued publishing the *Whig* from Confederate-occupied Knoxville. In 1862, due to the Parson's ceaseless condemnation of the Confederacy, his paper was suppressed, and in the spring of 1863 its publisher was exiled to western Tennessee (which was under federal occupation). There Brownlow again crossed paths with Andrew Johnson, now the state's military governor, and the two suffered through an uneasy alliance. Brownlow returned to Knoxville late in 1863 when federal forces moved into East Tennessee and he renamed his paper the *Knoxville Whig and Rebel Ventilator.*

Johnson's purpose in Tennessee was to create a new civil government under Lincoln's program of Reconstruction. Not until spring 1865 was civil government restored in Tennessee, and the new civil governor was none other than "Parson" Brownlow. Having been elected vice president, Andrew Johnson left Tennessee for Washington, leaving his state in the hands of his oldest enemy. With the war over, the two rivals went their separate ways in terms of policy as well. At first, once Johnson became president, there was some cooperation, as Brownlow asked Johnson for advice on administrative matters and requested presidential pardons for various Tennesseans. But, although President Johnson sought reconciliation and a speedy Restoration,

Governor Brownlow was not about to forgive or forget. He and the state legislature disfranchised most former Confederates and barred them from holding office. Unforgiving and unforgiven, with the vindictiveness of an angry god, Brownlow punished those he believed responsible for the war. When Johnson called on Southern states to reject the Fourteenth Amendment, Brownlow used strong-arm tactics and questionable parliamentary procedures to ensure the amendment's ratification in Tennessee; he addressed his ratification notice to the "dead dog in the White House." Tennessee was the only ex-Confederate state to avoid Military Reconstruction. The state was readmitted to Congress in 1866, and Brownlow was reelected in 1867.

But Tennessee's Unionists had a tenuous hold on power. The Fourteenth Amendment had enfranchised the state's blacks, but the Ku Klux Klan, which first appeared in 1866 in Pulaski, Tennessee, was so effective at intimidating black voters that President Johnson had to order the U.S. Army into the state. Brownlow also turned to state militia units, often comprised of black men, to enforce law and order. According to some, 1868 and 1869 saw civil war in Tennessee, with Brownlow blaming former Confederates but Johnson blaming Brownlow's militia.

Perhaps sensing their control slipping away, Republicans and former Whigs in the General Assembly elected Brownlow to the U.S. Senate in 1869, replacing Johnson's son-in-law David T. Patterson. But Brownlow's elevation to the Senate was anticlimactic, and his six-year term was unremarkable. Decades of hard living, mental and physical exertion, and bitter personal rivalries had left Brownlow weary and haggard. His voice nearly gone and his frame weakened, the Parson suffered one more blow as he left the Senate: he was succeeded by Andrew Johnson in 1875. Brownlow returned to Knoxville and his newspaper and died in 1877.

See also: Bell, John; Black Suffrage; Democratic Party; Fourteenth Amendment; Harris, Isham Green; Military Governor of Tennessee, Johnson as; Patterson, David Trotter; Postpresidential Career; Presidential Reconstruction; Readmission of Southern States; Reconstruction; Religion, Johnson's Attitude toward; Secession Referendums; Senator, Johnson as; State Legislator, Johnson as; Whig Party.

References: Alexander, Thomas B., *Political Reconstruction in Tennessee* (1950); Coulter, E. Merton, *William G. Brownlow, Fighting Parson of the Southern Highlands* (1937); Graf, LeRoy P., Haskins, Ralph W., and Bergeron, Paul H., eds., *The Papers of Andrew Johnson* vols. 2, 8, 9, 12–14 (1967–2000); Patton, James Welch, *Unionism and Reconstruction in Tennessee, 1860–1869* (1934).

Butler, Benjamin Franklin (1818–1893)

Benjamin Franklin Butler, an outspoken opponent of Andrew Johnson for much of the latter's presidential career, was born in Deerfield, New Hampshire. Butler was the third child of John Butler and his second wife, Charlotte Ellison. John Butler, a War of 1812 veteran and a privateer (or pirate), died when his son was only four months old. Because the family was left in impoverished circumstances, Butler began his education at home but attended several academies later. His mother ran a boardinghouse for mill workers in Lowell, Massachusetts, beginning in 1828.

Butler attended Waterville (later Colby) College in Waterville, Maine. He was supposed to become a Baptist minister but theological studies disagreed with him, and he preferred physics and chemistry. After graduating in 1838, Butler read law and was admitted to the bar in 1840.

As a lawyer, Butler apparently had a phenomenal memory and a thorough knowledge of the law. He willingly took the minor cases of the Lowell mill girls and soon became known as a friend of labor, although he also took cases from the mill owners. He used the letter as opposed to the spirit of the law when technicalities were to the benefit of his client, but he also did exhaustive research on complicated aspects of various cases. He had a sharp and snide wit, which he used on many occasions, and was frequently involved in controversies.

In May 1844 Butler married an actress, Sarah Hildreth (d. 1876), who then retired from the stage. The couple had four children: Paul (1845–1850), Blanche (b. 1847), Paul (b. 1854), and Ben Israel (b. 1856). Blanche married Adelbert Ames, the Reconstruction-era senator from and governor of Mississippi.

Despite his residence in a Whig district, Butler became involved in Democratic politics in 1840, at the same time as he became a lawyer. His first major political campaign was for a ten-hour workday. The legislature compromised with an eleven and one-fourth hour workday, but Butler made some enemies among the manufacturers. During the antebellum period he served a term each in the Massachusetts state house (1853) and state senate (1859). He was also a delegate in 1860 to the Democratic national conventions, where he supported the candidacy of John C. Breckinridge.

When war was declared, Butler promptly became a brigadier general of Massachusetts militia and in April 1861 occupied Annapolis. He then captured Baltimore in order to keep the state of Maryland in the Union. As these actions were not authorized by Abraham Lincoln's administration in Washington, due to the federal government's delicate relationship with Maryland, Butler was summoned to Washington and made a major general of volunteers. Butler's only military experience had been leading local militia and he was clearly a "political" general who managed to substitute a great deal of gall for military wisdom throughout the war.

Butler was assigned to command at Fort Monroe, Virginia, where he first used the term "contraband of war" to describe the status of slaves who had fled from their Confederate masters to the protection of the military. After a defeat at Big Bethel, Butler was removed from command. He led a poorly executed but successful attack on Forts Hatteras and Clark at Hatteras Inlet.

Then, after recruiting troops in Massachusetts, Butler commanded the occupying forces at New Orleans from May to December 1862, where his administration was harsh. He is probably best known for his order that women of New Orleans should be treated as prostitutes if they harassed Union soldiers, an order that aroused widespread wrath in Louisiana and the rest of the Confederacy. Butler's orders requiring the oath of allegiance from foreign consuls, as well as other activities such as censoring their mail, angered the international community. Rumors of corruption were associated with Butler (he allegedly stole spoons) and confirmed with some of his associates. Finally Lincoln removed Butler from command in December 1862.

Butler soon became commander of the Army of the James (Virginia) in 1863. In 1864 his forces were unable to help Ulysses S. Grant with the capture of Petersburg and Richmond because they became blocked at Bermuda Hundred. Butler was also defeated in an attempt to capture Fort Fisher at Wilmington, North Carolina. He was removed from command in January 1865, which made Butler angry at Grant for several years.

When Abraham Lincoln was assassinated, Butler said that it was a providential removal because Lincoln would have made the peace too easy on the South. At first Butler believed that Andrew Johnson would be just the sort of president required. Apparently he called on Johnson a number of times to give advice and wrote a lengthy letter replying to a question of Johnson's about the legal status of Robert E. Lee's army as prisoners of war and under parole. Some of Butler's friends wrote Johnson letters urging the president to give Butler a cabinet post, but Johnson appears not to have ever considered doing so. When Johnson later offered Butler the postmastership of Salem, Massachusetts, Butler turned it down about August 10, 1866, because he opposed Johnson's new National Union Party and did not believe that Johnson's policies toward the South were correct.

By the end of the War, Butler had allied himself with the Radical Republicans and soon became one of their leaders in the attempt to impeach Johnson. In October 1866 Butler spoke in Cincinnati, Ohio, giving reasons why Johnson should be impeached. These Radical sentiments apparently helped Butler's election to the U.S. House of Representatives, where he eventually served five terms (1867–1875, 1877–1879). He headed a special committee to investigate the assassination of Lincoln, but its real purpose was to collect evidence that would implicate Johnson. To this end, Butler and James M. Ashley pressured relatives and other people associated with Mary Surratt in an attempt to acquire such evidence. Butler also was active in the Committee on Reconstruction, which headed the final, successful drive for impeachment. Butler was chosen to be one of the seven house managers to prosecute the impeachment trial. He also wrote the tenth charge, which accused Johnson of trying to bring Congress into disrepute by his criticisms.

When the impeachment trial opened on March 30, 1868, Butler made the opening speech. Because Butler was well-known for his colorful theatrics, many people were eager to hear him. He spoke for four hours on technicalities and precedents of impeachment, disappointing those who had come for drama. During presentations of the defense witnesses, Butler objected to virtually everything, frequently engaging in ridicule, harassment, and abuse. Johnson's defense team was not intimidated, however, and Johnson was narrowly acquitted, despite Butler's best efforts. Butler immediately claimed that some of the senators voting for acquittal had been bribed. He formed an investigating committee, but no evidence of bribery was found.

Despite his earlier animosity toward Grant, Butler became a supporter of the president. After several unsuccessful attempts to be elected governor of Massachusetts, Butler finally succeeded in 1882 on a Greenback-Democratic coalition ticket, but he served only one term. Butler retired from politics after he was the unsuccessful Greenback candidate for president in 1884. He practiced law, wrote his memoirs (1892), and died suddenly in Washington, D.C., in 1893.

See also: Ashley, James Mitchell; Congressional Reconstruction; Grant, Ulysses Simpson; Impeachment; Impeachment Defense Counsel; Impeachment Managers; Joint Committee on Reconstruction; Lincoln, Abraham; National Union Convention and Party; Republican Party; Surratt, Mary (Elizabeth) Eugenia Jenkins.
References: Graf, LeRoy P., Haskins, Ralph W., and Bergeron, Paul H., eds., *The Papers of Andrew Johnson* vols. 5, 7–8, 11–13 (1967–2000); Holzman, Robert S., *Stormy Ben Butler* (1954); Trefousse, Hans L., *Ben Butler: The South Called Him Beast!* (1957).

Cabinet Members

When Johnson assumed the presidency, he retained Abraham Lincoln's seven cabinet members. Over the course of Johnson's term, some of these original officials resigned because of political disagreements or for other reasons. Johnson's attempt, in alleged violation of the Tenure of Office Act, to remove Edwin M. Stanton led to Johnson's impeachment. Johnson's cabinet members were as follows:

Secretary of State: William H. Seward (1865–1869)

Secretary of the Treasury: Hugh McCulloch (1865–1869)

Secretary of War: Edwin M. Stanton (1865–1868); Ulysses S. Grant (interim, 1867–1868); Lorenzo Thomas (interim, 1868); John M. Schofield (1868–1869)

Attorney General: James Speed (1865–1866); Henry Stanbery (1866–1868); Orville H. Browning (interim, 1868); William M. Evarts (1868–1869)

Postmaster General: William Dennison (1865–1866); Alexander W. Randall (1866–1869)

Secretary of the Navy: Gideon Welles (1865–1869)

Secretary of the Interior: John P. Usher (1865); James Harlan (1865–1866); Orville H. Browning (1866–1869)

See also: Each individual officeholder; Tenure of Office Act.
References: Graf, LeRoy P., Haskins, Ralph W., and Bergeron, Paul H., eds., *The Papers of Andrew Johnson* vols. 8–15 (1967–2000); Trefousse, Hans L., *Andrew Johnson: A Biography* (1989).

Canby, Edward Richard Sprigg (1817–1873)

Although Edward Richard Sprigg Canby was born in Kentucky, he moved to Indiana with his family when he was quite young. After some local schooling, he attended West Point and graduated thirtieth of the thirty-one in the class of 1839. He immediately returned to Indiana where, on August 1, 1839, he married Louisa Hawkins. Canby served in Florida against the Seminoles, assisted with the removal of other Southeastern Indians to Arkansas, and was involved in troop recruitment. During the Mexican-American War he served as assistant adjutant general and unofficial chief of staff for the 2nd Infantry Brigade under Colonel Bennet Riley in the Mexico City campaign and received two brevets.

After more service on the Pacific Coast and the frontier, Canby was stationed at Fort Defiance, New Mexico Territory, when the Civil War broke out. Made commander of the Department of New Mexico, his main object was to prevent the troops of Confederate General Henry H. Sibley from reaching and conquering California. Although defeated by Sibley's forces at the battle of Valverde in January 1862, Canby was ultimately victorious by drawing the Confederates away from their supplies. Assigned to a staff post in Washington, D.C., in March 1862, he spent a year and a half there, except for the four months he commanded in New York City to bring order after the July 1863 draft riots. In this staff position Canby corresponded with Tennessee's military governor, Andrew Johnson, about various administrative matters. In May 1864 Canby was given command of the Military Division of West Mississippi, a large district including Texas, Louisiana, and Florida, where he replaced General Nathaniel P. Banks. Working with the naval forces under Admiral David G. Farragut, Canby captured the forts protecting Mobile Bay and, on April 12, 1865, he captured Mobile itself. He accepted the surrenders of the forces of Generals Richard Taylor and Edmund Kirby Smith in May 1865.

In July 1865 Canby's command was defined as restricted to Louisiana so as not to conflict with the broader command of General Philip H. Sheridan. Hugh Kennedy, the mayor of New Orleans, wrote a series of letters to President Andrew Johnson in the summer and fall of 1865 complaining about Canby and his interference in the civil affairs of New Orleans, such as confiscating city property and suspending a meeting of the school board, which prevented these civil affairs from functioning properly, Kennedy thought. Canby, however, was trying to carry out appropriate Reconstruction policy, and in March 1866 he suspended newly elected Mayor John T. Monroe and Alderman James O. Nixon who, because of their Confederate connections, needed individual pardons, which Johnson promptly issued.

Sheridan had been doing a number of things deliberately to aggravate Canby, and on May 5, 1866, Canby requested a transfer out of the department. During the summer he became the commander of the Department of Washington. Then in August 1867 he was assigned to command the Second Military District—North and South Carolina—relieving the controversial General Daniel E. Sickles, whom Johnson had removed. Not surprisingly, Canby generated some controversy and protests from governors who did not want a military presence in their states. South Carolina governor James L. Orr complained about an order defining qualifications for jury duty, and in December 1867 North Carolina governor Jonathan Worth complained about the military arrest and imprisonment of various persons, arrests that Worth believed interfered with the state's civil court proceedings. Canby served in command of the Second Military District until August 1868, when he was ordered back to Washington.

Ordered to Texas in late 1868, Canby commanded there until April 1869, when he was assigned to Virginia, where he created controversy by requiring all the newly elected state officials to take the test oath. Although local authorities complained, as they would have about anybody seeking to carry out Reconstruction legislation, Canby was essentially a moderate whom Johnson could use to bring a calming influence in controversial positions. Canby's last assignment was as commander of the Department of the Columbia (1870–1873), which included Washington Territory and Oregon. Canby was murdered in northern California on April 11, 1873, by Captain Jack, a Modoc Indian, during a negotiation meeting.

See also: Indians; Military Districts; Military Governor of Tennessee, Johnson as; Pardons (Individual); Sheridan, Philip Henry; Sickles, Daniel Edgar.

References: Dawson, Joseph G., III, *Army Generals and Reconstruction* (1982); Graf, LeRoy P., Haskins, Ralph W., and Bergeron, Paul H., eds., *The Papers of Andrew Johnson* vols. 5–6, 8–10, 12–13 (1967–2000); Heyman, Max L., Jr.,

Prudent Soldier: A Biography of Major General E.R.S. Canby, 1817–1873 (1959); Warner, Ezra J., *Generals in Blue* (1964).

Chase, Salmon Portland (1808–1873)

Salmon Portland Chase, who had held numerous political offices previously, was chief justice of the Supreme Court of the United States during Andrew Johnson's term. Born in Cornish, New Hampshire, Salmon was the eighth of the eleven children of Ithamar and Jeanette Ralston Chase. When Salmon was nine years old, his father died and the child was sent to live with his uncle Philander Chase, the Episcopal bishop of Ohio. Salmon attended several schools and graduated from Dartmouth in 1826. For a time Chase conducted a boy's school in Washington, D.C., and then studied law with William Wirt. Admitted to the bar in 1829, Chase moved to Cincinnati to practice, where he also became involved in literary and antislavery activities.

Chase was married three times: to Catherine Jane Garniss (1811–1835) in 1834, to Eliza Ann Smith (1821–1845) in 1839, and to Sarah Bella Dunlop Ludlow (ca. 1820–1852) in 1846. Each of these women died of some disease. Among them they produced six daughters, but only two survived childhood. Catherine Jane (1840–1899), known as Kate, served as her father's hostess, worked to further his political career, and married Rhode Island politician William Sprague. Janet Ralston (Nettie) (1847–1925), Kate's half-sister, illustrated children's books and married William S. Hoyt of New York City.

During the 1830s and 1840s Chase became well known for his legal defenses of fugitive slaves and the persons who aided them. His antislavery policies affected his choice of political party and during the course of his life he switched parties a number of times. Originally a Whig, he joined the Liberty Party in 1840 and later moved on to the Free-Soil; then the Free, or Independent, Democrats; and in 1855, the Republicans. But by the election of 1868 he was seeking the Democratic presidential nomination.

Chase held several Ohio political offices including U.S. senator (1849–1855, 1861) and governor (1855–1859). He wanted very much to be the Republican presidential candidate in 1856, 1860, and 1864, but, although his candidacy was often discussed, he never had much actual support. Instead Abraham Lincoln asked him to be secretary of the treasury, an office Chase held from March 1861 to July 1864. In this difficult post he was responsible for financing the Union war effort during much of the Civil War. He resigned as a result of increasing friction with Lincoln. Nevertheless, when Supreme Court chief justice Roger B. Taney died, Lincoln appointed Chase as Taney's successor. Chase held this office from December 1864 to May 1873 and, as a result, played an important role during Johnson's presidency.

As chief justice, Chase administered the vice presidential oath to Johnson on March 4, 1865. Chase wrote to his friend Susan Walker afterward that he was "grieved" by Johnson's inebriation because he honored Johnson "as one who risked every thing for his convictions." On April 15, at the Kirkwood House hotel in Washington, D.C., Chase administered the presidential oath of office to Johnson as he succeeded the assassinated Abraham Lincoln. During the first few weeks of Johnson's presidency, Chase met with Johnson several times to discuss Reconstruction policy, giving advice, which the president chose not to heed. From May 1 to June 22 Chase toured various parts of the newly defeated South, traveling down the east coast and up the Mississippi River. He attempted to promote black suffrage, an idea that appealed to the blacks but not the whites. He wrote seven letters to Johnson describing conditions and encouraging black enfranchisement. Several of Johnson's friends wrote to warn Johnson that Chase was already campaigning for the 1868 presidential nomination, an accusation that was doubtless true to an extent, as Chase was always working toward his presidential goal.

Johnson wanted to meet with Chase in August 1865, hoping to discuss a trial for former Confederate president Jefferson Davis who was imprisoned at Fort Monroe. Chase replied that he did not believe that it was proper for the president and chief justice to discuss the case. In fact, Chase did all he could to delay Davis's trial. As the Supreme Court justice assigned to the circuit in Virginia, Chase would not hold a court term in the fall of 1865 because there was not enough time before the Supreme Court session, but also because Chase did not feel that it was appropriate to hold court in a place that was still under martial law. By November 1867 it seemed that Davis would finally be brought to trial, but again Chase was unable to attend, and in the spring of 1868 he was occupied with Johnson's impeachment trial. Public opinion had changed as people realized that Davis had no part in the assassination conspiracy and many no longer believed a trial to be necessary. In December 1869 Chase dismissed the case.

As chief justice, Chase presided over a court made up of men with conflicting political opinions. He tried to serve as a unifying factor, especially by personally doing a lot of hard work to prepare for hearing the cases. The Court generally took a moderate position on Reconstruction issues, believing that the questions were mostly political and did not require judicial involvement. The Court also tried to avoid being intimidated by Congress.

Chase held a very important position during Johnson's impeachment trial because the Constitution requires the chief justice to preside over the Senate in such cases. Chase

and the Senate had several disagreements over procedure, and the Senate determined many of its operating rules without consulting Chase, much to his annoyance. Although he stated his opinion to friends only, Chase did not believe that Johnson should have been impeached. He thought that Johnson had the right to disobey a law that he deemed unconstitutional in order to bring a test case before the Supreme Court. This was what Johnson had attempted to do with the Tenure of Office Act by dismissing Edwin M. Stanton. Chase wanted the Senate to "render an honest and impartial judgment" and said that he did not try to influence the votes of any of the senators. He was satisfied with Johnson's acquittal.

There was much talk during 1868 about Chase as a possible presidential candidate, and a number of Johnson's correspondents considered a Chase candidacy as a serious possibility. Although Chase's daughter, Kate Sprague, and some other friends worked for his nomination at the Democratic National Convention in New York in July, Chase had virtually no serious support and got hardly any votes on any of the ballots. Some people proposed that he should be a third-party candidate, but Chase did not attempt it.

In August 1870 Chase had a stroke and then, in the fall, a heart attack, but was well enough to return to Washington, D.C., to attend court in January 1871. It was clear, however, that his mental processes were not as sharp as previously. Despite that he was in poor health, he wanted to run for president in 1872, but he received no support. Chase's health further declined after he was improperly dressed for the inclement weather when he swore in the president at Ulysses S. Grant's second inauguration on March 4, 1873. He died on May 7, 1873, from a stroke.

See also: Black Suffrage; Davis, Jefferson; Democratic Convention; Election of 1864; Election of 1868; Grant, Ulysses Simpson; Impeachment; Lincoln, Abraham; *McCardle, Ex parte; Milligan, Ex parte;* Stanton, Edwin McMasters; Tenure of Office Act.

References: Blue, Frederick J., *Salmon P. Chase:*

A Life in Politics (1987); Graf, LeRoy P., Haskins, Ralph W., and Bergeron, Paul H., eds., *The Papers of Andrew Johnson* vols. 8–9, 13–14 (1967–2000); Niven, John, *Salmon P. Chase: A Biography* (1995); Niven, John et al., eds., *The Salmon P. Chase Papers* vols. 1–5 (1993–1998); Simpson, Brooks D., Graf, LeRoy P., and Muldowny, John, eds., *Advice after Appomattox: Letters to Andrew Johnson, 1865–1866* (1987); Trefousse, Hans L., *Andrew Johnson: A Biography* (1989); Waugh, John C., *Reelecting Lincoln: The Battle for the 1864 Presidency* (1997).

Civil Rights Act (1866)

When it became law on April 9, 1866, the Civil Rights Act was the first federal statute to define citizenship and safeguard civil rights within the states. "All persons born in the United States and not subject to any foreign power, excluding Indians not taxed" were declared to be citizens of the United States. As such, all citizens, and included among these were black Americans, should enjoy the same civil rights and privileges anywhere within the United States and its territories. From this point onward, national citizenship overrode state citizenship, with the federal government protecting the benefits of citizenship from state discrimination. These benefits included the right to sue (and be sued); the right to testify in court; the right to make contracts; the right to inherit, purchase, sell, or lease property; and the right of citizens to be secure in their person and property.

The stipulations in the act were directed toward two serious obstacles to achieving black civil rights: the 1857 decision in *Scott v. San[d]ford* and the recently passed Black Codes. The act effectively nullified the *Dred Scott* decision by affirming that blacks were indeed citizens. As for the codes, they became illegal after the act's new definition of federal civil rights. Still, this legislation was considered moderate by most because it never addressed black political rights. Although federal courts assumed jurisdiction over violations, states that did not pass offensive or illegal statutes avoided federal involvement. Many friends, both moderate Republicans and Democrats, advised Johnson to sign the measure because relations between the president and Congress had been deteriorating. Johnson's recent veto of the Freedmen's Bureau Bill and his hostile treatment of Congress in his Washington's Birthday Speech had made matters worse. But Johnson, insisting that Congress had no right to legislate for unrepresented states, especially when this legislation violated constitutionally accepted state powers, vetoed the Civil Rights Bill on March 27, 1866.

Congress passed the bill over Johnson's veto on April 9, what some historians have called the first override of the veto of a major piece of legislation. Still, unresolved issues remained. The president was clearly opposed to even a moderate and limited program of black civil rights. Johnson's refusal to adapt or compromise resulted in two developments: first, more Republicans found themselves leaning toward a more "radical" approach to Reconstruction, and second, Congress decided to grant and guarantee national citizenship by another means, the Fourteenth Amendment.

See also: Black Codes; Congressional Reconstruction; Constitution, Johnson's Attitude toward; Fourteenth Amendment; Freedmen's Bureau Bills (and Vetoes); Joint Committee on Reconstruction; Presidential Reconstruction; Reconstruction; Republican Party; Vetoes. For excerpts of the 1866 Civil Rights Act, see Appendix I.

References: Beale, Howard K., *The Critical Year: 1866* (1958 [1930]); Belz, Herman, *Emancipation and Equal Rights: Politics and Constitutionalism in the Civil War Era* (1978); Belz, Herman, *A New Birth of Freedom: The Republican Party and Freedmen's Rights, 1861–1866* (1976); Kendrick, Benjamin B., *The Journal of the Joint Committee of Fifteen on Reconstruction* (1914).

Colorado (Admission to Statehood)

Half of the area that eventually became the state of Colorado was acquired by the United States as part of the Louisiana Purchase in 1803. The rest was included in the land ceded to the United States in 1848 after the Mexican-American War. In the 1850s the future Colorado was considered a part of the Kansas and Nebraska Territories, with Arapahoe County (the Denver area) belonging to Kansas. However, as a result of a gold rush during 1858–1860, a separate Colorado Territory was created on February 28, 1861.

In 1864 Congress passed enabling acts to allow Nevada, Nebraska, and Colorado to each prepare a constitution and establish a state government. Nevada quickly completed its organization and became a state that same year, but Nebraska took until 1867. Some citizens of Colorado saw advantages to statehood whereas others believed that retaining territorial status would be better financially because the small population would not have to support its own government. In 1864 those who opposed statehood won when the citizens voted down the proposed state constitution. But the next year a new constitution passed by 155 votes, causing antistatehood forces to charge their opponents with election fraud.

Because the constitution had passed, a bill to admit Colorado to statehood was introduced in Congress in January 1866 and almost immediately met with two main objections. The first concern was the limited population of the prospective state, while a second problem, particularly troublesome in the middle of Reconstruction, was that the state constitution permitted only white men to vote. However, both houses of Congress did pass the statehood bill by early May 1866.

Meanwhile, in April 1866 the Senate had overridden Johnson's veto of the Civil Rights Bill by two votes. Apparently, in an attempt to gain more support for his program and cancel out the small radical majority, Johnson met with the two senators-elect from Colorado, John Evans and Jerome Chaffee, and indicated a willingness to admit Colorado to statehood if Evans and Chaffee would then support his Reconstruction measures in the Senate. Colorado's pro-statehood forces alleged that Johnson consequently vetoed the statehood bill because Chaffee and Evans would not commit themselves to support him.

Whatever the case may have been, Johnson vetoed the Colorado Statehood Bill on May 15, 1866. Like Congress, he had two major objections to the bill, and, also like Congress, his first objection was the small population, estimated to be 30,000. He believed that the residents, mostly recent arrivals and temporary settlers, would be better served by remaining a territory without the additional taxation that statehood would bring. In addition, he thought it would be unfair and unequal for a state with only 30,000 residents to have a representative and two senators in Congress when such a populous state as New York, with four million citizens, had "only" thirty-one representatives and two senators.

Johnson's second objection was that "it is not satisfactorily established that a majority of the citizens of Colorado desire or are prepared" to become a state. He claimed that in the election of 1864 the citizens voted statehood down by a large majority (but it was actually only 112). Therefore, he did not think it "entirely safe" to accept the vote taken a year later and not, he claimed, by congressional authority, which gave statehood a 155-vote majority.

According to his sources, the population of Colorado was actually declining rather than growing and so Johnson wanted either a census taken to determine the actual population or a congressionally authorized election to determine whether the people really did want statehood. He felt that the country should be cautious about admitting new states when eleven old ones, those of the former Confederacy, were still unrepresented in Congress.

Congress did not override this veto. However, by his action Johnson offended a number of pro-statehood moderate Republicans in Colorado, who no longer supported him thereafter.

A group of Colorado blacks, angry with Colorado's suffrage restriction, had petitioned the territorial governor and even members of Congress for the right to vote. This agitation eventually helped influence Congress to pass in January 1867 the Territorial Suffrage Act, which prohibited territorial restriction of suffrage based on color. It also motivated Congress in the same month to add the "Edmunds Amendment," named for Vermont senator George Edmunds, to new bills for the admission of Colorado and Nebraska. This amendment, also called the "fundamental condition," required that the prospective states amend their constitutions to include equal male suffrage.

Johnson promptly vetoed both statehood bills. In his second rejection of statehood for Colorado, dated January 28, 1867, the president complained that, except for the Edmunds Amendment, this was the same bill he had vetoed previously, and, in fact, he found even more objections to the bill now than he had the first time. He pointed out the conflict over suffrage between the territorial/state and federal legislation and claimed that Congress was exceeding its authority in the way that it was attempting to make Colorado a state.

Johnson pointed out that the territorial legislature had sent a protest (which he included in his message) against statehood because they claimed "a right to a voice in the selection of the character of our government" and because the population was too small "to support the expenses of a State government." Johnson then elaborated on the population issue. A census had

been taken in the fall of 1866 that showed the population to be slightly less than 28,000, a figure that Johnson accepted and based his calculations upon. (In reality this census was of questionable accuracy because the population of a number of counties had been only estimated, not counted.) He claimed that no state should be admitted with a lower population than 127,000, at that time the number required for a congressional district. If Colorado were admitted, there would be no reason to deny admission to other underpopulated territories such as Montana and Idaho.

Congress overrode Johnson's veto of the Nebraska Statehood Bill and that territory became a state. But Congress sustained Johnson's veto for Colorado because the population did seem to be small and many residents opposed statehood. Consequently, Colorado remained a territory for the time being and was not admitted to statehood until August 1, 1876, during Ulysses S. Grant's second term and the centennial of the United States.

See also: Black Suffrage; Nebraska (Admission to Statehood); Territorial Affairs.
References: Berwanger, Eugene H., *The West and Reconstruction* (1981); Graf, LeRoy P., Haskins, Ralph W., and Bergeron, Paul H., eds., *The Papers of Andrew Johnson* vols. 10–11 (1967–2000); Sprague, Marshall, *Colorado: A Bicentennial History* (1976); Trefousse, Hans L., *Andrew Johnson: A Biography* (1989).

Command of the Army Act
See Army Appropriations Act (1867)

Congressional Reconstruction

By 1864, once Northerners felt reasonably sure that the Confederacy would be defeated, another war, this one within Washington, D.C., itself, began. The struggle was over the manner and control of Reconstruction. President Abraham Lincoln, operating under the authority of commander-in-chief during wartime and the presidential prerogative of clemency, believed that the executive should control the postwar readmission process. His program, called the Ten Percent Plan, quickly met with congressional hostility. Members of Congress argued that the plan was too lenient, antidemocratic, and violated *their* right to control Reconstruction. Because Reconstruction involved representation in Congress, congressional Republicans argued that the legislature should direct it. Their response to Lincoln was the Wade-Davis Bill, which Lincoln pocket-vetoed. Congress, in reply, refused to seat representatives from Louisiana and Arkansas, states already "reconstructed" according to Lincoln's plan.

The accession of Andrew Johnson to the presidency filled Republicans with a hope that soon faded. Johnson was even more lenient than was Lincoln, and he was equally adamant about presidential control of readmission. Because Congress was not in session when Johnson became president in April, he initiated his own Reconstruction program. It was not until December 1865 that the national legislature reconvened and surveyed the damage.

Developments in the South, including the creation of Black Codes, widespread violence toward blacks and Unionists, and the election of former Confederates to Congress, forced many in Congress to question the value of Union victory. Accordingly, in December 1865 Congress refused to seat the Southern representatives, defying Johnson and his Reconstruction process. At the same time, congressional Republicans laid the groundwork for their own program by forming the Joint Committee of Fifteen on Reconstruction (usually called the Joint Committee on Reconstruction). Congress and the Committee imagined a moderate program designed to punish, at least temporarily, certain Confederates, protect basic civil rights for blacks in the South, and ex-

tend limited federal services to help freedpeople adjust to their new lives.

In February and March of 1866 the Committee presented, and Congress soon passed, the Freedmen's Bureau Bill and the Civil Rights Bill. As before, states protected basic civil rights—which now also pertained to blacks—but the national government possessed a corrective authority to intervene if states discriminated. President Johnson believed that the bills were a violation of traditional state sovereignty, an unwise use of federal funds, and an illegal use of the military (as a temporary system of justice under the Freedmen's Act). He vetoed both bills; Congress passed the Civil Rights Bill over his veto and passed a revised Freedmen's Bureau Bill over another veto the following July.

Johnson's actions, although rendered irrelevant by Congress, had profound effects. The president's opposition to moderate pieces of legislation, and his acerbic veto messages assailing Congress for its violations of the Constitution, helped create a coalition in Congress that had not previously existed. Even worse, Johnson did not restrict his condemnation of Congress to official channels, and his Washington's Birthday Speech further alienated Congress. Many Republicans, whom historians call "moderates," had believed that Johnson would accept a program that did not stress black political rights, confiscation of property, or permanent political disabilities. Yet Johnson had rejected this moderate proposal, increasing the influence of those "radicals" who saw Johnson as an unyielding obstructionist from the start. Johnson's vetoes also indicated that the executive, and perhaps even the South, would be an obstacle to any new Reconstruction initiative.

This conclusion led directly to the passage of the Fourteenth Amendment, Congress's one-step approach to Reconstruction. The amendment encompassed most of the Republican goals, including citizenship for blacks, limited imposition of disabilities on former Confederates, and the nationalization of civil rights. It also went further, cajoling states into either enfranchising blacks or facing a reduction in representation. Better still, the amendment was beyond Johnson's veto power and, with the understanding that ratification would bring readmission, held the promise of quick adoption.

Johnson reacted swiftly to the amendment's passage in June of 1866. Angered at congressional hypocrisy—Republicans demanded that states ratify a measure while insisting that those states were out of the Union—and arguing that the amendment again violated the bounds of state sovereignty, Johnson advised the former Confederate states to reject the amendment. Each one did, with the exception of his own state of Tennessee.

Congressional Republicans took the landslide victories in the fall of 1866 as an indication that the public supported their approach, and Johnson's interference with the ratification process drove members of Congress to further close ranks against him. When Congress unveiled its new Reconstruction program in the spring of 1867, it had none of the cajoling and compromise evident earlier; this was a new blueprint for the South, designed by Congress and imposed by the military.

Despite the earlier measures, historians often cite March 2, 1867, as the beginning of Congressional (or Radical) Reconstruction. That day saw the passage of three important laws: the First Military Reconstruction Act, the Army Appropriations Act (which contained the Command of the Army Act), and the Tenure of Office Act. President Johnson saw these acts as an unconstitutional usurpation of civil power by the military and of executive privilege by the legislature, and he vetoed the First Reconstruction Act and the Tenure of Office Act. As Republican framers of the act had anticipated, he could not bring himself to veto the appropriations measure. Nonetheless, Congress passed both bills over his vetoes. The Thirty-Ninth Congress then came to a close, but not before calling into session the Fortieth Congress, to begin immediately after the Thirty-Ninth adjourned. This Congress, elected in 1866 and holding a veto-proof majority, would hold three regular sessions in order to prevent President Johnson from acting when Congress was not sitting.

These laws created a framework that effectively shifted all restoration issues to Congress. Under the new program, army officers in the South oversaw the registering of voters, the calling of conventions, the writing of new state constitutions, and even the administering of justice. Once state conventions, based on universal male suffrage, had created new constitutions that abolished slavery and allowed for black suffrage, states were to hold elections to establish new governments. Their legislatures were then required to ratify the Fourteenth Amendment before Congress would readmit their representatives. The Reconstruction Acts also reasserted Congress's authority over disfranchisement and pardoning power, which had been left in limbo by the delay in ratifying the Fourteenth Amendment. Over the next year the Fortieth Congress would pass three Supplemental Reconstruction Acts, clarifying and extending the military's role in voter registration and the supervision of civil officials, and closing electoral loopholes affecting the state conventions.

The laws passed alongside the Reconstruction Acts were designed to protect Congress's program from executive meddling. The Tenure of Office Act forbade the president from removing officials without the consent of the Senate, and the Command of the Army Act forced the president to issue all army orders through the general-in-chief, Ulysses S. Grant. Still, President Johnson did his best to obstruct the process, by removing from command military officers who displayed Radical tendencies in executing the congressional directives.

By mid-June 1868 seven states had successfully met these criteria and had their representatives readmitted to Congress: Arkansas, Alabama, Florida, Georgia, Louisiana, North Carolina, and South Carolina. In these states new governments replaced the Johnson governments and their military supervisors. After blacks were expelled from the Georgia legislature in September 1868, Congress placed the state back under military control; not until 1870 did Georgia and the remaining three states, Texas, Virginia, and Mississippi, return to the Union and Congress. By that point Congress also required the ratification of the Fifteenth Amendment for readmission.

Congressional Reconstruction involved more than the legislation enacted to return the Southern states to Congress. It was in some ways a general outline designed to revamp the South; reconfigure the relationship of the legislative, executive, and judicial branches of government; and secure political control of the South and Congress for the Republican Party. For instance, in early 1868, when the Supreme Court prepared to consider *Ex parte McCardle,* Congress, fearful that an adverse decision would jeopardize its Reconstruction agenda, promptly removed the case from the Court's jurisdiction. Similarly, the impeachment and trial of President Johnson was an effort to remove an obstacle to fundamental social and political change. The charges that Johnson had violated the Tenure of Office Act are dubious, but Article XI of the Articles of Impeachment, which claimed that Johnson interfered with the laws of Congress and sought to prevent their execution, was not far wrong. The Radicals' attempt at conviction failed, but this was a moot point; by mid-1868 Johnson was a lame duck, Republicans firmly controlled Congress and the Reconstruction process, and all indications were that they would soon control the presidency as well.

Broadly conceived, Congressional Reconstruction involved more than the relationship between certain states and the Union. The Military Reconstruction Acts and the Fourteenth and Fifteenth Amendments fundamentally altered Southern, and American, society. Nor did Congressional Reconstruction end with readmission to Congress, for the process of economic rehabilitation and the new racial dynamics of U.S. politics forced the federal government to intervene in the former Confederate states for several years. Congressional Republicans had hoped to establish a self-sustaining process that would allow a return to a traditional state-and-federal balance of power. Instead, myriad problems plagued the new governments of the South, ranging from inexperience and corruption to economic disasters to reactionary Conservative violence. In the end, Congressional Reconstruction proved a fleeting experiment, and by the late 1870s the former Confederate states were controlled by the same class of men that President Johnson had allowed back into power a decade earlier.

See also: Amnesty Proclamations; Army Appropriations Act; Black Codes; Black Suffrage; Blacks (Slave and Free), Johnson's Attitude toward; Civil Rights Act; Conservatives; Constitution, Johnson's Attitude toward; Democratic Party; Election of 1866; Fifteenth Amendment; Fourteenth Amendment; Freedmen's Bureau Bills (and Vetoes); Governors, Provisional; Impeachment; Joint Committee on Reconstruction; Military Districts; Military Reconstruction Acts; Pardons (Individual); Presidential Reconstruction; Readmission of Southern States; Reconstruction; Republican Party; Tenure of Office Act; Thirteenth Amendment; Vetoes; Washington's Birthday Speech.

References: Benedict, Michael Les, *A Compromise of Principle: Congressional Republicans and Reconstruction, 1863–1869* (1974); Foner, Eric, *Reconstruction: America's Unfinished Revolution, 1863–1877* (1988); Perman, Michael, *Reunion without Compromise: The South and Reconstruction, 1865–1868* (1973); Trefousse, Hans L., *The Radical Republicans: Lincoln's Vanguard for Racial Justice* (1969).

Congressman, Johnson as (1843–1853)

While Andrew Johnson was serving his term in the Tennessee state senate (1841–1843), the legislature was involved in adjusting the legislative and congressional districts in the state. Johnson was appointed chair of the joint committee to lay out the districts. The results in East Tennessee were that the legislative districts favored the Whigs, whereas the First Congressional District (Johnson, Carter, Sullivan, Washington, Hawkins, Greene, and Cocke counties) had a majority of Democrats. It is not known whether Johnson deliberately helped to make this happen, but he benefited from the situation for ten years.

In 1843 Johnson engaged in quite a few political maneuvers, such as replacing long-term pro-Whig Greeneville postmaster William Dickson, in order to unseat the incumbent congressman, Abraham McClellan of Blountville, and get the Democratic nomination for himself. Johnson ran against John A. Aiken of Jonesboro, and despite the vituperative newspaper criticisms by Whig editor William G. "Parson" Brownlow, Johnson was victorious 5,495 to 4,892.

Johnson went to Washington without his wife, Eliza, but he took his oldest child, Martha, so that she could attend school in Georgetown. Not much involved in capitol social activities, Johnson spent a lot of time in the Library of Congress improving his education. It was in this period that he discovered Joseph Addison's *Cato,* which became one of Johnson's very favorite literary works and from which he liked to quote.

While in Congress, Johnson was a Democrat, but because of his own extreme adherence to Jeffersonian-Jacksonian principles, he was frequently at odds with many of the other Democrats in Congress. Although most Democrats agreed with Johnson in opposing many types of internal improvements and tariffs, Johnson took these things to extremes. As he had done in the state legislature, he opposed what he considered to be any type of unnecessary public expenditure. Consequently he voted against many measures that would cost money, such as much-needed funds to refurbish the White House and compensation for the victims of a gun explosion on the navy's USS *Princeton.* He also introduced a resolution to reduce the number of government clerks. Johnson was a member of the committee on claims, so he spent a lot of time working on these compensation cases. He also presented various petitions for his constituents. As a typical Southern Democrat, Johnson favored the acquisition of Texas and the expansion of slavery.

In 1845 Brookins Campbell, Johnson's two-time adversary for the state legislature, challenged Johnson's renomination, but the latter managed to be renominated anyway. The Whigs chose Brownlow to oppose Johnson. Brownlow took full advantage of the columns of his newspaper, the *Whig,* to vigorously castigate Johnson, particularly charging that Johnson was an abolitionist and an infidel. Nevertheless, Johnson won by a vote of 6,068 to 4,715.

During his second term in Congress, Johnson continued as an advocate of poor workingmen and "mechanics" against the aristocrats. He had a run-in with Jefferson Davis when Johnson understood some comments Davis made in a speech to be insulting to tailors. Johnson continued to oppose internal improvements and to advocate economy in government spending. It was at this time that Johnson became an outspoken opponent of the Smithsonian Institution because it would cost the government much more than Smithson's bequest. In conjunction with his support for the protection and expansion of slavery and the admission of Texas, Johnson supported the Mexican-American War. He opposed the Wilmot Proviso, which would have prevented slavery in any territory acquired from Mexico. Johnson tried to get military commissions for such Tennessee friends as Sam Milligan and helped to organize Tennessee regiments. However, he opposed raising the soldier's pay from $8 to $10 per month. On March 27, 1846, Johnson first introduced his Homestead Bill, which he would continue to push throughout the rest of his terms in the House and his years in the Senate.

During this term in office Johnson became increasingly alienated from President James K. Polk, even though they were both from the same party and state. These problems were partly a result of Polk's realizing that Johnson had originally supported Lewis Cass of Michigan for the Democratic nomination in 1844. Johnson had campaigned for Polk after the latter's nomination, but the president had failed to give Johnson the patronage opportunities the congressman thought he deserved. On February 2, 1847, Johnson made a speech in Congress denouncing the Polk administration. This was actually a campaign maneuver for reelection back home, because Johnson expected to be running against Landon C. Haynes, a Democrat. But Johnson miscalculated, giving the Whigs an advantage. They nominated Oliver P. Temple, a young lawyer, who set out to appeal to Johnson's enemies within his own party by pointing out his inconsistencies. The 1847 congressional race was the closest of the five and Johnson won only 5,658 to 5,342.

During his third term, Johnson continued his obsession with economy and his vendetta against the Smithsonian. He was still trying to reduce the number of government clerks or, failing that, their salaries; he opposed spending money for a memorial grave marker for the recently deceased John Quincy Adams; and he denied that Congress had the power to appropriate money to pave the streets of Washington, D.C. Although as a state legislator Johnson had opposed railroad expansion, as a congressman, he favored assistance for the East Tennessee and Virginia Railroad Company to provide better transportation for his constituents. He also continued to support the Mexican-American War and the expansion of slavery. In December 1848 Johnson introduced his Homestead Bill once more.

In 1849 Johnson was again renominated, despite the efforts of Brookins Campbell. His Whig opponent was Nathaniel G. Taylor, who would later be commissioner of Indian affairs under Johnson. Johnson was victorious 6,068 to 5,060.

During Johnson's fourth term, Congress was consumed by the issues ultimately resolved in the Compromise of 1850. Johnson actually proposed a compromise himself: admit California; legalize the provisional governments in Utah and New Mexico; pass a stronger fugitive slave law; and give Washington, D.C., back to Maryland, where slavery was legal, thus solving questions about ending slavery there. Johnson's recommendations were not followed, although some of them resembled the final solution. The only provision of the actual Compromise of 1850 that Johnson did not support was ending the slave trade in Washington, D.C., because he still wanted to return that city to Maryland. Johnson continued to push for his Homestead Bill. In February 1851 he introduced a bill to provide for the direct election of various public officials, such as judges.

In his fifth and last congressional campaign (1851), Johnson's opponent was Democrat Landon C. Haynes. Although it was a difficult campaign, Johnson won 6,538 to 4,844. During this final term, Johnson continued to advocate extreme government economy and once again introduced his bills for direct election of government officials. He finally saw a measure of success for his Homestead Bill on May 12, 1852, when it passed the House 107 to 56. But it soon died in a Senate committee.

In 1852 the Tennessee legislature, which had a Whig majority, gerrymandered the First Congressional District to make it a Whig rather than a Democratic district. As a result, Johnson successfully ran for governor instead.

Johnson attempted reelection to the House of Representatives once more, in 1872. When the regular Democratic Convention nominated Benjamin F. Cheatham, the representative of the Confederate military faction for Tennessee's new at-large seat, Johnson decided to run as an independent. The third candidate in the race was the Republican, Horace Maynard. The three campaigned around the state, sometimes jointly. It was no surprise that Johnson ran a poor third, but he split the Democratic vote so that Maynard won. Johnson's supporters rejoiced in the defeat of Cheatham and believed that Johnson had made a great contribution to that defeat.

See also: Brownlow, William Gannaway "Parson"; Constitutional Amendments, Proposed; Davis, Jefferson; Democratic Party; Governor, Civilian, Johnson as; Homestead Act; Johnson, Eliza McCardle; Maynard, Horace; Milligan, Sam; Patronage; Patterson, Martha Johnson; Polk, James Knox; Postpresidential Career; Railroads; Senator, Johnson as; State Legislator, Johnson as; Taylor, Nathaniel Green; Temple, Oliver Perry; Whig Party.

References: Congressional Quarterly's *Guide to U.S. Elections* (1975); Graf, LeRoy P., Haskins, Ralph W., and Bergeron, Paul H., eds., *The Papers of Andrew Johnson* vols. 1–2, 16 (1967–2000); Trefousse, Hans L., *Andrew Johnson: A Biography* (1989).

Conquered Provinces Theory

See Reconstruction

Conservatives

During Andrew Johnson's lifetime, the term "conservative" had many meanings and referred to a variety of groups who held similar, but not identical, goals, attitudes, and ideals. The term "conservative" was used for and by many of them because at their core they shared a common approach to government, a common understanding of the U.S. Constitution, and a common conception of the nature of humanity.

One of the earliest philosophers of conservatism was John Locke (1632–1704). Locke's conservatism included a limited government, the support of property rights, and the supremacy of a representative legislature over a single ruler. Locke argued that whereas liberals condone revolution, popular sovereignty, and natural rights, conservatives are more moderate and try to restrain power from both above and below. Suspicious of human nature and pessimistic in their views toward human virtues, conservatives distrusted both one-person rule and open democracy.

Perhaps conservatism's greatest theorist was Edmund Burke (1729–1797), who built upon Locke's ideas. Burke defined conservatism as a defense against major changes in the political, social, and economic institutions of a society. Conservatives, according to Burke, support the status quo but do not oppose all change. Instead they believe that stability can be maintained only if changes are introduced slowly and carefully, so that society can gradually absorb and react to its new character. In fact, the term "conservative" comes from the French *conservateur*, a name given to French writers of the nineteenth century who looked back longingly at the monarchies, political stability, and privilege of the eighteenth century.

In the United States, conservatism only rarely appeared in political rhetoric before the late 1830s. Surprisingly, despite the later connection between the Democratic Party and conservatism, the first politicians who used the term regularly were the Whigs. The Whig Party appeared as a response to the authoritarian nature of Andrew Jackson, whom they called "King Andrew I." Whigs also had strong reservations about the expanding democratic process, which Jackson and his Democratic Party initiated.

So, although Whigs opposed Jackson's alleged abuse of executive power, they also feared the extension of suffrage to what they called the "Mob." Claiming that they were the true heirs of the Founding Fathers and protectors of the Constitution, Whigs argued that Democrats were destroying the very fabric of society.

By the 1850s the Whig Party had dissolved under the acid of sectional interests, in particular slavery. Now the Democrats began to call themselves conservatives, charging that the newly formed Republican Party sought to upset the status quo. Democratic spokesmen appealed to everything from the Bible to the U.S. Constitution in defense of slavery, local control instead of national centralization, the natural inequality of races, and states' rights. But there were gradations within the party. Northern Democrats Lewis Cass and Stephen Douglas, for example, advocated popular sovereignty in the territories, an idea opposed by most Southern conservative Democrats. The most conservative Democrats believed in natural differences among genders, races, and classes and held that government attempts to modify this status quo were unconstitutional and dangerous. Southern conservatives became convinced that their class system, their plantation system, their national power, and even their property (slaves) were in jeopardy.

During 1860–1861, eleven Southern states embarked on a conservative revolution, a desperate gamble to try to keep Northern changes from sweeping the South, changes such as antislavery sentiments and legislation, industrial capitalism, and foreign immigration. Not all Southerners favored secession or even slavery itself, but most who finally supported the Confederacy could be classified as conservatives because they opposed changing the social, political, and economic systems. But the dynamic nature of war soon revealed conservative elements in the North as well, where the pressures and issues of a civil war exposed a spectrum of political viewpoints.

Early in the war a few radical thinkers such as abolitionist William Lloyd Garrison and Senator Charles Sumner envisioned emancipation as a war aim. They considered men such as Abraham Lincoln and Secretary of State William H. Seward to be conservatives because these officials held more limited views of the war and its aims. Yet to others Lincoln was a dangerous radical, bent on usurping power and destroying the Constitution. Northerners who opposed the war effort, ranging from the pro-Southern Copperheads to the more moderate Peace Democrats, considered themselves true conservatives and believed that Lincoln's wartime suppression of civil liberties as well as his party's financial and military policies were far more illegal and treasonous than secession. These Northern conservatives saw the Confiscation Acts, Congress's emancipation of District of Columbia and then territorial blacks, and Lincoln's Emancipation Proclamation as federal attempts to destroy the Constitution and secure total control of the government.

When Andrew Johnson became president in April 1865, he appeared to be all things to all people. To more radical elements in the Republican Party, his antisecession stance, experience as military governor of Tennessee, and apparent openness to black suffrage suggested that he might deal harshly with former rebels. But Northern and Southern conservatives, including former Confederates, Northern Peace Democrats and Copperheads, and even conservative Republicans, saw Johnson differently. He was, after all, not a Republican, but a Democrat who had been elected vice president on the Union (not Republican) Party platform. A Southerner, former slaveholder, fiscal conservative, and states' rights supporter in the Jacksonian tradition, Johnson might be amenable to a new coalition. Before the war, Johnson had detested secession-minded planters as much as abolitionists; perhaps he would agree to a new, "conservative" party, one based on old Whigs,

Southern Unionist Democrats, Northern War Democrats, and conservative Republicans. From late 1865 on, these groups began to use the term "conservative" to identify themselves because they wanted to appear as the forces of moderation and reconciliation, defending the Constitution and the states against revolutionary changes. Also, many conservative Republicans and even Peace Democrats sought to avoid the "Democratic" designation, as it denoted treason and rebellion.

Conservative elements in the North and South were encouraged by Johnson's May 29, 1865, proclamation for North Carolina that excluded blacks from voting in the restoration process. His selection of former Unionists as provisional governors indicated his moderate approach to Reconstruction. Johnson also hinted that any changes in suffrage needed to come from the states, not the federal government. The new president made other conservative gestures as well, such as removing black troops from the Southern states and restricting the confiscation of former Confederates' property. With congressional Radicals such as Thaddeus Stevens and Charles Sumner already agitating for black suffrage, conservatives hoped that the Northern public would see Johnson as the voice of moderation and repudiate congressional challenges to the established order.

Johnson's 1866 vetoes of the Freedmen's Bureau Bill and the Civil Rights Bill drew the dividing line between conservatives and those intent on creating a new nation. While the president's belligerent stance drove many moderate Republicans into the Radical ranks, it also encouraged conservatives who now truly believed that Johnson had the courage to oppose rapid change in American society. On March 29, 1866, Northern conservatives founded the National Johnson Constitutional Union Club, lead by Montgomery Blair, which spearheaded the drive to block the Radical's revolution. By summer, conservative clubs had appeared across the North, and in a June meeting with conservatives Alexander Randall, Orville Browning, Senator Edgar Cowan, and Senator James R. Doolittle, President Johnson expressed his desire to see a new party emerge for the fall elections.

The National Union Party had problems from the beginning. Some conservatives opposed the idea, including the influential Manton Marble, proprietor of the *New York World,* who argued that the Democratic Party, rather than a new party, was the only hope for staving off Radical dominance. Hoping that the new party would attract both Southern and Northern moderates, moderate Republicans were outraged when Copperheads were invited. Even the notorious Clement Vallandigham was elected to the proposed August convention in Philadelphia, although he declined to attend on advice from friends. Worse was the growing evidence that Johnson's conservative approach to the South was a failure, as indicated by the New Orleans riot of July 31, 1866. In this light, speeches at the convention seemed inconsistent with reality, with men such as Henry J. Raymond of the *New York Times* declaring that the South was at peace and blacks would be served best if left to the care of state governments. Coming on the heels of the convention, Johnson's ill-fated Swing-around-the-Circle campaign tour only exacerbated the National Union movement's problems. Their inability to compromise and inflexibility on constitutional issues cost the conservatives dearly, and the elections of 1866 ushered in a Radical-dominated Congress.

Conservative defeat in the congressional elections of 1866 had two results. First, Congress had popular support to begin reorganizing the South on its terms, and second, conservatives realized that if they did not adapt to the times they might well become obsolete. In early 1867 some conservatives demonstrated that they had learned that total opposition was ineffectual. President Johnson, trying to forestall the imposition of black suffrage on the South, worked out the "Southern (or North Carolina) Plan" with several Southern governors as a compromise. This plan substituted a new constitutional amendment for the pending Fourteenth Amendment. This substitute omitted the exclusion of former Confederates from office, but included a repudiation of secession. The new amendment approved of black suffrage in theory, but remanded the decision to the states and suggested that suffrage be based upon literacy and property qualifications (not applicable to anyone already voting). But the plan met with little support because too many moderate Republicans had followed the Radical lead, whereas many Southerners opposed conceding so much to blacks and their Republican allies. Furthermore, some Southern conservatives had stopped following Johnson; many blamed him for the devastating defeats in the fall of 1866, and it soon became evident that he was also to blame for the next great disaster, the coming of Congressional Reconstruction. Johnson's advice to former Confederate states that they should reject the Fourteenth Amendment did not rally conservative Northerners or throw Radical Republicans into chaos; instead it resulted in a complete restructuring of Southern society.

The passage of the Military Reconstruction Acts in the spring of 1867 brought momentous changes to the South. Most historians date the appearance of Conservative *parties* (rather than conservatives) to the implementation of Congressional (or Military) Reconstruction, for here Southern conservatives coalesced into autonomous, state-oriented parties, rather than just being ambiguous allies of Northerners who had similar goals. In fact, in many former Confederate states the designation "Conservative" became the official party name, replacing "Democratic," which carried treasonous connotations. Composed of everything from secession Democrats to Unionist Democrats and former

Whigs, these Conservative parties broke with their parallels in the North. After failing to build a new national coalition, following the misguided advice of President Johnson, and watching more Northern conservatives and moderates move to the left, conservative Southerners understood that they needed to stand on their own. The party name "Conservative" was indicative of a *negative* approach, one that opposed universal suffrage, ex-Confederate disfranchisement, and federal intervention in social and racial affairs.

Even here, however, there were variations across Conservative parties. In some states, such as South Carolina and Virginia, there was an early attempt by Conservatives to win over new black voters, relying on antebellum ties and threats of a new slavery to "Northern adventurers." The Conservative parties' constituencies and interests varied as well. In South Carolina and Texas, for example, agrarians and old planters adhered to an antebellum economy, whereas in Alabama and Virginia, former planters embraced Northern industrialism and railroad development.

But a common theme united the Conservatives: opposition to federal control over racial matters. Even in states where Conservatives sought to cooperate with the new black electorate, the goal was to control it in order to maintain white supremacy. The temporary courting of black votes (as by Wade Hampton in South Carolina) was done for expediency, not a genuine interest in the welfare of blacks. By 1868 Conservatives in every former Confederate state except Virginia were actively seeking to defeat the new state constitutions, which would permanently enfranchise blacks and entrench a Southern Republican Party (in Virginia the Conservative Party managed to legally assume power). Defeating the new state constitutions would prevent restoration and continue military rule; Conservatives preferred this over black Republican domination.

Once again Conservative ideals were swept aside in favor of liberal reforms. By the summer of 1868 nearly every Southern state was under a new constitution and a Republican government. Although distraught, Conservatives believed that Radical dominance would lead to corruption, racial intermarriage, and racial equality, all of which would convince Northerners that black suffrage was a mistake. Again Conservatives were to be disappointed, for although very few Northerners eagerly embraced black voting, by 1868 they were prepared to impose it upon the South rather than return former Confederates to power.

Southern Conservatives were not completely friendless. Their views on black suffrage were shared by many conservative Republicans and Northern Democrats. However, the election of 1868 demonstrated that these groups, even allied with Southern Conservatives, were politically impotent. The ticket of Horatio Seymour and General Francis P. Blair, Jr., overplayed its conservatism, especially after Blair made it clear that he opposed Congressional Reconstruction and would overturn Southern governments by force if necessary. On the other hand, the Republicans and their candidate, Ulysses S. Grant, took a moderate stand and largely avoided the controversial issue of black suffrage. Republicans did not avoid attacking the Democrats for their role in causing the Civil War, and using the Democratic designation made this inevitable, as Southern Conservatives had predicted.

Democratic defeat in 1868 reinforced the earlier supposition that Southern Conservatives could expect no help from the North. Beginning in 1869, with Republicans in control of both Congress and the presidency, Southern Conservatives found other ways to reexert control in their states. Fraud, economic blackmail (not hiring blacks who voted Republican), and outright violence by such organizations as the Ku Klux Klan curtailed the black turnout substantially. In 1871 Tennessee joined Virginia as a "redeemed" state, meaning that Conservatives had regained control of the state government. The Conservatives captured state after state with the last three, Louisiana, Florida, and South Carolina, falling in 1877.

Historians have characterized these "redeemers" by many names, including "conservatives," "Bourbons," "traditionalists," and "irreconcilables." To be sure, many differences existed across the states, and even within state Conservative parties. In some states, Conservatives sought to reestablish antebellum planter control, whereas in others a growing merchant middle class accepted Northern capitalism and industrialism. But at their core, Conservative parties were blood kin: they nearly always combined former Whigs and Democrats (except for South Carolina, which had no antebellum Whig organization to speak of) who wished to avoid the reactionary policies of the "unreconstructed" rebels, but who also opposed the egalitarian dogma of Republicans. Despite economic, class, and social differences, all the Conservative parties espoused home rule and white supremacy, which included white social superiority, white control of land and labor, and white domination in politics.

Despite their failures during Reconstruction, conservatives were not without their victories. One could argue that conservatives in Congress played pivotal roles; after all, Northern conservatives watered down the Military Reconstruction Acts and constitutional amendments and saved President Johnson from conviction at his impeachment trial. Of course the truculence of Southern conservatives, including President Andrew Johnson, brought about much of Congressional Reconstruction, but it was also Southern conservatives who played the largest role in determining the future of the postwar South. Congressional Reconstruction was a brief and largely unsuccessful experiment. Instead, white conservative Southerners would decide the

South's course. Their attitudes about race, the economy, the North, and even the Civil War and Reconstruction determined the shape of the South for generations to come.

See also: Amnesty Proclamations; Bennett, James Gordon (Jr. and Sr.); Bingham, John Armor; Black Suffrage; Black Troops in the South; Browning, Orville Hickman; Civil Rights Act; Congressional Reconstruction; Constitution, Johnson's Attitude toward; Democratic Convention; Democratic Party; Doolittle, James Rood; Election of 1866; Election of 1868; Elections of 1867; Fourteenth Amendment; Hancock, Winfield Scott; Jackson, Andrew; Military Reconstruction Acts; National Union Convention and Party; New Orleans Riot; Presidential Reconstruction; Randall, Alexander Williams; Republican Party; Schofield, John McAllister; Seymour, Horatio; Swing-around-the-Circle; Whig Party.

References: Benedict, Michael Les, *A Compromise of Principle: Congressional Republicans and Reconstruction, 1863–1869* (1974); Cooper, William J., Jr., *The Conservative Regime: South Carolina, 1877–1890* (1968); Donald, David Herbert, *The Politics of Reconstruction, 1863–1867* (1965); Gambill, Edward L., *Conservative Ordeal: Northern Democrats and Reconstruction, 1865–1868* (1981); Maddex, Jack P., Jr., *The Virginia Conservatives, 1867–1879: A Study in Reconstruction Politics* (1970); Perman, Michael, *Reunion without Compromise: The South and Reconstruction, 1865–1868* (1973); Sigler, Jay A., ed., *The Conservative Tradition in American Thought* (1969); Silber, Nina, *The Romance of Reunion: Northerners and the South, 1865–1900* (1993); Silbey, Joel H., *The American Political Nation, 1838–1893* (1991); Woodward, C. Vann, *Origins of the New South, 1877–1913* (1951).

Constitution, Johnson's Attitude toward

For Andrew Johnson, the U.S. Constitution was a rigid blueprint for American society, designed to protect the nation from the dangers of passing fads or foolish trends. After all, Johnson's United States was a nation in transition. The world of the nation's Founding Fathers was being swept away by the onset of early industrialism, the market revolution, the rise of antislavery and abolitionism, and the growth of the Whig Party (and later the Republican Party) with its activist ideas of federal intervention. Johnson feared that such changes could threaten democracy and disrupt the opportunities afforded young men who hoped to share in the wealth and political process. According to Johnson, the writers of the Constitution had crafted a system that protected opportunity so that all male citizens had an equal stake and an equal chance. Given a fair chance, the common man could rise above his station and, in the United States, achieve great things; Johnson himself was an example.

Johnson dedicated his political life to guarding the sanctity of the U.S. Constitution because it protected the people against tyranny, the oppression of the wealthy, excessive and unwarranted taxation, and self-interested business monopolies. In Johnson's life the states were the primary defenders of the Constitution and the primary focus of a citizen's loyalty: state citizenship was supreme, the state set voting qualifications, and states dictated federal policy because state legislatures elected U.S. senators.

As a result, Johnson the legislator tried to protect the needs of the many and opposed changes that benefited the few. As a state representative in the 1830s, Johnson opposed many internal improvements, such as aid to railroads, because they would create unfair monopolies. Instead, he pushed for spending on education, which would benefit all citizens equally; this stance cost him reelection. Johnson opposed the National Bank, and later, as a U.S. Representative, he argued against high protective tariffs. He feared that the federal government was developing a program to benefit bankers and large manufacturers at the expense of farmers and artisans. In comparison, in 1846 he introduced his Homestead Bill. Johnson believed that his bill, which did not become law until 1862, was a constitutional extension of federal power: it cost taxpayers nothing, favored no class or geographic region, and did not sap American self-reliance because occupants retained the land only if they worked it.

But most of his arguments opposed extending federal power. For instance, he supported the Gag Rule and contended that Congress had no authority to prevent the expansion of slavery into the new western territories. Slavery, after all, involved the sacred element of private property and was protected by the U.S. Constitution. Even as late as December 1860, Johnson refused to yield on slavery. He offered an "unamendable amendment" that would allay Southern fears with further constitutional guarantees covering slavery. Here again his constitutionalism was flexible because he would bend the guidelines to prevent a greater danger; he would alter the Constitution to prevent secession and protect the Union.

When finally forced to choose between states' rights and the Union, Johnson chose the Union. In a stirring two-day speech in the Senate on December 18 and 19, 1860, Johnson argued that secession was unconstitutional and that differences needed to be worked out within the Union. Secession, and the war that must follow, were not the result of democratic processes, but were brought on by a handful of troublemakers, North and South. Johnson stood by the Constitution and the Union: "In saving the Union, we save this, the greatest Government on earth."

Thus Johnson embarked on an end-justifies-the-means approach when the Union was in danger. His rejection of secession, his support of the Lincoln administration, his unprecedented role as military governor, and his emancipation of Tennessee slaves were done to protect the Union, which best protected the rights and opportunities of the people; in this he was convinced that he followed the spirit, if not the letter, of the Constitution. Yet the war must be restrained also, so as to not damage the Constitution. In July 1861, Johnson sponsored the War Aims Resolution (also known as the Crittenden-Johnson Resolution), which stated that the war was being fought to restore the Union and not to abolish slavery or for "any purpose of conquest or subjugation" nor to "interfere with the rights or established institutions of those States." The federal government sought to defend the Constitution and preserve the "dignity, equality, and rights of the several States unimpaired." The resolution passed 30 to 5 in the Senate, and a similar one passed overwhelmingly in the House.

Johnson's position as military governor of Tennessee fit in well with his views. Although at first his new role seemed inconsistent with his narrow constitutionalism, Johnson stood for popular government, and it was his duty to restore the state to a republican form of government as guaranteed by the U.S. Constitution. He ousted from office Confederates and their sympathizers, disfranchised the disloyal, held elections, supervised conventions, and forwarded various resolutions to the public for ratification. By early 1865 a new state government began to take shape, with only minimal interference by federal authorities. When Johnson left for Washington to become vice president, Tennesseans were under a new government and a new constitution, both of their own making.

This experience colored Johnson's perceptions of Reconstruction. If, during wartime, a state could be allowed the traditional powers afforded it under the Constitution—judging the qualifications of its voters, for instance—why during peacetime should the situation be different? When Johnson took control of Reconstruction in the spring of 1865, he attempted to return the nation to its federal system as quickly as possible, leaving state powers to the states, and federal powers to the federal government.

Johnson intended to keep the states as the true power base within the republic. Whereas many Northerners and Republicans believed that the war had irrevocably shifted power to the federal level, Johnson tried to keep an antebellum balance of power between the state and national levels. His amnesty proclamations were based upon the executive's pardon power as denoted in the Constitution; he had exercised such power as state governor and had insisted that Lincoln use it during the war. Johnson's appointment of provisional governors may have been unprecedented, but their role was to restart traditional processes of democratic government within the states. Johnson also avoided interfering in areas traditionally left to the states, such as suffrage qualifications or civil rights.

Congress eventually overturned Johnson's program in favor of an expanded federal role. Historians contend that Johnson could have prevented this by capitalizing on divisions between moderate and Radical Republicans. But historians misunderstand Johnson, for he saw no difference in the two groups. Unable to compromise on the Constitution, he perceived both groups as "radical" because each was ready, to varying extents, to alter the balance of power between the state and federal governments. The president's string of vetoes was consistent with his view of this traditional balance of power. "My policy," a phrase Johnson used countless times, represented a stiff defense of states' rights and opposition to the expansion of federal power. His 1866 vetoes of two Freedmen's Bureau Bills and the Civil Rights Bill, his opposition to the Fourteenth Amendment, and his 1867 vetoes of the Military Reconstruction Acts were based upon a traditional approach to the Constitution: military subordination to civil authority, an aversion to class-specific legislation, and a reliance upon the states (not the federal government) as the source and protector of citizens' rights. Although Johnson's racism certainly played a role in his vetoes, one should remember that he signed into law the Southern Homestead Act, which opened federal land to blacks as well as whites. Eventually Johnson's battle with Congress led to his impeachment, ostensibly for the violation of the Tenure of Office Act. As with the Civil War and his alleged interference with Congressional Reconstruction afterward, Johnson bent the Constitution to prevent, in his view, a greater constitutional calamity. The final break—Johnson's defiance of the Tenure Act—occurred because he and his entire cabinet believed the law to be unconstitutional because it infringed upon the powers and rights of the executive.

But a Congress that was able to impeach Johnson was not able to convict and remove him. A handful of Republicans came to the same conclusion, that a balance of power needed to be maintained at the federal level. Indeed, Johnson overstepped his authority in many ways, but Republicans realized that removing him was a greater threat to constitutional order than allowing him to remain. Just as Johnson had spent his life defending the Constitution, so it, in the end, had saved him. It comes as no surprise that the most sacred of American documents was buried with him.

See also: Amnesty Proclamations; Black Codes; Black Suffrage; Blacks (Slave and Free), Johnson's Attitude toward; Civil Rights Act; Congressional Reconstruction; Congressman, Johnson as; Conservatives; Constitutional Amendments, Proposed; Crittenden-Johnson Resolution; Democratic Party; District of Columbia Franchise; Finances, Johnson's Attitude toward Governmental; Fourteenth Amendment; Freedmen's Bureau Bills (and Vetoes); Funeral of Johnson; Governors, Provisional; Historical Attitudes toward Johnson; Homestead Act; Impeachment; *McCardle, Ex parte;* Military Governor of Tennessee, Johnson as; Military Reconstruction Acts; *Milligan, Ex parte;* Pardons (Individual); Presidential Reconstruction; Reconstruction; Republican Party; Secession, Johnson's Attitude toward; Senator, Johnson as; Tenure of Office Act; Thirteenth Amendment.

References: Graf, LeRoy P., Haskins, Ralph W., and Bergeron, Paul H., eds., *The Papers of Andrew Johnson* vol. 4 (1967–2000); McKitrick, Eric L., *Andrew Johnson and Reconstruction* (1960); McPherson, Edward, *The Political History of the United States of America during the Great Rebellion* 2nd ed. (1865); Sefton, James E., *Andrew Johnson and the Uses of Constitutional Power* (1980); Trefousse, Hans. L., *Impeachment of a President: Andrew Johnson, the Blacks, and Reconstruction* (1975).

Constitutional Amendments, Proposed

An apostle of a narrowly interpreted, inflexible Constitution, Andrew Johnson nonetheless advocated throughout his political career certain changes to the U.S. Constitution. As with other convictions, such as fiscal conservatism or his Homestead Bill, Johnson's devotion to his constitutional amendments reflected a stubborn fidelity to his value system.

Throughout his career Johnson sought ways to prevent a powerful government from treading on the rights of its citizens. Keeping the government tied to popular will, the essence of a democracy, was central to Johnson's republican philosophy. For Johnson, one of the best ways to ensure responsible and responsive government was to have it directly elected by the people. Johnson first proposed his constitutional amendments as a U.S. Representative in 1851. The amendments provided for the direct election of U.S. senators (rather than their election by state legislatures), a twelve-year term limit on all federal judges (including Supreme Court justices), and the modification of the electoral college. Johnson proposed eliminating the electoral college as it then existed because it served to distill the popular vote and place presidential elections in the hands of a few electors. Instead, Johnson envisioned electoral districts in each state, equivalent to the total number of federal senators and congressional representatives from that state. Each district represented one vote, so a candidate with a majority of votes in a particular district received the vote; the candidate with the national majority of these "electoral" votes became president. Johnson's proposition was defeated, and it failed the following year as well. As U.S. senator, he continued to agitate for the changes, but more pressing matters held the public's and Congress's attention.

Those matters came to a boil in the winter of 1860 after the election of Republican Abraham Lincoln. Still in the Senate, Johnson suddenly found a national audience for his constitutional amendments. Arguing that his modifications could avoid secession and war, in December of 1860 he presented a series of "unamendable amendments" to the Constitution. These included the direct election of the president (similar to his 1850s plan), who would serve a single six-year term. Likewise, federal judges would be restricted to one twelve-year term. Senators would be elected directly by the state citizenry. New wrinkles appeared with the threat of secession: the persons elected president and vice president would alternate between free and slave states. With the election of Lincoln in 1860, the next election would automatically fall to a Southern nominee. Territories would be divided among the slave and free states; states that did not assist in enforcing the Fugitive Slave Law would be assessed financial penalties; and Congress could not interfere with slavery in the District of Columbia, with the interstate slave trade, or with the three-fifths apportionment for Congress. Johnson's rousing "speech on secession," which occurred on December 18 and 19, was a plea for the acceptance of his amendments. As before, Johnson's suggestions fell on deaf ears.

Not until the waning months of his presidency did Johnson again attempt to alter the Constitution. Still hopeful of restraining the burgeoning power of the federal government, and basking in the glow of Senate acquittal, President Johnson made one last appeal in the summer of 1868. With the help of Judge Alfred O. P. Nicholson of Tennessee, who was staying in the White House, Johnson formulated another set of amendments for congressional consideration.

Some cabinet members disapproved the move, fearing that it would only anger Republicans who were still smoldering over defeat in the Senate trial. Secretary of the

Navy Gideon Welles, perhaps Johnson's most loyal supporter in the cabinet, opposed the amendments altogether. He rejected both the six-year presidential term and the single-term limit and favored keeping the electoral college and the legislative election of senators. Johnson's system, he feared, would favor more populous states, whereas the election of senators by state legislatures was by design: U.S. representatives represent the people and are elected by them. Senators represent the *states* and thus should be elected by legislatures. Welles feared that Johnson was making a pitch for the 1868 candidacy by trying to gain popular support in the wake of his rejection by the Democratic nominating convention. Secretary of State William H. Seward also opposed the amendments and cogently noted that if a presidential term had been six years, the Senate probably would have convicted Johnson.

Nonetheless, on July 18, 1868, Johnson forwarded his message to Congress. Johnson's proposal began by pointing out that Andrew Jackson first suggested a direct election of the president. From there Johnson examined the many flaws in the current system. For instance, electors were not required to follow the popular will, and the rise of party politics and nominating conventions restricted the opportunities for individuals to run for office. Direct election would open the field wide and prevent interference with popular sentiment. In a new amendment, Johnson also proposed a change in the line of presidential succession, suggesting that a person from the executive branch of government, rather than one from the legislative branch, follow the vice president. Johnson argued that the current system allowed for a consolidation of the executive and legislative powers never intended by the nation's Founders. He then followed with his usual suggestions regarding the direct election of senators and term limits for federal judges. Both the House and Senate received Johnson's proposals po-

litely and then referred them to judiciary committees, where the president's hopes languished for a while and then died.

Just as Johnson was unsuccessful in blocking constitutional amendments he opposed, he was unable to succeed in getting support for changes he desired. As late as 1873, in a speech while in Washington, Johnson reiterated the need for term limits and direct elections. Ironically, he would return to Washington again, in 1875, having been elected senator by the legislature of Tennessee.

See also: Cabinet Members; Congressman, Johnson as; Constitution, Johnson's Attitude toward; Crittenden-Johnson Resolution; Democratic Convention; District of Columbia Franchise; Lincoln, Abraham; Nicholson, Alfred Osborne Pope; Postpresidential Career; Secession, Johnson's Attitude toward; Senator, Johnson as; Seward, William Henry; Welles, Gideon.

References: Beale, Howard K., ed., *Diary of Gideon Welles* vol. 1 (1960 [1911]); Graf, Leroy P., Haskins, Ralph W., and Bergeron, Paul H., eds., *The Papers of Andrew Johnson* vols. 4, 14 (1967–2000); Sefton, James E., *Andrew Johnson and the Uses of Constitutional Power* (1980); Trefousse, Hans L., *Andrew Johnson: A Biography* (1989).

Consumption
See Tuberculosis

Cooper, Edmund (1821–1911)

Confidant and at times private secretary of Andrew Johnson, Edmund Cooper was born in Franklin, Tennessee, on September 11, 1821. He graduated from Jackson College, Columbia, Tennessee, in 1839 and in 1841 graduated from Harvard Law School. Promptly admitted to the bar, he began his law practice that same year in Shelbyville, Tennessee. In 1844 he married Mary E. Stephens (d. 1863), with whom he had three children. After several years as a widower, in 1868 Cooper married Lucy

Bonner, with whom he had one son. By 1856 Cooper had helped to organize the Bank of Shelbyville and was serving as its president.

Cooper's first political position was a seat in the Tennessee state house of representatives. Elected as a Whig, he served from 1849 to 1851. In 1861 Cooper was elected as a Unionist to the state convention to discuss secession, but he did not serve because the voters did not approve calling the convention to which they elected delegates.

Cooper's activities during the Civil War are not entirely clear. Certainly he was a devoted Unionist who spoke at Unionist meetings, sometimes on the platform with Military Governor Andrew Johnson in 1862. It is not known when Cooper and Johnson met, but they seem to have been friends already by the spring of 1862. In August of that year, Johnson appointed Cooper, along with Tennessee ex-governor William B. Campbell, as commissioners to visit Tennessee prisoners of war to determine who should be released or exchanged. Some time soon after this, Cooper was himself captured by the Confederates and in about November 1862 was exchanged for a rabid rebel Nashville lawyer, Turner S. Foster. Perhaps about this time Cooper was appointed one of Johnson's private secretaries, but it is not clear when the appointment was made or how long Cooper served.

Wherever else Cooper may have been during his career, he was frequently back in Shelbyville attending to his law practice. In 1863 Cooper, as a loyal slaveholder, was concerned that two of his menservants, who were "*absolutely necessary* for my comfort and convenience," might be impressed by Union recruiters of black troops who were then in Shelbyville. He asked Johnson to make sure that this did not happen.

In 1865 Cooper was again elected, as a Unionist, to the lower house of the Tennessee legislature and served in the session of April 3–June 12. During this period he was very conservative about the issue of disfranchisement, working to avoid the massive disfranchisement espoused by Governor William G. Brownlow and earning the governor's wrath by so doing.

Cooper resigned his state legislative seat after his election to the U.S. House of Representatives in August 1865. Like the rest of the Tennessee congressional delegation, Cooper had to wait nearly a year for admittance to the national legislative body. During this period Cooper seems to have spent some time as one of Johnson's four or five private secretaries, apparently in charge of appointments, and, at least for a time, taking Robert Johnson's place.

However long he served, Cooper was secretary long enough to have interacted with quite a few people who later wrote letters to Johnson that "Col. Cooper told them" some particular information (Cooper is not known to have had military experience and probably received the same rank held by Johnson's other secretaries who were detached from actual military service). Known to be close to Johnson, Cooper served as a conduit for people who wanted to get information to Johnson. Many wrote to Cooper asking him to pass on their concerns to the president. Many also used Cooper as a reference, saying that Cooper could tell Johnson who they were. Cooper also wrote numerous letters of recommendation for office seekers. When Cooper was finally admitted to his congressional seat on July 24, 1866, William G. Moore, already one of Johnson's secretaries, took over Cooper's duties.

Cooper actually served in the House only until March 3, 1867. He was not reelected in 1867 and in fact lost badly. He was opposed to black suffrage, and Governor Brownlow determined to defeat Cooper by interfering with voter registration in Cooper's district so that qualified whites were not registered and the district contained a majority of black voters. Brownlow also sent two companies of state militia to that district.

Cooper returned to Shelbyville and his law practice, but in September 1867 Johnson asked him to come to Washington, where Cooper stayed for some months as presidential "companion and friend." He may or may not have functioned as an aide or secretary. In late November 1867 Johnson nominated Cooper to be assistant secretary of the treasury. The Senate rejected Cooper's nomination on January 9, 1868, based on some 1863 law. However, Hugh McCulloch, secretary of the treasury, argued, based on precedent, that the law did not apply in this case and Cooper retained his post until shortly after Johnson left the presidency in March 1869. Cooper apparently remained with Johnson throughout the impeachment crisis. In July 1868 he attended the New York Democratic Convention, where he was one of those who worked hardest to promote Johnson's nomination. His reports to Johnson from the meeting were blunt, "Every body speaks kindly—but no more." They proposed only a complimentary resolution to Johnson. Ultimately the convention nominated Horatio Seymour. On July 5, while Cooper was still in New York, Johnson nominated him to replace Edward A. Rollins as commissioner of internal revenue. However, like all Johnson's nominees for this post, Cooper was rejected, but he did continue as assistant secretary of the treasury.

In 1869 Cooper was elected, as a Democrat, to a seat in the Tennessee state senate. Thus he would have a chance to help the legislature elect a senator for Tennessee. Johnson wanted very much to return to the Senate, but he had much opposition in Tennessee, both from the Radical Republicans and from former Confederates. The legislature began to vote on October 19. Two days later Johnson led with 48 votes, 4 votes short of a majority. However, on October 22, his opponents held a caucus and decided to unite behind Henry Cooper, a judge and the brother of Edmund. Unquestionably Edmund Cooper was in a very awkward position, being forced to choose between his brother and his close friend. Either choice was sure to cause difficulties. Ultimately Cooper supported his brother, who won by a vote of 55 to 51.

Johnson was deeply hurt by Cooper's "betrayal" and never forgave him. When he was campaigning for a Senate seat in 1874, Johnson frequently mentioned various notables in history who had suffered from traitors: George Washington had Benedict Arnold, Thomas Jefferson had Aaron Burr, Julius Caesar had Brutus, Jesus had Judas and Peter. Then Johnson proclaimed that he too had his Edmund and Henry (who had traitorously kept him from a Senate seat).

Edmund Cooper seems to have sacrificed his own political life to support his brother. His only further official position was as a Democratic presidential elector in 1876. He practiced law in Shelbyville until his retirement and died in that town on July 21, 1911.

See also: Brownlow, William Gannaway "Parson"; Democratic Convention; Johnson, Robert; McCulloch, Hugh; Military Governor of Tennessee, Johnson as; Patronage; Secretaries; Senator, Johnson as; Seymour, Horatio.
References: Graf, LeRoy P., Haskins, Ralph W., and Bergeron, Paul H., eds., *The Papers of Andrew Johnson* vols. 2, 4–6, 8, 10–16 (1967–2000); McBride, Robert M., et al., comps., *Biographical Directory of the Tennessee General Assembly* vol. 1 (1975–1991); Trefousse, Hans L., *Andrew Johnson: A Biography* (1989).

Coyle, John Francis (ca. 1822–fl. 1900)

Little is known about John Francis Coyle's early life beyond that he was a native of Washington, D.C., and was apparently well acquainted with some notable families such as those of Francis P. Blair and John Wilkes Booth. In 1848 he married Baltimore belle Kate Dowson (ca. 1826–1869) and they had two children, Annie (ca.

1849–fl. 1880) and Frank (ca. 1852–1909). From at least 1858 Coyle worked as a clerk and bookkeeper at the *National Intelligencer*.

The *Intelligencer* was a venerable, formerly Whig, newspaper in Washington, D.C., edited from 1812 to 1860 by William Winston Seaton and his brother-in-law Joseph Gales, Jr. After Gales died in 1860, Seaton, by this time seventy-five years old, ran the paper alone until late 1864. The paper recorded the daily activities of Congress and had a wide circulation before the Civil War, especially in Virginia. Although early in the war the *Intelligencer* took a fairly neutral tone, Seaton broke with Abraham Lincoln over the Emancipation Proclamation and supported George B. McClellan in the 1864 presidential race. The paper lost much of its remaining circulation to the pro-Lincoln *Chronicle*. At the end of December 1864, Coyle bought the paper in partnership with Chauncey H. Snow (fl. 1874) and immediately turned it into an extremely pro-Lincoln sheet.

On the morning of April 14, 1865, Coyle happened to run into John Wilkes Booth, whom he had known since the actor was a boy, and they shared "refreshments" in a nearby restaurant. Later in the day Booth wrote a letter to Coyle and gave it to the actor John Matthews, a friend of Coyle's, to be delivered the following day for publication in the *Intelligencer*. After he heard about the assassination, Matthews read the letter, burned it because he believed it would cause trouble for Coyle, and did not tell the editor about it until November 1865. Coyle, however, was harassed by the authorities because he had been seen talking to Booth on the day of the assassination and because there were rumors about the letter. Coyle did not reveal this information until 1898.

Coyle used the *Intelligencer* to support President Andrew Johnson and his policy. One other paper described the *Intelligencer* as Johnson's "official organ." Coyle also gave Johnson frequent advice on various political issues and on who should be appointed to what positions. At times, Coyle traveled to New York and New Orleans and reported to Johnson what opinions the president's "friends" in those locations expressed and what actions they wished Johnson to take.

Coyle hoped that Johnson would support the newspaper by giving the contracts to publish announcements for the various government departments to the *Intelligencer* rather than to its rival, the *Chronicle*. He also wanted Johnson to appoint candidates for offices who would give the *Intelligencer* their printing work. By July 1868 Coyle and Snow were deeply in debt and pleaded with Johnson to make these requested appointments in order to help them out of their desperate financial crisis. Coyle made clear that he did not expect a personal donation from Johnson but appropriate patronage, which he felt the *Intelligencer* had never received, despite the opinions to the contrary of some of Johnson's informants. Apparently the situation was resolved in some way that kept Coyle as Johnson's loyal friend and supporter. Evidence indicates that Johnson also provided Coyle with one or more loans. The *Intelligencer* supported the Democratic candidates Horatio Seymour and Frank P. Blair, Jr., in the presidential election of 1868.

When Johnson left the White House in March 1869, he and his family went to stay with the Coyles for two weeks. During this time Coyle accompanied Johnson to Baltimore for the grand banquet held in the former president's honor on March 11.

After Johnson returned to Greeneville, Tennessee, Coyle wrote to him explaining how certain money would be spent to pay off debts, including one to Johnson, apparently related to a receivership of the paper. But within a matter of months Coyle's life fell apart. On June 13, 1869, Coyle's wife Kate, who had also been Johnson's friend and occasional correspondent, died unexpectedly. Although she had suffered from a chronic illness, apparently for years, she became seriously sick only two days before her death. Then, on June 25, the *Intelligencer* folded, allegedly because of a printers' strike, which Coyle and Snow were unable to avert because of their financial straits. At the end of June, Coyle requested a further loan of $500 from Johnson to pay the debts associated with his wife's death and to help him to support his children.

Coyle's later life remains obscure. He held a variety of jobs in New York (for an asphalt paving company, for example) and Washington, D.C., and remained active in Democratic politics. On a few occasions he wrote to Johnson. He died sometime between 1900 and 1909.

See also: Blair, Francis Preston (Jr. and Sr.); Election of 1864; Election of 1868; Elections of 1867; Finances, Personal; Lincoln, Abraham; Lincoln Assassination Conspirators; Patronage.
References: 1860 Census, District of Columbia, Washington, 4th Ward, 266; Graf, LeRoy P., Haskins, Ralph W., and Bergeron, Paul H., eds., *The Papers of Andrew Johnson* vols. 10, 12–16 (1967–2000); Harper, Robert S., *Lincoln and the Press* (1951); Maione, Michael, and Hall, James O., "Why Seward? The Attack on the Night of April 14, 1865," *Lincoln Herald* 100 (Spring 1998): 29–34; *New York Times,* Dec. 18, 1909; Washington, D.C., city directories (1858–1868, 1898–1900); *Washington, D.C. Evening Star,* June 14 and 25, 1869; *Washington Post,* Apr. 17, 1898.

Crittenden-Johnson Resolution (1861)

The Crittenden-Johnson Resolution, also known as the War Aims Resolution, was passed by both houses of Congress in July 1861 in an attempt to define essentially conservative goals for the Union effort during the Civil War. The resolution was introduced in the House of Representatives on July 22 by John J. Crittenden of Kentucky (who is better known for his efforts to arrange a compromise between the North and South during the secession crisis of 1860–1861). The resolution passed the House the same day.

Andrew Johnson introduced a similar resolution in the Senate on July 24, although it was not considered until the next day. Johnson's version read: "*Resolved:* That the present deplorable civil war has been forced upon the country by the disunionists of the southern States now in revolt against the constitutional Government and in arms around the capital; that in this national emergency Congress, banishing all feeling of mere passion or resentment, will recollect only its duty to the whole country; that this war is not prosecuted upon our part in any spirit of oppression, nor for any purpose of conquest or subjugation, nor for the purpose of overthrowing or interfering with the rights or established institutions of those States, but to defend and maintain the supremacy of the Constitution and all laws made in pursuance thereof, and to preserve the Union, with all the dignity, equality, and rights of the several States unimpaired; that as soon as these objects are accomplished the war ought to cease."

The resolution was introduced just after the Union loss at First Bull Run (or Manassas) on July 21 and there was therefore special concern about Southerners being "in arms around the capital." Although the resolution initially provoked some heated debate in the Senate, eventually most were willing to define limited purposes for the war. As Johnson summarized it, the goals of the war were simply "to preserve the Constitution, to enforce the laws, and to preserve the Government." The Senate passed the resolution 30 to 5 on July 25. Later many Republican Congress members repudiated such limited purposes, and with Abraham Lincoln's Emancipation Proclamation the abolition of slavery also became a stated goal of the war.

Although Johnson himself would free the slaves in Tennessee, he never really went beyond these early conservative goals and they remained his purpose throughout the rest of his life. Echoes of the Crittenden-Johnson Resolution can be found in many of his later proclamations and speeches, for example, the Third Amnesty Proclamation of July 4, 1868, and his Knoxville speech of April 3, 1869, after he had left the presidency.

See also: Amnesty Proclamations; Blacks (Slave and Free), Johnson's Attitude toward; Constitution, Johnson's Attitude toward; Secession, Johnson's Attitude toward; Senator, Johnson as.

References: Graf, LeRoy P., "Andrew Johnson and the Coming of the War," *Tennessee Historical Quarterly* 19 (Sept. 1960): 208–221; Graf, LeRoy P., Haskins, Ralph W., and Bergeron, Paul H., eds., *The Papers of Andrew Johnson* vols. 4, 14, 15 (1967–2000); McPherson, James M., *Ordeal by Fire: The Civil War and Reconstruction* (1982).

Curtis, Benjamin Robbins (1809–1874)

One of Andrew Johnson's defense counsel, Benjamin Robbins Curtis, a native of Watertown, Massachusetts, was left fatherless at an early age. His widowed mother managed to earn enough money to prepare her son for Harvard and send him there in 1825. He graduated second in his class and attended the Harvard Law School for a time, but left in 1831 to take over an attorney's practice in Northfield, Massachusetts. About this time he married his cousin Eliza Maria Woodward (d. 1844). In 1834 he became a law partner to his distant cousin Charles Pelham Curtis in Boston, and they worked together for seventeen years. After the death of his first wife, Benjamin Curtis married his partner's daughter, Anna Wroe Curtis (d. 1860), in 1846.

Although Curtis had only a limited involvement in politics, he was a Whig supporting Daniel Webster and opposing the Free Soil Party in the late 1840s and early 1850s. He did serve in the Massachusetts house of representatives in 1851. In that same year Curtis, though only forty-one

years old, was appointed an associate justice of the U.S. Supreme Court. He wrote one of the two dissenting opinions in the *Dred Scott* case (1857), and after a disagreement with Chief Justice Roger B. Taney about the case, Curtis resigned from the Court in 1857.

Curtis had a notable and lucrative law practice after his resignation from the Court. He also married Maria Malleville Allen in 1861 after the death of his second wife. Although sympathizing publicly with the National Union Party in 1866, he apparently remained a conservative Republican. He had written to Johnson about cases involving former Supreme Court justice John A. Campbell and the dismissed General Fitz John Porter, before being selected to serve as one of Andrew Johnson's defense counsel during the impeachment.

Curtis made the opening speech for Johnson's defense on April 9, 1868. He clearly laid out the reasons why Secretary of War Edwin M. Stanton was not covered by the Tenure of Office Act; why Johnson had a right to test the constitutionality of a law; and why two of the articles attempted to restrict Johnson's freedom of speech, simply because he had a different opinion, which was not a criminal act. This was considered to be the best speech Curtis ever gave. He did not remain in Washington, D.C., for Johnson's entire trial, however, but returned to Boston for business on April 30, where he became ill.

After the successful conclusion of the impeachment trial, the Senate refused to confirm Henry Stanbery's reappointment as attorney general. Johnson then offered the post to Curtis who declined on June 8, 1868. He explained that he did not want a political office (perhaps as a result of his bad experience with the Supreme Court, although he did not say so). But he made certain that Johnson understood that he did not decline because he had any objection to Johnson's policies. He did not. Rather, he was committed to meeting the needs of his legal clients. Curtis's legal practice occupied him for the rest of his life and he is not known to have had any further contact with Johnson.

See also: Impeachment; Impeachment Defense Counsel; National Union Convention and Party; Stanbery, Henry; Stanton, Edwin McMasters; Tenure of Office Act.

References: Graf, LeRoy P., Haskins, Ralph W., and Bergeron, Paul H., eds., *The Papers of Andrew Johnson* vols. 8, 11, 14 (1967–2000); Trefousse, Hans L., *Andrew Johnson: A Biography* (1989).

Daughtry, Mary
See Johnson (Daughtry), Mary McDonough "Polly"

Daughtry, Turner (fl. 1840)

Andrew Johnson's stepfather, Turner Daughtry, has remained an obscure figure. His last name was spelled a variety of ways—Dougherty, Dotery, Dottery, etc.—and we have chosen the variation most frequently used in reputable sources. Perhaps from Sampson County, North Carolina, Daughtry was a propertyless voter and resident of Raleigh, North Carolina, who participated in the city watch, a type of police effort. He married Johnson's widowed mother, Mary McDonough Johnson, on May 6, 1812, and soon owned a lot valued in various years at $50 and $150. The Daughtrys had no children of their own.

In 1826 Turner and Mary Daughtry moved to Tennessee with Andrew Johnson, about the same time as Mary's other son, William P. Johnson, settled there. They located in Greeneville, where Daughtry served as an alderman in 1829. In a few years Andrew purchased a farm near Greeneville for his mother and stepfather.

Daughtry reportedly enjoyed watching his stepson's political contests.

Daughtry's date of death is not known, although he reportedly died of pneumonia while Andrew Johnson was in Congress. Daughtry was no longer living by the time of the 1850 census. He was probably buried in Old Harmony Cemetery, Greeneville, where many of the graves were unmarked or have been lost.

> **See also:** Greeneville, Tennessee; Johnson (Daughtry), Mary McDonough "Polly"; Johnson, William P.
> **References:** Andrew Johnson Project, Knoxville, TN, Johnson family files; Trefousse, Hans L., *Andrew Johnson: A Biography* (1989).

Davis, Jefferson (1807–1889)

Confederate president Jefferson Davis had several prewar conflicts with Andrew Johnson while both were in Congress and was at Johnson's mercy while imprisoned at Fort Monroe in Virginia after the Civil War. The future Confederate leader, the tenth child of Samuel Emory Davis and Jane Cook Davis, was born June 3, 1807 (or possibly 1808), in Kentucky and given the middle name Finis because he was the last child, although he never used that name. The family moved briefly to Louisiana and then to Mississippi. His father was extremely reserved and Jefferson developed a much closer relationship with his oldest brother Joseph Emory Davis (1784–1870), who functioned as a father figure for Jefferson for many years. When he was only nine, Jefferson was sent away to school in Kentucky, where he remained for several years. After more schooling in Mississippi, Jefferson attended Transylvania University in Kentucky for a year and then went to West Point. He graduated in 1828 and, because of his relatively low ranking (twenty-third of thirty-three), became a second lieutenant in the infantry.

Davis was not particularly happy in the military as he was on duty at several small, isolated forts in Wisconsin and Illinois. After several years of courting, he married Sarah Knox Taylor, daughter of his commanding officer, Zachary Taylor, on June 17, 1835. At this time Davis resigned from the army, intending to become a planter at "Brierfield," land purchased for him in Mississippi by his brother Joseph. No sooner had the couple arrived at their new home than both Jefferson and Sarah became very ill, probably with malaria. Sarah died on September 15, 1835. Jefferson needed several months to recover and had relapses for the rest of his life.

Davis continued as a planter and began to become interested in politics about 1840. He lost his first campaign for state representative in 1843 but he ran well for the Democrats on very short notice. On February 26, 1845, he married Varina Howell, with whom he eventually had six children (the four sons all predeceased him). That same year Davis was elected one of Mississippi's representatives in Congress. He threw himself fully into all the details of his office, unable to distinguish between the important and the trivial, and worked himself to exhaustion without allowing himself any opportunity for relaxation. (He would display these characteristics as Confederate president as well.)

In May 1846, as the Mexican-American War began, Davis told the Congress that a military education was necessary to lead troops; it could not be done as effectively by "mechanics," such as blacksmiths and tailors, who had no military training. Not surprisingly, the tailor Andrew Johnson, then serving his second term in the House of Representatives, was offended and engaged in a dispute with Davis. Soon thereafter Davis volunteered to lead Mississippi troops in the field, despite that he was in Congress. Elected colonel of the 1st Mississippi Volunteers, he left on July 4, 1846, to join his regiment. He played important roles in the battles of Monterrey and Buena Vista, where he served under his former father-in-law Zachary Taylor. At Buena Vista Davis was wounded in the foot and had to use crutches for the next two years. He was mustered out after a year of service and, now a war hero, was elected to the U.S. Senate, taking his seat in December 1847.

In July 1848 Davis gave a major Senate speech favoring slavery expansion, but he took little part in the presidential campaign of 1848 because he was a Democrat, but his close friend, the presidential candidate Zachary Taylor, was a Whig. When Henry Clay of Kentucky presented the proposals eventually known as the Compromise of 1850, Davis promptly opposed them and continued to do so, speaking about some part of the proposals fifty-four times, more than any other senator. Davis always ended his speeches with threats of disunion over the slavery issue and, after John C. Calhoun's death in 1850, became the leading Senate spokesman of Southern views. He did not propose new legislation but reacted to the proposals of others, always on the defensive, claiming that he and the South were under attack.

In 1851 Davis resigned his Senate seat to run for governor of Mississippi, a contest he narrowly lost. When Franklin Pierce became president in 1853, he selected Davis as his secretary of war. Davis was extremely involved in the War Department, which led to disputes with some of his subordinates who, after years of relatively inactive secretaries, were used to doing things their own way. Davis also attempted to introduce camels for military use in the southwestern deserts, but the experiment proved short-lived because the soldiers preferred horses and mules. Davis's term as secretary of war ended with the conclusion of the Pierce administration on March 4, 1857, but the legislature of Mississippi promptly reelected Davis to the Senate, where he served until January 1861, when Mississippi seceded.

During his term in the Senate, Davis had other conflicts with Andrew Johnson. One, in 1859, concerned who was to choose the furniture for the Senate committee rooms in the refurbished capitol building. Johnson and Davis took opposite sides on a number of other issues as well: Johnson was always more reluctant than Davis to vote funds for government projects; Johnson vigorously promoted the Homestead Act, which Davis opposed; Johnson opposed the transcontinental railroad, which Davis favored; and, of course, they ultimately differed about secession. Late in 1860, during a speech, Davis called Johnson a "miscreant." A rumor spread that, as a result of the insult, Johnson had shot and killed Davis, but, obviously, it was not true.

In February 1860 Davis introduced a series of resolutions in the Senate calling for congressional protection of slavery, which caused much heated debate. Once the Southern states began to secede, their leaders sought advice from Davis, the foremost Southern spokesman. Mississippi governor John J. Pettus made Davis major general of the Army of Mississippi. It seems that Davis wanted to be general-in-chief of all of the Southern armies. Instead, in February 1861, he was chosen provisional president of the new Confederacy by the unanimous vote of the representatives of the six seceded states assembled at Montgomery, Alabama. A few months later Davis was elected to a full six-year term.

While Davis was perhaps the best person available to be president of the new nation, there were many respects in which he was not really a good choice for the job. He was not a politician—he was unable to be more than barely civil to people he disliked, even if they could be useful to the Confederacy. He showed favoritism in appointments and was fiercely loyal to his friends, expecting the same loyalty back from them. When someone was "disloyal," Davis considered him an enemy, never forgetting or forgiving any affront. He carried on personal feuds with generals and members of Congress, thereby damaging the Confederate cause. Yet he also damaged the cause by his loyalty to his friends such as General Braxton Bragg, commander of the Army of Tennessee, and Lucius Northrop, head of the commissary department, leaving them in their posts long after they had proved their ineffectiveness.

Davis was also very inflexible. Apparently insecure, he often had trouble making a decision after carefully considering the issue from all sides. Once he made up his mind, he refused to change it. When he had made a decision or figured something out, he knew he was right and expected everyone to agree with him. He was unable and unwilling to admit that he ever made a mistake. He was also overly detail-oriented, focusing on the minutia of the War Department and unable to distinguish what was important. In addition, Davis suffered from chronic poor health, which made him ill-tempered and affected his ability to perform his duties.

Nevertheless, despite all these liabilities, Davis did have a certain dignity, which caused people to respect him. He developed an excellent working relationship with Robert E. Lee, no doubt strengthening that general in command of the Army of Northern Virginia by providing as much support as possible. Davis also oversaw the whole administrative arm of the Confederate government and should receive credit that the government was able to perform as well as it did for as long as it did. Of course, since he was president, people tended to blame Davis for everything that went wrong in the Confederacy, regardless of whether he had any direct connection with it or not.

Davis refused to accept the collapse of the Confederacy as reality and wanted to continue on with guerrilla warfare, but his generals refused. Davis was captured by Union cavalry near Irwinville, Georgia, on May 10, 1865. He was imprisoned at Fort Monroe, Virginia, where he was held in close confinement and even, for five days, forced to wear leg irons.

Davis was one of the Confederates accused of complicity in the assassination of Abraham Lincoln, which accounted, in part, for his initial harsh treatment at the fort. As Davis told one of his captors, Andrew Johnson, of all people, should know that rumors of Davis's involvement were lies because, thanks to their previous poor relationship, "I would a thousand times rather have Abraham Lincoln to deal with, as President of the United States, than to have *him*." Davis was never mistreated, but the stress of his confinement led to serious deterioration of his health. This problem was reported at length by his doctor, John J. Craven, who also wrote a book on the subject, *Prison Life of Jefferson Davis,* ghostwritten, with numerous fictional additions, by journalist Charles G. Halpine. Johnson even sent treasury secretary Hugh McCulloch to check to see that Davis was not being mistreated. After a few months Davis was moved to more comfortable quarters and permitted to see legal counsel and his Episcopalian minister, Reverend Charles Minnegerode of Richmond. However, for a full year Johnson did not grant permission for Davis to see his wife.

No sooner had Davis been arrested than Johnson began to receive mail about the Confederate leader. Some were glad that Davis had been captured and hoped that he would soon be tried and hanged. Others urged clemency because Davis was merely a "*servant* of the people." Some even threatened to assassinate Johnson if Davis were hanged. The government, at least at first, intended to bring Davis to trial. But as the postassassination excitement died down and it became evident that the testimony showing Davis's complicity was perjured, there was less enthusiasm for a trial. In addition, the question of jurisdiction arose. Should it be a military or a civil trial, and if civil, where should it be held? His indictment, rather a trumped-up charge, claimed that Davis had committed treason by inciting citizens (meaning soldiers) to resist the lawful authority of the United States (Ulysses S. Grant's army) at a specific date and place. Although several attempts were made to try Davis in Virginia, where the alleged treason had occurred, the trial was always postponed. Finally, two years after his capture, Davis was released on a writ of habeas corpus by the Virginia court. In December 1868 Chief Justice Salmon P. Chase of the United States Supreme Court dismissed the indictment.

After his release, Davis and his family lived in genteel poverty. He suffered from poor health and was rarely able to find remunerative work, although he served as figurehead president of an insurance company, which failed within a few years. In 1877 Davis began to write his memoirs with the help of several other people. Finally finished in 1881, the two-volume *Rise and Fall of the Confederate Government* was not very well written and apparently earned Davis no money. Jefferson Davis died of pneumonia in New Orleans on December 6, 1889.

See also: Chase, Salmon Portland; Congressman, Johnson as; Homestead Act; Lincoln, Abraham; McCulloch, Hugh; Senator, Johnson as.

References: Davis, William C., *Jefferson Davis: The Man and His Hour* (1991); Graf, LeRoy P., Haskins, Ralph W., and Bergeron, Paul H., *The Papers of Andrew Johnson* vols. 1, 3–4, 6, 8–11 (1967–2000).

Death of Johnson (July 31, 1875)

Ever since his near-fatal bout with cholera during the summer of 1873, Andrew Johnson had not been in the best of health. He was also tired from the stresses of campaigning for his election to the Senate in January 1875 and his short time in Washington, D.C., for the Senate session. In late July 1875 Johnson planned to go to Carter County, Tennessee, to the farm of his daughter Mary Johnson Stover Brown. In her continual search for improved health, Johnson's wife, Eliza, had gone to Mary's home about six weeks previously and Johnson wished to visit her and rest a bit before going back to Washington.

Early on the morning of July 28, Johnson boarded the train, where he met several friends and conversed with them extensively about his presidency. He blamed Edwin M. Stanton for most of the political troubles of Reconstruction and assured his audience that he had never seen the request for clemency for Mary Surratt until well after her execution. He claimed that after he heard about Abraham Lincoln's assassination he had spent much time considering how to conduct the affairs of state so that an objective historian, 100 years later, would be able to say, "He pursued the right course."

Arriving at Carter Station (or Depot) about 8:30 in the morning, Johnson, after an apparent delay, was met by Mary's carriage and driven the six miles to the Stover farm, arriving between 11:00 A.M. and noon. Although Johnson was tired from his trip, he kept up a continual conversation with his family about domestic matters. After a hearty lunch, Johnson went upstairs to his room. About 3:00 P.M. he was sitting in a chair talking to his granddaughter Lillie Stover. Something outside momentarily attracted her attention and as she looked out the window she heard a thud. Turning, she discovered that her grandfather had fallen out of the chair and she called for help.

Johnson's speech was slurred and his left side paralyzed from a stroke, yet once he was made as comfortable as possible in bed, he refused to allow his family to send for a doctor. He seemed to have no sense of the seriousness of his illness and believed that he would soon get over the attack. He kept talking extensively about domestic matters, even though he was in considerable pain. When the members of the Masonic lodge in Elizabethton, two miles away, heard about Johnson's illness, they sent attendants to help care for their afflicted brother.

Concerned that Johnson showed little improvement, his family called in several doctors from Elizabethton about twenty-four hours after the initial stroke. They attempted "to revive the deadened powers of their distinguished patient." But what little progress was made was soon destroyed by a second stroke, even more devastating than the first, which left Johnson unconscious. His other children, Martha Johnson Patterson and Andrew Johnson, Jr., arrived about 8:00 P.M. in the evening on July 30 with two family doctors from Greeneville, but Johnson did not recognize them or respond to treatment. He died about 2:30 A.M. on Saturday, July 31, 1875.

See also: Funeral of Johnson; Grandchildren; Health of Johnson; Johnson, Andrew, Jr., "Frank"; Johnson, Eliza McCardle; Masonic Order; Patterson, Martha Johnson; Senator, Johnson as; Stanton, Edwin McMasters; Stover (Brown), Mary Johnson; Surratt, Mary (Elizabeth) Eugenia Jenkins.
References: *Greeneville (Tennessee) Intelligencer,* August 6, 1875; Trefousse, Hans L., *Andrew Johnson: A Biography* (1989).

Democratic Convention (1868)

The Democrats and conservatives who gathered at Tammany Hall in New York City on July 4, 1868, knew that their party was in trouble. The previous

May the Republican Party announced its ticket of General Ulysses S. Grant and Speaker of the House Schuyler Colfax, thus joining the most popular man in the country with a lifelong politician. The Democratic Party knew that ticket would be hard to beat, especially by a party carrying the blame for secession and civil war. Even worse, the party's national leader, President Andrew Johnson, had been impeached and had only narrowly escaped conviction. As a result, there was no obvious candidate when the convention began.

There were individuals interested in the presidential candidacy, however, starting with George H. Pendleton of Ohio. The Democratic vice presidential candidate in 1864, Pendleton was a Unionist who opposed many of Lincoln's policies, including the Emancipation Proclamation. Central to his bid for nomination was his financial plan, which endorsed repaying bondholders (those who had bought government bonds to help fund the Union war effort) with greenbacks, government script, rather than the gold they had been promised. Called the "Ohio Plan," this idea met with support in some midwestern states but was opposed by eastern bankers and many influential bondholders.

Among those who supported redeeming government bonds with gold was General Francis P. Blair, Jr., of Missouri, a Union soldier, War Democrat, and Andrew Johnson confidant, who openly opposed Congressional Reconstruction. Some leading Democrats believed that they needed a military hero to counter Grant's popularity. But in June 1868 an embarrassing letter to James O. Broadhead, in which Blair advocated using force to overturn Republican governments in the South, made him appear too extreme for many Northern Democrats.

Another popular military figure was Pennsylvanian Winfield S. Hancock, who won over conservatives, and Andrew Johnson, by his moderation while he was commander of the Fifth Military District. Hancock's removal of Radical Republican officeholders and support of the civil courts, rather than military ones, brought him into conflict with his superior, Ulysses S. Grant, but earned him the admiration of the Democratic Party.

Similarly, the moderation displayed by Chief Justice Salmon P. Chase during the impeachment trial made the former secretary of the treasury a potential candidate. Although ambitious and brilliant, Chase was a long shot for the nomination because he was an ardent advocate of black suffrage. The Southern states that had been readmitted were sending delegates to New York, so Chase's chances were slim. Still, his opposition to much of Congressional Reconstruction, his support of hard money policies, and his advocacy of universal amnesty made him a contender.

New Yorker Horatio Seymour was rumored to be a candidate, but he had retired from politics and claimed he wanted to stay that way. While governor during the Civil War, Seymour was called a Copperhead, a traitor, and even a Confederate spy for opposing many of Lincoln's policies. But because of his connections to the powerful New York Democratic Party, which largely controlled the national executive committee, and his lifelong advocacy of conservative principles, Seymour was sought after by many to lead the party.

The party's nominal leader, Andrew Johnson, was not without his supporters either. Although rendered ineffectual by a veto-proof Republican Congress and the stigma of impeachment, Johnson still had a cadre of followers who hoped he would receive the presidential nomination. Johnson's opinion on the nomination is difficult to discern, as he seemed to favor Winfield Hancock at one point and Salmon P. Chase at another. It is also likely that, at times, he envisioned his own nomination. In a July 2 response to a group of New York Democrats, Johnson claimed that he was "not ambitious of further service—I may say indeed of further endurance in that elevated and responsible position, unless by a call so general and unequivocal that it would be an endorsement by the people of my endeavors to defend the Constitution." If such a call came, he would certainly accept; if not, then he would "cordially acquiesce—as has been my habit—in the decision of the American people." While Johnson did not actively campaign for the nomination, he was not indifferent to the convention's proceedings: he issued the Third Amnesty Proclamation on July 4, the day the convention opened; he had friends report from New York on the deliberations; and he eventually allowed his letter to the New York City Democrats to be published in the newspapers (which occurred on July 7).

The convention opened harmoniously enough, with August Belmont, the national chairman, delivering the welcoming address on July 4. The Declaration of Independence was read, and committee assignments were made. A friend of Johnson's, William Wales, had hoped in vain that the convention would read the Third Amnesty Proclamation. The convention then adjourned until Monday, July 6. That day Horatio Seymour was named chairman of the convention, and the convention decided to adopt the platform before the voting on candidates, probably because the delegates could come to a consensus on a platform more easily than they could a nominee.

Committees took over from that point and on July 7 presented the platform to the convention. The party called for the immediate restoration of all states to their rights within the Union, a universal amnesty, an agreement that suffrage would be left for individual states to decide, and the abolition of the Freedmen's Bureau. The platform endorsed the Ohio Plan and called for reform in government, a reduction of the armed forces, and the independence of the judicial and executive branches—a message aimed at the Republican Congress. Demo-crats also demanded that foreign powers recognize naturalized citizenship, which Great Britain had refused to do. The conservative platform was easily adopted, yet few were really happy with it. Southerners wanted an explicit statement in support of white-only suffrage (which did not occur), some Northern War Democrats disagreed with the overt criticisms of Congress, and hard-money proponents bristled over the Ohio Plan. Other resolutions followed the acceptance of the platform, including one praising Andrew Johnson and another calling the Reconstruction Acts "unconstitutional, revolutionary, and void."

Balloting on the nomination began the same day. Under the rules adopted, the nominee needed two-thirds of the 317 votes. The first ballot had Pendleton in a comfortable lead with 105 votes, followed by President Johnson with 65, mostly from Southern delegates. Other candidates included Sanford E. Church, Hancock, Asa Packer, James R. Doolittle, and Reverdy Johnson. Four more ballots resulted in small gains for Pendleton, a decline in support for Johnson, and readjustments among the many states that were waiting for some dominant candidate to appear. On the fourth ballot Seymour's name was offered, but the chairman declined the honor. Johnson confidant William W. Warden had predicted that no major figure, such as Pendleton or Chase, would get the nomination, but rather "some one not now *prominently* before the Convention" would receive it. As it became clear that Pendleton was not the unanimous choice and the delegates were biding time, Warden's opinion seemed valid. Warden, among others, had also insisted that Johnson publish his letter to the New York City Democrats; it appeared on the 7th, but had no impact on the voting.

The following day, July 8, began with Indiana switching its support to Thomas A. Hendricks, dooming Pendleton. Once it was clear that Pendleton had peaked, other states abandoned him as well. The big beneficiary was Winfield Hancock, who had garnered 144 votes by the eighteenth ballot. Johnson was left with only single-digit support; as he wrote to George H. Parker on the 8th, "I have experienced ingratitude so often, that any result will not surprise me." Just as it appeared a stampede might be forming for Hancock, Chairman Seymour adjourned the session, apparently to allow New Yorkers who opposed Hancock time to regroup.

Overnight, key states plotted strategy for the coming day. Pendleton agreed to formally withdraw, but the Ohio delegation could not decide on an alternate candidate. New York, currently supporting Hendricks to block Hancock, concurred in the advice of their leader, Horatio Seymour, to support Chase if Hendricks began to fade.

On July 9 Ohio made its move, voting for Asa Packer of Pennsylvania to lure that state's votes away from its other native son, Hancock. This resulted in a steady decline in Hancock's support, with much of the attention turning to Hendricks—thus thwarting Seymour's plan to nominate Chase.

After several ballots followed this trend, Ohio delegates Clement Vallandigham and George McCook nominated the chairman, Horatio Seymour, and called on the convention to ignore his refusals. The New York delegation seconded their calls. On the twenty-second ballot Ohio changed its vote to Seymour, and a stampede began. A group of friends collected the protesting Seymour and ushered him out of the convention. Within minutes Seymour was the unanimous choice as nominee, earning all 317 votes; he accepted the following evening.

The selection of the vice presidential nominee went much quicker, perhaps because the delegates were drained by the previous days' events. In addition, the need for a balanced ticket eliminated many possibilities and narrowed the field. The nomination fell to Francis P. Blair, Jr., the Union general and Midwesterner, despite his vitriolic opposition to Congressional Recon-

struction. His nomination was unanimous on the first ballot.

The confusion and party infighting that plagued the Democratic Party did not dissipate with the nomination of the ticket. In fact, the ticket demonstrated the many problems faced by the party: the platform advocated the Ohio Plan, yet Seymour openly opposed it; the party hoped to reach out to conservative Republicans, yet Seymour's war record and Blair's attacks on Congressional Reconstruction made that impossible. Barely a month after the convention closed, influential Democrats were already calling for a change in the ticket. No change occurred, but it probably would not have made a difference anyway. In the November election the Republican ticket of Grant and Colfax won 214 of the 294 possible electoral votes, and the Democratic Party's woes continued.

See also: Amnesty Proclamations; Blair, Francis Preston (Jr. and Sr.); Chase, Salmon Portland; Congressional Reconstruction; Conservatives; Democratic Party; Doolittle, James Rood; Election of 1868; Grant, Ulysses Simpson; Hancock, Winfield Scott; Johnson, Reverdy; Military Districts; Seymour, Horatio.

References: Bradley, Erwin Stanley, *The Triumph of Militant Republicanism: A Study of Pennsylvania and Presidential Politics, 1860–1872* (1964); Coleman, Charles H., *The Election of 1868: The Democratic Effort to Regain Control* (1933); Gambill, Edward L., *Conservative Ordeal: Northern Democrats and Reconstruction, 1865–1868* (1981); Graf, LeRoy P., Haskins, Ralph W., and Bergeron, Paul H., eds., *The Papers of Andrew Johnson* vol. 14 (1967–2000); *Official Proceedings of the National Democratic Convention, held at New York, July 4–9, 1868* (1868); Stebbins, Homer Adolph, *A Political History of the State of New York, 1865–1869* (1913).

Democratic Party

The Democratic Party of Johnson's day traced its roots back to the Democratic-Republicans of Thomas Jefferson. Jeffersonians favored a society of independent artisans and yeoman farmers, protected from government oppression by defensive local governments and a weak federal one. After emerging from a revolution caused in part by an overbearing government, Jeffersonians believed that the government that governed least, governed best. Arrayed against the Jeffersonians were Alexander Hamilton's Federalists, who believed that the future of the United States lay in commercial, banking, and urban interests, and they sought a more powerful central government to promote these.

The Democratic-Republicans ascended to power with the election of Jefferson to the presidency in 1800 and dominated politics after the Federalists self-destructed in the War of 1812. But the one-party system did not last long because the presidential election of 1824 split the party when Henry Clay's support of John Quincy Adams cost Andrew Jackson the victory.

Jackson and his followers, who felt they had been swindled out of the presidency by a "corrupt bargain," prepared for the election of 1828 under the original name, Democratic Republicans. They claimed that they represented the same issues, values, and people as had Jefferson. Their opponents, led by Clay and Adams, called themselves the National Republicans and called for an expansion of the federal government to assist industrial and mercantile interests.

Jackson was elected in 1828, and his party—which in 1832 formally began using the title "Democratic"—won every election until 1860 save two (1840 and 1848). Democrats were largely conservative in their political, economic, and social outlook, opposing paper money, a national bank, the expansion of federal powers, a loose reading of the U.S. Constitution, and protective tariffs.

Early in his political career Andrew Johnson allied himself with Jackson and the Democrats because they promoted the same small-town, artisan, limited-government interests that he held dear. As a state representative in the 1830s, Johnson consistently opposed state aid to railroads, even though it would benefit East Tennessee, and his opposition cost him reelection. He also fought against excessive government expenditures, official privilege (the exemption of judges from road labor), and a national bank.

As a member of Congress, Johnson adamantly opposed internal improvements, high tariffs, increasing the size of the federal bureaucracy, and military expenditures. Like other Democrats (and many Americans of all parties), he supported the Mexican-American War and territorial expansion. Here Johnson shared the internal contradiction that characterized his party: although Southern Democrats decried a powerful central government, they supported an activist government when it came to promoting and protecting slavery.

But by midcentury a rift had developed in the Democratic Party as slavery and its expansion became even more controversial. Southern Democrats believed that Congress was obligated to protect slavery where it existed and to help it flourish in new territories, but was constitutionally prohibited from restricting it. Southern Democrats also supported the enforcement of the Fugitive Slave Law (1793, revised 1850) and pushed through the unprecedented Gag Rule, all of which Johnson supported. Yet, although Democrats comprised the only national party by 1860, it was a party torn along sectional lines; the Whig Party (formerly the National Republicans) had collapsed, and the new Republican Party had adherents only in the West and North.

In the presidential election of 1860 the Democratic Party split along regional lines over the expansion of slavery into the territories. Northern Democrats under Stephen A. Douglas supported popular sovereignty, whereas Southern Democrats nominated John C. Breckinridge on a platform of government protection for slavery in the South and in the territories. This split, along with the fourth-party effort of

John Bell and the Constitutional Unionists, helped Abraham Lincoln win the election (although even had his opponents united, Lincoln would still have had enough electoral votes to become president). Johnson, who had hoped to serve as a compromise candidate, ended up unenthusiastically backing Breckinridge.

The election of Lincoln brought secession, civil war, and further turmoil to the Democratic Party. As a national party, it had adherents in both the North and South, but the issues of free labor, Union, and defending the Constitution meant that most Democrats followed their region rather than their party. The South was nearly solidly Democratic because the party defended states' rights and opposed federal interference in slavery. Conversely in the North, many Democrats—including Andrew Johnson, even though he was from a Confederate state—were War Democrats, or members of the Democratic Party who actively and enthusiastically supported the Lincoln administration's prosecution of the war to restore the Union. Fewer Northern Democrats were Peace Democrats, who called for a peaceful, noncoercive resolution to the crisis, even if it meant permanent separation. An extreme element of the Peace Democrats was represented by the Copperheads, who openly opposed the Lincoln administration and even sought to sabotage the Union war effort.

Even though many Democrats, such as Johnson, earnestly supported the Union war effort, the stigma of secession and the Civil War nearly destroyed the Democratic Party. Andrew Johnson, however, never left his party; elected vice president in 1864 on the Union Party ticket, he still clung to his Democratic Party principles. Knowing that the war had damaged his party, Johnson did what he could to help restore the party to life after his elevation to the presidency in 1865. His conciliatory Restoration policy, liberal pardons, and ardent defense of a lim-

ited federal government and extensive states' rights harkened back to the heyday of the Democratic Party.

Ironically, it was not Johnson who resurrected the Democratic Party, but time and the policies of the Republicans. At first, congressional disfranchisement of former Confederates and the enfranchisement of black American men further devastated the power of the Democratic Party. But as Reconstruction wore on, the Northern public tired of black rights and incompetent Southern Republican governments and turned toward economic development and Western expansion. Factional issues faded in the light of national undertakings, and white solidarity overrode interest in black rights. By 1874 Republican corruption, economic distress, and a backlash against black rights allowed Democrats to regain control of Congress, but another Democrat—Johnson left office in 1869—would not hold the executive chair until Grover Cleveland took office in 1885.

See also: Amnesty Proclamations; Blacks (Slave and Free), Johnson's Attitude toward; Congressional Reconstruction; Congressman, Johnson as; Conservatives; Constitution, Johnson's Attitude toward; Election of 1864; Finances, Johnson's Attitude toward Governmental; Jackson, Andrew; Joint Select Committee on the Conduct of the War; Lincoln, Abraham; National Union Party; Pardons (Individual); Polk, James Knox; Presidential Reconstruction; Republican Party; Secession, Johnson's Attitude toward; Senator, Johnson as; State Legislator, Johnson as; Whig Party.

References: Bowers, Claude G., *Making Democracy a Reality: Jefferson, Jackson, and Polk* (1954); Dell, Christopher, *Lincoln and the War Democrats: The Grand Erosion of Conservative Tradition* (1975); Kent, Frank R., *The Democratic Party: A History* (1928); Remini, Robert V., *Andrew Jackson and the Course of American Democracy, 1833–1845* (1984); Silbey, Joel H., *A Respectable Minority: The Democratic Party in the Civil War Era* (1977); Trefousse, Hans L., *Andrew Johnson: A Biography* (1989).

Dennison, William
(1815–1882)

A native of Cincinnati, William Dennison graduated from Miami University of Ohio in 1835 and then read law with Nathaniel G. Pendleton. Admitted to the bar in 1840, Dennison practiced law only until 1848, becoming involved in politics and business instead.

Soon after 1840 Dennison married and settled in Columbus, Ohio. He became a bank president and member of the city council, while investing in several railroads and also in an iron rolling mill. Despite that he lost much financially during the Panic of 1873, he acquired quite a sizable fortune.

From the beginning of his political career Dennison was opposed to the annexation of Texas and the extension of slavery into the territories. Initially a Whig, he was elected to the Ohio state senate in 1848 and served a single term. He remained a Whig through 1852 but was one of the first Ohio leaders to join and help organize the Republican Party. He was chairman of the Ohio delegation at the 1856 Philadelphia Republican Convention, which nominated John C. Frémont for the presidency.

In 1859 Dennison received the Republican gubernatorial nomination largely because all the other state party leaders were already in Congress. Elected to the office, he was governor of Ohio when the Civil War broke out. In April 1861, when Lincoln called for 75,000 troops to put down the rebellion, Dennison immediately and successfully began working to raise regiments from Ohio. In fact, he raised more than Ohio's quota, which worsened the state's already severe problems supplying its troops. Eager to protect Ohio from possible invasion, he agitated for permission to invade Kentucky and western Virginia. Although President Abraham Lincoln would not allow an invasion of Kentucky, Ohio troops under George B. McClellan were permitted to go to Wheeling, Virginia, to protect a convention of Unionists from Confederate attack. Dennison also exercised substantial control over railroads, telegraph lines, and express companies in Ohio to keep contraband goods and information from getting to the South.

But Dennison was not a popular governor. His manner tended to be impersonal, austere, and aristocratic, and his speeches were long-winded (even by nineteenth-century standards) and stiff. The common people could not relate to him. Even worse, the press tended to persecute him and to blame him for all the deficiencies of Ohio's war effort, even when the problems were really the fault of the federal War Department or some other person. As a result, Dennison was not nominated for a second term in 1861, even though the confusion and supply problems caused by gearing up for war had been largely fixed by the end of the year. Although some historians have considered Dennison to be the most inept of the North's Civil War governors, in fact, given the few months of the war that he was in office, his record compares favorably with other governors during that period.

In 1864 Dennison served as chairman of the National Union Party Convention in Baltimore, which renominated Abraham Lincoln for president and chose Andrew Johnson as his running mate. Then, in September 1864, Lincoln reluctantly agreed to the Radical Republicans' demand that he remove controversial Postmaster General Montgomery Blair from his cabinet. Lincoln appointed William Dennison as Blair's replacement, and he planned to keep Dennison during his second term even though the Ohioan was becoming more closely associated with the Radicals.

After Lincoln's assassination Johnson kept the same cabinet members, including Dennison. But Dennison's ideas differed from Johnson's policy. Dennison favored black suffrage and publicly supported the Union Republican candidates in some spring 1866 elections, angering and confusing some of Johnson's Democratic supporters. But the break finally came in June 1866 when Dennison, along with Secretary of the Interior James Harlan and Attorney General James Speed, refused to participate in the call for a National Union Party Convention in Philadelphia, and all three resigned. Johnson appointed Alexander W. Randall of Wisconsin to replace Dennison in July 1866.

Although still involved in politics—mentioned for the vice presidency in 1872 and 1880 and defeated by James A. Garfield for the Senate in 1880—Dennison was primarily involved with his business pursuits for the rest of his life. He died in Columbus after an eighteen-month illness.

See also: Black Suffrage; Cabinet Members; Election of 1864; Harlan, James; Lincoln, Abraham; National Union Convention and Party; National Union Party; Panic of 1873; Randall, Alexander Williams; Republican Party; Speed, James.

References: Abbott, Richard H., *Ohio's War Governors* (1962); Donald, David Herbert, *Lincoln* (1995); Graf, LeRoy P., Haskins, Ralph W., and Bergeron, Paul H., eds., *The Papers of Andrew Johnson* vols. 4, 7, 10, 13 (1967–2000); Schaefer, James A., "Governor William Dennison and Military Preparations in Ohio, 1861," *Lincoln Herald* 78 (no. 2, 1976): 52–61; Trefousse, Hans L., *Andrew Johnson: A Biography* (1989).

District of Columbia Franchise

Although Andrew Johnson believed that the states could, and even should, give the vote to blacks who were educated or met certain property qualifications, he opposed federal enforcement of black suffrage on any states or territories. In December 1865 the cities of Washington and Georgetown, District of Columbia, held a referendum on introducing black suffrage in the district and overwhelmingly defeated the idea. However, in December 1866, both the Senate and the House passed an act granting suffrage to all male citizens of the district over the age of twenty-one, who had resided there at least a year, had no criminal convictions, and had not voluntarily supported the rebellion. This permitted blacks to vote and disfranchised former Confederates. Secretary of War Edwin M. Stanton believed that this was constitutional because Congress was the legislative body for the district.

Johnson, on the other hand, did not believe the legislation was appropriate and vetoed it on January 5, 1867. He said that, although Congress had the right to legislate for the district, Congress still needed to take into account the desires of the District of Columbia residents, and they had already opposed the extension of the franchise. It was not fair for representatives of states where black suffrage was prohibited or restricted to impose it on someone else, nor should the district be used for an experiment. Johnson reminded Congress that the blacks were only recently slaves and they were not yet ready to be informed voters and officeholders. Giving blacks in Washington the right to vote would bring a rapid influx of blacks into the capitol, where they already made up a third of the population and many were unemployed. Imposing black suffrage in Washington could be seen as a prelude to forcing it on the states, leading to race hatred. Blacks did not need protection in Washington any more than they needed it in Indiana or Pennsylvania, nor was their vote necessary to maintain a loyal government. Johnson believed that black suffrage would weaken the government system by adding a lot of voters who did not know what they were doing and might be corruptly influenced.

Despite Johnson's opinion, his veto was overridden by the Senate on January 7, followed by the House on the eighth, and black suffrage went into effect in the District of Columbia.

See also: Black Suffrage; Blacks (Slave and Free), Johnson's Attitude toward; Congressional Reconstruction; Stanton, Edwin McMasters; Vetoes.

References: Graf, LeRoy P., Haskins, Ralph W., and Bergeron, Paul H., eds., *The Papers of Andrew Johnson* vol. 11 (1967–2000).

Doolittle, James Rood
(1815–1897)

An important Senate supporter of President Andrew Johnson, James Rood Doolittle, the son of Reuben and Sarah Rood Doolittle, was born in Hampton, New York, and grew up on a farm. He attended local schools, Middleburg Academy in Vermont, and Hobart College in Geneva, New York, from which he graduated in 1834. He read law and was admitted to the bar in 1837, practicing first in Rochester and then in Warsaw, New York, where he was district attorney of Wyoming County (1847–1850).

In 1837 he married Mary L. Cutting and they eventually had six children. Doolittle became involved in Democratic politics, campaigning for James K. Polk in 1844. In 1847, as a member of the so-called Barnburner faction, Doolittle introduced the resolution at the New York state convention that slavery should not expand into free territories.

In 1851 Doolittle moved to Racine, Wisconsin, and was judge of the first judicial circuit court (1853–1856). Unhappy about the repeal of the Missouri Compromise and the consequent possibility of the spread of slavery into free territory, Doolittle officially joined the Republican Party in 1856 and was soon elected to the Senate, where he served from March 4, 1857, until March 3, 1869.

Doolittle became acquainted with Andrew Johnson when they were both in the Senate. Doolittle was a strong supporter of Johnson's Homestead Act, although Johnson was unhappy when Doolittle associated the act with the slavery issue (homesteads would discourage the spread of slavery) because Johnson thought the issues should be kept separate. In December 1860 Doolittle was appointed to the Senate Committee of Thirteen to consider various compromise proposals as the Southern states began to secede. Doolittle was among those who voted against the Crittenden Compromise, the most promising of the suggestions, and the committee failed to agree on any compromise proposal. A friend and advisor of Abraham Lincoln during the Civil War, Doolittle supported Lincoln's reelection in 1864.

Doolittle, as one of the Committee of Arrangements for the inauguration on March 4, 1865, was Johnson's escort to the Senate Chamber and thus witnessed the vice president's unfortunate inebriated performance. But this did not prevent Doolittle from supporting Johnson, whom he believed was trying to carry out Lincoln's plan. As early as September 1865 Doolittle was criticized by the Wisconsin press for attending a Union convention and presenting resolutions supportive of Johnson's Reconstruction policy. During this period Doolittle made various patronage requests, and Johnson made at least some of the desired appointments. Doolittle was one of the leaders of the National Union Party movement in 1866, signing the call for the convention, serving on the executive committee, and then as permanent chairman of the convention. In the fall of 1866, when Johnson began his Swing-around-the-Circle tour to defend his policies, Doolittle urged the president not to make any "extemporaneous speeches," as this type of speech injured Johnson's position in ways that prepared speeches did not do. Doolittle joined Johnson's entourage at Buffalo, New York, but was unable to prevent the president from making impromptu speeches, which damaged Johnson's cause just as Doolittle had feared.

Doolittle served as chairman of the Senate Committee on Indian Affairs for a number of years and also chaired a joint committee of three (beginning in March

1865) whose purpose was to examine the condition of the Indian tribes and see how they were treated by civilian and military authorities. The committee traveled extensively in Kansas and elsewhere on the plains, empowered to make treaties to end Indian hostilities and provide security to white settlers. Their report on Indian affairs, published in January 1867, urged that the western states and territories be divided into five districts, each with its own inspecting commission. Other congressmen, however, wanted to see Indian affairs transferred to the control of the War Department rather than to the Interior Department, and the suggestions were not acted upon.

In the conflicts between Johnson and Congress that would lead to Johnson's impeachment, Doolittle, although still a Republican, was a firm supporter of Johnson. For months he had urged the removal of Secretary of War Edwin M. Stanton, whom Doolittle saw as a weak link in Johnson's cabinet. During the debate on the Tenure of Office Act, Doolittle pointed out that the act did not apply to Stanton, and some senators agreed who would later urge the impeachment of Johnson because he had removed Stanton. Doolittle was one of ten moderate or conservative Republicans who voted to acquit Johnson of the charges on which he was impeached. Doolittle was not reelected to the Senate and he left office at the same time as Johnson left the presidency. There was no known contact between the two after this point, although Doolittle's son wrote Johnson a letter of congratulations on his election to the Senate in 1875.

Doolittle returned to Racine, Wisconsin, but he also established a law office in Chicago, where he practiced with his son until his death. He became a Democrat and was soundly defeated for several political offices. Wisconsin Republicans were unable to forgive him for his support of Johnson.

See also: Drunkenness; Election of 1866; Homestead Act; Impeachment; Indians; National Union Convention and Party; Senator, Johnson as; Stanton, Edwin McMasters; Swing-around-the-Circle; Tenure of Office Act; Vice President, Johnson as.

References: Albright, Claude, "Dixon, Doolittle, and Norton: The Forgotten Republican Votes," *Wisconsin Magazine of History* 59 (Winter 1975–1976): 91–100; Graf, LeRoy P., Haskins, Ralph W., and Bergeron, Paul H., eds., *The Papers of Andrew Johnson* vols. 3–4, 7, 9–16 (1967–2000); Milton, George Fort, *The Age of Hate: Andrew Johnson and the Radicals* (1965 [1930]); Trefousse, Hans L., *Andrew Johnson: A Biography* (1989); Wagstaff, Thomas, "The Arm-in-Arm Convention," *Civil War History* 14 (June 1968): 101–119.

Douglass, Frederick (1817– or 1818–1895)

*T*he most notable black abolitionist of the nineteenth century, Frederick Douglass was born Frederick Augustus Washington Bailey on a plantation near Easton, in Talbot County on the Eastern Shore of Maryland. The son of a slave woman and a white man, Douglass was separated from his mother at an early age and was sent to Baltimore to be a house servant. There, by various stratagems, he learned to read and write. These new skills led to his dissatisfaction with slavery and his determination to escape eventually. After a period as a field hand on several Eastern Shore plantations, Douglass was sent back to Baltimore, where he learned the trade of caulking ships.

In 1838 Douglass, aided by a borrowed "seaman's protection" (a type of identity paper), escaped slavery by posing as a free black sailor on shore leave. He soon married Anna Murray, a Baltimore free black woman who had helped him to escape. They settled in New Bedford, Massachusetts, and he changed his last name to Douglass. The couple eventually had five children.

In 1841 Douglass became involved with the antislavery movement as a lecturer, able to give personal testimony about the evils of slavery. In 1845 he wrote *Narrative of the Life of Frederick Douglass, an American Slave,* a book designed to aid the antislavery cause and to demonstrate to doubters that in fact he had been a slave. Later on he wrote more extended versions of his autobiography: *My Bondage and My Freedom* (1855) and *Life and Times of Frederick Douglass* (1881, 1892). The publication of his *Narrative* put Douglass at risk because he was still officially a fugitive slave. He promptly took refuge in Britain, where he spoke frequently for the cause. In 1846 British abolitionists raised approximately $1,250 and purchased Douglass's freedom. Back in the United States, Douglass moved to Rochester, New York, and began to publish a newspaper, the *North Star,* which changed its name to *Frederick Douglass' Paper* in 1851.

During the Civil War, Douglass, long famous as an antislavery orator, recruited black men, including several of his own sons, to serve as soldiers in the Union army. Douglass had two private meetings in the White House with President Abraham Lincoln in which he felt that Lincoln treated him as an equal.

Such was not his experience with President Andrew Johnson, however. On February 7, 1866, Douglass was part of a delegation to see the president sent by the Convention of Colored Men then meeting in Washington, D.C., to protest the passage of restrictive Black Codes in many of the Southern states. Douglass and the other delegates asked Johnson to assist blacks to get equal rights as citizens, especially the right to vote. Johnson was angered by these black men telling him what to do. He said that his "course" should already have "given evidence" that he was a "friend of humanity." His "all" had been "perilled in that cause." He believed that granting the right to vote was the prerogative of the states and should depend on the will of the majority, brusquely brushing aside the comment from one delegate that South Carolina had a black majority. Johnson believed that if the Southerners were forced to accept black suffrage there would be race warfare between the blacks and the poor whites, to the detriment of the blacks. Johnson even suggested that emigration would be better for the blacks. The delegation, seeing the intractability of the president, soon left, and published a letter to the president in the *Washington Chronicle,* expressing their views to which Johnson had refused to listen. The following day Johnson reiterated his perspective (for publication) to a correspondent of the *New York Times.*

Douglass spent some time traveling and speaking in favor of black suffrage. He also hoped in 1867 to be appointed to head the Freedmen's Bureau, but nothing came of it besides some negotiations carried out by Johnson's black steward William Slade. In 1868 Douglass campaigned for the Republican presidential nominee, Ulysses S. Grant, whom he was sure would do more to help the blacks. Douglass was very pleased by the ratification of the Fifteenth Amendment in 1870.

After an arsonist burned his home in Rochester in June 1872, Douglass moved his family to Washington, D.C., where he had been spending most of his time anyway as editor of the *New National Era.* In 1877 Rutherford B. Hayes appointed Douglass marshal of the District of Columbia, the first time a black man had received an appointment requiring Senate confirmation. In this post he helped blacks to gain control of certain low-level government positions. But James A. Garfield removed Douglass in 1881 and made him recorder of deeds instead. On August 4, 1882, Douglass's wife Anna died of a stroke and in January 1884 Douglass married Helen Pitts, a forty-six-year-old white woman who worked as a clerk in the recorder's office. This interracial marriage caused much comment as well as opposition from most of their family members. During 1889–1891 Douglass served as U.S. minister to Haiti. He suddenly collapsed and died at his home in Washington on February 20, 1895.

See also: Black Codes; Black Suffrage; Black Troops in the South; Blacks (Slave and Free), Johnson's Attitude toward; Election of 1868;

Fifteenth Amendment; Grant, Ulysses Simpson; Lincoln, Abraham.

References: Douglass, Frederick, *Narrative of the Life of Frederick Douglass, an American Slave* (1960 [1845]); Graf, LeRoy P., Haskins, Ralph W., and Bergeron, Paul H., eds., *The Papers of Andrew Johnson* vol. 10 (1967–2000); McFeely, William S., *Frederick Douglass* (1991); Preston, Dickson J., *Young Frederick Douglass: The Maryland Years* (1980).

Drunkenness

Opponents of Andrew Johnson frequently charged him with drunkenness during his presidency. All of these charges were false except for one incident. That Johnson was inebriated at his vice presidential inauguration provided the basis for later suspicion and accusations.

By the time Johnson got to Washington, D.C., for the inauguration, he was in poor health. He arrived at the Capitol building on the morning of March 4, 1865, and stopped at the vice president's office, where he visited with the outgoing official, Hannibal Hamlin, and the latter's son. Because Johnson was not well, he asked Hamlin for some whiskey to fortify himself. Over a short period, Johnson drank three glasses of undiluted whiskey. Although this might not have affected him under ordinary circumstances, his illness and the heat of the crowded Senate chamber combined with the whiskey to cause obvious inebriation.

In addition to both houses of Congress, the chamber was occupied by the members of the Supreme Court, the cabinet, and the diplomatic corps, as well as various female guests who had come to watch the vice president be sworn in. (Abraham Lincoln would be inaugurated as president outside the Capitol later in the day.)

In his speech Johnson stressed his "plebeian" roots and the fact that, nevertheless, the people had elected him to the vice presidency. He also emphasized that every government official present, and he named some of them specifically, received his power from the people. Most printed versions of Johnson's speech tended to disguise his drunkenness by briefly mentioning the topics he spoke about and claiming that there was so much noise in the galleries that the reporter was unable to hear the speech distinctly.

The spectacle of a drunken vice president horrified and embarrassed the audience. Some of Johnson's opponents in the press called for his resignation or impeachment, and others made a variety of unkind remarks. Abraham Lincoln appeared less concerned. Although he acknowledged that Johnson had "made a bad slip," nevertheless he had known Johnson for many years and could positively state, "Andy ain't a drunkard." Other friends also affirmed that Johnson did drink alcoholic beverages, especially whiskey, and sometimes in quantity, but they had never seen him drunk. (Many men drank whiskey during this period because it was cheaper and more available than most other beverages, so Johnson's habits were not unusual.) Apparently he could drink or not, as he chose, and so was not an alcoholic. Unfortunately, the same could not be said of Johnson's three sons, each of whom became an alcoholic in early adulthood.

This single instance of public intoxication at his inauguration as vice president haunted Johnson throughout his presidency. A Nevada senator claimed that Johnson was drunk on the day he assumed the presidency after Lincoln's assassination, a story refuted by more reliable witnesses. Many more people suggested that Johnson was drunk when he delivered his tactless Washington's Birthday Speech on February 22, 1866, or harangued his listeners in some of the speeches during his Swing-around-the-Circle tour later in the same year. But Johnson was not intoxicated. He was merely falling back into ingrained stump-speaking habits, developed over many years of campaigning in Tennessee.

His actions did not conform to many people's ideas about how a president should behave and thus led to unfounded speculation and rumors.

See also: Hamlin, Hannibal; Health of Johnson; Johnson, Andrew, Jr., "Frank"; Johnson, Charles; Johnson, Robert; Lincoln, Abraham; Swing-around-the-Circle; Vice President, Johnson as; Washington's Birthday Speech.

References: Graf, Leroy P., Haskins, Ralph W., and Bergeron, Paul H., eds., *The Papers of Andrew Johnson* vols. 7, 10 (1967–2000); Trefousse, Hans L., *Andrew Johnson: A Biography* (1989).

Education, Johnson's Attitude toward

*T*hat Andrew Johnson had a very informal education himself colored his attitudes about education for others. In a speech to a group of visiting children from the Washington Sunday School Union on May 29, 1865, Johnson said that parents and teachers cannot educate a child but are only the means a person uses to educate himself or herself. No one would be educated unless they educated themselves.

Johnson was most definitely an advocate of public education for both boys and girls. As he said in the speech to the Sunday School children, every boy is a potential president of the United States and each girl could be a president's wife. They should prepare themselves morally, intellectually, and socially for such a position. In a speech at the opening of the Tennessee state agricultural fair on October 12, 1857, Johnson encouraged Tennesseans to educate their daughters to be teachers in order to end complaints that all schoolteachers came from the North. Although neither of Johnson's own daughters became teachers, they both had education beyond the basics—Martha at Miss English's School in Georgetown, D.C., and Mary at the Odd Fellows Female Institute in Rogersville, Tennessee.

When Johnson became governor of Tennessee in 1853, he used his first biennial message to the state legislature to advocate educational improvements for Tennessee children, claiming that the continuation of democratic institutions depended on education for the masses. The common schools in Tennessee were very bad because of underfunding. Johnson suggested that, as a remedy, the legislature should levy a school tax. The legislature took his advice and on February 28, 1854, passed an act levying both poll and property taxes specifically to fund education.

But Johnson was not an advocate of all forms of education. While he was in Congress, he was a continual opponent of the Smithsonian Institution, frequently complaining that it was an inappropriate or wasteful use of funds. He also urged the abolition of the naval academy at Annapolis and the military academy at West Point, suggesting replacing them with state military institutions.

Perhaps Johnson's educational viewpoint can be summarized by some remarks that he made in his first inaugural address as governor on October 17, 1853. He complained about young men whose snobbish literary education made them undemocratic and caused them to look down on the rest of humankind. Johnson was opposed to any type of education that could be considered elitist. He believed that education should be practical and should also teach reverence for the Constitution. Johnson made sure that all his sons had education beyond the basics, just like his daughters. But he did not attempt to send them to prestigious schools, nor did he insist that they graduate. Frank (Andrew Jr.) attended Georgetown College for several years while Johnson was president, but did not finish the program there, or at any other college, after Johnson left Washington. This anti-elitist or antiaristocracy viewpoint explains why Johnson could be both the "father" of education in Tennessee and opposed to the Smithsonian.

See also: Apprenticeship; Congressman, Johnson as; Education of Johnson; Governor (Civilian), Johnson as; Johnson, Andrew, Jr., "Frank"; Johnson, Charles; Johnson, Robert; Patterson, Martha Johnson; Stover (Brown), Mary Johnson.

References: Graf, LeRoy P., "Andrew Johnson and Learning," *Phi Kappa Phi Journal* (Fall 1962): 3–14; Graf, LeRoy P., Haskins, Ralph W., and Bergeron, Paul H., eds., *The Papers of Andrew Johnson* vols. 2, 8, 12, 16 (1967–2000).

Education of Johnson

Andrew Johnson was unique among U.S. presidents because he never attended a day of school. His parents were evidently illiterate. Yet somehow Johnson managed to learn to read and write, became an excellent tailor, and developed popular oratorical skills. Although he learned much by studying on his own, he nevertheless had help at times.

Several people have been credited with or claimed credit for teaching Johnson to read. James J. Selby, to whom Johnson was apprenticed, was legally responsible for being sure that his apprentices were taught to read and write, but there is no evidence that he did the teaching himself in Johnson's case. In fact, in a speech years later (1864), Johnson claimed that Selby had pretty much failed in this part of the contract.

James Litchford, the foreman of Selby's shop, thought that he was the one who had taught Johnson to read, certainly a reasonable possibility if Selby delegated the responsibility. Another story credited an elderly neighbor man who burned charcoal for a living with helping Johnson point out and name the alphabet and said that a servant girl taught Johnson to write. This account may also be true. Given the informality of Johnson's education, several people may have helped him at various points.

One claimant for the honor of teaching Johnson to read, Mary Elizabeth Shelton, of Columbia, Tennessee, probably did not. Her husband, James R. Shelton, a tailor, had briefly befriended and employed Johnson about 1826, but by then Johnson was already literate. While appreciating and acknowledging her care for him years before, Johnson himself denied that she taught him to read.

Biographical accounts of Johnson's life have frequently credited his wife Eliza with teaching him to read and write. But once again, he was already literate when he met her. Undoubtedly she encouraged him in his efforts to improve his writing, which came slowly because correspondence was not often necessary for a tailor and village alderman. Although his handwriting eventually became quite good (until he injured his arm in 1857), his spelling remained somewhat lacking.

Johnson began to develop his tailoring skills as an apprentice to James J. Selby beginning in either 1818 or 1822. Foreman James Litchford certainly helped to instruct Johnson and there may have been other journeyman tailors who at times supervised or in other ways contributed to Johnson's knowledge of making men's clothing. Johnson surely had a strong basic understanding of tailoring by the time he ran away from his apprenticeship in June 1824. He was able to get a job as a journeyman tailor first in Carthage, North Carolina, and then in Laurens, South Carolina, where he was commissioned to make a wedding coat for the local schoolteacher. Johnson then moved west, spending a few months in Mooresville, Alabama, where tailor Joseph Sloss taught him how to cut out and make frock suits. He then worked for James Shelton in Columbia, Tennessee, for a few months, and a bit later worked in Rutledge, Tennessee, as well. Each of these jobs, though only a few months in duration, helped to hone Johnson's skills. By the time he opened his own tailor shop in 1827 in Greeneville, Tennessee, he was quite an experienced tailor, although only eighteen years old.

As with writing, the oratorical skills that Johnson developed were the product of experience and informal lessons rather than schooling. One of the earliest factors influencing Johnson's oratorical style was the reading he heard while an apprentice. Especially influential was *The American Speaker* (also known as *United States Speaker* or *Columbian Orator*), a collection of speeches by English and American statesmen that was read to the tailors by Dr. William Hall. Johnson loved this book so much that Hall eventually gave it to him and he treasured it for the rest of his life. Johnson certainly was also influenced by political debates that he heard in both Selby's shop and his own. Finally, Johnson read whatever books on politics and oratory he was able to find on his own. From these he learned certain famous stories from antiquity that he used and reused in numerous speeches.

See also: Apprenticeship; Greeneville, Tennessee; Johnson, Eliza McCardle.

References: Graf, LeRoy P., Haskins, Ralph W., and Bergeron, Paul H., eds., *The Papers of Andrew Johnson* vols. 1, 6, 7 (1967–2000); Trefousse, Hans L., *Andrew Johnson: A Biography* (1989).

Election of 1864

Because 1864 was a presidential election year, both parties began to consider potential candidates in late 1863 and early 1864. By this time the Republicans were calling themselves the National Union Party in an attempt to include War Democrats, who wanted the Civil War prosecuted to Union victory and were uncomfortable being allied with the members of the peace wing of the party who wanted immediate, negotiated peace.

The Republicans had little chance of nominating any other presidential candidate besides Abraham Lincoln but some Radical Republicans wanted to nominate others and even attempted to do so. Some Radicals favored politician and general Benjamin F. Butler. An attempt to promote Secretary of the Treasury Salmon P. Chase for president failed in the spring of 1864. Others suggested General Ulysses S. Grant, but, to Lincoln's relief, Grant claimed to be uninterested. It also helped that Grant was given the rarely awarded rank of lieutenant general and put in charge of all the Union armies. The most serious threat came from the partisans of General John C. Frémont, whose 1861 order freeing the slaves of secessionists in Missouri had caused Lincoln to remove him from command. Frémont's supporters, calling themselves the Radical Democracy, held a convention on May 31, 1864, in Cleveland, Ohio, and nominated Frémont for the presidency. Frémont accepted the nomination but eventually withdrew his candidacy.

The Republican, or National Union, Convention met in Baltimore, Maryland, beginning on June 7, 1864. On June 8 the convention nominated Lincoln as expected. But the choice of a vice presidential candidate became more complex. Hannibal Hamlin, the current vice president, was a fairly radical Republican from Maine. For various reasons many Republicans thought that a War Democrat for vice president would give the ticket more widespread appeal. Lincoln seems to have been ambivalent about the choice, open to retaining Hamlin or having another candidate, such as Andrew Johnson. Many historians of Johnson and the Civil War period have accepted a story told by newspaper journalist Alexander K. McClure, in which he and three other friends of Lincoln maneuvered in the convention to get Johnson nominated because Lincoln wished it. As historian Don E. Fehrenbacher has shown in an important article published in 1995, the conspiratorial thesis for the nomination of Johnson is based on very weak evidence, mostly the 1891, and later, reminiscences of McClure himself.

Other evidence suggests that Lincoln really did not interfere. Johnson was nominated in part because the New England states and New York, which could have been expected to support Hamlin, did not support him. In addition, because of the desire to include War Democrats, Johnson seemed to be the perfect candidate. He would appeal to Democrats and border-state Southerners but also to Radicals because of his firm stand against the rebels. He was also a heroic figure for his refusal to leave the Senate when his state seceded. His heroism had been played up at the convention, especially in the very effective speech by Horace Maynard seconding Johnson's nomination, which some considered an important factor in defeating Hamlin for the nomination.

On the first ballot Johnson led with 200 votes, followed by 150 for Hamlin, 108 for Daniel S. Dickinson of New York, and 61 for various other candidates. Although Johnson did not have a majority, it was clear that the convention was leaning toward him. The Kentucky delegation was the first to switch its votes to Johnson and was followed by others in quick succession. The votes of the Pennsylvania delegation gave Johnson the majority he needed, but delegations continued to switch until the count

stood 494 votes for Johnson, 17 for Hamlin, and 9 for Dickinson. At this point the nomination was declared unanimous. Although some Republicans, such as Thaddeus Stevens, deplored Johnson's nomination, most were satisfied with the Lincoln-Johnson ticket.

The Democrats held their convention very late in the season. It did not begin until August 29 in Chicago. The party selected General George B. McClellan as its presidential candidate but declared the war a failure and gave McClellan a peace platform which he, in fact, opposed, angering the Peace Democrats.

During the summer of 1864 the prospects seemed dismal for the Republicans as the troops fought many battles with heavy Union losses. However, in August, forces under Admiral David G. Farragut captured Mobile Bay, and in September General William T. Sherman's troops captured Atlanta, and General Philip H. Sheridan's forces defeated the Confederates under Jubal Early in the Shenandoah Valley. These victories positively influenced the election in favor of the Republicans (National Union Party).

In September the state elections in Vermont and Maine went for the National Union candidates, as did the October elections in the crucial states of Ohio, Indiana, and Pennsylvania. These were accurate indicators of the presidential election in November. Johnson contributed to the outcome by campaigning in Tennessee (whose votes ultimately would not be counted) and Indiana. Many soldiers were permitted to vote in the field or furloughed to vote at home if their states would not permit absentee ballots. This soldier vote was overwhelmingly for the Lincoln-Johnson ticket, but did not decide the election. Lincoln received a total of 2,213,665 votes to McClellan's 1,802,237. The electoral vote was 212 for Lincoln to 21 for McClellan (the votes of New Jersey, Kentucky, and Delaware). As a result of the election, Andrew Johnson assumed the vice presidency on March 4, 1865.

See also: Butler, Benjamin Franklin; Chase, Salmon Portland; Democratic Party; Grant, Ulysses Simpson; Hamlin, Hannibal; Lincoln, Abraham; Maynard, Horace; Military Governor of Tennessee, Johnson as; National Union Party; Republican Party; Senator, Johnson as; Sheridan, Philip Henry; Sherman, William Tecumseh; Stevens, Thaddeus; Vice President, Johnson as.

References: Fehrenbacher, Don E., "The Making of a Myth: Lincoln and the Vice-Presidential Nomination in 1864," *Civil War History* 41 (Dec. 1995): 273–290; Graf, LeRoy P., Haskins, Ralph W., and Bergeron, Paul H., eds., *The Papers of Andrew Johnson* vol. 6 (1967–2000); Trefousse, Hans L., *Andrew Johnson: A Biography* (1989); Waugh, John C., *Reelecting Lincoln: The Battle for the 1864 Presidency* (1997).

Election of 1866

When the congressional election year 1866 arrived, allies of Andrew Johnson were concerned that supporters of the president needed to be elected. To this end, to avoid the stigma attached to the Democratic Party as a party of either rebels or Northern supporters of rebellion, Johnson and his advisors determined to organize a new party. The National Union Party took its name from its predecessor in 1864. However, although the 1864 party was a coalition mainly of all types of Republicans with some War Democrats, the Democrats predominated in the 1866 party, which was a coalition of Democrats and conservative Republicans.

In June, Johnson's advisors issued a call for a National Union Convention to meet at Philadelphia. Its purpose was to promote unity and harmony in support of Johnson and his Reconstruction policies. In fact, Johnson began to use support for the convention as a test for patronage purposes. Three of his cabinet members refused to support the convention and resigned, as did some other officeholders such as Hannibal

Hamlin, the collector of customs at Boston. The convention itself, held August 14–16, 1866, provided a notable symbol of unity when the delegates from South Carolina and Massachusetts entered the hall together arm-in-arm. However, it accomplished little else besides passing ten resolutions supportive of Johnson and the right of the Southern states to be represented in Congress, which became the party's platform.

A number of his correspondents wrote to Johnson with enthusiasm about the convention. But many more of the general population opposed the convention and the party because the majority of its members seemed to be former rebels and their supporters. Some well-meaning correspondents urged Johnson to steer clear of the party for this reason. Radical Republicans decided to call their own Southern Loyalists Convention to meet in Philadelphia in early September to counteract the National Union Party. Ironically, the Loyalist meeting split between Northern and Southern Unionists because the Southerners favored black suffrage and the Northerners did not. The Johnson forces then called a Soldier's and Sailor's Convention to meet at Cleveland and the Radical Republicans held a similar meeting at Pittsburgh, where Benjamin F. Butler gave a vehement speech and suggested that Johnson should be impeached. In general, however, none of these later conventions seemed to have a great impact.

Of far greater importance to the election were the riot in New Orleans on July 30 and Johnson's Swing-around-the-Circle campaign from August 29 to September 15. The New Orleans riot, which occurred when the 1864 Louisiana constitutional convention was recalled into session, resulted in a massacre of white and black convention attenders and spectators by white opponents and the city police. Here was direct evidence of violence against nonviolent gatherings of blacks and Unionists in the South, where Johnson was claiming that everything was peaceful. Even worse for Johnson's reputation was his refusal to sympathize with the victims of the riot. Instead, he blamed Congress and the attitudes of certain of its members for the riot and suppressed the section of General Philip H. Sheridan's report that called it a massacre by the police.

Johnson's Swing-around-the-Circle was a trip to Chicago for the dedication of a monument to Illinois's deceased Democratic senator Stephen A. Douglas. However, Johnson used the trip as an opportunity to bring his ideas to the people, giving speeches at numerous large cities and smaller towns. Unfortunately, Johnson could not resist his background as a stump speaker and the opportunity to respond to hecklers who interrupted some of his speeches. As a result, Johnson appeared very undignified and unpresidential, behavior that was reported in newspapers nationwide, actually losing support for Johnson rather than gaining it.

The trend toward the Republicans was first evident in a great victory by that party in Maine in early September. In fact, the rest of the fall elections showed an overwhelming support for the Republicans and defeat for pro-Johnson candidates. The Republicans gained a two-thirds majority in both houses of Congress and would now be able to control Reconstruction, replacing Johnson's program with their own.

See also: Black Suffrage; Butler, Benjamin Franklin; Cabinet Members; Congressional Reconstruction; Democratic Party; Hamlin, Hannibal; National Union Convention and Party; National Union Party; New Orleans Riot; Patronage; Presidential Reconstruction; Republican Party; Sheridan, Philip Henry; Swing-around-the-Circle.

References: Graf, LeRoy P., Haskins, Ralph W., and Bergeron, Paul H., eds., *The Papers of Andrew Johnson* vol. 11 (1967–2000); Trefousse, Hans L., *Andrew Johnson: A Biography* (1989); Wagstaff, Thomas, "The Arm-in-Arm Convention," *Civil War History* 14 (June 1968): 101–119.

Election of 1868

The election of 1868 would determine the successor of Andrew Johnson as president of the United States. Johnson, of course, hoped that that person would be himself. As early as 1864 there had been considerable popular support for giving the Republican nomination to General Ulysses S. Grant, thanks to his leadership in a number of Union military victories. Much to Abraham Lincoln's relief, however, Grant had indicated that he was not interested in the nomination. Grant did, after all, still have the war to win. By 1868 that situation had changed.

Although Grant had no political experience, his military success had made him the ideal candidate in the eyes of most Republicans. By late 1867 everyone except the most ardent Radicals was sure that Grant would be the Republican candidate in 1868. In fact, many believed that, after the Democratic victories in 1867, Grant was the only candidate with a chance to bring Republican victory. Grant's public break with Johnson, shown when the general had allowed Edwin M. Stanton to resume his office as secretary of war when the Senate refused to agree with Stanton's removal, made Grant a hero even to the Radicals. Johnson's acquittal in the impeachment trial also helped Grant's candidacy because some people had been concerned that, if Johnson were removed and replaced by Benjamin Wade, Wade would receive the Republican nomination.

Grant was, however, very reluctant to run for president. He recognized his own political inexperience. He also knew that he would be leaving a secure position as general-in-chief for the instability of political office-holding, an important concern because of his limited financial resources. Grant also knew that unexpected political situations could diminish his reputation. Yet by the time of his nomination, Grant was at least resigned to the idea because he dreaded the possibility that a Democrat, such as George H. Pendleton of Ohio, would be elected and would undo the results of the Union victory. Many people had told Grant that his candidacy was essential for Republicans to win. Therefore, when the Republican convention met in Chicago and nominated Grant unanimously on May 21, 1868, Grant accepted the candidacy.

The Democratic Convention did not meet until July 4, 1868. In this case there was no leading candidate, not even the incumbent, Andrew Johnson. Although popular with many ordinary Democrats, Johnson was not popular with the party leaders, who resented his running with Lincoln in 1864 and his failure to use patronage to the Democrats' advantage. In addition to Johnson and Pendleton, possible candidates included General Francis P. Blair, Jr., of Missouri, General Winfield Scott Hancock of Pennsylvania, Chief Justice Salmon P. Chase of Ohio, and former New York governor Horatio Seymour, who did not wish to be a candidate. Nevertheless, on the twenty-second ballot, Seymour was chosen, with Blair as his vice presidential running mate. This pair turned out to be a poor choice and made campaigning easy for the Republicans, who had many opportunities to "wave the bloody shirt," contrasting Republican war efforts with Democratic opposition to the Union cause. In fact, Seymour had opposed the war, and Blair made a number of tactless statements in opposition to Reconstruction. Far from appealing to Republican voters, the Democratic candidates drove a number of their own party members, including some of Johnson's cabinet members, to vote for Grant.

Johnson was disappointed at what he considered the ingratitude of the Democratic Party in failing to nominate him, but he paid no attention to correspondents who urged him to establish a third party or try to replace Seymour. Although he politely endorsed Seymour, Johnson was not at all involved in the campaign until late

October. Then, after the Democrats lost badly in the October state elections in Ohio, Pennsylvania, and Indiana, Seymour decided to go out and campaign himself, something that presidential candidates usually did not do during this period. On October 22 Johnson wrote a rather melodramatic note to Seymour, which was published in the newspapers, urging Seymour to personally expose the evil activities of "all the enemies of constitutional government." Johnson's note surely had no effect on the election.

There was considerable violence in the Southern states by the Ku Klux Klan and similar groups against black and white Republicans in order to discourage them from voting. In Louisiana, General Lovell H. Rousseau, commanding the military there, urged blacks, for their own protection, not to vote, rather than offering military guards at the polls. Nevertheless, Grant was elected, receiving 3,598,235 popular and 286 electoral votes to Seymour's 2,706,829 and 80, respectively.

See also: Blair, Francis Preston (Jr. and Sr.); Chase, Salmon Portland; Democratic Convention; Democratic Party; Grant, Ulysses Simpson; Hancock, Winfield Scott; Impeachment; Lincoln, Abraham; Patronage; Republican Party; Rousseau, Lovell Harrison; Seymour, Horatio; Stanton, Edwin McMasters; Wade, Benjamin Franklin.

References: Foner, Eric, *Reconstruction: America's Unfinished Revolution, 1863–1877* (1988); Graf, LeRoy P., Haskins, Ralph W., and Bergeron, Paul H., eds., *The Papers of Andrew Johnson* vols. 14–15 (1967–2000); Simpson, Brooks D., *"Let Us Have Peace": Ulysses S. Grant and the Politics of War and Reconstruction, 1861–1868* (1991); Trefousse, Hans L., *Andrew Johnson: A Biography* (1989).

Elections of 1867

*T*he elections in the fall of 1867 focused on state and local offices and issues, rather than on the election of congressmen or the president. In the South the elections involved voting to approve calling a constitutional convention, as well as electing delegates to attend the convention. In these elections the Republicans were overwhelmingly successful, both in getting convention approval and in delegate selection, thanks to a high black voter turnout in the Southern states.

In the North the elections included a broader spectrum of officials, such as governors and legislators, as well as referendums on enfranchising blacks in Ohio, Minnesota, and Kansas. Kansas voters also were considering suffrage for women. Not confined to any particular date, various states held their elections in September, October, or November.

Just before the elections began, Johnson on September 3, 1867, issued a proclamation that the army should support law and order in the Carolinas as defined by the civil courts there. He issued another proclamation on September 7 granting amnesty to all but the leading Confederates. Whether these proclamations had any influence on the outcome of the election is not clear, but the Democrats won resounding victories everywhere in the North. All the attempts to extend suffrage, to blacks or women, were defeated. Although the Democratic gubernatorial candidate in Ohio was narrowly defeated, the legislature there gained a majority of Democrats, making it clear that they would not reelect the Radical Republican Benjamin F. Wade to the Senate, leaving his term to expire in 1869. In Pennsylvania, Democrats also won most of the executive and judicial offices.

Similar results elsewhere led many correspondents to congratulate Johnson throughout the fall. These results also led to a certain Democratic overconfidence. Some believed that these victories would permanently squelch the idea of impeachment, a perspective that Johnson may also have espoused, leading him to remove Secretary of War Edwin M. Stanton even after the Senate had insisted on his reinstatement. It also led others to suggest that the Democrats

could be certain of victory in the presidential election of 1868.

The Republicans drew their own conclusions from the Democratic victory. Some blamed the defeat on the fact that Johnson had not been impeached and redoubled their efforts to bring this about. Others believed that the race issue, particularly equal suffrage for blacks, had caused the defeat, and they began to tone down any further appeals for racial equality. Many Republicans also became certain that the only possible way to win the presidential contest in 1868 would be to have Ulysses S. Grant as the candidate.

See also: Amnesty Proclamations; Black Suffrage; Democratic Party; Election of 1868; Grant, Ulysses Simpson; Republican Party; Stanton, Edwin McMasters; Wade, Benjamin Franklin.
References: Foner, Eric, *Reconstruction: America's Unfinished Revolution, 1863–1877* (1988); Graf, LeRoy P., Haskins, Ralph W., and Bergeron, Paul H., eds., *The Papers of Andrew Johnson* vol. 13 (1967–2000); Trefousse, Hans L., *Andrew Johnson: A Biography* (1989).

Evarts, William Maxwell (1818–1901)

William M. Evarts, a member of Andrew Johnson's defense counsel and also one of his attorney generals, was born in Boston. He attended Boston Latin School and graduated from Yale University with honors in 1837. He read law in several offices and attended Harvard Law School before being admitted to the New York bar in 1841. He soon went into partnership with several other lawyers and remained with the noted firm for nearly sixty years. On August 30, 1843, Evarts married Helen Minerva Wardner. They became the parents of twelve children.

Evarts's first political appointment was as assistant U.S. attorney for the southern district of New York (1849–1853). Originally a Whig, Evarts became a Republican and was chairman of the New York delegation to the 1860 Chicago convention, which nominated Lincoln, although Evarts backed William H. Seward. During the Civil War, Evarts made several trips to England (1863–1864) to try to get the British to stop building ships for the Confederacy.

Evarts had been critical of Andrew Johnson in the recent past and was a supporter of Ulysses S. Grant for the presidency. Consequently, Johnson's advisors saw the astute lawyer as a good person to have on a bipartisan impeachment defense team. Evarts believed that a president could be impeached only for a criminal act that directly interfered with the fundamental aspects of the government or the public interest. Evarts gave the longest speech of all at Johnson's trial. His summary argument lasted four days (April 28–May 1). Evarts was also involved in negotiations with the moderate Republicans to get all parties to agree on General John M. Schofield for secretary of war and to demonstrate that Johnson would not interfere with the Military Reconstruction Acts. These negotiations helped to bring about Johnson's acquittal by a very narrow margin.

After the trial, the Senate refused to confirm Henry Stanbery's renomination as attorney general. Then Benjamin R. Curtis turned down the job. Finally, Evarts agreed to take the post, so Johnson nominated him on June 23, 1868, and the Senate confirmed him on July 15.

Like Stanbery and other attorney generals, Evarts was responsible for giving official opinions on the appropriateness or legality of federal government actions. Evarts issued opinions on the eight-hour workday law, which applied to artisans at certain government military installations; the Jefferson Davis case; when railroad companies should be paid for completed work; and the possibility of certain military officers being restored to their original rank after being reduced in rank by a military commission. Evarts also recommended several individu-

als for patronage posts and encouraged the pardon of a man imprisoned for a minor liquor violation.

When Johnson left the presidency, Evarts returned to a notable legal and political career. He was involved in the arbitration of the *Alabama* Claims with Britain (1871–1872); was a defense attorney in the notorious *Theodore Tilton v. Henry Ward Beecher* case (1875), during which he took eight days to deliver his summary speech; and was chief counsel for the Republican Party in the 1876–1877 dispute over the presidential election returns of Samuel J. Tilden and Rutherford B. Hayes. When Hayes became president, he selected Evarts to be his secretary of state (1877–1881). Evarts then served as U.S. senator from New York (1885–1891). Ill health, particularly progressive blindness, caused him to retire from public life some years before his death in New York City.

See also: *Alabama* Claims; Curtis, Benjamin Robbins; Davis, Jefferson; Impeachment; Impeachment Defense Counsel; Patronage; Republican Party; Schofield, John McAllister; Seward, William Henry; Stanbery, Henry.

References: Benedict, Michael Les, *The Impeachment and Trial of Andrew Johnson* (1973); Evarts, William Maxwell, *Arguments and Speeches of William Maxwell Evarts* vol. 1 (1919); Graf, LeRoy P., Haskins, Ralph W., and Bergeron, Paul H., eds., *The Papers of Andrew Johnson* vols. 14–15 (1967–2000); Trefousse, Hans L., *Andrew Johnson: A Biography* (1989).

Ewing, Thomas, Jr. (1829–1896)

Ewing, Thomas, Sr. (1789–1871)

Born in West Liberty, Virginia (now West Virginia), Thomas Ewing, Sr., moved with his family to Waterford, Ohio, in 1792, and to Ames Township (Athens County), Ohio, around 1798. Taught at home by an older sister, Ewing was a quick learner and a voracious reader. He attended Ohio University while still employed at a salt works and was among the first to graduate from that institution, receiving his degree in 1815. Ewing studied law and was admitted to the bar in 1816, whereupon he relocated to Lancaster, Ohio, to practice law.

Although Ohio was developing rapidly, it still suffered from a dearth of skilled professionals, so Ewing's ability became well known and he earned repute throughout the West. His household grew as well; he married Maria Wills Boyle in 1820, and the two had seven children, including Thomas Jr. (eight children if one adds William Tecumseh Sherman, whom the Ewings adopted in the late 1820s and who received an appointment to West Point through Senator Ewing). In the early 1820s Ewing served as Fairfield County's prosecuting attorney and used that as a stepping stone into politics. Defeated for the state legislature in 1823, Ewing rebounded in 1830 and won a seat in the U.S. Senate, serving from 1831 to 1837. Embracing the new Whig Party's platform of internal improvements and anti-Jacksonianism, Ewing pushed for higher tariffs and the recharter of the Bank of the United States. Senator Ewing was also a catalyst for the reorganization of the postal department and the settlement of the Ohio–Michigan border dispute.

Defeated for reelection in 1836, Ewing returned to his law practice until 1841, when he was appointed secretary of the treasury by the first Whig president, William Henry Harrison. Ewing remained in the cabinet after Harrison's death, but the new president, John Tyler, so resisted Ewing's financial policies that the latter resigned. He went back to Lancaster, but returned to Washington in 1849, when President Zachary Taylor asked him to take over, and basically organize, what became the Department of the Interior. With Taylor's death in 1850, Ewing resigned his cabinet post, but received an appointment to the Senate to fill an unexpired term (1850–1851). He left Washington and returned again to his law practice. A staunch Unionist, the elder Ewing held no government post during the Civil War, but advised President Lincoln on western matters and legal issues and was among those who urged Lincoln to release the Confederate commissioners during the *Trent* Affair.

Thomas Ewing, Jr., played an even more prominent role in the Civil War than his father did. The fifth child and fourth son of Thomas Sr. and Maria Wills Boyle Ewing, Thomas Jr. was born in Lancaster, Ohio, and attended preparatory school there. At the age of twenty he accompanied his father to Washington, D.C., and became a private secretary to President Taylor while his father served as secretary of the interior. Thomas Jr. left executive service along with his father, but remained in the capital city for two years as a claims clerk. He then moved to Providence, Rhode Island, and attended Brown University. He graduated in 1854, returned to Ohio, entered Cincinnati Law School, and by late 1855 had passed the bar. In early 1856 Ewing married Ellen Cox, and the two headed west to Leavenworth, Kansas, where Ewing added his name to the law firm of Ewing, Sherman, and McCook.

At this time, the drama unfolding in Kansas between proslavery and antislavery forces captivated the nation. Ewing, an outspoken opponent of slavery, became a leading figure in the state's attempt to remain "free" (making slavery illegal in the state) and was responsible for exposing many of the frauds associated with the 1858 Lecompton Constitution. Realizing that his state's fight was the nation's struggle as well, he spoke out in 1860–1861 against secession, but also worked toward compromise to preserve the Union. In January 1861, his Unionism and legal background led to his selection as the first chief justice of the state supreme court, but he resigned in 1862 to fight in the Civil War.

In September 1862 Ewing recruited, and became colonel of, the 11th Kansas Volunteer Cavalry. Ewing participated in brutal campaigns in Arkansas and Kansas and commanded the St. Louis District during the 1864 invasion of Missouri by Confederate general Sterling Price. For his performance Ewing was brevetted major general of volunteers in 1865, after which he resigned. After the war he resided in Washington, D.C., where he practiced law. During the trial of the Lincoln assassination conspirators, the younger Ewing served as defense counsel for Dr. Samuel A. Mudd, Samuel B. Arnold, and Edward Spangler.

Both Thomas Sr. and Thomas Jr. served as unofficial advisors to President Andrew Johnson, even though neither held public office during the Johnson administration. As former Whigs, floating between the War Democrats and the conservative Republicans, the Ewings potentially represented the core of a new Johnsonian party. All three men were devoted to the Union, and all supported Lincoln's lenient plan of postwar reconstruction. Even the younger Ewing, who had witnessed warfare at its most vicious in the West, believed that reconciliation with minimal federal interference was the most practical approach to Reconstruction.

Because of their similar views, the Ewings wrote and visited Johnson frequently, offering advice on the president's travels, veto messages, speeches, and political and military appointments. In several instances remarks and suggestions made by the elder Ewing appeared in Johnson speeches. There are also instances when Johnson seemingly complied with the Ewings' advice, although the results may have been coincidental, including: Thomas Sr.'s call for the removal of General John Pope; his warning against using Jeremiah S. Black as defense counsel during the impeachment trial; Thomas Jr.'s advice on complying with the Tenure of Office Act via a written explanation of the suspension of Secretary of War Edwin M.

Stanton; and Thomas Jr.'s insistence on having Johnson veto an 1869 bill for funding public credit.

Eager to have in his corner conservative war heroes and national figures of unimpeachable character, the president considered bringing both Ewings into his administration. As early as the fall of 1867, Johnson toyed with the idea of replacing General Ulysses S. Grant as interim secretary of war with either Ewing and sounded out Thomas Jr. for the head of the Treasury Department in place of the incumbent Hugh McCulloch (the elder Ewing opposed the appointment), but the Senate refused to act on the nomination. The only nomination to succeed was that of Hugh Boyle Ewing, an older brother of Thomas Jr., who was sent as minister to The Hague in 1866.

By the time Johnson left office, the Ewings had fully embraced the Democratic Party. Thomas Sr. never held a public office again, choosing instead to continue practicing law. In October 1869 he suffered a seizure while arguing a case before the Supreme Court (and had himself baptized on the courtroom floor). He retired to Lancaster, Ohio, where he died in October 1871.

The younger Ewing remained active in politics. He was sent as a Democrat to the Ohio constitutional convention in 1873–1874 and served two terms in Congress (1877–1881). He stayed in the East, moved to New York City, and opened a law practice. He died in a streetcar accident in January 1896.

See also: Black, Jeremiah Sullivan; Cabinet Members; Congressional Reconstruction; Conservatives; Democratic Party; Grant, Ulysses Simpson; Impeachment; Jackson, Andrew; Lincoln, Abraham; Lincoln Assassination Conspirators; McCulloch, Hugh; Mudd, Samuel Alexander; Patronage; Pope, John; Presidential Reconstruction; Presidential Travels; Sherman, William Tecumseh; Stanbery, Henry; Stanton, Edwin McMasters; Tenure of Office Act; Whig Party.

References: GedCom Genealogy database at http://www.my-gedcom/db/page/longacre/ 34062 used 7/3/00; Graf, LeRoy P., Haskins, Ralph W., and Bergeron, Paul H., eds., *The Papers of Andrew Johnson* vols. 13–15 (1967–2000); Kansas State Historical Society at http://www.kshs.org/ms/ewing.htm used 7/3/00; Katz, Bernard S., and Vencil, C. Daniel, eds., *Biographical Dictionary of the United States Secretaries of the Treasury, 1789–1995* (1996); Taylor, David Gene, "The Business and Political Career of Thomas Ewing, Jr.: A Study of Frustrated Ambition" (Ph.D. Dissertation: University of Kansas, 1970).

Ex parte McCardle

See McCardle, Ex parte

Ex parte Milligan

See Milligan, Ex parte

Farewell Address (1869)

As Andrew Johnson left the presidency, he addressed the people of the United States one final time. This was not a speech, however, but a written document, dated March 4, 1869, and published in the newspapers and in pamphlet form.

Johnson made clear immediately that he wished to vindicate his administration. Rather than retaining the large army remaining from the Civil War and using it for foreign adventures to reunite the country in a common cause, such as driving the French out of Mexico, as many urged him to do, he had disbanded the excess troops. He also backed away from the wartime presidential powers assumed by Abraham Lincoln and vetoed the "almost unlimited additional powers" granted to him by the Civil Rights and Freedmen's Bureau bills. By these actions Johnson refrained from increasing the "public burden" or sacrificing lives "to visions of false glory." Instead, he claimed that his acts showed "that my sole ambition has been to restore the Union of the States, faithfully to execute the office of President, and, to the best of my ability, to preserve, protect, and defend the Constitution." He said he should not be blamed if party factions have caused his policy to be used to further divide the country rather than reunite it.

Johnson called the Civil War "a stupendous and deplorable mistake" caused by misunderstandings between the two sections. Remembering "the frightful cost of the arbitrament of the sword" should cause all Americans to "cling closer than ever to the Constitution as our only safeguard" and to seek to preserve peace between the sections.

Recent events in the United States, as well as examples from ancient history, showed the dangers of "a departure from the letter and spirit of the Constitution." After citing the traumas of ancient Rome under the general and tyrant Sulla in the first century B.C., Johnson claimed that similar things have happened in the United States. "Conscription, confiscation, loss of personal liberty, the subjugation of States to military rule, and disfranchisement," all begun as military necessities, have now been accepted as normal.

Johnson then discussed at great length the "encroachments on the Constitution" enacted by a two-thirds majority in Congress, which he was powerless to prevent. These "encroachments" have meddled with the constitutional balance of power between the three branches of the federal government by changing judicial jurisdiction simply to protect certain favored legislation, and by failing to consider presidential vetoes respectfully. Johnson predicted that the government "may be wholly sub-verted and overthrown" by this partisan congressional majority unless the Constitution is amended to alter the way presidential vetoes are treated.

But Johnson was only beginning his criticism. He then lambasted the congressmen as "pretended patriots" who have "persistently sought to enflame the prejudices engendered between the sections" and "to retard the restoration of peace and harmony." They constantly attacked the liberties of the people and the powers of the president, he said. He then enumerated the ways in which Congress had diminished the chief executive's Constitutional powers: removing his supreme command of the army and navy; "making subordinate officers independent of and able to defy their chief" because he could not remove them; robbing the president of his pardoning power; and conspiring to impeach, arrest, and remove the president. Congress also increased the debt by recklessly spending money; kept a large standing army to oppress the people; "engaged in class legislation" by encouraging monopolies; failed to act on important treaties; reduced the people of ten states "to a condition more intolerable than that from which the patriots of the Revolution rebelled"; deprived people of their right to protection and a proper trial; and impeached the president, who was loyal to the Union, but failed to bring Jefferson Davis, leader of the rebellion, to trial. All of this "illustrates the extremity of party management and inconsistency on the one hand, and of faction, vindictiveness, and intolerance on the other."

According to Johnson, the war ended both slavery and the alleged right of secession, but it preserved the Constitution intact, including the right of the states to determine the qualifications of their own voters, a right that Congress had been trying to usurp. The people must require the three branches of the federal government to stay within their constitutional limits and to remember that the states do still retain important rights. He particularly urged young men just eligible to participate in elections to remember and act upon these things.

Johnson believed that his policy was correct and that he had nothing to regret about his term. He concluded by urging the country to forget the past and return to the principle "The Constitution and the Union, one and inseparable."

Many people did not think very much of Johnson's final effort to vindicate himself while still in office. Although a few of his friends wrote congratulatory letters, the *New York Herald* accurately remarked that Johnson's words "smell of chagrin, distrust, ill nature, and bad blood" and were better suited to stump speaking in Tennessee than as the farewell message of the nation's chief executive.

See also: Congressional Reconstruction; Constitution, Johnson's Attitude toward; Davis, Jefferson; Impeachment; Mexico; Presidential Reconstruction; Reconstruction; Republican Party; Vetoes.

References: Graf, LeRoy P., Haskins, Ralph W., and Bergeron, Paul H., eds., *The Papers of Andrew Johnson* vol. 15 (1967–2000); Trefousse, Hans L., *Andrew Johnson: A Biography* (1989).

Fenians

The Fenian movement, an attempt to free Ireland from British domination by attacking Britain's North American possession, Canada, affected foreign relations during Andrew Johnson's presidency. In the 1840s the devastating potato famine and the unsuccessful Irish rebellion against the British in 1848 had caused more than one million Irish to leave the country, the majority of them coming to the United States. Most came for economic reasons but some were political exiles who strongly resented British rule of Ireland and vowed to overthrow it.

The Irish Revolutionary Brotherhood was founded in March 1858 in Dublin, Ireland, with the goal of overthrowing British rule. That autumn the Irish Revolutionary Brotherhood was also established in the United States with the particular purpose of raising funds for Irish liberation. The U.S. branch changed its name to the Fenian Brotherhood in 1859 in honor of an ancient Irish hero, Finn MacCumhal (d. A.D. 283), and a specially trained militia named after him. The Fenian movement grew slowly but benefited from the Civil War when 150,000–175,000 Irish-Americans fought in the Union army and gained military experience. The Fenians also gained sympathy from those Northerners who were convinced that the British were pro-Confederate.

At the end of the war many demobilizing Irish-Americans joined the Fenian Brotherhood with the prospect of forming an army to attack Canada. Meanwhile, in September 1865, the British raided the Irish Revolutionary Brotherhood headquarters in Ireland, suppressing its newspaper, imprisoning most of its staff, and capturing an American ship bringing supplies and men to support the proposed insurrection. This essentially ended hopes of revolution from within Ireland and left any remaining possibility of Irish liberation with the Fenians in the United States.

By this time the Fenians had split into several factions. The leadership of the "men of action" thought that Canada could be captured easily with enough men and arms. The Canadians would be won to the Fenian cause and Canada would serve as a base for Fenian operations in Ireland. Failing that, perhaps the British and Americans could be provoked into going to war, which would allegedly benefit the Irish.

Rumors of Fenian invasion bothered the Canadians in 1865–1866, but U.S. secretary of state William H. Seward thought the Fenian threat was greatly exaggerated. To some extent this was true because the Feni-

ans split into two factions in late 1865. But both factions began to plan separate invasions of Canada. The American Fenians were further provoked when, on February 17, 1866, the British Parliament suspended the writ of habeas corpus in Ireland to prevent further nationalistic violence and promptly arrested hundreds of Fenians, including 150 naturalized U.S. citizens of Irish heritage. Over time a number of these Irish-Americans wrote to Andrew Johnson complaining about the lack of assistance they received from the local U.S. consul and asking Johnson's aid in getting their release.

The Fenian situation was a touchy one for Johnson. He wanted to be sure that the Fenians did not violate certain neutrality laws that the United States had signed. On the other hand, Johnson did not want to take any unnecessary restrictive action, based simply on threats, and thereby alienate the large Irish-American voting population, which usually voted Democratic, in a crucial congressional election year.

Fenian raids against Canada finally took place in mid-April and early June 1866. Although a Fenian force briefly defeated some Canadian militia in June, all the invasions were dismal failures as a result of manpower and supply shortages, ineffective leadership, and lack of coordination. Hundreds of Fenians were arrested in the United States and Canada and a number were imprisoned in Canada.

The U.S. government finally took a direct stand against the Fenians on June 6, 1866, when Johnson issued a neutrality proclamation, warning all Americans against taking part in illegal invasions. The government also sent General George G. Meade with U.S. troops to the border areas to discourage invasions and arrest returning invaders.

All the Fenians arrested by U.S. forces were soon released and never brought to trial. The Canadians also released some of their prisoners, but beginning in October 1866, after the initial excitement had died down, fifty-six Fenians were brought to trial. During the trials several citizens as well as Fenian prisoners wrote to Johnson requesting his intervention. Eventually Johnson did ask Seward to intercede for the prisoners. Twenty-five Fenians were convicted and some were sentenced to be hanged, but none met that fate. All sentences were commuted to twenty years of imprisonment at hard labor. But no Fenians served their whole term. One prisoner died in 1869. The rest were released at various times from 1867 to 1872.

See also: Election of 1866; Foreign Affairs; Seward, William Henry.

References: Graf, LeRoy P., Haskins, Ralph W., and Bergeron, Paul H., eds., *The Papers of Andrew Johnson* vols. 10–11, 13–14 (1967–2000); Jenkins, Brian, *Fenians and Anglo-American Relations during Reconstruction* (1969); Neidhardt, W.S., *Fenianism in North America* (1973).

Fifteenth Amendment

The Fifteenth Amendment, which prohibited the use of race as a voting qualification, was the last of the three Reconstruction amendments. Passed by Congress in February 1869 and ratified in March 1870, it represented the capstone of the Republican Reconstruction program.

As with many Republican initiatives during Reconstruction, the Fifteenth Amendment was the result of an evolutionary process. Because the abolition of slavery and the passage of the Civil Rights Act would increase Southern representation in Congress, Republicans sought to counterbalance this by cajoling Southern states into allowing black suffrage via the Fourteenth Amendment. Other factors driving the decision to enfranchise Southern blacks were the desires to create a new Southern Republican Party, counterbalance white conservative voters, and reward former slaves for their wartime loyalty and service. After the former Confederate states rejected the Fourteenth Amendment, Congress imposed black suffrage on the South through the Military Reconstruction Acts, which required new state constitutions to enfranchise black males.

The enfranchising of blacks was not, however, limited to the South. Congress also extended the franchise to the District of Columbia (January 1867) and all federal territories (also January 1867) and even imposed it on Nebraska for the territory to become a state (February 1867). Although black suffrage seemed to be gaining momentum, most states of the West and Midwest still opposed enfranchising blacks, and state referendums to grant suffrage were repeatedly and decisively defeated. When Republicans fared badly in the elections of 1867, many moderates blamed the drop-off in support on the specter of black voting.

By 1868 many moderate Republicans were reevaluating the risks involved in granting black suffrage across the North. The presidential election, which resulted in a Republican victory, was not as one-sided as had been predicted; Ulysses S. Grant had won the popular vote by only 300,000 votes, but that was with the aid of more than 400,000 votes from Southern blacks. Congressional Republicans began to consider the advantages of enfranchising Northern blacks, which seemed appropriate in the light of the current double-standard at work in the former Confederate states. In the South itself, white intimidation, terrorism, and economic coercion had actually diminished the black vote, worrying congressional Republicans that state provisions guaranteeing voting rights might not last long. The answer seemed to be an amendment to the Constitution, which future state governments could not alter and state populations could not reject. An amendment would permanently protect black voting in the South, create a new Republican bloc in the North, and reinvigorate the Republican Party nationally.

In January of 1869 two proposals appeared in Congress providing for the extension of suffrage to blacks nationally: George S. Boutwell presented his amendment in the House of Representatives and William M. Stewart offered his in the Senate. Republicans in both Houses (the few Democrats could not affect the outcome) quarreled over voting qualifications and the issue of overtly mentioning the right to office-holding. The final version, which blended both proposals and passed Congress on February 26, 1869, was both moderate and revolutionary, and really satisfied no one. Radicals who advocated black suffrage complained about the negative phrasing of the first section, that the right to vote "shall not be denied . . . on account of race, color, or previous condition of servitude." This did not guarantee suffrage, but instead made illegal only certain types of voting discrimination. But the proposal did make it legal for black males to vote nationally, barring nonracial qualifications (such as literacy or paying a poll tax), an incredible accomplishment considering the status of American blacks and the racism of most American whites. Supporters of black voting placed their hopes in the second section, which allowed Congress "to enforce this article by appropriate legislation," thus granting Congress a power heretofore left to the states, the regulation of suffrage.

The ratification process, which required acceptance by three-quarters of the state legislatures for the amendment to take effect, began in March 1869. The New England states quickly ratified it, for many already permitted some form of black suffrage and the black population there was minimal. In the South ratification also proceeded quickly, as many states were under Republican control and had enfranchised blacks through their constitutions; even for Conservatives, the amendment would only force the North to live by the same standards. In fact Virginia, Texas, Mississippi, and Georgia were required to ratify the amendment for readmission, so they had little

choice anyway. Some Midwest states were dragged into supporting the amendment by powerful politicians who saw a personal advantage in courting the black vote. Opposition was strongest in the West, where the fear of enfranchising the growing Chinese immigrant population resulted in only one state, Nevada, ratifying it. In March 1870 the Fifteenth Amendment became part of the U.S. Constitution.

Historians still debate the goals and successes of the Fifteenth Amendment. Certainly its impact on the South was fleeting. Black and white Republicans in the South were never secure in the exercise of their voting rights, and measures such as the Enforcement Act of 1870 and the Ku Klux Klan Act of 1871, passed under the second section of the Fifteenth Amendment, were never fully implemented and eventually declared unconstitutional.

After the demise of the Reconstruction governments in the late 1870s, Southern Conservatives rewrote their constitutions to include literacy, property, and tax qualifications for voting, which legally disfranchised much of the black population; these restrictions were within the letter of the law because the amendment only prohibited discrimination based upon race.

The amendment was not, however, a total failure. In the North most states continued to abide by the spirit of the law, and since one of the amendment's central purposes was to enfranchise Northern blacks, this was a victory. But the full impact of the amendment, and the true implementation of its intent, would not come until the second Reconstruction of the 1960s.

See also: Black Suffrage; Blacks (Slave and Free), Johnson's Attitude toward; Chase, Salmon Portland; Congressional Reconstruction; Conservatives; Constitution, Johnson's Attitude toward; Democratic Party; District of Columbia Franchise; Douglass, Frederick; Election of 1868; Elections of 1867; Fourteenth Amendment; Military Reconstruction Acts; Nebraska (Admission to Statehood); Readmission of Southern States; Reconstruction; Republican Party; Stevens,

Thaddeus. For complete text of the Fifteenth Amendment, see Appendix I.

References: Gillette, William, *The Right to Vote: Politics and the Passage of the Fifteenth Amendment* (1965); Kaczorowski, Robert J., *The Politics of Judicial Interpretation: The Federal Courts, Department of Justice and Civil Rights, 1866–1876* (1985); McPherson, James M., *The Struggle for Equality: Abolitionists and the Negro in the Civil War and Reconstruction* (1964).

Finances, Johnson's Attitude toward Governmental

Andrew Johnson's attitude toward governmental finances was evident as early as his service in the state legislature (1835–1837, 1839–1843) and can be summarized in one word: economy. Both in the state house and the state senate Johnson voted against measures that would cost his constituents money, such as more funding for the insane asylum and money to pay the expenses of the legislature. In his first term in the house (1835–1837) he voted against legislation to expand railroads, angering his constituents and losing his bid for reelection in 1837.

During his ten years in the U.S. House of Representatives (1843–1853), Johnson consistently opposed any expenditures that he considered to be unnecessary, generally anything that would benefit the wealthy but not the lower classes. He voted against measures for funds to refurbish the White House, to compensate victims of a gun explosion on the navy's USS *Princeton,* and to raise soldier's monthly pay. Johnson was especially opposed to accepting money to establish the Smithsonian Institution because then the government would have to continue to support it, a long-term wasteful expense, which would benefit only the upper classes. Johnson became an outspoken continual opponent of the Smithsonian. He strongly advocated and frequently introduced a Homestead Bill, which, rather than reducing government income by distributing lands free or nearly so, would, he claimed, be a source of increased government income.

While Johnson was governor of Tennessee (1853–1857), he actually advocated a tax increase for public education. He also, in a foreshadowing of what he would do as president, began each of his biennial messages with a discussion of the state debt, which he urged the legislators to reduce.

As U.S. senator (1857–1862), Johnson continued his parsimonious ways, voting against funds to erect a commemorative statue to George Washington and an appropriation for observing a solar eclipse. He opposed virtually all appropriations (except a few for Tennessee) or at the least questioned them, no matter what they were for.

As president, Johnson had far more opportunities to expound on financial economy. The Civil War had been extremely costly, according to Johnson's calculations, costing about twice the total amount of money previously spent by the federal government from its founding until 1861. The debts resulting from the war were very large and the expenditures of the government after the war (maintaining the military during Reconstruction, for example) were also astronomical, from Johnson's perspective. In his annual messages and some other speeches, he would give a history of the nation's finances since the Revolution in order to emphasize the huge national debt. His goal was to see it paid off as quickly as possible because the government was wasting money on interest payments to bondholders and, in order to make those payments, was taxing the people oppressively.

Even after his term as president, Johnson continued to speak out on financial matters, especially railing at the bondholders, whose interest payments were made in gold, while the government paid everyone else with depreciated currency.

See also: Annual Messages; Congressman, Johnson as; Education, Johnson's Attitude toward; Governor (Civilian), Johnson as; Homestead Act;

Postpresidential Career; Senator, Johnson as; State Legislator, Johnson as.

References: Graf, LeRoy P., Haskins, Ralph W., and Bergeron, Paul H., eds., *The Papers of Andrew Johnson* vols. 1–16 (1967–2000); Trefousse, Hans L., *Andrew Johnson: A Biography* (1989).

Finances, Personal

Although Andrew Johnson began life in poverty, when he died in 1875 he was one of Greeneville, Tennessee's, wealthiest citizens. While Johnson practiced his trade as a tailor, he not only made quality clothing, but he saved his earnings and invested wisely. He was able to purchase a building for the tailor shop on July 30, 1830, and on February 24, 1831, he bought a house. There are some conflicting accounts about what houses he owned and lived in, but in September 1851 he bought a large brick home on Main Street, paying the owner $950 plus his previous home. Now called the "Homestead," this property included surrounding land, a spring, and outbuildings.

Johnson's investments went beyond simply a place for himself and his family to live, although the full extent of the investments cannot be known. These investments included at least five slaves, although these people served a practical function as house servants and Johnson did not buy and sell slaves for profit. By 1843, when Johnson completed his term in the state legislature and then was elected to Congress, he had no need to return to tailoring. He could even afford to send his daughter Martha to a private school in Georgetown, D.C., while he was in Congress.

In November 1852 Johnson purchased twenty-three acres from John Maloney (the area that is now the National Cemetery where Johnson is buried). At various times he also purchased several small offices. He apparently invested in some railroads as well. It is not known exactly what other property he owned, but in the late 1850s Johnson was buying and selling quite a bit of real estate in the Greeneville area. His sons Charles and Robert acted as his agents while Johnson held political posts in Nashville and Washington, D.C.

At the time of the Civil War, the Confederates confiscated Johnson's home, which they used for a hospital, damaging the property in the process. As a result of this, and the confiscation of Johnson's trunks from the person with whom he had stored them, Johnson and his family lost most of their personal effects that they did not have with them. Johnson, however, continued to make shrewd investments somewhere because by the end of his presidency Johnson had the funds to enlarge and rehabilitate the house and replace its furnishings.

After his return to Greeneville, Johnson bought a commercial building and other property in the town and the surrounding area. He had sizable investments in Tennessee state bonds and large deposits in banks in Washington, D.C., and Knoxville. In addition, he loaned money to various friends, not always successfully. In the several years before his death he loaned more than $5,000 to James P. Snapp for a cotton factory in Union County. Snapp was unable to repay the debt and in the late 1870s the property became a part of Johnson's estate, managed first by Johnson's son Andrew Jr. (Frank) and then by his grandson Andrew Johnson Patterson.

The Panic of 1873 dealt a blow to Johnson's investments when the First National Bank in Washington, D.C., failed in September 1873. Johnson lost $73,000; however, over the next several years, most of it was repaid to Johnson in installments.

Johnson died without a will on July 31, 1875. The Tennessee Supreme Court assessed his net worth as $152,651.55, but some estimates are higher. Johnson's wife, as administrator, did nothing to settle the estate before her own death in January 1876. Even Frank was unable to settle it before he died in 1879. Litigation over Johnson's estate thus continued into the 1880s.

See also: Congressman, Johnson as; Death of Johnson; Governor (Civilian), Johnson as; Grandchildren; Greeneville, Tennessee; Johnson, Andrew, Jr., "Frank"; Johnson, Charles; Johnson, Eliza McCardle; Johnson, Robert; Panic of 1873; Postpresidential Career; Slaves, Owned by Johnson; State Legislator, Johnson as.

References: Connally, Ernest Allen, "The Andrew Johnson Homestead at Greeneville, Tennessee," *East Tennessee Historical Society Publications* 29 (1957): 118–140; Graf, LeRoy P., Haskins, Ralph W., and Bergeron, Paul H., eds., *The Papers of Andrew Johnson* vols. 1–16 (1967–2000); Lawing, Hugh, "Andrew Johnson National Monument," *Tennessee Historical Quarterly* 20 (June 1961): 103–119; Trefousse, Hans L., *Andrew Johnson: A Biography* (1989).

Foreign Affairs

During his term as president, Andrew Johnson, understandably, concentrated on domestic issues, especially those associated with Reconstruction. But at times he also had to deal with various international matters. Most of the significant foreign issues are considered in individual entries and merely summarized here.

Two important situations confronted Johnson early in his presidency. During the American Civil War, French troops had invaded neighboring Mexico and seated an emperor, Maximilian, on the throne. Many of the Radical Republicans as well as members of the military favored a U.S. invasion to drive the French out. Johnson, however, sided with Secretary of State William H. Seward in favoring other forms of persuasion rather than force. In 1867 the French troops were withdrawn and Maximilian was captured and executed by Mexican nationalists.

The other situation was the Fenian movement, an organization of Irish and Irish-Americans intent on overthrowing British rule in Ireland. This organization appealed to many Union army veterans who became involved in several unsuccessful attempts to invade Canada because it was Britain's closest possession. The Fenians created several types of problems for Johnson because he could not approve activities that violated U.S. neutrality treaties, but did not want to alienate Democratic voters of Irish-American heritage. Secretary of State Seward did eventually intercede for Fenians imprisoned in both Canada and Ireland.

Another issue that soon arose with Britain was the matter of the so-called *Alabama* Claims. The United States was seeking compensation for commercial losses sustained during the Civil War that resulted from the activities of British-built Confederate commerce raiders such as the CSS *Alabama*. Years of discussion culminated in a treaty in January 1869, but the Senate rejected it and the situation was not resolved until 1871.

The matter of the rights of naturalized citizens of the United States when they visited their native country became a concern with both naturalized British and German citizens. The British refused to acknowledge that anyone could give up their British citizenship, which caused particular problems for naturalized Irish, a number of whom were arrested in Ireland in connection with Fenian activities. The various Germanic states also refused to accept American naturalization, and visiting German-Americans were frequently subjected to fines and the military service that they had not done before they left the country. U.S. minister George Bancroft negotiated a treaty with the Germanic states in February 1868, ratified by the Senate in July 1868, which attempted to resolve the problem by determining that five years of continuous residence in the United States (or Germany) would be sufficient for naturalization. A number of people found this treaty controversial.

In July 1866, communications with Europe drastically speeded up because of the successful completion of the transatlantic telegraph cable. Andrew Johnson and Queen Victoria of Britain were the first heads of state to exchange messages through it. In 1867 the purchase of Alaska from Russia significantly enlarged U.S. territory. Finally, the controversy over the right to work the resources of the guano island of Alta Vela, a possession of Santo Domingo, became a situation affecting Johnson in 1867–1868. Such a minor issue assumed larger proportions because its chief partisan, Jeremiah S. Black, pestered Johnson about the issue and refused to serve as one of Johnson's defense counsel during the impeachment trial because Johnson would not take action about Alta Vela.

Throughout his presidency Johnson made foreign affairs–related patronage appointments such as ministers and other legation personnel. Johnson rewarded several of his supporters with diplomatic posts, for example, Reverdy Johnson, Lewis D. Campbell, and George Bancroft. Few foreign posts were available, however, compared with those in the United States and the territories.

Each year Johnson discussed foreign affairs in part of his annual message. He used this opportunity to mention significant foreign matters, treaties negotiated, and problems pending and resolved that affected the United States.

See also: *Alabama* Claims; Alaska, Purchase of; Alta Vela; Annual Messages; Black, Jeremiah Sullivan; Fenians; Impeachment; Johnson, Reverdy; Mexico; Patronage; Seward, William Henry; Sumner, Charles; Transatlantic Cable.
References: Graf, LeRoy P., Haskins, Ralph W., and Bergeron, Paul H., eds., *The Papers of Andrew Johnson* vols. 8–15 (1967–2000).

Forney, John Wien (1817–1881)

*B*orn in Lancaster, Pennsylvania, John Wien Forney had a limited education before beginning to work in a store when he was thirteen. Apprenticed at a newspaper office three years later, Forney was editor and part owner of another paper at the age of twenty. This was only the first of a number of successful newspaper enterprises with which Forney was involved in Pennsylvania and Washington, D.C.

In 1840 Forney married Elizabeth Mathilda Reitzel. He also soon became involved in politics as a Democrat and supporter of Pennsylvania politician James Buchanan. Forney served as clerk of the U.S. House of Representatives (1851–1856) and, with Alfred O.P. Nicholson, was a partner in the Washington *Daily Union* (1854–1856). In 1857 Forney established the *Philadelphia Press,* originally to support Buchanan. But when the president failed to reward Forney with the patronage he believed was his due, and when the Democratic leadership divided over Kansas and other issues, Forney became a Republican. He held the post of secretary of the Senate for some years (1861–1868) while continuing to publish the *Press* as well as a new paper, the *Washington Chronicle,* which he began in 1861.

In the mid-1860s Forney claimed that he had been a supporter of Andrew Johnson for more than twenty years. It is known that both Johnson and Forney spoke at a political meeting at the Washington navy yard on July 7, 1852. Forney also wrote a favorable biographical sketch of Johnson, which he printed in the *Press* in September 1857. Benjamin C. Truman, sometime aide to Johnson while the latter was military governor of Tennessee, was also employed by Forney as a reporter for the *Press* and the *Chronicle.* At times during the Civil War, Forney apparently did some maneuvering in Washington, D.C., to get support and supplies for Johnson, visiting President Abraham Lincoln and Secretary of War Edwin M. Stanton as the case required. He also wrote a number of editorials supporting Johnson and was active at the 1864 National Union Party Convention in Baltimore, helping to get the vice presidential nomination for Johnson.

As soon as Lincoln and Johnson were elected, Forney began to make patronage requests of Johnson, urging him to see that the Union Democrats got their share of patronage and were not crowded out by "Old Whigs and Republican partisans." He also asked Johnson to restore to him some patronage rights that Hannibal Hamlin had switched from the secretary of the Senate to the sergeant-at-arms. As Johnson tried to decide whether to stay in Tennessee until after inauguration day, Forney informed him that six previous vice presidents had missed their ceremony. But he urged Johnson to arrive in time because he was "the representative of the Democratic element without which neither Abraham Lincoln nor yourself could have been chosen," and he should be present to help shape government policy in ways desired by the National Union Party. Forney attended the inauguration and published only a vague report of Johnson's inebriated speech, attempting to protect his friend from criticism.

When Johnson succeeded to the presidency, Forney, as his friend of many years, felt entitled to give Johnson advice on various matters, especially about patronage posts in Pennsylvania. In a letter of October 22, 1865, Forney complained, "Although I have recommended several, you have not appointed one of my personal friends." Johnson nominated Forney's candidate in this case.

Forney also had the ability to make enemies. One Albert B. Sloanaker, a Pennsylvanian who found his desire for office frustrated by Forney, called him a "political sycophant," a "political prostitute," and a "political whelp." By early 1866 Forney and Johnson also had become enemies. Apparently the cause of the rupture was Johnson's veto of the Freedmen's Bureau and Civil Rights bills in February and March 1866. With these vetoes Johnson became a traitor to the Union Republican Party, from Forney's perspective. The president conspired to bring Southern traitors back to power and became "the persecutor of the colored race." Johnson also made matters worse in his Washington's Birthday Speech of February 22, 1866. He had been criticizing Radical Republicans Thaddeus Stevens, Charles Sumner, and Wendell Phillips as persons attempting to destroy the federal government. When someone asked about Forney, Johnson responded, "In reply to that I will simply say I do not waste my ammunition upon dead ducks." Some friends of Johnson who had cause to mention Forney in their correspondence thereafter referred to him as the "dead duck." Forney was offended and his newspapers were among those most critical of Johnson for the remainder of his presidency.

Forney sold the *Washington Chronicle* in 1870 and returned to Philadelphia. He continued to engage in journalism, wrote several books, traveled, and gave lectures.

See also: Black Suffrage; Civil Rights Act; Drunkenness; Election of 1864; Freedmen's Bureau Bills (and Vetoes); Hamlin, Hannibal; Lincoln, Abraham; Military Governor of Tennessee, Johnson as; National Union Party; Nicholson, Alfred Osborne Pope; Patronage; Stanton, Edwin McMasters; Stevens, Thaddeus; Sumner, Charles; Truman, Benjamin Cummings; Trumbull, Lyman; Vetoes; Vice President, Johnson as; Washington's Birthday Speech.
References: Graf, LeRoy P., Haskins, Ralph W., and Bergeron, Paul H., *The Papers of Andrew Johnson* vols. 2, 4, 6–10 (1967–2000).

Fourteenth Amendment

*T*he most studied and most controversial amendment to the U.S. Constitution, the Fourteenth Amendment was an attempt by Congress to resolve the dilemma of Reconstruction while staying within conventional bounds of the federal-and-state balance of power. As some have put it, the amendment represented a sort of peace treaty. Although created by a Republican Congress, the amendment's carrot-and-stick approach to civil and voting rights offered

Southern states considerable latitude in directing their own affairs. When Congress passed the amendment in 1866, many believed that the former Confederate states would ratify it and be readmitted to the Union, and with that Reconstruction would end; instead, Reconstruction, and a whole new constitutional era, was just beginning.

The Fourteenth Amendment was the product of the Joint Committee of Fifteen on Reconstruction, which was concerned about the vulnerability of the Civil Rights Act of 1866. Because the civil rights guaranteed in that act could fall before court decisions or future congressional action, Republicans decided to alter the Constitution itself, and so safeguard rights, especially those of black Americans, for posterity. The amendment defined national citizenship for the first time, something previously left to the states, by declaring all persons born or naturalized in the United States to be U.S. citizens; this included black Americans, thus formally overturning the *Dred Scott* decision. The amendment also placed certain rights under federal jurisdiction—"nationalized" them—which allowed for federal action in case of infringement by a state. Thus, the crucial due process and equal protection clauses redefined who would guarantee civil rights, while the amendment redefined citizenship itself.

Section II tackled the problem of representation. Slaves had been counted as three-fifths of a person for representation; after emancipation blacks were fully counted for purposes of representation, even though they had no political power. Thus emancipation would increase Southern representation in Congress by some twelve seats. Congressional Republicans hoped to prevent this by threatening to reduce the representation of any state that denied the vote to any man over twenty-one years of age. Southern states faced a choice, and Republicans sensed a win–win situation. Former Confederates would either voluntarily extend the vote to blacks or lose seats in Con-

gress. The wisdom of this section is questionable because Congress never imposed the reduction clause, despite clear evidence of voting discrimination. Yet the clause was largely responsible for the failure of ratification among several *Northern* states.

Section III disfranchised Confederates who had taken an oath to the United States before the war, but stated that Congress could remove these disabilities by passing individual pardons. Section IV declared the Confederate debt invalid and void, and Section V was the standard "enforcement provision," which provided Congress with the authority to pass legislation to enforce the amendment.

The amendment passed Congress on June 16, 1866, and was immediately submitted for ratification, with the inference that ratification by former Confederate states would bring readmission. President Andrew Johnson attacked the inconsistency inherent in this process. Congress was compelling states to ratify a measure that those states had never debated or voted upon because they were unrepresented in Congress. Further, Johnson argued that the amendment itself was unconstitutional, as it upset the traditional balance between state and federal powers. The president made the most of suspicions that ratification would *not* bring readmission and advised Southern states to reject the amendment. Only his own state, Tennessee, ratified it (July 19) and was readmitted to the Union. The other Southern states' rejection of the amendment helped lead to Republican victories in the elections of 1866. The resulting Republican-dominated Congress opted for more stringent and coercive measures, embodied in the Military Reconstruction Acts of 1867. The new governments created under military and congressional supervision still faced the Fourteenth Amendment as a condition of readmission. Not until the summer of 1868 did the requisite three-quarters of the states ratify the amendment, and it became part of the Constitution on July 28, 1868.

Controversy over the amendment did not recede after its ratification. Its passage in 1866 had already set several significant precedents relating to congressional authority and intent. The protection of basic civil rights, traditionally a state function, was transferred to the federal government. For instance, the enforcement acts that were passed under the Grant administration, aimed at punishing such groups as the Ku Klux Klan for violating civil and political rights, were based upon the Fourteenth Amendment. Similarly, here Congress first broached the issue of black suffrage; when the former Confederate states rejected the voluntary option of enfranchising blacks, Radicals imposed it themselves with the Military Reconstruction Acts. Reviving dormant ideas from the Wade-Davis Bill, Congress also designated itself arbiter of "loyalty" and took control of the amnesty and pardon process, which both Lincoln and Johnson believed was an executive function. The amendment redefined "participation in rebellion" as a legislative issue and authorized Congress to disfranchise rebels, declare amnesty, and grant pardons. Johnson continued to issue amnesties and individual pardons for former Confederates, but because Congress controlled elections and office-holding, Johnson's proclamations were largely meaningless.

The amendment's impact continued to expand after Reconstruction. By the mid-1870s the Supreme Court began curtailing the amendment's jurisdiction concerning state discriminatory action. This only added more controversy, in the form of the famous conspiracy theory, the belief that the amendment had really been designed to protect corporations (which by the 1880s were legally regarded as persons) from state interference. Decades of probusiness rulings followed, generating corresponding regulatory measures by Congress in response.

Not until after World War II did the amendment's focus shift back to blacks and civil rights, when Justice Hugo Black advocated the "incorporation" argument, which maintains that the Fourteenth Amendment incorporates the Bill of Rights, and, in turn, projects them as restraints upon the states. Scholars still debate whether this was the original intent. Nonetheless, this view provided the legal foundation for much of the civil rights legislation of the so-called Second Reconstruction of the 1960s, as well as the basis for the constitutional right to abortion, the elimination of religion from public schools, and the foundation for many anti–capital punishment arguments. So the amendment has, in effect, reversed the Bill of Rights, a situation that Johnson had feared from the beginning; under the incorporation argument, the Fourteenth Amendment takes restrictions once placed upon the federal government and now directs them toward the states. In this way, legal concepts have evolved into accepted law through court decisions and legal interpretations, rather than through legislative action.

See also: Amnesty Proclamations; Black Codes; Black Suffrage; Congressional Reconstruction; Election of 1866; Joint Committee on Reconstruction; Pardons (Individual); Readmission of Southern States; Reconstruction; Republican Party. For complete text of the Fourteenth Amendment, see Appendix I.

References: Belz, Herman, *Emancipation and Equal Rights: Politics and Constitutionalism in the Civil War Era* (1978); Curtis, Michael Kent, *No State Shall Abridge: The Fourteenth Amendment and the Bill of Rights* (1986); Dorris, Jonathan Truman, *Pardon and Amnesty under Lincoln and Johnson: The Restoration of the Confederates to Their Rights and Privileges, 1861–1898* (1953); Kaczorowski, Robert J., *The Nationalization of Civil Rights: Constitutional Theory and Practice in a Racist Society, 1866–1883* (1987); Maltz, Earl M., *Civil Rights, the Constitution, and Congress, 1863–1869* (1990).

Freedmen, Johnson's Attitude toward

See Blacks (Slave and Free), Johnson's Attitude toward

Freedmen's Bureau Bills (and Vetoes)

On February 19, 1866, President Andrew Johnson vetoed the Freedmen's Bureau Bill and set forth his fundamental objections to Republicans' attempts to legislate for the former Confederate states. From this veto onward, the president and Congress would follow increasingly divergent paths over Reconstruction policy.

Congress created the Bureau of Refugees, Freedmen, and Abandoned Lands on March 3, 1865. Run largely by the U.S. Army, the Freedmen's Bureau was an attempt to provide for former slaves during the war and ease their transition into freedom. Designed originally as a war measure, the bureau was scheduled to expire one year after the end of the war. By late 1865, as the former Confederate states instituted devices (such as Black Codes) to restrict blacks' economic and legal rights, congressional Republicans decided to extend the Bureau's life so that former slaves could continue receiving legal, economic, and material assistance.

Authored by Lyman Trumbull, with the assistance of Bureau Commissioner General Oliver O. Howard, the Freedmen's Bureau Bill was considered by most Republicans to be moderate in nature (Radicals such as Thaddeus Stevens criticized it for not going further). The bill allowed the agency to continue indefinitely, authorized the president to set aside tracts of land for blacks to rent or own, and created a national appropriation for the bureau's funding. The bill expanded the number of bureau employees (both military and civilian), set aside funds for black schools, and continued in force the military courts that oversaw cases involving discrimination against blacks. Congress passed the bill and sent it to Johnson on February 13, 1866.

The president was already working on what became his first veto. Johnson consulted with Bureau Adjutant General Joseph S. Fullerton, Secretary of State William H. Seward, Navy Secretary Gideon Welles, and Congressmen James R. Doolittle and Edgar Cowan. Johnson's veto came on February 19, 1866. The president's objections were based in his strict understanding of the U.S. Constitution, his ardent opposition to the use of the military during peacetime, and his resistance to federal encroachment in areas traditionally controlled by the states. Johnson called the bill "class" legislation because it extended legal and economic assistance to a particular segment of society. To a former tailor who never attended school, such a bill was unfair and unnecessary and sapped the ability of freedpeople to become a "self-sustaining population." Similarly, Johnson's arguments against renting and giving land to freedpeople reflected his limited-government attitude, his opposition to class-specific legislation, and his ability to appeal to white racial prejudices: why should the federal government provide land for former slaves, Johnson argued, when it has never done so for whites? In addition, Johnson protested the use of "arbitrary tribunals" and "military jurisdiction" when civil courts were operating, brushing aside the argument that civil courts discriminated against freedpeople.

But Johnson went beyond the details of the bill and challenged Congress directly. As he would do in later vetoes, Johnson maintained that the legislation, aimed largely at the South, was unconstitutional because Congress had no right to legislate for unrepresented states. Republicans found this rejection of congressional authority the most offensive and most dangerous part of the veto because it denied Congress's right to legislate for the South until the states were readmitted—basically nullifying any congressional program.

Several moderate Republicans, hoping to work with Johnson on a compromise program of Reconstruction, voted with Democrats and other conservatives to uphold the president's veto by a vote of 30 to 18. Republicans, including Lyman Trumbull, began working on another bureau bill, one that would be even more moderate than the first. Instead of an indefinite life-span, the bureau was extended for only two years. Whereas the first bill allowed the purchase or rental of confiscated property in the South, the new bill provided for return of most land to its former owners; instead, land previously belonging to the federal government would be opened to freedpeople under the Southern Homestead Act (signed into law by Johnson on June 21, 1866). Similarly, the authors watered down the military-judicial functions; cases involving discrimination could now be transferred to federal courts under the recently passed Civil Rights Act. Like the original bill, the new bill provided funding for schools, assistant commissioners, and the purchase of clothing, tools, and other necessities. With the alterations, the framers hoped that this bill would either receive Johnson's approval or be able to garner enough votes to override a veto. On June 26 the Senate agreed to the House's revised Freedmen's Bureau Bill.

But Johnson never intended to cooperate, as shown though his antagonistic Washington's Birthday Speech, veto of the Civil Rights Bill, and attempts to discredit the bureau through biased fact-finding trips. On July 16, 1866, Johnson vetoed the second Freedmen's Bureau Bill, sending in a much shorter message that referred Congress to his February veto for detailed arguments. The objections were the same: the bill was an unnecessary and unconstitutional piece of "class legislation" that used military tribunals and federal funds to benefit a particular group. Now alienated by his refusal to cooperate, moderate and Radical congressmen united and passed the bill the same day that Johnson vetoed it.

Johnson's vetoes demonstrated that he was unwilling to compromise on any aspect of Reconstruction, and his intransigence helped unite the Republican Party on a program of action. In July 1868 Congress passed two more Freedmen's Bureau Bills, the first extending the bureau until January 1, 1869, and the second guaranteeing the tenure of Commissioner Howard. By that time the bureau already had passed its prime. The agency had provided economic and legal assistance in the first years of freedom and established a solid base for education. But, partly as a result of Johnson's opposition, a lack of funding and personnel prevented the bureau from ever having the impact that Johnson feared.

See also: Blacks (Slave and Free), Attitude toward; Civil Rights Act; Congressional Reconstruction; Constitution; Johnson's Attitude toward; Doolittle, James Rood; *Milligan, Ex parte;* Republican Party; Trumbull, Lyman; Vetoes; Washington's Birthday Speech.

References: Benedict, Michael Les, *A Compromise of Principle: Congressional Republicans and Reconstruction, 1863–1869* (1974); Bentley, George R., *A History of the Freedmen's Bureau* (1955); Cox, John H., and Cox, LaWanda, "Andrew Johnson and His Ghost Writers: An Analysis of the Freedmen's Bureau and Civil Rights Veto Messages," *Mississippi Valley Historical Review* 48 (Dec. 1961): 460–479; Oubre, Claude F., *Forty Acres and a Mule: The Freedmen's Bureau and Black Land Ownership* (1978).

Funeral of Johnson

Andrew Johnson died about 2:30 on the morning of Saturday, July 31, 1875, from the effects of two strokes suffered at his daughter Mary Johnson Stover Brown's farm in Carter County, Tennessee. Members of the Masonic order took charge of the body, wrapping it in blankets packed with ice and then placing it in a pine box for transportation back to Greeneville. The body left the farm early Saturday morning in a wagon and was placed on the train at Carter's Depot. Local citizens were at Jonesboro and other stations along the route to express their sorrow. At Home Depot Johnson's grandchildren Andrew and Mary Belle

Patterson, the only close family members who had not been in Carter County when Johnson died, boarded the train.

Many citizens, as well as the members of Masonic Lodge No. 119, of which Johnson had been a member, met the train in Greeneville. Here the Masons received the body with the appropriate ceremonies of the order; placed it on a wagon draped in mourning; and, while bells tolled, escorted the corpse to the Johnson residence. Because Johnson had often expressed his desire to be wrapped for burial in "the flag of his country" and to hold or have his head rest on the U.S. Constitution (accounts vary), his body was prepared for burial in this way. The corpse was then placed in a large casket decorated with silver Masonic symbols and a silver label engraved "ANDREW JOHNSON, AGED 67 YEARS." The casket was placed in the parlor with a Masonic guard, and a steady stream of friends and neighbors paid their respects until Monday noon, when the body was moved to the courthouse for further lying in state and visitation.

Meanwhile, citizens had draped Greeneville buildings, including the courthouse, Johnson's office, and his tailor shop, with long strips of black and sometimes white cloth. They had also held a meeting at 8:00 A.M. on Monday, August 2, to express their sorrow and plan the funeral, for which purpose they appointed a committee headed by H.H. Ingersoll. They also responded to messages from Nashville and Knoxville, each requesting that Johnson be buried in their city. The Greeneville meeting passed a resolution expressing their belief that Johnson should be buried in the town that had been his home for nearly half a century. This had been Johnson's wish and his family's as well.

Many prominent Tennessee politicians, including Governor James D. Porter and other officeholders, attended Johnson's funeral on Tuesday, August 3. Thousands of common people came as well, as did more than ten newspaper correspondents. Most of Johnson's immediate family members were also there: his children Martha Patterson and Andrew Johnson, Jr., his sons-in-law David T. Patterson and William R. Brown, and his grandchildren Andrew and Mary Belle Patterson, and Lillie, Sarah, and Andrew Stover. Only his wife, Eliza, who was too ill, and his daughter Mary Stover Brown, who stayed in Carter County to care for her mother, were unable to attend.

Around 10:00 A.M. a special train from Knoxville brought the Dickinson Light Guards and their band and also the Coeur de Lion Commandery of the Knights Templar, who were to join the local Johnson Guards and Masonic lodge in the ceremonies. After everyone who desired to do so had paid their respects, eighteen pallbearers moved the casket from the courthouse to the hearse as they walked through a line of Knights Templar who stood with swords crossed while the band played a funeral piece.

The procession to the grave site was led by a group of marshals, followed in succession by the Johnson Guards, the Greene County Patrons of Husbandry, the Odd Fellows, Dickinson's Light Guards and band (which played funeral marches all the way), the Masons, the hearse pulled by four horses, the pallbearers and Knights Templar, Johnson's family members, the governor and other public officials, the choir, and, finally, other citizens. The route to the grave site was at least half a mile long and lined with crowds of people on each side. The grave site, on top of a hill that Johnson had purchased in 1852, afforded a good view of the surrounding area.

The funeral ceremonies were Masonic, the first conducted by the Knights Templar and the second by the Master Masons. They included various symbolic actions and readings. Songs were performed by a Masonic choir and an ensemble of eight male voices. The casket was lowered into the grave, which contained a zinc-lined box and cemented walls to preserve the casket for later reinterment in a planned family vault. After the grave was filled, Mrs. W.D. Williams of Greeneville laid a large bouquet of white lilies and roses tied together with white ribbons inscribed "THE PEOPLE'S FRIEND" and "HE SLEEPETH," on the grave. No member of the clergy had a formal part in the ceremonies.

A tailor's association, wanting to honor the only tailor who had ever become president, asked permission to provide a monument for Johnson's grave. However, when time passed and no marker was forthcoming, Johnson's children erected a monument, a large marble obelisk topped by an American eagle and decorated with a Bible and the U.S. Constitution. Johnson's old friend George W. Jones spoke when the monument was dedicated on June 5, 1878.

See also: Constitution, Johnson's Attitude toward; Death of Johnson; Grandchildren; Greeneville, Tennessee; Johnson, Andrew, Jr., "Frank"; Johnson, Eliza, McCardle; Masonic Order; Patterson, Martha Johnson; Religion, Johnson's Attitude toward; Stover (Brown), Mary Johnson.

References: *Greeneville (Tennessee) Intelligencer,* Aug. 6, 1875; Trefousse, Hans L., *Andrew Johnson: A Biography* (1989).

Governor (Civilian), Johnson as (1853–1857)

Andrew Johnson served two terms as governor of Tennessee after completing five terms in the U.S. House of Representatives. No doubt Johnson would have remained in Congress had not the Whigs in the state legislature, led by Gustavus A. Henry, gerrymandered (or, as Johnson put it, "Henrymandered") his safe Democratic district into one with a Whig majority in 1852. There was some sentiment for Johnson to be elected governor even before he decided to run. Despite efforts by a caucus of Johnson's Democratic enemies to derail his nomination, the Democratic state convention nominated him unanimously in April 1853. That same month the Whigs nominated Henry as their candidate.

Both candidates campaigned across the state, beginning with a joint debate in Sparta, Tennessee, on June 1. Large crowds came to hear the campaigners. Johnson proposed such reforms as the direct election of the president, vice president, and senators and term limits for U.S. Supreme Court justices (Johnson would continue to promote these amendments to the Constitution until his death). He also discussed his pet Homestead Bill, which Henry also favored. Johnson stressed the need for im-

proved public schools, an issue that Henry ignored. Johnson also defended his past political record, which was vigorously denounced by such Whigs as newspaper editor William G. "Parson" Brownlow, who supported Henry. The biggest controversy of the campaign was the "Henrymandering" issue. Johnson won with 63,413 votes to Henry's 61,163, but the legislature had a slight Whig majority, which would hinder Johnson's ability to see his program enacted.

Johnson was inaugurated on October 17, 1853, at McKendree Church in Nashville. His inaugural address has been called the Jacob's Ladder address. In it he stressed the principles of democracy and claimed that "democracy is a ladder, corresponding in politics, to the one spiritual which Jacob saw in his vision: one up which all, in proportion to their merit, may ascend." This speech brought Johnson criticism from his enemies for years to come. (Johnson's analogy was also weak because Jacob's vision in Genesis 28 involved angels and had nothing to do with the progressive merits of humankind.) He also discussed other issues.

Johnson's first biennial message, of December 19, 1853, addressed such concerns as the state debt, a tax for road maintenance rather than forcing the poorest citizens to do the work for free, the need for a tax to support public education, the need for penitentiary reforms so that the inmates were not being taught trades to compete with honest mechanics, and the need for judicious spending on internal improvements. Although the legislature did not do many of the things that Johnson requested, in February 1854 they did pass a bill levying several types of taxes to support education. They also established an Agriculture Bureau and passed an act to support railroad expansion. A state library and geological survey were also established.

As governor of Tennessee, Johnson had rather limited powers. He could not veto laws or do much to enforce them, and he had only limited appointments to make. His duties included sending a biennial message to the legislature (which only met every other year), pardoning prisoners (Johnson pardoned more than did previous governors), and overseeing the administration of the penitentiary and the Bank of Tennessee. He also dealt with extradition requests, made payments to railroads for mileage completed, and issued proclamations of various sorts. Johnson was the first Tennessee governor to devote most of his time to being governor, and on the few occasions when he went home to Greeneville for a few weeks, he was castigated by the Whig press.

By 1855 the Whig Party was in decline and many Whigs in Tennessee were joining, or at least allying with, the American Party, usually called the Know-Nothings. This party included a number of secret membership rituals and was dedicated to keeping immigrants and Roman Catholics out of political offices, and even restricting their entry into the country. The Whig/Know-Nothing candidate for governor in 1855 was Meredith P. Gentry. Andrew Johnson somewhat reluctantly became the Democratic candidate.

By agreement the campaign began on May 1 with a joint debate in Murfreesboro. Although Johnson discussed other issues, he harshly attacked the Know-Nothings, opposing religious tests for public office

and urging freedom of religion, a constitutional right, for everyone. It was a grueling campaign for the candidates. They were scheduled to hold sixty meetings but the campaign ended a few days early, on July 26, when Gentry became ill in Knoxville. To the surprise of many, and the chagrin of the Know-Nothings, Johnson won the election on August 2 by somewhat more than 2,100 votes.

Johnson's second inauguration was a quiet and brief ceremony on October 23 at which he gave a short address. His concerns were similar to those he had expressed in 1853. He also faced a Whig-majority legislature, which again ignored much of his proposed legislation. Johnson was in Nashville the entire winter of 1855–1856 and missed the marriage of his daughter Martha to his good friend David T. Patterson on December 13, 1855. Just before Johnson was due to return to Greeneville in April 1856, he took $1,200 out of the bank and slept with it under his pillow. On the night of April 13, 1856, a fire burned Johnson's hotel, the Nashville Inn. While he assisted a woman to safety, the fire destroyed his personal effects and money.

During the summer of 1856, beginning with a mass meeting in Nashville in July when he delivered a three-hour speech, Johnson campaigned for the Democratic presidential candidate, James Buchanan, even though he did not think Buchanan was the best candidate. Johnson's speeches helped to give the Democratic candidate a majority vote in Tennessee for the first time since 1832.

Early in 1857 Johnson went to Washington, D.C., on several business matters. Coming back by way of Georgia, Johnson severely injured his right arm when his train derailed between Augusta and Atlanta. This injury would bother him for the rest of his life. Although many Democrats wanted Johnson to run for a third term, Johnson declined because he was more interested in a Senate seat if a Democratic-majority legislature could be elected in 1857. Consequently, Johnson campaigned for the Democratic gubernatorial candidate, Isham G. Harris (even though he did not like Harris much), as well as any legislators who supported his senatorial aspirations. Johnson's participation in the campaign was somewhat hampered by ill health, however.

The Democrats won both the governorship and the legislative majority in August 1857. On October 8 the legislature elected Johnson U.S. senator. Isham Harris was inaugurated as governor on November 3.

See also: Brownlow, William Gannaway "Parson"; Congressman, Johnson as; Constitutional Amendments, Proposed; Democratic Party; Education, Johnson's Attitude toward; Greeneville, Tennessee; Harris, Isham Green; Health of Johnson; Homestead Act; Patterson, David Trotter; Patterson, Martha Johnson; Senator, Johnson as; Whig Party.

References: Bentley, Hubert Blair, "Andrew Johnson, Governor of Tennessee, 1853–57" (Ph.D. Dissertation: University of Tennessee, 1972); Caskey, W.M., "First Administration of Governor Andrew Johnson," *East Tennessee Historical Society Publications* 1 (1929): 43–59; Caskey, W.M., "The Second Administration of Governor Andrew Johnson," *East Tennessee Historical Society Publications* 2 (1930): 34–54; Graf, LeRoy P., Haskins, Ralph W., and Bergeron, Paul H., eds., *The Papers of Andrew Johnson* vol. 2 (1967–2000); Trefousse, Hans L., *Andrew Johnson: A Biography* (1989).

Governor, Military
See Military Governor of Tennessee

Governors, Provisional

President Andrew Johnson appointed provisional governors in seven former Confederate states as part of his Presidential Reconstruction plans. (The other four states already had governors because of Abraham Lincoln's Reconstruction policies.) Each of the affected states received a provisional governor when Johnson issued a proclamation establishing that state's government. The provisional governors had important patronage responsibilities, filling many vacant local and state government positions, often with former Confederates. The governors also oversaw the election of delegates to their state constitutional convention, the meeting of that convention, and the election of a legislature and governor. In no state did they encourage black suffrage. The term of the provisional governor ended when the elected governor assumed his office. Most served until about December 1865, although the new Texas governor did not take office until August 1866. All Johnson's appointees had originally opposed secession. They all could be considered "loyal," Johnson's major criterion, but some had served in the Confederate government and would have been unable to take the "Ironclad Oath."

The first provisional governor was William W. Holden (1818–1892), the controversial North Carolina editor and politician, who was appointed governor of North Carolina on May 29, 1865. He was succeeded by Jonathan Worth, who was inaugurated on December 15 and took office on December 28. Mississippi was the second state to have its government established. William L. Sharkey (1798–1873), a Vicksburg lawyer with legislative and judicial experience, was appointed on June 13, 1865. His successor, Benjamin G. Humphreys, was inaugurated on October 16 but did not take office until December 25.

Both Georgia and Texas were organized on June 17. James Johnson (1811–1891) was a Columbus, Georgia, lawyer and former congressman who later served as collector of customs and state superior court judge. Charles J. Jenkins was inaugurated as his successor on December 14 and assumed office on December 19. Andrew Johnson's appointment of Andrew Jackson Hamilton (1815–1875) as provisional governor of Texas was his second controversial appointment (Holden was the first). About 1847 Hamilton, a lawyer, had moved from Alabama to Texas, where he had been state attorney general, a state legislator, and a member of Congress. A Unionist who fled to the North during the Civil War, Hamilton had been appointed military governor of Texas by Lincoln (similar to Andrew Johnson's appointment in Tennessee) in 1862 and many Texans did not like him as a result. James W. Throckmorton was inaugurated on August 6, 1866, and took office on August 13.

On June 21, 1865, Lewis E. Parsons (1818–1895), a lawyer born in New York and who since 1841 had lived in Alabama, where he served in the legislature, was appointed provisional governor of Alabama. He was succeeded by Robert M. Patton who was inaugurated on December 13 and took office on December 20. Benjamin F. Perry (1805–1886), an editor and Unionist who had served in South Carolina's Confederate legislature, became South Carolina's provisional governor on June 30, 1865. James L. Orr, elected to succeed him, was inaugurated on November 29 and took office on December 21.

Florida was the last Confederate state to have its provisional government established. William Marvin (1808–1902), a New York lawyer who had moved to Florida and served as its territorial district attorney and later as a U.S. district judge, was appointed provisional governor on July 13. David S. Walker was inaugurated as his successor on December 20, 1865, taking office on January 18, 1866.

See also: Black Suffrage; Lincoln, Abraham; Military Governor of Tennessee, Johnson as; Presidential Reconstruction.

References: Foner, Eric, *Reconstruction: America's Unfinished Revolution, 1863–1877* (1988); Graf, LeRoy P., Haskins, Ralph W., and Bergeron, Paul H., eds., *The Papers of Andrew Johnson* vols. 8–9 (1967–2000).

Grandchildren

Andrew Johnson had five grandchildren—Lillie, Sarah, and Andrew Stover, the children of his daughter Mary; and Andrew and Belle Patterson, the children of his daughter Martha. His sons Charles and Robert did not marry, and Frank's (Andrew Jr.'s) marriage produced no children. These five grandchildren, who ranged in age from five to ten when Johnson became president, resided in the White House, with occasional exceptions, during his term. The first White House Easter egg hunt was held for these grandchildren. On several occasions the young residents of Washington, D.C., were invited to children's parties at the president's home. In fact, Johnson celebrated his sixtieth birthday, on December 29, 1868, with a party for 300 children.

Lillie Stover, who was named Eliza Johnson Stover in honor of her grandmother but never used her full name, was born to Daniel and Mary Johnson Stover on May 11, 1855, in Carter County, Tennessee. She spent most of her early years at the Stover farm there but left with her parents and other family members in October 1862 when they were forced out of the area by the Confederates. Lillie traveled with her mother, grandmother, and siblings to towns in Indiana and Kentucky, seeking improvement in her grandmother's health. The family finally joined Andrew Johnson in Nashville, where he was military governor. Here Lillie's father died of tuberculosis in December 1864.

Lillie was reputedly Andrew Johnson's favorite grandchild, ·perhaps because she was the first. Reportedly he wanted to take her to Europe and have her educated in French and German after he left the presidency, but these things did not happen. Apparently she attended a convent school in Nashville for a time and became a Catholic. On July 28, 1875, Andrew Johnson went to Carter County to visit. Lillie accompanied him to his room after lunch, where they were apparently discussing her forthcoming marriage when Johnson collapsed from a stroke and died on July 31.

On October 14, 1875, Lillie married Thomas Maloney in Carter County. Maloney (1846–1907), a Union cavalry veteran and lawyer, had been serving as Johnson's secretary and coediting the *Greeneville Intelligencer* with Frank Johnson. The couple resided in Greeneville. They had no children and apparently did not have a happy marriage. No evidence has been located pertaining to their divorce, but it probably occurred in 1883 after Mary Stover's death. Lillie resumed her maiden name and Maloney moved to Ohio, where in 1884 he married Flora Hope, who was twenty years his junior. The couple had one daughter, Theodosia, and moved to Utah, where Maloney was active in the legal profession until his death from pneumonia.

After Lillie's sister Sarah died of tuberculosis in 1886, Lillie raised her two small nephews for several years. But in late 1891 Lillie, having tuberculosis herself, entered a sanatorium in Knoxville, where she spent the last eleven months of her life. She died on November 5, 1892, surrounded by her aunt, Martha Johnson Patterson; her brother-in-law, William B. Bachman; Bachman's second wife; and Lillie's two nephews. Lillie Stover was buried on Monument Hill in Greeneville.

Sarah Drake Stover, named for her paternal grandmother, Sarah Murray Drake Stover, was born in Carter County on June 27, 1857. She too spent her early childhood there, was a refugee during the war, suffered the loss of her father when she was only seven and a half, and lived in the White House. After the presidential period she attended St. Bernard Academy, a convent school in Nashville. There she became a Catholic and was confirmed in St. Mary's Cathedral, Nashville, on May 6, 1877, choosing Mary Clare as her confirmation name in honor of the mother superior of the convent. Sarah kept a diary during 1876–1877 in which she recorded much teenage angst but also her genuine religious struggles. She lamented the absence of a Catholic church in Carter County, and saw no comfort in attending a Protestant one. When her mother sent her to a Protestant school in Binghamton, New York, she left without her mother's permission and returned to the convent, making her mother angry. During the fall of 1877 Sarah was seriously considering becoming a nun. However, in a diary entry of July 1878, some months after the rest of her diary, Sarah seemed to have fallen for someone she considered "the best of men." Perhaps this was William Bruce Bachman (1852–1922), a Sullivan County teacher, whom she married on June 7, 1881, at the Hattie House in Knoxville in a ceremony conducted by Father Francis T. Marron.

The Bachmans had two sons, Andrew Johnson Bachman (1882–1955) and Samuel Bernard Bachman (1884–1914). Sarah died of the tuberculosis, so common in her family, before her younger son was two years old. The two boys were raised by their Aunt Lillie for several years until she herself was confined to a sanatorium by tuberculosis. At this point the two boys apparently went to live with their father and his second wife, the former Lula May Peterson, at "Stover Hall," the Union Depot home built by Mary Stover. It burned in 1906, but slowly enough to permit the rescue of the Johnson-Stover heirlooms and papers. These were placed in the new house, built on the same site and called "Long Shadows." Sarah's son Andrew married Ethel Crockett Irwin (b. 1892) on September 8, 1920. They had no children. Andrew's brother Samuel died unmarried on April 3, 1914, yet another victim of tuberculosis. Because Andrew and Samuel Bachman were the last Johnson descendants of the Stover line, "Long Shadows" and the Johnson-Stover papers and relics were inherited by the descendants of their half-siblings, the four children of William B. Bachman's second marriage.

The third Stover child, and the youngest of Johnson's grandchildren, was Andrew Johnson Stover. Born in Carter County on March 6, 1860, he was hardly more than a baby when his family left Carter County and only five when he went to live in the White House. Andrew Stover remains the most mysterious of Johnson's grandchildren. Nothing is known about his education or his occupation, if he had one. According to one family tradition, he was "kicked in the head by a mule" and consequently was not quite "right." Whether Andrew was literally kicked in the head or whether this was a figure of speech is not clear. There was certainly some problem because when his mother Mary Stover drew up her will in 1882, she left most of her property to her two daughters. She placed Lillie in charge of a trust for Andrew—the proceeds of a large farm in Texas. These provisions were to be in effect until Andrew reached the age of forty. A gold watch was to be held in trust for him until "he becomes a sober steady man," but if he did not reform, the trust would go to his heirs or next of kin at his death. Mary also willed that in case Andrew, "owing to his habits or improvident acts should waste his estate or come to want," his sisters should provide him with the necessities of life. Evidently, whether through injury or his own intemperate habits (similar to the alcoholism that had so plagued his three uncles), Andrew Stover was not a responsible person. But he long outlived his sisters and became a hermit, dying of pneumonia on January 25, 1923, near Elizabethton, Tennessee. He was also buried on Monument Hill in Greeneville.

Andrew Johnson Patterson, the older child of Martha Johnson and David Trotter Patterson, ultimately was the most successful of the Johnson grandchildren. He was born in Greeneville on February 25, 1857. Because David Patterson was a Confederate judge, his family stayed in Greeneville until Union troops occupied parts of East Tennessee. In October 1863 the Pattersons were able to join the rest of the Johnson family in Nashville. Andrew apparently played quite a bit with his uncle, Frank Johnson, who was about four and a half years Andrew Patterson's senior. Young Patterson, of course, lived in the White House during Johnson's presidency while his mother, Martha, was official White House hostess and his father was a senator from Tennessee. Andrew was educated at Tusculum College in Greeneville and studied law for some time, although he never practiced it. Instead he managed cotton factories in Union Depot (Bluff City), Jonesboro, and Greeneville, Tennessee. He was elected as a Democrat from Sullivan County to the Tennessee state house of representatives and served a single term (1889–1891). His other political post was an appointment by Grover Cleveland as U.S. consul in British Guiana (1894–1898).

On December 19, 1889, at Limestone, Tennessee, Andrew Patterson married Martha Ellen (Mattie) Barkley (1864–1948). The couple had one daughter, Margaret Johnson Patterson (Bartlett) (1903–1992). In 1898 Andrew and Mattie Patterson moved to the Johnson home in Greeneville to care for Andrew's mother, Martha Johnson Patterson, who was an invalid for several years before her death.

Because of Andrew Patterson's life in the White House and his otherwise frequent contact with his grandfather, who died when Patterson was eighteen, the latter had a fund of family stories that he used to recount to anyone who cared to listen. He converted his wife and daughter to the cause of preserving the family heritage, which they carried on after his death. The last surviving grandchild of Andrew Johnson, Andrew Johnson Patterson died in the family home on June 25, 1932, after several months of declining health. He was buried in the family plot on Monument Hill.

Mary Belle Patterson (usually called Belle), Andrew's younger sister, was born at Greeneville on November 11, 1859. Like her brother and Stover cousins, she experienced the dislocations of the Civil War and the pleasures of childhood in the White House. She attended school in Binghamton, New York, and was known to suffer from asthma. On February 17, 1886, she married John Landstreet of Loudon County, Virginia, and the following year their daughter Martha Belle Patterson Landstreet (1887–1969) was born on August 6 at Port Richmond, New York. Mary Belle, however, had tuberculosis and her husband took her to California in the hope that a change of climate would restore her health. It did not, and she died in Auburn, California, on July 9, 1891. Her body was returned to Greeneville for burial on Monument Hill.

For a number of years Martha Belle Landstreet was raised by her grandmother, Martha Patterson, in the Johnson home in Greeneville. However, as Martha Patterson's health declined, her granddaughter went to live with her father in Richmond, Virginia. Here in 1907 she married Robert Josiah Willingham, Jr. (1875–1953). They had two daughters, Martha Belle Willingham (Colt) and Elizabeth Landstreet Willingham (Crump). Both of these daughters married and had children. As a result, all Andrew Johnson descendants living in 2000 are descendants of his granddaughter Mary Belle Patterson.

See also: Bartlett, Margaret Johnson Patterson; Death of Johnson; Greeneville, Tennessee; Johnson, Andrew, Jr., "Frank"; Johnson, Charles; Johnson, Eliza McCardle; Patterson, David Trotter; Patterson, Martha Johnson; Stover, Daniel; Stover (Brown), Mary Johnson; Tuberculosis.

References: Andrew Johnson National Historic Site, Greeneville, TN: Patterson files, Mary Johnson Stover will, Sarah Stover diary, Stover files; Andrew Johnson Project, Knoxville, TN: Patterson files, Stover files; *Burke's Presidential Families of the United States of America* (1975); Graf, LeRoy P., Haskins, Ralph W., and Bergeron, Paul H., eds., *The Papers of Andrew Johnson* vols. 6, 16

(1967–2000); *Greeneville (Tennessee) Sun,* June 27, 1932; *History of the Bench and Bar of Utah* (1913); *Knoxville Journal,* Nov. 6, 1892, June 27, 1932; *Knoxville Sentinel,* Jan. 28, 1923; McGuire, Robert M., and Robison, Dan M., *Biographical Directory of the Tennessee General Assembly* vol. 2 (1979); 1900 Census, Utah, Weber County, Harrisville, Enumeration District 180, p. 5.

Grant, Ulysses Simpson (1822–1885)

Civil War general and hero, Ulysses Simpson Grant commanded the Union army and served as interim secretary of war during Andrew Johnson's presidency. Increasingly at odds over policy, the two became avowed enemies by early 1868, and Johnson was extremely critical of Grant during the latter's own presidency.

Grant, the son of Jesse Root and Hannah Simpson Grant, was born at Point Pleasant, Ohio. Baptized Hiram Ulysses Grant, he was called by his middle name. He grew up in Georgetown, Ohio, where he liked working on his father's farm, especially with horses, but despised his father's main business, a tannery. Educated in local schools, Grant was a mediocre student, but by a fluke won admission to West Point. The nominating congressman mistakenly listed him as Ulysses Simpson (Simpson being his mother's maiden name) and Grant kept the new name. At West Point Grant was also mediocre except in mathematics and horsemanship, but he graduated in 1843. Because there was no vacancy in the cavalry, Grant was assigned to the infantry and served in Missouri and Louisiana until the Mexican-American War broke out. His regiment was sent to Mexico in September 1845. He saw action with the forces of both Zachary Taylor and Winfield Scott and won brevets of first lieutenant and captain for his bravery in the Mexico City campaign.

On August 22, 1848, Grant married Julia Dent, the sister of his West Point roommate.

The couple apparently had an excellent, supportive relationship and produced four children. In 1851, when Grant was ordered to the Pacific Coast, he had to leave his family behind because of the difficulties of travel and his low pay. Bored and frustrated in his new posts, Grant began to drink. When ordered by his strict commanding officer to reform or resign, Grant resigned in July 1854.

For the next few years Grant worked as a farmer, real estate agent, and custom house clerk, always without success. At times Grant's father and father-in-law had to provide assistance. Finally, Grant ended up clerking for two of his brothers in a Galena, Illinois, leather store.

This dismal situation changed with the onset of the Civil War. Beginning as a colonel of volunteers, Grant soon became a brigadier general and by the end of the war was the highest ranking officer in the entire U.S. Army with the title of full general. He was victorious at Forts Henry and Donelson, Shiloh, and Vicksburg in the West, and his 1864 campaigns in the East resulted in the surrender of Robert E. Lee and his army at Appomattox Court House, Virginia, on April 9, 1865.

Of importance here is the relationship between Grant as commander of the army and Andrew Johnson, president and, constitutionally, commander-in-chief. Grant had had a good working relationship with Abraham Lincoln and he expected to have the same with Johnson. They had already had some contact during the war when Johnson was military governor of Tennessee and Grant was in western Tennessee. They corresponded about various prisoners, for example. But as Johnson's Reconstruction policies became clearer, Grant became concerned that the Southerners who caused the war would so quickly return to power that the results of the war would be lost and thousands of Union soldiers would have died in vain. Therefore, Grant began to work in secret, for example, in letters to

friends and certain subordinates, to oppose Johnson's policies and support those of Congress.

In public, however, Grant refused to speak out against Johnson and attempted to give respect to the president's position, even though Grant came to like him less and less personally. Grant became the subject of a tug of war for his support between Johnson and his followers and the Radical Republicans. Johnson persuaded Grant to go along on the Swing-around-the-Circle in 1866 to try to show the country that Grant supported Johnson, much to Grant's distress. Radical-inspired crowds called for Grant, at the expense of Johnson, but Grant largely maintained silence. He may also have become inebriated at some point.

Johnson tried to get Grant out of Washington in the fall of 1866 by sending him to Mexico with the newly appointed minister Lewis D. Campbell. Apparently Johnson was hoping to get Secretary of War Edwin M. Stanton to resign and to replace him with General William T. Sherman, who favored Johnson's policies. But Grant would not leave, Stanton did not resign, and Sherman refused to have anything to do with a political post in Washington. Sherman eventually went on the fruitless trip to Mexico.

Thanks to the Command of the Army Act, a part of the Army Appropriations Act passed by Congress in 1867, all orders and instructions from the president and Stanton had to be issued through Grant, placing him firmly in control of the army. About the same time, Congress also passed the Tenure of Office Act and the First Military Reconstruction Act, taking the control of Reconstruction matters away from Johnson.

On August 12, 1867, after a long period of conflict with his secretary of war, Johnson suspended Stanton from office, while Congress was not in session. Grant reluctantly agreed to serve as secretary of war ad interim because he did not want Johnson to appoint someone who might interfere with the army. Also in August, Johnson wanted to remove Grant's good friend General Philip H. Sheridan from command of the Fifth Military District, essentially for enforcing the Military Reconstruction Acts too stringently (an enforcement that Grant supported). Grant protested to Johnson that the removal would have a bad effect on the public because the Northern people loved Sheridan and did not want him removed. Grant reminded Johnson that "the will of the people is the law of the land" in a republic. Johnson fired back a missive on August 19 answering and contradicting each of Grant's arguments, emphasizing that the *Constitution* is the law of the land. Johnson soon removed Sheridan.

According to the Tenure of Office Act, Johnson had to notify the Senate why he had suspended Stanton from office. This he did in December 1867, soon after Congress reassembled. On January 13 the Senate declined to consent to Stanton's removal and Grant handed the office back to Stanton. This action made Johnson furious because he believed that Grant had made an agreement not to turn back the office, in order to test the constitutionality of the Tenure of Office Act. Grant wanted no part of a legal challenge, especially one that would ally him with Johnson rather than with Congress. The angry letters written by both Johnson and Grant were publicized and led to a final break between the two.

Johnson's removal of Stanton in February 1868 led to the president's impeachment, which Grant favored. At the same time, the Republican National Convention was meeting in Chicago. Many Republicans had believed for some time that their only real chance for success in 1868 would be to have Grant as their presidential candidate. Grant was reluctant to run for a number of reasons: he hated the maneuverings of politics, he feared what politics might do to his reputation, and he was reluctant to give up a secure financial position as general-in-chief for one where he would be out of a job in eight years at most. But he finally accepted the nomination because he believed that it was his duty to run. He was afraid that the results of the Civil War would be lost if a Democrat won. Grant, as was traditional at the time, did not campaign for himself. He was elected in November 1868 over the Democrat Horatio Seymour.

The enmity between Johnson and Grant continued to the end of Johnson's life. Grant refused to allow his children to attend the big children's party that Johnson held to celebrate his own sixtieth birthday in December 1868. Johnson refused to attend Grant's inauguration. Johnson also made insulting comments about Grant in speeches and newspaper interviews. He repeatedly called Grant a "little fellow" who was not very bright, was controlled by others, and had lied to Johnson. Johnson ridiculed the idea that Grant was a second George Washington, as some were calling him, and castigated the president for receiving all sorts of gifts from various people. Even in his Senate speech in March 1875, Johnson was critical of Grant.

Grant has never received high marks for his presidency from historians either, although Brooks Simpson has recently presented a much more positive perspective in several books. Grant, as already mentioned, disliked politics and was not skilled at them. He also tended to appoint friends and relatives to posts for which they were not qualified, leading to government corruption. A number of Republicans came to oppose Grant so much that they withdrew and formed a separate party, the Liberal Republicans, in 1872. However, when that party allied with the Democrats and nominated Horace Greeley, an unsuitable candidate, many "liberals" were disillusioned, and Grant won reelection by a huge majority.

At the end of his second term, Grant and his family went to Europe for a time. After his return to the United States, financial catastrophe and business failure left the family impoverished. Finally, fighting throat cancer, Grant wrote his *Personal Memoirs* (1885–

1886), which he finished just before his death on July 23, 1885. The book was a phenomenal success and earned about $450,000 for his family.

See also: Army Appropriations Act; Congressional Reconstruction; Constitution, Johnson's Attitude toward; Election of 1868; Impeachment; Lincoln, Abraham; Mexico; Military Districts; Military Governor of Tennessee, Johnson as; Military Reconstruction Acts; Newspaper Interviews; Postpresidential Career; Presidential Reconstruction; Republican Party; Senator, Johnson as; Seymour, Horatio; Sheridan, Philip Henry; Stanton, Edwin McMasters; Swing-around-the-Circle; Tenure of Office Act.

References: Graf, LeRoy P., Haskins, Ralph W., and Bergeron, Paul H., eds., *The Papers of Andrew Johnson* vols. 5–16 (1967–2000); Grant, Ulysses S., *Personal Memoirs* (1885–1886); Hesseltine, William B., *Ulysses S. Grant, Politician* (1935); Hyman, Harold M., "Johnson, Stanton, and Grant: A Reconsideration of the Army's Role in the Events Leading to Impeachment," *American Historical Review* 66 (Jan. 1960): 85–100; Simon, John Y., ed., *The Papers of Ulysses S. Grant* 24 vols. to date (1967–); Simpson, Brooks D., *"Let Us Have Peace": Ulysses S. Grant and the Politics of War and Reconstruction, 1861–1868* (1991); Simpson, Brooks D., *The Reconstruction Presidents* (1998).

"Grasp of War"
See Reconstruction

Greeneville, Tennessee

Greeneville, a small town in Greene County in East Tennessee, became Andrew Johnson's home in 1826 and remained so until his death in 1875, even though at times political offices or the exigencies of the Civil War caused him to actually live in Nashville or Washington, D.C.

Much of what became the downtown area of Greeneville was acquired in 1783 by Robert Kerr, who built a house near what was called the Big Spring and soon deeded fifty acres for the establishment of the town as a county seat. Several stores opened and a log courthouse was constructed in 1785. The town was officially established and the streets laid out in 1786. Both the town and the county were named for the Revolutionary War hero, General Nathanael Greene. The area was at first a part of North Carolina and a number of its residents were active in trying to establish the abortive state of Franklin in the mid-1780s. When Tennessee became a state in 1796, Greene County was a part of it.

Although exact population records for 1826, the year Andrew Johnson arrived, have not been found, Greeneville was certainly no larger than it was in 1834, when, as described in the *Tennessee Gazetteer,* the town had a population of 500. It also boasted two taverns, four stores, three physicians, four lawyers, a Presbyterian and a Methodist church, a large brick courthouse, a stone jail, a large spring, and a grist mill.

Johnson apparently decided to settle in Greeneville because he found work as a tailor and because he fell in love with Eliza McCardle, whom he married in May 1827. They resided behind his tailor shop in the back room of a two-room building on Main Street. On July 30, 1830, at a public auction, Johnson bought for $51 the building that became famous as his tailor shop. He may have lived in a small frame house behind the shop (accounts vary) until he built a small two-story brick house (known to some as the "Kerbaugh House") across the street in 1838. In September 1851 Johnson purchased the large house on Main Street, which came to be known as the "Homestead." It was apparently built in 1849–1851 by its previous owner, James Brannon. Johnson paid $950 for it in addition to deeding Brannon his previous home across from the tailor shop. The new home was an eight-room structure, two stories high on the front, with a single story ell over two basement rooms projecting from the back. Johnson seems to have had some remodeling or finishing work done on the inside about the time he purchased it. During and after the Civil War, soldiers of both sides occupied the home as a hospital and for other purposes from at least March 22, 1862, to at least January 26, 1868. These dates can be determined from graffiti left in the house by the soldiers.

As Johnson prepared to leave the presidency and return to Greeneville, he had extensive renovations done to the home. This included adding a second story to the ell to enlarge the house and wallpapering most of the rooms. Johnson's daughter Mary Stover returned to Greeneville early to superintend the refurbishing. Because many of the Johnson's household furnishings had been lost or stolen during the war, the family purchased many items in Washington in the last months of their stay.

In addition to the homes that he owned at various times, Johnson invested in other Greeneville property. He purchased small neighboring offices in 1852 and 1856. In 1870 he bought a parcel of land adjoining the "Homestead" from his son-in-law David Patterson. In the 1870s Johnson also bought several pieces of property from his friend William Lowry. Undoubtedly Johnson owned other local real estate but it is not possible to know exactly what it was.

In the early nineteenth century Greeneville was governed by an annually elected board of seven aldermen who then selected one of their number to be mayor. Johnson was elected alderman each year from 1829 to 1837, although he resigned in 1835 when he was elected to the state legislature. He served as mayor in 1834 and 1837.

The *Tennessee State Gazetteer,* published in 1876, a few months after Johnson's death, showed how much Greeneville had changed in the fifty years since Johnson had moved there. Although the town was still small, its population had tripled to 1,500. Its business interests had grown as well and now consisted of ten general stores, three groceries, two druggists, two hardware dealers, one farm implement dealer, one jeweler, one harness shop, one furniture factory, one pump factory, one flour mill, three hotels, and two weekly newspapers.

There were also ten churches, six for whites and four for blacks.

Johnson bought the hilly tract of land outside the town, which became his final resting place, from John Maloney on November 11, 1852, many years before he needed it. According to family tradition, Johnson liked to go there for rest and meditation. One of the highest hills in the area and providing an excellent view, it was known as Signal Hill during the Civil War but later as Monument Hill after it became Johnson's cemetery. At his death in 1875 Andrew Johnson was the first person buried there, soon followed by his wife, Eliza, in January 1876. His surviving children apparently had the bodies of his sons Charles and Robert moved from previous burial places to the hill sometime before the Johnson monument was dedicated in 1878. After considerable litigation over Johnson's estate, his daughter Martha Patterson became the owner of the cemetery during the rest of her life. In 1906 the secretary of war accepted fifteen acres to use as a national cemetery, which was administered by the army until 1942 and then became part of the historic site. As a result of this dual purpose, Johnson and his extended family are buried on the crown of the hill (the final burial was his great-granddaughter Margaret Johnson Patterson Bartlett in 1992), and veterans are buried all over the rest of the hill.

Because Johnson died without a will, there was much litigation about his estate for many years. Johnson's daughter Martha, his last surviving child, eventually inherited the home. After making extensive changes in 1885 to modernize the structure, she lived there until her death in 1901. Her son Andrew Johnson Patterson, his wife Mattie, and daughter Margaret then resided in the home for years. All were concerned about preserving the memories and memorabilia of Andrew Johnson.

The tailor shop had remained in the family over the years, being used, among other things, as a residence and a shop by some of Johnson's former slaves. In 1921 the state of Tennessee purchased the tailor shop for $5,000 and soon enclosed it in a protective structure, which the state administered until it was given to the federal government in 1941.

The "Homestead" itself remained the family residence, but, thanks to the activities of Margaret Johnson Patterson Bartlett and her mother Mattie Patterson, in 1935 Congress voted to grant national monument status to the Johnson sites in Greeneville as soon as the federal government acquired the title to both the "Homestead" and the tailor shop. This happened when the government bought the "Homestead" from the family in 1942 for $44,000. (The government had already acquired the tailor shop the previous year.) On April 27, 1942, Franklin D. Roosevelt, by presidential proclamation, established the Andrew Johnson National Monument, consisting of the "Homestead," tailor shop, and cemetery, under the auspices of the National Park Service.

Although it administered the home, the Park Service was unable to begin renovations to remove Victorian era additions until 1956. The goal was to return the home to its 1869–1875 look rather than to the prewar period. There were several reasons for this, but probably most important was that most of the postwar furnishings were still available whereas many prewar items had disappeared. The restoration was completed in 1958. The visitor center was also constructed during this period, with exhibits that were renovated in 1997–1998.

In 1963 the monument was renamed the Andrew Johnson National Historic Site. The following year the Park Service acquired Johnson's earlier home ("Kerbaugh House"). Although for years it was mainly used for offices, the lower floor was redesigned with a number of exhibits during the 1997–1998 renovations. A small park across the street has a statue of Johnson, placed there in 1995. Residents of Greene-

ville have, in recent times, also attempted to capitalize on their illustrious former citizen by naming a motel, a bank, and several other businesses after Johnson.

See also: Bartlett, Margaret Johnson Patterson; Finances, Personal; Funeral of Johnson; Grandchildren; Johnson, Charles; Johnson, Eliza McCardle; Johnson, Robert; Offices Held; Patterson, Martha Johnson; Postpresidential Career; Stover (Brown), Mary Johnson.

References: Connally, Ernest Allen, "The Andrew Johnson Homestead at Greeneville, Tennessee," *East Tennessee Historical Society Publications* 29 (1957): 118–140; Doughty, Richard Harrison, *Greeneville: One Hundred Year Portrait, 1775–1875* (1975); Graf, LeRoy P., Haskins, Ralph W., and Bergeron, Paul H., eds., *The Papers of Andrew Johnson* vol. 16 (1967–2000); Andrew Johnson Project, Knoxville, TN: Greeneville file; Lawing, Hugh, "Andrew Johnson National Monument," *Tennessee Historical Quarterly* 20 (June 1961): 103–119; *Nashville Daily American,* June 6, 1878; *Tennessee Gazetteer* (1834); *Tennessee State Gazetteer* (1876).

Groesbeck, William Slocum (1815–1897)

William Slocum Groesbeck, Ohio attorney and one of Andrew Johnson's defense counsel, was born in New York state but moved with his parents to Cincinnati when he was a small child. Educated at Augusta College, Augusta, Kentucky, and Miami University, Oxford, Ohio, where he graduated with honors, Groesbeck was admitted to the bar in 1836. On November 12, 1837, he married Elizabeth Burnet (d. 1889), and the couple had three sons and two daughters.

Groesbeck developed a successful legal practice and invested in Cincinnati real estate. He was a member of the Ohio state constitutional convention (1850–1851) and the commission to codify the state laws (1852). As a Democrat he was elected to a single term in the U.S. House of Representatives (1857–1859). He attended the unsuccessful peace convention in Washington in early 1861. A noted orator in Cincinnati,

Groesbeck received Andrew Johnson there with a brief welcoming speech on June 19, 1861. Johnson, who had just escaped from the secessionist upheaval in Tennessee, then gave a speech himself.

During the Civil War, Groesbeck was one of the leading War Democrats in Ohio. He was elected to a seat in the state senate (1862–1864). In November 1865, after Johnson became president, Groesbeck wrote the president a letter giving his thoughts on military commissions and urging Johnson to avoid trying Jefferson Davis by one. Groesbeck was a supporter of the National Union Party in 1866 and a delegate to its convention in Philadelphia.

When he was impeached by the U.S. House of Representatives in 1868, Johnson selected Groesbeck as one of his defense counsel. Groesbeck believed that impeachment charges must be based on actual indictable crimes and argued that Johnson had the right to have a law tested by the Supreme Court. In addition, he insisted that the Tenure of Office Act did not apply to Edwin M. Stanton, who was Abraham Lincoln's appointee for secretary of war.

On June 5, 1868, after the conclusion of the trial, Groesbeck wrote Johnson a note. Grateful for the president's acquittal, Groesbeck remarked, "It will always be to me a pleasant recollection, that I served you in the recent trial." Groesbeck also wrote Johnson a number of letters about pardons and patronage appointments. He was an Independent Liberal Republican candidate for president in 1872 but received little support. An advocate of civil service reform, Groesbeck was also an authority on the bimetallic currency issue. He spent a number of years in retirement before his death.

See also: Davis, Jefferson; Impeachment; Impeachment Defense Counsel; National Union Convention and Party; Pardons (Individual); Patronage; Stanton, Edwin McMasters; Tenure of Office Act.

References: Benedict, Michael Les, *The Impeachment and Trial of Andrew Johnson* (1973); Graf, LeRoy P., Haskins, Ralph W., and Bergeron, Paul H., eds., *The Papers of Andrew Johnson* vols. 4, 9, 14–16 (1967–2000).

Hamlin, Hannibal (1809–1891)

Maine politician and Andrew Johnson's predecessor as vice president, Hannibal Hamlin was born about six months after Abraham Lincoln in Paris Hill, Maine. He attended the local school and then Hebron Academy for a year. Hamlin's father intended that his son should attend college, but some family problems arose and then the father died. So Hannibal ended up doing surveying, running a newspaper, and teaching school for brief periods of time, before running the family farm while studying law. He spent a year under Samuel Fessenden, a noted lawyer who was ardently antislavery and probably influenced Hamlin's views. In 1833 Hamlin was admitted to the bar and set up a law practice in Hampden, Maine. That December he married Sarah Jane Emery (d. 1855) and they had four children (their oldest son died at age nine).

Hamlin rather quickly became involved in politics as a Jacksonian Democrat. He served in the state house of representatives from 1836 to 1841 and was its speaker in 1837, 1839, and 1840. He then served two terms in the U.S. House of Representatives (1843–1847). Strongly antislavery, Hamlin backed the Wilmot Proviso. He had hoped to be elected to the U.S. Senate in 1846 but was outmaneuvered in the legislature by his opponents. His local supporters reelected him to another term in the state house instead in 1847. When Maine's other senator, John Fairfield, died from the complications of a quack medical treatment, Hamlin was elected to the seat in May 1848. Reelected to a full term in 1850, Hamlin nearly resigned in 1855 when his wife was dying of tuberculosis.

Hamlin had been becoming increasingly frustrated with the Democratic Party, especially when President Franklin Pierce tried to pressure him to support the Kansas-Nebraska Act (1854), which Hamlin strongly opposed. In 1856, in a Senate speech, Hamlin announced that he was joining the Republican Party. After an exciting campaign, Hamlin was elected governor of Maine, a post he accepted briefly with the understanding that he would hold office for only a few weeks, until he was reelected to the Senate early in 1857. On September 25, 1856, in the midst of all this political excitement, Hamlin married his deceased wife's much younger half-sister, Ellen Vesta Emery, and this happy marriage produced two sons.

While in the Senate, Hamlin was an advocate of the rights of American fishermen, supported the construction of a transcontinental railroad, and spoke out against slavery and the slave power while opposing the admission of Kansas as a slave state. Although Hamlin had not wanted the Republican vice presidential nomination in 1860, his supporters worked hard to get it for him at the convention in Chicago. He was an appropriate candidate for a number of reasons: he was a friend of William H. Seward, who was instrumental in choosing the vice presidential nominee; he gave a geographical balance to the ticket, being from Maine while Abraham Lincoln was from Illinois; he was a former Democrat, whereas Lincoln was a former Whig; and Hamlin had a strong record of opposition to slavery expansion. His choice, although a surprise to Hamlin, was popular with the Republicans.

Elected in November 1860, Hamlin resigned from his Senate seat in January 1861. Although he was instrumental in helping Lincoln choose his cabinet members, Hamlin had few other responsibilities during his term besides presiding over the Senate. These duties bored Hamlin because he could not participate in debate or voting (except in case of a tie) and he could do little to influence patronage. He was often absent from the Senate for months at a time. Hamlin identified with the Radical Republicans, urging Lincoln to emancipate the slaves and use black men as soldiers, both of which the president eventually did.

Hamlin expected renomination in 1864 but the situation had changed. Many Republicans now thought that their ticket would be stronger with a border-state War Democrat vice presidential candidate such as Andrew Johnson. Lincoln apparently did not indicate a strong preference for any candidate, even keeping Hamlin, determining not to interfere with the choice of the convention. In addition, Hamlin lost because the delegates from New York and New England, where he should have been strongest, did not support him. Hamlin was disappointed. On inauguration day, March 4, 1865, Hamlin met Johnson at the vice presidential office. When the ailing Johnson asked for whiskey to strengthen himself, Hamlin had to send out for some since he did not drink alcoholic beverages himself and had had them banned from the Capitol building. Hamlin acknowledged some possible fault for Johnson's drunkenness at the ceremony but certainly had not done anything deliberate.

Lincoln intended to nominate Hamlin for another position and Hamlin chose collector of customs for the port of Boston. Because Lincoln was assassinated before he could make the nomination, Johnson nominated Hamlin in August 1865. He resigned a year later because he could not agree with the new National Union Party that Johnson was promoting.

After two years as president of a Maine railroad company, Hamlin was elected again to the U.S. Senate in 1869 and was there when Andrew Johnson returned to the Senate in March 1875. Hamlin served until 1881. In that year President James Garfield appointed Hamlin minister to Spain, a position he held until 1882. Hamlin retired to Maine, where he died, apparently of heart problems, in 1891.

See also: Democratic Party; Drunkenness; Election of 1864; Lincoln, Abraham; National Union Convention and Party; National Union Party; Republican Party; Vice President, Johnson as.

References: Fehrenbacher, Don E., "The Making of a Myth: Lincoln and the Vice-Presidential Nomination in 1864," *Civil War History* 41 (Dec. 1995): 273–290; Graf, LeRoy P., Haskins, Ralph W., and Bergeron, Paul H., eds., *The Papers of Andrew Johnson* vols. 10–11 (1967–2000); Hunt, H. Draper, *Hannibal Hamlin of Maine: Lincoln's First Vice-President* (1969); Waugh, John C., *Reelecting Lincoln: The Battle for the 1864 Presidency* (1997).

Hancock, Winfield Scott (1824–1886)

Future general Winfield Scott Hancock and his twin brother Hilary were born near Norristown, Pennsylvania, on February 14, 1824. Hilary, later a lawyer like the boys' father, practiced in Minneapolis and became an alcoholic. After being educated in the Norristown schools, Winfield went to West Point, where he graduated eighteenth of twenty-five in the class of 1844, a class that began with 100 students.

Hancock made the army his career. After two years on the frontier in Texas, he served in the army of the person he was named for, Winfield Scott, during the Mexican-American War, earning several brevets for his actions in various battles of the Mexico City campaign. Hancock then served in Florida during the Seminole War; in Kansas during the unrest there; in an expedition against the Mormons in Utah; and as a quartermaster in California, where he was stationed when the Civil War broke out. In 1850 he married Almira Russell of St. Louis, and they had two children.

Thanks to his military experience, Hancock was immediately appointed brigadier general of volunteers and given a brigade to command when he arrived on the east coast in September 1861. He took part in the Peninsula Campaign and the battle of Antietam, where he became commander of a division. Hancock led his troops well at Fredericksburg and Chancellorsville, but is best known for his leadership at Gettysburg, where he held on to strategic ground and his troops resisted Pickett's Charge. Hancock was wounded in the thigh during this battle and was absent from the battlefront while he recuperated for several months. He led his corps in the Army of the Potomac's battles of 1864, but was assigned to recruiting duty in November because his wound reopened.

At the end of the Civil War, Hancock was stationed in Winchester, Virginia, but the new president, Andrew Johnson, called him to Washington, D.C., to help restore order after Abraham Lincoln was assassinated. As commander of the Middle Military Division, Hancock was in charge of the prisoners accused of conspiring to assassinate Lincoln and also had to hang the four who were sentenced to death. Hancock hoped for a last minute reprieve for Mary Surratt and stationed messengers along the route from the White House, but no stay of execution came.

In April 1866 Congress passed a resolution thanking Hancock for his actions at Gettysburg. He also became a major general and in August was given command of the Department of the Missouri. There he encountered numerous problems with the Indians in Kansas and Colorado. In part, the difficulties resulted from misunderstandings and mistrust between Hancock and the Indians. Hancock had little patience with them and no knowledge of their customs. In April 1867 Hancock so alarmed the residents of an Indian village that they fled rather than meet to talk with him. In retaliation Hancock had their village burned. This destruction helped to provoke an increase in Indian raids, usually against isolated settlers and travelers.

On August 26, 1867, Johnson ordered Hancock to take command of the Fifth Military District (Louisiana and Texas) to replace the controversial General Philip H. Sheridan. As a result of the danger from a yellow fever epidemic, Hancock did not arrive in New Orleans until late in November. His assignment to the post was popular with Southern whites even before he arrived, and his popularity only increased when he publicly announced that he would respect the civilian governments and courts rather than making numerous removals of officeholders, as his predecessor had done. Johnson approved of this conservative order and sent a message to Congress requesting that body to give Hancock some sort of public commendation, but Congress did not do so. In February 1868 Hancock removed nine members of the New Orleans city council from office for electing an official in alleged violation of one of Sheridan's orders. When Ulysses S. Grant, commander of the army, told Hancock to suspend the order rather than supporting him in his actions, Hancock asked to be relieved from his post because he believed that his "usefulness as Commander of this District is destroyed." At Johnson's request, Hancock was assigned to head the Military District of the Atlantic, headquartered in Washington, D.C. But this lasted only as long as Johnson was president.

Although Hancock was a strong contender for the Democratic presidential nomination in 1868, Horatio Seymour received the nomination, only to be defeated by the Republican candidate, Ulysses S. Grant. Hancock had served under Grant during the Civil War, but their good relationship soured when Grant countermanded Hancock's order in 1868. Hancock was uncomfortable with Grant, who proceeded to take offense and ultimately banished Hancock to command unimportant departments, such as the Department of Dakota (1870–1872), despite Hancock's higher rank. Later, as commander of the Department of the East, Hancock was in charge of Grant's funeral ceremonies in August 1885, which were conducted smoothly, thanks to Hancock's careful planning.

In 1880 Hancock received the Democratic presidential nomination and barely lost to another Union army veteran, James A. Garfield. Hancock died February 9, 1886, after a short illness complicated by diabetes.

See also: Democratic Convention; Election of 1868; Grant, Ulysses Simpson; Indians; Lincoln, Abraham; Lincoln Assassination Conspirators; Mudd, Samuel Alexander; Seymour, Horatio; Sheridan, Philip Henry; Surratt, Mary (Elizabeth) Eugenia Jenkins.

References: Graf, LeRoy P., Haskins, Ralph W., and Bergeron, Paul H., eds., *The Papers of Andrew Johnson* vols. 8–9, 11–15 (1967–2000); Jordan, David M., *Winfield Scott Hancock: A Soldier's Life* (1988); Warner, Ezra J., *Generals in Blue* (1964).

Harlan, James (1820–1899)

Born in Clark County, Illinois, James Harlan moved with his family to Parke County, Indiana, a frontier area, when he was four years old. He was able to supplement his frontier education with other reading and, after teaching school, he entered Indiana Asbury (later DePauw) University in 1841, graduating in 1845. In this same year he married Ann Eliza Peck and the couple soon moved to Iowa, where Harlan became principal of Iowa City College. A Whig, Harlan was unfairly defeated in his first political contest (for superintendent of public instruction) in 1847. Soon after this, he began to study law, and was admitted to the bar in 1850. He did not immediately give up his education career; he headed Iowa Conference University (later Iowa Wesleyan) from 1853 to 1855.

Harlan's political career began because of his support for Free Soil antislavery ideas. Elected to the U.S. Senate as a Republican in 1857, he was reelected in 1860, concentrating on such western concerns as homesteads, college land grants, and the transcontinental railroad. He also supported Abraham Lincoln's war measures. The two men were good friends, and Harlan's daughter Mary eventually married Lincoln's oldest son, Robert Todd, in September 1868. As Lincoln chose cabinet members for his second term of office, he planned to replace Secretary of the Interior John P. Usher with Harlan, effective May 15, 1865.

However, a month before this transition was to take place, Lincoln was assassinated. Because of pressure from Usher's friends, Harlan offered not to take the post, but Johnson insisted that the cabinet be as Lincoln desired and refused to accept Harlan's offer. Johnson also knew Harlan from the Senate and had been pleased with Harlan's understanding and management of a new Homestead Bill, a cause dear to Johnson, in April 1860.

Nevertheless, Harlan's tenure as secretary of the interior was not satisfactory either for him or Johnson. To economize in his department, Harlan dismissed a number of employees, including one clerk in the Indian office who would eventually be a famous poet, Walt Whitman. These dismissals and other policies made Harlan some enemies and caused accusations of improper appointments and other corruption. Although cleared of these charges, Harlan still found that his reputation was damaged. Johnson did not think much of Harlan either, but the break finally came because Harlan, who leaned increasingly toward the Radical Republicans, opposed the National Union Party in 1866 and refused to participate in the call for its convention. Harlan offered to resign whenever Johnson wanted. The president requested the resignation at the end of July, to take effect September 1, and Orville H. Browning replaced Harlan in the Interior Department.

Harlan was elected to the Senate again in 1866 and thus was a member during Johnson's impeachment trial. He voted guilty on all the articles of impeachment that the Senate considered. Harlan's political career came to an end with his defeat for reelection in 1872. Although he was a candidate again for both senator and governor, he was always defeated. In 1873 Judge Advocate General Joseph Holt published a letter claiming that Johnson had indeed seen the request for clemency for Mary Surratt, signed by a number of the officers of the military commission that tried her, and he had signed the order for her execution anyway. Harlan contributed a letter, which Holt quoted to support his claim against Johnson. Harlan's last official post was as a member of the second *Alabama* Claims court (1882–1886).

See also: *Alabama* Claims; Browning, Orville Hickman; Holt, Joseph; Homestead Act; Impeachment; Lincoln, Abraham; National Union Convention and Party; Surratt, Mary (Elizabeth) Eugenia Jenkins; Usher, John Palmer.

References: Graf, LeRoy P., Haskins, Ralph W., and Bergeron, Paul H., eds., *The Papers of Andrew Johnson* vols. 3, 8, 10, 13 (1967–2000); Trefousse, Hans L., *Andrew Johnson: A Biography* (1989).

Harris, Isham Green (1818–1897)

Isham Green Harris, the youngest son in a family of eleven, was born near Tullahoma, in Franklin County, Tennessee. His parents, Isham Green Harris and Lucy Davidson Harris, had emigrated some years earlier from North Carolina, believing that the frontier offered more opportunity. Young Isham attended common schools until he was fourteen, when he left to earn money to help his struggling family. He moved to Paris, Tennessee, where an older brother had a law practice. There young Isham worked as a clerk during the day and read law at night.

After spending several years in Paris, Harris relocated to Ripley, Mississippi, where he prospered as a merchant. He soon returned to Paris, where he was admitted to the bar in 1841 and began his own law practice. There he also met Martha Maria Travis, who had moved to Tennessee from Virginia. They married in 1843 and eventually had eight children.

His law practice led Harris into political circles and he was elected as a Democrat to the state senate in 1847 and the U.S. House of Representatives in 1849 and 1851. He declined to run in 1853 and instead moved to Memphis to concentrate on his law practice. Before long he had returned to politics and was elected governor in 1857 on a program of state's rights and the expansion of slavery. Harris was elected for two more terms, in 1859 and 1861, despite Unionist opposition from the eastern regions of the state. But a majority of Tennesseans supported Harris and his promises to stand against the threat of federal encroachments on private property, especially slaves.

Harris's opportunity to prove his mettle came in early 1861, after the secession of several Deep South states from the Union. Tennessee, at the urging of Harris, held a referendum on secession in February 1861, but voters decided to reject separation and stay in the Union. With the firing on Fort Sumter in April 1861, Harris, who had been pushing for secession since late 1860, sensed a shift in public opinion and took the initiative. First, Harris defied Lincoln and his call for troops, responding instead that Tennesseans would fight in support of their "Southern brethren." He then wrote to Confederate president Jefferson Davis, asking for military support; Confederate soldiers were in the state by late spring. On May 6, at Harris's urging, the state legislature passed an ordinance of secession, declaring the state independent of the United States. The next day another plan of Harris's came to fruition, as the state entered into a "military league" with the Confederate States of America. A month later, on June 8, the voting population legitimized these actions when it approved a formal declaration of secession. In July Tennessee joined the Confederate States of America, and in August Harris was elected governor for the third time. Technically, he remained governor until March 1865, when William G. Brownlow was inaugurated governor.

Governor Harris spent little of this term in Tennessee. As Union forces moved into the state in early 1862, Harris removed with the government to Memphis; the legislature adjourned soon after. By the time Andrew Johnson had taken over as military governor of Tennessee, an irate Harris had joined the Confederate army as a member of General Albert Sidney Johnston's staff. Legends have it that when Johnston was fatally shot at Shiloh he fell into Harris's arms. Harris later served on the staffs of Confederate Generals Pierre G.T. Beauregard, Braxton Bragg, Joseph Johnston, and John Bell Hood and saw action at Stone's River, Chickamauga, Missionary Ridge, Atlanta, and Franklin.

With the collapse of the Confederacy, the Brownlow government offered $5,000 for Harris's capture, holding him personally responsible for Tennessee's secession and ensuing devastation. Harris fled to Mexico, along with several other high-ranking Confederate politicians and generals. His family joined him briefly, but then returned to Tennessee when, in 1867, Harris left for England. He remained there until the reward offer was dropped, then in late 1867 he made his way back to Memphis and his law practice.

A decade later, with Democrats again controlling the state government, Harris returned to politics and Washington, D.C. He was elected to the Senate in 1877, 1883, 1889, and 1895 and died during his fourth term. After lying in state in Washington and Nashville, he was buried in Memphis.

See also: Brownlow, William Gannaway "Parson"; Democratic Party; Lincoln, Abraham; Military Governor of Tennessee, Johnson as; Secession Referendums.

References: Horn, Stanley F., "Isham G. Harris in the Pre-War Years," *Tennessee Historical Quarterly* 19 (Sept. 1960): 195–207; Looney, John Thomas, "Isham G. Harris of Tennessee, Bourbon Senator, 1877–1897" (M.A. Thesis: University of Tennessee, 1970); McBride, Robert M., et al., comps., *Biographical Directory of the Tennessee General Assembly* vol. 1 (1975–1991); McLeary, Ila, "The Life of Isham G. Harris" (M.A. Thesis: University of Tennessee, 1930).

Health of Johnson

Andrew Johnson, although generally a fairly healthy man, had illnesses that may have affected his actions at several critical times in his career. Periodically during the 1850s Johnson would mention to correspondents that his health was not very good, but he rarely was specific about the nature of his problem. In June 1856 Johnson told his son Robert that he planned to take some "Arnold's Union Pills," which Johnson considered a "Sovereign [sic] remedy with me for all complaints." (He was still using the product in 1860.) In October of 1856 Johnson did a testimonial for Professor Muller's "Improved Spectacles," which Johnson claimed "excell [sic] any I have ever tried."

Early in 1857 Johnson went to Washington, D.C., on gubernatorial business. On February 1, on the way home, his train was involved in a serious accident about seventeen miles east of Augusta, Georgia. Apparently, as a result of an obstruction on the track, several cars, including Johnson's, were derailed and went over an embankment variously described as thirty to sixty feet high. Johnson's right arm was seriously broken near the elbow. Sources conflict about the amount of treatment Johnson had in Atlanta before he arrived in Nashville on February 3, suffering great pain. A few months later he had to have the arm rebroken, but it did little good, nor did consultations with several noted Philadelphia surgeons. Although Johnson regained some use of the arm, he had trouble with it for the rest of his life. During the time that he held official positions, Johnson had secretaries, so he needed to do very little writing himself. However, after his presidency, he was without a secretary at times. In a number of instances he apologized to his correspondents for writing in pencil, but explained that it was necessary because of his arm problems.

During the Civil War Johnson was ill a number of times. In the spring of 1863 he had a bad cold with a sore throat and hoarseness aggravated by a lot of public speaking. During the summer he had a "violent bilious attack" and was ill again in September. But Johnson had a far more important illness in February and March 1865. The exact nature of his illness is not clear, but he was confined to his room by February 16 and had to cancel a speech to the American Union Commission on February 22. A reporter who heard his remarks in Cincinnati on February 27 noted that Johnson was hard to hear and understand.

Johnson arrived in Washington, D.C., on March 3, still unwell. The next day, on his way to the inauguration, Johnson attempted to strengthen himself with several glasses of straight whiskey, resulting in his unfortunate inebriation. After the ceremonies Johnson convalesced at the home of Francis P. Blair, Sr., in Silver Spring, Maryland, and he did not return to Washington until March 11.

Johnson had another crucial illness in 1865, lasting from June 27 to July 6, which kept him from attending a monument dedication at Gettysburg on July 4. Even worse, it probably kept him from being as attentive as he otherwise would have been to the results of the military commission that tried the Lincoln assassination conspirators. If Judge Advocate General Joseph Holt *did* show Andrew Johnson the petition from five commission members urging clemency for Mary Surratt, as Holt later claimed he had done, Johnson might not have noticed it simply because he was so unwell.

Johnson had more illnesses while he was in the White House, including an attack of kidney stones (often called "the gravel") in the early spring of 1867. This problem plagued Johnson with some frequency. He had another serious attack in late March 1869, just after he returned to Greeneville, causing his family members to bring his physician, Basil Norris, from Washington, D.C. A number of correspondents recommended various cures, mineral waters, and doctors who had helped them with similar problems. In June of that year Johnson's speech at Gallatin, Tennessee, was delayed for an hour while he recovered from a "partial attack" of the same malady.

About the end of June 1870, Johnson was bitten or stung by an insect, and this prevented his being in Knoxville for the July 4 celebration. However, he did not suffer any severe illness until the end of June 1873. At this time he contracted cholera during an epidemic that swept Tennessee and other parts of the nation. Once he became ill, Johnson was taken to the farm of his daughter, Martha Patterson, where he slowly improved. Although Johnson recovered from this illness, it had a permanent effect on his health. It also had a permanent effect on his speechmaking abilities, although this may be more evident to modern readers than it was to listeners at the time. Although Johnson's speeches were usually long and appear tedious to the reader, there is a certain sharpness about them that is hard to define but is clearly missing after Johnson's episode of cholera. Probably one of the best examples of this change is his speech in Washington, D.C., on October 23, 1873.

In speeches during the spring of 1874 Johnson several times referred to his poor health preventing him from speaking much, but, despite his protestations, he managed to give a lengthy speech. Early in 1875, after Johnson was elected to the Senate, he was clearly very tired. He arrived in Washington just in time for the beginning of the session and refused all offers of a welcoming celebration and speech opportunity. After he returned to Greeneville he continued to be rather unwell and seemed to be trying to put his affairs in order before going back to Washington. While visiting his daughter Mary Stover in Carter County at the end of July, Johnson had a stroke. Despite medical treatment, Johnson had another stroke or two and died early in the morning on July 31, 1875.

See also: Death of Johnson; Drunkenness; Holt, Joseph; Lincoln Assassination Conspirators; Patterson, Martha Johnson; Physical Description of Andrew Johnson; Postpresidential Career; Religion, Johnson's Attitude toward; Senator, Johnson as; Stover (Brown), Mary Johnson; Surratt, Mary (Elizabeth) Eugenia Jenkins.

References: Graf, LeRoy P., Haskins, Ralph W., and Bergeron, Paul H., eds., *The Papers of Andrew Johnson* vols. 1–3, 6–8, 15–16 (1967–2000); *Nashville Union and American,* June 9, 1869; Trefousse, Hans L., *Andrew Johnson: A Biography* (1989).

Historic Sites Associated with Johnson

See Greeneville, Tennessee

Historical Attitudes toward Johnson

Historical attitudes toward Andrew Johnson (and Reconstruction in general) have varied over the years. Scholars assessing historical writings (a study known as historiography) have divided these writings into periods when a certain attitude tended to prevail.

While Johnson was president, Radical Republicans denounced him as a terrible president and person who deserved to be impeached, although they ultimately were unable to convict him and remove him from office. On the other hand, Democrats and Conservatives wrote Johnson, during his presidency and at the time he left, that upon "sober second thought" (once the emotions had died down) the people would consider Johnson to be one of the country's greatest presidents. This never happened, although it probably came closest in 1956 when Clinton Rossiter, in his book *The American Presidency,* considered Johnson one of six "near great" presidents, following seven "great" ones. In contrast, in early 2000 a C-SPAN survey of presidential leadership ranked Andrew Johnson fortieth of forty-one presidents, only ahead of James Buchanan. Undoubtedly, these results were affected by many contemporary factors, such as political correctness, otherwise it is difficult to imagine how William Henry Harrison, who served only one month, or Warren G. Harding, whose associates and subordinates were notorious for their corruption, could rank ahead of Johnson. Nevertheless, these contrasting estimations are indicative of historical changes in attitude, and especially the importance of changes in attitudes about racial matters, to assessing Johnson and his presidency.

During the period from 1869, when Johnson left the presidency, until 1899, the end of the century, most discussions of Johnson and his term were found in the published memoirs, diaries, and letters of his contemporaries. Johnson was usually mentioned in passing and was never the focus of the work. Many of these writers were Northerners and Republicans, and their comments tended to express their personal biases and emotions in ways unfavorable to Johnson. In the 1870s these writers mainly reflected the Radical opinions, but, beginning with Hugh McCulloch's *Men and Measures of Half a Century* (1888), some writers began to be more sympathetic while still acknowledging that Johnson had various faults, such as making unwise comments. The most favorable account of Johnson published in the period was Laura C. Holloway's *The Ladies of the White House* (1870).

By the late 1800s the common view held that Johnson's Reconstruction plan was good because it was originally Abraham Lincoln's but that it failed because of Johnson's mistakes and character flaws. These new attitudes became possible as people began to write about Reconstruction who were too young to have been involved in it and consequently had no related emotional biases. They also had some new sources to use as Johnson's papers became available in the Library of Congress and as the *Diary* of Gideon Welles was published. In addition, conditions in the South after the end of Congressional Reconstruction showed that the Republican plan had not worked either. As Northern racism became more outspoken, thanks to imperialism and the labeling of nonwestern peoples as inferiors who needed to be controlled by whites, views of Johnson became more positive while the reputation of the Radicals declined.

During the 1900–1926 period, the trend toward a more positive attitude about John-son continued. Fewer memoirs were published but more works were written by historians and interest in the Reconstruction period grew. Particularly important as a leader and teacher of this group of "nationalist" or "traditional" historians was William A. Dunning of Columbia University who published *Reconstruction, Political and Economic* in 1907. He and his students promulgated a very pro-Southern perspective, which stressed the allegedly incompetent Negro-dominated governments forced on the South by the vindictive Radical Republicans in Congress who wanted to dominate and humble the South and used military occupation for that purpose. This military Reconstruction resulted in great distress in the South and some violence. Andrew Johnson, who opposed Congress and its plans unsuccessfully, was regarded as a hero. This so-called "Dunning School" of interpretation remained commonly accepted until the 1960s.

From 1927 to 1932 Johnson was studied more intensively and pictured more positively than at any time before or since. The rash of works published at this time included three major biographies and two other influential books on Reconstruction. One reason for the increased interest in Johnson was the October 25, 1926, Supreme Court decision in *Myers v. United States*. In this case an Oregon postmaster claimed that it was illegal for President Woodrow Wilson to remove him from office. In a 6 to 3 vote the court ruled that the president had the right to remove public officials he had appointed with the advice and consent of the Senate. This ruling suggested that Johnson had legally removed Edwin M. Stanton and that the Tenure of Office Act was unconstitutional. Not surprisingly, two of Johnson's new biographers were lawyers: Robert W. Winston, who wrote *Andrew Johnson, Plebeian and Patriot* (1928), and Lloyd Paul Stryker, author of *Andrew Johnson, a Study in Courage* (1929). The third biographer was George Fort Milton, author of *The Age of Hate: Andrew Johnson and the Radicals* (1930).

All three biographers announced their determination to vindicate Johnson from Radical slander and long-term misunderstanding. All three showed Johnson's heroic rise from poverty, his self-education, his democracy and attempts to help the average citizen, as well as his devotion to the Union and the Constitution. All three authors approved Johnson's Reconstruction program, which they identified with Lincoln's; supported Johnson's opposition to black suffrage; and harshly criticized the Radicals. Stryker found the fewest faults in Johnson and depicted his enemies as the most evil. At least one historian considered Winston's biography to be the most balanced. Milton's included much detailed information.

The other important books of the period—Claude Bowers's *The Tragic Era* (1929) and Howard K. Beale's *The Critical Year* (1930), which discussed the election of 1866—shared the same viewpoint as the three biographies. Although authors of this period admitted that Johnson was sometimes tactless and indecisive, they stressed his courage, devotion to the Union, and other good qualities. These authors believed that, even though Johnson made some mistakes, the primary causes of the failure of Reconstruction under Johnson were the machinations of the Radicals and circumstances beyond Johnson's control (such as the New Orleans riot in 1866).

During the 1933–1959 period, interest in Johnson and Reconstruction declined, but most historians still approved of Johnson, with a few exceptions such as the noted black historian W.E.B. Du Bois, whose *Black Reconstruction* was published in 1935. It was not until the late 1950s–early 1960s that a number of historians, often referred to as "revisionists," began to offer a different perspective on Johnson and Reconstruction, usually centered on questions pertaining to blacks, such as attitudes toward black suffrage and black participation

in Reconstruction events. This perspective was the result of the renewed concern for black civil rights in the 1960s. Because Johnson did not favor suffrage or any special assistance for the freedpeople, most historians in this period saw him as the villain and favored the Radicals who worked for black civil rights. Eric L. McKitrick's *Andrew Johnson and Reconstruction* (1960) was the first important reexamination of Johnson's presidency during this period. John Hope Franklin's more general study, *Reconstruction: After the Civil War* (1961), was also extremely important.

From the 1960s through the 1990s, historians, in addition to the focus on blacks, concentrated on the conflicts of "ideology" or perspectives between Johnson and his supporters and the Radicals. Some historians (called "postrevisionists") in the 1970s were skeptical of Reconstruction generally and stressed the continuity between the pre–Civil War South and the postwar South, suggesting that the war and Reconstruction made almost no real difference. At least some of the historians of this later period have been criticized for "presentism," judging the past by the issues and standards of the present time. Although it would be impossible for a historian to remove all traces of the present from his or her perspective, "presentism" has definitely affected the views of Johnson expressed in the late twentieth century.

Two historians in this period who have been more sympathetic and balanced toward Johnson than most are James E. Sefton in *Andrew Johnson and the Uses of Constitutional Power* (1980) and Albert Castel in *The Presidency of Andrew Johnson* (1979). Both tried to view Johnson from the perspective of his own time and what was possible then. Sefton saw Johnson as true to his own constitutional principles.

These books and several others deal with various aspects of Johnson's life and presidency, but the only full biography written in the late twentieth century is Hans L. Trefousse's *Andrew Johnson: A Biography* (1989). Trefousse wrote about Johnson after several decades of writing biographies of his Radical Republican enemies, such as Benjamin F. Butler and Benjamin F. Wade. Although Trefousse tried to be fair to Johnson, it is clear that the president was not Trefousse's favorite person. Although this is the best biography of Johnson available, it is stronger on the pre-presidential years than during the presidency, mainly because Trefousse was able to use the pre-presidential volumes of *The Papers of Andrew Johnson*. (Volume 8 of *The Papers,* the first presidential volume, was published the same year as Trefousse's biography.)

Preparatory work for *The Papers of Andrew Johnson* began at the University of Tennessee, Knoxville, in 1956. The first volume was published in 1967 and the sixteenth and last in 2000. Each volume covers a specific period of Johnson's life and seeks to present a representative selection of letters addressed to Johnson as well as letters and other documents written by him (when they are available, as extant Johnson writings are rather sparse in some periods). The editors of *The Papers of Andrew Johnson* have tried to include a balanced selection for research purposes that presents both Johnson's strengths and weaknesses as accurately as possible.

In 1998 and 1999 there was a flurry of renewed interest in Johnson when President Bill Clinton was impeached and tried. Although newspapers, magazines, and other media addressed the issue incessantly, 2000 is too early to see any scholarly assessments of the issue or whether attitudes toward Andrew Johnson have been changed at all.

See also: Black Suffrage; Blacks (Slave and Free), Johnson's Attitude toward; Butler, Benjamin Franklin; Congressional Reconstruction; Constitution, Johnson's Attitude toward; Election of 1866; Impeachment; Lincoln, Abraham; McCulloch, Hugh; New Orleans Riot; Presidential Reconstruction; Reconstruction; Republican Party; Tenure of Office Act; Wade, Benjamin Franklin; Welles, Gideon.

References: Alexander, Roberta Sue, "Presidential Reconstruction: Ideology and Change," in Anderson, Eric, and Moss, Alfred A., Jr., eds., *The Facts of Reconstruction: Essays in Honor of John Hope Franklin* (1991); Foner, Eric, "Reconstruction Revisited," *Reviews in American History* 10 (Dec. 1982): 82–100; Graf, LeRoy P., Haskins, Ralph W., and Bergeron, Paul H., eds., *The Papers of Andrew Johnson* vols. 1–16 (1967–2000); Hays, Willard, "Andrew Johnson's Reputation," *East Tennessee Historical Society Publications* 31 (1959): 1–31; 32 (1960): 18–50; Kincaid, Larry, "Victims of Circumstance: An Interpretation of Changing Attitudes toward Republican Policy Makers and Reconstruction," *Journal of American History* 57 (June 1970): 48–66; Notaro, Carmen Anthony, "History of the Biographic Treatment of Andrew Johnson in the Twentieth Century," *Tennessee Historical Quarterly* 24 (Summer 1965): 143–155; Perman, Michael, "Solving the Riddle of Andrew Johnson," *Journal of East Tennessee History* 62 (1990): 105–114; Sefton, James E., "The Impeachment of Andrew Johnson: A Century of Writing," *Civil War History* 14 (June 1968): 120–147; "American Presidents: Viewer Survey Results—Historians," http://www.americanpresidents.org/survey/historians/overall.asp, printed 2/29/00. Complete citations for the most useful books mentioned in this article can be found in the Bibliography.

Holt, Joseph (1807–1894)

*J*oseph Holt was the judge advocate general of the army during Andrew Johnson's term, serving as the chief prosecutor at the trial of the Abraham Lincoln assassination conspirators and provoking a quarrel with Johnson over the Mary Surratt case. Holt was born in Kentucky and educated at St. Joseph's and Centre colleges. By the age of twenty-one he was a practicing lawyer in Elizabethtown, Kentucky, but in 1832 moved to Louisville, where he briefly helped to edit the *Louisville Advertiser.* He was in demand as a Democratic Party speaker and spent two years as a district attorney there.

In 1835 Holt moved to Port Gibson, Mississippi, where he was involved again in Democratic politics and served as counsel for the city of Vicksburg in a noted case involving the heirs of the city's founder. At some point Holt married Mary Harrison, who died of tuberculosis. Holt also contracted the disease and in 1842 returned to Louisville to recuperate. He was married a second time, to Margaret Wickliffe, but was not much involved in politics until 1856. As a reward for Holt's work in that campaign, President James Buchanan made him commissioner of patents (1857–1859). Holt joined Buchanan's cabinet as postmaster general (1859–1861) and then became secretary of war when John B. Floyd left the cabinet (1861). Holt was opposed to secession and urged Buchanan to take a firm stand against the departing Southern states.

During the spring and summer of 1861 Holt opposed Kentucky's declaration of neutrality and any concessions to the Confederacy, writing letters for publication to promote Union sentiment in his home state. He also campaigned in New York and Massachusetts to gain support for the Union war effort. Although Holt was a Democrat, he strongly supported the Lincoln administration and the war. Lincoln appointed him to the new office of judge advocate general of the army on September 3, 1862. Over the course of the rest of the war Holt and Lincoln were in frequent communication about numerous military cases involving court-martials, pardons, and dismissals. Holt would advise Lincoln on whether sentences should be carried out or the culprit pardoned. Lincoln tended to be merciful in more cases than Holt. Already by the time of his cabinet service with Buchanan, Holt was notable for his disagreeable personality, which did not improve during the Civil War. When Edward Bates submitted his resignation as attorney general in November 1864, Holt declined the proffered appointment and remained as judge advocate general.

After Lincoln's assassination, Holt was the one who preferred charges against the alleged assassination conspirators. He was the chief prosecutor and found the witnesses, some of whom perjured themselves in their testimony and were afterward tried and imprisoned for it. Widely regarded as vindictive, Holt was determined to get the alleged conspirators convicted and he was successful. He was not successful in developing any connection between them and Confederate president Jefferson Davis, however, which he also wished to establish, even by using questionable evidence.

The most controversial part of Holt's career related to Mary Surratt, one of the alleged conspirators. Although she undoubtedly knew the conspirators, she probably had little or nothing to do with the assassination itself. Yet she was convicted on circumstantial evidence and sentenced to be hanged along with three more obvious male culprits. At the time there was considerable sentiment that her sentence should be commuted to life imprisonment, if for no other reason than that she was a woman. Five of the generals on the military commission signed a petition with this request. The commission finished its work on June 30, 1865. On July 5 Johnson was well enough, after a debilitating attack of kidney stones, to see Holt, who brought the sentences and his own recommendations that they be carried out because "the proceedings were regular," the defendants had good lawyers, there were hundreds of witnesses, and the evidence justified the sentences. Holt would later allege that Johnson saw the generals' petition for Mary Surratt attached to the findings and ordered the execution on July 7 anyway. Johnson claimed that he did not know anything about the petition until 1867, when he was reviewing the papers in the case. There was considerable discussion of the petition in the press in 1867, much to Holt's distress. Given Johnson's illness, he probably did not pay very much attention to any of the papers put before him. Holt even wrote the endorsement agreeing to the sentences and Johnson merely signed it. However, because Holt was determined to have the conspirators convicted and punished, it is entirely possible that he could have avoided bringing the petition or could have folded it is such a way that Johnson would not see it. Whatever happened, this issue became a public dispute in 1873.

Before that point, Holt continued as judge advocate general throughout Johnson's presidency, with the same duties and roles as he had performed under Lincoln—heading the military justice system and referring court-martial outcomes to Johnson with recommendations. Holt was also the government prosecutor in the trial of Henry Wirz, who was hanged for his role as commandant at Andersonville prison. Holt remained in his post during Ulysses S. Grant's term until December 1, 1875, when he retired because of his age.

It has not been possible to determine what caused Holt to instigate a public conflict with Johnson in August 1873. Johnson thought that Holt was trying to get himself noticed so that he would be appointed chief justice of the Supreme Court to replace the recently deceased Salmon P. Chase. But the Ulysses S. Grant papers show no evidence that Holt was considered or recommended for the post. Whatever his motivation, Holt was determined to defend himself from Johnson's "calumny," "perfidy," and other uncomplimentary terms, even though there evidently was no recent criticism of Holt by Johnson.

Holt carried out his defense by writing a long letter to the editor of the *Washington Chronicle,* which published the letter on August 26, 1873. The missive was mainly a collection of other letters, written to Holt by various people, which, he claimed, presented his "innocence" of failing to show the Mary Surratt clemency petition to Johnson. He based his case on the hearsay testimony from John A. Bingham that Secretary of State William H. Seward and Secretary of War Edwin M. Stanton (both deceased by 1873) had said that the petition was discussed in a cabinet meeting and all were united in opposing commutation of the sentence. Holt based much of his argument on weak, after-the-fact evidence. The earliest letters that Holt collected were written in 1868, three years after the Surratt trial and execution. He could not seem to comprehend that anyone else might have had the idea that Mary Surratt's case should be commuted because of her gender unless they had seen the petition.

Johnson pointed out that fallacy when he refuted Holt's charges in a letter to the editor of the *Chronicle.* The letter was dated November 11, 1873, and published the next day. Johnson had consulted with former secretary of the navy Gideon Welles, whose diary indicated that because of Johnson's illness there was no cabinet meeting between the end of the trial and the execution of the assassination conspirators. Johnson also commented in detail on other aspects of Holt's evidence.

Holt replied with another venomous letter published on December 1. It included a lengthy, vituperative tirade against Johnson. Each of Johnson's comments was negated with such phrases as "web of misrepresentations," "gross perversions," and "malignant insinuations." From Holt's perspective, he had suffered "relentless aspersion" from Johnson for eight years, and nothing Johnson ever said could possibly be true. Johnson realized this and, having made his defense once, did not bother to reply to Holt's second letter. However, Holt's charges did provoke quite a few comments in the letters of other persons to Johnson during the fall of 1873.

Even in his retirement, after Johnson's death, Holt was still determined to salvage his reputation, as he saw it. In July 1888 he published in the *North American Review* an article that consisted of letters from Holt harassing Johnson's former attorney general, James Speed, to give Holt information, which Speed either did not want to give him or did not have. Most of the time, however, Holt's retirement was apparently quiet. He died in Washington, D.C., after a misstep on some stairs.

See also: Bingham, John Armor; Chase, Salmon Portland; Davis, Jefferson; Health of Johnson; Lincoln, Abraham; Lincoln Assassination Conspirators; Postpresidential Career; Seward, William Henry; Speed, James; Stanton, Edwin McMasters; Surratt, Mary (Elizabeth) Eugenia Jenkins; Welles, Gideon; Wirz, Henry.

References: Basler, Roy P., ed., *The Collected Works of Abraham Lincoln* vols. 4–8 (1953); George, Joseph, Jr., "Subornation of Perjury at the Lincoln Conspiracy Trial? Joseph Holt, Robert Purdy, and the Lon Letter," *Civil War History* 38 (Sept. 1992): 232–241; Graf, LeRoy P., Haskins, Ralph W., and Bergeron, Paul H., eds., *The Papers of Andrew Johnson* vols. 4, 8–10, 12–16 (1967–2000); Holt, Joseph, "New Facts about Mrs. Surratt," *North American Review* 147 (July 1888): 83–94; Levin, H., ed., *The Lawyers and Lawmakers of Kentucky* (1897); Milton, George Fort, *The Age of Hate: Andrew Johnson and the Radicals* (1965 [1930]); Smith, Elbert B., *The Presidency of James Buchanan* (1975); *Washington Chronicle,* Aug. 26, Nov. 12, Dec. 1, 1873; *Washington Evening Star,* Oct. 13, 1873.

Homestead Act

The idea of a Homestead Act was extremely important to Andrew Johnson and he devoted much of his time while a member of the U.S. House of Representatives and the U.S. Senate to efforts to see such an act passed. The basic premise of the Homestead Act was that a low-income, landless, white male head of household would receive vacant land from the public domain (usually 160 acres) at no cost, or a very minimal charge, provided he lived on it for some period of time (usually five years) and made improvements, such as building a house and planting crops. Over the course of the eighteen years that such measures periodically were under consideration, numerous variations were suggested, but the basic principles remained the same.

Andrew Johnson first proposed a Homestead Bill in the House of Representatives on March 27, 1846. Although it was read and ordered to committee, nothing further was done with the bill at this time. Johnson introduced homestead bills repeatedly over the years. He was advocating one in 1850 during the period when the bills of the Compromise of 1850 were under discussion. In April 1852 Johnson complained that his Homestead Bill should have been passed rather than a bill that granted 48,000,000 acres as bounties to U.S. Army veterans. Johnson said that people who passed that land grant bill had no grounds to complain that a homestead bill was unconstitutional because the federal government has financial obligations based on the proceeds from land sales. In fact, Johnson believed that his Homestead Bill would actually raise federal revenue rather than lower it, by giving landowners the resources with which to make other purchases. Not surprisingly, Johnson's opponents attached various amendments to his bill in an attempt to kill it. However, the Homestead Bill passed the House on May 12, 1852, but it died in a Senate committee.

When Johnson became governor of Tennessee in 1853, he was unable to take an active part in furthering passage of a homestead bill. Nevertheless, he mentioned its importance and, whenever he was able to speak about the topic, urged Tennessee's federal legislators to vote for such a bill.

In 1857 Johnson became a U.S. senator and introduced a homestead bill in that branch of the legislature on December 22, 1857. As a leading supporter of homestead legislation, Johnson was an anomaly among Southerners. Many Southerners did not like the Homestead Bill because it was not useful for slaveholders. In addition, they were concerned that the bill would reduce land sales revenue and cause the federal government to raise the tariff in order to compensate. As a result, Johnson's main opponents were other Southerners, whereas his allies were the Republicans of the North and Midwest. Although Johnson delivered an impassioned speech on May 20, 1858, addressing all the objections to the Homestead Bill, the Senate voted to postpone consideration of the bill until the next session.

Johnson continued to work for his pet bill, introducing it again in December 1859. Finally, in June 1860, after amendments and compromises moderated some parts of the bill, both houses of Congress passed homestead legislation, only to have it vetoed by President James Buchanan. An angry Johnson delivered a lengthy Senate speech on June 23, 1860, in response to Buchanan's veto, but the Senate was unable to override the veto. Johnson introduced yet another Homestead Bill in December 1860 but it received little attention because most members of Congress were much more concerned about the secession crisis. Johnson, having become military governor of Tennessee, was no longer in the Senate when the Homestead Act became a law in May 1862. Ironically, after Johnson's many years of work for homestead legislation, when the bill finally passed, the Republicans received the credit.

Johnson never ceased to be interested in the Homestead Act. While he was president, he wrote four annual messages to be delivered in Congress. Each year, as part of his comments on the report of the secretary of the interior, he made sure to note how many acres of land had been distributed under the Homestead Act.

See also: Annual Messages; Congressman, Johnson as; Constitution, Johnson's Attitude toward; Governor (Civilian), Johnson as; Senator, Johnson as; Territorial Affairs.

References: Graf, LeRoy P., Haskins, Ralph W., and Bergeron, Paul H., eds., *The Papers of Andrew Johnson* vols. 1–4, 7, 9–11, 13, 15 (1967–2000); Trefousse, Hans L., *Andrew Johnson: A Biography* (1989).

House Judiciary Committee

Because the U.S. Constitution gives the U.S. House of Representatives the responsibility of impeaching federal officials, should this become necessary, the House determined to refer all resolutions urging the impeachment of President Andrew Johnson to its Judiciary Committee. Although people had mentioned and even pushed the idea of impeaching Johnson for some months, the first actual impeachment resolution was introduced by Ohio representative James M. Ashley on January 7, 1867. Because Ashley made a number of charges against Johnson, the role of the Judiciary Committee was to investigate the accusations to see if Johnson had committed these offenses and then to determine if the offenses were impeachable.

The Judiciary Committee that met in January 1867 was a balanced group, not controlled by the Radicals. All of its members were lawyers. Its chairman, James F. Wilson (1828–1895) of Iowa, was a moderate Republican who served in the U.S. House (1861–1869) and U.S. Senate (1883–1895). Other moderate Republicans included Frederick E. Woodbridge (1818–1888) of Vermont, who was in the U.S. House (1863–1869); New Yorker Daniel Morris (1812–1889), who served in the House (1863–1867); and Francis Thomas (1799–1876) of Maryland, who sat in the House (1831–1841 and 1861–1869). The four Radical Republicans were George S. Boutwell (1818–1905) from Massachusetts, who served in both the House (1863–1869) and Senate (1873–1877); Thomas Williams (1806–1872) of Pennsylvania, who served in the House (1863–1869); Burton C. Cook (1819–1894) of Illinois, who served in the House (1865–1871); and William Lawrence (1819–1899) of Ohio, who served in the House (1865–1871 and 1873–1877). The single Democrat on the committee was Andrew J. Rogers (1828–1900) of New Jersey, who was in the House (1863–1867).

The committee began secret investigations immediately (detective Allan Pinkerton was able to keep Johnson informed of their activities, however). Ashley and others were trying to prove that Johnson had had improper correspondence with Jefferson Davis; had sold offices; had taken money from the U.S. treasury without congressional approval; had appointed provisional governors in the South illegally; and had unlawfully dealt with railroads, which the federal government had seized during the Civil War. They called a number of witnesses, from the questionable, such as the controversial detective Lafayette Baker and several unsuccessful office seekers, to cabinet members Hugh McCulloch and Edwin M. Stanton, as well as Judge Advocate General Joseph Holt. The committee found little relevant information and they simply reported that the investigation should be continued.

After the new Congress convened on March 4, 1867, there were changes to the House Judiciary Committee. Morris and Rogers had not been reelected and Cook apparently switched committee assignments. The new members were John C. Churchill (1821–1905), a New York Republican, serving his first of two House terms (1867–1871); and Democrats Charles A. Eldredge (1820–1896) of Wisconsin, who served in the House (1863–1875); and Samuel S. Marshall (1821–1890) from Illinois, who served in the House (1855–1859 and 1865–1875).

This reorganized committee continued the investigation, fishing into every aspect of Johnson's personal and political affairs in the hope of finding something impeachable. They even investigated his bank account, which made Johnson very angry. The committee called witnesses about Johnson's veto messages, the return of land to former Confederates, pardons, appointments, the diary of Abraham Lincoln assassin John Wilkes Booth, the New Orleans riot, and the failure of the federal government to try Jefferson Davis. Still, the committee had no conclusive impeachable evidence and voted to adjourn on June 3, 1867.

The committee convened a third time about the impeachment matter on June 26, 1867. But further examination, even of the idea that Johnson had been involved in Lincoln's assassination, brought out no more impeachable issues and the committee reported that it could not be ready with an impeachment charge before the next congressional session. But Johnson's suspension of Edwin M. Stanton as secretary of war in August, and his removal of Philip H. Sheridan and Daniel E. Sickles as commanders of two of the military districts, as well as the Democratic victories in the fall elections, all provoked further investigations by the committee in November. This time, unlike the three previous investigations, the committee recommended impeachment, by a vote of 5 to 4. Churchill switched his vote to impeachment, whereas Wilson, Woodbridge, Eldredge, and Marshall continued to oppose impeachment. The majority report, written by Williams, charged Johnson with, among other offenses, pardoning traitors, being the cause of the New Orleans riot, and defying Congress. Wilson and Woodbridge agreed that Johnson had done these things, but did not believe that they were impeachable offenses.

Boutwell introduced the impeachment resolution in the House on December 5, 1867. However, many of the members of the House believed that Johnson had to commit an indictable crime before he could be impeached and there was no evidence that he had done so. As a result, the resolution was defeated by a vote of 108 to 57.

After Johnson removed Stanton in February 1868, John Covode of Pennsylvania brought another impeachment resolution to the House. This time it was referred to the Committee on Reconstruction, headed by Thaddeus Stevens, rather than to the Judiciary Committee. After the resolution passed on February 24, 1868, Judiciary Committee members Wilson and Boutwell served on the committee to draw up the impeachment charges. They and Williams were also among the impeachment managers who prosecuted Johnson at his trial. But the Judiciary Committee as an entity had no further involvement with Johnson's impeachment and trial.

See also: Ashley, James Mitchell; Butler, Benjamin Franklin; Davis, Jefferson; Elections of 1867; Holt, Joseph; Impeachment; Impeachment Managers; Lincoln Assassination Conspirators; McCulloch, Hugh; Military Districts; New Orleans Riot; Pardons (Individual); Sheridan, Philip Henry; Sickles, Daniel Edgar; Stanton, Edwin McMasters; Stevens, Thaddeus.

References: *Biographical Directory of the United States Congress* (1989); Trefousse, Hans L., *Andrew Johnson: A Biography* (1989); Trefousse, Hans L., *Impeachment of a President: Andrew Johnson, the Blacks, and Reconstruction* (1975).

Impeachment

On February 24, 1868, the U.S. House of Representatives formally impeached President Andrew Johnson of "high crimes and misdemeanors," making Johnson the first president to face this form of indictment. Impeachment opened the way for a trial in the U.S. Senate, a confrontation that capped a three-year battle between congressional Republicans and the chief executive. At stake was the course of Reconstruction, the balance of power among the branches of the federal government, and the 1868 presidency.

At first, the movement for impeachment was limited to a few Radical Republicans. In December 1866 the House voted down a call for an impeachment inquiry by Ohio representative James M. Ashley, who believed that the president was implicated in the assassination of his predecessor, Abraham Lincoln. In early January 1867, after Johnson's veto of the District of Columbia black suffrage bill, more Republicans became concerned over the future of Reconstruction. Elections in the fall of 1866 ensured Republicans of a majority in both houses of Congress, so party leaders prepared to embark on a new Reconstruction program.

In January 1867, fearing that Johnson would continue to obstruct congressional initiatives, the House Judiciary Committee began an impeachment investigation of the president. The House controlled the investigation because the U.S. Constitution stipulated that "the House of Representatives shall have the sole power of impeachment" (Article I, Section 1). Should the committee recommend impeachment and the House vote in favor of it, the case would be tried in the Senate because "the Senate shall have the sole power to try all impeachments. . . . When the President of the United States is tried, the Chief Justice shall preside; and no person shall be convicted without the concurrence of two-thirds of the members present" (Article I, Section 3). But the investigation was unprecedented, and congressmen had little to guide them beyond the ambiguous wording of Article II, Section 4: "The President, Vice President, and all civil officers of the United States shall be removed from office on impeachment for, and on conviction of, treason, bribery, or other high crimes and misdemeanors."

The president's chief critics, including representatives Ashley, Thaddeus Stevens, George S. Boutwell, and Benjamin F. Butler, described Johnson's defiance and interference. They charged Johnson with complicity in the assassination of Lincoln and the "murder" of assassination conspirator Mary Surratt, bribery, drunkenness, and even treason. They cited the president's unprecedented appointment of provisional governors in the former Confederate states, his liberal amnesty and pardon policies toward former Confederates, and his failure to protect the lives and rights of former slaves and white Unionists in the South. Congress had accepted the new state governments created under Johnson's system (although not their federal representatives) but in 1866 had passed two Freedmen's Bureau Bills and the Civil Rights Bill, drawn up by moderate Republican Lyman Trumbull. These met with executive hostility and vetoes. By late summer Johnson had deliberately scuttled what might have been the war's "peace treaty," the Fourteenth Amendment.

In 1867, with the promise of a genuine Republican Reconstruction agenda, some congressional Republicans believed that removing the president was the only way to protect Congress's program. By March the program had taken shape in the form of the Military Reconstruction Acts, the Command of the Army Act, and the Tenure of Office Act. But the U.S. Army was supervising Reconstruction, and its commander-in-chief was President Andrew Johnson. By late spring 1867, Johnson had ordered the reinstatement of civil officers removed by the army; threatened to remove generals who were too enthusiastic in enforcing congressional directives; and had his attorney general, Henry Stanbery, deliver an official opinion of the Reconstruction Acts that virtually nullified them.

By midsummer a special summer session of Congress convened to hear the report of the House Judiciary Committee. Despite President Johnson's deliberate thwarting of congressional intentions, there was no abuse of power, treason, or any actual crime. At this time, the committee voted 5 to 4 against bringing formal charges of impeachment; nonetheless, the investigation would continue.

Johnson also continued in his attempt to dismantle the Reconstruction Acts. On August 5 the president asked for the resignation of his secretary of war, Edwin M. Stan-

ton, who had allied with the Radicals long before. Stanton refused to resign, so on August 12 Johnson suspended him and appointed General Ulysses S. Grant as secretary of war ad interim (because Congress was not in session, the suspension was allowed under the Tenure of Office Act). Then on August 26, Johnson removed General Daniel Sickles from command of the Carolinas and General Philip H. Sheridan from the Fifth District for interfering in Southern state governments, that is, enforcing the Reconstruction Acts.

Talk of impeachment was again in the air when Congress reconvened in November 1867: was it necessary, was it prudent, was it legitimate? Two somewhat contradictory conclusions seemed to emerge from the discussion. First, many people in and out of the government agreed that a law needed to be broken in order that impeachment be authorized; thus far, it was difficult to argue that the president had actually broken any law. Second, U.S. precedent and legal scholarship indicated that the issue was not, and should not be, whether or not an official acted morally or legally. The issue should be whether the executive had in some way abused the powers granted to him, an argument that dated back to *The Federalist* papers in 1788.

Congress took a step toward impeachment when, on November 25, the Judiciary Committee reported 5 to 4 in favor of impeachment. The debate that followed centered around one point: had the president broken the law? Evidently the answer was no, because on December 7 the impeachment resolution was defeated, with only a minority of Republicans voting for it. Some historians claim that fall state elections across the North and West, in which the Democratic Party made significant gains, cooled the fires of impeachment. Congressional Republicans would not embark on an unprecedented, controversial undertaking without significant public approval or evidence of criminal activity. But impeachment was not dead. In fact, interest and support were growing, and Johnson's actions were not the only cause.

Republicans were concerned about the presidential election of 1868, now less than a year away. If Johnson remained in office through 1868, he could use his patronage powers, combined with his position as commander-in-chief, to defeat the ratification in the South of the new Reconstruction Act constitutions and governments. Southern states would not be readmitted, and this could affect the election itself. Radicals were especially anxious, not only because Johnson was opposed to their interracial society but also because they favored for president men such as Chief Justice Salmon P. Chase and Senate president pro tempore Benjamin F. Wade. The choice of the moderates, General Ulysses S. Grant, was still clearly the front-runner, but if Radicals could remove Johnson, then Benjamin Wade would become president (there was no vice president after Johnson's accession). Although the Radical Wade hoped to become president, he recognized his unpopularity and suggested that if he replaced Johnson he could work for Chase's election.

The impeachment movement received further impetus from President Johnson. Encouraged by the failure of the impeachment vote, he removed from command John Pope (in Virginia) and Edward Ord (Arkansas and Mississippi) and replaced them with conservative generals. Then, on December 12, in compliance with the Tenure of Office Act, he sent to the Senate his reasons for suspending Stanton. The Tenure of Office Act stipulated that officials appointed with the "advise and consent of the Senate" could not be removed without Senate approval. This protection lasted for the term of the president under whom they were appointed and one month thereafter. The act was designed to protect federal officeholders from Johnson's ax, but no one was sure if cabinet members were included. But in his explanation, Johnson never claimed that Stanton was excluded from the act, and the letter suggested that the suspension was done in compliance with it.

On January 10, 1868, the Senate Committee on Military Affairs refused to "advise and consent" to the suspension, and on January 13 the Senate voted to do the same. The same day, the House Committee on Reconstruction, which had taken control of the impeachment investigation, voted against recommending impeachment for the suspension of Stanton. It seemed clear that Congress expected the secretary of war to return to his office.

The next day, in direct defiance of the wishes of Congress, Johnson fired Stanton and appointed Adjutant General of the Army Lorenzo Thomas as secretary of war ad interim. It appeared as though Johnson believed that the tenure law was unconstitutional and hoped to test its constitutionality in court; this is difficult, however, to reconcile with his earlier adherence to the requirements of the law. For Radicals, the president had broken the law in two ways. First, he had removed Stanton from office in violation of the Tenure of Office Act and in opposition to the advise and consent of the Senate. Second, he had appointed Thomas secretary of war ad interim while Congress was in session. On February 22 the Reconstruction Committee recommended that the president be impeached for "high crimes and misdemeanors." This was the Constitution's wording, because as yet no specific charges existed. On February 24 the House voted 128 to 47 to impeach President Johnson, with every Republican voting "aye." The Speaker then designated a committee to draw up formal articles of impeachment, the charges, and these were handed over to the impeachment managers, seven House Republicans chosen by caucus on March 2 to prosecute the case. These were Benjamin F. Butler, Thaddeus Stevens, Thomas Williams, John A. Bingham, James F. Wilson, George S. Boutwell, and John A. Logan.

After debate and modification, on March 3 the House agreed on eleven articles of impeachment. Eight charged the president with violating the Tenure of Office Act by appointing Thomas and removing Stanton, one (drafted by Benjamin F. Butler) referred to Johnson's attempts to "bring Congress into ridicule and disrepute" by his public criticism and slander of Congress, one charged Johnson with breaking the Command of the Army Act, and the last (drafted by Thaddeus Stevens) charged him with willful interference and obstruction of the Reconstruction Acts.

The articles were sent to Johnson with a request for a written reply. The president was also allowed time to assemble a defense staff and prepare his case. As counsel, Johnson selected Henry Stanbery (who resigned as attorney general to defend the president), Benjamin R. Curtis, William S. Groesbeck, William M. Evarts, and Thomas A.R. Nelson.

Meanwhile the Senate had been preparing for its role as high court of impeachment. On March 2, the Senate finalized the rules for holding court and reiterated that an "aye" vote from two-thirds of those present was necessary for conviction and removal. After several postponements, the Senate trial opened on March 30, 1868. Salmon P. Chase, chief justice of the United States, presided, with the House managers acting as prosecution opposite Johnson's defense counsel. The Senate sat as the jury, and the galleries were open to guests who were able to secure tickets to the Senate. The president, on advice of his counsel, never appeared at the trial. For six weeks the opposing sides argued over issues great and small, ranging from the nature of presidential rights and authority and the powers of Congress to details over the wording of a telegram or the substance of a conversation.

As the trial dragged on, Republican leaders designated May 12 for a vote, hoping to conclude the trial—and convict the president—before the Republican National Convention in late May.

With a key Republican senator, Jacob Howard of Michigan, ill, the Senate moved the vote back to May 16. The Senate had ruled that each article would be voted upon individually, with the order of articles to be determined on the day of the vote. On May 16, Senate Republicans decided to vote on Article XI first, believing that the charge of obstructing Congress had the most support. Chief Justice Chase asked each senator, "How say ye?" The vote was 35 guilty and 19 not guilty, one vote shy of the two-thirds necessary for conviction. For the not-guilty vote, the twelve Senate Democrats had been joined by seven Republicans: William Pitt Fessenden, James W. Grimes, Joseph S. Fowler, Lyman Trumbull, Edmund Ross, John B. Henderson, and Peter G. Van Winkle.

Reeling from the defeat, Republicans adjourned to gather their forces and convince the seven "recusants" to vote for conviction. The Senate reassembled as high court of impeachment on May 26 and began voting on Article II, which charged Johnson with violating the Tenure of Office Act by removing Stanton. The vote was exactly the same as on Article XI, 35 guilty, 19 not guilty. Next the Senate took up Article III, which indicted Johnson for appointing Thomas in Stanton's place. The vote was again 35 to 19, one vote shy of conviction. Because other articles charged Johnson with *conspiring* to violate the Tenure of Office Act, and because the Senate had already ruled that he *did not* violate the law, conviction on the other articles seemed impossible. On May 26 the Senate adjourned as high court of impeachment, and the trial was over. Johnson remained as president, and Edwin M. Stanton vacated the War Office.

Why had impeachment failed to bring conviction? One reason was the weakness of the charges; no one was sure that the Tenure of Office Act applied to Stanton. (Interestingly, Congress modified the act under the Grant administration, giving the president more latitude in removing officials. The Supreme Court ruled the Tenure of Office Act unconstitutional in 1926.) There was also a real fear among moderate Republicans of Benjamin Wade's becoming president. Wade was an extremist who had alienated nearly everyone during his senatorial career. His brief control of the presidency might jeopardize the nomination of Ulysses S. Grant, the moderates' choice. Also working in Johnson's favor was his defense team, a politically balanced group comprising some of the nation's best legal minds: two moderate Republicans, two War Democrats, and one conservative Democrat. Not only were their legal arguments excellent, their advice to Johnson was crucial as well: they kept Johnson out of the courtroom and warned him against making any speeches or public addresses.

In line with this, Johnson also helped his cause by trying to cooperate with Congress. On May 4 he received the new constitutions for South Carolina and Arkansas, completed under the congressional system, and forwarded them to Congress with no comments, delays, or reservations. Then, while Thomas and Stanton were still fighting over the secretary's office, Johnson nominated John Schofield, a moderate general, as secretary of war. Schofield had dutifully enforced the Reconstruction Acts in Virginia (after replacing John Pope), and Johnson followed appropriate procedure by transmitting the nomination to the Senate for approval.

See also: Army Appropriations Act; Ashley, James Mitchell; Butler, Benjamin Franklin; Cabinet Members; Chase, Salmon Portland; Congressional Reconstruction; Curtis, Benjamin Robbins; Election of 1866; Election of 1868; Elections of 1867; Evarts, William Maxwell; Fourteenth Amendment; Grant, Ulysses Simpson; Groesbeck, William Slocum; House Judiciary Committee; Impeachment Defense Counsel; Impeachment Managers; Military Reconstruction Acts; Nelson, Thomas Amis Rogers; Pope, John; Presidential Reconstruction; Reconstruction; Republican Party; Ross, Edmund Gibson;

Schofield, John McAllister; Sheridan, Philip Henry; Sickles, Daniel Edgar; Stanbery, Henry; Stanton, Edwin McMasters; Stevens, Thaddeus; Surratt, Mary (Elizabeth) Eugenia Jenkins; Tenure of Office Act; Thomas, Lorenzo; Wade, Benjamin Franklin. For excerpts from the Articles of Impeachment, as well as excerpts from President Johnson's reply, see Appendix II.

References: Benedict, Michael Les, *The Impeachment and Trial of Andrew Johnson* (1973); DeWitt, David Miller, *The Impeachment and Trial of Andrew Johnson, Seventeenth President of the United States: A History* (1903); Smith, Gene, *High Crimes and Misdemeanors: The Impeachment and Trial of Andrew Johnson* (1977); Trefousse, Hans L., *Impeachment of a President: Andrew Johnson, the Blacks, and Reconstruction* (1975); *Trial of Andrew Johnson . . . 3 vols.* (1868).

Impeachment Defense Counsel

After the U.S. House of Representatives passed a resolution on February 24, 1868, impeaching Andrew Johnson, the president needed to select attorneys to serve as his defense counsel. He received advice from his cabinet, from other trusted friends such as Reverdy Johnson and Thomas Ewing, Sr., and from some members of the general public. A number urged Johnson to employ Republican lawyers and avoid Democrats who had been his active supporters. Some also urged Johnson to avoid including former attorney general Jeremiah S. Black, whom the president had actually already selected. Black's known attitudes and personality could injure Johnson's cause, these advisors believed. Black resigned from Johnson's defense on March 9 because of differences of opinion about the Alta Vela case.

Ultimately Johnson's defense team had five members. Benjamin Robbins Curtis of Boston was a Republican and former associate justice of the U.S. Supreme Court. William Maxwell Evarts, a noted New York lawyer, was also a Republican and a supporter of Ulysses S. Grant for president. William Slocum Groesbeck of Ohio, a War Democrat, had previously given Johnson some legal advice. Johnson chose Thomas

Amis Rogers Nelson of Tennessee as the replacement for Black. Nelson had been a Whig opponent of Johnson's during the 1840s, but after they campaigned against secession together, they remained close colleagues. The last member of the group was Henry Stanbery, who resigned as Johnson's attorney general on March 11, 1868, in order to serve in the president's defense without possible conflict of interest.

One of the first and perhaps most important things that the defense did for Johnson was to insist that the president not appear at the trial in person and that he not give any further newspaper interviews. They all recognized Johnson's tendency to damage his own cause by impromptu comments. At times Johnson became irritated with his attorneys and what he saw as their weak defense of his case. He threatened to conduct his own defense, but he never actually did.

Johnson and his counsel submitted their reply to the Articles of Impeachment in a missive to the Senate on March 23. The trial itself began on March 30 and during the first few days the prosecution submitted its case. The defense began on April 9 with Curtis giving what is considered as one of the best speeches of his career. He pointed out that the Tenure of Office Act did not apply to Secretary of War Edwin M. Stanton because he had been appointed by Abraham Lincoln. Curtis further stated that Johnson had the right to test the constitutionality of a law. He pointed out that two articles were attempts to restrict Johnson's freedom of speech and that to have a difference of opinion was not a criminal act. Even Benjamin F. Butler, one of the most active of the prosecuting impeachment managers, admitted that Curtis had left little for the other defense attorneys to say.

Nevertheless, all five gave speeches at various points. Some discussed the issue of what exactly was an impeachable offense. Others tried to direct the questioning of such witnesses as William T. Sherman and

Gideon Welles to demonstrate Johnson's intent to test the constitutionality of the Tenure of Office Act. Many of the senators objected to this type of question, but it was relevant to Johnson's defense.

All five lawyers did not remain equally active throughout the trial. Stanbery became ill on April 14 and had to remain at home for several weeks. About the time that Stanbery recovered, Curtis left for Boston on April 30. He intended to take care of business matters but also became ill and apparently did not return to Washington before the end of the trial.

Meanwhile, Evarts was active in negotiating with some of the conservative Republican senators for the nomination of General John M. Schofield as secretary of war and assuring the senators that Johnson would not meddle with the Military Reconstruction Acts. Finally, when three of the impeachment articles were voted upon on May 16 and 26, the defense strategy paid off. Johnson was narrowly acquitted.

See also: Alta Vela; Black, Jeremiah Sullivan; Butler, Benjamin Franklin; Curtis, Benjamin Robbins; Evarts, William Maxwell; Ewing, Thomas (Jr. and Sr.); Groesbeck, William Slocum; Impeachment; Impeachment Managers; Johnson, Reverdy; Military Reconstruction Acts; Nelson, Thomas Amis Rogers; Newspaper Interviews; Schofield, John McAllister; Sherman, William Tecumseh; Stanbery, Henry; Stanton, Edwin McMasters; Tenure of Office Act; Welles, Gideon.

References: Benedict, Michael Les, *The Impeachment and Trial of Andrew Johnson* (1973); Graf, LeRoy P., Haskins, Ralph W., and Bergeron, Paul H., eds., *The Papers of Andrew Johnson* vols. 13–14 (1967–2000); Trefousse, Hans L., *Andrew Johnson: A Biography* (1989).

Impeachment Managers

*T*he seven impeachment managers were selected by the U.S. House of Representatives to act essentially as the prosecuting attorneys for Andrew Johnson's impeachment trial. When the House voted on February 24, 1868, to impeach Johnson, they actually had no specific charges available and a committee had to be appointed to draw them up. At the same time, a caucus selected the managers, who were approved on March 2, 1868.

Three of the members, John A. Bingham of Ohio, Benjamin F. Butler of Massachusetts, and Thaddeus Stevens of Pennsylvania, are discussed individually in this volume. George Sewel Boutwell (1818–1905) of Massachusetts, a lawyer, held numerous state political offices including governor (1851–1852), was the first federal commissioner of internal revenue (1862–1863), served slightly more than three terms in the U.S. House of Representatives (1863–March 12, 1869), was secretary of the treasury under Ulysses S. Grant (1869–1873), and filled a U.S. Senate seat vacancy (1873–1877). John Alexander Logan (1826–1886), an Illinois lawyer, was a member of the Illinois house of representatives (1852–1853, 1856–1857), the U.S. House of Representatives (1859–1862, 1867–1871), and the U.S. Senate (1871–1877, 1879–1886). He also fought in the Mexican-American War and the Union army during the Civil War, where he achieved the rank of major general of volunteers. Thomas Williams (1806–1872), a Pennsylvania lawyer, served in the state senate (1838–1841) and the U.S. House of Representatives (1863–1869). James Falconer Wilson (1828–1895) of Iowa was also a lawyer. After serving in the state house of representatives (1857, 1859) and the state senate (1859–1861), Wilson was a member of the U.S. House of Representatives (1861–1869) and the U.S. Senate (1883–1895).

Boutwell, Williams, and Wilson were members of the House Judiciary Committee (Wilson chaired it) when the committee several times considered impeachment for Johnson. Bingham, Boutwell, Logan, Stevens, and Wilson were on the committee that drew up the eleven impeachment charges. Bingham, after much debate, became the chairman of the impeachment managers.

The managers presented the Articles of Impeachment to the Senate on March 4, 1868. Johnson was due to answer them on March 13 and on that date a large crowd gathered, but only Johnson's attorneys came, requesting forty days to prepare their reply. Butler objected vigorously and the defense was given ten days.

The actual trial began on March 30. Johnson never attended in person but was defended by a team of five attorneys. Butler gave the opening speech, a technical presentation that disappointed those who had come for entertainment. The managers presented a series of witnesses for the prosecution who gave little information that was not already known.

Benjamin R. Curtis opened for the defense on April 9–10 in a speech that clearly argued Johnson's lawful intentions. The defense then presented its witnesses, whose testimony was frequently objected to by the managers, especially Butler. The closing arguments were presented April 22–May 6, including speeches by Boutwell (April 22–23), Stevens (April 27), Williams (April 27–28), and Bingham (May 4–6). But the prosecution's case was weak in many respects and Johnson was acquitted by one vote on May 16 and 26, 1868. Although Butler tried to prove that some of the senators who voted for acquittal had been bribed, he was unable to find any evidence to support the accusation.

See also: Bingham, John Armor; Butler, Benjamin Franklin; Curtis, Benjamin Robbins; Evarts, William Maxwell; Groesbeck, William Slocum; House Judiciary Committee; Impeachment; Impeachment Defense Counsel; Stanbery, Henry; Stevens, Thaddeus.

References: Benedict, Michael Les, *The Impeachment and Trial of Andrew Johnson* (1973); *Biographical Directory of the United States Congress* (1989); Trefousse, Hans L., *Impeachment of a President: Andrew Johnson, the Blacks, and Reconstruction* (1975).

Indians

As president, Andrew Johnson was much more concerned about Reconstruction than he was about Indian affairs. Nevertheless, with the post–Civil War expansion of western settlement and the construction of the transcontinental railroad, the resulting Indian unrest required Johnson's attention at times.

Johnson had some exposure to Indian affairs during his years in the U.S. House of Representatives and Senate. In most cases this either related to patronage matters (people wanted his assistance to get a job in the Indian service) or it involved voting on Indian appropriations. In May 1858 Johnson urged his Senate colleagues to consider the Indian appropriations bill in its scheduled order, after the Homestead Bill, which was Johnson's pet legislation.

Patronage requests naturally increased once Johnson became president. Of course there were requests to appoint or remove Indian agents for the various tribes as well as superintendents of the districts. But there were also requests for the appointment of a commissioner of Indian affairs who was in charge of Indian matters under the supervision of the secretary of the interior, an arrangement that led to some conflict. Four men served as commissioner during Johnson's term: William P. Dole, Abraham Lincoln's commissioner since 1861, served only until July 1865; Dennis N. Cooley, Dole's successor, served until November 1, 1866; Lewis V. Bogy, whose nomination was not confirmed by the Senate, served until March 1867; and his successor, Nathaniel G. Taylor, served for the rest of Johnson's term.

Johnson received many complaints, most often from territorial governors, delegates, or other officials rather than private citizens, about Indian depredations in the western states and territories. Texas, Colorado, Kansas, Montana, Nebraska, the Dakotas, Wyoming, and New Mexico all experienced raids or threats of attack. Sometimes the correspondent gave details of livestock stolen and persons murdered or kidnapped. At other times the letter writer pled for more federal troops or the authorization to raise a local militia at federal expense.

One of the most publicized of the attacks was the Fetterman Massacre near Fort Phil Kearny, Nebraska Territory, on December 21, 1866. This fort was one of three constructed to protect the Bozeman Trail to Montana, which ran through Indian hunting grounds and caused a great deal of upheaval. The ambush, which killed Brevet Colonel William J. Fetterman and the eighty other men in his party, was one of the Indian efforts to force the closure of the three forts, which the army vacated in August 1868, as a result of the Fort Laramie treaty.

Indians also wrote to Andrew Johnson, sometimes by dictating to their agent or another interpreter. Tribal matters of concern to these correspondents included retaining an agent threatened with removal or urging the removal of an unscrupulous agent. Some persons wanted Johnson to intervene in a tribal factional struggle, which was particularly true of the Cherokees. In several cases Indian leaders wanted to come to Washington, D.C., to meet with Johnson personally. Although some delegations were allowed to do this, others were unable to visit because the Interior Department refused to give them permission or to pay their expenses.

During Johnson's term several commissions were sent to various parts of the West to attempt treaty negotiations with the disgruntled Indians. Among them were commissions headed by Senator James R. Doolittle and Dakota governor Newton Edmunds in 1865, and an 1867–1868 peace commission including Indian commissioner Nathaniel G. Taylor and General William T. Sherman. Some treaty negotiations were unsuccessful because the Indians involved were out hunting or for other reasons refused to come to the meeting place. In other cases, treaties were negotiated that usually involved the cession of Indian land to the federal government and the confinement of the Indians on reservations. As he said in his Fourth Annual Message (1868), Johnson approved of putting Indians on reservations "where they may be encouraged to abandon their nomadic habits and engage in agricultural and industrial pursuits." Unfortunately, the federal government was often slow to provide as promised for the reservation Indians, and a shortage of supplies, leading at times to the prospect of actual starvation, was a cause of some Indian outbreaks.

Any Indian unrest also stimulated further debate over whether the War or Interior Department should be in control of Indian affairs. The War Department, which was always in favor of solving any Indian problem by the use of military force, destroyed a number of villages and killed nonhostile as well as offending Indians in several battles during Johnson's term. The Interior Department, which had been overseeing the Indian Bureau since its establishment, was generally in favor of negotiated solutions to difficulties. By the end of Johnson's term, negotiations had contributed to the establishment of a fragile peace.

See also: Annual Messages; Browning, Orville Hickman; Doolittle, James Rood; Patronage; Sherman, William Tecumseh; Taylor, Nathaniel Green; Territorial Affairs.

References: Graf, LeRoy P., Haskins, Ralph W., and Bergeron, Paul H., eds., *The Papers of Andrew Johnson* vols. 2–3, 8–15 (1967–2000).

Jackson, Andrew (1767–1845)

Andrew Jackson, seventh president of the United States, had a tremendous influence on the political ideas of Andrew Johnson. Jackson was born in poverty in the Waxhaw District of South Carolina soon after the death of his father. His mother and two older brothers all died during the Revolutionary War. Jackson, though only a child, fought in the Battle of Hanging Rock and was imprisoned by the British. After a brief time as a schoolteacher, Jackson read law and was admitted to the bar in 1787. He soon moved to Jonesboro on the western frontier of North Carolina and was appointed solicitor of the western district. He retained the same office when the area became part of Tennessee and he served in the constitutional convention for the new state.

Jackson soon moved west to the Nashville area, where he practiced law, engaged in land speculation, and aspired to become a gentleman farmer on the plantation that he named "The Hermitage." In the early 1790s Jackson married Rachel Donelson Robards, without either of them realizing that her divorce from Lewis Robards was not yet final. This mistake was the source of scandal and accusations against Jackson at various points in his political career, especially during the presidential election of 1828. The Jacksons had no children of their own, but they adopted one of Rachel's nephews, whom they called Andrew Jackson, Jr.

Jackson served in the U.S. House of Representatives (December 5, 1796–September 1797) and U.S. Senate (September 1797–April 1798, March 4, 1823–October 14, 1825), each time resigning long before the end of his term. He also held such local offices as judge of the Tennessee Supreme Court (1798–1804) and major general of the state militia. It was the militia connection that finally brought Jackson fame. He led Tennessee troops against the Creek Indians after the latter massacred the people who had taken refuge at Fort Mims, Mississippi Territory (now Alabama). Jackson and his forces defeated the Creeks at the Battle of Horseshoe Bend (March 27, 1814), forcing the Creeks to cede land to the federal government.

The victory also brought Jackson a commission as major general in the U.S. Army. This caused him to be sent to New Orleans to defend that city against the British. Jackson led a motley force of militia, Creoles, blacks, and pirates in thoroughly defeating the British forces on January 8, 1815, after the treaty ending the War of 1812 actually had already been signed. Nevertheless, Jackson became a major national hero, a reputation only enhanced for most people in 1818 when Jackson pursued some Seminole Indians into Spanish Florida and captured the town of Pensacola, creating an international incident.

In 1824 Jackson, John Quincy Adams, Henry Clay, and William H. Crawford were candidates in a four-way presidential contest. Although Jackson had the most popular votes, no candidate had a majority of electoral votes, so the election had to be decided by the House of Representatives, which eventually chose Adams. Jackson campaigned in one way or another for the next four years and was elected in 1828, with reelection in 1832.

There were three major issues during Jackson's presidency. When South Carolina objected to tariff measures and passed legislation to nullify them (declare them null and void in the state of South Carolina), Jackson sent troops to enforce the legislation, proclaiming that the Union must and shall be preserved. During this time as well, Jackson worked for removal of the Cherokee Indians from Georgia, North Carolina, and Tennessee to Indian Territory (now Oklahoma), although they were not actually removed until Martin Van Buren's term. The third issue was the contest with Nicholas Biddle over the renewal of the charter of the Bank of the United States, an institution that Jackson abhorred. His destruction of the bank resulted in some long-term financial problems for the United States. At the conclusion of his presidency, Jackson retired to "The Hermitage," where he died; he was buried in the garden.

Jackson had a tremendous influence on Andrew Johnson. When Johnson began his political career, Jackson was president and headed the Democratic Party, of which Johnson became a staunch member. Despite a local legend, there is no indication that the two ever met or corresponded. In 1844 Johnson was one of many persons who signed a petition to Jackson, his only known contact. Nevertheless, Johnson saw Jackson as his model in many respects and frequently cited Jackson's example in various situations. During the Civil War, Johnson, the Unionist, often referred to Jackson's support of the Union in the 1830s. In speeches delivered in 1863–1864 Johnson frequently pictured Jackson turning over in his grave, extending his long, pointing finger, and exclaiming, "The Federal Union—it must be preserved!"

During his presidency, Johnson, in his veto of the Tenure of Office Act, for example, justified his own removal of officeholders by pointing out that Jackson had also done so. Johnson did not cease to cite Jackson once he left the presidency either. Johnson proposed and supported several constitutional amendments, including popular election of the president and vice president and a single term for the president. Johnson often cited Jackson's 1829 advocacy of these same principles. Johnson also used the example of Jackson's attack on monopolies and his attitude toward the so-called money power as Johnson ranted against bondholders and financial controllers of the country. Johnson kept a portrait of Jackson hanging on his parlor wall in Greeneville.

Not only did Johnson cite Jackson, but contemporaries compared Johnson to Jackson for his firmness, his Unionism, and his focus on the Constitution.

See also: Constitutional Amendments, Proposed; Democratic Party; Finances, Johnson's Attitude toward Governmental; Historical Attitudes toward Johnson; Patronage; Postpresidential Career; Secession, Johnson's Attitude toward; Tenure of Office Act; Vetoes.

References: Graf, LeRoy P., Haskins, Ralph W., and Bergeron, Paul H., eds., *The Papers of Andrew Johnson* vols. 5–6, 12–16 (1967–2000); Remini, Robert V., *Andrew Jackson* 3 vols. (1977–1984).

Johnson, Andrew, Jr., "Frank" (1852–1879)

The third son and fifth and last child of Andrew and Eliza McCardle Johnson, Andrew Johnson, Jr., was born on August 5, 1852. Known to family and friends as Frank, he was eighteen and a half years younger than his nearest sibling, Robert, and less than three years older than his niece Lillie Stover. His father was often absent during Frank's childhood, either serving in Nashville as governor or in Washington, D.C., as senator. His mother began to suffer from tuberculosis while he was quite young. Little is known about his early education but it was certainly quite irregular during the Civil War because Frank refugeed with his mother. First they stayed with his sister Mary Stover in Carter County, Tennessee, and then spent time in Indiana and Kentucky for his mother's health before finally joining his father, then serving as military governor, in Nashville.

Frank apparently attended the Vermont Episcopal School in Burlington in 1865–1866. During 1867–1869 he was a student at Georgetown College, a Catholic school in Georgetown, D.C. After the conclusion of his presidency, Andrew Johnson returned to Washington, D.C., to see his son and to attend the Georgetown graduation on July 1, 1869. Friends prevented him from actually attending the graduation, however, because President Ulysses S. Grant was there to present the awards to the students and no one wanted an unpleasant scene.

Frank did not graduate from Georgetown nor did he apparently have any further education after 1869. He did not seem to have much career ambition either, but he may have been in poor health. He spent some time at his sister Mary's farm, perhaps assisting with its management. By the fall of 1874 he and his father's sometime secretary, Thomas Maloney, were editing the *Greeneville Intelligencer,* a newspaper doubt-less established to support his father's candidacy for the Senate. The newspaper ceased publication within a year after Andrew Johnson's death in 1875.

After the death of his mother in January 1876, Frank Johnson became executor of his father's estate. He farmed in Carter County and then managed a cotton factory in Union Depot, Sullivan County, Tennessee, which became the property of Andrew Johnson's heirs as a result of one of their father's investments. On November 25, 1875, Frank married Kate Mae (or May) Rumbough, usually called Bessie, of North Carolina. Their marriage was subject to severe strains as Frank followed in the footsteps of his older brothers and drank to excess. Although he had written a letter to his mother in April 1869, just after his brother Robert's death, promising never to let intoxicating liquors pass his lips, he was unable to keep this promise. A year after their marriage, Bessie Johnson went home for a time because of her husband's drinking. Perhaps there was a connection between Frank's alcoholism and his worsening tuberculosis. He died of the disease on March 12, 1879, at his home in Union Depot, and his body was brought to Greeneville for burial with other family members already interred on Monument Hill.

After Frank Johnson's death his sisters, Martha Patterson and Mary Stover, had a dispute with his widow over rights to the Johnson home in Greeneville. About 1885 the litigation was resolved by a compromise. In 1886 Bessie Johnson married Colonel Daniel B. Safford of New York. They had two children and eventually settled in Hot Springs, North Carolina.

See also: Finances, Personal; Grandchildren; Greeneville, Tennessee; Johnson, Eliza McCardle; Johnson, Robert; Patterson, Martha Johnson; Stover (Brown), Mary Johnson; Tuberculosis.

References: Andrew Johnson National Historic Site, Greeneville, TN; files Andrew Johnson Project, Knoxville, TN; Andrew Johnson, Jr., "Frank" file, Sarah Stover diary, Stover family file; Graf, LeRoy P., Haskins, Ralph W., and Bergeron, Paul

H., eds., *The Papers of Andrew Johnson* vols. 6, 16 (1967–2000); *Knoxville Chronicle,* Mar. 20, 1879; *New York Tribune,* July 2, 1869; Trefousse, Hans L., *Andrew Johnson: A Biography* (1989).

Johnson, Charles (1830–1863)

Charles Johnson, the second child and oldest son of Andrew and Eliza Mc-Cardle Johnson, was born in Greeneville, Tennessee, on February 19, 1830. About 1847 he may have attended Franklin College, a "manual labor school" near Nashville that specialized in business and agricultural subjects. In any case, by early 1849 Charles Johnson and J.B.R. Lyon were coediting the *Greeneville Spy,* a paper established by Andrew Johnson. Although he held the position for more than a year, Charles seems not to have been very interested in editing. By the late 1850s he had become a partner, with Greeneville postmaster Elbert Biggs, in a drug store venture. He also assisted his younger brother Robert in making many real estate and business transactions for their father when he was absent in Nashville or Washington, D.C.

Although Andrew Johnson was concerned about his son's career struggles and evident lack of ambition, he was even more worried about Charles's tendency to heavy drinking. Charles managed to remain sober for periods of time, but had a serious lapse in the spring of 1860, when he accompanied Robert to the Democratic National Convention in Charleston, South Carolina. Soon after they reached the city, Charles went on a binge, which Robert was unable to prevent or control. Robert claimed that he was barely able to get him back to Greeneville, and when they arrived Charles returned to drinking.

Charles was a Unionist during the secession crisis but at one time he took the Confederate oath of allegiance, apparently in an unsuccessful attempt to preserve family property. In October 1862 he accompanied his mother, brother Andrew Jr. (Frank), and sister Mary Stover and her family to Nashville when the Confederates forced them to leave East Tennessee. At some point Charles must have had some medical training because in the fall of 1862 he was able to accept an appointment as assistant surgeon of the 10th Tennessee Infantry.

The regiment was stationed near Nashville when, on April 4, 1863, Charles fell from his horse and was killed under circumstances that were never quite clear. On April 7, after the body was embalmed by Alanson W. Kelly, a funeral procession, including Charles's regiment and part of Robert Johnson's cavalry, took the body to Mt. Olivet Cemetery, where it was placed in a vault. Robert was probably the only family member to attend the funeral since Andrew Sr. was in Washington, D.C.; Eliza, Frank, and Mary were in Kentucky; and Martha was across enemy lines in Greeneville. Some years later Charles was reinterred in the national cemetery at Greeneville, on the hilltop where his parents were already buried.

See also: Johnson, Andrew, Jr., "Frank"; Johnson, Eliza McCardle; Johnson, Robert; Patterson, Martha Johnson; Stover (Brown), Mary Johnson.
References: Graf, LeRoy P., Haskins, Ralph W., and Bergeron, Paul H., eds., *The Papers of Andrew Johnson* vols. 1–6, 14 (1967–2000); Trefousse, Hans L., *Andrew Johnson: A Biography* (1989).

Johnson, Eliza McCardle (1810–1876)

The daughter of John McCardle and Sarah Phillips McCardle, Eliza McCardle was born October 10, 1810. Her father, a Greeneville, Tennessee, shoemaker, at one time also kept an inn in nearby Warrensburg. After his death in 1826, Eliza helped her mother make quilts. Eliza met Andrew Johnson soon after he arrived in Greeneville in September 1826 and, according to tradition, she immediately announced to friends that some day she would marry Johnson. Whether this tradition is true or not, on May 17, 1827, sixteen-and-a-half-year-old Eliza and eighteen-year-old Andrew were married by a justice of the peace in Warrensburg.

Eliza Johnson was better educated than most of the women in her town, having attended Rhea Academy in Greeneville for a time. Traditional accounts claim that Eliza taught Andrew to read, but actually he was already literate. She may have taught him to write, but, whatever the case, she encouraged his further education and helped him develop his oratorical skills.

Considered to have a modest, retiring temperament, Eliza's personality contrasted sharply with her husband's more aggressive, outgoing nature. She seems to have sought to provide a calming, supportive, comfortable home atmosphere for him. Despite frequent, lengthy periods of separation while Andrew held political office in Nashville or Washington, D.C., the couple were apparently devoted to each other and Andrew was always concerned for her well-being. The Johnsons had five children: Martha (1828), Charles (1830), Mary (1832), Robert (1834), and Andrew Jr., known as Frank (1852).

Initially the Johnsons lived in a two-room frame house in Greeneville, using one room for living space and the other for Andrew's tailor shop. In 1831 they were able to buy a brick home with a separate building for the tailoring business. They bought a larger house in 1851. Eliza apparently managed the family financial affairs competently during Andrew's many absences.

Sometime during the 1850s Eliza contracted tuberculosis. Although her health periodically worsened or improved for the rest of her life, she generally remained an invalid, traveling only when necessary and rarely appearing at public events.

When Tennessee seceded in the spring of 1861, Eliza was still in Greeneville, where she suffered much harassment as the wife of a prominent Unionist. Forced by the Confederates to leave town, she and Frank stayed with her daughter Mary Stover in Carter County, Tennessee, until October 1862, when Eliza was again compelled to leave. Confederate General Nathan Bedford Forrest at first refused to let her through his lines to join her husband, by then military governor of Tennessee, in Nashville.

After Johnson assumed the presidency, Eliza finally went to Washington, D.C. However, she remained in her room most of the time, allowing the duties of White House hostess to devolve upon her older daughter, Martha Patterson, often assisted by Mary Stover, as both daughters and their children lived in the White House during much of Johnson's term.

After the Johnsons left the White House, they returned to Greeneville, where Eliza's health remained poor. By the spring of 1875 her condition was steadily deteriorating and was too precarious for her even to attend her husband's funeral when he died that summer. A few months later, on January 15, 1876, Eliza died at her daughter Mary's home in Carter County.

See also: Education of Johnson; Grandchildren; Greeneville, Tennessee; Johnson, Andrew, Jr., "Frank"; Johnson, Charles; Johnson, Robert; Patterson, Martha Johnson; Stover (Brown), Mary Johnson.

References: Graf, LeRoy P., Haskins, Ralph W., and Bergeron, Paul H., eds., *The Papers of Andrew Johnson* vols. 1–16 (1967–2000); Holloway, Laura Carter, *The Ladies of the White House* (1870); Trefousse, Hans L., *Andrew Johnson: A Biography* (1989); Young, Nancy Beck, "Eliza (McCardle) Johnson," in Gould, Lewis L., ed., *American First Ladies: Their Lives and Their Legacy* (1996).

Johnson, Jacob (1778–1812)

Born in rural North Carolina on April 17, 1778, Jacob Johnson came from a line of yeoman farmers owning land in Virginia. This property was lost by Jacob's father, William Johnson, Sr., leaving Jacob landless and illiterate. By 1800 he had moved to Raleigh, where he worked in the stables and as a handyman at Casso's Tavern. There he met and courted the tavern's laundress, Mary McDonough, and the two were married on September 9, 1801. The couple had three children: William P. (1804–1865), Elizabeth (1806–d. infancy), and Andrew (1808–1875).

During the years after his marriage Johnson held a variety of odd jobs: bartender (1806), janitor at the state capitol building (1808), porter at the State Bank of North Carolina (1810), constable (1811), sexton of Bethel Presbyterian Church, and official town bell ringer. He was also captain in the town watch (1811).

Sometime in late 1811 (no source ever gives a date), Johnson was watching a canoe with three passengers paddling around on Hunters' Mill Pond when the boat tipped over, dumping the men, who could not swim, into the water. Johnson jumped in and rescued Raleigh *Star* publisher Thomas Henderson and his friends. But the experience apparently made Johnson seriously ill. One very cold day, as he was ringing the bell for a funeral, he collapsed. Taken home, Johnson died on January 4, 1812. He was buried under a simple tombstone marked "JJ."

All contemporary sources describe Jacob Johnson as an honest, industrious, friendly, well-respected citizen. But after his son Andrew became a political figure in Tennessee, various scurrilous rumors circulated, especially during congressional elections in the early 1840s. Spread particularly by journalist and Johnson opponent William G. Brownlow, some rumors claimed that Andrew was actually the son of one or another Raleigh lawyer, and Brownlow bluntly called Jacob Johnson a chicken thief. These aspersions upset Andrew so much that he traveled to Raleigh to investigate the truth of his father's reputation and later included a defense of Jacob as part of a lengthy pamphlet response to various other slanders by Brownlow.

In 1867 Raleigh citizens decided to put a marker on Jacob Johnson's grave more appropriate for the father of a president. At the invitation of the mayor, governor, and other North Carolinians, Andrew Johnson attended the dedication ceremony of the ten-foot red limestone shaft on June 4, 1867.

See also: Brownlow, William G. "Parson"; Johnson (Daughtry), Mary McDonough "Polly"; Presidential Travels; University of North Carolina.

References: Graf, LeRoy P., Haskins, Ralph W., and Bergeron, Paul H., eds., *The Papers of Andrew Johnson* vols. 1, 12 (1967–2000); Trefousse, Hans L., *Andrew Johnson: A Biography* (1989).

Johnson, Martha
See Patterson, Martha Johnson

Johnson, Mary
See Stover (Brown), Mary Johnson

Johnson (Daughtry), Mary McDonough "Polly" (1782–1856)

Mary McDonough, born July 17, 1782, was the daughter of Andrew McDonough, a Revolutionary War veteran, and his first wife, whose name is unknown. Usually known as "Polly," their daughter was a weaver who also worked as a laundress at Casso's Tavern, an inn in Raleigh, North Carolina, and sometimes as a seamstress for a millinery shop. On September 9, 1801, she married Jacob Johnson, a handyman at the tavern, and the couple had three children: William P. (1804–1865), Elizabeth (1806–d. infancy), and Andrew (1808–1875).

On January 4, 1812, Jacob died from the effects of exposure received when he saved several fellow townsmen from drowning. A few months later, on May 6, the widow married Turner Daughtry, a propertyless resident of Raleigh, whose occupation is not known. Although Daughtry soon acquired a town lot, the couple remained poor. They had no children. They apprenticed Mary's sons to learn a trade, William to a printer at first, and then to a tailor, in which apprenticeship he was eventually joined by his brother Andrew.

Both boys left their apprenticeships early and the family moved to eastern Tennessee in 1826, all but William settling permanently in Greeneville. Andrew's tailoring business flourished and he was able to buy a farm for his mother and stepfather. In the early 1850s, sometime after the death of Turner Daughtry, Mary went to live with Andrew's family in their home on Greeneville's Main Street, and she remained with them until her death on February 13, 1856. She was originally buried in the Old Harmony Cemetery, Greeneville, but her remains were later moved to the family cemetery on Monument Hill.

See also: Apprenticeship; Daughtry, Turner; Johnson, Jacob; Johnson, William P.
References: Trefousse, Hans L., *Andrew Johnson: A Biography* (1989).

Johnson, Reverdy (1796–1876)

Noted lawyer, Maryland senator, and Andrew Johnson supporter, Reverdy Johnson was no relation to the president. The son of John and Deborah Ghieselen Johnson, Reverdy graduated from St. John's College at Annapolis (1811) and was admitted to the bar in 1815. In 1817 he began practicing law in Baltimore and remained active and prominent in the legal profession there for nearly sixty years. On November 16, 1819, he married Mary Mackall Bowie (ca. 1804–1873), whose grandfather had been a Maryland governor.

In the 1820s Johnson worked with Thomas Harris, clerk of the Maryland Court of Appeals, to compile the reports of the cases of that court (1800–1827). He was involved in a number of important cases over the years, probably the most notable of which was the case of the slave Dred Scott (1857) in which Johnson served as an attorney for Scott's owners and was credited with winning the case for them.

Johnson held a number of political offices. As a Whig, he served in the state senate (1821–1829), the U.S. Senate (1845–1849), and as U.S. attorney general (1849–1850) under President Zachary Taylor. Soon after Taylor's death, Johnson became a Democrat but he was never completely comfortable in the party. Although Johnson sympathized with the South and favored conciliation, participating in the peace convention in Washington, D.C., in 1861, he opposed secession. He was a member of the Maryland state house of representatives (1860–1861) and then became a U.S. senator again (1863–1868).

As a senator, Reverdy Johnson was an important supporter of President Andrew Johnson. He first offered his support in a note of April 24, 1865, shortly after Andrew Johnson succeeded to the presidency. Over the course of Johnson's presidential term, Reverdy Johnson, who had nearly illegible handwriting, made many patronage suggestions, to some of which the president agreed. Other people, writing Johnson on patronage matters, often gave Reverdy Johnson's name as a reference. In August 1866 Reverdy Johnson attended the National Union Party Convention in Philadelphia and was the chairman of the committee that brought a copy of the proceedings to Andrew Johnson. As a member of the Senate who supported Andrew Johnson, Reverdy Johnson was particularly important to the president during the impeachment trial, by giving legal and other advice, by negotiating with some of the other senators, and by voting that Andrew Johnson was not guilty of the charges considered.

Shortly after the impeachment, the president nominated Reverdy Johnson to be U.S. minister to Great Britain. He was confirmed by the Senate in June 1868. When Reverdy Johnson left for Europe the following month, he had several important matters to negotiate with the British: the naturalization of British subjects who moved to the United States (a long-standing problem); the jurisdiction over the San Juan Islands in Puget Sound off Washington Territory and British Columbia; and the settlement of the *Alabama* Claims for damages done to U.S. shipping by British-built Confederate vessels during the Civil War. Many Americans were angry with Reverdy Johnson because they believed that he was too easy on the British. Although Johnson negotiated agreements on all the issues, Secretary of State William H. Seward insisted on treaty revisions. Even then, the Senate did not ratify any of the agreements, mainly because they were negotiated by an Andrew Johnson supporter. However, later treaties, based on these, were eventually passed.

After Ulysses S. Grant assumed the presidency, Reverdy Johnson resumed his law practice in Baltimore. When Andrew Johnson was reelected to the Senate in 1875, Reverdy Johnson accompanied his friend to the swearing-in ceremony. Reverdy Johnson died February 10, 1876, from injuries sustained in an accidental fall.

See also: *Alabama* Claims; Foreign Affairs; Grant, Ulysses Simpson; Impeachment; National Union Convention and Party; Patronage; Senator, Johnson as; Seward, William Henry.

References: Graf, LeRoy P., Haskins, Ralph W., and Bergeron, Paul H., eds., *The Papers of Andrew Johnson* vols. 5, 7–8, 10–11, 13–15 (1967–2000); Trefousse, Hans L., *Andrew Johnson: A Biography* (1989).

Johnson, Robert (1834–1869)

Robert Johnson, the second son and fourth child of Andrew and Eliza Johnson, was born in Greeneville, Tennessee, on February 22, 1834. He was the "baby" of the family until the birth of his brother Frank (Andrew Jr.) eighteen years later. Little is known about Robert's education. In late 1850 or early 1851 he went to Franklin College in Nashville but he came right home, making various excuses. At some point he worked as a clerk in Pleasant M. Craigmiles's store, read law with Robert McFarland, and was licensed to practice the legal profession in February 1856. While Andrew Johnson was governor of Tennessee, Robert clerked for him at times and also, working with his older brother Charles, managed many of Andrew Johnson's business affairs, such as buying property.

Not surprisingly, Robert Johnson got involved in politics and was elected to represent four counties in the Tennessee state legislature for the 1859–1861 session. He attended the Democratic presidential nominating conventions in 1856 and 1860, convinced that the 1860 convention in Charleston would nominate his father, which it did not. In Charleston, he found himself responsible for his brother Charles who went on a drinking spree for most of the convention.

During the secession winter of 1860–1861, Robert Johnson was a Unionist and spoke in opposition to calling a secession convention. Once Tennessee seceded, he, fearing arrest, fled. Robert Carter, a Greeneville farmer, hid him for four months and he also stayed with one or more of the guerrilla groups in the mountains until he was finally able to escape to Kentucky in February 1862. By March, Colonel Robert Johnson was raising a regiment, the 4th Tennessee Infantry (U.S.A.), composed mainly of other East Tennessee refugees like himself. His muster record lists him as five feet six inches tall, with "florid" complexion, dark eyes, and brown hair. During the summer the regiment was changed from infantry into the 1st Tennessee Cavalry (U.S.A.), but Johnson was rarely in command of his regiment and was never in a battle because he was usually absent on recruiting service or some other task.

In April 1863 Robert Johnson was the only family member in Nashville and thus the only one to attend the funeral of his brother Charles, who had died of a fall from his horse. Whether Robert had been drinking before his brother's death is not known, but he certainly did afterward and it cost him the command of a brigade of cavalry. General William S. Rosecrans even specifically told Robert to stop drinking. But Robert's promise to Rosecrans was one of many similar vows that he made and broke. Sometime during the war he seems to have gone from being a legislator and person responsible for his father's business affairs to an alcoholic who was apparently never able to please his father and was quite a family problem. The reason for this change is not known, although it is possible that poor health may have been a factor. As early as 1856 Robert suffered hemorrhaging from the lungs, probably a symptom of tuberculosis. Alcohol was used as a remedy for many afflictions during this period and medicinal use of alcohol may have caused or contributed to Robert's problem. In any case, he resigned his cavalry post in May 1864 and became a secretary for his father, who was military governor of Tennessee.

When Andrew Johnson became vice president, Robert Johnson stayed behind in Nashville, packing up his father's books and papers. At the time that Lincoln was assassinated, Robert was too drunk to realize what had happened or that his father was now president. Andrew Johnson wanted all of his family members to join him in Washington, D.C., as soon as possible. His son, however, despite his father's wishes, lingered in Nashville and Greeneville with the papers and did not get to Washington until August 1865.

From November 1865 to April 1866 and from September 1866 to at least May 1867, Robert served as one of his father's secretaries. But he never seemed to be far enough from the bottle. Secretary of the Navy Gideon Welles arranged for him to go on a trip with the USS *Chattanooga* in the summer or fall of 1866 with a minor diplomatic task, to investigate the "slave coolie trade." Robert did not go, however, in part because it took so long to repair and outfit the ship that its departure date kept being delayed for several months. From July to October 1868 he was confined in a Washington, D.C., asylum to cure his alcohol habit. He was given a good deal of freedom and spent time with various young women friends who came to visit. But he was definitely in the bad graces of his father, and his only family visitors were his sister Martha Patterson and her daughter Belle. As soon as he was released from the asylum, he began drinking again. He was forcibly returned to the asylum several times, all of which is painfully detailed in a diary that he kept.

Although Robert Johnson seems to have been an attractive and personable man when sober, he never married. He seems to have seriously considered the possibility in 1860 but without success. Nevertheless, he was extremely interested in attractive women in almost an adolescent way, always on the lookout for them, even when he attended chapel at the asylum, as is evident from his diary entries. He seems, also from the diary entries, to have been quite well-read, but very frustrated because of his inability to control his drinking or to please his father.

At the conclusion of his father's presidency, Robert went home to Greeneville with the family. On April 22, 1869, he apparently took an overdose of laudanum and died in his sleep. Andrew Johnson was on a campaign tour, stopping in Athens, Alabama, when he received a telegram with the news of his son's demise. He hurried back to Greeneville to be present for Robert's burial with Masonic honors on April 24. It is not known in which Greeneville cemetery he was initially interred, but sometime after the death of his father his remains were moved to Monument Hill.

See also: Drunkenness; Grandchildren; Greeneville, Tennessee; Johnson, Charles; Military Governor of Tennessee, Johnson as; Patterson, Martha Johnson; Secretaries; Tuberculosis; Welles, Gideon.

References: Andrew Johnson Project, Knoxville, TN: Robert Johnson file and diary; Compiled Service Records, RG 94, National Archives, Robert Johnson file; Graf, LeRoy P., Haskins, Ralph W., and Bergeron, Paul H., eds., *The Papers of Andrew Johnson* vols. 1–3, 5–8, 15 (1967–2000); Holloway, Laura Carter, *The Ladies of the White House* (1870); Trefousse, Hans L., *Andrew Johnson: A Biography* (1989).

Johnson, William P. (1804–1865)

The son of Jacob and Mary McDonough Johnson, William P. Johnson, the only surviving sibling of Andrew Johnson, was born in Raleigh, North Carolina, on October 10, 1804. No one knows what his middle name was. Sometime not long after the death of his father in January 1812, William was apprenticed to Colonel Thomas Henderson, editor of the *Raleigh Star* and one of the men whose life Jacob Johnson had saved. When Henderson moved several years later, William was apprenticed to a Raleigh tailor, James J. Selby. Eventually William's brother Andrew joined him as an apprentice to Selby.

The two boys looked different physically, William having light hair, a fair complexion, and freckles, whereas his brother had black hair and a darker skin tone. These details appear in a June 1824 newspaper advertisement soliciting the return of the two boys who had run away from their apprenticeship after playing a prank on a neighbor. The runaways went first to Carthage, North Carolina, for a few months and then to Laurens, South Carolina, where they probably worked as tailors for a year or more before briefly returning to Raleigh.

William Johnson moved to Tennessee in 1826, at approximately the same time as his brother, mother, and stepfather, but whether he actually went with them or moved there first has been a matter of some debate. Although he was apprenticed as a printer and a tailor, he practiced the trade of carpenter as an adult, but it is not known where he learned these skills. In 1828 he made a tailoring table for Andrew.

On February 23, 1832, William Johnson married Sarah Giddings McDonough (1816–1882), who apparently was his first cousin. The couple ultimately had eleven children: Jane (1832–1855), Laura (1833–1834), Jacob (1835–1835), Andrew Jr. (1836–1897), James V. (1838–1919), Devolco (1840–1854), Elizabeth (1842–1905), Olive (1845–1864), Nathan (1847–1929), Albert (1852–1866), and William (1857–1933). Unlike his brother, William Johnson did not remain in Tennessee. He apparently never owned property nor was able to do much more than scrape by financially, living in Georgia and Alabama in the 1840s and 1850s before finally settling in Columbia, Texas, about 1857.

During the Civil War, William was a Unionist and apparently did not participate on either side. In June–July 1865 he visited his brother at the White House for three weeks and received a political appointment—as surveyor of the port of Velasco, Texas, at the mouth of the Brazos River—a rather insignificant post, but one that would support his family.

In early October 1865, William Johnson accidentally shot himself in the arm while hunting. Medical attention was unavailable for several days and the arm finally had to be amputated. Gangrene set in, however, and he died on October 24, 1865, leaving his family impoverished.

See also: Apprenticeship; Johnson, Jacob; Johnson (Daughtry), Mary McDonough "Polly"; Nephews.

References: Graf, LeRoy P., Haskins, Ralph W., and Bergeron, Paul H., eds., *The Papers of Andrew*

Johnson vols. 1, 3–4, 6, 8–9 (1967–2000); Muir, Andrew Forest, "William P. Johnson, Southern Proletarian and Unionist," *Tennessee Historical Quarterly* 15 (Dec. 1956): 330–338; Trefousse, Hans L., *Andrew Johnson: A Biography* (1989).

Joint Committee on Reconstruction

The Joint Committee on Reconstruction (also known as the Committee of Fifteen or the Joint Committee of Fifteen on Reconstruction) was established by Congress in December 1865 to develop a Congressional Reconstruction plan because most Republicans did not like the provisions already instituted by President Andrew Johnson.

The committee consisted of six senators and nine members of the House of Representatives. Republican senator William P. Fessenden of Maine was the chairman of the entire committee. The other senators were: James W. Grimes (Republican, Iowa), Ira Harris (Republican, New York), Jacob M. Howard (Republican, Michigan), George H. Williams (Republican, Oregon), and Reverdy Johnson (Democrat, Maryland). The nine representatives were chaired by Thaddeus Stevens (Republican, Pennsylvania), who has sometimes been mistakenly called the chairman of the whole committee. The other representatives were: Elihu B. Washburne (Republican, Illinois), Justin S. Morrill (Republican, Vermont), John A. Bingham (Republican, Ohio), Roscoe Conkling (Republican, New York), George S. Boutwell (Republican, Massachusetts), Henry T. Blow (Republican, Missouri), Andrew J. Rogers (Democrat, New Jersey), and Henry Grider (Democrat, Kentucky). For the second session of the Thirty-Ninth Congress, beginning in December 1866, Washburne asked to be excused from the committee and was replaced by John F. Farnsworth (Republican, Illinois). Henry Grider died on September 7, 1866, and was replaced by Elijah Hise (Democrat, Kentucky).

The committee was controversial from the beginning. Andrew Johnson and other opponents saw it as a "conspiracy" and a secret group trying to force its plans on Congress and to dictate administration policies.

Although the committee was established and selected in December 1865, it did not meet until January 6, 1866. Its most important task was to prepare a proposal for a constitutional amendment that would deal with citizenship issues and several other concerns. To get more evidence about postwar conditions in the South, the committee subdivided into four groups of three to take testimony about these conditions (Fessenden, Reverdy Johnson, and Stevens did not serve on a subcommittee). From January 17 to May 19, 1866 (but mostly in February), the subcommittee members interviewed 136 men and one woman (Clara Barton), most of whom were already in the Washington, D.C., area. They also received some written testimony. Those testifying included Southern-born or resident Unionists, Northern travelers, U.S. Army and Freedmen's Bureau personnel, and a limited number of former Confederates and Virginia blacks. More people testified about Virginia than about any other state, but each seceded state was discussed by at least three persons. The intention of the committee was not to get a balanced view of the South, but to show the way that Johnson's Reconstruction policy had failed and thus demonstrate a need for a new policy by Congress.

The committee used the information to back its amendment proposal, which it delivered to Congress on April 30. After much discussion and adjustment, both houses passed the Fourteenth Amendment by June 13, 1866. The committee also issued a report of the testimony collected, and a number of Republican candidates used it to good advantage in the election of 1866.

The committee expired on March 3, 1867, with the end of the Thirty-Ninth Congress. Thanks to the election of Republican majorities in both houses in the fall of 1866 and the passage of the First Military Reconstruction Act just before the session ended, Reconstruction was now in congressional hands and the committee was no longer needed.

See also: Bingham, John Armor; Congressional Reconstruction; Election of 1866; Fourteenth Amendment; Johnson, Reverdy; Military Reconstruction Acts; Presidential Reconstruction; Republican Party; Stevens, Thaddeus.
References: Clark, John G., "Historians and the Joint Committee on Reconstruction," *Historian* 23 (May 1961): 348–361; Kendrick, Benjamin B., *The Journal of the Joint Committee of Fifteen on Reconstruction* (1914); Lowe, Richard, "The Joint Committee on Reconstruction: Some Clarifications," *Southern Studies* 3 (Spring 1992): 55–65.

Joint Select Committee on the Conduct of the War

Senator Andrew Johnson was one of the original seven members of Congress's Joint Select Committee on the Conduct of the War. The Union war effort was going very badly in 1861. Northern troops had suffered several defeats. In addition, generals were moving very slowly against the enemy and President Abraham Lincoln was not taking the actions espoused by Radical Republicans. In fact, the president had even retracted General John C. Frémont's proclamation freeing the slaves of Confederates in Missouri. Believing that the situation required closer congressional oversight, Congress established a somewhat bipartisan committee in December 1861. The three senators on the committee included, in addition to the Tennessee Democrat Johnson, two Radical Republicans, Zachariah Chandler of Michigan and Benjamin F. Wade of Ohio, who was also chairman of the committee. The four members from the House of Representatives were Republicans

George W. Julian of Indiana, John Covode of Pennsylvania, and Daniel W. Gooch of Massachusetts, and Democrat Moses F. Odell of New York.

Johnson was probably chosen because he was an outspoken War Democrat, who frequently denounced secession, most notably in his Senate speech of December 1860. In addition, Johnson had worked with Wade before in an attempt to get a homestead bill passed. Johnson proved to be a very active committee member during his few months of service. He was, in fact, glad to serve on the committee because he hoped to use the committee to prod the government to send troops to drive the Confederates out of his home area of East Tennessee, a hope that went unrealized.

None of the committee members, Johnson included, had any military background. Consequently, the members' ignorance led them to unrealistic expectations of what generals could and should do. They did not understand the effect of new rifled weapons and minié balls in frontal assaults, the importance of entrenchment, or that the war simply could not be won in a single battle. These attitudes were typical of Northern civilians, but committee members might have been expected to become better informed over time. This did not happen, however, and the committee even discriminated against West Point–educated professional soldiers.

These attitudes affected what cases the committee chose to investigate. The committee did expose corruption and inefficiency, as in the matter of ice contracts for the medical department. They also investigated crimes against humanity, calling attention to the massacre of black soldiers at Fort Pillow and the massacre of Indians at Sand Creek, Colorado Territory. However, most of the committee's efforts went into trying to affix blame for various Union debacles such as First Bull Run and Ball's Bluff. This usually meant prosecution of professional generals who, for partisan reasons, the committee assumed to be disloyal because they moved cautiously, favored conciliation of Southern civilians rather than confiscation of their property, and were members of the Democratic Party. One of their most important targets was General George B. McClellan. The committee also tried to get important military appointments for their Republican allies who favored emancipation but were not particularly competent generals, such as John C. Frémont, Joseph Hooker, and Benjamin F. Butler. These maneuvers by the committee contributed to distrust between civilian and military leaders and to factions in the military, which were counterproductive to the war effort. The committee was constantly trying to get Lincoln to make the changes they wished, but were successful only when Lincoln had some reason of his own for doing so.

During Johnson's tenure on the committee, it investigated the role of General Robert Patterson in the Union defeat at First Bull Run. Although Patterson certainly contributed to the loss, he was by no means solely to blame, as the Radicals tried to prove. Johnson also participated in the attack on McClellan, whom Johnson did not like because the general was friendly with the Peace Democrats (Johnson was a member of the War faction) and seemed to be a possible Democratic rival for the presidential nomination in 1864. Johnson served with Benjamin Wade as a member of a subcommittee that met with Secretary of War Edwin M. Stanton and McClellan to try to get the blockade of Washington, D.C., removed from the mouth of the Potomac River.

In early March 1862 Johnson was appointed military governor of Tennessee and therefore he resigned from the committee on March 12. He was replaced by Joseph Wright of Indiana, who was later succeeded by Benjamin F. Harding of Oregon, and finally by Charles R. Buckalew of Pennsylvania (all Democrats). But Johnson still retained an interest in the committee's doings.

In fact, he was in Washington, D.C., during March 1863 and, although no longer a member, he helped to prepare the committee's very negative report on McClellan.

After Lincoln's assassination in April 1865, the Radical Republicans on the committee were pleased to have their former colleague installed in the White House. Wade, Julian, and Chandler rushed to see Johnson with the intention of becoming his political advisors and forestalling the influence of the conservative members of his cabinet. They were gratified by Johnson's tough rhetoric at their initial meeting, when he proclaimed that "treason must be made infamous and traitors must be impoverished." But it soon became clear that Johnson was not a Radical. He proved far more conciliatory toward the South than Lincoln was, uninterested in black civil rights, and an extremely strict constructionist of the Constitution. He also insisted that the president, not Congress, should be in charge of Reconstruction. As a result, Benjamin Wade, Zachariah Chandler, and George Julian became some of Johnson's most determined foes during his presidency. The Committee on the Conduct of the War adjourned on May 22, 1865. In December 1865, Republicans disgruntled with Johnson's presidential program of Reconstruction, followed the precedent that they had set with the wartime committee and established the Joint Committee on Reconstruction.

See also: Butler, Benjamin Franklin; Constitution, Johnson's Attitude toward; Democratic Party; Joint Committee on Reconstruction; Lincoln, Abraham; Military Governor of Tennessee, Johnson as; Republican Party; Secession, Johnson's Attitude toward; Senator, Johnson as; Wade, Benjamin Franklin.

References: Tap, Bruce, *Over Lincoln's Shoulder: The Committee on the Conduct of the War* (1998); Williams, T. Harry, "Andrew Johnson as a Member of the Committee on the Conduct of the War," *East Tennessee Historical Society Publications* 12 (1940): 70–83.

L

Lincoln, Abraham (1809–1865)

Abraham Lincoln, whom Andrew Johnson succeeded as president, was born in Hardin County, Kentucky, and moved with his family to Indiana in 1816 and then to Illinois in 1830. His mother, Nancy Hanks Lincoln, died when her son was only nine, and young Lincoln was much influenced by his stepmother, Sarah Bush Johnston Lincoln. At best, Lincoln had a few scattered months of formal schooling and was mostly self-educated. After leaving his father's farm, Lincoln worked as a surveyor, storekeeper, and postmaster of New Salem, Illinois (1833–1836), while reading law. He was admitted to the bar in 1836.

In April–June 1832 Lincoln served as a captain and private with volunteer troops in the Black Hawk War. He was elected to four terms in the Illinois state house of representatives (1834, 1836, 1838, 1840) and one term in the U.S. House of Representatives (1847–1849). He campaigned unsuccessfully for the U.S. Senate as a Whig in 1855 and a Republican in 1858.

He moved his law practice in 1837 to Springfield, Illinois. There he met Mary Todd of Kentucky, who was living with her relatives Ninian and Elizabeth Todd Edwards. After a tempestuous courtship Abraham Lincoln and Mary Todd were married in November 1842. They had four sons, but only the oldest, Robert Todd Lincoln, survived to adulthood.

In 1860 Abraham Lincoln was the first Republican to be elected president of the United States. From the Southern perspective, his election was unacceptable after a decade of increasing tensions that focused on issues relating to the expansion of slavery in the territories, as well as other matters that divided the North and the South. As a result of the election, eleven Southern states withdrew from the Union and formed the Confederate States of America. Not surprisingly, the whole country was soon involved in a bloody civil war.

Andrew Johnson refused to resign his seat in the U.S. Senate when his state, Tennessee, seceded. He was perceived as a hero by Unionists and Republicans, even though he was a Democrat. Lincoln and Johnson had met in 1847 when both were members of Congress. After substantial amounts of Tennessee came under Union control in early 1862, Lincoln selected Johnson for the difficult position of military governor of the state. The two communicated frequently through personal representatives, such as Horace Maynard, who went to Washington, D.C., in April 1862 and met with Lincoln about Johnson's concerns.

Lincoln and Johnson also exchanged a good many direct missives, as well as communicating through Secretary of War Edwin M. Stanton since many of Johnson's concerns pertained to the military situation in Tennessee.

During the National Union Party (Republican) Convention in Baltimore, Maryland, in June 1864, Lincoln was renominated for president. There was a move to replace the current vice president, Hannibal Hamlin, with a candidate who would appeal to the War Democrats associated with the party. Andrew Johnson was the ideal candidate. Although Lincoln was favorable to Johnson as a running mate, he probably did not maneuver to have Johnson nominated, recent studies have shown.

These two candidates were elected in November 1864 and inaugurated on March 4, 1865. Although Johnson embarrassed Lincoln severely with his inebriated speech at the inauguration, Lincoln defended his vice president, protesting that, although Johnson had made a bad mistake, he was not a drunkard. Nevertheless, Lincoln and Johnson had no contact besides letters until a meeting on April 14, 1865, the day Lincoln was assassinated, precipitating Johnson into the presidency. Although Johnson would claim to be following Lincoln's plans for Reconstruction, he had no more than the general knowledge available to the public about what the plans actually were. Because Lincoln and Johnson were so different in personality, attitudes, and flexibility, Reconstruction under Johnson was doubtless very different than it would have been under Lincoln.

See also: Congressman, Johnson as; Drunkenness; Election of 1864; Hamlin, Hannibal; Lincoln, Mary (Ann) Todd; Lincoln Assassination Conspirators; Maynard, Horace; Military Governor of Tennessee, Johnson as; National Union Party; Presidential Reconstruction; Reconstruction; Republican Party; Secession, Johnson's Attitude toward; Senator, Johnson as; Stanton, Edwin McMasters; Vice President, Johnson as; Whig Party.

References: Donald, David Herbert, *Lincoln* (1995); Fehrenbacher, Don E., "The Making of a Myth: Lincoln and the Vice-Presidential Nomination in 1864," *Civil War History* 41 (Dec. 1995): 273–290; Graf, LeRoy P., Haskins, Ralph W., and Bergeron, Paul H., eds., *The Papers of Andrew Johnson* vols. 5–7 (1967–2000); Hunt, H. Draper, *Hannibal Hamlin of Maine: Lincoln's First Vice-President* (1969); Waugh, John C., *Reelecting Lincoln: The Battle for the 1864 Presidency* (1997).

Lincoln Assassination Conspirators

Throughout his presidency Abraham Lincoln received numerous anonymous threats against his life. After he was assassinated in Ford's Theatre on April 14, 1865, the priority of the federal government was to find out who had done this deed. Many suspects were arrested and imprisoned for varying lengths of time, including John T. Ford, the owner of the theater. The new president, Andrew Johnson, issued a proclamation offering rewards for the arrest of several high-level Confederate officials. But soon attention began to focus on a particular group of suspects.

These conspirators, led by the actor John Wilkes Booth (1838–1865), had been planning for at least six months to kidnap Lincoln and hold him captive as a hostage for Southern prisoners of war. The band of conspirators included George A. Atzerodt (1835–1865), a Maryland carriage painter and ferry operator for Confederate couriers; David Edgar Herold (1842–1865), a Washington, D.C., pharmacist's assistant; Lewis Paine (or Payne, also known as Louis Thornton Powell) (1844–1865), son of a Baptist minister and a former Confederate soldier; Samuel Arnold (1834–1906), a former schoolmate of Booth's who had been a Confederate soldier and farm hand; John Harrison Surratt (1844–1916), a Confederate courier and long-time friend of Booth; and Michael O'Laughlin (ca. 1837–1867), a feed-store clerk and former neighbor of Booth.

Booth and his associates made several unsuccessful kidnap attempts while Lincoln was riding around Washington unescorted. After an attack on Lincoln's carriage, which turned out to be occupied by someone else, O'Laughlin, Arnold, and Surratt dropped out of the conspiracy. With the fall of Richmond and the defeat of Robert E. Lee and his army in early April 1865, the conspirators, having now no place to take Lincoln if they kidnapped him, settled on assassination in desperation as a last way to help or avenge the South. According to his diary, Booth developed his plan on the afternoon of April 14, 1865. He would shoot Lincoln while the president watched a play at Ford's Theatre. Meanwhile Atzerodt was to kill vice president Andrew Johnson and Paine was to slay Secretary of State William H. Seward, thus causing chaos at the highest levels of government. Booth succeeded in his attempt and Paine managed to seriously wound Seward, his son, and a nurse, but Atzerodt lost his nerve and fled Washington, D.C.

Atzerodt, Paine, Arnold, and O'Laughlin were quickly captured, along with Edmund (also called Edman or Edward) Spangler (1825–1875), a carpenter at Ford's Theatre who was suspected of aiding Booth there; Mary E. Surratt (1823–1865), mother of John Surratt and owner of a Washington, D.C., boardinghouse where the conspirators had met; and Samuel A. Mudd (1833–1883), a Maryland physician who had set the leg that Booth had broken by jumping to the theater stage after he shot Lincoln. On April 26 Booth and Herold were cornered in a Virginia tobacco barn, where Booth was shot and Herold captured.

The conspirators were promptly tried by a military commission (May 9–June 30, 1865). Many correspondents warned Johnson that the accused should have a civil trial and there were numerous arguments for or against a military trial. Generally, the military trial was justified because Lincoln was the commander-in-chief and his death came as a result of the war, which was just

ending. The mood of the country favored a quick trial and the speedy execution of anyone implicated in the president's death. Recent historians have suggested that the outcome of the trial by military commission was probably the same as it would have been in a civil trial. Although there was little doubt about the guilt of such conspirators as Paine, the evidence against some of the others consisted of circumstantial and even perjured testimony. Spangler, who was certainly acquainted with Booth, was probably merely in the wrong place at the wrong time. Mudd, as a doctor should, had treated an injured man who came to his door, a man who was doing his best to hide his identity, even if Mudd was acquainted with him previously.

The military tribunal found all eight conspirators guilty to some degree and sentenced Herold, Paine, Atzerodt, and Mary Surratt to be hanged on July 7, a week after the end of the trial. The other four, Arnold, O'Laughlin, Spangler, and Mudd, found guilty of lesser crimes, were sentenced to lengthy or life imprisonment at hard labor at Fort Jefferson in the Dry Tortugas, islands near Key West, Florida. While handing down the sentences, five members of the military court urged clemency for Mary Surratt. Most people at the time believed that she was guilty of aiding the conspiracy, but many of them were opposed to the execution of a woman. The court addressed the clemency request to Johnson as the only official who could lessen the sentence to life imprisonment, but he later claimed that he had never seen it and thus allowed her execution to be carried out. Judge Advocate General Joseph Holt, the government's prosecuting attorney, claimed that he had shown the paper to Johnson. This dispute has never been resolved. Some people, especially by the time of Johnson's impeachment crisis, accused Johnson of the murder of Mary Surratt, and the issue surfaced again in 1873 when Holt published a letter in his own defense.

John Surratt, who was probably not in Washington at the time of the assassination, managed to flee the country and was located in 1866 in Italy, where he was serving in the troops guarding the Pope. Returned to the United States, he was tried by a civil court in the spring of 1867, a period of much calmer emotions than 1865, and after two juries failed to agree on his guilt, he was released.

As members of the House of Representatives's Judiciary Committee attempted to find charges on which to impeach Johnson in 1867, they sought to connect him with Lincoln's assassination. There were various reports of attempts by committee agents to solicit perjured testimony from John Surratt and others, and at least one perjurer, Charles Dunham (also known as Sanford Conover), spent time in prison. There is no evidence of Johnson's complicity in the conspiracy.

Soon after the trial and imprisonment of the remaining conspirators, Johnson began to receive requests for their pardon, especially the pardon of Samuel Mudd, who was depicted as a doctor merely doing his duty. In addition, some urged his freedom based on his selfless service during a yellow fever epidemic in 1867 after the post surgeon died of the fever. Johnson did not, however, pardon Mudd, Spangler, and Arnold until February 1869, just before he left office. (O'Laughlin had died during the yellow fever epidemic in 1867.) At the same time, Johnson also granted permission for the families of Booth, Mary Surratt, Herold, and Atzerodt to remove the bodies of their deceased relatives from their initial burial place at the Washington Arsenal to burial grounds of the families's choosing. (Apparently no one claimed Paine's body.)

The question of more widespread Confederate involvement in the plot, particularly by secret agents in Canada and high government officials such as Jefferson Davis, has been much debated ever since 1865. Most historians have concluded that

Davis was not involved, but there may well have been some financial assistance from Canadian operatives. In the 1980s and 1990s William Tidwell, a former agent for the Central Intelligence Agency, has developed some controversial theories about the role of the Confederate secret service in the plot to kidnap Lincoln.

See also: Bingham, John Armor; Ewing, Thomas, Jr.; Holt, Joseph; Lincoln, Abraham; Mudd, Samuel Alexander; Pardons (Individual); Surratt, Mary (Elizabeth) Eugenia Jenkins.

References: Carter, Samuel, III, *The Riddle of Dr. Mudd* (1974); Graf, LeRoy P., Haskins, Ralph W., and Bergeron, Paul H., eds., *The Papers of Andrew Johnson* vols. 8–16 (1967–2000); Hanchett, William, *The Lincoln Murder Conspiracies* (1983); Kunhardt, Dorothy Meserve, and Kunhardt, Philip B., Jr., *Twenty Days* (1965); Miscellaneous publications of the Surratt Society, Surratt House Museum, Clinton, MD; Tidwell, William A., *April '65: Confederate Covert Action and the American Civil War* (1995); Tidwell, William A., Hall, James O., and Gaddy, David Winfred, *Come Retribution: The Confederate Secret Service and the Assassination of Lincoln* (1988); Turner, Thomas Reed, *Beware the People Weeping: Public Opinion and the Assassination of Abraham Lincoln* (1982).

Lincoln, Mary (Ann) Todd (1818–1882)

Mary Ann Todd Lincoln, wife of Abraham Lincoln, Andrew Johnson's predecessor as president, had little use for Johnson and delayed his occupation of the White House in 1865. Born in Lexington, Kentucky, Mary Ann Todd was the third child and third daughter of Robert Smith Todd, a wealthy businessman and politician, and Eliza Parker, Todd's first wife. Eliza died of puerperal fever, a childbirth-related infection, when Mary was six and a half years old. As a middle child of six surviving children, Mary got little positive attention and seems to have been a particular target of her stepmother Betsey Humphreys Todd, who had nine more Todd children. Mary even lost her middle name when a younger sister was named Ann.

Mary's father believed that girls should have a good education and Mary had nine years at Lexington academies, which was about twice as long as educated girls usually received. Mary spent three or four years at a boarding school in town to keep her away from her stepmother, who was intensely disliked by all six of her stepchildren.

In 1839 Mary went to Springfield, Illinois, to live with her oldest sister, Elizabeth Todd Edwards, and her husband Ninian. She soon became acquainted with Abraham Lincoln, a rising lawyer who had none of her social skills or wealthy, educated background. They shared an interest in politics and developed a deep love for one another, despite Elizabeth Edwards's attempts to discourage the match. Their engagement was broken by a quarrel on January 1, 1841, and they remained estranged until 1842. A reconciliation arranged by a mutual friend led to their marriage on November 4, 1842.

The Lincolns had four sons: Robert Todd (1843–1926), the only one who survived to adulthood; Edward Baker (1846–1850), who died of tuberculosis; William Wallace (1850–1862), who died of typhoid fever while Lincoln was president; and Thomas "Tad" (1853–1871), who died of pleurisy, a lung disease. Lincoln spent as much as a third of the year away from Springfield on legal business, leaving Mary to raise the children and manage the household.

When Lincoln became president, Mary believed that she should have a wardrobe suitable for a first lady and that the White House should be elegantly redecorated. In carrying out both plans she caused controversy. The White House was much in need of refurbishing, but her expensive tastes caused her to exceed the budget. Some also questioned the appropriateness of such extravagance during wartime. Mary Lincoln was more active in the public eye than any previous first lady and this also caused controversy and media criticism. Few noted such positive things as her visits to hospitalized soldiers or that she ran the president's household efficiently on a budget little larger than she had had in Springfield.

Mary Lincoln was in the diplomatic gallery for her husband's second inauguration and witnessed Andrew Johnson's vice presidential inauguration fiasco. She was disgusted with Johnson because he had embarrassed her husband.

After Lincoln was assassinated, Mary was inconsolable and remained in bed at the White House for weeks, unable to cope with any noise, and did not leave until May 22, when she went to Chicago. Meanwhile, Johnson had his office at the Treasury Department and lived at the home of Massachusetts congressman Samuel Hooper, who resided at the corner of H and 15th Streets. Johnson moved his office to the White House in late May, but did not live there until June. When his family arrived, they spent the summer at the Soldiers Home outside Washington, which the Lincolns had also used as a summer residence.

Mary Lincoln complained that Johnson's behavior toward her was "brutal" because he did not call on her nor send her a letter of condolence, although he did forward resolutions of sympathy from Congress in January 1866. He also did not buy the Lincoln carriages, although Robert Lincoln offered them at his mother's request. Mary believed that Johnson had conspired with John Wilkes Booth to assassinate Lincoln and made this accusation directly to Secretary of War Edwin M. Stanton.

In the fall of 1866 when Andrew Johnson came to Chicago to dedicate the Stephen A. Douglas monument, the excuse for Johnson's Swing-around-the-Circle tour, Mary Lincoln left Chicago to avoid him. When the president went on to Springfield to visit Lincoln's tomb, Mary was offended by his "vanity and presumption" in doing so.

Mary always remained a sufferer and dressed in mourning. She lived in Europe for several years and for a time in 1875 was confined in an insane asylum in Illinois at the instigation of her son Robert. Evidence makes it clear that Mary was not insane. However, she could be quite eccentric, and historian Jean Baker makes a good case for the idea that Mary had the personality disorder of narcissism. She spent her later years estranged from Robert and in poor health with near-blinding cataracts, spinal difficulties, and kidney problems. She died from a stroke on July 16, 1882.

See also: Drunkenness; Lincoln, Abraham; Lincoln Assassination Conspirators; Swing-around-the-Circle; Vice President, Johnson as.

References: Baker, Jean H., *Mary Todd Lincoln: A Biography* (1987); Graf, LeRoy P., Haskins, Ralph W., and Bergeron, Paul H., eds., *The Papers of Andrew Johnson* vols. 7–8 (1967–2000); Trefousse, Hans L., *Andrew Johnson: A Biography* (1989).

Masonic Order

The Free and Accepted Masons, also called the Masonic Order or Freemasonry, is the largest secret society in the world. It possesses no central authority, but is divided among national units and further subdivided into regional ones, called lodges. The organization itself is based in custom and tradition, with elaborate rites and rituals that allegedly originated with the stonemasons and cathedral builders of medieval Europe.

Central to the order is the complex system of degrees, which create an internal hierarchy. Each local lodge confers three degrees, corresponding to the medieval guild classifications of apprentice (First Degree), journeyman (Second Degree), and master (Third Degree, or Master Mason). From here the order splits into two rites (or branches), called the Scottish Rite and the York (or Royal Arch) Rite. The Scottish Rite has thirty degrees above the Master level, whereas the York Rite has ten higher degrees. The highest York degree is the Order of the Knights Templar, which is equivalent to the thirty-third degree of the Scottish Rite. Associated with the Masons are the Ancient Egyptian Arabic Order of the Nobles of the Mystic Shrine, more commonly called the Shriners (who are ordinarily thirty-second level Masons).

Freemasonry also has chapters for boys (De Molay) and female relatives (the Order of the Eastern Star), as well as several girls' organizations (such as Job's Daughters).

The true origins of Freemasonry remain a mystery. Earliest evidence places the organization in England in the fourteenth century, although some Masonic historians claim that the group can be traced back to ancient times. The first lodge in the American colonies appeared in 1730, and many leading figures of the republic were Masons, including George Washington, Benjamin Franklin, and Paul Revere. Considering the Mason's principles, this seems appropriate: Freemasonry advocated liberal ideas of the most classical sort, such as religious toleration, loyalty to local government, and political moderation.

This connection to liberal ideas damaged Freemasonry's image in the conservative environment of nineteenth century Europe. At the same time, Masons came under attack in the United States; their secretive nature seemed the antithesis of U.S. democracy and, although they professed Christian values, they opposed the formal structures of organized churches. Yet despite the rise of an Anti-Masonic Party in the 1830s, largely in the Northern states, Masons continued to flourish; James Monroe, Andrew Jackson, and James K. Polk were all Masons. So too was Andrew Johnson, although some of the details of his membership are in dispute because the records of his lodge were destroyed during the Civil War. At least two sources claim that Johnson entered the Masonic Order in 1851 through Greeneville Lodge No. 119, the same lodge as Andrew Jackson. Evidently Johnson followed both rites (which was rather uncommon); he was initiated into the Scottish Rite, but held York degrees as well.

Johnson's Masonic membership was no secret, and as president he demonstrated a public support for the order. For instance, on November 20, 1866, he declared a holiday for Masons employed by the federal government in Washington so that they could attend the laying of a cornerstone for a new Masonic Hall in Baltimore. Johnson even canceled a cabinet meeting so he could attend. On May 23, 1867, Johnson received Masons at the White House after the opening of a new chapter in the District of Columbia. In fact, Johnson's elevation to thirty-second degree Mason, Scottish Rite, occurred in the White House. On June 20, 1867, Azariah T.C. Peterson of Minnesota, a thirty-third degree Mason and Grand Prior of the Supreme Council, and Benjamin Brown French, a thirty-third degree Mason of Washington, D.C., conferred degrees four through thirty-two on the president.

Four days later Johnson took part in the dedication of a new Masonic Temple in Boston. A lodge from New York had brought with them the "Washington Bible," the Bible upon which George Washington took the oath of office at his first inauguration. Legend has it that, in a dramatic gesture of patriotic and Masonic solidarity, Johnson carefully placed his hand upon the very page Washington used when taking the oath. At a banquet later that night, the president expressed his belief that "the great principles of Masonry are synonymous and identical with the great principles of free government."

Johnson's Masonic connections even crept into the impeachment drama. At the height of the impeachment trial, on May 20, 1868, the president granted leave to federal employees who wished to attend the laying of the cornerstone of a new Masonic Temple in Washington, and Johnson himself marched in the parade. Masonic historians have even claimed that impeachment itself was the result of anti-Masonic prejudice. Johnson's bitterest enemy was Pennsylvania representative Thaddeus Stevens, who, as a state legislator in the 1830s, had proposed a bill to make secret societies illegal, a bill aimed particularly at the Masonic order. Some Masons not only argue that impeachment was solely an attempt to destroy Masonry in the executive branch, but they also claim that Johnson's acquittal was a result of his Masonic membership. The man usually accorded the honor of saving Johnson, Edmund G. Ross of Kansas, was a Mason (Topeka Lodge No. 17) and he could not break his oath and do harm to another Mason. There is little evidence to support any of these theories.

Johnson's Masonic involvement decreased only slightly during his postpresidential years. We know of his status as a Knight Templar (the highest degree of the York Rite) because a photograph taken by C.C. Giers of Nashville in April 1869 shows Johnson with his Knight's sash, cap, and sword. Only a few weeks later Johnson's son Robert, also a Mason, died. Robert was buried with Masonic honors after a service conducted by both a minister and a Mason from the Greeneville Lodge. Even after Johnson left the White House, total strangers, using secret Masonic symbols and codes, wrote to him asking for financial assistance and help procuring pardons. It is not known how seriously Johnson took his Masonic obligations to assist other Masons.

Because Johnson was never affiliated with any organized church, it is not surprising that his funeral was a traditional Knights Templar service. After his death in Carter County, Tennessee, in July 1875, his body was returned to Greeneville. For a time the casket rested in the assembly room of the Masonic Hall. The funeral was conducted by the Coeur de Lion Commandery of Knoxville and included both a procession of Knights Templars and a Masonic Band. Joining the Templars from Knoxville and the Greeneville Masons were Masonic lodges from Knoxville and Jonesboro. Typical of Andrew Johnson, he stayed with his causes and his beliefs until the end.

See also: Death of Johnson; Funeral of Johnson; Greeneville, Tennessee; Impeachment; Impeachment Managers; Jackson, Andrew; Johnson, Robert; Polk, James Knox; Religion, Johnson's Attitude toward; Ross, Edmund Gibson; Stevens, Thaddeus.

References: Denslow, Ray V., *Freemasonry and the Presidency, U.S.A.* (1952); Doughty, Richard Harrison, *Greeneville: One Hundred Year Portrait, 1775–1875* (1975); Graf, LeRoy P., Haskins, Ralph W., and Bergeron, Paul H., eds., *The Papers of Andrew Johnson* vols. 10–12, 14 (1967–2000); *Nashville Daily Banner,* May 1, 1869; Winston, Robert W., *Andrew Johnson: Plebeian and Patriot* (1928).

Maynard, Horace (1814–1882)

Horace Maynard was born in Westboro, Massachusetts, and after graduating from Amherst College (Massachusetts) in 1838, he moved to Knoxville, Tennessee. There he served as tutor and then professor of mathematics (1839–1844) at East Tennessee College (now the University of Tennessee). During this period he studied law. Upon admission to the bar in 1844, Maynard gave up his teaching career and began to practice law.

On August 30, 1840, Maynard's twenty-sixth birthday, he married Laura Ann Washburn of Royalton, Vermont. Eventually the couple had seven children, at least one of whom became a lawyer like his father.

Maynard's first attempt to run for political office, a seat in Congress, ended in defeat in 1853. But he was elected from the second district (Knoxville) in 1857, 1859, and 1861. His Whig Party background put Maynard and Andrew Johnson in opposing parties. However, because both were devoted Unionists, they worked together in 1860–1861, unsuccessfully, to prevent the secession of Tennessee from the Union. Maynard was reelected during the tumultuous summer of 1861. Unlike his Unionist colleague Thomas A.R. Nelson, Maynard was able to escape from Tennessee to Washington, D.C., where he and Senator Johnson agitated for assistance for the Unionists of East Tennessee. Although they advocated federal military advances into the area, other priorities of the government and military leaders prevented such action until 1863.

When Johnson was appointed military governor of Tennessee, Maynard was one of his traveling companions to Nashville in March 1862. Maynard returned to Washington on April 20 and during the rest of April and May served as Johnson's contact with President Abraham Lincoln and Secretary of War Edwin M. Stanton, relaying Johnson's concerns to these government officials while also keeping Johnson up to date on what was happening in Washington. Maynard also communicated Johnson's patronage requests to the appropriate persons and discussed what should be done with captured rebels from Tennessee. Although Maynard visited Washington several more times during the war, he was attorney general of Tennessee during the latter part of the conflict (1863–1865). He spent part of his tenure at home in Knoxville after Union forces regained control there in 1863. From this location he was able to report to Johnson about conditions in East Tennessee.

During the early months after Johnson became president, Maynard continued to report on Tennessee conditions. Maynard was disappointed when the state legislature did not elect him to the U.S. Senate and expected to return to his law practice in Knoxville. However, in August 1865 he was elected to the U.S. Congress. Despite his Unionist background, he was not permitted to take his seat until July 24, 1866, when Tennessee was officially readmitted to the Union. After some wavering, by late 1866 Maynard had sided with the Radical Republicans and had ceased to be a supporter of Andrew Johnson.

Although Maynard was again defeated for a U.S. Senate seat in 1867, he continued to be reelected to Congress. In 1872 Maynard, running as a Republican, was engaged in a three-way contest with Benjamin F. Cheatham (Democrat) and Andrew Johnson (Independent) for Tennessee's at-large congressional seat. They held joint debates at various locations. Although Johnson ran a poor third, he was somewhat satisfied in splitting the Democratic vote leading to the defeat of Cheatham, the candidate of the Confederate military clique. The victorious Maynard served in the House until March 1875. He was then the U.S. minister to Turkey (1875–1880) and postmaster general (1880–1881) in the cabinet of Rutherford B. Hayes. Maynard died in Knoxville.

See also: Lincoln, Abraham; Military Governor of Tennessee, Johnson as; Nelson, Thomas Amis Rogers; Patronage; Secession, Johnson's Attitude toward; Senator, Johnson as; Stanton, Edwin Mc-Masters; Whig Party.

References: Graf, LeRoy P., Haskins, Ralph W., and Bergeron, Paul H., eds., *The Papers of Andrew Johnson* vols. 5–8 (1967–2000); Rothrock, Mary U., ed., *The French Broad-Holston Country: A History of Knox County, Tennessee* (1946); Trefousse, Hans L., *Andrew Johnson: A Biography* (1989).

McCardle, Ex parte

*T*he Supreme Court case *Ex parte McCardle,* during Andrew Johnson's presidency, concerned the constitutionality of the First Military Reconstruction Act. William H. McCardle was the editor of the *Vicksburg Times* in Mississippi. In 1867 he wrote a number of editorials highly critical of General Edward O.C. Ord, the commander of the Fourth Military District (Mississippi and Arkansas). Irritated by this criticism, Ord had McCardle arrested on November 8, 1867, and charged with disturbing the peace, inciting rebellion, libel, and impeding Reconstruction. McCardle was supposed to be tried by a military commission twelve days later, but he got a circuit court judge to issue a writ of habeas corpus. McCardle appeared in the civil court on November 22. Although Judge Robert A. Hill decided that the First Military Reconstruction Act of March 2, 1867, which permitted district commanders to arrest disturbers of the peace and try them by a military commission, was constitutional, he sent an appeal of the decision on to the Supreme Court.

On January 21, 1868, the Supreme Court decided to speed up hearing the case rather than letting it wait for months or even years. Because the case concerned the constitutionality of the First Military Reconstruction Act, Radical Republicans were alarmed, and the government's prosecuting attorneys attempted to have the case dismissed because the Supreme Court supposedly did not have jurisdiction in the case. But the court decided to hear it anyway.

The merits of the case were argued before the Supreme Court on March 2–5 and 9, 1868, during the same time as the preparations for Johnson's impeachment trial. McCardle's defense attorneys, who included Jeremiah S. Black, argued that libel was a state, not a federal, offense; that McCardle had been denied his constitutional right to a jury trial; that the court in *Ex parte Milligan* had determined that military commission trials for civilians were unconstitutional; and that the First Military Reconstruction Act was unconstitutional because it deprived people of their rights, violated the Thirteenth Amendment, and destroyed the constitutional system of checks and balances. Also, the actions of the federal government showed that Mississippi was considered a state before March 2, 1867, when the act was passed, and, by passing the act and sending in troops to control the military district, Congress was acting in a revolutionary manner.

The three government prosecutors, who included Senator Lyman Trumbull, insisted that Mississippi did not have a recognized state government and it was the right and responsibility of the federal government to help it organize one. Congress had the sole power to determine how to do this and it had chosen the Reconstruction Acts as that method. Congress had declared war in 1861 and the war was not over until Congress said so. Therefore it was military necessity to send troops into Mississippi and the other Southern states. Furthermore, the Supreme Court had no jurisdiction because, according to the First Military Reconstruction Act, there could be no habeas corpus appeal from a person in military custody for a military offense, as McCardle allegedly was.

Meanwhile, the Radical Republicans in Congress decided to try to pass legislation to handicap the Court. This, with Johnson's prospective removal by the impeachment process, would leave Congress more powerful. The Judiciary Act of March 27, 1868, was an innocuous bill allowing for an easier appeals process for money and property cases. The Radicals added an amendment that would repeal a part of the Judiciary Act of February 5, 1867, which permitted appeal to the Supreme Court in habeas corpus cases. Any such cases now before the Supreme Court would be dismissed. This meant the McCardle case. The bill was rushed through both houses of Congress before the Democrats realized what was happening.

Johnson held the bill as long as he was able to legally, waiting for the Supreme Court to act, but it did not do so. Johnson vetoed the bill on March 25, 1868, pointing out the incongruity of easing property appeals while prohibiting them for personal liberty cases. When the Supreme Court finally ruled on the case on April 12, 1869, it decided that Congress had the right to change a court's jurisdiction, and therefore the case was dismissed. The government did not prosecute McCardle further and the case was dropped because General Ord was no longer in Mississippi. The Supreme Court never ruled on the constitutionality of the Congressional Reconstruction program.

See also: Black, Jeremiah Sullivan; Congressional Reconstruction; Constitution, Johnson's Attitude toward; Military Districts; Military Reconstruction Acts; *Milligan, Ex parte;* Republican Party; Thirteenth Amendment; Trumbull, Lyman; Vetoes.

References: Eubank, Sever L., "The McCardle Case: A Challenge to Radical Reconstruction," *Journal of Mississippi History* 18 (Apr. 1956): 111–127; Fairman, Charles, *History of the Supreme Court of the United States vol. 6: Reconstruction and Reunion, 1864–88* (1971); Graf, LeRoy P., Haskins, Ralph W., and Bergeron, Paul H., eds., *The Papers of Andrew Johnson* vol. 13 (1967–2000).

McCulloch, Hugh (1808–1895)

Hugh McCulloch, born at Kennebunk, Maine, attended Bowdoin College but did not graduate. (After he was awarded an honorary A.M. in 1863, he was counted as a member of the class of 1829.) He taught school and studied law in Boston. In 1833, a year after he was admitted to the bar, McCulloch moved to Fort Wayne, Indiana, where he married Susan Mann in 1838. The couple had at least two sons and two daughters.

McCulloch did not remain a lawyer long because, in 1835, he became involved in banking, as the cashier and manager of the Bank of Indiana branch in Fort Wayne, a position he held until he became president of the bank (1856–1863). McCulloch was apparently an excellent banker, keeping his institution afloat during the panics of 1837 and 1857.

In 1863 Secretary of the Treasury Salmon P. Chase selected McCulloch to be comptroller of the currency, helping to organize the national banking system. Chase resigned in 1864 and was briefly replaced by William P. Fessenden, who resigned at the beginning of Abraham Lincoln's second term. Lincoln chose McCulloch for the treasury post and the secretary stayed on when Andrew Johnson succeeded the assassinated Lincoln. McCulloch attended Johnson's swearing in, and Johnson's first cabinet meeting was held in McCulloch's office.

McCulloch had first noticed Johnson during the Civil War because of Johnson's strong Unionist stand. Then military governor of Tennessee, Johnson made a speaking tour to Ohio and Indiana, where McCulloch was impressed by Johnson. McCulloch did not attend Lincoln and Johnson's inauguration on March 4, 1865, but when he commented to Lincoln about Johnson's inebriation, Lincoln assured McCulloch that Johnson was not a drunkard. Years later, when McCulloch wrote his autobiography, *Men and Measures of Half a Century* (1889), he also attested to the fact that in four years of working closely with the president he never saw him drunk, but he pointed out that Johnson's extemporaneous, stump-speaking style made him appear drunk at times. On several occasions, such as on Washington's Birthday in 1866 and before the Swing-around-the-Circle tour later that year, McCulloch urged Johnson to avoid impromptu speaking, but the president ignored the advice.

With the end of the Civil War, McCulloch had to make plans to deal with a very large national debt. His fiscal policies were conservative: to pay off the bonds, contract the currency (reduce the amount of money in circulation), and return to the gold standard. He did not agree with Johnson's idea to pay the bondholders in currency, as everyone else was paid, rather than in gold.

Throughout Johnson's presidency, Johnson and McCulloch discussed and exchanged many notes about patronage matters, as there were many offices to be distributed, particularly in the Internal Revenue Department and the customs service. Both men also had to consider the desires of representatives, senators, and other influential politicians from the affected state before a nomination could be made. Sometimes people urged Johnson and McCulloch to remove an officeholder whom the advisors considered to be unsatisfactory.

Each year, McCulloch made an annual report and Johnson discussed important aspects of it in his annual message. McCulloch also sometimes gave Johnson advice on particular political situations, such as opposing the idea of removing General Philip Sheridan as commander of the Fifth Military District (Louisiana and Texas).

By 1867 Johnson was receiving complaints about McCulloch from various sources. Some persons were unhappy that McCulloch had not made the patronage changes that they had recommended. Others saw McCulloch as an opponent of Johnson's policy and a hypocrite in his cabinet. Many critical things were published about McCulloch in the press, especially in 1868. Some persons speculated that the opposition to McCulloch was led by a group of New York City businessmen and officials who were fraudulently avoiding paying whiskey taxes and whom the Treasury Department was attempting to prosecute. A number of people advised Johnson to remove McCulloch from office. Johnson's lieutenants at the Democratic Convention in New York in 1868 reported that many of the delegates would not seriously consider nominating Johnson for president because he had not removed McCulloch. But the treasury secretary had numerous supporters in the banking world and Johnson had no better prospective replacement, so McCulloch remained in office until the end of Johnson's term in 1869.

For several years after 1869 McCulloch was a partner with Jay Cooke in a London banking firm, which survived the Panic of 1873, when Cooke's enterprises in the United States failed. McCulloch was briefly secretary of the treasury again at the end of

Chester A. Arthur's term (1884–1885). McCulloch died at his home in Maryland in 1895.

See also: Annual Messages; Chase, Salmon Portland; Democratic Convention; Drunkenness; Finances, Johnson's Attitude toward Governmental; Lincoln, Abraham; Military Districts; Military Governor of Tennessee, Johnson as; Panic of 1873; Patronage; Sheridan, Philip Henry; Swing-around-the-Circle; Washington's Birthday Speech.

References: Graf, LeRoy P., Haskins, Ralph W., and Bergeron, Paul H., eds., *The Papers of Andrew Johnson* vols. 8–15 (1967–2000); McCulloch, Hugh, *Men and Measures of Half a Century* (1889); Schell, Herbert S., "Hugh McCulloch and the Treasury Department, 1865–1869," *Mississippi Valley Historical Review* 17 (Dec. 1930): 404–421; Trefousse, Hans L., *Andrew Johnson: A Biography* (1989).

Memphis Riot (1866)

*T*he Memphis and New Orleans riots provided ammunition for the opponents of Andrew Johnson's Reconstruction policy, leading to the defeat of his National Union Party in the 1866 fall elections and the passing of the Military Reconstruction Acts.

In 1866 Memphis was a fairly rowdy town with several factors contributing to a potential for violence. The Civil War and emancipation had brought many social changes to Memphis. After the city fell to Union forces in 1862, several "contraband" camps for escaped slaves were established near Fort Pickering in south Memphis. This led to permanent large concentrations of blacks in the area, whereas before the war blacks had been fewer in number and scattered throughout the city. Numbers also grew when blacks moved from the countryside to the protection of the fort after the war. In addition, a number of black troops were stationed at the fort, aggravating the white population by their very existence, as well as occasional misbehavior.

Most white Memphis residents were extremely racist and remained defiantly seces-

sionist even after the end of the war. A large part of the working class population was Irish in heritage. Because many former Confederates were disfranchised by Tennessee law, the Irish voters were able to control the city government, electing an Irish mayor and all five aldermen. In addition, nearly all of the firefighters and police were Irish, with police brutality and incompetence being notorious. The Irish hated the blacks because both groups were competing for the same jobs. Many Irish would attack blacks at the slightest provocation, and conflicts with the black soldiers were frequent. The newspapers tended to make matters worse by always printing the most sensational aspects of any event, seemingly in a deliberate attempt to inflame emotions. They would later blame the Memphis riot on "northern fanatics, idle Negroes, and the black troops."

On April 30, 1866, the War Department was mustering out the last of the black troops in Memphis, but most of them were planning to remain in the city, where they had settled their families. There was a clash between the police and some blacks in south Memphis on that day. It is not clear who fired the first shot and evidence indicates that the blacks sometimes harassed their white foes. However, the events of May 1 and 2, the days of the actual riot, were largely a series of attacks by white policemen and citizens on blacks and their property, wherever they might be. The mayor could not bring order because he was intoxicated most of the time. The federal army commander was slow to dispatch troops to the scene. When the white troops did finally arrive, they failed to arrest any white rioters. Witnesses attested to the innocence of most of the black victims, but the white rioters, many of whom were known, could not be brought to justice, either because they had fled or because no white jury would convict them.

During the course of the riot forty-six blacks and two whites were killed, and seventy to eighty other people of both races were injured. Five black women were raped. Property destruction was also widespread. Four black churches, twelve schoolhouses, and ninety-one homes were burned by the rioters.

Andrew Johnson did not even express sympathy for the victims of the riot. Because of the failure of civilian and military authorities to bring the rioters to justice, the riot, along with that in New Orleans in July, became prime Republican campaign material in the fall, contributing to the defeat of many of the candidates of the National Union Party. Newly elected Republicans in Congress joined with Republicans already there to pass much legislation shifting control of Reconstruction from President Andrew Johnson to Congress. The legislation included a number of acts designed to protect the civil rights of blacks.

See also: Black Troops in the South; Congressional Reconstruction; Election of 1866; Military Reconstruction Acts; National Union Convention and Party; New Orleans Riot; Presidential Reconstruction; Reconstruction; Swing-around-the-Circle; Tenure of Office Act.

References: Graf, LeRoy P., Haskins, Ralph W., and Bergeron, Paul H., eds., *The Papers of Andrew Johnson* vols. 10, 11 (1967–2000); Lovett, Bobby L., "Memphis Riots: White Reaction to Blacks in Memphis, May 1865-July 1866," *Tennessee Historical Quarterly* 38 (Spring 1979): 9–33; Rable, George, "Memphis: The First Modern Race Riot," *Geoscience and Man* 19 (June 1978): 123–127.

Mexico

The main concern about Mexico during Andrew Johnson's term as president was that Mexico had an emperor, Maximilian, who had been placed and kept in power by French troops. This was contrary to U.S. principles enunciated in the Monroe Doctrine in 1823 (no European country could develop any new colonies in the Americas).

The problem began in 1861 when Mex-

icans were not paying their debts to foreign creditors and the Mexican government was too unstable to be helpful. In order to collect these debts, the British, Spanish, and French sent troops to Mexico. Britain and Spain negotiated a settlement in 1862 and withdrew their troops. But the French emperor, Napoleon III, made impossible demands and sent more troops until there were 35,000 in Mexico in 1863. They seized Mexico City and overthrew the president, Benito Juarez, in June 1863. Napoleon replaced Juarez with an emperor, the former archduke of Austria, Ferdinand Maximilian, who had to renounce his claim to the Austrian throne in order to become Mexican emperor. Maximilian liked Mexico very much and assumed many Mexican customs. But he was unsuccessful in establishing control and always had to be backed by the French troops, who were continually in conflict with the forces of Juarez.

Maximilian hoped to have an alliance with the Confederate States of America, but Napoleon was cautious about the possibility of a war with the United States, which a Confederate alliance might provoke. William H. Seward, the U.S. secretary of state, also negotiated carefully, hinting that the United States *might* recognize Maximilian if Napoleon did not recognize the Confederates. In fact, Napoleon became more concerned about events in Europe, and not only did not recognize the Confederacy but also began to pay less attention to Mexico.

After the United States won the Civil War, the United States sent a number of troops, commanded by General Philip H. Sheridan, to the Texas-Mexico border to exert pressure by their presence. Commanding General Ulysses S. Grant favored direct U.S. military intervention in Mexico and was quite pushy about it in 1865. Although Johnson wanted the French troops out of Mexico, he sided with Secretary of State Seward, who wanted to negotiate and leave direct intervention as a last resort. In fact, in his farewell address in March 1869, Johnson pointed out with some pride that he had resisted this pressure for military involvement.

Johnson nominated his old friend Lewis D. Campbell of Ohio as minister to Mexico in late 1865, but at this point there was nowhere for such an official to go. Johnson wrote several letters to Napoleon in January 1866 stating that he had not authorized any U.S. military incursions into Mexico (U.S. soldiers had apparently helped Juarez supporters to capture a border town). But, he pointed out, such problems could be avoided if the French troops were withdrawn, an action that would be good for both France and the United States. Meanwhile, Grant and others were agitating for the United States to sell arms to the Juarez forces. This would be a violation of U.S. neutrality, however. Grant arranged a clandestine meeting in April 1866 between Johnson and the Mexican ambassador Matias Romero. They developed a deal in which the U.S. government would sell weapons to a civilian merchant, who would in turn sell them to the Mexicans.

Also in April 1866, Johnson and Napoleon III made an agreement that called for the withdrawal of French troops in three groups: in November 1866, March 1867, and November 1867. As a result, in the fall of 1866 Johnson prepared to send Campbell to Mexico. Johnson wanted Grant to accompany the ambassador, but Grant refused to go, so General William T. Sherman went instead. The trip was largely futile because Campbell and Sherman failed to locate Juarez. In addition, Napoleon delayed the troop withdrawal until 1867. When the French troops finally left, Maximilian was captured by the Juarez forces and shot by a firing squad on June 19, 1867. Juarez resumed control of the Mexican government.

During the rest of his term, Johnson was involved with patronage matters related to Mexico. In June 1867 Campbell resigned as ambassador and was eventually replaced by General William S. Rosecrans, who was confirmed by the Senate in July 1868. The other patronage requests related to a treaty signed by the United States and Mexico on July 4, 1868, setting up a commission to deal with claims presented by both U.S. and Mexican citizens since 1848. Many people wanted that commissioner's post. However, ratification of the treaty was not completed until January 1869 and the legislation to put it into effect was not passed until April 1869, so Johnson had left office before a commissioner was appointed.

See also: Farewell Address; Foreign Affairs; Grant, Ulysses Simpson; Patronage; Seward, William Henry; Sheridan, Philip Henry; Sherman, William Tecumseh.

References: Graf, LeRoy P., Haskins, Ralph W., and Bergeron, Paul H., eds., *The Papers of Andrew Johnson* vols. 8–12, 14–15 (1967–2000); Hanna, Alfred Jackson, and Hanna, Kathryn Abbey, *Napoleon III and Mexico: American Triumph over Monarchy* (1971); Krauze, Enrique (Heifetz, Hank, trans.), *Mexico, Biography of Power: A History of Modern Mexico, 1810–1996* (1997); McPherson, James M., *Ordeal by Fire: The Civil War and Reconstruction* (1982).

Military Districts

As a result of the First Military Reconstruction Act, passed by Congress on March 2, 1867, and then repassed over President Andrew Johnson's veto, ten of the eleven former Confederate states were divided into military districts. Tennessee was exempted because the state approved the Fourteenth Amendment and thus was not subject to further Reconstruction measures. There were five military districts: First District—Virginia; Second District—North and South Carolina; Third District—Georgia, Alabama, and Florida; Fourth District—Arkansas and Mississippi; and Fifth District—Louisiana and Texas. Although civil governments were not abolished in these states, each district had a military commander who, when necessary, was superior to state officials and could remove them for such causes as obstructing Reconstruction. The commander also supervised the distribution and use of troops in the district to keep order, voter registration, and the process of electing a constitutional convention to draw up a state governing document satisfactory to Congress. Once this constitution had been ratified by the voters and a new government installed, the military commander would be relieved of his duties and the district would be abolished.

Despite his opposition to the First Military Reconstruction Act, Andrew Johnson was responsible for appointing generals as commanders for the districts. He based his appointments mainly on the suggestions of Ulysses S. Grant, the commanding general of the army. Johnson's initial appointments were: First District—John M. Schofield; Second District—Daniel E. Sickles; Third District—George H. Thomas, who was transferred before taking command and was replaced by John Pope; Fourth District—Edward O.C. Ord; and Fifth District—Philip H. Sheridan. Although few people in the South liked the idea of military districts, they found some of the commanders more acceptable than others.

In the First District, John M. Schofield commanded from March 1867 to June 1, 1868, when he became Johnson's secretary of war. George Stoneman then commanded until March 1869. He was briefly replaced by L.S. Webb in March and April 1869, and then Edward R.S. Canby, who commanded from April 1869 to January 27, 1870. At this point Virginia was readmitted to the Union and civil government was restored.

Daniel E. Sickles of the Second District was one of the more controversial commanders because he tried to enforce the Military Reconstruction Acts stringently. He was removed from command on August 26, 1867, and replaced by Edward R.S. Canby, who served until July 24, 1868, when civil government was restored.

In the Third District, John Pope also provoked much controversy and Andrew Johnson received many letters of complaint requesting Pope's removal. Johnson removed Pope on December 28, 1867, and on January 2, 1868, he replaced Pope with George G. Meade. Although Alabama was restored to the Union in June 1868 and Georgia and Florida followed in July, Meade remained in the former Third District until March 1869, in command of troops still required in the area to keep the peace.

Edward O.C. Ord commanded the Fourth District until December 28, 1867, when he was replaced by Irvin McDowell. By July 1868, when Alvan Gillem replaced McDowell, Arkansas had already been readmitted to the Union and the Fourth District consisted of Mississippi only.

The Fifth District saw more commanders, at least temporarily, than any other district. Its first commander, Philip H. Sheridan, was certainly one of the most controversial commanders. He removed many officeholders and enforced the Military Reconstruction Acts strictly. After receiving many requests for Sheridan's removal, Johnson acted on August 26, 1867, at the same time as he removed Sickles in the Second District. Although Winfield S. Hancock was appointed to command the district, he did not arrive until November 28, 1867, because of the threat of yellow fever. Temporary command was exercised by Charles Griffin, who soon succumbed to the yellow fever epidemic, and then Joseph A. Mower. Hancock was transferred at his own request on March 18, 1868. He was temporarily replaced by Joseph J. Reynolds, and then Robert C. Buchanan until July 28, 1868. When Reynolds resumed command in July, Louisiana had been restored to statehood and the Fifth District consisted of Texas alone. Texans had considerable difficulty preparing and approving their constitution. But even when Texas was finally restored to statehood, troops remained there, as they did in the other states, to quell violence.

See also: Canby, Edward Richard Sprigg; Fourteenth Amendment; Hancock, Winfield Scott; Military Reconstruction Acts; Pope, John; Readmission of Southern States; Schofield, John McAllister; Sheridan, Philip Henry; Sickles, Daniel Edgar.

References: *American Annual Cyclopaedia* (1867, 1868); Graf, LeRoy P., Haskins, Ralph W., and Bergeron, Paul H., eds., *The Papers of Andrew Johnson* vols. 12–13 (1967–2000); Heyman, Max L., Jr., *Prudent Soldier: A Biography of Major General E.R.S. Canby, 1817–1873* (1959); McDonough, James L., "John Schofield as Military Director of Reconstruction in Virginia," *Civil War History* 15 (Fall 1969): 237–256.

Military Governor of Tennessee, Johnson as (1862–1865)

*I*n February of 1862, after the Union victories in western Tennessee, President Abraham Lincoln embarked on a plan to rescue that state from Confederate control and restore it to its proper relationship within the Union. Tennessee was the first state to undergo "wartime Reconstruction," and central to this process was the military governor of the state, Andrew Johnson. In March of 1862 Lincoln, through Secretary of War Edwin M. Stanton, notified then-Senator Johnson of his appointment as military governor, to be in charge of reconstituting a loyal government for Tennessee.

Johnson resigned his Senate seat, and arrived in Nashville on March 12, 1862, trading, as one friend wrote, "the soft cushioned seat in the Senate for the jolting saddle of the war horse." Johnson's position was unprecedented in U.S. history: he was appointed directly by the president and answerable only to him. (After Lincoln selected Johnson, Congress appointed Johnson brigadier general, but otherwise Congress was not involved.) Lincoln granted Johnson sweeping powers to remove and appoint officials, suspend the writ of habeas corpus, and call and supervise elections. Johnson's mission was "to carry into full and fair effect the 4th. Section of

the 4th. Article of the Constitution of the United States," which guaranteed every state a republican form of government. In other words, Johnson was to eliminate rebels from all local and state governmental positions and create a loyal (pro-Union) state government. This had to be accomplished in a pro-Confederate area, with active military operations still occurring in the vicinity and with the pro-Union portion of the state (the east) still under Confederate control.

Johnson seemed the obvious man for the task: a Tennessean who had been governor for two terms. President Lincoln believed that Johnson's working-class roots and staunch Unionism would be a catalyst for a resurgence of "national" feeling among the state's rank-and-file. Johnson's slaveholding background might lure prominent men back to the flag, providing evidence that the Lincoln administration was not (initially) in favor of emancipation. The choice of a man from a seceded state demonstrated that Lincoln, like Johnson, did not believe that the states had left the Union.

But Johnson's qualifications were no match for this dilemma. The Confederate state government of Isham Harris continued to claim legitimacy, having first relocated to Memphis and then to Chattanooga. Much of the state was still under Confederate military occupation, and the other areas, including Nashville, faced constant guerrilla and cavalry threats. Nashville itself was hardly secure, and although U.S. forces were present, Johnson faced the constant danger of kidnapping or assassination. In fact, the fortifications around the capitol building were so elaborate that the building took on the name "Fort Andrew Johnson." Even his partner in this venture, the U.S. Army, was of little help, and their relationship was characterized more by antagonism and rivalry than cooperation.

As was occurring at the national level, a new political party was forming in Tennessee, one drawn along Unionist lines regardless of earlier affiliations. Thus, Military Governor Johnson found himself at odds with many former Democratic allies while embracing former Whig opponents, such as his longtime enemy (but fervent Unionist) William G. Brownlow. Many former Whigs received positions in his temporary government. Johnson ruled the state himself because no loyal legislature existed until he called an election for it. But there were positions that needed filling immediately. Former opponent Edward H. East became secretary of state, and Whigs Horace Maynard and Edmund Cooper became attorney general and Johnson's private secretary, respectively.

Confederates who refused to take an oath of allegiance to the United States were eliminated from politics. In April 1862, not long after Johnson's arrival, much of Nashville's government refused to take the oath. Johnson removed them all, arrested the mayor, and appointed councilmen and aldermen of his choosing, who then elected a new mayor. Each fall Johnson appointed new boards of councilmen and aldermen, and another election occurred. Johnson closed newspapers that supported the Confederate cause, and even jailed ministers who spoke sympathetically about the Confederacy. Bankers, editors, and publishers found themselves under arrest, with some being shipped North to Camp Chase, Ohio, if they refused to take the oath.

Such harshness was necessary at the upper levels of government, but in his March 1862 "Appeal to the People of Tennessee," Johnson indicated that leniency and forgiveness awaited the common people. His mission, he told Tennesseans, was to preserve public property, provide protection under the law, and restore the government to its loyal antebellum status.

The military governor even embarked on a stump speaking tour across Middle and West Tennessee, offering amnesty to all those who had been duped by planters and secessionist leaders. He was threatened by Confederate cavalry, his train was nearly attacked, and he encountered a cool reception at most stops. So few individuals were interested that Johnson's optimism was shaken, and he found himself offering (with Lincoln's approval) amnesty and parole to Tennessee Confederates who were prisoners of war in Northern camps. Further evidence of hostility toward Johnson and the Union came in May 1862 when a "rebel" was elected judge in Nashville; Johnson had the man arrested and replaced with his Unionist opponent, but it demonstrated the antagonism that existed.

By the summer of 1862 Johnson was taking a harder line, as evidenced by a July 4th speech, which contained the famous line "treason must be made odious and traitors impoverished." Johnson continued to remove local officials and jail businessmen and approved of an army plan to confiscate rebel property for army use. Such actions angered Confederate Tennesseans, so Johnson had his doubts when President Lincoln pushed him to hold elections in the "secure" congressional districts of western Tennessee. Johnson arranged for elections in December 1862, but the combination of cavalry raids by Confederate general Nathan Bedford Forrest and antipathy by local voters resulted in a low turnout; rebel sympathizers won anyway, but Congress rejected the results. Such was the case for most "secure" areas of the state, and so Johnson himself continued to appoint judges, mayors, councilmen, and other local officials.

The U.S. Army was nearly as much trouble as the Confederate one. Since Johnson's arrival in Nashville, there had been problems of authority and jurisdiction between the military governor and General Don Carlos Buell, commanding the Army of the Ohio. Buell and his superior, General Henry W. Halleck, commander of Union armies in the West, believed that generals were responsible for waging war and that politicians had to stand aside and wait for the peace. Johnson and his superior, Abraham Lincoln, conceived of the war differently and believed that offering amnesty and beginning Reconstruction as soon as possible would weaken the enemy war effort. But with the war still being waged, the two commanders in Tennessee struggled over resources, personnel, and troop allocation. For instance, Johnson wanted soldiers on hand to enforce his pronouncements and arrests, defend the capitol, and protect railroads and Unionists' property. When Buell resisted, Johnson penned letters to Secretary of War Stanton or President Lincoln. Although Lincoln once told his military governor that acceding to all his requests would mean placing him in command of the western armies, the president usually backed Johnson.

Relations slowly improved after October 1862, when Buell was removed and the Union army in Tennessee came under the direction of William S. Rosecrans, commander of the Army of the Cumberland. At first the situation remained strained, as Nashville grew in size and importance, with contrabands (ex-slaves) and refugees streaming in and Union forces using it as a base of operations. Johnson had his own civil courts in operation, and in early 1863 Halleck ordered the military not to interfere in civil cases. But because army courts continued to operate until 1864, Johnson flooded Washington with requests for stays of execution and alterations in military sentences; in nearly every case Lincoln overruled the army in favor of his governor. Johnson also protested when Rosecrans developed his own military police units and in March 1863 requested authority from Washington to take control of all military forces in Nashville. Rosecrans refused; however, renewed operations in East Tennessee in 1863 kept the general away from Nashville. This allowed Johnson to create his own "Home Guards," and later the administration detached a brigade of Union forces for the governor's use. But having the authority led to other problems, such as competing with the army for supplies, weapons, and even recruits.

Another controversial issue, one that came to dominate all others, was slavery. Johnson, an unswerving Unionist, believed that the sole purpose of the war was to preserve intact the United States. As a Union-occupied city, Nashville became a haven for runaway slaves, and both military commanders and Johnson used former slaves—and current resident slaves for that matter—to help construct defenses and repair roads. Yet Tennessee still permitted slavery, and even the Emancipation Proclamation of January 1, 1863, did not alter that. But Johnson was becoming convinced that slavery was central to the Confederate war effort and that only by destroying slavery could the rebellion and its causes be completely eradicated.

By 1863 Johnson was openly criticizing slavery. In an August speech in Nashville, Johnson directly blamed slavery for secession and civil war, calling it a "cancer on our society." Through 1863 Johnson's attacks on slavery became more pronounced and more frequent, even though he clearly opposed it on practical grounds, and had no desire to grant citizenship or political rights to blacks. By early 1864 the military governor was advocating a state convention to end slavery and calling on Congress to pass an amendment to abolish it. In June of 1864 the reconstituted Republican Party, calling itself the National Union Party, nominated Johnson as the vice presidential candidate for the 1864 election; certainly his newfound opposition to slavery helped him win support among the Republicans. In October Johnson openly embraced emancipation as a war aim and officially abolished slavery in Tennessee, earning the title the "Moses of the Colored Men."

Johnson was less enthusiastic over the recruiting of former slaves and other blacks for military service. In March 1863 President Lincoln had advised Johnson that the "colored population is the great available, and yet unavailed of, force for restoring the Union" and that "men of your ability and position, [should] go to this work" of putting blacks into uniform. If Johnson, an "eminent citizen of a slave-state" and "a slave-holder," took the lead, surely other Southerners would follow. Not until late 1863—and after many more letters from Lincoln—did Johnson move toward enlisting blacks, and even then he offered $300 to slave owners who voluntarily manumitted their slaves. Once enrolled in the army, blacks were paid a salary and guaranteed freedom after their service. (General Orders No. 329 of October 1863, which came on the heels of Johnson's proposal, formally authorized black recruitment in Maryland, Missouri, and Tennessee and included the $300 payment.)

Emancipation and enlisting blacks fit well into Lincoln's policy, but made restoring Tennessee even more difficult as it split Johnson's Unionists. By the middle of 1863 radical Unionists wanted immediate emancipation, the elimination of Confederates from any role in government, and the confiscation of rebel property. More conservative Unionists stuck to the original goal of the war—the preservation of the Union—and opposed the expansion of war aims. Johnson specifically declared that only "unconditional Union men" could play a role in the restoration of the state. In January 1864, after Confederate forces had been driven from East Tennessee, Johnson ordered county elections to take place in March. The qualifications that Johnson required for voters went far beyond the requirements established by Lincoln in the president's "Ten Percent Plan" of December 1863. Those wishing to participate in the elections (white men over twenty-one) had to take a new oath, declaring that they desired the suppression of the rebellion and the success of the Union armies and that they would assist in achieving these results. Both rebels and Unionists complained, but Lincoln backed Johnson—even though it negated the president's amnesty.

Because organizational problems and Confederate guerrilla activity interfered with the elections, Johnson decided that the results were invalid. Another proposal followed in the late summer. On August 2, 1864, a mass meeting of Union men in Nashville called for a September convention to discuss Restoration. Local elections and Johnson appointments filled the seats at the September convention, which called for a constitutional convention to meet in Nashville in 1865 to revise the state constitution and select new state officers. In December 1864 the decisive Union victory at the battle of Franklin, just south of Nashville, ended the Confederate threat in Tennessee. It finally seemed like Reconstruction was progressing.

On January 9, 1865, at what some historians have called the pinnacle of his career, Johnson spoke to the 500 delegates assembled at the constitutional convention in Nashville. The military governor—and vice president elect since November of 1864—called on those present to put aside former differences and come together to create a new state, one without slavery. On February 22 the convention completed its revisions of the 1835 state constitution, including amendments voiding secession, abolishing slavery, and rejecting the Confederacy. Those permitted to vote under Johnson's guidelines went to the polls in late February to ratify the constitution, officially ending slavery in Tennessee. "Thank God the tyrant's rod is broken" was President Lincoln's reaction. On March 4, voters elected a new legislature and a new governor (William G. Brownlow).

Andrew Johnson was not present, however. Although he asked permission to stay in Tennessee until the new government was installed, Lincoln ordered him to Washington for the inauguration. Johnson left Tennessee during the last week of February and arrived at the nation's capitol on March 1, three days before the inauguration. Andrew Johnson left behind him a war-torn state, a fledgling state government, and a vindictive population, only to embark on a far more controversial phase of his life.

See also: Black Troops in the South; Blacks (Slave and Free), Johnson's Attitude toward; Brownlow, William Gannaway "Parson"; Constitution, Johnson's Attitude toward; Cooper, Edmund; Democratic Party; Election of 1864; Harris, Isham Green; Johnson, Eliza McCardle; Lincoln, Abraham; Maynard, Horace; Milligan, Sam; "Moses of the Colored Men" Speech; National Union Party; Nelson, Thomas Amis Rogers; Nicholson, Alfred Osborne Pope; Reconstruction; Secession, Johnson's Attitude toward; Stanton, Edwin McMasters; Temple, Oliver Perry; Vice President, Johnson as.

References: Basler, Roy P., ed., *The Collected Works of Abraham Lincoln* vols. 6–8 (1953–1955); Durham, Walter T., *Nashville: The Occupied City* (1985); Durham, Walter T., *Reluctant Partners: Nashville and the Union, July 1, 1863 to June 30, 1865* (1987); Graf, LeRoy P., Haskins, Ralph W., and Bergeron, Paul H., eds., *The Papers of Andrew Johnson* vols. 5–7 (1967–2000); Maslowski, Peter, *Treason Must Be Made Odious: Military Occupation and Wartime Reconstruction in Nashville, Tennessee, 1862–65* (1978); Sefton, James E., *Andrew Johnson and the Uses of Constitutional Power* (1980).

Military Reconstruction Acts

Converging developments in 1866 led Congress to craft a wholly new Reconstruction program. On one hand, President Johnson's opposition to moderate measures and Southern hostility to blacks, Unionists, and the Fourteenth Amendment clearly indicated that Congress faced serious obstacles in protecting civil rights in the South. On the other hand, congressional overrides of the Civil Rights and Freedmen's Bureau Bill vetoes demonstrated a growing solidarity among Republicans. This power bloc was enhanced by sweeping Republican victories in the 1866 congressional elections, which meant that the next Congress would be virtually veto-proof.

Seeing that the president and his Southern governments were uncooperative, and knowing that it now held nearly unopposable power, the Republican Congress dis-

carded cooperation and opted for coercion. In four Military Reconstruction Acts, Congress established an intrusive, involuntary system designed to readmit the Southern states along lines of Congress's choosing.

Predicated on the theory that the former Confederate states were now "conquered provinces," the First Military Reconstruction Act, passed March 2, 1867, divided the South into five military districts, each commanded by a major general appointed by President Johnson. The First District was Virginia; the Second District included North and South Carolina; the Third covered Georgia, Florida, and Alabama; the Fourth was Arkansas and Mississippi; and Louisiana and Texas comprised the Fifth District. Tennessee was not included because it had rejected Johnson's advice and ratified the Fourteenth Amendment. Some historians view the new boundaries as eliminating state identities, but in fact state designations continued, state courts continued to operate, state officials continued to hold their positions, and even the governments created under Johnson's Presidential Reconstruction remained. These governments were, however, declared "provisional," existing only until new ones were established under congressional guidelines.

The March 2 act spelled out these guidelines. Officers of the U.S. Army would oversee the election of delegates to state conventions. As these elections were to be based upon universal male suffrage, the First Military Reconstruction Act was the first national measure to allow blacks to vote. These conventions were to produce new state constitutions, which included universal male suffrage, and present their constitutions to a public vote. Once accepted, a new governor and legislature could be elected, the Fourteenth Amendment ratified, and the state could take its place in Congress.

The same day, March 2, Congress passed two other measures designed to limit the president's interference. The Army Appropriations Act contained the Command of the Army Act, which stated that all orders to the army had to pass through the secretary of war or the general-in-chief. Because both men, Edwin M. Stanton and Ulysses S. Grant, respectively, had Republican sympathies, Congress could effectively keep its eye on Johnson. Congress also passed the Tenure of Office Act, which prohibited, without Senate approval, the removal of officeholders who had been appointed with the Senate's consent.

Johnson signed the Army Appropriations Act—although he submitted a "protest" over the Command of the Army rider—but vetoed both other bills. He charged that they were unconstitutional extensions of federal power into areas of state jurisdiction. Worse yet, the Reconstruction Act created a military despotism that was inimical to American values and traditions and under which army officers had authority over duly-elected civil officials. Johnson also pointed out the inconsistency of treating these states as "out of the Union" while declaring that the war proved that the Union was indivisible. Johnson's vetoes were quickly overridden the same day, and the acts became law.

The measures were not foolproof, Congress soon learned. Because Johnson appointed the military commanders, he could also transfer or remove them, which he did when they appeared overly enthusiastic in their execution of Congress's measures. By the end of 1867 only one of the original five commanders, John M. Schofield, was still in place; Johnson had removed Philip H. Sheridan, Daniel E. Sickles, John Pope, and Edward O.C. Ord.

Congress's program also hit snags as a result of Southern intransigence, as Johnson's governors deliberately procrastinated to avoid enfranchising blacks. On March 23, 1867, the Fortieth Congress, called into session immediately by its predecessor, passed—over Johnson's veto—the First Supplemental Military Reconstruction Act (sometimes called the Second Military Re-

construction Act), which authorized the military to take over the voting process by creating registration boards, directing actual registration, and preventing certain categories of former Confederates from registering. The new law also set forth time frames for the elections and the conventions. Realizing the impotence of his veto power (the act passed over his veto easily) President Johnson had his attorney general, Henry Stanbery, write a narrow legal opinion of the new law, which seriously limited the powers of the military officers.

With army officers confused over who to register and who to exclude, and Southern civil officials beginning to interfere as a result, Republicans in Congress added teeth to their program. On July 19, 1867, Congress passed the Second Supplemental Military Reconstruction Act (or Third Reconstruction Act) designed to close some of these loopholes. In direct defiance of the president and his attorney general, the act specifically stated that it and "its predecessors" were to be "construed liberally" and went on to explain some of what that construction meant: military officers had authority over every civil official in their districts, could remove any civil official who impeded the implementation of Congressional Reconstruction measures, and could appoint others in their stead. Voting eligibility was carefully explained, but in cases of ambiguity military officers and their chosen registrars were given sweeping authority to determine who was eligible and who was not. Officers could even exclude persons who took the loyalty oath if they believed them to be lying. President Johnson, outraged by the blatant disregard for civil supremacy, vetoed the bill, but Congress easily passed the bill over his opposition.

As registration, voting, and the calling of conventions proceeded, some Southerners found another loophole. The original Reconstruction Act provided that the new constitutions needed to be approved by a majority *of those registered.* So, conservative whites in several states registered in great numbers, if military officials allowed them, but boycotted the vote on the constitution. This would defeat the constitution and black suffrage, but of course extend the military's presence.

The constitution in Alabama failed in this way, and in South Carolina the vote was dangerously close. Congress reacted by passing, on March 11, 1868, the Third Supplemental Military Reconstruction Act (Fourth Reconstruction Act), which stipulated that only a majority *of those voting,* not registered, was necessary to carry the constitution.

By late June of 1868 seven states had met these requirements, and under the "Omnibus Bill" they were readmitted to Congress. Arkansas, Alabama, Florida, Georgia, Louisiana, North Carolina, and South Carolina were officially restored. The other three former Confederate states, Mississippi, Texas, and Virginia, remained under military guidance because of problems with their state constitutions. Not until 1870 were these readmitted, along with Georgia, which Congress had returned to military control after conservative whites drove elected blacks from the legislature.

Although some historians and Southerners, past and present, have complained about the oppression of the Military Reconstruction Acts, these were not severe nor radical measures. The situation was temporary, with clear guidelines on how to escape military supervision. With the exception of voter registration, military officers were not to interfere with civil functions unless laws were being broken; for instance, state and local courts operated unhindered unless authorities violated the Civil Rights Act, in which case military courts entered the picture.

Courts, police, and tax collection all continued under Johnson's governments. In fact, some Radicals, such as Thaddeus Stevens, believed that these laws were too moderate. Despite the extent of the rebellion and the current power of Congress, there was no confiscation of land, no sweeping military trials of former rebels, no redistribution of land to the freedpeople, no redrawing of existing state borders. Most accounts of the hardships suffered under "military rule" are exaggerated because it lasted only a brief time, and the governments it inaugurated did not last much longer.

See also: Army Appropriations Act; Black Codes; Black Suffrage; Congressional Reconstruction; Constitution, Johnson's Attitude toward; Election of 1866; Fourteenth Amendment; Grant, Ulysses Simpson; Joint Committee on Reconstruction; Military Districts; Presidential Reconstruction; Readmission of Southern States; Reconstruction; Republican Party; Stanbery, Henry; Stanton, Edwin McMasters; Tenure of Office Act; Vetoes. For the complete text of the First Military Reconstruction Act, see Appendix II.

References: Benedict, Michael Les, *A Compromise of Principle: Congressional Republicans and Reconstruction, 1863–1869* (1974); Graf, LeRoy P., Haskins, Ralph W., and Bergeron, Paul H., eds., *The Papers of Andrew Johnson* vols. 12–14 (1967–2000); Perman, Michael, *Reunion without Compromise: The South and Reconstruction, 1865–1868* (1973); Sefton, James E., *The United States Army and Reconstruction, 1865–1877* (1967).

Milligan, Ex parte

*T*he important civil liberties case, *Ex parte Milligan,* was decided by the Supreme Court during Andrew Johnson's term as president. It involved issues such as the suspension of the writ of habeas corpus and the trial of civilians by military commissions.

The writ of habeas corpus is an idea that the writers of the Constitution borrowed from English common law. It simply means that when a person is arrested, his or her lawyer may go before a court to request a writ of habeas corpus. When a judge issues such a writ, the judge is asking the imprisoning authority to explain why the prisoner is being held. If the judge finds the reason insufficient, the judge can order the prisoner released. To suspend the writ means that the government can continue to hold a prisoner without giving any reasons.

The U.S. Constitution in Article I, Section 9, clause 2, says that the writ "shall not be suspended, unless when in cases of Rebellion or invasion the public Safety may require it." This clause is found in the section of the Constitution that lists things that Congress may not do. But the Constitution is not really clear about who *may* suspend the writ—Congress or the president—during a rebellion or invasion. This matter became a major issue during the Civil War, which was clearly a rebellion. Early in the war, Congress was not in session. In April 1861 when Virginia seceded from the Union, riots broke out in Baltimore, and Washington, D.C., was unprotected. Abraham Lincoln, based on his interpretation of his war powers, and with great reluctance, authorized the suspension of the writ in Maryland on April 27. Over the course of the war, Lincoln would authorize the suspension of the writ at other times and places as well, which caused considerable controversy and objections from Chief Justice Roger B. Taney.

On March 3, 1863, Congress passed the Habeas Corpus Act, which recognized the right of the president to suspend the writ during the rebellion and the right of the Supreme Court to hear cases on appeal. This implied that civilians arrested as a result of Lincoln's suspension of the writ should be tried in civilian courts rather than by military commissions. But military commission trials continued, especially in the Western states. The case of *Ex parte Milligan* emerged from one of these cases in Indiana.

In the Indianapolis area there were a number of secret societies associated with political party membership. One of these was the Sons of Liberty, a Democratic group. Harrison H. Dodd was apparently the ringleader of a vague conspiracy by some of these Sons of Liberty to stage an armed uprising in the Chicago area during the Democratic Na-

tional Convention in 1864 and to free Confederate prisoners of war from nearby Camp Douglas. Other plans discussed involved capturing Union weapons and kidnapping the governor of Indiana. No actual attempt was made to do any of these things, but Dodd, when arrested, had 400 revolvers. Six other men were also arrested in connection with the "conspiracy." One man was released and one became a state witness, but the rest were tried by a military commission, in part because of issues connected with the election of 1864. Dodd fled to Canada during his trial and was sentenced to death in absentia. Three of the other four were found guilty, although all they had done was talk, and were sentenced to death. After various delays, Andrew Johnson approved their sentences, which were to be carried out on May 19, 1865.

On May 10 attorneys for Lambdin P. Milligan and the two other men filed for a writ of habeas corpus. The execution was delayed and their sentences were then commuted to life imprisonment at hard labor. The Supreme Court decided to consider the case in March 1866 and to allow the attorneys for both sides to present longer arguments than usual. The government prosecutors were Attorney General James Speed, Benjamin F. Butler, and future attorney general Henry Stanbery. The four defense attorneys included future president James A. Garfield and Jeremiah S. Black. The court listened to arguments March 6–13, 1866, and ruled on April 3 that a military commission had had no jurisdiction to try and sentence Milligan and his colleagues. On December 17, 1866, Justice David Davis and Chief Justice Salmon P. Chase issued two opinions elaborating on their decision in the *Milligan* case. They said that several laws showed that neither the president nor Congress could authorize military trials for civilians, even during wartime, in areas where civil courts were operating, such as Indiana. They also ruled that suspension of the writ of habeas corpus merely permitted the government to detain people, not to try them in some other way when the civil courts were open.

Milligan was released. He later sued for damages for illegal imprisonment and was awarded $5.

See also: Black, Jeremiah Sullivan; Butler, Benjamin Franklin; Chase, Salmon Portland; Election of 1864; *McCardle, Ex parte;* Speed, James; Stanbery, Henry.

References: Fairman, Charles, *History of the Supreme Court of the United States, vol. 6: Reconstruction and Reunion, 1864–88* (1971); Gambone, Joseph G., "*Ex parte Milligan:* The Restoration of Judicial Prestige?" *Civil War History* 16 (Sept. 1970): 246–259; Rehnquist, William H., *All the Laws but One: Civil Liberties in Wartime* (1998); Stampp, Kenneth M., "The Milligan Case and the Election of 1864 in Indiana," *Mississippi Valley Historical Review* 31 (June 1944): 41–58.

Milligan, Sam (1814–1874)

A native of Greene County, Tennessee, Andrew Johnson confidant Sam Milligan was educated at Greeneville and Tusculum Colleges. Johnson seems to have become acquainted with Milligan in the late 1820s when Johnson belonged to the Greeneville College debating society, and they became close friends. In 1838 Johnson made a coat for Milligan. After teaching school for a time, Milligan read law with Robert J. McKinney. He was admitted to the bar in 1844, setting up his practice in Greeneville. (In the 1850s he used Johnson's old tailor shop as his law office.)

Milligan was a member of the Tennessee house of representatives (1841–1847). In 1842 Milligan in the house and Johnson in the senate cooperated to introduce a bill to divide the state into congressional districts based solely on voting population without considering the three-fifths figure normally added for the black population. But the bill was tabled. During the Mexican-American War, Milligan served as a major in the Quartermaster Department, dealing with commissary stores, and was stationed in Mexico for a time. After the war, in 1849,

Milligan married Elizabeth Howard (1826–1909) by whom he had three children.

In 1850 Milligan briefly edited the *Greeneville Spy,* a newspaper supporting and supported by Johnson. The latter tried several times to get political appointments for Milligan, usually without success. In 1852 Governor Johnson appointed Milligan to be inspector general on his military staff. Milligan would rather have had a congressional seat and was disappointed when Nathaniel G. Taylor defeated him for a vacancy in 1854.

At various times during the 1850s to 1870s Johnson and Milligan exchanged extensive correspondence. Clearly Johnson regarded Milligan as an important political confidant and discussed his future political plans. Milligan also wrote to Johnson giving him advice and local information. He promoted Johnson's candidacy for the 1860 Democratic presidential nomination, but without success.

Himself a Unionist, Milligan attended the Washington Peace Conference in 1861. After Tennessee seceded, Milligan apparently remained in Greeneville, where he handled various legal matters for Johnson and his family. He finally had to flee to a Union-controlled area in 1864 and went to Nashville, where he served as a clerk in Military Governor Johnson's office and as commissioner of banks. Johnson appointed Milligan to the state supreme court in 1865, a post he held until 1868.

When Johnson became president, Milligan wrote letters encouraging Johnson in his presidential role and occasionally also sent letters of recommendation for office seekers. He also apparently tried to help Johnson's son Robert, when the young man was in Greeneville with a drinking problem. Although Johnson tried to appoint Milligan to several foreign posts, Milligan had to turn them down because of family concerns. In 1868, however, Milligan accepted an appointment as a judge of the U.S. Court of Claims, a post he held until his death. After Johnson left the presidency and returned to

Greeneville, Milligan continued to write to him about events in Washington.

Milligan suffered from a kidney disease for about a month before he died. During Milligan's final illness, Johnson, who was visiting Washington on business, went to see him. Milligan died in Washington on April 7, 1874. Johnson attended his funeral in Greeneville, where the judge was buried.

See also: Governor (Civilian), Johnson as; Greeneville, Tennessee; Johnson, Robert; Military Governor of Tennessee, Johnson as; Patronage; Taylor, Nathaniel Green.
References: Graf, LeRoy P., Haskins, Ralph W., and Bergeron, Paul H., eds., *The Papers of Andrew Johnson* vols. 1–5, 7–12, 14–16 (1967–2000).

Moore, William George (1829–1898)

William George Moore, confidential secretary of Andrew Johnson during most of his presidency, was born in Washington, D.C., on November 30, 1829. Little else is known about his early years or his personal life, but he was a clerk at the capitol before the Civil War began. He served in various positions (finally as sergeant) in the National Rifles, District of Columbia Volunteers, from April 15 to July 15, 1861, and then became a clerk in the War Department for the rest of the war. Afterward he held the rank of major in the volunteers and ultimately was breveted lieutenant colonel and colonel, thus he is usually called Colonel Moore in the Johnson correspondence.

He began to serve as one of Johnson's secretaries in November 1865 and stayed until the end of Johnson's presidency. He quickly became one of Johnson's most trusted assistants and confidants, frequently serving as a conduit for messages to Johnson and penning Johnson's replies. During the crisis relating to Edwin M. Stanton, Moore himself carried important messages, including the request for Stanton's resignation as secretary of war. He also traveled with Johnson to North Carolina and New England in the summer of 1867. Moore testified at Johnson's impeachment trial, called both by the prosecution and the defense on various questions. During 1866–1868 Moore kept a diary and notes about events during Johnson's presidency and the opinions that Johnson expressed. These records have been extremely helpful to historians.

After Johnson's presidency Moore remained in the army as a paymaster, stationed at Fort Leavenworth, Kansas, to deliver wages to remote army posts. He left his wife, Mary G., and at least a son and a daughter in Washington, D.C., so the children might continue their education. This separation may explain why Moore resigned from the army in April 1870 and returned to Washington, D.C., where he became a notary public. During 1873 and 1874 Moore assisted Johnson with several important matters. He met with officials at the failed First National Bank and relayed information to Johnson about measures being taken to deal with Johnson's large account. Moore also provided Johnson with recollections about the accusations related to the Mary Surratt case made by Judge Advocate General Joseph Holt in his letters to the Washington *Chronicle*. Moore remained in Washington and served as major and superintendent of the District of Columbia police from December 1886 until his death on July 12, 1898.

See also: Finances, Personal; Holt, Joseph; Impeachment; Panic of 1873; Patronage; Presidential Travels; Secretaries; Surratt, Mary (Elizabeth) Eugenia Jenkins; University of North Carolina.
References: Graf, LeRoy P., Haskins, Ralph W., and Bergeron, Paul H., eds., *The Papers of Andrew Johnson* vols. 11–16 (1967–2000); Sioussat, St. George L., "Notes of Colonel W.G. Moore, Private Secretary to President Johnson, 1866–1868," *American Historical Review* 19 (Oct. 1913): 98–132; Trefousse, Hans L., *Andrew Johnson, A Biography* (1989); U.S. Censuses, Washington, D.C.: 1860, 3rd Ward, p. 100; 1880, 37th Enumeration District, p. 9; Washington, D.C., directories, 1855–1885.

"Moses of the Colored Men" Speech (1864)

On the evening of October 24, 1864, a crowd of blacks held a torchlight procession in Nashville, Tennessee, campaigning for the Union Party candidates Abraham Lincoln and Andrew Johnson. They ended at the state capitol building, where they called for a speech from Johnson, the vice presidential candidate and military governor of Tennessee.

In his speech from the capitol steps, Johnson addressed the fact that Lincoln's Emancipation Proclamation had not freed the slaves in Tennessee (apparently at least in part because of Johnson's urging, although he omitted any mention of that from the speech). Because he believed that "the hour has come when the last vestiges of it [slavery] must be removed," he announced that "I, Andrew Johnson, do hereby proclaim freedom, full, broad and unconditional, to every man in Tennessee!"

He went on to chastise some of the wealthy Confederate-sympathizing planters in the Nashville area, suggesting that the division of their property among small farmers would be good for society, although he gave no orders to that effect. He also charged that the aristocrats who complained about the "negro equality" that allegedly would result from emancipation had in fact been practicing such equality themselves as evidenced by the number of mulatto children in their households. Johnson promised the blacks that "henceforth the sanctity of God's holy law of marriage shall be respected in your persons."

"Looking at this vast crowd of colored people," Johnson continued, "and reflecting through what a storm of persecution and obloquy they are compelled to pass, I am almost induced to wish that, as in the days of old, a Moses might arise who should lead them safely to their promised land of freedom and happiness."

When the crowd shouted "You are our Moses!" and "We want no other Moses but you," Johnson replied, "Well, then, humble and unworthy as I am, if no other better shall be found, I will indeed be your Moses, and lead you through the Red Sea of war and bondage, to a fairer future of liberty and peace." He intended "to stay and fight this great battle of truth and justice to a triumphant end. Rebellion and slavery shall, by God's good help, no longer pollute our State."

Although the blacks who heard the speech responded with great enthusiasm, others then and since have suggested that Johnson was either inebriated or a hypocrite, given his earlier and later attitudes toward blacks. But historian David W. Bowen, in his study of the question, has suggested that Johnson adapted his views with changing circumstances in order to remain the leader of the Tennessee Unionists and continue in favor with the Lincoln administration. Controversial at the time, the speech raised the hopes of blacks, which were quickly deflated by Johnson's failure as president to act in defense of the freedmen.

See also: Blacks (Slave and Free), Johnson's Attitude toward; Election of 1864; Military Governor of Tennessee, Johnson as.

References: Bowen, David Warren, *Andrew Johnson and the Negro* (1989); Graf, LeRoy P., Haskins, Ralph W., and Bergeron, Paul H., eds., *The Papers of Andrew Johnson* vol. 7 (1967–2000); Trefousse, Hans L., *Andrew Johnson: A Biography* (1989).

Mudd, Samuel Alexander (1833–1883)

Born on a Maryland plantation, Samuel Alexander Mudd attended Frederick College, Frederick, Maryland, and then Georgetown College, Georgetown, District of Columbia, from which he graduated in 1854. After obtaining a degree from the school of medicine associated with the university in Baltimore in 1856, he apprenticed with his cousin George Mudd. He married a neighbor, Sarah Frances Dyer, in 1857 and established himself as a physician and tobacco farmer near Bryantown, Maryland, in the area where his relatives had lived for several generations. The couple eventually had nine children.

During the Civil War, Maryland was a hotbed of strife between Unionists and Confederate sympathizers. Federal soldiers frequently annoyed the residents of Mudd's region, which was also much-traveled by Confederate couriers. Mudd's neighbors believed him to be a Unionist and there is no evidence that he participated in the Confederate underground except in one instance when he briefly hid his brother-in-law and two friends. He did not join any army but continued to farm and practice medicine, although his profits declined.

After John Wilkes Booth shot Abraham Lincoln in the presidential box of Ford's Theatre on April 14, 1865, Booth jumped to the stage and broke his leg. Escaping Washington, Booth remembered a doctor on his route, Samuel Mudd. Booth and David Herold arrived at Mudd's home very early in the morning on April 15 requesting treatment. Because Booth had met Mudd several times before, he kept his head bundled up or his face toward the wall, disguised his voice, and used an assumed name during the hours he was at the Mudd's.

Arrested more than a week after Booth's visit, Mudd was imprisoned with many other suspects in Washington. Mudd and seven others who were believed to be among the most guilty of the prisoners were tried by a military commission (May 9–June 30, 1865), as ordered by President Andrew Johnson. Defended by Thomas Ewing, Jr., Mudd, like the other suspects, did not testify in court. Convicted on ill-defined charges, Mudd was sentenced to life imprisonment at hard labor at Fort Jefferson in the Dry Tortugas, a chain of islands near Key West, Florida.

Almost immediately Sarah Mudd and Thomas Ewing began to provide affidavits and plead for Mudd's release, but Andrew Johnson refused to consider it. Eventually, numerous other people wrote to Johnson in behalf of Mudd, arguing that Mudd had merely been doing his duty as a doctor when he set Booth's leg. In addition, some correspondents urged Mudd's freedom because of his selfless service to the Fort Jefferson garrison during a terrible yellow fever epidemic in 1867 in which the post surgeon had died. During the final days of his term, Johnson pardoned Mudd on February 8, 1869. The pardon arrived at Fort Jefferson on March 8 and Mudd was released from confinement but could not be transported to Key West until three days later. Physically weakened, Mudd reached home on March 20. He continued to farm and practice medicine in reduced economic circumstances for the rest of his life.

Long after his death, Mudd's case has continued to generate controversy as family members have sought to persuade the federal government to declare him innocent. In 1993 the University of Richmond even staged a mock trial with distinguished lawyers to debate the case.

See also: Ewing, Thomas (Jr. and Sr.); Lincoln Assassination Conspirators; Pardons (Individual).

References: Carter, Samuel III, *The Riddle of Dr. Mudd* (1974); Graf, LeRoy P., Haskins, Ralph W., and Bergeron, Paul H., eds., *The Papers of Andrew Johnson* vols. 8–15 (1967–2000); Hanchett, William, *The Lincoln Murder Conspiracies* (1983); Turner, Thomas Reed, *Beware the People Weeping: Public Opinion and the Assassination of Abraham Lincoln* (1982); Jones, John Paul, ed., *Dr. Mudd and the Lincoln Assassination: The Case Reopened* (1995).

National Union Convention and Party (1866)

The National Union Party was organized in 1866 by Democratic and conservative Republican supporters of Andrew Johnson. The purpose of the coalition was to elect Johnson supporters to Congress in 1866 and to elect Johnson himself to the presidency in 1868.

Union-Johnson clubs were already forming around the country by late 1865, but the movement was slowed by Radical Republican opposition to Johnson's Reconstruction plans and the passage over Johnson's vetoes of the Freedmen's Bureau and Civil Rights bills. Johnson and his supporters decided to concentrate on the 1866 election and in early June called a convention. Johnson was very involved in the plans, but ultimately organization devolved upon the executive committee, composed of former governor Alexander W. Randall of Wisconsin (soon to be postmaster general); Senator James R. Doolittle of Wisconsin; Orville H. Browning of Illinois (soon to be secretary of the interior); Senator Edgar A. Cowan of Pennsylvania; and Montgomery Blair of Maryland (formerly Abraham Lincoln's postmaster general).

The call for the convention, issued on June 25, 1866, defended Johnson's Reconstruction policy, as well as the rights of the Southern states to determine their own voters and to have representatives in Congress. Delegates espousing these principles, from all states and territories, were invited to the convention. Johnson began to use this call to weed out those officeholders who opposed him. Cabinet members were requested to support the call for the convention. Secretary of the Interior James Harlan, Postmaster General William Dennison, and Attorney General James Speed resigned rather than support the convention and were replaced by Orville H. Browning, Alexander W. Randall, and Henry Stanbery, respectively. Secretary of War Edwin M. Stanton refused both to support the convention and to resign. A circular was sent to other officeholders asking their written approval of the convention. A number of them, including Boston collector of customs Hannibal Hamlin, wrote to Johnson resigning their posts because they refused to support a party that seemed to be composed "almost exclusively of those actively engaged in the late rebellion," a party that was clearly opposed to the "Union Republican" party, which these officeholders supported.

Selection of delegates to the convention caused some problems. Correspondents advised Johnson to have nothing to do with the party because so many former disunionists were active in it. Others complained about the difficulties of getting a balance of Republican and Democratic delegates. Worst of all, from the conservative Republican viewpoint, was the selection of Clement L. Vallandigham, the infamous Copperhead Democrat, as one of Ohio's delegates. Some of the convention leaders tried to convince Vallandigham not to attend.

The convention met in Philadelphia in a large, hastily erected, and still unfinished building on Girard Avenue nicknamed "the wigwam." Randall called the meeting to order around noon on August 14. Then the delegates vigorously cheered and applauded the arm-in-arm entrance of Governor James L. Orr of South Carolina and General Darius N. Couch of Massachusetts, followed by the rest of the delegates from their respective states in a show of unity that many observers found touching. General John A. Dix was named temporary chairman of the convention and gave a speech. The leadership, the committees appointed, and all aspects of the schedule were carefully arranged by the executive committee because the purpose of the convention was not to encourage discussion but to display unified support for Johnson and his Reconstruction policy. Randall and Browning reported to Johnson daily on events at the convention.

One of the few things that did not go according to plan was staged by Clement Vallandigham. Although he picked up his delegate ticket, he did not actually attend the convention. However, on the second day, Vallandigham sent a letter, read by another delegate, in which he stated that he did not believe the convention had the right to exclude him, but he believed that the convention was too important for him not to be willing to sacrifice his own personal desires.

On the third day, August 16, the convention met and adopted ten resolutions supportive of Johnson and his policy, which served as a platform for their party. Then the convention adjourned. On August 17 the party executive committee issued a call for supporters to hold mass meetings everywhere, but little of this occurred.

The following day, August 18, a committee consisting of two delegates from each state and one from each territory called on Johnson to present him with a copy of the convention proceedings. Johnson made a short speech in reply in which he claimed to have been overcome by emotion when he read of the Massachusetts and South Carolina delegates entering the convention arm-in-arm. He criticized Congress for not "promoting reconciliation and harmony" by its legislation and once again took his stand as a supporter of the Constitution. He proclaimed the Philadelphia convention more important than any that had occurred since 1787.

Response to the convention, not surprisingly, varied. Convention delegates used the opportunity to make numerous patronage requests of Johnson. The president also received a number of letters approving the convention. Radical Republicans, however, organized a Southern Loyalists Convention in Philadelphia. As more and more Democrats supported Johnson in the National Union Party, moderate and conservative Republicans left the coalition until it was primarily a Democratic organization, unlike the 1864 party whose name it had taken. Johnson responded to criticism of himself and the party by embarking on his Swing-around-the-Circle tour to defend his policies before the people. However, his speeches did not strengthen the party, and it lost badly in the fall 1866 election, giving the Radical Republicans a congressional majority.

See also: Blair, Francis Preston (Jr. and Sr.); Browning, Orville Hickman; Cabinet Members; Civil Rights Act; Constitution, Johnson's Attitude toward; Democratic Party; Dennison, William; Doolittle, James Rood; Freedmen's Bureau Bills (and Vetoes): Hamlin, Hannibal; Harlan, James; National Union Party; Patronage; Presidential Reconstruction; Randall, Alexander Williams; Readmission of Southern States; Reconstruction;

Republican Party; Speed, James; Stanbery, Henry; Stanton, Edwin McMasters; Swing-around-the-Circle.

References: Graf, LeRoy P., Haskins, Ralph W., and Bergeron, Paul H., eds., *The Papers of Andrew Johnson* vols. 10–11 (1967–2000); Trefousse, Hans L., *Andrew Johnson: A Biography* (1989); Wagstaff, Thomas, "The Arm-in-Arm Convention," *Civil War History* 14 (June 1968): 101–119.

National Union Party (1864)

The National Union Party was the name used by the Republican Party in 1864 to broaden their appeal to include War Democrats (those Democrats who supported the Republican administration in the war effort) and others who would not want to vote for the Democratic candidate, especially one running on a peace platform, but who were reluctant to vote for anyone labeled Republican.

The idea of a Union Party dated to January 1861 when Francis P. "Frank" Blair, Jr., of Missouri organized a party of all types of Unionists in St. Louis. Similar coalitions spread to all the Northern states by the state elections of 1862, but because they were local, informal, unstructured, and weak some thought that they may even have contributed to the Republican defeats in those contests.

Desiring to unify all the prowar factions, the Republicans at the national level temporarily changed to the National Union Party. Although this angered many Radical Republicans, it did permit Andrew Johnson, a War Democrat, to be the party's vice presidential candidate in 1864. The party soon after resumed the Republican title. The National Union Party of 1866, while using the same name, was essentially a conservative Democratic organization.

See also: Election of 1864; Election of 1866; Lincoln, Abraham; National Union Convention and Party.

References: Waugh, John C., *Reelecting Lincoln: The Battle for the 1864 Presidency* (1997).

Naturalization
See Foreign Affairs

Nebraska (Admission to Statehood)

Nebraska became a territory in 1854 as a result of the controversial Kansas-Nebraska Act, although it was not troubled by the violence over the question of slavery expansion that plagued its sister territory. Over the next decade Nebraska grew in population and its land values rose as it became evident that the Union Pacific Railroad, the eastern section of the transcontinental railroad, would be routed through the territory.

On April 19, 1864, Congress passed an act authorizing the people of Nebraska Territory to prepare a constitution and establish a state government. But there was considerable opposition to the idea of statehood from Democrats who had various partisan jealousies and from others who feared that the territory, then with an estimated population of 30,000, could not afford the expenses of state government. The constitutional convention that met that year adjourned without even drafting a constitution because the majority of the delegates opposed statehood.

By 1866 opposition to statehood had declined somewhat, partly because the population had grown (possibly even doubled) and partly because Kansas and Colorado were agitating to have the railroad line run farther south than Nebraska, a calamity that Nebraska statehood might avert. Still, there was enough opposition to cause the pro-statehood leaders to maneuver to have the territorial legislature function as the constitutional convention and thus avoid a problem such as had occurred in 1864. The legislature approved a previously drafted constitution and submitted the controversial document to the people in a June 1866 election. The vigorous, partisan campaign resulted in a narrow victory, by only 100 votes, for the pro-state constitutional forces. Charges of fraud were largely ignored by the federal government and in July, near the end of the session, Congress passed a bill to admit Nebraska. Not about to add another Republican state to the forces of his opponents, Andrew Johnson pocket-vetoed the bill. As a result, those Nebraska Republicans who previously had been neutral in the conflict between Johnson and Congress now openly sided with Congress.

In December 1866 Congress reassembled and Ohio senator Benjamin F. Wade introduced another Nebraska statehood bill. While conservative opponents again complained that the population was too small and the method of drawing up a constitution was too peculiar, some radicals opposed admission because the Nebraska constitution specified that voters should be "white." Consequently, in January 1867, the Senate passed a measure known as the "Edmunds Amendment" or the "fundamental condition," which it attached to the Nebraska Statehood Bill as well as to that of Colorado, which was applying at the same time. Named for Senator George Edmunds of Vermont, the amendment required that the constitutions of Nebraska and Colorado provide for equal suffrage for blacks before the territories could be admitted to statehood. This time Johnson explicitly vetoed the Nebraska Statehood Bill on January 29, 1867, objecting that the "fundamental condition" was unconstitutional because Congress could not regulate the franchise of a state; the people of Nebraska had been given no chance to vote on the issue of equal suffrage.

Congress promptly repassed the Nebraska Statehood Bill over Johnson's veto and the Nebraska legislature, meeting in special session, unanimously approved the "fundamental condition" on February 21. As a result, on March 1, 1867, Johnson was compelled to proclaim Nebraska the thirty-seventh state.

It was clear that Reconstruction issues reached even to the frontier. Nebraska was the only state admitted with the "fundamental condition." Other new states would not enter the Union until after the Fifteenth Amendment, granting equal suffrage to blacks, was ratified in 1870.

See also: Black Suffrage; Colorado (Admission to Statehood); Territorial Affairs.

References: Berwanger, Eugene H., *The West and Reconstruction* (1981); Graf, LeRoy P., Haskins, Ralph W., and Bergeron, Paul H., eds., *The Papers of Andrew Johnson* vols. 10–11 (1967–2000); Olsen, James C., *History of Nebraska* (1955); Potts, James B., "Nebraska Statehood and Reconstruction," *Nebraska History* 69 (Summer 1988): 73–83; Richardson, James D., comp., *A Compilation of the Messages and Papers of the Presidents, 1789–1897* vol. 6 (1896–1899); Trefousse, Hans L., *Andrew Johnson: A Biography* (1989).

Nelson, Thomas Amis Rogers (1812–1873)

Thomas Amis Rogers Nelson, a Whig opponent of Andrew Johnson but later a Unionist ally, was born in Roane County, Tennessee, but soon moved to Knoxville with his family. He attended East Tennessee College (the predecessor of the University of Tennessee) and graduated in 1828. When his family moved to Elizabethton in Carter County, Nelson went along and clerked in his father's store until 1831, when he went to Knoxville to read law. Admitted to the bar in 1832, before his twenty-first birthday, he returned to Elizabethton to practice law and served as solicitor for upper East Tennessee (1832–1836), a position that helped his career. In 1836, with his father and other family members, Nelson opposed the Andrew Jackson–selected presidential candidate of the Democrats, Martin Van Buren, and helped to give Carter County a Whig majority.

On July 30, 1839, Nelson married Anne Elizabeth Stuart (ca. 1817–1850) and moved to Jonesboro. They had six children, born 1840–1849. After Anne's death, Nelson married Mary Jones in August 1852, by whom he had five children, born 1853–ca. 1858.

Because Nelson was selected as a Whig presidential elector in 1840, 1844, and 1848, he was involved in considerable campaigning for the candidates. In 1840 and 1848 this included debates with Andrew Johnson, who was campaigning for the Democratic candidates. After two unsuccessful attempts to be elected to the U.S. Senate, Nelson was elected in 1859 to the U.S. House, where he took a strong Unionist stand, as did his Senate colleague Andrew Johnson. On December 7, 1859, Nelson made a speech denouncing slavery agitation and advocating Unionism. He circulated many copies of the speech to his constituents. It generated quite a bit of controversy because these opinions were considered by some to be disloyal to the South.

In 1860 Nelson attended the Constitutional Union Party Convention in Baltimore and was an elector for its moderate presidential candidate John Bell. Once again, Nelson did a lot of campaigning. After Abraham Lincoln was elected in November, both Nelson and Johnson participated in a Union meeting in Greeneville on November 24, supporting a resolution favoring a Union of equal states with equal rights. When Nelson returned to Washington for the congressional session, he served on the House's "committee of thirty-three" to recommend possible ways to reconcile the sectional controversy. He proposed three amendments to the Constitution, but eventually withdrew them in favor of the proposal known as the Crittenden Compromise. After the adjournment of Congress and a personal meeting with Lincoln, which satisfied Nelson about the president's attitude toward the South, Nelson returned to Tennessee. Here he was involved in an intensive campaign to keep Tennessee in the Union, making one or two speeches daily in East Tennessee. The pace of the campaign picked up after Tennessee governor Isham G. Harris called the state legislature into session and asked that body to secede from the Union. Although the legislators did do this on May 6, they insisted that the people be able to vote on the issue in a referendum scheduled for June 8. From late April until the election Nelson and Johnson canvassed jointly, stressing that as a Whig and a Democrat they had frequently campaigned against one another but now they were working together to preserve the Union. During the campaign they endured frequent verbal harassment and even physical threats. They also participated in the Unionist East Tennessee Convention in Knoxville (May 30–31, 1861), of which Nelson was president.

Although East Tennessee defeated secession by a 2 to 1 margin, the rest of the state approved of it with more than an eighty percent majority. Nelson called for the East Tennessee Convention to assemble again, this time at Greeneville. Meeting June 17–20, 1861, the delegates unsuccessfully petitioned the state legislature to permit them to set up a separate state in East Tennessee. Although Tennessee had seceded by this time, Nelson's constituents reelected him to the U.S. House. However, when Nelson attempted to leave Tennessee, he was arrested by the Confederates and taken to Richmond. Several days of imprisonment there persuaded Nelson to announce, on his return to East Tennessee on parole, that the people should no longer oppose Confederate authority. Although he promised to abide by Tennessee's decision to secede, he did not promise to promote the Confederacy, and he did not do so. He suffered harassment from both occupying rebels and federals.

After the end of the war, Nelson occasionally sent requests for patronage or pardons to Johnson, who was now president. In 1866 Nelson was involved with the National Union Party effort in Tennessee. His greatest service to Johnson came in 1868 when he was one of the president's defense counsel during the impeachment trial. Nelson was chairman of the Tennessee delegation to the Democratic National Convention in New York City in 1868 and nominated Johnson for president, although Horatio Seymour eventually won the nomination.

In 1870–1871 Nelson served as one of the justices of the Tennessee Supreme Court, but he resigned in November 1871. One of his last activities was serving as president of the young men's library association in Knoxville. Nelson died of cholera during the epidemic in the summer of 1873.

See also: Bell, John; Democratic Convention; Greeneville, Tennessee; Harris, Isham Green; Impeachment Defense Counsel; National Union Convention and Party; Secession Referendums; Senator, Johnson as; Seymour, Horatio; Whig Party.

References: Alexander, Thomas B., *Thomas A.R. Nelson of East Tennessee* (1956); Graf, LeRoy P., Haskins, Ralph W., and Bergeron, Paul H., eds., *The Papers of Andrew Johnson* vols. 1–5, 7–8, 11–12, 14–16 (1967–2000).

Nephews

Seven of the eleven children of Andrew Johnson's only brother, William, were boys. However, many of them died young or had little contact with their uncle. Only Andrew Johnson, Jr., and James Johnson seem to have communicated with Andrew Johnson very often.

Andrew Johnson, Jr. (May 21, 1836–January 3 or 31, 1897), the fourth child and second son of William P. Johnson and his wife Sarah Giddings McDonough Johnson, was born in Greeneville, Tennessee. Because his older brother died when less than a year old, Andrew was, in effect, the oldest son. By 1840 the family had moved to La-Grange, Georgia, where Andrew grew up and became a carpenter. His family moved to Alabama and then to Texas, and he may have gone with them for a time at least.

However, by 1860 he was back in Greene County, Tennessee, working at his trade.

Andrew Jr. was a Unionist and briefly joined a home guard unit, although he claimed never to have been a guerrilla. Apparently captured for a brief time in November 1861, he was arrested by Confederate partisan rangers in November 1862 on a charge of disloyalty to the Confederacy. Andrew refused to take a loyalty oath or to be conscripted into the Confederate army. He wanted to leave the Confederacy. Instead, he spent more than a year in prison at Knoxville, Tennessee; Salisbury, North Carolina; and, finally, for at least six months, in Castle Thunder at Richmond, Virginia. Andrew Johnson, military governor of Tennessee, received a number of letters from men who had been imprisoned with his nephew. When they won their release, they wrote to the governor reporting about conditions in Castle Thunder and urging Johnson to arrange his nephew's release. In fact, Governor Johnson did write several letters for this purpose. Andrew Jr. was exchanged in early December 1863. Later in the month he was appointed agency aid to the office of the surveyor of customs and worked in Kentucky or Tennessee at $3 per day, a wage increased a year later to $3.60.

After the war, in May 1865, the Tennessee legislature elected Andrew Jr. to be keeper of the state penitentiary at a salary of $2,000 per year, plus board for his family. However, as the legislature soon determined to restructure the institution and appoint new supervisors, Andrew Jr. was removed from office in May 1866. After a stint as a tax commissioner for the Internal Revenue Service in the Nashville area (1866–1868), Andrew Jr. was appointed a special agent for Tennessee, a post he combined with farming and apparently held intermittently until at least 1880.

Sometime before 1870 Andrew Jr. married an Irish-born woman named Julia (ca. 1837–fl.1883), who had a daughter Ellen (ca. 1857–1872). Julia served as postmistress at Goodlettsville, Tennessee, near Nashville, at least during 1877–1883. In 1875, after Ellen's untimely death, Andrew Jr. and Julia, who had no children of their own, adopted a daughter, Anna (b. ca. 1870). She outlived both of her adoptive parents and in court contested her father's will, which left all of his estate to his third wife, whom he had married in 1896, only a year before his death.

James Johnson (February 3, 1838–March 10, 1919) was the fifth child of William and Sarah Johnson and less than two years younger than his brother Andrew Jr. He too was born in Tennessee, grew up in Georgia, and may have migrated with his family to Alabama and Texas, but he was not with his family in Texas in 1860. What he did during the Civil War is not known, but in 1865 he was appointed deputy keeper of the penitentiary (assistant to his older brother) at a salary of $800 per year and with board for his family. Sometime during this period he married Sue (b. ca. 1843), a South Carolina native who died sometime before the 1880 census, leaving James with five children: Jessie (b. 1867), James V. (b. 1869), Katie B. (b. 1872), Cassie (b. 1874), and Van Leer (b. 1876).

When William P. Johnson died in Texas in October 1865 from the complications of an accidental gunshot wound, James went to Texas to help settle his father's affairs. On his return to Nashville he wrote to his uncle, President Johnson, explaining that it was now his and his brother Andrew's responsibility to support their mother and younger siblings. However, James was unable to support his family with his present job, and so he asked President Johnson for another position. Johnson appointed his nephew assessor of internal revenue at Sabine Pass, Texas, replacing James's maternal uncle, Benjamin F. McDonough, who was unable to serve because he could not take the "test oath" because he had been a Confederate customs collector. James remained in Texas until at least May 1868. By 1870 he was farming in Goodlettsville, Tennessee, and was still thus occupied in 1880.

See also: Johnson, William P.; Military Governor of Tennessee, Johnson as; Patronage.

References: Andrew Johnson Project, Knoxville, TN: Andrew Johnson, Jr., William P. Johnson files; Censuses: 1860, Tennessee, Greene County, Timber Ridge, p. 115; 1860, Texas, Brazoria County, Columbia, pp. 40–41; 1870, Tennessee, Davidson County, 20th Civil Dist., Goodlettsville, pp. 23, 33; 1880 Tennessee, Davidson County, 20th Dist., Goodlettsville, p. 11; Graf, LeRoy P., Haskins, Ralph W., and Bergeron, Paul H., eds., *The Papers of Andrew Johnson* vols. 3, 6, 8–11, 14, 16 (1967–2000); *Nashville American,* Nov. 9, 1899.

New Orleans Riot (1866)

*I*n 1864, under the auspices of Abraham Lincoln's Reconstruction plan, General Nathaniel P. Banks conducted an election in the Louisiana parishes (counties) then under Federal control, to choose delegates to a convention to write a new state constitution. Before the convention adjourned, it passed a resolution allowing the convention's president to call it back into session if necessary, probably in case the voters did not approve the constitution. However, the resolution did not contain any time limit so that, when Unionists, dissatisfied with Louisiana's largely former Confederate government, wanted to recall the convention two years later, it was technically legal to do so.

Some of the convention leaders invited those who had previously served as delegates to meet at the Mechanics' Institute in New Orleans on July 26, 1866. Because of much protest on the part of opponents of the convention and the consequent fear of violence, only forty members appeared, short of a quorum, and the meeting was adjourned until July 30.

At this point, opposition to the convention escalated. Opponents claimed that the convention was not representative, which was true because delegates had not yet been elected from parishes under Confederate control in 1864. Opponents also tended to be former Confederate whites whose allies were currently in power and who were particularly alarmed about the recent passage of the Civil Rights Act, which outlawed the Black Codes that they felt were necessary to control the freedmen. In fact, the main cause of opposition was the intent of the convention to add provisions to the constitution permitting blacks to vote.

Unionist and radical supporters of the convention held a mass meeting, a common political event of the time, on the evening of July 27. A number of speakers addressed the crowd, which included many blacks. Though critics later called the speeches "incendiary" and claimed that they incited the riot, in fact they were, at worst, a bit intemperate and only urged the blacks to defend themselves if necessary.

Opponents of the convention tried hard to stop it from meeting. Lieutenant Governor Albert Voorhies and Attorney General Andrew S. Herron tried to get the district criminal court to prevent the meeting, if necessary by arresting the members of the convention. They telegraphed President Andrew Johnson to inquire whether the military forces in Louisiana would obstruct the court process. Johnson replied that Herron could ask the military commander for "sufficient force to sustain the civil authority in suppressing all illegal or unlawful assemblies who usurp or assume to exorcise [sic] any power or authority without first having obtained the consent of the people of the State."

Absalom Baird, in command of the troops at New Orleans in the absence of Philip H. Sheridan, the district commander, was in a predicament. Mayor John T. Monroe told Baird that the convention violated municipal ordinances and he would have it "dispersed." Baird prohibited this and also refused to allow the sheriff to arrest the delegates. But he did agree to have troops on hand in case of necessity. Unfortunately, he thought the meeting was supposed to begin on July 30 at 6:00 P.M. rather than at noon.

When convention members met at noon, they still did not have a quorum, so after a prayer they adjourned for an hour. During that hour a procession of blacks, with a U.S. flag and a small band or a single drummer (accounts vary) at their head, marched toward the Mechanics' Institute to support the convention. A white man fired a revolver at them as they crossed Canal Street but no one was hurt. By 12:30 P.M., 300 to 400 blacks had gathered outside the Institute while perhaps thirty whites were inside. About 1:00 P.M. fighting broke out. Apparently the city police and firefighters, along with certain white citizens, had previously organized and armed themselves for an attack. Perhaps a tenth of the convention delegates and their black supporters were armed. Once the police opened fire, blacks ran into the Institute for shelter but it was of little use as the police charged the building and were only temporarily beaten back with chairs. Many who tried to surrender were shot or stabbed. Those who jumped out of the windows to try to save themselves were pursued and many blacks were shot or severely beaten. By 2:40 P.M. Baird's troops had arrived, the riot was over, and martial law had been declared.

Baird ordered Dr. Albert Hartsuff, army assistant surgeon in charge of a nearby hospital, to assemble a list of casualties. After examining all the killed and wounded he could find, Hartsuff reported thirty-seven convention-goers or supporters killed (thirty-four of them black), forty-eight seriously wounded (forty black), and eighty-eight slightly wounded (seventy-nine black), with possibly as many as ten more blacks killed and twenty wounded of whom he could get no positive evidence. A number of the dead were "pounded almost to a jelly." The police and their allies had one killed and ten slightly wounded. These statistics support the view of those who blamed the police for what they called a massacre.

Louisianans downplayed the riot, blaming it generally on a conspiracy backed by Radical Republicans and its specific outbreak on the "armed mob" supporting the convention. The police, from this perspective, were acting in self defense.

Although there had actually been more blacks killed in the South before the riot than during it, these had been scattered incidents in place and time and so did not have the same impact on Northern public opinion as the numerous casualties at New Orleans. It was clear that, despite President Johnson's assertions, the South had not been peacefully restored and was not law abiding. Something would have to be done to protect the blacks in the South.

Nor did Johnson's response to the riot help his own situation. He had opposed the convention before it met, accusing it of attempting to usurp power. He never expressed any sympathy for the victims of the riot. Instead he took the advice of Connecticut senator James Dixon that blame should be deflected from the administration or the conservatives would lose many votes in the forthcoming congressional election. On September 8, 1866, while Johnson was on his Swing-around-the-Circle campaign trip, he considered the riot in his St. Louis speech. He blamed the riot on the Radical Congress, claiming that they "substantially planned" it, that the Congress was working with the convention—every member of which was a traitor to the U.S. Constitution—in the hope that once the new government was established Congress would choose it over the one previously and legitimately organized in order to enfranchise blacks and disfranchise whites.

These ill-considered remarks were widely published in Northern newspapers and resulted both in criticism of Johnson and in damage to his cause. The riot and the reaction to it contributed to the failure of Johnson's National Union Party coalition in the congressional elections in the fall of 1866, leading to the election of an overwhelming majority of Radical Republicans who soon passed the pieces of legislation establishing Congressional Reconstruction, some of which were designed to protect blacks from resentful Southern whites. Eventually the House Judiciary Committee, seeking information on which to impeach Johnson, investigated the riot and held Johnson responsible for it, but this was not one of the charges actually used to impeach him.

See also: Black Codes; Black Suffrage; Civil Rights Act; Election of 1866; Impeachment; Memphis Riot; National Union Convention and Party; Republican Party; Sheridan, Philip Henry; Swing-around-the-Circle.
References: Graf, LeRoy P., Haskins, Ralph W., and Bergeron, Paul H., eds., *The Papers of Andrew Johnson* vols. 10–11 (1967–2000); Reynolds, Donald E., "The New Orleans Riot of 1866, Reconsidered," *Louisiana History* 5 (Winter 1964): 5–27; Taylor, Joe Gray, *Louisiana Reconstructed, 1863–1877* (1974); Trefousse, Hans L., *Andrew Johnson: A Biography* (1989); Vandal, Gilles, *The New Orleans Riot of 1866: Anatomy of a Tragedy* (1983).

Newspaper Interviews

Interviews with newspaper correspondents proved to be a good way for Andrew Johnson to get his views to the general public both during his presidency and afterward. Although the twenty-nine interviews printed in *The Papers of Andrew Johnson,* volumes 9–16, are probably not an exhaustive compilation of interviews, they include all the major ones and are certainly representative of any others that may have occurred.

The first known interview was conducted by George L. Stearns on October 3, 1865, and printed in the *New York Times* on October 23. The final interview, with Melville E. Stone on March 7, 1875, was printed in the *New York Herald* on March 8. Johnson gave the most interviews in 1867 (six) and 1868 (five) because of various Reconstruction issues, including the removal of several officials, and the resulting impeachment crisis. In other years Johnson gave one to three interviews. Some of the names of the correspondents are unknown (nine) but those who have been identified include, in addition to Stearns (one) and Stone (one): Alexander K. McClure (one), Louis J. Jennings (one), Charles G. Halpine (two), Joseph B. McCullagh (four), Jerome B. Stillson (two), Alexander H. Evans (one), Augustus J. Ricks (one), Louis J. DuPré (one), John Mulroy (one), Horace V. Redfield (one), a Mr. O'Connor (one), C.W. Charlton (one), and either Hiram J. Ramsdell or Zebulon L. White (one).

Once the interviews were printed, they were soon reprinted in many other newspapers, but they were first published in the *New York Times* (one), *Washington Morning Chronicle* (one), *The Times* (London) (two), *Augusta Constitutionalist* (one), *National Intelligencer* (one), *Cincinnati Commercial* (six), *Boston Post* (two), *New York World* (three), *New York Herald* (six), *Memphis Appeal* (two), *Washington Evening Star* (one), *Knoxville Press and Herald* (one), *Nashville Republican Banner* (one), and *New York Tribune* (one).

Although Johnson most frequently used speeches to spread his views, his interviews usually tended to be more informative and concise. Some were primarily direct quotations whereas others were summaries of what Johnson had to say. Not surprisingly, the correspondents tended to interview Johnson on whatever issues were current at the time. These varied from perspectives on numerous aspects of Reconstruction to questions of national finances and Johnson's postpresidential political campaigns. Some of the interviewers also included physical descriptions of Johnson and, after the presidency, described his home in Greeneville.

See also: Finances, Johnson's Attitude toward Governmental; Greeneville, Tennessee; Impeachment; Physical Description of Andrew Johnson; Postpresidential Career; Reconstruction.

References: Graf, LeRoy P., Haskins, Ralph W., and Bergeron, Paul H., eds., *The Papers of Andrew Johnson* vols. 9–16 (1967–2000).

Nicholson, Alfred Osborne Pope (1808–1876)

Alfred Osborne Pope Nicholson, a close friend of Andrew Johnson and a fellow U.S. senator before the Civil War, was born in Williamson County, Tennessee. Nicholson's father died when the boy was about four. As a teenager, Nicholson attended the Old Brick Academy in Columbia, Tennessee, and then the University of North Carolina at Chapel Hill, from which he graduated in 1827. Nicholson studied medicine, as was customary, with several doctors in Columbia and attended a course of lectures (1828–1829) at the Jefferson Medical College in Philadelphia. On June 17, 1829, Nicholson married Caroline O'Reilly (1811–1894), the daughter of one of his physician mentors. Between 1831 and 1851 they had eight children (five sons and three daughters).

Nicholson soon became interested in being a lawyer rather than a doctor, so he studied law and was admitted to the bar in 1830. He also opened a printing office and edited the *Western Mercury,* a weekly paper (1832–1835). A Democrat, he served in the Tennessee house of representatives (1833–1839) while also working with Robert L. Caruthers on the *Compilation of the Tennessee Statutes.* It is not clear exactly when Andrew Johnson and Nicholson met, but they campaigned together in 1840 for Democratic presidential candidate Martin Van Buren, who was defeated by William Henry Harrison. On December 19, 1840, Felix Grundy, one of Tennessee's U.S. senators, died. On December 25, Tennessee governor James K. Polk appointed Nicholson to Grundy's place, making Nicholson the youngest U.S. senator at the time. He served until February 7, 1842, when the Whig-controlled legislature did not elect him and, in fact, failed to elect any senator for two years.

Elected to the state senate (1843–1845), Nicholson moved his family in 1844 from

Columbia to Nashville, where they remained until 1850. He campaigned for James K. Polk's election to the presidency in 1844 and edited the *Nashville Union* (1845–1846) and, for a time, the weekly *Democratic Statesman*. Nicholson and Johnson had been part of a movement to nominate Lewis Cass of Michigan as the Democratic presidential candidate in 1844. Although the movement was not successful then, Cass was nominated in 1848. Nicholson received a letter from Cass, which became famous. In this letter Cass defined his idea of "popular sovereignty," that the people living in a territory should be able to decide whether they wanted to have slavery or not.

Over the course of the 1840s and 1850s Johnson and Nicholson exchanged some lengthy letters on political matters. While he was in Congress, Johnson asked Nicholson to support his Homestead Act at home in Tennessee, which Nicholson did. Nicholson campaigned for Franklin Pierce for president in 1852, but when Pierce won, Nicholson turned down the offer of the cabinet position of postmaster general. In 1853 or 1854 Nicholson became editor of the *Washington Union,* the paper of the Pierce administration, in partnership with John W. Forney. They were also elected as public printers of the United States for several years. Nicholson sold the paper in November 1856 after James Buchanan was elected and returned to Tennessee about March 1857.

Nicholson had visited Tennessee during the summer of 1855 to campaign for Johnson's reelection as governor. In 1857 both campaigned for the election of Isham G. Harris as governor. In addition to Harris's victory, a legislature with a Democratic majority was elected. That legislature elected both Johnson and Nicholson to U.S. Senate seats. Johnson took his seat immediately, but Nicholson did not assume his until 1859, when John Bell's term expired. While both were senators, Nicholson continued to support Johnson's homestead ideas.

Some time around 1860 Johnson and Nicholson began to be somewhat estranged. Although both campaigned for John C. Breckinridge for president in 1860, Johnson's heart was not really in the campaign because he remained a firm Unionist. Nicholson, however, espoused a more Southern rights Democratic position. He saw Abraham Lincoln's election as a declaration of war on slavery. He left Washington, D.C., in March 1861 and, unlike Johnson, he did not return to his Senate seat. Therefore, he was officially expelled by the Senate in July 1861.

Nicholson took no part in the Civil War, but he was twice imprisoned as a Confederate sympathizer (1862, 1865). Because he refused to take an oath of allegiance to the United States, Nicholson spent most of the war exiled from Tennessee, staying with relatives of his wife near Florence, Alabama. Johnson granted him a special pardon on August 28, 1865, to relieve him from indictment on conspiracy charges brought because he had been a U.S. senator.

After the war Nicholson resumed his law practice. He attended the National Union Party Convention in Philadelphia in 1866. During Johnson's presidency the relationship between the two seems gradually to have improved and there are an increased number of letters from Nicholson in 1868 discussing the Tennessee political situation and even making patronage recommendations. Nicholson was a delegate to the Tennessee constitutional convention (1870), where he gave an effective speech urging that black suffrage be retained. In 1870 he was also elected chief justice of the Tennessee supreme court, a post he held until failing health forced his retirement in January 1876, just weeks before his death in March.

See also: Bell, John; Black Suffrage; Congressman, Johnson as; Democratic Party; Forney, John Wien; Governor (Civilian), Johnson as; Harris, Isham Green; Homestead Act; Lincoln, Abraham; National Union Convention and Party; Pardons

(Individual); Polk, James Knox; Secession, Johnson's Attitude toward; Senator, Johnson as.

References: Clark, Patricia P., "A.O.P. Nicholson of Tennessee: Editor, Statesman, and Jurist" (M.A. Thesis: University of Tennessee, 1965); Graf, LeRoy P., Haskins, Ralph W., and Bergeron, Paul H., eds., *The Papers of Andrew Johnson* vols. 1–5, 7–9, 14 (1967–2000).

Offices Held

From 1829, when Andrew Johnson was first elected to a local position, until 1869, when he left the presidency, Johnson was rarely without some type of public office. His political career began in late 1829 when some of his working-class friends elected the tailor to be one of Greeneville's aldermen. In that period the town had several aldermen who met with the mayor as the town council, deciding about such issues as street repairs, taxes, regulation of outhouses, and granting liquor licenses. Many of the meetings were held at Johnson's tailor shop while he was in office. He was reelected as alderman annually (1830–1837) and served as mayor in 1834 and 1837. (In Greeneville the aldermen were elected in November or December of each year. At their early January meeting they selected the person who would be mayor.) Johnson was still an alderman when he was elected to the state house of representatives as the "floater" for Greene and Washington counties in 1835.

Johnson ran for reelection to the legislature in 1837 but was defeated, primarily because he had voted against some railroad bills, which his constituents thought would benefit East Tennessee. This was Johnson's only election defeat until after his presidency. He was, however, reelected in 1839

and then elected to the state senate in 1841. In 1843 Johnson was elected to the first of his five terms in the U.S. House of Representatives, where he served March 4, 1843–March 3, 1853. Thanks to maneuvering by his political enemies, who gerrymandered his district to give it a Whig majority, Johnson, a Democrat, had no chance for reelection in 1853. Instead he successfully ran for governor and was reelected in 1855.

On October 8, 1857, the Tennessee legislature elected the outgoing governor to the U.S. Senate, where he served until March 4, 1862, when Abraham Lincoln appointed him military governor of Tennessee. Johnson resigned the military governorship in order to become vice president on March 4, 1865. Only one vice president of the United States, John Tyler, held the office for a shorter period than Johnson, who, six weeks later, assumed the presidency on April 15 after Lincoln's assassination.

Johnson's often controversial presidency, discussed in many entries in this volume, concluded on March 4, 1869, when, failing even to be nominated for election to his own term, Johnson was succeeded by Ulysses S. Grant. Narrowly defeated for the U.S. Senate by Henry Cooper in October 1869, Johnson also met defeat for Tennessee's at-large seat in the House of Representatives in 1872. Consequently, Johnson was out of office for nearly six years, until his four-vote majority victory in the Senate race in January 1875. Johnson was unable to fully enjoy his final victory, however, because he was able to attend only one short Senate session (March 1875) before he died of a stroke on July 31, 1875.

See also: Congressman, Johnson as; Democratic Convention; Election of 1864; Election of 1868; Governor (Civilian), Johnson as; Grant, Ulysses Simpson; Lincoln, Abraham; Military Governor of Tennessee, Johnson as; Senator, Johnson as; State Legislator, Johnson as; Vice President, Johnson as.

References: Graf, LeRoy P., Haskins, Ralph W., and Bergeron, Paul H., eds., *The Papers of Andrew Johnson* vols. 1–16 (1967–2000); Trefousse, Hans L., *Andrew Johnson: A Biography* (1989).

Panic of 1873

The Panic of 1873, a major national economic collapse, resulted in a large financial loss for Andrew Johnson. During the late 1860s and early 1870s the country was involved in a railroad boom. With the completion of the transcontinental railroad in May 1869, railroads were projected or under construction in many parts of the country. But by 1872 there was a decline in manufacturing as well as in railroad construction. In April 1873, Johnson, who was involved in a variety of financial investments, predicted an economic crash and was only a few months off in his projections.

In the fall of 1873 a number of businesses, which had overextended themselves, failed. When the prominent bankers Jay Cooke and Company suspended business on September 18, 1873, as a result of problems associated with their heavy investments in the Northern Pacific Railroad, the stock market fell and numerous other banks failed or suspended payment. This included the First National Bank of Washington, directed by Jay Cooke's brother Henry D. Cooke, Sr., and where Johnson had deposited $73,000. Almost immediately newspapers across the country announced Johnson's loss, but he hastened to assure people that he was not impoverished by the loss, thanks to other investments.

By mid-October Johnson had gone to Washington to make his claim. Fortunately, he and the bank were able to work out a payment plan. Johnson received $21,000 in November and other amounts periodically after that. By the time of Johnson's death in 1875, most of the money had been repaid.

As a result of the Panic of 1873, the United States suffered an economic depression for six years.

See also: Finances, Personal; Postpresidential Career; Railroads.
References: Graf, LeRoy P., Haskins, Ralph W., and Bergeron, Paul H., eds, *The Papers of Andrew Johnson* vol. 16 (1967–2000); Unger, Irwin, *The Greenback Era: A Social and Political History of American Finance, 1865–1879* (1964).

Pardons (Individual)

Because the United States never recognized the Confederate States of America as an independent political entity, it viewed citizens who supported the Confederacy as rebels fighting against the U.S. government. Any restoration of the Union had to take into account some sort of punishment and, eventually, some sort of forgiveness. Presidents Abraham Lincoln and Andrew Johnson shared two beliefs on this point. First, treason and rebellion were the acts of individuals, not states, so the U.S.

government needed to deal with restoring the loyalty of those individuals. There was no reason to complicate matters with constitutional debates over the status of the states themselves. Second, both presidents believed that most Southerners were basically loyal and had been duped or forced into supporting the rebellion.

Thus the Restoration programs of Lincoln and Johnson shared several components; chief among them was a tendency toward leniency. Because most former Confederates were not serious threats to the Union, they could resume their places as U.S. citizens, complete with all rights and privileges, with little trouble. Under Lincoln's Ten Percent Plan of December 8, 1863, once ten percent of a state's 1860 voters took the oath of loyalty, most citizens, even those not involved in the oath taking, were relieved of any culpability in the rebellion. President Johnson's four amnesty proclamations were even less taxing: Johnson extended clemency to hundreds of thousands of ex-Confederates who had to do nothing to have their disabilities relieved.

But another common element in these two programs was that each omitted certain groups of individuals from the more general forgiveness. This again reflected the presidents' biases and underlying perceptions of the white South: a small group of individuals bore responsibility for the war, and those persons could regain their rights as citizens only by personally applying for a pardon. Without a pardon, a person could not vote or hold political office, acquire or transfer property, obtain copyrights or patents, or sue in court. Unpardoned individuals also feared for their property because the threat of confiscation loomed large during the war and immediately after it. Subsequently, those not covered by an amnesty faced severe economic hardships, as the Southern economy was in shambles and they could not secure loans or credit.

In his Reconstruction proclamations of December 1863 and March 1864 President

Lincoln excluded seven categories of persons from a general amnesty. These were civil and diplomatic officers of the Confederacy, anyone who left a U.S. judicial position to join the Confederacy, all Confederate military officers over the rank of colonel in the army or lieutenant in the navy, any person who left Congress to join the Confederacy, those who had resigned commissions in the U.S. military to join the Confederacy, anyone who had treated black soldiers as other than legitimate prisoners of war, and those persons under arrest or indictment. According to the U.S. Constitution, the pardoning power was an executive function. So in order to enjoy the full privileges of citizenship, any person in the exempted classes needed to apply directly to the president for a pardon. This usually involved taking an oath of allegiance before a U.S. commissioner, justice of the peace, or marshal. This oath was forwarded to Washington, D.C., and eventually to the president, who would approve or deny the pardon. Apparently Lincoln was very lenient and pardoned nearly all exempted persons who applied.

President Andrew Johnson's first amnesty proclamation, issued May 29, 1865, contained twice the number of exempted classes as Lincoln's. In addition to the seven groups excluded by his predecessor, Johnson denied amnesty to those persons who had left the continent in order to assist the Confederacy, any Confederate who had graduated from West Point or Annapolis, all former Confederate governors, those who left the North and headed South to assist in the rebellion, persons who had been involved in the destruction of U.S. commerce, those persons possessing personal wealth of $20,000 or more in 1860, and anyone who had violated a previous oath of allegiance. The thirteenth exception, aimed at the wealthy elite of the Old South, drew the most criticism. Secretary of State William H. Seward and General Ulysses S. Grant opposed it, but Johnson would not budge. This exemption excluded more persons than all other classes combined, a number estimated at between 60,000 and 80,000 people.

But, as with Lincoln, individuals in the excluded classes could apply to the president for a pardon, and "such clemency will be liberally extended as may be consistent with the facts of the case and the peace and dignity of the United States." On June 7, 1865, Attorney General James Speed issued guidelines for pardon applications. An oath of loyalty had to be subscribed before an officer of the U.S. military, a civil officer of a loyal state, or a registrar appointed by President Johnson. The oath was then forwarded to the provisional governor of the applicant's state, who, after examination, might or might not forward the applicant's oath and accompanying letters of support to the U.S. attorney general. The attorney general then organized the material, checked it for completeness, and sent it on to the president.

The Southern governors played a crucial role in the pardoning process. On May 29, 1865, the same day that Johnson issued his first amnesty proclamation, he also issued instructions for the Restoration of the government of North Carolina. This was followed shortly by proclamations for the governments of Mississippi, Georgia, Texas, Alabama, and South Carolina (Louisiana, Arkansas, Tennessee, and Virginia were functioning under directives from wartime Reconstruction). The governors of all these states had complete authority in deciding which applications went on to Washington and which languished on the governor's desk. Governors such as Andrew J. Hamilton of Texas and William W. Holden of North Carolina exercised their power ruthlessly; some 300 applications were found in Holden's office when he left the position. Others, such as Benjamin F. Perry of South Carolina and William L. Sharkey of Mississippi, forwarded nearly all applications to the president; Perry claimed to have sent between 2,000 and 3,000 applications during his first six months in office. The gover-

nors, who had friends to be reinstated and rivals to be punished, used their power for both personal and political ends. With few exceptions Johnson approved nearly every application he received, making one historian conclude that it was the governors, and not Johnson, who really controlled the pardoning process. In fact, in the fall of 1865, many individuals who had not yet been pardoned were elected to Southern state conventions. Johnson merely informed his governors that, if one of these delegates needed a pardon, the governor could just say the word and Johnson would issue it.

The president believed that the governors were better qualified to determine who was needed for the state government, who was being honest in their application, and who really constituted a threat to the Union. Johnson's amnesties readmitted to full citizenship those who would be central to a new national party, comprised of moderate Democrats and former Whigs. Confederate and secessionist leaders were extremists, so if a governor disregarded an application, there was no damage to Johnson's plans.

The pardon application process irritated some while providing a temporary livelihood for others. Department heads complained that the president spent too much time reviewing pardon applications. By the fall of 1865, with the coming of Southern conventions to create new state governments, so many applications were flooding in that a pardon clerk, Matthew F. Pleasants, had to be placed in the attorney general's office. Papers reported that by October the president was issuing hundreds of pardons a day. At the same time, the chief of the National Protective Police (later the Secret Service), General Lafayette C. Baker, criticized the whole system of pardon seekers and pardon brokers. Local Washingtonians even complained that petitioners and brokers were filling up the hotels and restaurants and cutting off access to the president. These pardon brokers, or pardon attorneys, were persons employed by an applicant to make sure the application reached the right people and received the proper consideration. With so many requests coming in, and so many officials and offices involved, materials could be misplaced, misfiled, or simply ignored. For about $150, a reasonable fee considering what was at stake, a pardon broker organized and supervised the application during its course. Prices went higher for special treatment; in one case a man who could learn nothing about his application paid a broker $500 to secure a successful outcome. The broker, who knew Johnson, met the president at a reception, presented the application, and received the signature on the spot. Pleasants, the pardon clerk, opposed the use of pardon brokers and by some accounts Johnson did as well, but the president always seemed to find time to meet them, especially women. There was talk briefly about creating a "pardon board," headed by Senator Henry Wilson, to alleviate the pressure on the attorney general's office and supervise brokers' activities, but it never materialized.

Despite his leniency, Johnson maintained control over the fate of the highest ranking Confederates. Although he did grant individual pardons liberally, there is little to the myth that Johnson craved the attention and power of having former planters and generals begging for mercy. As both a civilian and military governor of Tennessee, Johnson was long accustomed to supplicants, of all classes, seeking clemency or favors. Johnson excluded the fourteen classes because he truly believed that these persons were either responsible for the war or sought to benefit from it. Furthermore, the exclusion forced these individuals—political, military, and social leaders—to personally demonstrate their allegiance to the Union and their rejection of secession. Johnson hoped that this would set an example for other former Confederates, amnestied or not, that the war was over and reconciliation had to begin.

As a result, Johnson temporarily withheld pardons from many prominent figures. Many high-ranking civil officials applied for pardons only months after Appomattox, but Johnson held them in limbo until he was prepared to extend them clemency. Not until the end of 1866 did Johnson pardon Confederate secretaries of the treasury Christopher C. Memminger and George A. Trenholm, and he kept Secretary of the Navy Stephen R. Mallory and Secretary of War James A. Seddon waiting until late 1867. A total of seventy-two generals received special pardons, but many others had to wait until Johnson's July 4, 1868, amnesty; for instance, generals James Longstreet, Edmund Kirby Smith, Howell Cobb, George Pickett, and Richard S. Ewell all petitioned for pardons, but were denied. (Ewell in fact came under four exceptions: one of rank, one for resigning a U.S. army commission, one for graduating from West Point, and one based upon his wealth.) Not until Johnson's July 4, 1868, amnesty were these officers, and many others, relieved of their disabilities. John C. Breckinridge and Jefferson Davis never received individual pardons, but instead came under Johnson's Christmas 1868 amnesty; Johnson made clear that these men would have been granted pardons had they only applied, which neither did.

The reverse happened to General Robert E. Lee, who applied for his pardon six months after surrendering. But his application was mishandled, and although most of his materials did reach Johnson, his oath was lost. Believing Lee sought a pardon but refused to take the oath, Johnson denied him clemency, and continued to deny it despite pleas by Ulysses S. Grant and other top Union generals. Although he never received an individual pardon, Lee was included under the provisions of the July 4, 1868, amnesty.

As contemporaries had argued, Lee had taken the oath, and proof appeared in 1970, when Lee's loyalty oath surfaced in the State Department files in the National Archives. Subscribed to on October 2, 1865, the oath revealed that Lee was indeed honorable and had not tried to circumvent the process. In recognition of this oversight, Congress formally relieved Lee of the disabilities imposed by the Fourteenth Amendment, and on August 5, 1975, President Gerald R. Ford signed a pardon for Lee, officially returning the general to full U.S. citizenship. Lee finally joined some 13,500 persons who received individual pardons.

See also: Amnesty Proclamations; Congressional Reconstruction; Davis, Jefferson; Fourteenth Amendment; Governors, Provisional; Lincoln, Abraham; Presidential Reconstruction; Speed, James.

References: Davis, William C., *Jefferson Davis: The Man and His Hour* (1991); Dorris, Jonathan Truman, *Pardon and Amnesty under Lincoln and Johnson: The Restoration of the Confederates to Their Rights and Privileges, 1861–1898* (1953); Perman, Michael, *Reunion without Compromise: The South and Reconstruction, 1865–1868* (1973); Thomas, Emory, *Robert E. Lee* (1995).

Patronage

The concept of patronage, the idea that an official should reward his supporters with offices and punish his opponents by removing them from office, is much older than the United States. In the United States the idea is most associated with Andrew Jackson and his "spoils system," the blatant proclamation that "to the victor belong the spoils." In fact, Jackson removed and appointed fewer officeholders than this philosophy would suggest.

Actually all presidents have been expected to use patronage and have done so to some extent. By the mid-nineteenth century, before the civil service reforms beginning in the 1880s, which made many offices subject to examination and merit-based appointment, there were hundreds of offices available, especially in the post office and treasury departments. These appointments became a burden to the president as hundreds of alleged supporters clamored for offices for themselves or their friends.

Patronage even contributed to the deaths of two presidents. William Henry Harrison's fatal cold (1841) worsened in part because he was overwhelmed by office seekers and unable to rest. James A. Garfield was assassinated (1881) by a disappointed office seeker, Charles Guiteau. But other presidents of the mid-nineteenth century were pestered by office seekers, and Andrew Johnson was no exception.

Presidents were expected particularly to pay attention to the requests of supportive senators and representatives who would make recommendations about the appointment of faithful party members in their own states. This expectation brought congressman Andrew Johnson into conflict with President James K. Polk in the mid-1840s when the latter failed to heed Johnson's patronage requests despite his devotion of his own time and money to Polk's campaign in 1844.

In the months after Johnson became president, his voluminous mail consisted mostly of requests for pardon or for appointment to office. Even after Johnson's impeachment and his failure to be nominated for president by the Democrats in 1868, he received many requests for posts. In fact, some people requested patronage even after Johnson was no longer in office.

Requests for office could come in many forms. Some supplicants visited Johnson in person, others wrote letters or did both. Thousands of such patronage-related letters survive. Some writers made straightforward requests for vacant offices. Some seekers first had to request that an office be vacated. They suggested the removal of the incumbent because he was a Radical Republican or he opposed Johnson's Reconstruction policy. Some requests for removal resorted to petty, tattletale tactics, such as reporting that the official showed disrespect for Johnson's picture, to demonstrate the supposed villainy of the incumbent.

At times Johnson received telegrams reporting the death of an officeholder that day with the request that the sender be appointed in place of the deceased. Some advisors wrote long letters detailing whom Johnson should remove or appoint to perhaps a dozen different offices in order to increase the number of Johnson supporters in their state. In some instances requests for removal were prompted by incompetence or corruption, but in the majority of cases the rationale was strictly partisan. Some of Johnson's advisors were political notables in their states, such as governors or members of Congress. More people were obscure individuals who took it upon themselves to give Johnson a piece of their mind. Some attempted to take advantage of political "debts" owed to them by Johnson and sought to have him appoint their friends, as did Edmund Ross after he voted for Johnson's acquittal during the impeachment trial. Most of the letter writers were men but some women also wrote in behalf of friends or relatives, or occasionally themselves, requesting such humble positions as treasury department clerk. Some well-connected applicants could procure as many as several dozen letters of recommendation in their behalf. It is no wonder that Johnson needed at least four secretaries.

It is impossible to know to what extent Johnson responded directly to patronage seekers. Some surviving letters have notations such as "file" or otherwise indicate that the missive was answered. No doubt Johnson simply ignored some requests. In other cases Johnson made promises or seems to have implied that he would take action but did not actually do so. For example, R. King Cutler of Louisiana for *months* visited and wrote to Johnson urging him to remove William P. Kellogg, the collector of customs at New Orleans. Despite all these pleas, Johnson never removed Kellogg, who eventually resigned to take a U.S. Senate seat.

In other instances Johnson did attempt to remove or appoint officeholders as requested. He nominated some of the men suggested by Edmund Ross, for example. In a number of cases in the South he replaced Unionists with former Confederates, angering many Republicans. But Johnson's freedom of action in patronage matters was soon restricted by Congress when the new Tenure of Office Act was passed to prevent him from removing certain officeholders. There were ways to get around the law, but an attempt to do so in the case of Edwin M. Stanton (even though the law did not actually apply to Stanton) provoked Johnson's impeachment. Johnson's opportunity to make appointments was also seriously impaired by the Senate, which confirmed fewer and fewer of his nominees as his term progressed. In many cases the Senate rejected the nominee; in others they tabled the nomination. Edward A. Rollins, the commissioner of internal revenue, resigned his post effective with the confirmation of his successor, but he remained in office for the rest of Johnson's term because the Senate refused to confirm any of Johnson's numerous nominees. Thus, Johnson's conflict with Congress over Reconstruction seriously restricted his ability to dispense patronage, especially during the latter part of his term.

See also: Impeachment; Polk, James Knox; Ross, Edmund Gibson; Stanton, Edwin McMasters; Tenure of Office Act.
References: Graf, LeRoy P., Haskins, Ralph W., and Bergeron, Paul H., eds., *The Papers of Andrew Johnson* vols. 1, 8–15 (1967–2000).

Patterson, Andrew Johnson
See Grandchildren

Patterson, David Trotter (1818–1891)

A friend and son-in-law of Andrew Johnson, David Trotter Patterson was born near Greeneville, Tennessee, on February 28, 1818, one of the twelve children of Andrew and Susan (Trotter) Patterson. During his adolescence he worked for several years in his father's paper mill. He also attended two years of college in Greenville, South Carolina, before returning to Tennessee to read law with Robert J. McKinney. Admitted to the bar in 1841, Patterson practiced law in Greeneville, becoming a friend and political associate of Johnson's. In 1844 Patterson wished to become attorney general for East Tennessee. Johnson personally presented Patterson's application to President John Tyler, but the latter chose someone else. In May 1854 Patterson was elected to an eight-year term as judge of Tennessee's first judicial circuit.

That Patterson also became a friend of other members of the Johnson family besides the father was evident when in October 1855 he asked for permission to marry Johnson's oldest daughter, Martha, who, at twenty-seven, was ten years Patterson's junior. The couple were married on December 13, 1855, at the Johnson home. Johnson himself was in Nashville and unable to attend. The Pattersons had two children: Andrew Johnson (February 25, 1857–June 25, 1932) and Mary Belle (November 11, 1859–July 9, 1891).

The Civil War brought many problems for Patterson, who was, like his father-in-law, both a lifelong Democrat and a Unionist. In November 1861 Patterson was arrested as a suspect in the bridge burnings carried out by some East Tennessee Unionists (including his brother-in-law Daniel Stover). Finally able to convince the Confederate authorities that he had not participated in the destruction, Patterson was released in December 1861 after taking a loyalty oath. Reelected in 1862, he continued to serve as circuit judge under the Confederates until Union troops occupied parts of East Tennessee in the fall of 1863. In October Patterson and his family were given transportation to enable them to join Military Governor Andrew Johnson and other family members in Nashville.

That Patterson had continued to serve as a judge under the Confederates made his Union sympathies suspect. But Patterson explained that he had retained the post after consultation with local Unionists, because as judge he could (and did) protect these Unionists from unjust political prosecutions such as were happening in other districts. Patterson was pardoned in March 1864 by President Abraham Lincoln.

In April 1865 the Tennessee legislature elected Patterson to the U.S. Senate for a term that expired on March 4, 1869. During this term, which overlapped with Johnson's presidency, Patterson lived in the White House with his family while Martha served as principal hostess for her father. Patterson supported his father-in-law's Reconstruction and other administration policies and voted for Johnson's acquittal during the impeachment trial.

The Pattersons returned to Tennessee from Washington in 1869 and took up residence on a farm that Johnson gave to Martha. It was located at Henderson Depot, or Henderson Station (which name Patterson soon had changed to Home), about six miles from Greeneville. Here Patterson raised stock and feed. He also owned part of the Home Woolen Company, was involved with a flour mill, had property in Washington, D.C., and owned a farm in Hawkins County. He died of heart failure near Greeneville on November 3, 1891, and was buried in the Johnson family plot on Monument Hill.

See also: Grandchildren; Greeneville, Tennessee; Impeachment; Patterson, Martha Johnson; Stover, Daniel. For the letter from Andrew Johnson to David T. Patterson, October 26, 1855, see Appendix II.
References: Graf, LeRoy P., Haskins, Ralph W., and Bergeron, Paul H., eds., *The Papers of Andrew Johnson* vols. 1–16 (1967–2000); *Knoxville Daily Journal,* Nov. 3, 1891; Speer, William S., *Sketches of Prominent Tennesseans* (1888).

Patterson, Martha Johnson
(1828–1901)

Martha, the oldest and favorite child of Andrew and Eliza (Mc-Cardle) Johnson, was born in Greeneville, Tennessee, on October 25, 1828. She attended various local schools, including one taught by Catherine M. Melville, who became a family friend. In 1844–1845 Martha was in Washington, D.C., with her father, who was then serving as a member of Congress. Martha attended Miss S.L. English's Female Seminary in Georgetown and developed a friendship with President James K. Polk and his wife.

On December 13, 1855, Martha married David Trotter Patterson (1818–1891), a lawyer and political friend of her father's. They had two children: Andrew Johnson (1857–1932) and Mary Belle (1859–1891). During the Civil War the Pattersons remained in Greeneville while David served as a Confederate judge. With the Union occupation of the area in the fall of 1863, the Pattersons joined Military Governor Andrew Johnson and other family members in Nashville.

Upon Abraham Lincoln's assassination, Andrew Johnson succeeded him in the presidency. Johnson was insistent that all of his family members join him in Washington as soon as possible. Martha and her children arrived with her mother, Eliza, and youngest brother Frank (Andrew Jr.) on June 19, 1865. The family members spent most of the summer of 1865 at the Soldier's Home on the outskirts of the city (a place also favored by Lincoln as a summer retreat) rather than in the White House.

Because Eliza Johnson was sick with tuberculosis, Martha Patterson took on the practical and ceremonial aspects of being first lady, assisted by Mary Johnson Stover, her widowed sister. Although the family had a number of servants, Martha oversaw everything; milked the two cows; and made all the butter, cream, and ice cream used in the White House. When Congress appropriated $30,000 for the purpose, Martha, emphasizing simplicity and economy, refurbished the presidential home, which had become quite shabby as a result of extensive use during the Civil War. She also reputedly held official receptions more economically than many of her predecessors. Because David Patterson was serving as a senator from Tennessee, Martha had additional social responsibilities. Various accounts reported that she was a very popular hostess.

Martha apparently had good relationships with her younger siblings. She and her daughter Belle were the only family members who went to see her brother Robert in the summer and fall of 1868 when he was confined to an asylum because of his alcoholism.

After Johnson's presidency ended, which coincided with the end of David Patterson's senatorial term, the Pattersons returned to East Tennessee, where they lived on the former Henderson farm in Home, about six miles from Greeneville. In 1873 Johnson deeded the farm, about 516 acres, to Martha. During that period she often came to visit her mother and helped care for her when Johnson was away from home on frequent political trips. Martha began to suffer from rheumatism during the 1870s.

An extremely difficult year for Martha was 1891, when her daughter Belle Patterson Landstreet died of tuberculosis in California in July and her husband David died of heart disease in November. Martha cherished and helped to raise her granddaughter Martha Belle Patterson Landstreet (1887–1969). She also promoted the memory of her father, Andrew Johnson. In 1898, as Martha's health deteriorated, her son Andrew and his wife Martha Ellen (Mattie) Barkley (1864–1948) came to live with her in the Johnson home in Greeneville. After several years of disability, Martha died on July 10, 1901 of dysentery complicated by chronic disease. She was buried in the family plot on Monument Hill.

See also: Grandchildren; Greeneville, Tennessee; Johnson, Eliza McCardle; Johnson, Robert; Lincoln, Abraham; Patterson, David Trotter; Polk, James Knox; Stover (Brown), Mary Johnson; Tuberculosis.

References: Graf, LeRoy P., Haskins, Ralph W., Bergeron, Paul H., eds., *The Papers of Andrew Johnson* vols. 1, 8, 16 (1967–2000); Holloway, Laura Carter, *The Ladies of the White House* (1870); *Knoxville Journal and Tribune,* July 11, 1901; *Knoxville Sentinel,* July 10, 1901; *Nashville Union and American,* November 10, 1874; Trefousse, Hans L., *Andrew Johnson: A Biography* (1989).

Patterson (Landstreet), Mary Belle

See Grandchildren

Physical Description of Andrew Johnson

The earliest surviving physical description of Andrew Johnson was printed in a Raleigh, North Carolina, newspaper on June 24, 1824, when the future president was fifteen and a half. The description was contained in tailor James J. Selby's advertisement for his runaway apprentices, William and Andrew Johnson. The advertisement reversed the descriptions of the brothers, but, properly attributed, Andrew was described as "of a dark complexion, black hair, eyes, and about 5 feet 4 or 5 inches."

As an adult, Johnson was five feet eight inches tall and in April 1865 weighed 178 pounds. He was usually described as well or strongly built, with thick black hair, a swarthy complexion, a prominent nose, and piercing eyes. He was always clean shaven and well dressed in the male fashions of the period. He rarely smiled, usually seeming calm and serious, although he could become very animated when discussing subjects he considered important. Most thought Johnson to be a pleasant conversationalist. By the end of his presidency, Johnson's hair had grayed "but otherwise there is nothing about him that would indicate his being over forty-five." (He was sixty.)

When Johnson returned to the Senate in March 1875, a *New York Tribune* reporter described the former president just a few months before his death. "Physically, Mr. Johnson has undergone less change during the past eight years than almost any senator upon the floor. His hair may be a shade lighter as it is undoubtedly somewhat thinner, but there is no evidence of baldness. There are neither hard lines nor deep wrinkles in his face, but his expression is a mixture of sadness and earnestness—an expression which has been habitual with him when in repose during the past ten years. His form is not bent, all his senses are acute, he is sound and strong, and, take him all in all, at the age of 67 he is a remarkably well-preserved man."

See also: Apprenticeship; Health of Johnson; Senator, Johnson as.

References: Graf, LeRoy P., Haskins, Ralph W., and Bergeron, Paul H., eds., *The Papers of Andrew Johnson* vols. 1, 15–16 (1967–2000); Milton, George Fort, *The Age of Hate: Andrew Johnson and the Radicals* (1965 [1930]); *New York Tribune,* Mar. 8, 1875; Trefousse, Hans L., *Andrew Johnson: A Biography* (1989).

Polk, James Knox (1795–1849)

Born in Mecklenburg County, North Carolina, future president James Knox Polk was the oldest of the ten children of Samuel and Jane Knox Polk. To improve their economic standing, the Polk family moved to Columbia, Tennessee, near Nashville, when Polk was nearly eleven. After some local education, he attended the University of North Carolina and in 1818 graduated at the top of his class. Polk returned to Tennessee, studied law with the noted Felix Grundy in Nashville, and began his own law practice in Columbia in 1820. But serving as clerk of the state senate whetted his appetite for politics and in 1823 he was elected to a term in the state legislature. On January 1, 1824, Polk married Sarah Childress of Murfreesboro, Tennessee. The couple had a happy marriage but they had no children.

In 1825, Polk, a Democrat, was elected to the first of seven successive terms in the U.S. House of Representatives (1825–1839), spending his last two terms as Speaker of the House (1835–1839). This was followed by a term as governor of Tennessee (1839–1841). Andrew Johnson, newly reelected to the state legislature in 1839, was appointed to a committee to welcome Polk, and, despite their difference in background, the two seem to have become allies for the time being. Johnson supported Polk as governor, and several letters from Johnson to Polk, discussing political matters, survive.

In the 1841 gubernatorial race Polk failed to be reelected. Even worse, he was defeated again in 1843. These losses caused Johnson, among others, to view Polk as a rather weak prospective Democratic presidential candidate in 1844, and Johnson favored Lewis Cass of Michigan instead. Nevertheless, the Democrats, meeting in convention in Baltimore, on the ninth ballot nominated Polk, the first "dark horse" candidate (an unexpected, compromise candidate). Once the nomination was made, Johnson actively campaigned for Polk, and when the latter defeated the Whig candidate, Henry Clay, Johnson, now a member of Congress, expected to have a say in patronage matters (seeing his supporters appointed to available offices) as a reward. But he was to be disappointed.

In fact, Polk and Johnson soon split over the patronage issue. At first Polk did grant some of Johnson's requests, but then paid less attention to them. Perhaps he did not know about Johnson's opposition to his nomination right away. In any case, because Johnson was very much annoyed at Polk's failure to heed his requests, he called at the White House on July 21, 1846, and told

Polk so, reminding the president of his support with time and money in the campaign of 1844. After an hour of futile discussion, Johnson was even angrier, complaining to a friend about Polk's terrible appointments and his ingratitude toward Johnson. Nevertheless, despite their personal conflict, Johnson supported Polk's actions during the key crisis of his administration—the Mexican-American War.

Polk was elected on a platform urging the annexation of Texas to the United States. Although some of the arrangements for the annexation were made by Congress under the outgoing president, John Tyler, the final steps took place during Polk's term. This annexation led almost immediately to war with Mexico, the country that was losing Texas and feared that it would lose more territory in the southwest. The conflict broke out over the issue of the southern boundary of Texas. Texas and the U.S. government claimed that the boundary was at the Rio Grande, whereas the Mexican government claimed that the Nueces River, about 100 miles north of the Rio Grande, was the border. Polk sent troops into the disputed area and, when Mexican soldiers attacked them, Polk claimed that American blood had been shed on American soil and thus persuaded Congress to declare war on Mexico in May 1846.

Over the next two years, U.S. forces under Zachary Taylor in northern Mexico and Winfield Scott campaigning from Vera Cruz to Mexico City fought with and defeated the Mexican forces. The treaty of Guadalupe Hidalgo (1848) gave the United States the additional territory it craved—California and New Mexico (present day California, Nevada, and Utah, most of Arizona and New Mexico, and parts of Colorado and Wyoming)—as well as the Texas boundary at the Rio Grande.

Polk's presidency is best known for the Mexican-American War and the resulting territorial acquisitions, but Polk's administration also saw the peaceful settlement of the Oregon territorial boundary question at the forty-ninth parallel (the present border between Washington state and British Columbia, Canada), the passage of a new lower tariff, and the reestablishment of the Independent Treasury (for control of federal funds without the use of banks). Polk is one of the few presidents who accomplished all of his stated goals.

Polk was not renominated in 1848, having pledged in 1844 to serve only one term. After this term ended on March 4, 1849, Polk returned to Tennessee, where he died in Nashville on June 15, possibly of cholera, less than four months after leaving office.

See also: Congressman, Johnson as; Patronage; Patterson, Martha Johnson.

References: Bergeron, Paul H., *The Presidency of James K. Polk* (1987); Eisenhower, John S.D., *So Far from God: The U.S. War with Mexico, 1846–1848* (1989); Graf, LeRoy P., Haskins, Ralph H., and Bergeron, Paul H., eds., *The Papers of Andrew Johnson* vol. 1 (1967–2000); Haynes, Sam W., *James K. Polk and the Expansionist Impulse* (1987); Levy, Leonard W., and Fisher, Louis, eds., *Encyclopedia of the American Presidency* 4 vols. (1994); Polk, James K., *The Diary of James K. Polk during His Presidency, 1845–1849* 4 vols. Quaife, Milo M., ed. (1910); Trefousse, Hans L., *Andrew Johnson: A Biography* (1989).

Pope, John (1822–1892)

Union general John Pope, who commanded the Third Military District for a time during Andrew Johnson's term, was born in Louisville, Kentucky. He graduated from West Point, seventeenth in his class, in 1842. After four years of assignments with the topographical engineers, he served with Zachary Taylor's army in Mexico, as a result of which he received two brevets. After the war he continued in the topographical engineers, mostly in the West. On September 15, 1859, Pope married Clara Pomeroy Horton, and they had two sons and two daughters.

Soon after the outbreak of the Civil War in 1861, Pope was appointed a brigadier general and ordered to join the forces of General John C. Frémont in Missouri. In March and April 1862 Pope commanded the army that captured New Madrid, Missouri, and Island No. 10, opening a portion of the Mississippi River to Union navigation. He was involved in the siege of Corinth, Mississippi, and then was ordered east to command the Army of Virginia in the Washington, D.C., area. His serious loss at the Battle of Second Manassas (or Bull Run), July 29–30, 1862, resulted from his failure to understand the military situation. Nevertheless, he blamed others for the defeat, including General Fitz John Porter, whom Pope had cashiered for alleged disobedience to orders. Porter later wrote several letters to President Andrew Johnson, as did several of Porter's supporters, asking for a new trial to present now-available Confederate evidence that proved that Pope had no idea of the situation and that Porter could not have carried out the orders. Pope opposed a new trial and Johnson did nothing for Porter. It was many years before Porter was finally vindicated.

As a result of Second Manassas, Pope was sent to Minnesota, where he commanded troops that put down a Sioux uprising. In January 1865 he was given command of the Military Division of the Missouri (Kansas and Missouri). The next year he was commanding the Department of New Mexico.

After Congress passed the First Military Reconstruction Act on March 2, 1867, Johnson had to appoint commanders for the five military districts. Based on Ulysses S. Grant's recommendations, Johnson selected Pope for the Third Military District (Alabama, Georgia, and Florida). In this post Pope was active in carrying out his interpretation of the Reconstruction Acts. He removed the mayor and other city officials of Mobile, Alabama, after there was a "riot" there in May 1867. He also issued General Orders No. 49, which forced civil officials to give their advertisements to pro–Reconstruction newspapers only. These and other attempts to enforce the Reconstruction Acts caused much opposition from residents of the affected states. Johnson received many letters asking that Pope be removed for various offenses, such as attempting to "Africanize" Alabama. Only one of Johnson's correspondents, a Georgia judge, said not to remove Pope. Although he did not agree with many things that Pope did, the writer thought that Pope was as good as anyone else would be. Even some of Johnson's advisors, such as Thomas Ewing, Sr., urged the president to remove Pope, which Johnson finally did in late December 1867. General George G. Meade replaced Pope, who was sent to the Department of the Lakes. Pope commanded various western departments until 1882, when he was retired because of his age. He died from nervous prostration in Ohio.

See also: Ewing, Thomas (Jr. and Sr.); Grant, Ulysses Simpson; Military Districts; Military Reconstruction Acts.

References: Cozzens, Peter, and Girardi, Robert I., eds., *The Military Memoirs of General John Pope* (1998); Graf, LeRoy P., Haskins, Ralph W., and Bergeron, Paul H., eds., *The Papers of Andrew Johnson* vols. 7, 10, 12–13 (1967–2000); Hennessy, John J., *Return to Bull Run: The Campaign and Battle of Second Manassas* (1993); Trefousse, Hans L., *Andrew Johnson: A Biography* (1989).

Postpresidential Career

On March 4, 1869, Andrew Johnson left the presidency and began a lengthy period during which he held no political office. He did not immediately leave Washington, but spent several weeks with John F. Coyle's family, taking a side trip to Baltimore on March 11 to attend a reception and testimonial dinner in his honor. On March 18 he left Washington with his wife and several other family members, giving speeches along the way to Greeneville, where the party arrived on March 20. Almost immediately Johnson became so ill with an attack of kidney stones that his family members sent for Dr. Basil Norris, Johnson's physician in Washington, D.C. Johnson recovered quickly but not before the rumor spread, and was printed in some newspapers, that Johnson was dead.

In most of Johnson's speeches in the spring of 1869 he quoted lines from Joseph Addison's play *Cato,* in which the noble Roman retired to his rural property to pray for his country. Johnson claimed that he was retiring to Greeneville for the same purpose and was seeking no office. But Johnson was almost immediately bored with small town life after his greater involvements in Washington, and he was soon speaking around Tennessee and even in northern Alabama. Here a telegram reached him reporting the April 22 death of his son Robert (from an overdose of laudanum), temporarily stopping his speaking tour.

In late June and early July, Johnson was in Washington, D.C., visiting his son Frank (Andrew Jr.) at Georgetown College and handing out awards at the commencement ceremonies of a girl's school. He also spoke at a number of places in Tennessee, allegedly not campaigning for himself but hoping that the legislators elected in August would, in turn, elect him to the Senate in October. In a very close election on October 22, Johnson was defeated (55 to 51) by an alliance of both his Radical Republican opponents and his former Confederate enemies.

Meanwhile, Johnson managed his finances and attempted, without success, to track down his trunks and papers taken by General James Longstreet's forces in 1864. He received many letters from people wanting various favors and also received numerous invitations to speak, and, in fact, to go on paid lecture tours. He also financially backed his friend John C. Burch in an unsuccessful attempt to purchase a West Tennessee newspaper, the *Memphis Appeal.* Early in 1870 they were similarly unsuccessful in purchasing the *Memphis Avalanche.*

Throughout 1870 Johnson was pestered by requests from autograph seekers. He continued to receive requests from people who wanted favors such as letters of recommendation or information about opportunities for settlement in Greeneville. One man proposed that his family should come to the United States from Switzerland at Johnson's expense and they would work as his servants. During the year, Johnson bought some Greeneville property from his old friend William Lowry. In late June or early July, a bite or sting that Johnson sustained apparently kept him from celebrating July 4 in Knoxville.

Johnson did not enjoy a particularly exciting year in 1871. He received his usual types of requests in the mail. On May 27 he was the featured speaker at the closing ceremonies of the Mechanic's Fair in Knoxville. He emphasized his own background as a "mechanic" (tailor) and denounced the use of prison labor and training as competition for honest mechanics and artisans.

In 1872 Johnson traveled out of state at least twice. He attended the April wedding of Josie Campbell, daughter of Johnson's good friend Lewis D. Campbell, and her groom Murray Millikin, who were married in Cincinnati. Then, in early June, Johnson traveled to Washington, D.C., where he testified before a congressional committee investigating the disappearance of some papers from Don Carlos Buell's court of inquiry in 1863. Although Johnson had quarreled with Buell, he knew nothing about the missing papers.

Johnson, however, traveled far more in 1872 inside the state of Tennessee as part of the congressional campaign. In March Johnson refused to run for the first district seat. However, in May, Tennessee was granted an additional at-large (statewide) seat and Johnson declared his candidacy. The Democrats selected General Benjamin F. Cheatham as their candidate. Before the war, he and Johnson had worked together,

but Cheatham had fought for the South and now was the representative of the Confederate military faction that had done so much to defeat Johnson's Senate hopes in 1869. The Republican candidate was Horace Maynard. Johnson ran as an independent candidate. He spoke in many places and often debated Cheatham, as well as Maynard occasionally. Johnson's opposition was strong and he came in a poor third. However, the votes cast for him were votes lost by Cheatham, and so Maynard won. As his supporters claimed, by his defeat Johnson had broken much of the power of the Confederate military "ring."

Although politics had been Johnson's focus in 1872, he occupied much of 1873 with business affairs. He had numerous investments in property, had loaned money, and had sizable bank accounts in Tennessee and Washington, D.C. In late June and early July, however, Johnson nearly lost his life when he contracted cholera as the epidemic swept through Tennessee. Taken to his daughter Martha's farm six miles from Greeneville, Johnson recovered, although he never fully regained his health.

In August, Judge Advocate General Joseph Holt published a vituperative letter in the *Washington Chronicle* defending himself from supposed aspersions cast upon him by Johnson. Holt claimed that, when he came to bring the papers authorizing the execution of the Lincoln assassination conspirators to Johnson to be signed, he *did* show Johnson the request for clemency for Mary Surratt, signed by five members of the military commission that tried her. Johnson had said that he never saw it until after Mary Surratt's execution. Holt had accumulated some belated "evidence" in his favor, which he printed in his article. But why he waited seven years to bring up the issue is a question that has not been answered. Johnson began to make plans to reply to Holt, contacting several of his earlier associates, such as former secretary of the navy Gideon Welles, for information.

Johnson's reply was delayed in part because in September Jay Cooke's banking house in New York failed, beginning the Panic of 1873. The First National Bank in Washington, D.C., an enterprise of the Cooke family, also failed on September 18 and Johnson lost the $73,000 he had deposited there. It was a serious financial blow, although Johnson had other investments and resources. He went to Washington in October to see what arrangements could be made. In fact, by the time of Johnson's death, much of the loss had been repaid.

On November 12, 1873, Johnson finally published his rebuttal to Holt. Although several friends offered him the use of their newspapers, Johnson chose to continue the debate in the *Washington Chronicle.* Holt published another vituperative letter in the issue of December 1, citing additional "evidence" recalled by his supporters years after the fact. Although he considered it, Johnson chose not to reply further.

Johnson's finances, both his other investments and the problems with the First National Bank, occupied much of his correspondence. He made another trip to Washington in April 1874 to collect a dividend from the bank. But as the year progressed he became increasingly involved in politics, speaking at various places to help his supporters be elected to the legislature in November. Despite an overwhelmingly Democratic legislature, Johnson still had great opposition to his Senate aspirations. It took 55 ballots over several days before the legislature finally elected Johnson to the Senate on January 26, 1875. At last the former president was "vindicated" and he received hundreds of congratulatory letters and telegrams from friends and strangers.

Although friends urged Johnson to get to Washington early for the Senate session and proposed to give him a grand reception, he chose to arrive just before the session began and even published a notice in the newspaper asking friends to visit him individually rather than arranging a large public gathering. During the Senate session, March 5–24, Johnson gave one speech, on the situation in Louisiana, where some Democratic legislators elected under questionable circumstances had been removed from the meeting hall by the military. Johnson remained in Washington until early April, still working with the First National Bank on his payments.

Johnson was clearly tired and not in the best of health when he reached Greeneville. He seemed to be trying to put his affairs in order before his planned return to the Senate in the fall. He did not, however, prepare a will. At the end of July he traveled up to Carter County to see his wife, who was staying with their daughter Mary Stover on her farm. Just hours after he arrived, Johnson suffered a stroke, followed by one or two more, from which he died on July 31, 1875.

See also: Cooper, Edmund; Coyle, John Francis; Death of Johnson; Finances, Personal; Greeneville, Tennessee; Health of Johnson; Holt, Joseph; Maynard, Horace; Moore, William George; Panic of 1873; Senator, Johnson as; Surratt, Mary (Elizabeth) Eugenia Jenkins; Welles, Gideon.

References: Andrew Johnson Project, Knoxville, TN: files; Graf, LeRoy P., Haskins, Ralph W., and Bergeron, Paul H., eds., *The Papers of Andrew Johnson* vols. 15–16 (1967–2000); Trefousse, Hans L., *Andrew Johnson: A Biography* (1989).

Presidential Reconstruction

Presidential Reconstruction usually refers to the period during which Andrew Johnson dominated the readmission process, beginning May 29, 1865, and continuing through the passage of the Military Reconstruction Acts in March 1867. But the phrase itself can be more broadly construed, encompassing the efforts of Abraham Lincoln during the war and the continuation of Johnson's Reconstruction governments until 1868.

Because Reconstruction involved a situation unprecedented in U.S. history, no one was really sure who should direct the process or what shape that process should assume. During the war, President Abraham Lincoln asserted his authority as wartime executive and issued his Ten Percent Plan (December 1863). In the occupied Confederate states, ten percent of 1860 voters would need to take an oath of allegiance. This would create an electorate that, under the eyes of the U.S. Army and a governor appointed by Lincoln, would then elect a convention and write a new constitution recognizing such federal wartime measures as the abolition of slavery in the territories and the Emancipation Proclamation. Beyond this, Lincoln made no mention of the status of slaves. By the war's end, four states were already being "reconstructed" under Lincoln's plan: Louisiana, Arkansas, Virginia (an aberration which actually began *before* the Ten Percent Plan), and Tennessee—which featured Andrew Johnson as wartime governor. Congress made clear, however, that this plan was unacceptable and that Congress would have a say in the readmission process. To drive the point home, Congress refused to seat the representatives from the two states that "completed" Reconstruction, Arkansas and Louisiana.

Soon after Johnson became president on April 15, 1865, he presented a plan reminiscent of, but not the same as, Lincoln's. Like Lincoln, Johnson believed Reconstruction to be an executive function, to be completed as quickly as possible and with a minimum of disruption. Johnson neither called Congress into session nor sought the advice of members of Congress before implementing his program. Also like Lincoln, Johnson saw Restoration (as he called it) as a purely political matter that could be addressed by loyalty oaths, new constitutions, and readmission to Congress. Neither president sought a social revolution, and both believed that a few planters—the famous "slave power conspiracy"—were behind the war. Both presidents held that individuals, not

states, committed treason, and, because the war had proven the Union indivisible, Restoration should be an easy matter.

Despite similarities, Johnson's plan was not the same as Lincoln's. An expert at gauging public opinion and maintaining his delicate constituency, Lincoln presented a conservative plan and, although many in Congress balked, the army, the South, and most of Northern opinion was behind him. Lincoln was a president at war, with enormous authority and sweeping powers, yet he declined to push their limits. Johnson, on the other hand, had no mandate; he was a vice president who became executive by assassination, taking over after the war had ended. Worse, Johnson seemed incapable of sensing the public's mood. Although his plan was slightly more demanding than Lincoln's (it required a majority of 1860 voters rather than ten percent), he did not possess the advantages of a president at war; the North and Congress were not interested in a rapid, superficial Restoration; and some former Confederates still seemed intent on defying the victorious national government. Further, because Lincoln's plan operated during wartime, no one really knows what sort of peacetime arrangement he would have made. It is hard to imagine Lincoln reacting to race riots and Black Codes in the indifferent manner of Johnson.

Johnson's version of Presidential Reconstruction began on May 29, 1865, with his Proclamation of Amnesty and Reconstruction, which recognized as valid four governments—Tennessee, Virginia, Arkansas, and Louisiana—established under Lincoln's plan. The plan required a majority (not ten percent) of the 1860 registered voters to take a loyalty oath. Fourteen categories of individuals could not receive amnesty in this way and needed to apply directly to Johnson for a personal pardon. These classes included high-ranking Confederate civil and military officers, persons who had taken an oath to the United States previous to the war, anyone currently under federal arrest or indictment, and—the class which receives the most historical attention—anyone with prewar holdings of $20,000 or more.

Johnson then appointed temporary governors to oversee the rest of the process of Restoration: William W. Holden for North Carolina, Benjamin F. Perry for South Carolina, William H. Sharkey for Mississippi, Andrew Jackson Hamilton for Texas, James Johnson for Georgia, Lewis E. Parsons for Alabama, and William Marvin for Florida. All were prewar Unionists and men of moderate views, but some had also supported their states after secession, even holding office in the Confederate state governments. Johnson wanted Unionists who were locally popular, because their credibility was necessary to ensure support for his plan. The governors oversaw the amnesty process, the registration of eligible voters (those who could vote in 1860), and then elections for state constitutional conventions. Johnson required these constitutions to acknowledge the results of the war: each had to abolish slavery, repudiate secession and the Confederate war debt, and officially ratify the Thirteenth Amendment. These were the results of the war and the issues that had led to it, and Johnson, a conservative, Southern, strict constructionist, had no intention of embarking on a political or social revolution in the South. His disqualifying of certain segments of Southern society was similarly designed to send a message to those leaders of the "slave power conspiracy," the wealthy planters Johnson blamed for secession and civil war. Once complete, the new constitution had to be put to public vote, followed by the election of new state officers (to replace Johnson's temporary appointments) and new federal representatives.

In retrospect, Johnson's program was doomed before it started. He had not learned from his predecessor's experience that Congress demanded a role in Reconstruction. Making matters worse, his conservative stance and Southern sympathies produced an executive who seemed ultra-sensitive to the feelings of defeated Confederates, yet indifferent to the problems and pains of former slaves and Southern Unionists. No state abided by his demands in their constitutional conventions; every state avoided one or more of his requirements, yet Johnson ignored this. Violence against former slaves and Unionists was rampant, but neither Johnson's appointed governors nor the governments elected under his plan seemed interested; nor in fact did Johnson, and he never pushed the states to see that security and justice prevailed. Similarly, when the states created and passed their so-called Black Codes, laws governing the life and labor of the freedpeople, Johnson saw only a tradition of the states' control over their own citizenry.

Perhaps the final blow came with the election of new federal representatives. The fourteen classes made ineligible under Johnson's May 1865 proclamation were not ineligible for long. Thousands applied directly to Johnson for pardons, either personally or through a pardon broker, and most of these applicants had their political disabilities promptly removed. By design, these were leaders of the Old South and the Confederacy, and even Johnson was surprised when many were elected to Congress; he had hoped that the common whites, men with the same roots as he, would repudiate the planter elite and elect commoners and Unionists. Johnson's naiveté was astounding; he had forgiven the planter class, so why would other Southerners reject them? Again, despite some misgivings, Johnson refused to interfere in the internal matters of the states, and he fully expected them to be readmitted to Congress.

The congressmen charged with accepting or rejecting the Southern representatives had been watching these developments with increasing apprehension. When Congress assembled in December 1865, it refused to admit the Southern representatives, serving notice that it rejected Johnson's entire program. Instead, Republicans in Congress created the Joint Committee of Fifteen on Reconstruction, the brains behind an entirely different Reconstruction program.

Johnson's final opportunity to save his plan of Restoration came with the congressional elections of 1866. During the year, Congress had begun inching toward its version of Reconstruction, with the Civil Rights and Freedmen's Bureau bills, and had demonstrated that it would override Johnson's vetoes. Johnson's only hope was for conservatives to take control of Congress. To this end he helped create the National Union Party, which advocated regional reconciliation and acknowledged an end to hostilities and the Restoration process. But continued violence in the South and Johnson's immature and unprofessional performance on his Swing-around-the-Circle campaign tour effectively killed a movement that had little support from the beginning. The elections of 1866 ushered in a Congress more than two-thirds Republican, essentially veto-proof, and spelled the real end of Presidential Reconstruction.

By 1867 Congress had effectively wrested control of Reconstruction away from President Johnson, sweeping away the Black Codes, disfranchising many former Confederates, and eventually replacing Johnson's governments altogether. Until the end of his administration Johnson insisted that congressional interference in a state's internal affairs was unconstitutional and that the pardon power lay with the executive. For this reason Johnson continued to issue pardons and proclaim amnesties, even though Congress—through the Military Reconstruction Acts and the Fourteenth Amendment—had stripped him of this power.

See also: Amnesty Proclamations; Black Codes; Black Suffrage; Blacks (Slave and Free), Johnson's Attitude toward; Congressional Reconstruction; Conservatives; Constitution, Johnson's Attitude toward; Election of 1866; Governors, Provisional; Joint Committee on Reconstruction; Lincoln, Abraham; Memphis Riot; Military Reconstruction Acts; National Union Convention and Party; New Orleans Riot; Pardons (Individual); Readmission of Southern States; Reconstruction; Swing-around-the-Circle; Thirteenth Amendment.

References: Carter, Dan T., *When the War Was Over: The Failure of Self-Reconstruction in the South, 1865–1867* (1985); Castel, Albert, *The Presidency of Andrew Johnson* (1979); Dorris, Jonathan Truman, *Pardon and Amnesty under Lincoln and Johnson: The Restoration of the Confederates to Their Rights and Privileges, 1861–1898* (1953); Graf, LeRoy P., Haskins, Ralph W., and Bergeron, Paul H., eds., *The Papers of Andrew Johnson* vols. 8–11 (1967–2000); McKitrick, Eric L., *Andrew Johnson and Reconstruction* (1960); Sefton, James E., *Andrew Johnson and the Uses of Constitutional Power* (1980); Trefousse, Hans L., *Andrew Johnson: A Biography* (1989).

Presidential Travels

As president, Andrew Johnson did not often leave Washington, D.C. In fact, he never even visited his home in Tennessee at any time during his term. His most extensive trip was the Swing-around-the-Circle (August 28–September 15, 1866), which is discussed in another entry. He also took a brief trip to Baltimore in November 1866 to attend a Masonic Temple cornerstone laying.

Johnson's other travels took place in 1867. In May, Johnson received an invitation from the mayor of Raleigh, North Carolina, to attend the dedication of a monument at the grave of Johnson's father on June 4. He also received invitations to attend the June 6 commencement at the University of North Carolina in Chapel Hill. The result was a trip to his native state by way of Richmond, Virginia.

Johnson left Washington on June 1 accompanied by Secretary of State William H. Seward, Postmaster General Alexander W. Randall, and presidential private secretary William G. Moore. They spent the night at the Spottswood House hotel in Richmond and attended St. Paul's Episcopal Church there the next morning. On Monday, June 3, the party traveled to Raleigh, where Johnson was greeted by the military governor General Daniel Sickles, the mayor William D. Haywood, and a crowd. Johnson delivered a speech there at the Yarborough House, where he was staying. He thanked the people for their welcome, expressed emotion at returning to his native state after some forty years, proclaimed his loyalty to the Constitution, and urged young men to work hard in order to rise in the world.

On June 4 Johnson attended the dedication of the monument to his father, Jacob Johnson, who had died when the president was only three. The monument, a ten-foot shaft of red limestone, was inscribed: "In memory of Jacob Johnson; an honest man, beloved and respected by all who knew him. Born —. Died January 1812, from a disease caused by an over-effort in saving the life of a friend." On June 6 Johnson attended commencement ceremonies at the University of North Carolina. The following day the party left Raleigh, spent the night in Richmond again, and returned to Washington, D.C., on June 8.

Johnson had another trip planned as well, to Boston and other places in the northeast. At least one of his friends urged Johnson not to go. The president had had an important reason to go to North Carolina, but he had no family connection to New England and Thomas Ewing, Jr., was concerned that there might be problems such as had occurred on the Swing-around-the-Circle campaign tour. Johnson went anyway and was respectfully received in each place where he stopped. He also avoided delivering political harangues.

Johnson and the same men with whom he had gone to North Carolina left Washington on June 21. They visited New York City; Springfield, Massachusetts; and then Boston. Here, in one of the highlights of the trip, Johnson participated in the dedication of the new Masonic temple at Tremont and Boylston Streets. The party then moved on to Philadelphia; Hartford, Connecticut; and New Haven, where he told the Yale students that he had chosen the wrong profession—he should have been a schoolteacher. Finally, visiting Baltimore and Annapolis, Johnson addressed the constitutional convention of the state of Maryland at Annapolis on June 29. Johnson spoke about how well he had been received, both in the North and in the South, and believed "that an era of good will is about to be inaugurated." Never touching on controversial topics, he discussed constitutional amendment procedures, and how years earlier George Washington had resigned his general's commission in Annapolis to return to civilian life. Johnson and his companions returned to Washington that day after a successful trip.

Johnson took one more short excursion in 1867. He went to the dedication on September 17 at Antietam battlefield, where he delivered very brief remarks. "My appearance on this occasion will be the speech that I will make," he said. He urged the audience to imitate the example of the soldiers in death "and live together in friendship and peace."

Despite invitations to visit various friends, Johnson made no further presidential trips. At first he could not leave during the impeachment threat and proceedings. Then he did not wish to leave while Congress was in session. Consequently, he remained in Washington until the end of his term.

See also: Ewing, Thomas (Jr. and Sr.); Johnson, Jacob; Moore, William George; Randall, Alexander Williams; Seward, William Henry; Sickles, Daniel Edgar; Swing-around-the-Circle; University of North Carolina.

References: Graf, LeRoy P., Haskins, Ralph W., and Bergeron, Paul H., eds., *The Papers of Andrew Johnson* vols. 11–13 (1967–2000); Trefousse, Hans L., *Andrew Johnson: A Biography* (1989).

R

Railroads

Railroads were an extremely important, expanding, and at times controversial, part of the economy during Andrew Johnson's political career. About 1860 there were 30,636 miles of railroad track in the United States, roughly two-thirds of it constructed during the 1850s. Much track was destroyed in the South, the area that had the least mileage, during the Civil War. The later 1860s, the period of Johnson's presidency, saw the construction of 16,090 miles, including most of the transcontinental railroad.

Andrew Johnson was never particularly in favor of government aid for so-called internal improvements such as railroads. He voted against some railroad charter bills during the 1835–1836 legislative session because he believed they were unconstitutional and encouraged monopolies, not to mention that they would create unemployment for teamsters and tavern owners. Despite Johnson's opposition, the legislature passed these bills and numerous others. By the time Johnson was governor in 1854, one of his concerns was the issuance of state bonds to support railroad construction in Tennessee. In some cases he approved issuing the bonds and in other cases he did not.

While Johnson was in the U.S. Senate in the late 1850s he was a strong advocate of a homestead bill, which would grant land to the landless poor. This goal contributed to his opposition to a transcontinental railroad because all the bills establishing such an enterprise offered the railroad vast amounts of land to help it pay construction expenses. Johnson, in a January 25, 1859, speech opposing the railroad, used the argument that government support of railroad construction could not be justified under the various articles of the Constitution cited, such as Congress's war powers or its right to control commerce or establish post roads. Consequently, such support was not constitutional. In addition, Johnson insisted that a transcontinental railroad would not protect California or encourage the preservation of the Union as its supporters alleged. He believed that far too much government money would be expended for the railroad and it was important to determine how the government was going to get that money in the first place. He also protested that so much land would be given to railroads when Congress refused to give much smaller amounts to actual settlers through a homestead act.

As military governor of Tennessee during the Civil War, Johnson was concerned about restoring destroyed railroads in the state and was at times authorized to have federal troops protect the railroad construction workers.

During Johnson's presidency, railroad issues often became patronage matters. Johnson could nominate the government directors for the Union Pacific Railroad and various other railroad commissioner posts and he received a number of requests to appoint certain people. He also received many letters asking him to support certain prospective railroad routes both inside and outside the United States.

In June 1862 both houses of Congress had finally approved a transcontinental railroad, but the Union Pacific company was not actually organized until October 1863. It built west from Omaha while the Central Pacific built east from San Francisco, beginning in January 1863. One of Johnson's concerns as president, especially as the rail lines moved toward completion, was at what points each railroad should be paid for finished sections of track. The Union Pacific particularly faced charges of shoddy workmanship and threats that funds would be withheld until the problems were fixed. Questions about these railroad subsidies were discussed in a number of cabinet meetings. The Central Pacific and the Union Pacific railroads were joined at Promontory Point, Utah, on May 10, 1869, just two months after Johnson left the presidency.

See also: Annual Messages; Governor (Civilian), Johnson as; Homestead Act; Military Governor of Tennessee, Johnson as; Patronage; Senator, Johnson as; State Legislator, Johnson as; Territorial Affairs.

References: Graf, LeRoy P., Haskins, Ralph W., and Bergeron, Paul H., eds., *The Papers of Andrew Johnson* vols. 1–3, 6, 11–15 (1967–2000); Ringwalt, J.L., *Development of Transportation Systems in the United States* (1888).

Randall, Alexander Williams (1819–1872)

Alexander Williams Randall was born in Ames, New York. He attended Cherry Valley Academy and then studied law under his father, Phineas Randall. In 1840 he moved west to Wisconsin Territory, where he practiced law in Prairieville (later renamed Waukesha). Two years later he married Mary C. Van Vechten of New York state. She died in 1858.

Randall quickly became involved in politics, at first as a Whig and then as a Democrat. His first political appointment (1845) was the postmastership of his town. This position provided him with some useful political connections. In 1846 he was a delegate to the state constitutional convention, where he set back his political career for several years by proposing a resolution in favor of black suffrage. By 1848 he had moved to the Free Soil wing of the Democratic Party and then became a Republican.

After a term in the state assembly and a few months filling an unexpired judicial term, Randall was elected governor of Wisconsin in 1857 and reelected in 1859 on the Republican ticket. When the Civil War broke out in April 1861, Randall, who had been urging preparedness for months, was an extremely efficient organizer of troops and had the first Wisconsin regiment ready to go to the front in six days. By the time he left office nine months later, Wisconsin had sent 25,000 soldiers to the Union army.

Unable to get a senatorship, Randall wanted a military appointment but Abraham Lincoln appointed him minister to Rome instead. Randall returned to the United States the next year still hoping for a military post. Again Lincoln gave him something else, first assistant postmaster general (1863). From this position Randall was an influential worker for Lincoln's reelection in 1864.

In early June 1866, even before he held a cabinet position, Randall traveled with President Andrew Johnson, Secretary of State William H. Seward, and Colonel William Moore, Johnson's secretary, to North Carolina to attend the unveiling of a monument to Johnson's father. Johnson also spoke at the commencement of the University of North Carolina and received an honorary degree.

When several of Johnson's cabinet members resigned in June 1866 because they opposed the call for a National Union Party convention, Johnson appointed Randall to the office of postmaster general, replacing William Dennison. Randall attended the National Union Party Convention in Philadelphia in August, where he opened the meeting on August 14 and wrote several letters to Johnson about convention events.

As postmaster general, Randall occupied one of the most important patronage-granting posts in the government. He constantly received requests and recommendations for postmasterships nationwide as well as other requests to remove postmasters, usually because their politics did not suit the writer of the letter. Some of Johnson's correspondents urged the president to revamp his cabinet, particularly removing Secretary of State Seward, Secretary of the Treasury Hugh McCulloch, and Randall, all of whom they considered to be obstructions to Johnson's policy. Johnson did not remove them, however.

Although one historian claims that Johnson had little confidence in Randall by sometime in 1867, nevertheless Randall was one of the president's staunchest supporters. He helped to raise funds to cover the cost of Johnson's impeachment defense and he attended the July 1868 Democratic National Convention in New York City, where he worked unsuccessfully for Johnson's nomination for president. On March 11, 1869, just after Johnson left office, Randall was one of only two of his former cabinet members to attend the grand banquet given in Johnson's honor in Baltimore.

Randall's loyalty to Johnson ruined his further prospects for a political career, so he moved to Elmira, New York, the hometown of his second wife, Helen M. Thomas, whom he had married in 1863. There he practiced law briefly until he died from cancer in 1872.

See also: Cabinet Members; Democratic Convention; Dennison, William; Impeachment; McCulloch, Hugh; Moore, William George; National Union Convention and Party; Patronage; Presidential Travels; Seward, William Henry.
References: Graf, LeRoy P., Haskins, Ralph W., and Bergeron, Paul H., eds., *The Papers of Andrew Johnson* vols. 11, 13–15 (1967–2000); Trefousse, Hans L., *Andrew Johnson: A Biography* (1989).

Readmission of Southern States

One of the major concerns of Andrew Johnson's presidency was the process by which the former Confederate states would be admitted to their normal place in the Union with full representation in Congress. There were several viewpoints about the status of the seceded states at the close of the Civil War. Perhaps the most extreme view was espoused by Thaddeus Stevens, who believed that the Southern states were now conquered provinces. The "state suicide" theory of Charles Sumner and some other Radical Republicans claimed that by seceding the Southern states had removed themselves from statehood; consequently, they were now territories subject to government by Congress and its appointees.

On the other hand, Andrew Johnson believed that states could not secede and consequently were not out of the Union. Individuals, not states, committed treason, therefore, individuals, not states, should be punished (hence the various exceptions to the Amnesty Proclamation of May 29, 1865). Thus, Johnson believed that Reconstruction, or "Restoration," should be a fairly simple and speedy process.

Also believing that he, not Congress, should be in charge of Reconstruction, Johnson issued a proclamation on May 29, 1865, granting amnesty to most former Confederates who swore an oath of loyalty to the United States. There were fourteen excepted classes of persons who had to apply to Johnson for individual pardons. On the same day, Johnson issued another proclamation establishing a provisional government for North Carolina, appointing as provisional governor William W. Holden. Holden was to call an election (only loyal persons and those who had received amnesty could vote) for delegates to a constitutional convention. Johnson soon issued similar proclamations for other states: Mississippi (June 13), Georgia and Texas (June 17), Alabama (June 21), South Carolina (June 30), and Florida (July 13). Tennessee, Louisiana, Virginia, and Arkansas already had Reconstruction governments established under Abraham Lincoln. The constitutions had to abolish slavery, repudiate secession and the Confederate debt, and ratify the Thirteenth Amendment.

Unfortunately for Johnson's plans, most of the Southern states were recalcitrant about carrying out Johnson's requirements, and Congress demanded a role in Reconstruction to make the process of readmission more difficult. In December 1865 Congress refused to seat the men elected by the Southern states because a number of these men had been influential Confederate leaders.

When Congress passed the Fourteenth Amendment (allowing blacks to be considered citizens) in 1866, the Southern states were expected to ratify it. But Johnson encouraged these states not to do so and none of them did except, ironically, the president's home state of Tennessee. Consequently, Tennessee was readmitted to the Union, its representatives were admitted to Congress, and it escaped the impact of Congressional Reconstruction as detailed in the four Military Reconstruction acts.

For a state to be readmitted to the Union, an election supervised by the military authorities had to be held to select delegates to a constitutional convention. The new state constitutions had to include universal male suffrage and to be approved by the electorate, as well as Congress. Once this was accomplished, the state could elect new state officials and a legislature. When the legislature had ratified the Fourteenth Amendment, the state would be readmitted and its representatives could take their seats in Congress.

Although these requirements were moderate and straightforward, misunderstandings and deliberate procrastination caused Congress to clarify their demands with three more Military Reconstruction acts. In late June 1868, seven states—Arkansas, Alabama, Florida, Georgia, Louisiana, North Carolina, and South Carolina—were readmitted. The other three states—Mississippi, Texas, and Virginia—had problems with their constitutions and were not readmitted until 1870 after they had also ratified the Fifteenth Amendment. In addition, Georgia was returned to military rule after conservative whites in the legislature ejected the black legislators. Georgia was admitted again in 1870.

See also: Amnesty Proclamations; Black Suffrage; Congressional Reconstruction; Fifteenth Amendment; Fourteenth Amendment; Governors, Provisional; Lincoln, Abraham; Military Districts; Military Reconstruction Acts; Pardons (Individual); Presidential Reconstruction; Reconstruction; Stevens, Thaddeus; Sumner, Charles; Thirteenth Amendment.

References: Foner, Eric, *Reconstruction: America's Unfinished Revolution, 1863–1877* (1988); Graf, LeRoy P., Haskins, Ralph W., and Bergeron, Paul H., eds., *The Papers of Andrew Johnson* vols. 8–15 (1967–2000).

Reconstruction

Reconstruction refers to the period of readjustment during and after the American Civil War when the nation struggled to define the place of the former Confederate states, former Confederates, and former slaves within the Union. Reconstructing the Union involved activity at several levels: the readmission of the seceded states, the restructuring of Southern society without slavery, and the physical rebuilding of a devastated region. The problem of how to treat the seceded states and their white and black citizens involved complex constitutional, political, social, and economic issues.

While the war was still raging, Reconstruction began politically with President Abraham Lincoln's Ten Percent Plan of December 1863. In Confederate states under federal occupation, once ten percent of the 1860 voters had taken a loyalty oath, formation of a new state government could begin. Lincoln's view of Reconstruction assumed executive direction, was fairly lenient, and accepted that the states themselves had never left the Union. The only attention paid to blacks was that new state constitutions had to recognize any war measures affecting blacks, such as emancipation. Some Republicans opposed both Lincoln's claim of executive control and his leniency, and by July 1864 had proposed an alternative, the Wade-Davis Bill. Congressional Republicans saw their plan pocket-vetoed by Lincoln, but they responded by refusing to seat federal representatives of the president's "reconstructed" states. By war's end Lincoln governments were in Louisiana, Tennessee, Arkansas, and Virginia, but congressional hostility was already apparent.

The elevation of Andrew Johnson to the presidency on April 15, 1865, did little to deflect that hostility. Despite threats of punishment for traitors, Johnson quickly demonstrated that, like Lincoln, he believed that the states were still part of the Union and that only individuals, not states, can commit treason. In fact Johnson avoided the term "Reconstruction," as it denoted some altering of the status quo; he used the term "Restoration," which implied a mere returning to a previous situation. (To avoid confusion, we use Reconstruction in our discussion.) Also like Lincoln, Johnson believed that Reconstruction was the executive's responsibility and he supported a minimalist approach, hoping that the traditional balance of power between the state and federal governments could be maintained.

Because Congress was not in session when Johnson became president, initially he was able to implement his Reconstruction program uncontested. With the exception of the abolition of slavery, Johnson's restored South looked much like the antebellum South. He appointed provisional governors to oversee the writing of new state constitutions and the formation of new state governments, issued no requirements regarding the protection of or provision for freed blacks, and supported the maintenance of an all-white electorate. President Johnson liberally granted pardons to those not covered by his amnesty proclamation of May 29, 1865, restoring political rights to thousands and ensuring that the Southern state governments and federal representatives would be more similar than different from their antebellum predecessors.

Congressional Republicans had already demonstrated that they would not accept total presidential control over any Reconstruction program or a quick and easy solution. When Congress reassembled in December 1865, the struggle for control of Reconstruction policy flared anew. Although not yet ready to abandon the president and his program, congressional Republicans were concerned about violence and abuse against blacks in the South and the ease with which former secessionists reclaimed power. By spring of 1866 a theory was gaining momentum. Called the "grasp of war" concept, it stated that a victor could hold the vanquished in a sort of limbo, the "grasp of war," until the winners had gained all they desired from the losers. Thus, it was the North's "right" to demand certain changes and actions from the South *before* readmitting the states to the Union. For some moderate Republicans, this meant guarantees of civil and legal rights to blacks, but a growing number of Radical Republicans sought political rights for blacks, punishment for former Confederates, and the establishment of a secure Southern Republican Party.

Radicals who favored a more severe Reconstruction policy proposed alternate theories to support their views. For instance Thaddeus Stevens, the influential representative from Pennsylvania, advocated the "conquered provinces" theory, which stated that rebellion had destroyed the previous relationship between the federal government and the Confederate states. The states and population of the former Confederacy were no more than a conquered land, to which the Constitution's rights and privileges did not apply. Congress could hold the region in its "grasp of war" indefinitely and had the authority to completely reshape the region; this might include black suffrage, the disfranchisement of former Confederates, confiscation of property, and even the redrawing of borders.

A variation of this was another radical proposal that operated on the "grasp of war" premise and assumed congressional jurisdiction. This was the "state suicide" theory of Massachusetts senator Charles Sumner, who argued that Southern states had deliberately and willingly severed themselves from the Union, committing treason and abrogating the relationship to the federal government. The simplest way of resolving the matter was to treat the Southern states as territories, under congressional control, and force them to meet certain criteria for admission to the United States just as new territories did.

But such plans were too revolutionary, so moderate Republicans tried to work from within Johnson's program by allowing his governments to remain but requiring additional modifications, such as acceptance of the Civil Rights Act, the Freedmen's Bureau Act, and the Fourteenth Amendment. When it became clear that neither the Southern states (with the exception of Tennessee) nor the president would compromise and accept these demands, moderate Republicans became more radical, and the Radicals took control of Reconstruction.

In early 1867 Congress officially rejected Johnson's program. The three Military Reconstruction Acts of 1867 (and one in 1868) were not the revolutionary measures that Stevens and Sumner had envisioned, but they did place Reconstruction firmly under congressional direction and encompass a list of demands binding upon the states. These measures, administered by the army, enfranchised black males and disfranchised many former Confederates, setting the stage for a Southern Republican Party. For readmission Congress required the states themselves to grant black suffrage through new constitutions, and each state had to ratify the Fourteenth Amendment. Arkansas, North Carolina, South Carolina, Virginia, Alabama, Texas, Mississippi, Florida, Georgia, and Louisiana all passed through Congressional or Military Reconstruction; Tennessee, which had ratified the Fourteenth Amendment, was readmitted without undergoing Congressional Reconstruction. By the end of 1868, six Southern states had been readmitted under congressional guidelines: Arkansas, South Carolina, North Carolina, Florida, Alabama, and Louisiana. Four others, Virginia, Texas, Mississippi, and Georgia, would be readmitted in 1870, after meeting the additional criteria of ratifying the Fifteenth Amendment.

President Johnson, believing that congressional measures were both unconstitutional and un-American, frequently criticized and even hindered congressional efforts. With a veto-proof Republican majority, Congress overrode veto after veto and finally impeached Johnson in February 1868 for violation of the Tenure of Office Act (1867). Although impeached by the House of Representatives, Johnson was not convicted by the Senate and thus remained in office to complete his term.

Congress, however, easily retained control of Reconstruction policy, and with the election of Ulysses S. Grant in 1868 the program seemed to offer even greater promise. Grant had sided with the Radicals in the congressional conflict with Johnson, and Republicans had every hope that the new president would fight for a new Union as ardently as he had fought for the old one.

The question of readmission to the Union was only one aspect of Reconstruction, and perhaps the least vexing one. For in the South itself other issues assumed greater importance, such as the creation of new governments, the physical rebuilding of devastated cities and ruined plantations, the development of a wage labor system to replace slavery, and the emergence of a new relationship between whites and blacks. Congressional Reconstruction gave rise to a new ruling class, made up of Northerners (carpetbaggers), Southerners who were Unionists or who accepted the new order (scalawags), and enfranchised blacks.

The social and political revolution in the South opened the way for adventurers and fortune seekers, and men of both races and political parties saw the upheaval and heavy economic speculation (as states were trying to restart their economies) as an opportunity to get rich quick. Corruption and fraud were rampant in Southern Republican governments, and there were certainly cases of wily whites taking advantage of uneducated blacks. But the extent of fraud was no worse than in some Northern governments at the time or in conservative Democratic governments that came to power in the 1870s. The changing social and economic nature of the nation made abuses nearly unavoidable. In addition, Southern Republican governments did achieve much; the heavy taxes that Democrats complained of went to repairing cities; constructing schools, roads, and railroads; and financing agricultural and commercial loans.

Nor was the extent of the revolution as grand as many conservative Southerners, and historians, maintained. Much to the chagrin of politicians such as Stevens and Sumner, Reconstruction did not permanently or totally revamp the South. Confiscation of land did not occur, so land, the basis of power in an agricultural society,

largely remained in white hands. Changes in the political structure were no less fleeting, for conservative Southerners reacted antagonistically to the Republican governments. Economic blackmail, voting fraud, and outright violence—by such groups as the Ku Klux Klan—kept Republicans away from the polls. As Southern white resistance intensified, Northern resilience dwindled.

At first the Grant administration seemed intent on protecting the gains made under Congressional Reconstruction, even using the U.S. Army and the Department of Justice to enforce political and civil rights. But in the 1870s the federal government and the Northern population steadily lost interest in the South. Supreme Court decisions such as the "slaughterhouse" cases, *U.S. v. Reese,* and *U.S. v. Cruikshank* limited the right of the federal government to enforce much of Congress's legislation. Other issues became more compelling, such as Indian troubles out West, corruption in the Grant administration, and the recession of 1873. By the presidential election of 1876 only three Southern states still had Republican governments—Florida, South Carolina, and Louisiana. In that fraud-ridden election a special electoral commission chose Republican Rutherford B. Hayes over Democrat Samuel B. Tilden. Hayes refused to be burdened with supporting Southern Republican governments and pulled military units out of Southern capitals. By April 1877, all former Confederate state governments were back in the hands of conservative Democrats.

But controversy and conflict did not end with the closing of Reconstruction, and soon historians were debating the ideals and impact of the period. The earliest Reconstruction studies viewed opposition to Reconstruction as justified and necessary. In the late nineteenth and early twentieth centuries, historians such as William Dunning, John Burgess, Claude Bowers, and E. Merton Coulter argued that Republican governments were corrupt and incompetent, supported only by a wrongly enfranchised inferior race and a tyrannical federal government. The Dunning School, as it came to be called, saw Andrew Johnson as a champion of the Constitution who tried to protect a misguided, but penitent, South.

By the middle of the twentieth century, changing demographics and racial views, resulting in part from the Second World War and a reaction to Nazism, forced scholars to reexamine Reconstruction policies. The racism and pro-Southern bias of the Dunning School faded and revisionists such as W.E.B. Du Bois, John and LaWanda Cox, and Richard Current began to see Congress, the freedmen, and even carpetbaggers in a more favorable light. These were heroes of the grandest liberal tradition, fighting for democracy, equality, and civil rights. Consequently Andrew Johnson lost considerable esteem and became a closed-minded bigot who did his best to block progress.

Soon this scholarly trend received modifications, as a wave of neo-revisionists questioned the accomplishments of the period altogether. During the so-called Second Reconstruction of the 1950s and 1960s, a new generation attempted, with their own successes and failures, to fulfill the promise of the first Reconstruction. In this environment, historians such as C. Vann Woodward, Harold Hyman, and Michael Les Benedict saw black civil and political rights as illusory, the Reconstruction amendments as a whitewash, and Republican control in Washington temporary and ineffectual. Did Reconstruction achieve anything at all, they asked? Or did it merely serve to antagonize the regions and races? Historians continue to debate this question and will no doubt continue to produce theories claiming to explain a period when idealism and promise coexisted alongside despair, greed, violence, and chaos.

See also: Army Appropriations Act; Black Codes; Black Suffrage; Blacks (Slave and Free), Johnson's Attitude toward; Civil Rights Act; Congressional Reconstruction; Conservatives; Constitution, Johnson's Attitude toward; Democratic Party; Election of 1866; Election of 1868; Fifteenth Amendment; Fourteenth Amendment; Freedmen's Bureau Bills (and Vetoes); Impeachment; Joint Committee on Reconstruction; *McCardle, Ex parte;* Military Districts; Military Reconstruction Acts; *Milligan, Ex parte;* Presidential Reconstruction; Readmission of Southern States; Republican Party; Tenure of Office Act; Thirteenth Amendment.

References: Benedict, Michael Les, *A Compromise of Principle: Congressional Republicans and Reconstruction, 1863–1869* (1974); Bowers, Claude G., *The Tragic Era: The Revolution after Lincoln* (1929); Burgess, John W., *Reconstruction and the Constitution, 1866–1876* (1902); Coulter, E. Merton, *The South during Reconstruction, 1865–1877* (1947); Cox, LaWanda, and Cox, John H., eds., *Reconstruction, the Negro, and the New South* (1973); Current, Richard N., ed., *Reconstruction, 1865–1877* (1965); Curry, Richard O., "The Civil War and Reconstruction, 1861–1877: A Critical Overview of Recent Trends and Interpretations," *Civil War History* 20 (Sept. 1974): 215–238; Du Bois, W.E.B., *The Souls of Black Folk: Essays and Sketches* (1903); Dunning, William, *Reconstruction, Political and Economic* (1905); Fleming, Walter L., *The Sequel of Appomattox: A Chronicle of the Reunion of the States* (1919); Foner, Eric, *Reconstruction: America's Unfinished Revolution, 1863–1877* (1988); Franklin, John Hope, *Reconstruction: After the Civil War* (1961); Gillette, William, *Retreat from Reconstruction, 1869–1879* (1979); Hyman, Harold, *A More Perfect Union: The Impact of the Civil War and Reconstruction on the Constitution* (1973); McKitrick, Eric L., *Andrew Johnson and Reconstruction* (1960); Perman, Michael, *Reunion without Compromise: The South and Reconstruction, 1865–1868* (1973); Trelease, Allen W., *White Terror: The Ku Klux Klan Conspiracy and Southern Reconstruction* (1971); Weisberger, Bernard A., "The Dark and Bloody Ground of Reconstruction Historiography," *Journal of Southern History* 25 (Nov. 1959): 427–447; Woodward, C. Vann, *Reunion and Reaction: The Compromise of 1877 and the End of Reconstruction* (1951).

Religion, Johnson's Attitude toward

Although Andrew Johnson at times attended church services, he was never a member of any particular religious denomination. Periodically, personal friends and general correspondents urged Johnson to be converted to Christianity, but he never gave any indication that he had had, or even desired, such an experience.

In 1839, early in his career, Johnson opposed a resolution calling for a minister to open each daily legislative session with prayer. This became the basis for charges by his political opponents that Johnson was an "infidel." Through his newspaper, William G. "Parson" Brownlow was Johnson's most vigorous and vituperative attacker, especially in the 1845 congressional campaign. Finally, in October 1845, Johnson wrote a lengthy pamphlet refuting Brownlow's charges and claiming that he never had "a solitary doubt" about "the great scheme of salvation, as founded, taught, and practiced by Jesus Christ himself." Johnson, however, demonstrated that his understanding of Christianity was not especially orthodox when he explained that "a belief in pure and unadulterated principles of Democracy, is a belief in the religion of our Saviour, . . . rewarding the virtuous and meritorious without any regard to station, to wealth, or distinction of birth." Perhaps it was this highly charged local religious atmosphere that caused Johnson to use more Biblical allusions and quotations in his earlier speeches than he did as president and after.

During the 1850s Johnson opposed the Know-Nothing Party. As he announced in a May 1855 speech at Murfreesboro, he believed that "all men have a natural and indefeasible right to worship Almighty God according to the dictates of their own conscience." He opposed the persecution of Catholics and foreigners and pointed out that Protestant heroes such as John Calvin, Martin Luther, John Wesley, and Roger Williams would all be considered foreigners. In general, Johnson opposed the idea of any particular established church and he believed that there should be no religious test for state or federal office.

Johnson tended to be eclectic in his church attendance, when he attended. People in Washington, D.C., thought that he favored the Methodist and Lutheran churches, but he was actually more Swedenborgian in his beliefs. Friends in Greeneville believed that he favored the Roman Catholics. His son Andrew Jr. (Frank) attended Georgetown College, a Catholic school, and his granddaughters Lillie and Sarah Stover attended convent schools and became devout Catholics. Johnson gave a $500 donation for the construction of Greeneville's St. Patrick's (Catholic) Church and sat in the front row for its dedication in 1870, but is not known to have attended it otherwise. He also sold land and gave a donation to the Cumberland Presbyterian Church in Greeneville. He contributed to several black churches as well.

In 1854 Johnson encouraged his son Robert to "let the foundation of your moral standard be justice, prudence, temperence [sic], virtue, self reliance and fortitude," for he thought that "a religion that does not embrace these as its leading elements is not of divine origin." After Johnson's death one newspaper, trying to assess his religious beliefs, accurately remarked that "it is only by putting together this and that that we can come to any conclusion at all." What the paper found "demonstrates, as do his thirty-two degrees in Masonry, that he did believe in God, but it is not in any way shown that he ever reached any very definite conclusion as to His nature."

Johnson's most often cited expression of his religious beliefs was written on June 29, 1873, when he had cholera, and found among his papers after his death. "All Seems gloom and dispair [sic]. I have performed my duty to my God, my country, and my family. I have nothing to fear. Approaching death to me is the mere shadow of God's protecting wing. Beneath it I almost feel sacred. Here I know can no evil come. Here I will rest in quiet and peace beyond the reach of calumny's poisoned shaft—the influence of envy and jealous enemies, where Treason and Traitors in state, back sliders and hypocrits [sic] in church can have no place—where the great fact will be realized that God is truth and gratitude, the highest attribute of man.

"Adieu—sic iter ad astra. Such is the way to the stars or immortality."

After Johnson died of a stroke two years later, he had a Masonic funeral with no involvement by the clergy of any denomination.

See also: Brownlow, William Gannaway "Parson"; Funeral of Johnson; Grandchildren; Greeneville, Tennessee; Johnson, Andrew, Jr., "Frank"; Masonic Order; State Legislator, Johnson as; Stover (Brown), Mary Johnson.

References: *Bristol (Tennessee) News,* Aug. 10, 1875; Doughty, Richard Harrison, *Greeneville: One Hundred Year Portrait, 1775–1875* (1975); Graf, LeRoy P., Haskins, Ralph W., and Bergeron, Paul H., eds., *The Papers of Andrew Johnson* vols. 1–3, 6–8, 16 (1967–2000); Trefousse, Hans L., *Andrew Johnson: A Biography* (1989).

Republican Party

The Republican Party appeared in 1854 in opposition to the Kansas-Nebraska Act and the extension of slavery into the territories. Named for the party founded originally by Thomas Jefferson, the Republican Party was a sectional one, comprised of antislavery Northern Democrats and Whigs, Free Soilers, and some abolitionists from the short-lived Liberty Party. The party advocated the Homestead Act, a national banking system, high tariffs, the promotion of industrial development, and, most importantly, opposition to the spread of slavery. Like many Southerners, Andrew Johnson saw the Republicans as disunionists and abolitionists whose agitation threatened the Union itself. Yet in 1860 Johnson, the Republicans, and their first victorious president Abraham Lincoln found themselves unified by that one cause, the preservation of the Union.

Although Republicans agreed on the necessity of preserving the Union, they differed on other wartime issues. As early as 1863 fissures appeared, most relating to the prosecution of the war, the extent of emancipation and black rights, and the Reconstruction that would follow victory. President Lincoln and more moderate Republicans hedged on the issue of black rights and openly espoused a lenient plan for the South after the war. Other leading Republicans were more radical, including Thaddeus Stevens, Charles Sumner, Benjamin F. Butler, and Benjamin Wade. They pushed for a more aggressive military policy, demanded abolition and federal protection for freed blacks, hinted at black political rights, and envisioned a punitive approach to Reconstruction. Although Andrew Johnson's views would eventually put him at odds with the Radicals, during the war his views on Unionism and the prosecution of the war dovetailed with theirs. As a result, Senator Johnson was appointed to the Joint Select Committee on the Conduct of the War, a body developed by Radicals to pursue a more aggressive military policy. Johnson's appointment as military governor of Tennessee in March of 1862 cut that tenure short, but his performance in Tennessee reinforced the Radical opinion of him.

The divisions in the Republican Party became more pronounced after the surrender of Confederate forces at Appomattox. Radical members of Congress, who opposed Lincoln's "with malice towards none" approach, greeted the accession of Johnson to the presidency as a stroke of Providence. These congressmen voiced plans for the confiscation of rebel land and its distribution to former slaves, the disfranchisement of former Confederates, and the extension of suffrage to blacks. Moderate Republicans feared a Northern backlash and supported only minimal federal initiatives on civil rights, while staunchly opposing confiscation. Neither faction had their say at the war's end, however, because Congress was not in session and President Johnson moved forward unilaterally with his program of Reconstruction. The rapidity and leniency of his policy alarmed not only Radicals, who had thought him an ally, but moderates as well. Johnson's policy allowed former Confederates to regain political power, allowed states to pass Black Codes, and completely ignored the plight of the freedpeople.

Hoping to reach a compromise, in 1866 moderate Republicans, through Senators Lyman Trumbull of Illinois and William Pitt Fessenden of Maine (who was Chair of the Joint Committee on Reconstruction), approached Johnson with two measures intended to protect and provide for the former slaves in the South. The first Freedmen's Bureau Bill and the Civil Rights Bill were moderate measures that fell short of Radical expectations, but met with Johnson's approval—or so moderates believed. Congress passed both measures, and Johnson vetoed them. Taken aback, moderates rewrote the Freedmen's Bureau Bill to incorporate some of the president's objections; Johnson vetoed the revised bill as well. The same summer, the Committee on Reconstruction delivered the Fourteenth Amendment, a moderate measure that excluded black suffrage and disfranchised only leading Confederates; many in Congress believed that Reconstruction could end if the president and the South accepted the amendment. Instead Johnson campaigned against its ratification, and every former Confederate state except Tennessee rejected it. Some historians see 1866 as a pivotal period in Reconstruction because Johnson had an opportunity to divide the Republican Party, quash the Radical element, and readmit the Southern states. Instead, his vetoes, his acerbic Washington's Birthday Speech, and his perceived chicanery convinced moderates that Johnson was intractable and drove them toward the Radical camp.

The passage of the Civil Rights Act and the Freedmen's Bureau Act over Johnson's vetoes, taken with the elections of 1866 and the coming of Congressional Reconstruc-

tion in 1867, create the image that the Republicans were a solid block, unified behind their opposition to Johnson and their support of black rights. Many historians still use the phrase "Radical Reconstruction" to characterize the period of intense congressional activity that began in March 1867. But this picture is not entirely accurate. Certainly by late 1866 moderate Republicans agreed with the Radical's desire to reverse Johnson's program and restrain the executive from causing further damage. The meager support given to Johnson's National Union Party by only the most conservative Republicans demonstrated this. Moderates also understood that any changes in federal policy, such as the extension or protection of black rights, needed to come from the legislative branch, not the executive. In this way, Johnson's obstinacy was partly responsible for the successes of the congressional program. But the factions continued to squabble over constitutional, ideological, and personal issues. As a result, most congressional legislation represented a compromise, although the Radicals, who were clearly in the minority, usually conceded more. The Military Reconstruction Acts, for example, were radical in their support for military law and the federal extension of suffrage, but had serious loopholes; did *not* overturn civil government, as many believe; and were temporary in nature. Also, the acts had no economic provisions, and Radicals continued to advocate the redistribution of land in the South. Similarly, the Fifteenth Amendment, with its limited and negative phrasing, granted suffrage to no one and completely ignored the issue of office-holding; it merely prohibited the use of race and color as qualifications for voting.

Some scholars also perceive impeachment as evidence for Radical control of Reconstruction. But Johnson's impeachment in February of 1868 was not the first attempt; earlier Radical efforts (under the sponsorship of James Ashley) had been defeated easily by moderates in the House of

Representatives. As with the developments in 1866, Johnson himself was largely to blame for driving House moderates and Radicals together for the successful impeachment vote. Still, this alliance did not hold, and Senate Radicals were unable to convict and remove Johnson. His removal would have assisted the potential presidential candidacies of two Radicals, Senator Benjamin Wade and Chief Justice Salmon P. Chase. Instead, Johnson retained the presidency, and the choice of the moderate Republicans, Ulysses S. Grant, remained the front-runner for president in 1868.

See also: Ashley, James Mitchell; Bingham, John Armor; Black Codes; Black Suffrage; Butler, Benjamin Franklin; Chase, Salmon Portland; Civil Rights Act; Congressional Reconstruction; Election of 1866; Election of 1868; Fifteenth Amendment; Fourteenth Amendment; Freedmen's Bureau Bills (and Vetoes); Grant, Ulysses Simpson; Impeachment; Joint Select Committee on the Conduct of the War; Joint Committee on Reconstruction; Lincoln, Abraham; Military Governor of Tennessee, Johnson as; Military Reconstruction Acts; National Union Convention and Party; Presidential Reconstruction; Stevens, Thaddeus; Sumner, Charles; Trumbull, Lyman; Wade, Benjamin Franklin; Washington's Birthday Speech.

References: Abbott, Richard H., *The First Southern Strategy: The Republican Party and the South, 1855–1877* (1986); Benedict, Michael Les, *A Compromise of Principle: Congressional Republicans and Reconstruction, 1863–1869* (1974); Cox, LaWanda F., and Cox, John H., *Politics, Principle, and Prejudice, 1865–1866: Dilemma of Reconstruction America* (1963); Gienapp, William E., *The Origins of the Republican Party, 1852–1856* (1987); Trefousse, Hans L., *Andrew Johnson: A Biography* (1989); Trefousse, Hans L., *The Radical Republicans: Lincoln's Vanguard for Racial Justice* (1969).

Restoration
See Presidential Reconstruction

Ross, Edmund Gibson (1826–1907)

*F*uture senator Edmund Gibson Ross, the son of Sylvester F. and Cynthia Rice Ross, was born in Ashland, Ohio, and apprenticed at the age of ten to a printer. After completing his apprenticeship, he worked as a journeyman printer for papers in Ohio, Indiana, Illinois, and Wisconsin. In 1848 he married Fanny M. Lathrop (d. 1899) of New York state and they had seven children. In 1856 Ross became a Republican and moved to Kansas with several family members, becoming involved in the free-state cause. He edited several antislavery newspapers and served in the Wyandotte (free-state) Constitutional Convention (1859). In 1862 Ross enlisted in the 11th Kansas Regiment and eventually rose to the rank of major. He fought in a number of battles in the trans-Mississippi west, most notably at Prairie Grove in Arkansas. After the war he returned to journalism and became editor of the *Laurence Tribune*.

In July 1866 James H. Lane, a senator from Kansas and a supporter of Andrew Johnson, committed suicide. Kansas governor Samuel Crawford, Ross's commanding officer during the Civil War, appointed Ross to the vacancy, mainly because the latter was a political unknown and the other potential candidates would have upset the various political factions in the state Republican Party. Ross arrived in Washington, D.C., in time for the last three days of the congressional session. Surprisingly, in January 1867 the state legislature elected Ross to the remainder of Lane's term. Later, opponents claimed that friends of Ross purchased the votes, but evidence was not conclusive.

Initially Ross was a Radical, opposed to Andrew Johnson and in favor of most of Congress's Reconstruction legislation. He disapproved of Johnson's removal of Edwin M. Stanton from the post of secretary of war, but he wanted Johnson to have a fair impeachment trial.

When two articles of impeachment were considered on May 16 and 26, 1868, seven Republicans joined with the Democrats in the Senate to acquit Johnson, saving him from conviction by a single vote. Historians and other observers have focused on Ross's vote as the crucial one and debated why he voted to acquit against the outspoken urgings of many of his Kansas constituents. At the time, some opponents claimed that Ross and the other six Republicans had been bribed, but there is no evidence of this. However, Ross was involved in some negotiations with certain senators who were willing to vote not guilty if Johnson would nominate John M. Schofield to be secretary of war. (The president did so.)

Part of the reason why attention has focused on Ross is because he had not declared his vote ahead of time, so when the balloting reached him it was evident what the final verdict would be because everyone already knew the position of the senators voting after him. There is evidence that, had Ross voted guilty, several other senators were prepared to vote not guilty so that Johnson would be acquitted. Attention has also been focused on Ross because he focused it on himself. He wrote three articles and a book in the 1890s that promoted the view that voting not guilty was a courageous act, equivalent to political suicide, done to save the nation from Radical Republican control and congressional domination of the executive department. This view was accepted by some historians and later widely popularized by a chapter in then-senator John F. Kennedy's Pulitzer Prize–winning book *Profiles in Courage* (1955).

Other historians have claimed that Ross voted for acquittal to secure his advantage in patronage matters. In fact there seems to be some truth to this perspective. The other Kansas senator, Samuel C. Pomeroy, and the state's representative, Sidney Clarke, had allied against Ross and, if Johnson were removed and replaced by Benjamin F. Wade, the two would have been in a good position to persuade Wade to remove Ross's supporters from office, replacing them with Pomeroy-Clarke supporters. After the impeachment trial, Ross wrote several letters to Johnson requesting the appointment of various of his own supporters to enable him to combat the Clarke-Pomeroy forces.

Ross's term in the Senate lasted until 1871 and during his term he attended well to the needs of his Kansas constituents. Bribery by political opponents prevented his renomination. Ross returned to his journalistic career, editing several Kansas papers for short periods of time. In 1872 Ross joined the Liberal Republicans because he had been poorly treated by the regular Republicans and he disliked their candidate, President Ulysses S. Grant. He soon switched to the Democratic Party, which was not very strong in Kansas, and was badly defeated as their candidate for governor in 1880.

In 1882 Ross moved to Albuquerque, New Mexico, where he worked as a journalist but also became involved in local business opportunities. He became an opponent of the "Santa Fe Ring," which controlled territorial politics. In 1885 President Grover Cleveland appointed Ross territorial governor. Because of his conflicts with the "ring," he had a stormy four-year term and was not reappointed by Benjamin Harrison nor by Cleveland when he resumed office in 1893. Ross remained in Albuquerque for the rest of his life. He left the Democratic Party in 1896 because he opposed its free silver policies. During the 1890s he wrote about Johnson's impeachment, focusing on the event that was the high point of his life.

See also: Impeachment; Republican Party; Schofield, John McAllister; Stanton, Edwin McMasters; Wade, Benjamin Franklin.

References: Berwanger, Eugene H., "Ross and the Impeachment: A New Look at a Critical Vote," *Kansas History* 1 (Winter 1978): 235–242;

Graf, LeRoy P., Haskins, Ralph W., and Berg-eron, Paul H., eds., *The Papers of Andrew Johnson* vol. 14 (1967–2000); Lamar, Howard R., "Edmund G. Ross as Governor of New Mexico Territory: A Reappraisal," *New Mexico Historical Review* 36 (July 1961): 177–209; Plummer, Mark A., "Profile in Courage? Edmund G. Ross and the Impeachment Trial," *Midwest Quarterly* 27 (Autumn 1985): 30–48; Roske, Ralph J., "The Seven Martyrs?" *American Historical Review* 64 (Jan. 1959): 323–330.

Rousseau, Lovell Harrison (1818–1869)

Lovell Harrison Rousseau, a soldier, politician, and Andrew Johnson supporter, was born near Stanford, Kentucky. He had some local education, but at fifteen he had to become a laborer constructing a turnpike in order to help support his family after his father died in a cholera epidemic. He studied law and in 1840 moved to Bloomfield, Indiana, where he was admitted to the bar in 1841. On July 5 of the same year he married Maria Antoinette Dozier (ca. 1829–ca. 1897). The couple had four children: Mary E. (d. 1869), Richard H. (ca. 1846–1881), a daughter (b. ca. 1848), and George L. (1852–1882).

Rousseau served in the Indiana state house of representatives (1844–1845); as captain in the 2nd Indiana Infantry during the Mexican-American War (1846–1847), during which he saw action in the battle of Buena Vista; and was in the Indiana state senate (1847–1849). Then Rousseau moved back to Kentucky, to Louisville, and practiced criminal law. He held a seat in the Kentucky state senate (1860–1861) but resigned it to raise a Union regiment because he was decidedly opposed to the secession movement. He was mustered in as colonel of the 3rd Kentucky Infantry (Union) on September 9, 1861, and in 1862 he was promoted to major general. He fought at Shiloh, Perryville, Stone's River (Murfreesboro), and in the Chickamauga campaign, although he was not in that battle. From November 1863 to November 1865 Rousseau commanded the district of Nashville, and it is doubtless in this capacity that he first encountered Military Governor Andrew Johnson, with whom he corresponded when military and civilian matters intersected. Although Rousseau was opposed to secession, he favored slavery, and some of the more antislavery army officers were unhappy with Rousseau's policies of permitting slaves to go with their owners if the slaves were "willing" and of canceling the sentences of certain citizens who had been convicted of abusing blacks. Rousseau sent information about Tennessee support for Johnson after he became president.

After losing a Kentucky election for the U.S. Senate in 1865, Rousseau resigned from the army and was elected to the U.S. House of Representatives. Although initially appearing to be a radical, Rousseau soon became much more conservative and a supporter of Johnson's policies. He made a number of patronage requests of Johnson, and a number of job applicants cited Rousseau as a reference when they requested a job. During an argument in a corridor of the Capitol, Rousseau beat Iowa representative Josiah B. Grinnell with a cane. Censured by the House for this violence, Rousseau resigned but was reelected by his constituents and served until the end of his term, March 3, 1867.

Rousseau reentered the army and became a brigadier general on March 28, 1867. In July Johnson sent him to New Orleans to observe the situation, particularly to report on General Philip H. Sheridan, the controversial commander of the district. Although the purpose of Rousseau's mission was secret, Sheridan complained to Ulysses S. Grant about Rousseau's conduct, allegedly interfering with Sheridan's duties and suggesting that the commander be removed, all without any apparent authority for Rousseau's actions.

Next, Rousseau was sent to Alaska,

where, as the agent of the U.S. government, he received the territory from the Russian commissioner. He then became commander of Washington Territory, where he remained until April 1868, on occasion sending Johnson observations about the political climate of the Pacific Coast.

A number of persons had written to Johnson at various times urging the president to assign Rousseau to command the troops in Louisiana. Rousseau assumed command of the department of Louisiana and Arkansas on September 15, 1868. The situation in Louisiana was tense because riots between white Democrats and black Republicans were continually expected as both campaigned for the candidates in the approaching 1868 election. Rousseau was able to keep the political situation under control through strategic deployment of his troops. He also took care to avoid offending the white Louisianans, even restoring some officeholders who had been removed by his predecessors.

On January 4, 1869, Rousseau was suddenly taken very ill with "congestion of the bowels" and died on January 7. His huge funeral demonstrated how much the New Orleans citizens loved him. Rousseau's death left his family in straitened circumstances, and his widow wrote several letters to Johnson asking that her sons be given military appointments. Although Johnson sent the nominations to the Senate, that body refused to approve them. In March 1869, however, they did grant Maria Rousseau a $30 monthly pension.

See also: Alaska, Purchase of; Election of 1868; Military Governor of Tennessee, Johnson as; Patronage; Readmission of Southern States; Sheridan, Philip Henry; Territorial Affairs.

References: Dawson, Joseph G., III, "General Lovell H. Rousseau and Louisiana Reconstruction," *Louisiana History* 20 (Fall 1979): 373–391; Graf, LeRoy P., Haskins, Ralph W., and Bergeron, Paul H., eds., *The Papers of Andrew Johnson* vols. 4, 6–7, 12–15 (1967–2000); Warner, Ezra J., *Generals in Blue* (1964); U.S. Census, Kentucky, 1860, Jefferson County, Louisville, 6th Ward, p. 92.

Schofield, John McAllister (1831–1906)

John McAllister Schofield, who became Andrew Johnson's secretary of war in June 1868, was born in Gerry, New York. His father was a Baptist minister who moved the family to Illinois in 1843 when he became a home missionary. Young Schofield was educated in the local public schools and spent one summer as a surveyor in Wisconsin and a winter as a district teacher before being appointed as a cadet at West Point. Schofield graduated seventh in the class of 1853. After being briefly stationed in South Carolina and Florida, he became assistant professor of natural and experimental philosophy at West Point in 1855. In June 1857, he married Harriet Bartlett (d. ca. 1889), daughter of the West Point philosophy professor. They had five children, of whom two sons and one daughter survived to adulthood.

In 1860 Schofield took a year's leave of absence to be professor of physics at Washington University in St. Louis, Missouri. However, with the outbreak of the Civil War he became involved in the organization of Union forces in Missouri, serving as a mustering officer, organizing a regiment, and serving as chief of staff to General Nathaniel Lyons before the latter was killed

at Wilson's Creek in August 1861. Becoming a brigadier general of volunteers in November 1861, Schofield held various commands, mostly in Missouri, until finally, in May 1863, he became commander of the Department of the Missouri.

From February 1864 Schofield commanded the XXIII Corps and the Army and Department of the Ohio, participating in William T. Sherman's Atlanta campaign. Rather than being part of the March to the Sea, Schofield and his troops were instrumental in defeating the Confederate forces of John Bell Hood at the battles of Franklin and Nashville in Tennessee in late 1864. Then transferred to North Carolina, Schofield helped Sherman in the final maneuvers against the Confederate Army of Tennessee under Joseph E. Johnston. After the Confederate defeat, Schofield commanded the Department of North Carolina briefly before being sent to France to negotiate the withdrawal of the French troops supporting Maximilian in Mexico.

When Schofield returned to the United States in August 1866, he was assigned to command the Department of the Potomac, which included Virginia. After the passage of the First Military Reconstruction Act in March 1867, Schofield became the commander of the First Military District, comprised of Virginia. In all his activities there, Schofield attempted to be moderate in his actions and attitudes, to be impartial toward both blacks and whites, to prevent government takeover by the radicals and unprepared freedmen, and to prepare Virginia for a return to normal status in the Union as soon as possible. James L. McDonough, the historian who has studied Schofield most extensively, considered him to be an outstanding administrator.

Schofield's moderate actions and attitudes made him a prospective replacement for Secretary of War Edwin M. Stanton and one on whom all sides could agree. Negotiations conducted in April of 1868 by William M. Evarts, one of Johnson's impeachment defense counsel and future attorney general, contributed to Johnson's acquittal. Schofield was nominated on April 24, confirmed after Johnson's acquittal, and became secretary of war on June 1, 1868. During his period of service, Schofield and Johnson often corresponded about War Department matters. Schofield resigned the post when Johnson left office.

Schofield continued his army career, commanding a number of different departments. In 1872 he visited Hawaii to examine its strategic value to the United States and recommended Pearl Harbor for a naval base. He was superintendent of West Point (1876–1881) and in 1888 became commanding general of the army. After several years as a widower, Schofield married Georgia Kilbourne of Iowa in 1891. He retired from the army in September 1895 because of his age and used his retirement to write an autobiography, *Forty-Six Years in the Army* (1897). Schofield died in St. Augustine, Florida, where he often spent winters, on March 4, 1906.

See also: Evarts, William Maxwell; Impeachment; Mexico; Military Districts; Military Reconstruction Acts; Sherman, William Tecumseh; Stanton, Edwin McMasters.

References: Graf, LeRoy P., Haskins, Ralph W., and Bergeron, Paul H., eds., *The Papers of Andrew Johnson* vols. 7, 14–15 (1967–2000); McDonough, James L., "John Schofield as Military Director of Reconstruction in Virginia," *Civil War History* 15 (Fall 1969): 237–256; McDonough, James L., *Schofield: Union General in the Civil War and Reconstruction* (1972); McDonough, James L., and Alderson, William T., "Republican Politics and the Impeachment of Andrew Johnson," *Tennessee Historical Quarterly* 26 (Summer 1967): 177–183.

Secession, Johnson's Attitude toward

Long before the Civil War, Andrew Johnson saw himself as a Southern Unionist Democrat, opposed to secession. In 1860 he tried to conciliate the Southern wing of his party by opposing Northern personal liberty laws and advocating protection for slavery in the territories. But once Abraham Lincoln was elected, Johnson opposed the virulent secession spirit and clearly declared his Unionism, while still hoping for reconciliation between the sections.

The most important way in which Johnson declared his Unionism was his "Speech on Secession," delivered in the Senate on December 18–19, 1860. On December 13 he had once again proposed some amendments to the Constitution (amendments that he had first offered in 1851): the president and vice president should be elected by the people, not the electoral college, with the offices alternating between the North and the South; senators should be directly elected by the people; the Supreme Court members should be appointed for a term of twelve years each with one-third of the terms expiring every four years and an equal number of Northern and Southern justices in each group. Instead of using the opportunity to speak further on his amendments, Johnson indicated his views "in reference to the questions that agitate and distract the public mind."

Johnson bluntly stated, "I am opposed to secession. I believe it is no remedy for the evils complained of. . . . I shall take other grounds while I try to accomplish the same end." He thought that "this battle ought to be fought not outside, but inside of the Union, and upon the battlements of the Constitution itself." He claimed that no state has the Constitutional right to secede because "the Constitution of the United States makes no provision for its own destruction." New York could not join the Union originally with reservations that would permit it to withdraw. So the only way for a state to get out of the Union was by mutual agreement of all the states or by revolution, not the action of an individual state.

Throughout his speech Johnson at some length quoted James Madison, Thomas Jefferson, John Marshall, and Andrew Jackson as authorities opposed to secession. He did not believe that the federal government had the right to "coerce" a state (as an entity), but it did have a right to enforce the laws against individuals in a state, as George Washington had done during the Whiskey Rebellion and Andrew Jackson had done during the Nullification Crisis with South Carolina in the early 1830s. Johnson showed that South Carolina was now breaking laws by trying to take forts that were federal property. This was clearly treason. He pointed out the absurdity of states such as California, Texas, and Florida, where much federal money had been spent, seceding whenever they pleased. The same should apply to any state. He believed that slavery could be preserved only by constitutional means within the Union. To break up the Union would ultimately bring an end to slavery.

Once the government had separated, Johnson asked, what was to prevent further separation until just a number of little states remained? He suggested that the South wanted to break up the Union just because its candidate was defeated in a perfectly legal election. Johnson insisted that the North too must preserve the guarantees of the Constitution and not violate them with personal liberty laws. As for Johnson, he intended to stand by the Constitution.

Not surprisingly, Southerners criticized his speech, whereas more support came from the North and West, especially in letters from a wide variety of private citizens. The press response was rather limited because Johnson was little known outside Tennessee, but some Northern legislators began to take an interest in Johnson and what he had to say. Thirty-six thousand people requested copies of the speech from the *Congressional Globe* and Johnson himself ordered 10,000 copies.

Johnson made two more speeches against secession, each more militant than the first. He delivered the "Speech on the Seceding States" in the Senate on February 5–6, 1861. "The Speech in Reply to Senator Lane," of March 2, 1861, was a response to critical remarks made by Oregon senator Joseph Lane, an extreme Southern sympathizer. By this time Johnson was less obscure and he received more supportive correspondence as well as press coverage. He was lauded as the "second Jackson" and a future president. Many organizations invited him to speak, offering as much as $125 per lecture. His support of the Union led to patronage opportunities, the military governorship of Tennessee, the vice presidency, and ultimately the presidency itself.

See also: Constitutional Amendments, Proposed; Democratic Party; Jackson, Andrew; Senator, Johnson as.

References: Graf, LeRoy P., "Andrew Johnson and the Coming of the War," *Tennessee Historical Quarterly* 19 (Sept. 1960): 208–221; Graf, LeRoy P., Haskins, Ralph W., and Bergeron, Paul H., eds., *The Papers of Andrew Johnson* vol. 4 (1967–2000).

Secession Referendums (Tennessee, 1861)

Andrew Johnson, a devoted Unionist, was an indefatigable campaigner in opposition to Tennessee's secession referendums. After Abraham Lincoln was elected president of the United States in November 1860, seven Southern states quickly seceded from the Union. Tennessee governor Isham G. Harris was eager to have Tennessee join them. But he knew that many Tennesseans were at least conditional Unionists and he could not simply ask for immediate secession. Instead Harris called a special session of the state legislature to meet on January 7, 1861. He asked the legislature to set up a referendum so that the people could vote on whether to call a secession convention. The legislature appointed February 9 as the date for the referendum and mandated the election of delegates in case the convention was approved.

Both Unionists and secessionists actively campaigned for their respective viewpoints. Unionists were strongest in the areas, such as East Tennessee, where there were few slaves and where a majority of the voters were Whigs (or Opposition, as they called themselves after the death of the national Whig Party in the early 1850s). Unionists argued that Lincoln had not even become president yet and Southerners should at least wait and see if he did anything to threaten slavery before withdrawing. Secessionists were strongest in the middle and western areas, where there were large slave-holding planters and where Democratic voters held a majority. The Unionists won, with fifty-five percent of the voters opposed to the convention. However, had the convention been held, three-quarters of the delegates would have been Unionists.

The turning point for Tennessee, as for three other border states, was Lincoln's April 15, 1861, call for troops after the Confederates captured Fort Sumter in South Carolina. Governor Harris bluntly told Lincoln that Tennessee would not provide any manpower to "coerce" its sister slave states. He also called for the legislature to meet again on April 25. This time Harris asked the legislature to declare Tennessee independent rather than wasting the time to call a special secession convention. Both

houses approved secession on May 6, but insisted that the people be allowed to vote on the proposal on June 8.

Although Unionists were not really able to campaign in Middle and West Tennessee, they campaigned vigorously in East Tennessee. Andrew Johnson opposed most of his Democratic colleagues and allied with his Whig former opponents, such as Thomas A.R. Nelson, Oliver P. Temple, and William G. Brownlow, to speak as many places as possible. In fact, Johnson and Nelson traveled together from late April to June 8, playing on the fact that, despite their past political differences, they were now working together to preserve the Union. It was an exhausting campaign and Johnson and Nelson were frequently heckled, verbally abused, and even physically threatened for their stand. Both also participated in the East Tennessee Convention, a meeting of Unionists in Knoxville on May 30–31 of which Nelson was the president.

The Unionists were successful in East Tennessee, defeating secession by a 2 to 1 vote, but this result was outweighed by the more than eighty percent majority in favor of secession in both Middle and West Tennessee. Although members of the East Tennessee Convention met in Greeneville June 17–20 and sent a resolution to the legislature asking that the Unionist counties be allowed to set up a separate state, the legislature unanimously vetoed the idea. Secessionists in East Tennessee began to persecute the Unionist leaders. Johnson fled the state. Nelson, who had just been reelected to the U.S. House of Representatives, attempted to do the same, but was captured by the Confederates and briefly imprisoned in Richmond. Nevertheless, Unionist sentiment continued strong in East Tennessee and created many problems for the Confederate government during the war.

See also: Bell, John; Brownlow, William Gannaway "Parson"; Democratic Party; Harris, Isham Green; Lincoln, Abraham; Nelson, Thomas Amis Rogers; Secession, Johnson's Attitude toward;

Senator, Johnson as; Temple, Oliver Perry; Whig Party.

References: Alexander, Thomas B., *Thomas A. R. Nelson of East Tennessee* (1956); Bergeron, Paul H., Ash, Stephen V., and Keith, Jeanette, *Tennesseans and Their History* (1999); Graf, LeRoy P., Haskins, Ralph W., and Bergeron, Paul H., eds., *The Papers of Andrew Johnson* vol. 4 (1967–2000).

Secretaries

Quite a number of men served Andrew Johnson as secretary from the early 1860s until his death in 1875. Some served for only a few weeks or months, whereas others worked with Johnson for years. Dates of service for some are uncertain. The names of thirteen secretaries are known, but there were undoubtedly others. Some of the more prominent secretaries are discussed in separate entries and receive only a passing mention here.

Johnson's earliest known secretary was William A. Browning (1835–1866). He was the son of Peregrine W. Browning, a Washington, D.C., tailor, and became secretary to Johnson during the summer of 1861 while Johnson was still a senator. When Johnson became military governor of Tennessee in 1862, Browning went with him and continued on as secretary even after Johnson became president. In December 1865 Browning was nominated to serve as secretary for the U.S. legation in Mexico, but he died in early 1866 before the appointment was confirmed.

Benjamin Cummings Truman, a newspaper reporter, apparently functioned intermittently as Johnson's private secretary, aide, and messenger in 1862. Tennessee politician Edmund Cooper also probably served as Johnson's secretary during some part of 1862. Robert Johnson, Andrew Johnson's second son, began to perform secretarial duties for his father in May 1864 and continued through the rest of Johnson's military governorship, staying behind in Nashville to pack up his father's papers when Johnson became vice president.

Andrew K. Long (ca. 1842–1878), the last known secretary from Johnson's pre-presidential years, was a native of Illinois who served in the 7th Pennsylvania Reserves (1861–1863) and as first lieutenant, Co. C, 12th Tennessee Cavalry, U.S. (1864–1865). He was a member of General Alvan C. Gillem's staff (1864) until in August he was detailed as secretary to Johnson. Long was appointed major and assistant adjutant general of U.S. Volunteers in September 1865, an appointment probably related to his continuing service to Johnson, which lasted until November 1867. He became a captain and worked in the commissary and subsistence department, stationed at least a part of the time in the Wyoming Territory, where his son was born in 1874. Long was back in Washington, D.C., when, on January 23, 1878, he committed suicide.

Although Browning and Long continued on as Johnson's secretaries when he became president, Johnson quickly added others to his staff. Reuben Delavan Mussey (1833–1892), a native of New Hampshire and a Dartmouth graduate (1854), taught school before becoming a newspaper reporter. Joining the regular army in 1861, Mussey became a captain in the 19th Infantry. In 1863 he became a recruiting officer for black troops, headquartered in Nashville, and eventually was supervisor of contrabands for Middle and East Tennessee. No doubt Mussey met Johnson while they were both in Nashville, as he wrote to the governor describing his recruiting plans. Mussey joined Johnson's secretarial staff in April 1865 and remained until November. He resigned officially because of some questions about his financial records while a recruiting officer. But Mussey, an ardent abolitionist, had major policy differences with Johnson over Reconstruction and was uncomfortable remaining part of an administration with which he disagreed. He also resigned from the army in December 1865, became a partner in the Cumberland Land Company of Tennessee, and in 1867 became a lawyer in Washington, D.C. Mussey later wrote a letter to Judge Advocate General Joseph Holt, which Holt used as evidence against Johnson in his 1873 letters about the Mary Surratt case.

Possibly succeeding Mussey, who at one time signed himself as "military secretary," West Point graduate (1861) Wright Rives (1838–1916) served as military secretary (in charge of all matters relating to military cases) for the rest of Johnson's presidency. Rives had requested appointment in April 1865 because of disabilities caused by typhoid fever during the siege of Corinth and Vicksburg, which prevented him from being on active duty. He also reminded Johnson that he was the son of John C. Rives, long-time editor of the *Washington Globe,* who had recently died. Rives had first applied for a staff post with Johnson in 1863 but was more successful in 1865.

In June 1865 Robert Morrow (1846–1873) also requested a position in which he could serve Johnson and support his widowed mother after the recent death of his father, Samuel Morrow, a Knoxville banker. Morrow had enlisted in the volunteers during the Civil War and had risen from captain to brevet colonel. Morrow became one of Johnson's secretaries in July 1865 and served until the end of Johnson's presidency. On several occasions, Morrow traveled to Knoxville, presumably to attend to business for his mother, and while there wrote Johnson letters discussing the political situation. After Morrow finished his duties with Johnson, he became an army paymaster in the West, where he committed suicide in San Francisco on November 27, 1873.

Although Edmund Cooper's dates of service with Johnson are not precisely clear, he did apparently serve as Johnson's secretary in charge of appointments from sometime in the fall of 1865, after Cooper's election to the House of Representatives, until he was admitted to his seat in July 1866. Cooper may also have carried out some secretarial duties in the fall of 1867, when he was in Washington, D.C., as a companion for Johnson.

During his father's presidency, Robert Johnson also served again as an official secretary from November 1865 to April 1866 and from September 1866 to at least May 1867. In part the purpose of this job was to keep Robert constructively employed and under supervision so that he would remain sober. But the plan did not work. Robert's alcoholism continued and he was finally sent to an asylum.

William G. Moore, one of Johnson's most trusted secretaries and confidants, served from November 1865 to March 1869. The last of Johnson's known secretaries during the presidency was William W. Warden (1827–1890), a lawyer and correspondent for several major daily newspapers. His secretarial term was brief, and probably an interim replacement, around May 1866. But Warden continued to be a strong supporter of Johnson's and worked hard, although unsuccessfully, for his presidential nomination by the Democratic National Convention in 1868.

While Johnson was president he could expect to have secretaries. But after his term expired he still needed a secretary because problems resulting from his old arm injury made extensive writing a chore. However, Johnson discovered that finding a secretary in Greeneville was not an easy task and he frequently complained to correspondents that he was without a secretary and had to do all his own writing. Sometime, apparently in late 1869 or 1870, Elbert C. Reeves (1841–1929) opened a law office in Greeneville. He and Johnson became good friends and Reeves served as Johnson's secretary at least part-time. Reeves edited the *Greeneville National Union* for awhile and in 1874 canvassed most Tennessee state legislators in support of Johnson's senatorial aspirations.

Another of Johnson's later part-time secretaries was his future grandson-in-law,

Thomas Maloney, a lawyer and coeditor of the *Greeneville Intelligencer* with Frank Johnson. Johnson's last secretary was Livingston Browning (ca. 1848–1904), a Washington, D.C., lawyer and a brother of Johnson's former secretary William A. Browning. Johnson hired Browning in March 1875 to attend to secretarial matters in Washington, D.C. They conducted some correspondence before Johnson's death at the end of July.

Johnson had numerous secretaries, and, while president, had more than twice as many secretaries as Abraham Lincoln, who had only two. Johnson's secretaries did all the paperwork tasks that would be expected of secretaries. They took dictation of letters that Johnson would sign and wrote out other messages at the request of Johnson, which they signed themselves. Before the days of any type of duplication process except the printing press, the secretaries copied numerous documents and letters by hand. They also served as go-betweens, both in person and through correspondence, for various people who wished to communicate with Johnson. The secretaries handled Johnson's schedule of appointments and also the masses of correspondence relating to patronage appointments as well as the pardons needed by many former Confederates. They filed the paperwork when Johnson was finished with it. Secretaries served as messengers for Johnson on numerous occasions and Moore accompanied the president on trips to North Carolina and New England. Moore seems to have been the only secretary who kept extensive notes about incidents during Johnson's presidency or the privately expressed opinions of the president himself. After Johnson left office, Moore gave him a copy of the notes.

See also: Cooper, Edmund; Democratic Convention; Grandchildren; Health of Johnson; Holt, Joseph; Johnson, Andrew, Jr., "Frank"; Johnson, Robert; Lincoln, Abraham; Military Governor of Tennessee, Johnson as; Moore, William George; Newspaper Interviews; Pardons (Individual); Patronage; Postpresidential Career; Presidential Travels; Senator, Johnson as; Surratt, Mary (Elizabeth) Eugenia Jenkins; Truman, Benjamin Cummings.

References: Graf, LeRoy P., Haskins, Ralph W., and Bergeron, Paul H., eds., *The Papers of Andrew Johnson* vols. 4–9, 11–16 (1967–2000); *Knoxville Weekly Chronicle,* December 10, 1873; Levstik, Frank R., "A View from Within: Reuben D. Mussey on Andrew Johnson and Reconstruction," *Historical New Hampshire* 27 (Fall 1972): 167–171; Pension Records, RG 15, National Archives, Elizabeth F. Long file; Sioussat, St. George L., "Notes of Colonel W.G. Moore, Private Secretary to President Johnson, 1866–1868," *American Historical Review* 19 (Oct. 1913): 98–132; Trefousse, Hans L., *Andrew Johnson, A Biography* (1989); U.S. Census, Washington, D.C., 1850, 4th Ward, p. 438; Washington, D.C., directories, 1867–1887; *Washington Post,* Aug. 5, 1904.

Selby, James J.
See Apprenticeship; Education of Johnson

Senator, Johnson as (1857–1862, 1875)

Andrew Johnson was elected to the U.S. Senate twice during his career. During his first term he was an outspoken Southern Unionist, remaining in the Senate when his state seceded. His election to a second term was considered to be a vindication of his previous political policies.

Johnson served as governor of Tennessee in 1853–1857. According to state law, he was eligible for one more two-year term. But Johnson, considering future political prospects, decided to be a candidate for the Senate instead. During this period, senators were elected by their state legislature, not directly by the public. Consequently, a candidate for senator would campaign for legislative candidates upon whose vote he could count. Thus, in 1857 Johnson campaigned vigorously for the Democratic gubernatorial candidate Isham Harris and Democratic legislators. When Harris won the governorship and the Democrats won the majority of seats in the legislature, many

Tennesseans saw the victory as an indication of support for Johnson's election to the Senate. On October 8, 1857, the legislature elected Johnson to the Senate by a vote of 57 to 38.

The congressional session began on December 7, 1857, and Johnson was sworn in. As a senator, Johnson continued his two major emphases from his terms in the House of Representatives: a homestead act and a stress on fiscal economy. He wasted no time in introducing his Homestead Bill again on December 22, 1857, just two weeks after he joined the Senate. By this time Southern Democrats had come to oppose the idea of giving away free land to farmers because it was of little use to slaveholders and it might cut down the revenue from land sales, forcing an increase in tariffs, a situation that Southern leaders strongly opposed. Instead Johnson, a Southern Democrat, found himself allied with Northern Republicans who supported a homestead act.

Despite various speeches by Johnson, in May 1858 the Senate voted to postpone the homestead matter until the next session. Johnson could not introduce the bill again until December 20, 1859, and it was finally passed May 10, 1860. After a compromise version passed both houses of Congress, President James Buchanan vetoed the Homestead Bill on June 22, 1860, and the Senate was unable to override the veto, much to Johnson's disgust. Johnson introduced a homestead measure once more in December 1860, but it was not considered because of the secession crisis.

When it came to government fiscal policy, Johnson was opposed to many things that he considered to be excessive expenditures, such as enlistment of more regular soldiers to put down Mormon unrest in Utah, certain pensions, erection of a statue honoring George Washington, the transcontinental railroad, and an appropriation to aid observing a solar eclipse. He also favored abolishing the franking privilege (members of Congress could send mail free with their signature in place of a postage stamp) and got into an argument with Jefferson Davis over the cost of furnishing the new congressional committee rooms.

Probably the most significant thing Johnson did as a senator, however, was to take a firm stand in support of the Union and to oppose secession. He made several major antisecession speeches (December 18–19, 1860, and February 5–6, 1861), which made him a hero in the North and a pariah in much of the South. He vigorously campaigned against secession in his own state, but when Tennessee seceded anyway, Johnson returned to his Senate seat, the only senator from a seceded state remaining in Congress. This contributed to his image as a Northern hero and to his appointment to the Joint Select Committee on the Conduct of the War. It also encouraged President Abraham Lincoln to rely on Johnson for Tennessee patronage suggestions, to appoint Johnson as military governor of Tennessee in March 1862, and to approve him as vice presidential nominee in 1864.

When Johnson left the presidency in March 1869 he protested that he was going to retire from political life to his "own vine and fig tree" in Greeneville. This retirement lasted a few weeks at most because Johnson was soon involved in political campaigning in Tennessee, specifically for a Senate seat. There was considerable popular support for Johnson, but a great deal of opposition from various party leaders. During the campaign, correspondents wrote to Johnson about his prospects for election as well as to warn him about several plots to prevent his election. In fact, although Johnson was leading for a number of ballots, a caucus of his opponents, representing both Radical Republicans and secessionists, settled on Henry Cooper, brother of Johnson's former secretary and protégé Edmund Cooper. Cooper was narrowly elected on October 22, 1869, by a vote of 55 to 51. Johnson was angered by this betrayal by Edmund Cooper and never forgave him, frequently referring in speeches to Henry and Edmund Cooper in the context of other heinous traitors, such as Judas in the New Testament.

After losing a race for the House of Representatives in 1872, Johnson again campaigned for the Senate in 1874–1875. In addition to making speeches himself, he sent out several friends, such as his sometime-secretary Elbert C. Reeves, to lobby various legislators. Johnson also spent a number of weeks in Nashville himself. Balloting by the legislature took several days because there were a number of candidates and no one was able to get a majority. Finally, on January 26, 1875, on the fifty-fifth ballot, Johnson was elected with 52 votes. The remaining 45 votes were scattered among five other candidates.

Johnson and his friends rejoiced in his vindication. Yet Johnson's health was not as good as it had been. When he went to Washington, D.C., for the special session in March 1875, he asked his friends not to hold a serenade or other celebration, preferring to meet with them quietly. This was an unusual action for Johnson. He was interviewed by correspondents of the *New York Tribune* on March 6 and the *New York Herald* on March 7. Johnson claimed to be in the Senate not for vengeance or as a party man, but as an independent to deal with current issues. Johnson made one speech during the session, on March 22, in which he was critical of President Ulysses S. Grant and also of political affairs in Louisiana, where federal troops had been called in to oust illegally seated Democratic members of the legislature. This was the only speech Johnson delivered during the short session and, in fact, the only one he delivered during his second Senate term. When Johnson left Washington, D.C., after the Senate adjourned he never returned because he died on July 31, 1875.

See also: Congressman, Johnson as; Cooper, Edmund; Crittenden-Johnson Resolution; Davis, Jefferson; Death of Johnson; Democratic Party; Election of 1864; Finances, Johnson's Attitude toward Governmental; Governor (Civilian), Johnson as; Grant, Ulysses Simpson; Greeneville, Tennessee; Harris, Isham Green; Health of Johnson; Homestead Act; Joint Select Committee on the Conduct of the War; Lincoln, Abraham; Military Governor of Tennessee, Johnson as; Newspaper Interviews; Postpresidential Career; Secession, Johnson's Attitude toward; Secession Referendums.

References: Graf, LeRoy P., Haskins, Ralph W., and Bergeron, Paul H., eds., *The Papers of Andrew Johnson* vols. 3, 16 (1967–2000); Russell, Robert G., "Prelude to the Presidency: The Election of Andrew Johnson to the Senate," *Tennessee Historical Quarterly* 26 (Summer 1967): 148–176; Trefousse, Hans L., *Andrew Johnson: A Biography* (1989).

Seward, William Henry (1801–1872)

Secretary of state under two presidents, William Henry Seward was born in Florida, a town in upstate New York. His parents, Samuel and Mary Jennings Seward, mindful of their son's weak constitution and sharp mind, decided early to furnish young Henry with a first-class education. As Seward's wealth and status grew, he repaid his parents and readily assisted his three brothers and his sister.

Seward graduated from Union College in 1820, read law, passed the bar in 1822, and entered a law practice in Auburn, New York, in 1823. He soon met and married Frances Adeline Miller, the daughter of his law partner. The couple had five children: Augustus Henry (b. 1826), Frederick William (b. 1830, who became an assistant to his father in the State Department), Cornelia (b. 1835, who died in infancy), William Henry, Jr. (b. 1840), and Frances Adeline (b. 1844).

Keeping abreast of politics, as many young lawyers did, Seward grew distrustful of the Jacksonian Democrats who emerged in the 1820s. A trip into the South, and the presence of slaves in his father's household, turned Seward toward antislavery, John

Quincy Adams, and the promise of internal improvements and national development. By the late 1820s Seward was mingling with anti-Jacksonians who would soon form the Whig Party, although his pro-immigration attitudes and anti-Masonic stances branded him as a radical and an extremist.

Mentored by New York newspaper mogul and Whig Thurlow Weed, Seward moderated his positions and won election to the state senate in 1830. He ran unsuccessfully for governor in 1834, after which he returned to a flourishing law practice. In 1838 Seward tried the gubernatorial alternative again, this time successfully. As governor he was an outspoken critic of slavery and became a national figure for refusing to enforce the fugitive slave law. In addition to provoking Southern resentment, he antagonized nativists by advocating public education for Catholic immigrants excluded by a school administration dominated by Protestants.

Seward returned to his law practice, but entered national politics in 1848 with his election to the U.S. Senate. Both conservative Whigs and Southern Democrats found him a difficult colleague because he had a penchant for fixating on the most sensitive issues. He bitterly opposed the Compromise of 1850 and the Kansas–Nebraska Act, spoke of a "higher law" than that of the Constitution, and warned that civil war, caused by slavery, would tear the nation apart. Seward was reelected as a Whig in 1854 and moved quickly into the Republican ranks. The phrase "irrepressible conflict" comes from an 1858 Seward speech and aptly demonstrates his sense of dramatics and destiny.

Ambitious and gifted, Seward's inflexibility removed him from consideration as a Republican candidate in 1856 and 1860. He backed the Republican nominees in both elections, and his dedication to Abraham Lincoln's campaign earned him the appointment as secretary of state. Seward, a political veteran who believed himself President Lincoln's intellectual superior, planned to be the "power behind the throne" and expected to casually usurp the executive's authority. His April 1861 memo "Some Thoughts for the President's Consideration" displayed typical arrogance and condescension, as the secretary proposed war against Spain and France, giving up Fort Sumter, and a gradual transfer of day-to-day responsibility from the president to the secretary of state.

As did other advisors, Seward learned that Lincoln was competent and clever, and the two developed a close relationship. Seward's views on the South softened until he and the president were in close conformity. Both favored an eventual but gradual emancipation, a wartime focus on preserving the Union, and a limited and conciliatory Reconstruction process. Historians give Seward credit for delaying the preliminary Emancipation Proclamation until after a Union victory, for securing passage of the Thirteenth Amendment in the House of Representatives, and for the creation of a national day of Thanksgiving. (Seward's was the political pressure that made magazine editor Sarah Josepha Hale's dream a reality in 1863.)

Like Lincoln, Seward found himself alienated from both Democrats and Radical Republicans, a handicap that carried through Andrew Johnson's administration. As a result, during Lincoln's term Radicals never ceased trying to maneuver Seward out of the cabinet, just as during Johnson's term Democrats sought to do the same.

Other characteristics also carried over from the Lincoln administration, such as Seward's careful handling of the French in Mexico, his expansionistic tendencies, and his arrogant-but-respectful handling of Great Britain, as seen in the *Trent* Affair and the *Alabama* Claims. Seward's cunning combination of nationalistic bluster and deference appeased the English and helped prevent foreign intervention.

Injured in a carriage accident early in 1865, the secretary was still recovering when attacked by Lewis Paine as part of the Lincoln assassination conspiracy. Paine's assault left Seward disfigured for life, and Lincoln's assassination left the federal government in the hands of Andrew Johnson. Johnson asked Seward to remain as secretary of state, perhaps knowing that Seward had played a key role in securing the Tennessean's nomination as vice president in 1864. Seward became one of Johnson's most trusted advisors. Seward agreed with Johnson's conciliatory approach to Reconstruction, although the former preferred a process that would allow more congressional input and a greater reliance on moderate Republicans, instead of Democrats. But Seward's views on the Constitution, the freedpeople, and the former Confederate states were consistent with Johnson's. Seward wrote the main draft of the First Freedmen's Bureau Bill veto, the Civil Rights Bill veto, and Johnson's annual messages of 1865 and 1866. He composed, nearly in its entirety, the president's veto of the Tenure of Office Bill and supported the president's ill-fated National Union Convention in 1866. In fact, Seward accompanied Johnson on the Swing-around-the-Circle, a trip instigated by an invitation that *Seward* had received to speak in Chicago.

But Johnson did not always heed Seward's advice. The president altered most of Seward's drafts, usually deleting conciliatory sections and adding more antagonistic language. Seward himself warned Johnson to resist attacking Congress during the Swing-around-the-Circle, and the secretary often found himself clarifying and qualifying his executive's comments. Seward opposed the removal of General Philip Sheridan and the suspension of Secretary of War Edwin M. Stanton, argued against issuing the July 4, 1868, Amnesty Proclamation, and urged Johnson to attend President Ulysses S. Grant's inauguration. Seward sought similarities between Johnson and his adversaries, but Johnson focused on differences.

As secretary of state, Seward was an expansionist, most famous for his purchase of Alaska in March 1867 (dubbed "Seward's Folly" by some contemporaries). Seward also acquired the Midway Islands and established diplomatic exchanges with China. He tried unsuccessfully to purchase the Danish West Indies and a port in the Dominican Republic. Johnson supported nearly all Seward's adventures, and the secretary defended Johnson to the very end.

Seward left office along with Johnson in 1869. Despite declining health, the former secretary toured the world for fourteen months and then retired to his home in Auburn, New York. He succumbed to what may have been amyotrophic lateral sclerosis (Lou Gehrig's disease) on October 10, 1872.

See also: *Alabama* Claims; Alaska, Purchase of; Amnesty Proclamations; Annual Messages; Blair, Francis Preston (Jr. and Sr.); Cabinet Members; Civil Rights Act; Election of 1866; Foreign Affairs; Freedmen's Bureau Bills (and Vetoes); Lincoln Assassination Conspirators; Mexico; National Union Convention and Party; Presidential Reconstruction; Sheridan, Philip Henry; Stanton, Edwin McMasters; Sumner, Charles; Swing-around-the-Circle; Tenure of Office Act; Thirteenth Amendment; Vetoes; Whig Party.
References: Paolino, Ernest N., *The Foundations of the American Empire: William Henry Seward and U.S. Foreign Policy* (1973); Taylor, John M., *William Henry Seward: Lincoln's Right Hand* (1991); Trefousse, Hans L., *Andrew Johnson: A Biography* (1989); Van Duesen, Glyndon G., *William Henry Seward* (1967).

Seymour, Horatio (1810–1886)

Horatio Seymour, Civil War governor of New York and Democratic presidential candidate in 1868, was born in Pompey Hill, New York, and moved with his family to Utica when he was nine years old. There he attended several schools before being sent for two years to a military academy in Middletown, Connecticut. He read law in Utica and was admitted to the bar in 1832. On his twenty-fifth birthday, May 31, 1835, Seymour married Mary Bleeker (d. 1886), a union that lasted for more than fifty years. The couple had no children.

Seymour began his political career in January 1833 when he became military secretary for New York governor William L. Marcy, a post Seymour held for six years. Marcy, however, continued on as his political mentor and friend for more than twenty years. In the 1830s and 1840s, when New York Democrats split into two factions, Seymour was a conservative ("Hunker," as opposed to "Barnburner"), but he frequently tried to influence the groups toward compromise. He was elected to the New York assembly for three terms (1842, 1844, 1845), serving as speaker during the last term. He was a promoter of canals and particularly a route to unite the Great Lakes with the Mississippi River. Seymour also served as mayor of Utica (1842–1843).

During his career Seymour was nominated six times for governor of New York and was elected to two terms (1852–1854, 1862–1864). He was not a reformer. Although opposed to slavery, Seymour was even more opposed to abolitionists and to federal interference with slavery. He expected the institution to die out eventually from the competition with free labor, which would be strengthened by immigration. He also opposed prohibition and the nativist opinions of the Know-Nothing Party in the 1850s. In 1860 certain Democrats wanted to nominate Seymour as a compromise presidential candidate. But Seymour withdrew his name from consideration. Although Seymour thought that Abraham Lincoln's election was a bad thing, he unsuccessfully urged compromise between the North and South and a popular vote on the Crittenden Compromise.

During the Civil War Seymour was a leader of the Peace Democrats. He opposed the Emancipation Proclamation, the arrest of the ultra-Southern-sympathizing Ohio Democrat Clement L. Vallandigham, and any war powers exercised by Lincoln that Seymour believed were not constitutional. Nevertheless, Seymour was loyal to the Union and dedicated to recruiting the soldiers necessary to fill New York's quota. Yet Seymour was opposed to the draft, and during the New York draft riots of 1863 his comments were misinterpreted by the press as disloyal. In 1864 in Chicago, Seymour presided over the Democratic National Convention, which nominated General George B. McClellan for president. Seymour was also a candidate for governor in 1864 but was defeated by the Republican candidate Reuben E. Fenton, at least in part because of tampering with the New York soldier's vote.

In 1868 Seymour was again selected to preside over the Democratic National Convention, this time in New York City. Andrew Johnson was among the many candidates competing for the nomination. Seymour, however, declined to be a candidate. Nevertheless, on July 22, 1868, on the twenty-second ballot, he was unanimously nominated as a compromise candidate and reluctantly accepted the nomination. Francis Preston Blair, Jr., the vice presidential nominee, did not help matters during the campaign, as his sometimes extreme statements were interpreted to indicate a desire to resume the Civil War.

Johnson and Seymour had very little contact at any time. John F. Coyle, editor of the *Washington National Intelligencer,* wrote to Johnson on August 20, 1868, with a message from Seymour, whom Coyle had recently interviewed. Seymour wanted to thank Johnson for all that the president had done for the country. Seymour wanted to reassure him that he had always admired Johnson and had expressed sympathy for him during the impeachment trial. If Seymour were elected, he would be "indebted" to Johnson for "counsel" from Johnson's presidential experience. Clearly this message was intended to convince Johnson to declare his support of Seymour and thus aid the Democratic campaign. Although Johnson certainly opposed the Republican candidate, Ulysses S. Grant, he did not do anything to campaign for Seymour until October 22. At that point he wrote a letter to Seymour that was widely published. Johnson had read that Seymour intended to campaign personally and the president urged Seymour to do it because of the current state of public affairs. He melodramatically proclaimed that the people should be "warned against the encroachments of despotic power now ready to enter the very gates of the citadel of liberty." This was Johnson's only campaign effort.

Seymour was defeated by a popular vote of 2,706,829 to 3,013,421 for Grant and an electoral vote of 80 to 214, respectively. In the 1870s Seymour helped Governor Samuel J. Tilden in his efforts to drive William M. Tweed from power in New York City and reform the Tammany Hall Democratic political organization. Seymour also wrote several magazine articles on political subjects. In his later years he suffered a sunstroke, increasing deafness, and general frailty. He died in Utica on February 12, 1886, after a short illness.

See also: Blair, Francis Preston (Jr. and Sr.); Coyle, John Francis; Democratic Convention; Democratic Party; Election of 1864; Election of 1868; Grant, Ulysses Simpson; Impeachment; Lincoln, Abraham.
References: Graf, LeRoy P., Haskins, Ralph W., and Bergeron, Paul H., eds., *The Papers of Andrew Johnson* vols. 3, 7, 14–15 (1967–2000); Mitchell, Stewart, *Horatio Seymour of New York* (1938).

Sheridan, Philip Henry (1831–1888)

*P*hilip Henry Sheridan, who as commander of the Fifth Military District disagreed with Andrew Johnson about Reconstruction policy, was the third of the six children of recent Irish immigrants John and Mary Meenagh Sheridan. Philip was probably born on March 6, 1831, in Albany, New York, although other birthplaces have also been listed. The family moved to Somerset, Ohio, when Sheridan was very small. There, Sheridan's father was a road and canal builder, and Philip attended local schools until the age of fourteen, when he quit to clerk in a general store. In 1848 he was admitted to West Point, where he survived mathematics thanks to tutoring by his roommate. After a fight with a cadet sergeant, Sheridan was suspended for a year and graduated with the class of 1853.

Assigned to the infantry, Sheridan served in Texas and against Indians in the Northwest before the Civil War. When that conflict broke out, he at first served as a quartermaster in Missouri and during the campaign to Corinth, Mississippi. He became colonel of the 2nd Michigan Cavalry in May 1862 but soon was made a brigadier general. He fought in such western theater battles as Booneville, Perryville, Stone's River, Chickamauga, and Chattanooga (where his troops led the charge up Missionary Ridge). Ulysses S. Grant then made him the commander of cavalry for the Army of the Potomac, and Sheridan fought at the Wilderness, Todd's Tavern, Spottsylvania Court House, Cold Harbor, Howe's Shop, and Trevilian Station. Ordered by Grant to destroy all potential enemy supplies in the Shenandoah Valley, Sheridan practiced a devastation so severe that Grant commented that even a crow flying over the Valley would have to bring his own rations. Sheridan's raids, plus the actions of his troops at Five Forks and Saylor's Creek, along with his capture of crucial Confederate supplies, led to Robert E. Lee's surrender of the Army of Northern Virginia at Appomattox Courthouse, Virginia, on April 9, 1865.

In May 1865 Sheridan was placed in command of the Military Division of the Southwest. After some adjustments this included Florida, Louisiana, and Texas. Sheridan was mainly concerned with Texas at this point, preparing for a possible invasion of Mexico to drive out the Emperor Maximilian and his French supporters. Sheridan's threatening actions did help convince the French to withdraw. By the fall of 1865 Sheridan became more interested in Reconstruction matters, particularly in Louisiana, which was commanded by his subordinate, Edward R.S. Canby. Sheridan and Canby had some conflict until Canby requested and received a transfer in May 1866.

Sheridan believed that the army was needed in Louisiana to protect Unionists and freedmen. He also thought that blacks needed and deserved voting rights to protect their new freedom. In most matters of Reconstruction Sheridan agreed with the Radical Republicans and thus came into conflict with President Andrew Johnson.

Despite the potential for unrest in Louisiana, Sheridan went to Texas because of a Mexican crisis and therefore was not in New Orleans when the riot occurred on July 30, 1866. He returned on August 1 and his investigation caused him to blame the reassembling of the constitutional convention as the immediate cause. But he blamed the mayor, John T. Monroe, and other local officials for not controlling the situation or bringing the guilty to justice, the thug-ridden police force for their violence, and the press for spurring on the unrest.

After the passage of the First Military Reconstruction Act on March 2, 1867, Johnson appointed Sheridan commander of the Fifth Military District comprised of Louisiana and Texas. Sheridan announced that he intended to enforce the Reconstruction Acts strictly and he did so, disfranchising more former Confederates than the act probably applied to, for example. He believed that the Second Military Reconstruction Act gave him the right to remove civil officeholders whom he saw as "impediments" to Reconstruction, and on March 27, 1867, he removed New Orleans mayor John T. Monroe, Louisiana attorney general

Andrew S. Herron, and first district judge Edmund Abell, all for in some way failing to prevent or to punish the perpetrators of the riot of July 1866. On June 3, Sheridan removed Louisiana governor J. Madison Wells (who did not vacate until forced to on June 7), followed by Texas governor James W. Throckmorton on July 30, and twenty-two New Orleans city councilmen on August 1.

Meanwhile, President Johnson was becoming increasingly unhappy with Sheridan, whose enforcement of the Reconstruction Acts was much more strict than Johnson desired or than Attorney General Henry Stanbery had ruled was necessary. Johnson had received many letters from persons in Louisiana complaining about Sheridan's allegedly tyrannical acts as commander of the Fifth District and urging his removal. In cabinet discussions on the subject, the cabinet members were split over whether Sheridan should be removed or not. In July 1867 Johnson even sent General Lovell H. Rousseau to New Orleans to check up on Sheridan and the situation.

When, on August 17, Johnson sent orders to commanding general Ulysses S. Grant to transfer Sheridan elsewhere, Grant protested. He thought that the transfer would have a bad effect on the Northern public, who loved Sheridan and did not want him removed. Despite Grant's opinion, which Johnson answered point by point, the president had determined to remove Sheridan and he did so, having him ordered to report to Fort Leavenworth, Kansas, immediately. Johnson had two official reasons: a "private" telegram from Sheridan to Grant of June 22, 1867, which was published in the *New York Tribune* on June 24 and was disrespectful of Johnson; and Sheridan's inappropriate (according to Johnson) exercise of power "in an arbitrary and offensive manner." General Daniel Sickles, commander of the Third District, was removed at the same time. Temporarily replaced by General Charles Griffin (who died of yellow fever within days), Sheridan left for Fort Leavenworth on September 5. Johnson received many letters of support for removing Sheridan.

After combating Indian warfare on the Plains, Sheridan spent time in Europe (1870–1871) and observed the Franco-Prussian War. Afterward, headquartered in Chicago, he helped bring order to the city after the terrible fire of October 8, 1871. In January 1875 President Ulysses S. Grant sent Sheridan to Louisiana once again to bring order out of partisan chaos in the state legislature, a situation that Andrew Johnson resoundingly criticized in the single speech he made during his brief time in the Senate in March 1875.

On June 3, 1875, in Chicago, Sheridan married Irene Rucker, who was only half his age and the daughter of an army quartermaster. They had three daughters and a son, none of whom married. In 1884, when William T. Sherman retired, Sheridan became commanding general of the army. In poor health from obesity and heart disease, Sheridan spent a year and a half writing his memoirs (published in 1888). He died August 5, 1888, the day after he had finished reading the proofs of his book, as the result of a series of heart attacks.

See also: Black Suffrage; Canby, Edward Richard Sprigg; Congressional Reconstruction; Grant, Ulysses Simpson; Indians; Military Districts; Military Reconstruction Acts; New Orleans Riot; Republican Party; Rousseau, Lovell Harrison; Sherman, William Tecumseh; Sickles, Daniel Edgar; Stanbery, Henry.
References: Dawson, Joseph G., III, *Army Generals and Reconstruction* (1982); Graf, LeRoy P., Haskins, Ralph W., and Bergeron, Paul H., *The Papers of Andrew Johnson* vols. 11–13 (1967–2000); Morris, Roy, Jr., *Sheridan: The Life and Wars of General Phil Sheridan* (1992).

Sherman, William Tecumseh (1820–1891)

A future Union general, William Tecumseh Sherman was the third son and sixth child of the eleven children of Charles Robert and Mary Hoyt Sherman. Born in Lancaster, Ohio, and named Tecumseh after a noted Shawnee chief, the boy was called "Cump" by family and friends. When his father died suddenly in 1829, the children were divided up among relatives and friends, and Tecumseh went to live with neighboring lawyer and politician Thomas Ewing, Sr., his wife Maria, and their children (eventually six). Although never officially adopted by his foster family, Sherman was raised as one of their own children and given the name William Tecumseh when he was baptized in the Catholic church. On May 1, 1850, after a seven-year engagement, Sherman married his foster sister Ellen Ewing (ca. 1824–1888). Her devout Catholicism, which Sherman did not share, and her closeness to her father, to whom Sherman awkwardly felt indebted, caused considerable stress in their marriage. They were often separated as a result of Sherman's military activities as well. Nevertheless, they eventually had four daughters and four sons, although two of the boys died young.

Sherman graduated from West Point in 1840, ranked sixth in his class. After being stationed in various places and serving in the Mexican-American War, Sherman resigned from the army in 1853 and managed a San Francisco bank, which failed in the Panic of 1857. After several other unsuccessful ventures, he became superintendent of a new military college in Louisiana (now Louisiana State University), but he resigned the post when Louisiana seceded in 1861.

Sherman rejoined the U.S. Army in May 1861, when he was appointed colonel of the 13th Infantry. Initially he had a number of problems that were worsened by hostile reports in the press, which resented Sherman's efforts to restrict information going to newspapermen who, Sherman believed, frequently revealed military secrets. Stationed in Kentucky in 1861, Sherman had some initial contact with Andrew Johnson, who urged Sherman to send troops into East Tennessee. But Sherman did not do so, to Johnson's disgust. Sherman led troops in the Shiloh, Vicksburg, and Missionary Ridge campaigns (1862–1863), for which he received military promotions through various grades of general. In December 1863, while visiting with General Ulysses S. Grant in Nashville, Sherman and a number of other generals called on Military Governor Johnson.

Sherman is best known for his 1864 campaigns. First he pursued the Confederates through northern Georgia, finally capturing Atlanta in early September, thereby helping to ensure the election of Abraham Lincoln and Andrew Johnson to the presidency and vice presidency in November. Sherman then led his troops through Georgia to Savannah, wreaking much destruction, and eventually moved into South Carolina and finally North Carolina, where he forced the surrender of Joseph E. Johnston's Confederate Army of Tennessee in April 1865. Because Sherman was an advocate of a hard war but a mild peace, his negotiations with Johnston resulted in an agreement considered too lenient and with too many political implications. The agreement was rejected by the cabinet and publicly denounced by Secretary of War Edwin M. Stanton, leading to hurt feelings on Sherman's part, as the general was quite sensitive.

In January 1865 Sherman had sought to make provision for the numerous blacks who had followed his army to the coast. He issued Field Orders No. 15, assigning abandoned lands on the Georgia and South Carolina sea islands to the blacks for cultivation. General Oliver O. Howard, head of the Freedmen's Bureau, exempted these lands from his July 28, 1865, order returning abandoned lands to their owners. Andrew Johnson, however, nullified both Sherman's and Howard's orders because he wanted owners to be able to claim all their land. But Congress overrode these provisions, permitting the freedmen to receive compensation for their improvements and to buy twenty-acre plots elsewhere, a process of adjustment that took years to complete.

Although Sherman believed in fair treatment for blacks, he did not believe in black suffrage or any other equal rights that would alienate Southern whites. Therefore, he approved of Johnson's vetoes of the Freedmen's Bureau bills and Johnson's policy in general, as it provided a lenient Reconstruction for the South. Sherman frequently made comments supportive of Johnson's policy, without realizing that as a military hero his words would have political impact. Consequently, Sherman tended to be annoyed by Johnson's attempts to make him a part of the president's administration, particularly rejecting several attempts to make him secretary of war in place of Stanton.

In the fall of 1866 Sherman traveled, on Johnson's order, to the Texas-Mexico border with Louis Campbell, the new U.S. ambassador to Mexico, in a largely futile effort to meet with representatives of the Mexican government. When Congress passed the Military Reconstruction Acts, Johnson considered Sherman as an appropriate head for the Fifth Military District (Louisiana and Texas). Sherman, however, refused to head any district, claiming instead to prefer taking a troop of cavalry west to fight Indians. In fact, he headed the military division west of the Mississippi River. Johnson was anxious to have Sherman stationed in Washington at the time of the impeachment crisis and attempted to make him commander of the new Military Division of the Atlantic, headquartered in the capital. Sherman, wanting nothing to do with politics, protested at length. After he testified at Johnson's trial that the president's purpose in asking him to become secretary of war was to test the Tenure of Office Act in the best interests of the country, Sherman was permitted to return to his headquarters in St. Louis.

When Ulysses S. Grant became president, Sherman succeeded him as commanding general of the army. But Sherman's feelings were badly hurt when almost immediately the bureaus under his command were put under the control of the secretary of war. Miserable, he returned to St. Louis and wrote his *Memoirs* (1875). The situation did not improve until 1876. Then Sherman returned to Washington and actively exercised his command until his retirement from the army in late 1883. His relationship with Grant never fully recovered, however.

Sherman continued to reject political involvement. When pressured to accept the Republican presidential nomination in 1884, he squelched the movement by stating that he would not accept the nomination nor serve if elected. Sherman died in New York City on February 14, 1891, after a cold turned to pneumonia, complicated by chronic asthma.

See also: Black Suffrage; Election of 1864; Ewing, Thomas (Jr. and Sr.); Foreign Affairs; Freedmen's Bureau Bills (and Vetoes); Grant, Ulysses Simpson; Impeachment; Indians; Mexico; Military Districts; Military Governor of Tennessee, Johnson as; Presidential Reconstruction; Stanton, Edwin McMasters; Tenure of Office Act; Territorial Affairs.

References: Graf, LeRoy P., Haskins, Ralph W., and Bergeron, Paul H., eds., *The Papers of Andrew Johnson* vols. 4, 5, 8, 10–15 (1967–2000); Marszalek, John F., *Sherman: A Soldier's Passion for Order* (1993); Sherman, William T., *Memoirs* (1875 and numerous reprints); Trefousse, Hans L., *Andrew Johnson: A Biography* (1989).

Sickles, Daniel Edgar (1819–1914)

Controversial general Daniel Edgar Sickles, whom Johnson removed from command of the Second Military District in 1867, was born in New York City in 1819. In his later years he gave his birth date as 1825 and people believed him because he looked much younger than he was. A bright and willful youth, he quit school and became a typesetter. He eventu-

ally attended New York University for a time but quit after the death of his mentor, Lorenzo L. DaPonte. Sickles then read law and was admitted to the bar in 1846. He also became involved in politics as a Tammany Hall Democrat and was elected to the state legislature in 1847.

Sickles was an elegant dresser, a theater attender, a connoisseur of food, a womanizer, and a crony of many politicians and influential men. He frequently did outrageous things, such as taking a prostitute along to Albany for the meeting of the state assembly. Because he spent money lavishly and was always in need of more, he was frequently accused of questionable financial dealings. On September 27, 1852, Sickles, then almost thirty-three, married Teresa Bagioli (1836–1867), a sixteen-year-old whom Sickles had known since she was an infant. They had a daughter, Laura, who was born while Sickles was in England, serving as secretary of legation (1853–1855) to James Buchanan, the U.S. minister there. After a term in the state senate (1856–1857), Sickles was elected to the U.S. House of Representatives (1857–1861).

In 1859 Sickles, although guilty of many marital infidelities himself, shot and killed Philip Barton Key (son of Francis Scott Key, author of "The Star-Spangled Banner"), his wife's lover. During the notorious trial that followed, Sickles was defended by Edwin M. Stanton, among others, and acquitted on the grounds of temporary insanity. Sickles then took his repentant wife back, which was regarded as an even greater scandal.

Soon after the Civil War broke out, Sickles volunteered to raise a regiment, and in fact recruited a brigade, becoming a brigadier general of volunteers as of September 1861. He was promoted to major general in November 1862. He led troops in the Peninsula campaign and at Antietam (Sharpsburg), Fredericksburg, and Chancellorsville. At Gettysburg on July 2, 1863, Sickles, contrary to orders, stationed his corps in the Peach Orchard, where they were decimated in an attack by Confederates under General James Longstreet. Sickles spent the rest of his life defending this action against strong criticism.

Sickles would also remember the second day at Gettysburg for another reason. Late in the battle he was struck in the right leg by a cannon ball and had to undergo an amputation in a field hospital. The severed leg was placed in a miniature coffin and Sickles donated it to the recently founded Army Medical Museum. In his later years he would often go there to visit his leg. (The bones can still be seen in Washington, D.C., in the National Museum of Health and Medicine, the successor to the Army Medical Museum.) This wound ended Sickles's battlefield service.

In May 1864 President Abraham Lincoln sent Sickles on a confidential mission to Union-held Southern areas, especially Tennessee, where he may have been either checking to see if Andrew Johnson's military governorship was as severe as reported or seeing if Johnson would be interested in the vice presidential nomination. Whatever Sickles's purpose, apparently he and Johnson, whom he had known while in Congress, took a sightseeing trip to "The Hermitage," the former home of Andrew Jackson near Nashville. The next year Sickles went on a government mission to Colombia in Latin America. When Sickles returned to the United States in July, Johnson appointed him military governor of South Carolina, where he remained until 1867, turning down an appointment as minister to The Hague in 1866.

Sickles's tenure in South Carolina generated a certain amount of controversy and a number of complaints, because of some of the orders he issued. But he created less controversy than he did as commander of the Second Military District, comprising both Carolinas, beginning in March 1867, under the provisions of the First Military Reconstruction Act. Most obnoxious were his orders overruling the civil courts, particularly in the area of debt collection. When Johnson traveled to North Carolina in June 1867, he was welcomed to Raleigh by Sickles. However, on August 26 Johnson ordered Sickles relieved from command of the Second Military District and replaced by Edward R.S. Canby. Sickles demanded a court of inquiry but Johnson declined to permit it because Sickles had already been allowed to publish his own version of the events leading to his removal. Sickles was ordered to New York City to await further orders, but he apparently received none and retired from the army with the rank of major general in April 1869.

President Ulysses S. Grant appointed Sickles minister to Spain in May 1869, a post he held until December 1873. While there Sickles, a widower since 1867, married Caroline de Creagh on November 28, 1871. The couple had a daughter and a son, but lived apart for decades and were reconciled to only a limited extent at the end of Sickles's life.

In his later years Sickles was very involved with the placing of commemorative monuments at Gettysburg. One reason for his election to the U.S. House of Representatives for another term (1893–1895) was his desire to promote preservation of the battlefield. Although a Democrat, Sickles actively campaigned for the Republican candidate, William McKinley, in 1896. Despite that he had inherited a fortune from his father, Sickles's extravagance had led to serious financial trouble by the time of his death from a stroke in 1914.

See also: Canby, Edward Richard Sprigg; Election of 1864; Grant, Ulysses Simpson; Lincoln, Abraham; Military Districts; Military Governor of Tennessee, Johnson as; Military Reconstruction Acts; Presidential Travels.

References: Graf, LeRoy P., Haskins, Ralph W., and Bergeron, Paul H., eds., *The Papers of Andrew Johnson* vols. 6, 10–13 (1967–2000); Swanberg, W.A., *Sickles the Incredible* (1956).

Slavery, Johnson's Attitude toward

See Blacks (Slave and Free), Johnson's Attitude toward

Slaves, Owned by Johnson

Although Andrew Johnson began his career in poverty, by 1842 he was wealthy enough to purchase a slave to serve as household help. The young woman, named Dolly, came from Parrottville, Tennessee, and was about fourteen years old. According to family tradition, she was going to be sold at auction when she saw Johnson, liked his looks, and asked him to buy her. He spent $500. Soon afterward Johnson bought her younger half-brother Sam. In all the censuses located, Dolly is listed as black and Sam is indicated as mulatto.

Exactly how many slaves Johnson owned has been a matter of some debate by historians. The 1850 census shows four slaves and that of 1860 shows five slaves in Johnson's household. A sale receipt exists for the 1857 purchase of a thirteen-year-old slave named Henry, who did not appear in the 1860 census. Historians have suggested that Johnson sold him, or Johnson may merely have been acting as an agent for some other purchaser. However, he may well have been the Henry who was one of Johnson's servants while he was military governor and president, although nothing further is known about him. Johnson himself muddied the waters when in various speeches he said that he owned anywhere from seven to ten slaves. In these same speeches he claimed to have bought a few slaves but never to have sold any. No doubt some of the inconsistencies resulted from a certain amount of oratorical exaggeration for effect. In any case, although the exact number of Johnson slaves cannot be determined, it was definitely a small number whose pur-

pose was primarily domestic service. By all accounts Johnson treated his slaves well.

A good bit has been discovered about the known Johnson slaves. Sam, who with his sister and her offspring took the last name Johnson when freed, was considered Johnson's favorite slave and apparently was rather spoiled. Martha Johnson Patterson claimed that Johnson was actually Sam's servant rather than the other way around. In January 1860 Johnson's oldest son, Charles, wrote to his father to complain about Sam. He had become quite an "independent gentleman" who talked back to Eliza Johnson, refusing to do the work that she had requested and desiring to be paid the full amount he earned for hiring his time, rather than just a portion of it. Although Charles thought that his father should sell the impudent Sam, Johnson did not do so. During the Civil War, Sam worked for a time for Robert C. Carter, a Greeneville farmer. This was probably in part an attempt to escape Confederate confiscation of Andrew Johnson's property, including his slaves. Eventually the slaves were taken to join the Johnsons in Nashville.

To the extent that slave marriages were recognized in the 1850s, Sam married a woman named Margaret. By 1870 the couple had five children. Thirty-five to forty years old at the time (the censuses vary), Sam supported his family by working as a house carpenter. He continued his connection with the Johnson family, buying some land in Greeneville from Andrew Johnson's heirs and living there in the 1880s. Some sources indicate that he was still living in 1901.

While she was Johnson's slave, Dolly, Sam's older sister, had three children—Liz, Florence, and William—who also became his slaves. Because Dolly was always listed as black and her children as mulatto, it is probable that their father was a white man (or possibly several white men since William was eleven years younger than his nearest sister). Nothing is known regarding this man and there are no rumors about the involvement of members of the Johnson family. After emancipation Dolly continued to work for the Johnsons in Greeneville. For a time she and William lived in the old Johnson tailor shop, where they baked and sold pies. Dolly probably died between 1875 and 1880 because by the latter date William was living in his oldest sister's household.

Liz or Lizzie (1846–fl.1900) was the oldest of Dolly's children. While they were young, Liz and her sister Florence were treated somewhat as pets by the Johnson family. In 1854 Johnson bought a little chair for them while he was on a trip to Nashville. Lizzie married George Forbey, a Greeneville farmer, and they eventually had at least nine children. In 1875 Lizzie and some of her children were living with Mary Stover Brown in Carter County, perhaps to help take care of Eliza Johnson, who was also staying at Mary's farm. That Lizzie continued to have a close relationship with the Johnsons after emancipation is evident from the names of some of her children. Lillie S. (b. 1869) and Belle P. (b. 1870) were obviously named for two of the Johnson granddaughters. At her death in 1883, Mary Stover willed Lizzie Forbey four acres of land in Greeneville. Lizzie and members of her extended family were living in Knoxville in 1900 but had either died or moved elsewhere by 1910.

Dolly's second daughter, Florence (ca. 1848–fl.1870), went to the White House to work for the Johnsons during the presidential period. She returned with them to Greeneville and in 1870 was living with her mother and brother. She seems to have disappeared from the record thereafter.

William (1859–1943) experienced slavery only as a small child. He did recall the benevolence of Andrew Johnson as a master and knew that he did not have to be afraid of being sold, as some of his playmates did. He reportedly learned to cook from Eliza Johnson and Martha Patterson, as well as his mother Dolly, whom he helped with her pie-baking business.

William later remembered as a young man sitting with the dying Andrew Johnson and holding his hand. After William's mother died he worked as a servant in Greeneville and then moved to Knoxville, where he worked as a chef or pastry cook in a number of restaurants. He was also briefly doorman for the Andrew Johnson Hotel.

In 1936 William was disappointed that he did not get to meet Franklin D. Roosevelt when the president came to East Tennessee for the dedication of Norris Dam. When Roosevelt heard about Johnson's former slave, he sent a secret service man to bring William to Washington, D.C., to visit Roosevelt in the White House. This trip was one of the highlights of William's life. He particularly treasured the silver-headed cane given to him by the president, refusing to let it out of his sight, even during his final illness. He died in a home for the aged in Knoxville in May 1943. Although all newspaper reports of the death of the last of Johnson's former slaves listed him as eighty-seven years old, consistent early census reports indicate that William was actually eighty-four.

See also: Blacks (Slave and Free), Johnson's Attitude toward; Death of Johnson; Grandchildren; Johnson, Charles; Johnson, Eliza McCardle; Patterson, Martha Johnson; Stover (Brown), Mary Johnson.

References: Andrew Johnson National Historic Site, Greeneville, Tennessee: Mary Johnson Stover will; Bowen, David Warren, *Andrew Johnson and the Negro* (1989); Graf, LeRoy P., Haskins, Ralph W., and Bergeron, Paul H., eds., *The Papers of Andrew Johnson* vols. 2–3, 5–7, 10, 15–16 (1967–2000); *Greeneville (Tennessee) Sun,* May 17, 1943; *Knoxville News-Sentinel,* May 17, 1943; U.S. Censuses, Tennessee: 1850 Greene County, Slave Schedules, p. 864; 1860 Greene County, Slave Schedules, p. 5; 1870 Greene County, 10th Civil District, Greeneville, p. 19; 1880 Greene County, Greeneville, p. 165; 1900 Knox County, Knoxville, Enumeration District 63, p. 16.

Speed, James (1812–1887)

James Speed was born near Louisville, Kentucky, attended local schools, and graduated from St. Joseph's College at Bardstown, Kentucky, about 1828. After two years of working for the county clerk's office in Louisville, Speed studied law at Transylvania University in Lexington. He began to practice law in Louisville in 1833, and in 1841 married Jane Cochran, a local woman, with whom he eventually had seven sons. That same year, Speed met Abraham Lincoln, who was visiting his good friend Joshua F. Speed, James Speed's brother, in Louisville. James Speed even loaned Lincoln some law books.

In 1847 Speed was elected to a term in the state legislature. In 1849, however, he was defeated for membership in the state constitutional convention. Part of the reason for this was his antislavery stance, an unpopular view in Kentucky, which he proclaimed in a series of letters in the *Kentucky Courier* in 1849. But he kept busy teaching law at the University of Louisville (1856–1858, 1872–1879) in addition to his practice.

During the secession crisis Speed wanted to preserve the Union, prevent war, and keep Kentucky neutral. He and his brother Joshua supplied Lincoln with advice on the Kentucky situation both during and after the secession crisis. From 1861 to 1863 Speed served in the state senate and then, in late 1864, Lincoln nominated him to replace Attorney General Edward Bates, who wished to retire because of his age (he was seventy-one).

After Lincoln's assassination Speed attended Andrew Johnson's swearing in at the Kirkwood House. Speed gave his official opinion that the assassination conspirators could be tried in a military court and, despite warnings from other advisors about the questionable legality of such a procedure, Johnson, with the approval of the rest of the cabinet, chose the military commission option.

As Johnson's attorney general, Speed was involved in many aspects of Reconstruction. He gave official opinions on a number of legal issues, including the need for an amnesty proclamation superseding Lincoln's, which would take into account the changed conditions at the end of the war. This resulted in Johnson's Proclamation of Pardon and Amnesty of May 29, 1865. Speed also pronounced an opinion about what powers the provisional governors of the Southern states did or did not have and determined the conditions under which legal proceedings against former Confederates could be dismissed. In addition, Speed assessed the validity of claims for compensation for wartime destruction of property, dealt with matters concerning captured property, and determined the jurisdictions of military and civil courts. In this regard he claimed that Jefferson Davis and other Confederate officials could be legally held as prisoners of war because they were captured during wartime. But he did not believe they could have a military trial. Instead they needed to have a civil trial in the state(s) where they committed their alleged treasonous act(s). Because the civil courts were not then operating in Virginia, Davis's trial was delayed and, in fact, the case never came to trial.

Speed and his office were also involved in receiving and processing the pardon applications that flowed in as a result of Johnson's amnesty proclamations. A special clerk had to be hired to deal with pardon matters, but at times the volume was still overwhelming and numerous people wrote to Johnson complaining that no action had been taken in their case.

But Speed and Johnson disagreed over much of the president's policy. Speed especially favored black suffrage and the Fourteenth Amendment, both of which Johnson opposed. Along with Secretary of the Interior James Harlan and Postmaster General William Dennison, Speed disapproved of the National Union Party Convention in

Philadelphia in 1866 and refused to participate in the call for it. He resigned as attorney general on July 17, 1866, and was replaced by Henry Stanbery.

Speed returned to Louisville, where he practiced law, taught at the University of Louisville law school, and was defeated in campaigns for the Senate and House of Representatives. In 1873 he wrote a letter to Joseph Holt about the controversial matter of whether Johnson had seen the petition favoring clemency for Mary Surratt in 1865. Holt used the letter to support his position that Johnson had seen the petition before Surratt was executed. But the letter said only that Speed himself had seen the petition (probably, as Johnson claimed, at the War Department) and Speed refused to discuss what went on in cabinet meetings, implying that the matter had been discussed there but not actually saying so.

Speed died at his home, "The Poplars," near Louisville, Kentucky.

See also: Amnesty Proclamations; Black Suffrage; Cabinet Members; Davis, Jefferson; Fourteenth Amendment; Holt, Joseph; Lincoln, Abraham; Lincoln Assassination Conspirators; National Union Convention and Party; Pardons (Individual); Reconstruction; Stanbery, Henry; Surratt, Mary (Elizabeth) Eugenia Jenkins.

References: Donald, David Herbert, *Lincoln* (1995); Graf, LeRoy P., Haskins, Ralph W., and Bergeron, Paul H., eds., *The Papers of Andrew Johnson* vols. 7–10, 13, 16 (1967–2000); Trefousse, Hans L., *Andrew Johnson: A Biography* (1989).

Stanbery, Henry (1803–1881)

Andrew Johnson's attorney general, Henry Stanbery, was born in New York City, but moved with his parents to Ohio when he was eleven. At the age of sixteen he graduated from Washington College in Pennsylvania. He read law and was admitted to the bar in 1824, joining Thomas Ewing, Sr., in partnership in Lancaster, Ohio, until 1831, when Ewing became a U.S. senator. In 1829 Stanbery married Frances E. Beecher (d. 1840), with whom he had five children. After she died, Stanbery married Cecelia Bond (fl. 1881) in 1841.

In 1846 Stanbery was elected attorney general of Ohio and moved to Columbus. He was an influential member of the Ohio state constitutional convention in 1850–1851. In 1853 he moved his law practice to Cincinnati. Initially a Whig, Stanbery later became a Republican, supporting Abraham Lincoln during his presidency, and then Andrew Johnson. In March 1866 Thomas Ewing, Sr., was among others who suggested Henry Stanbery as a replacement for Johnson's attorney general James Speed, whom they considered rather weak. However, on April 16 Johnson nominated Stanbery for a vacancy on the Supreme Court. At the time, Congress was working on a bill to reduce the size of the Court, so the Senate apparently did not even consider the nomination. Instead, once Speed resigned because he would not support the National Union Party, Johnson nominated Stanbery on July 20. He was confirmed by the Senate three days later.

As attorney general Stanbery had the responsibility of giving official legal opinions on a variety of subjects such as pardon questions, the payment of claims to loyal persons, other property matters, and what to do about a trial for Jefferson Davis when the circuit court was not going to meet in Virginia in the fall. Stanbery helped prepare Johnson's veto of the First Military Reconstruction Act. In May 1867 Stanbery prepared an official opinion on the Reconstruction Act, an opinion that caused considerable controversy and provoked many Radical Republicans to consider him an obstructionist. Interpreting the law as narrowly as possible, Stanbery believed that the military commanders could only keep the peace and punish criminals, not interfere with the provisional governments or civilian courts by removing officials who displeased them. Voting registrars had to accept the oaths of Southerners at face value and not investigate to see whether the prospective voter had committed perjury. Stanbery's opinion was supported by all of Johnson's cabinet except Secretary of War Edwin M. Stanton, and even he agreed with most of it.

After the U.S. House of Representatives impeached Johnson, Stanbery resigned from his cabinet post on March 11, 1868, so that he could serve as one of Johnson's defense counsel without possible conflict of interest. (Secretary of the Interior Orville H. Browning served as interim attorney general.) Although active at the beginning of the trial, Stanbery became ill on April 14 and was confined to his home for several weeks, unable to return to the proceedings until the end of April or early May. Once Johnson had been acquitted, he, on May 27, renominated Stanbery to be attorney general. The Senate rejected the nomination on June 2. After Benjamin R. Curtis declined the offered post, William M. Evarts, another of Johnson's defense counsel, was successfully nominated and confirmed.

Stanbery returned to his successful law practice in Cincinnati. Occasionally he wrote Johnson a letter, including a congratulatory note when Johnson was reelected to the Senate. About 1878 Stanbery retired from his law practice because of failing eyesight and died in New York City.

See also: Browning, Orville Hickman; Curtis, Benjamin Robbins; Davis, Jefferson; Evarts, William Maxwell; Ewing, Thomas (Jr. and Sr.); Impeachment; Impeachment Defense Counsel; Military Reconstruction Acts; National Union Convention and Party; Republican Party; Speed, James; Stanton, Edwin McMasters.

References: Benedict, Michael Les, *The Impeachment and Trial of Andrew Johnson* (1973); Graf, LeRoy P., Haskins, Ralph W., and Bergeron, Paul H., eds., *The Papers of Andrew Johnson* vols. 10–14, 16 (1967–2000); Trefousse, Hans L., *Andrew Johnson: A Biography* (1989).

Stanton, Edwin McMasters (1814–1869)

Born in Steubenville, Ohio, Edwin McMasters Stanton was the eldest child of David and Lucy Norman Stanton. Bright and quick-witted, Edwin developed asthma at a young age, and suffered respiratory seizures throughout his life. Some contemporaries and historians attribute his bouts with depression and irascible disposition to this ailment.

As a youth Stanton attended Kenyon College in Gambier, Ohio (he left before receiving a degree), and read law under several local lawyers. He passed the bar in 1835, but being under the legal age, had to wait another year before commencing practice. Soon he was flourishing personally and professionally. In 1836 he married Mary Lamson, and his law partner, a rising local Democrat, turned most of the practice over to Stanton. Stanton met and grew to respect fellow Ohioan Salmon P. Chase, but the two, although sharing antislavery views, differed greatly on which political party was best suited to protect the Union and limit slavery's expansion. In 1837 the Stantons' first child was born, a daughter they named Lucy. But here the good fortune seemed to end. His daughter died in 1841, and, although a son arrived later that same year, Stanton's wife Mary died several years later, in 1844.

In 1847 Stanton shifted his practice to Pittsburgh, where he hoped to enlarge his client base and escape the painful memories of Ohio. A relatively inactive Democrat, Stanton deliberately kept his antislavery views private to protect his growing law practice, and in 1850 he was admitted to practice before the Supreme Court. He served as counsel with Abraham Lincoln in *McCormick v. Manny,* and, although Lincoln came away impressed with the Ohioan, Stanton overtly snubbed the humble Illinois lawyer. Considered by peers to be ambitious and materialistic, Stanton moved in 1856 to Washington, D.C., hoping to concentrate on cases before the Supreme Court. During this time, Stanton married Ellen Hutchison, and the two had three children. In 1859 Stanton became the first to use successfully a temporary insanity defense, thus saving Daniel Sickles from punishment on the charge of murdering Philip Barton Key, who was having an affair with Sickles's wife (Key was the son of Francis Scott Key, author of "The Star-Spangled Banner").

In December 1860, as the secession crisis intensified, President James Buchanan reorganized his cabinet and asked Stanton to be attorney general. Placing the public good (Stanton was a devout Unionist) before his personal situation, Stanton left a $50,000-a-year practice to enter the lame-duck administration. Eager to preserve the Union—and perhaps his cabinet post—Stanton passed information along regarding White House activities to prominent congressmen and President-elect Abraham Lincoln, hoping to undercut Buchanan's timidity and spur forceful action. Diffident toward Lincoln, Stanton left his post with Lincoln's accession in the spring of 1861, but soon found himself involved with the new administration as legal advisor to Secretary of War Simon Cameron. By January of 1862 Cameron's department was wracked by charges of fraud and inefficiency, and Lincoln removed the secretary. For one of the few times in Lincoln's administration, two great rivals, Secretary of the Treasury Salmon P. Chase and Secretary of State William H. Seward, agreed with one another; both suggested Stanton for the position of secretary of war.

The new secretary was neither personable nor approachable, but was efficient, honest, and dedicated to the point of fanaticism. He worked tirelessly to bring order out of chaos and created the largest, best-equipped, and best-supplied army the United States had ever seen. In doing so he earned the sobriquet "tyrant," for he seemed master of his own kingdom. He enlarged the War Department building and staff, took control of railroads, investigated and prosecuted irregularities in government, standardized military contracts, censored the press, directed the security service, and even relocated the main telegraph to the War Department (not even the White House had its own telegraph). He dealt directly with congressmen, state and local leaders, generals, and contractors. His brusque, demanding nature offended many of them, but he placed pragmatism above etiquette.

But Stanton was not inflexible, and he modified his views toward both Lincoln and the Democratic Party during the war. As the war progressed, the secretary of war came to trust and admire Lincoln, while his opinion of the Democratic Party took a turn for the worse. His Unionism, his anti-slavery attitude, and his uncompromising devotion to Union victory made him vengeful and paranoid toward Democrats and the South, a sentiment he would harbor after the war's end. Yet, during wartime such dedication to the cause made for a good working relationship with Senator Andrew Johnson, who served on the Joint Select Committee on the Conduct of the War (which reported to Stanton). After Lincoln appointed Johnson military governor of Tennessee in early 1862, Stanton advised Johnson on raising troops, pardoning suspected Confederates, and recruiting blacks for the army.

Secretary of War Stanton played a central role in the aftermath of one of the war's final episodes, the assassination of President Lincoln. Stanton believed that the Confederate government was behind the conspiracy, and he used every weapon in his power to root out the attackers and their accomplices. Stanton authorized the use of a military tribunal to try the suspects and apparently supported death sentences for many involved (although Judge Advocate General

Joseph Holt later claimed that the secretary favored clemency for Mary Surratt).

The assassination of Lincoln further confirmed Stanton's cynical view toward Southerners. The secretary at first misjudged President Andrew Johnson because he believed that the president's war record augured for a Reconstruction program that would be punitive toward former Confederates and sympathetic toward former slaves. But from the summer of 1865 forward, relations deteriorated between the executive and his secretary of war. Although Stanton's manuscripts are extensive, he died in 1869 and so was unable to compile his own account of the tumultuous Johnson administration. It is clear that Stanton opposed the president's amnesty proclamations and pardon policy, and that the secretary was leaking information about cabinet meetings by late 1865. By early 1866 Johnson's friends were agitating for Stanton's removal because the army operated the Freedmen's Bureau and enforced law and order across the South. Johnson suspected that Stanton was in collusion with Radical Republicans who were resisting Presidential Reconstruction, but he was hesitant to move against his secretary of war.

Any hope of rapprochement between the two men vanished in 1867, after the passage of the Military Reconstruction Acts. Once Congress assumed responsibility for Reconstruction, Stanton actively supported the new program. Stanton did not concur in Johnson's vetoes, contradicted Attorney General Henry Stanbery's opinion that the acts were unconstitutional, and attempted to protect generals who enforced congressional directives, contrary to Johnson's demands. Ironically, the only veto Stanton supported (he even helped to author it) was Johnson's veto of the Tenure of Office Act, which many believed was passed to protect Stanton from removal by the president. A fundamental question now arose: did the president have the right to discharge subordinates who did not execute his policy?

Stanton believed that he had an obligation to obey his conscience and Congress, and thus ensure that the fruits of Union victory were fully realized. Johnson, on the other hand, held fast to his view of the Constitution and his belief that reconciliation was necessary, not revenge or revolution.

By August 1867 Johnson was convinced that his secretary of war was guilty of insubordination that bordered on treason. Early in the month, reports circulated that there had been a clemency petition for Mary Surratt, and Stanton claimed that the president had known about it. Johnson denied this, but took it as confirmation that his secretary could not be trusted. On August 5 the president asked for Stanton's resignation. Stanton refused to tender it, so in accordance with the Tenure of Office Act (Congress was not in session), the president formally suspended him from office on August 12 and appointed General Ulysses S. Grant secretary of war ad interim.

After Congress reconvened and Republicans failed in their attempt to pass an impeachment resolution, Johnson forwarded his explanation for Stanton's suspension to the Senate. On January 13 the Senate voted not to "advise and consent" to Stanton's suspension, and General Grant, unsure of his standing, gave the office back to his predecessor. Still eager to be rid of Stanton and convinced of the Tenure of Office Act's unconstitutionality, Johnson reacted to the Senate decision by firing Stanton. The president appointed Adjutant General of the Army Lorenzo Thomas as secretary of war ad interim. Stanton, encouraged by Radicals in the House and Senate, refused to surrender his office and even had Thomas arrested.

Johnson's blatant disregard for the Senate's decision prompted another impeachment vote. On February 24 the House impeached the president for "high crimes and misdemeanors" and soon drew up eleven charges, eight of which dealt with the firing of Stanton and the appointing of Thomas. During the Senate trial, President Johnson, in a daring and potentially disastrous move, sent the name of General John M. Schofield as a replacement for Stanton. Although Johnson's Republican adversaries liked Schofield, a central issue in the Senate trial was that Stanton was the secretary of war and could not be removed by the executive without senatorial consent. Johnson emerged victorious from this engagement on May 26, when the Senate adjourned after failing to convict the president. Defeated, Stanton surrendered his office the same day, and on May 30 the Senate confirmed Schofield as his successor; both the Senate and Stanton claimed that he "relinquished" the office to avoid admitting that Johnson had the authority to fire him.

Having survived the chaos of Civil War and Reconstruction, Stanton now directed his energies to a new goal, to become a justice of the Supreme Court. Stanton campaigned fiercely for Grant in 1868 and was rewarded in December 1869 with an appointment to the U.S. Supreme Court. Sadly, the stresses of government service had aggravated his asthma, and he was already in ill health when he received the nomination. Four days after his confirmation, on December 23, 1869, Stanton suffered a debilitating asthmatic attack and died the following day.

See also: Cabinet Members; Chase, Salmon Portland; Congressional Reconstruction; Davis, Jefferson; Democratic Party; Election of 1868; Grant, Ulysses Simpson; Holt, Joseph; Impeachment; Joint Select Committee on the Conduct of the War; Lincoln, Abraham; Lincoln Assassination Conspirators; Military Districts; Military Governor of Tennessee, Johnson as; Military Reconstruction Acts; Mudd, Samuel Alexander; Pope, John; Presidential Reconstruction; Republican Party; Schofield, John McAllister; Senator, Johnson as; Seward, William Henry; Sheridan, Philip Henry; Sickles, Daniel Edgar; Stanbery, Henry; Surratt, Mary (Elizabeth) Eugenia Jenkins; Tenure of Office Act; Thomas, Lorenzo.

References: Hendrick, Burton J., *Lincoln's War Cabinet* (1946); Neely, Mark E., ed., *The Abraham Lincoln Encyclopedia* (1982); Thomas, Benjamin P., and Hyman, Harold M., *Stanton: The Life and Times of Lincoln's Secretary of War* (1962); Trefousse, Hans L., *Andrew Johnson: A Biography*

(1989); Trefousse, Hans L., *The Radical Republicans: Lincoln's Vanguard for Racial Justice* (1969).

State Legislator, Johnson as (1835–1837, 1839–1843)

After serving as alderman and mayor of Greeneville, Andrew Johnson was elected to two terms in the Tennessee state house and one in the state senate. When he took his seat in the house in October 1835 Johnson was not clearly aligned with any political party and, in fact, appeared to be an independent with Whig inclinations. During his first term (1835–1837), he was a member of the committee on county districts and of a special committee to consider the repeal of the Common School Act of 1836. Over the course of the session, he moved various resolutions, bills, amendments, or other actions, many of which were rejected, although some were acted upon. In short, he was involved in the typical activities of a state legislator of the period. Johnson was an avid supporter of measures for economy in government, opposing many bills that would cost his constituents money, such as more funding for the insane asylum and even the money to pay the expenses of the legislature. Johnson was also very much opposed to measures expanding railroads because, he said, they put innkeepers and non-rail methods of transportation out of business. Unfortunately, this stand conflicted with the desires of his constituents, who were eager to have railroad service in East Tennessee. As a result, Johnson was defeated by Brookins Campbell in the election of 1837.

It was not until 1839 that Johnson finally declared himself a Democrat. In that year he ran against Brookins Campbell, also a Democrat, for the second time. In this election Johnson won, in part because of the bad economic effects of the Panic of 1837. During his second house term (1839–

1841), again representing Greene and Washington Counties, Johnson voted for all the measures that supported the Democratic administration of President Martin Van Buren. Johnson was generally hostile to legislation that favored banks and always voted for economy in government, just as he did during his first term. He was a member of several committees; perhaps the most important was that which investigated the condition of the common school fund. The report charged that there had been "official mismanagement" of the school funds. Johnson also opposed opening the legislative sessions with daily prayers by a minister.

In 1841 Johnson was elected to a term in the state senate (1841–1843) representing Greene and Hawkins Counties. He was named a member of standing committees on finance, internal improvements, the penitentiary, and public roads, and served on other committees as well. He was one of the leaders of the group known as the "immortal thirteen," thirteen (eventually twelve) state senators who, for the whole session, refused to meet in joint session with the house to elect two U.S. senators from Tennessee. Because the legislature had just a slight Whig majority, two Whigs would be elected. The twelve Democrats refused to attend and thus prevented a quorum. As a result, Tennessee had no U.S. senators for two years and the Whigs capitalized on the controversy, winning control of both houses of the legislature in 1843.

The legislature did consider other business during the session as well. During discussions on a permanent capitol for the state, Johnson persistently opposed Nashville and advocated Knoxville, to no avail. He also favored the creation of a new state, to be called Frankland, out of portions of East Tennessee, Western North Carolina, Northern Georgia, and Southwestern Virginia. Although nothing came of this either, it showed Johnson's concern for the particular needs of his constituents, which often differed from those of the other sec-

tions of Tennessee. Once again Johnson proposed many bills and amendments, with mixed results. He continued to vote as a Jacksonian Democrat and to advocate economy in government. On February 5, 1842, he received his pay of $508 for the legislative session plus $88 for mileage. In October–November 1842 Johnson attended a special session of the legislature that dealt with issues of revising the electoral districts of the state. Johnson did not return to the state legislature the next year because in 1843 he was elected to the U.S. House of Representatives.

See also: Congressman, Johnson as; Education, Johnson's Attitude toward; Finances, Johnson's Attitude toward Governmental; Religion, Johnson's Attitude toward; Whig Party.
References: Graf, LeRoy P., Haskins, Ralph W., and Bergeron, Paul H., eds., *The Papers of Andrew Johnson* vol. 1 (1967–2000); Macaulay, Alexander S., Jr., "Growing Pains: The Immortal Thirteen, the Destructive Twelve, and the Emergence of Two-Party Politics in Antebellum Tennessee," *Journal of East Tennessee History* 70 (1998): 1–33; Trefousse, Hans L., *Andrew Johnson: A Biography* (1989).

Stevens, Thaddeus (1792–1868)

A native of Vermont, Thaddeus Stevens was born with a clubfoot, a disability that bothered him throughout his life and may have contributed to his irritable personality. He was educated at a local academy and then at Dartmouth, from which he graduated in 1814. After a brief teaching career, during which he also read law, he was admitted to the bar and settled in Gettysburg, Pennsylvania, to practice. He soon became a noted lawyer in the area. In addition to his prosperous legal career, he bought considerable property in Gettysburg, as well as the Caledonia Forge and several other holdings related to the iron business. He helped found the local library and was elected to the first of his five terms on the town council in 1822. Although he never married, Stevens helped to raise two nephews after the death of their father.

Stevens's earliest political involvement on a wider scale was as a member of the Anti-Masonic Party, a cause he avidly espoused from about 1829 to the late 1830s. Under these auspices he was first elected in 1833 to the Pennsylvania legislature, where he was active in support of free public education. (He served in the legislature in 1834–1835, 1837, and 1841 as well.) By 1840 Stevens was campaigning for the Whig presidential candidate, William Henry Harrison, although Stevens tended to put his own particular slant on Whig principles rather than following the orthodox party policy.

In 1842 Stevens moved with his law practice to the larger town of Lancaster, Pennsylvania. From this new location he was first elected to the U.S. House of Representatives in 1848 and ultimately served nearly seven terms (1849–1853, 1859–1868), first as a Whig and then as a Republican of the most radical sort.

Beginning in 1861 Stevens was chairman of the House Ways and Means Committee, which, because of his responsibilities for scheduling discussion and dealing with national finances, was a very powerful position. Although many considered Stevens to be the "dictator" or "tyrant" of the House during the Civil War and Reconstruction, there was never a majority of Radical Republicans in the House to support him, so, although Stevens expressed his opinions freely, he was often unable to turn them into legislation. His position caused him to work closely with the secretary of the treasury to get legislation passed to finance the war. Stevens was outspoken in his antislavery stance, as he had been before the war, and was very much in favor of using black men as soldiers on an equal basis with whites. He was also a strong advocate of confiscating the property of certain Confederates in order to pay Union war expenses and provide for the needs of the freedmen. He advocated this well before his own Caledonia Forge was destroyed by rebel raiders during the Gettysburg campaign, and the idea of confiscation was not a matter of revenge for his own personal losses, as some accused.

By the end of the war Stevens had become even more radical, especially on the issue of the reconstruction of the South. He believed that the South, having withdrawn from the Union, was not to be governed by the Constitution (which would not apply to an area outside the country), but by certain general laws of war. Therefore, the South should be treated as a conquered province and the requirements for its return to the Union should be determined by the Congress not the president. This view, of course, caused conflict between Stevens and both Presidents Abraham Lincoln and Andrew Johnson.

At the Republican National Convention in Baltimore in 1864 Stevens favored the renomination of Vice President Hannibal Hamlin. He did not agree with the nomination of Andrew Johnson because the candidate came from Tennessee, which, from Stevens's perspective, was a rebel province outside the Union. Because Congress was not in session when Lincoln was assassinated, Stevens was at home in Lancaster. When he heard the news, he recalled the disastrous presidencies of John Tyler and Millard Fillmore, vice presidents who had succeeded deceased chief executives William Henry Harrison and Zachary Taylor, respectively. Thus Stevens had a poor opinion of Johnson from the very beginning of the latter's administration.

Nevertheless, Stevens at first attempted to work with Johnson, writing and urging the new president to call a special session of Congress to deal with Reconstruction questions. This Johnson did not do and, in fact, he took Reconstruction matters into his own hands with his Amnesty Proclamation of May 29, 1865, an announcement that appalled Stevens and represented everything he was trying to avoid. Johnson also paid no attention to Stevens's request asking him not to issue pardons until Congress was in session. Consequently, Stevens decided that Johnson was hopeless and the only way to retrieve the situation was for the Radical Republicans in Congress to provide the leadership.

Stevens's opinion was confirmed by widespread violence against the freedmen and the passage of restrictive Black Codes in the Southern states, actions that seemed to result from Johnson's lenient policies. Stevens proposed the establishment of the Joint Committee on Reconstruction and served on it. He also headed the House Committee on Appropriations, a powerful assignment. Stevens used these positions and any other opportunity to try to prevent Johnson's Reconstruction plan from taking effect. He was particularly concerned about the rights of blacks and Southern Unionists as he received many alarming reports about their treatment that were reinforced by accounts of the riot in Memphis in May 1866 followed by one in New Orleans in July.

As a congressman, Stevens was also interested in other government affairs that did not pertain to Reconstruction. He criticized the administration's cautious treatment of Maximilian and the Mexican situation, but supported the purchase of Alaska. He was a supporter of the transcontinental railroad, high protectionist tariffs, an eight-hour workday for laborers, and more pay for low-level government workers, as well as protection for the Indians and suffrage for blacks. He was far ahead of public opinion on many issues and often urged measures that were too radical for Congress to pass.

Meanwhile, Johnson, in his Washington's Birthday Speech (February 22, 1866) publicly and intemperately listed Stevens and several others as persons whom Johnson saw "as being opposed to the fundamental principles of this government, and as now laboring to destroy them." He also abused Stevens in his Swing-around-the-Circle speeches in the fall of 1866. Stevens, however, had many uncomplimentary things to say about Johnson in some of his own speeches, once even suggesting that God had sent Johnson as a plague on the country instead of the lice, which had afflicted the ancient Egyptians. Stevens and Johnson were both stubborn men utterly devoted to and inflexible in support of their own principles—which happened to be totally opposed to each other.

Among the bills introduced by Stevens to help curb Johnson's Reconstruction activities were the Tenure of Office Act, the Army Appropriations Bill, and three of the four Military Reconstruction Acts. He also desired Johnson's impeachment, which he urged unsuccessfully for some time.

Johnson's removal of Secretary of War Edwin M. Stanton in alleged violation of the Tenure of Office Act, and his refusal to reinstate Stanton when the removal was not accepted by the Senate, was the catalyst for impeachment proceedings in the spring of 1868. Although named one of the impeachment managers, Stevens was not able to take the leading role he would have liked because his health, which had been deteriorating for the previous several years, was very precarious. Some historians have suggested that the outcome of the trial might have been different had Stevens been well enough to head the effort rather than leaving it to Benjamin F. Butler. After Johnson was acquitted in May, Stevens sought, without success, to introduce five new charges.

Thaddeus Stevens survived the congressional session by only a couple weeks, dying in Washington, D.C., about midnight on August 11–12, 1868. After lying in state in the Capitol building in Washington, D.C., he was buried in Lancaster, Pennsylvania, in Schreiner's Cemetery, which he chose because the cemetery permitted blacks to be buried there also.

See also: Alaska, Purchase of; Amnesty Proclamations; Army Appropriations Act; Black Suffrage; Butler, Benjamin Franklin; Congressional Reconstruction; Hamlin, Hannibal; Impeachment; Impeachment Managers; Joint Committee on Reconstruction; Memphis Riot; Mexico; Military Reconstruction Acts; New Orleans Riot; Reconstruction; Republican Party; Swing-around-the-Circle; Tenure of Office Act; Washington's Birthday Speech.

References: Brodie, Fawn M., *Thaddeus Stevens: Scourge of the South* (1959); Graf, LeRoy P., Haskins, Ralph W., and Bergeron, Paul H., eds., *The Papers of Andrew Johnson* vols. 6–14 (1967–2000); Palmer, Beverly Wilson, and Ochoa, Holly Byers, *The Selected Papers of Thaddeus Stevens* 2 vols. (1997–1998); Trefousse, Hans L., *Andrew Johnson: A Biography* (1989); Trefousse, Hans L., *Thaddeus Stevens: Nineteenth Century Egalitarian* (1997).

Stover, Andrew Johnson
See Grandchildren

Stover, Daniel (1826–1864)

*L*ittle is known about Daniel Stover's life before his marriage to Andrew Johnson's daughter Mary on April 17, 1852, except that on April 19 his father, William Stover, made out a deed of gift, giving his son six slaves (a woman and possibly her children), for the payment of $1. He deeded Daniel five tracts of land valued at $3,700, as well as various household and farming goods, which he would inherit when his parents died. These gifts were no doubt intended to help Daniel set up his new household. He was apparently, however, already a successful farmer in the Watauga Valley of Carter County, Tennessee, near Elizabethton. Daniel and Mary Stover had three children: Eliza Johnson Stover, the oldest of Andrew Johnson's grandchildren, and always called "Lillie" (1855–1892); Sarah Drake Stover (1857–1886); and Andrew Johnson Stover (1860–1923).

In December 1859 Stover borrowed $600 from his father-in-law, Andrew Johnson, with the intention of paying it back in a year, but for reasons not now known, he was unable to do so. In 1860 Stover was appointed one of the census takers for that year. A staunch Unionist during the secession crisis, Stover was a delegate to anti-secession conventions in Knoxville and Greeneville in May and June 1861.

During the Civil War, Stover participated in some guerrilla operations in East Tennessee including a bridge burning, which led to brutal Confederate retaliation against East Tennessee Unionists. Commissioned a colonel in 1862, Stover organized at Louisville, Kentucky, the 4th Tennessee Infantry (U.S.A.), a regiment of displaced East Tennessee Unionists, who reported for duty at Nashville in August 1863. However, Stover soon became so ill with tuberculosis that he had to give up his command. His attending physician blamed Stover's illness on "the exposure and hardship, incident to his service as a volunteer in the mountains of East Tennessee." His "persistence afterward in the performance of his duties" caused his condition to deteriorate until Stover died of "pulmonary consumption" on December 18, 1864, in the home where Military Governor Johnson was living in Nashville. Stover's body was placed in a vault in Mount Olivet Cemetery, where his brother-in-law Charles Johnson was already interred. In October 1865 he was buried in a private plot in Carter County, the location of which was only rediscovered in the late 1990s.

Apparently Stover died intestate except for a few directions about the use of funds for the benefit of his wife and children. A sale of his property—oil can, horn, dishes, etc.—took place on October 3, 1865, and raised $990.62 for his estate. In the fall of 1869, Andrew Johnson tried to collect the $600 borrowed by Stover before the war, and the Stover estate, then without funds, petitioned the court for permission to sell eighty-five acres of land to pay this debt. It is not clear, however, whether Johnson ever was paid.

See also: Grandchildren; Stover (Brown), Mary Johnson; Tuberculosis.

References: Andrew Johnson Project, Knoxville, TN: Stover files; Graf, LeRoy P., Haskins, Ralph E., and Bergeron, Paul H., eds., *The Papers of Andrew Johnson* vols. 3–4, 6–7, 9 (1967–2000); *Greeneville (Tennessee) Sun,* Oct. 16, 1998; Trefousse, Hans L., *Andrew Johnson: A Biography* (1989).

Stover (Maloney), Eliza Johnson "Lillie"

See Grandchildren

Stover (Brown), Mary Johnson (1832–1883)

Mary Johnson, born May 8, 1832, was the third child and second daughter of Andrew and Eliza (McCardle) Johnson. Although little is known about her childhood, she did attend the Odd Fellows' Female Institute at Rogersville, Tennessee, where she was in the "middle" class in 1850–1851. On April 7, 1852, she married Daniel Stover (1826–1864) of Carter County and they moved to his farm in the Watauga Valley. In the mid-1850s, however, Mary would have preferred to live nearer to Greeneville to have more social contacts. The couple had three children: Eliza Johnson Stover, who was always called "Lillie" (1855–1892), Sarah Drake Stover (1857–1886), and Andrew Johnson Stover (1860–1923).

When the Civil War broke out, Daniel Stover was a staunch Unionist and took part in some bridge burnings to frustrate Confederate supply efforts. As a result of these activities, Stover had to hide out in nearby mountainous areas, apparently contracting the beginnings of the tuberculosis from which he eventually died. For some time Mary and her small children seemed to be safe enough on their farm. When her mother, Eliza Johnson, and brother Frank (Andrew Jr.) were forced to leave Greene-

ville, they came to the Stover farm for refuge. In October 1862, Mary and Daniel Stover and their three children, along with Eliza and Frank Johnson, left East Tennessee, escorted by Mary's older brother Charles Johnson. After some unpleasant experiences, they were able to cross into Union territory. Efforts to improve Eliza's health took Mary and Eliza to Vevay, Indiana, and Louisville, Kentucky. As was the case for years, Eliza's health worsened and improved periodically, but eventually she was well enough for the family to join Andrew Johnson, then military governor, in Nashville.

Unfortunately, the person who became seriously ill was Daniel Stover, whose worsening health forced him to resign his post as colonel of the 4th Tennessee Infantry (U.S.A.). He died of tuberculosis on December 18, 1864, in the Nashville home where Governor Johnson was living, leaving to Mary all his money for the support of herself and the children.

When the war ended and Andrew Johnson suddenly became president as a result of the assassination of Abraham Lincoln, Johnson wanted all of his family to join him in Washington, D.C. Mary wanted to return with her children to her home in Carter County, and, in fact, did so. But Johnson was especially adamant that she come to Washington because he was concerned about the Stover family's safety in a very rural and robber-infested area. Mary and her family did come to the White House in the summer of 1865. Although she made several trips back to Tennessee during the course of Johnson's presidency, Mary otherwise aided her sister Martha Patterson as hostess at White House functions. In early February 1869 Mary and her children left Washington before the rest of the family in order to prepare the Johnson home in Greeneville for occupation.

The Johnsons had barely gotten resettled when Mary married a Greeneville neighbor, William Ramsey Brown (ca. 1816–

1902), a dry goods merchant and widower with four children. The private family ceremony took place at the Johnson home on the evening of April 20, 1869. It was not, however, a successful marriage and the couple were soon estranged, living separately for a number of years. Rumors suggest that William Brown was abusive or mismanaged the Stover children's inheritance. However, the only concrete evidence comes from the divorce papers. Mary complained that Brown had not provided properly for her. In the spring of 1872 she had gone to Carter County with his encouragement to manage the Watauga farm in the interests of her children. Brown had taken her up there and abandoned her without enough furniture or the necessaries of life until her father sent her some money. She said that Brown told her to remain on the farm because his store could not support both his family and hers. Each of Mary's complaints (when read in the original documents) appear fairly weak and were satisfactorily refuted by Brown in his response. But the situation must have been well known or the oral testimony presented to Judge E.E. Gillenwaters must have been more convincing. Mary applied for the divorce on February 14, 1876, just a month after the death of her mother, her last surviving parent. Brown responded to the complaints on February 17, and the divorce was granted on February 19, restoring to Mary her Stover name and her rights as a single woman.

Over the last few years of Mary's life she accumulated a considerable amount of property in Tennessee and Texas. Some of it was certainly her share of Andrew Johnson's estate. However, because he died without a will and settlement of the estate took some time, it is impossible to tell just how much she inherited. One property that she did inherit was an interest in the Holston Cotton Mills in Union Depot (later Bluff City), Tennessee. Johnson had invested in this factory in the 1870s and Frank Johnson managed it until his death in 1879. Mary built a large brick home there, which was called "Stover Hall." It eventually became the home of her son-in-law William B. Bachman and his second family, until the house burned in 1906.

When Mary wrote her will a few months before she died, she left most of her property to her two married daughters, who were to share the property equally and have rights of sale without any interference from their husbands. She did leave some property to her son Andrew, with provisions for his sisters to provide for him if necessary. For whatever reason, he apparently was not able to manage his own affairs in a responsible manner. Mary died at her home in Union Depot on April 19, 1883, "after a brief illness." A casket and hearse were sent to retrieve the body and she was buried with other family members previously interred on Monument Hill in Greeneville.

See also: Grandchildren; Greeneville, Tennessee; Johnson, Andrew, Jr., "Frank"; Johnson, Charles; Johnson, Eliza McCardle; Patterson, Martha Johnson; Stover, Daniel; Tuberculosis.

References: Andrew Johnson National Historic Site, Greeneville, TN: Brown divorce papers, Mary Stover will; Andrew Johnson Project, Knoxville, TN: Stover folders; *Bristol Herald Courier and Virginia-Tennessean*, June 3, 1979; 1870 Census, Tennessee, Greene County, 10th Dist., Greeneville, p. 17; 1880 Census, Tennessee, Greene County, Greeneville, p. 160; Graf, LeRoy P., Haskins, Ralph W., and Bergeron, Paul H., eds., *The Papers of Andrew Johnson* vols. 1–2, 4, 6, 8, 16 (1967–2000); *Knoxville Daily Chronicle*, April 22, 1883; *Philadelphia Press*, June 30, 1868; *Washington Daily Morning Chronicle*, Oct. 5, 1865; *Washington Evening Star*, Feb. 5, 1869.

Stover (Bachman), Sarah Drake
See Grandchildren

Sumner, Charles (1811–1874)

*T*he son of Charles Pinckney Sumner and Relief Jacob Sumner, young Charles was the oldest son of nine children. Reared by an antislavery lawyer-turned-sheriff and an abolitionist mother, Sumner developed an idealistic, even fanatical, devotion to justice and equality. Sumner attended Boston Latin School (1821–1826) and Harvard College (1826–1830). He graduated from Harvard Law School (1833) and was admitted to the bar in 1834. Unhappy practicing law, he hoped to teach at Harvard Law School, where he could focus on ideals and theory, rather than the cold, dry facts. He did lecture briefly at Harvard, wrote legal texts, and edited a law review.

Bored and disappointed, in late 1837 Sumner traveled to Europe, where he studied law and languages, and returned to Boston in 1840. His law practice offered little personal or financial reward, and he found his interests, be they the racial integration of public schools, penal reform, or hopeless pinings after married women, to be unsuccessful and alienating to Boston politicians and socialites.

Despite—or because of—his lack of political affiliation, Sumner was chosen to deliver the Independence Day oration in Boston in 1845. A pacifist, he denounced the Mexican-American War, opposed the annexation of Texas, and decried the possible expansion of slavery. Although many admired his style and vigor, the listeners, mostly veterans of one conflict or another, were offended. Sumner's first public address was microcosmic of the political career it generated: Sumner, in his adherence to principle, was indifferent to audience, environment, or timing. Nonetheless, the oration led to a brief flirtation with the Conscience Whigs, a faction within the party that ardently opposed the spread of slavery. By 1850 Sumner and other Conscience Whigs had drifted into the Free Soil Party,

which, in coalition with Democrats in the Massachusetts legislature, elected Sumner to the first of four terms in the U.S. Senate in January 1851 (he assumed Daniel Webster's seat).

This sudden rise to national position did not inhibit Sumner, who lashed out in the Senate against the Compromise of 1850, the Fugitive Slave Law, and, later, the Kansas-Nebraska Act. His attacks on the bills—and then the laws—were so vicious that Southern senators suggested that he be expelled for treason. By 1854–1855 his principles placed him at the forefront of the Massachusetts Republican Party, but his antagonistic, obstinate tone made enemies as well. On May 22, 1856, two days after an especially vehement address called the "Crime against Kansas," Sumner was assaulted at his Senate desk by South Carolina congressman Preston Brooks, nephew to Senator Andrew P. Butler, also of South Carolina. From the perspective of Brooks and many other Southerners, Sumner had insulted Butler and had to be chastised; Brooks attacked Sumner with a gutta-percha cane and left the senator severely injured and barely conscious.

Sumner spent three years in convalescence, first in Boston (where he was reelected to his Senate seat in 1857) and then in Europe. He returned to the United States in late 1859 and, despite chronic pain and recurring illnesses, was as outspoken as ever. He voiced concerns over Abraham Lincoln's nomination in 1860 and actually welcomed secession when it came in late 1860 and early 1861. A student of international affairs, Sumner believed that secession would bring emancipation because the Confederate States of America could not survive on its own, and certainly not if confronted with war. This placed Sumner at odds with Tennessee senator Andrew Johnson because Sumner opposed the Crittenden-Johnson Resolution of 1861 (also known as the War Aims Resolution).

Sumner was more moderate and more

successful in his foreign policy goals than in his domestic ones. The Lincoln administration helped Sumner become chairman of the powerful Senate Committee on Foreign Relations, a post he would hold for ten years. He emerged as an able rival to Secretary of State William H. Seward and at times functioned as President Lincoln's chief foreign affairs advisor. Eager to avoid antagonizing European powers, Sumner played a central role in defusing the *Trent* Affair, as he pushed for the rapid release of the Confederate commissioners. The senator prevented hostile moves against the French in Mexico, yet blocked measures in support of Maximilian's government as well.

But Sumner's domestic agenda remained extreme and, in his view, unfulfilled. As early as October 1861 he openly advocated emancipation and by early 1862 proposed his "state suicide" theory, which argued that the Confederate states had voided their statehood status and thus had reverted to territories (and thereby were under the direction of Congress). With the Union victories of 1863, Sumner even feared that the war would end too soon, before his goals of abolition, suffrage, and equality were achieved. The Massachusetts legislature elected him to a third term in January 1863, and, although he saw some of his goals come to fruition, he played little or no role in the process: the Emancipation Proclamation, the creation of the Freedmen's Bureau, and the Thirteenth Amendment all developed without his aid, a theme that continued through Reconstruction. In addition, his approval for these measures was halfhearted because this idealist believed that most Republican initiatives were deficient and conservative. For instance, he rejected both Lincoln's Ten Percent Plan and the Wade-Davis Bill, as neither guaranteed equal rights or black suffrage. A close personal friend of Lincoln's (Mary Todd Lincoln had a great liking for the senator also), Sumner nonetheless grew apart politically from the president and his conciliatory views.

After Lincoln's assassination—Sumner remained at the deathbed through the night—the senator moved quickly to discuss affairs with the new president. Sumner had a natural distaste for Johnson, a Southerner and slaveholder, and, in fact, Sumner had called for Johnson's resignation after the latter's inebriated inaugural address upon assuming the vice presidency. Still, Johnson's service as military governor of Tennessee impressed Sumner, especially Johnson's handling of Confederates and support for emancipation. After meeting with the new president on April 15 and 16, Sumner believed that Johnson held similar views on equal rights, punishment for former Confederate officials, and even black suffrage.

Sumner reacted with shock to Johnson's May 29, 1865, Amnesty Proclamation, but, along with other Republicans, did nothing through the summer. Outraged and defiant, Sumner pledged in late 1865 to oppose Johnson and his Southern governments, seeing both as obstacles to the potential fruits of Union victory. Sumner also believed that Reconstruction was a congressional, not executive, function. Gradually more Republicans came to agree, as through 1866 President Johnson alienated the party by rejecting moderate legislation. In fact, Sumner accepted it as a badge of honor when Johnson named him as a threat to the Union in the president's February 1866 Washington's Birthday Speech. Slowly Congress moved into areas first probed by Radical Republicans such as Sumner and Representative Thaddeus Stevens, through the Civil Rights Act, the bill to enfranchise blacks in the District of Columbia, the requirement for black suffrage in Colorado and Nebraska, and the passage of the Military Reconstruction Acts. Still, Sumner's support for these measures was halfhearted because he sought more sweeping changes. He pushed for black educational guarantees, black suffrage in the North, and the redistribution of land in the South.

His domestic life seemed similarly unfulfilled. A bachelor until 1866, he began courting Alice Mason Hooper, a widow thirty years his junior, in the spring of that year. They married in October, but problems abounded, including differences in age and interests, financial difficulties (unlike many politicians, Sumner had abandoned his law practice and had no second income), and rumors of his wife's infidelity. The two separated in 1867 and divorced in 1873.

As his brief marriage collapsed, his missions in the Senate seemed to gain momentum. In 1867 Sumner was pivotal in securing ratification for the purchase of Alaska, which he had at first opposed as a result of Seward's secretive handling of the negotiations. More important, other senators and representatives began seeing the necessity of what he had advocated since late 1866: the impeachment and removal of President Johnson. Sumner, ever the principled theorist, saw impeachment as a political, not a legal, mechanism, and thus was confounded by colleagues who would not act against the president without a law being broken. When Johnson removed Secretary of War Edwin M. Stanton on February 21, 1868, Sumner was thrilled and relieved and immediately sent the one-word telegram "Stick" to the embattled secretary. Yet once again Sumner was denied a major role in the unfolding drama: the House of Representatives impeached the president, drew up the charges afterward, and selected the trial managers. Sumner voted guilty at the trial, but watched in horror each time as the president escaped removal. Sumner was among the first to charge Kansas senator Edmund Ross with receiving a bribe and supported Senator Benjamin F. Butler's investigations into Johnson's finances.

Sumner showed little enthusiasm for the election of 1868 and believed that Republican nominee Ulysses S. Grant was a poor agent for Reconstruction. Neither the new administration nor Congress had tolerance for Sumner's extremist views, and his position as longest sitting senator, after his fourth election in January 1869, brought little clout. Sumner opposed the Fifteenth Amendment, advocated funding the U.S. debt, and lobbied for a pension for Mary Todd Lincoln. Now that Congress considered issues of impeachment and black suffrage closed, Sumner turned to his civil rights bill as his new obsession. At the time of his death, his bill would still be languishing in Congress.

Only as the chair of the Senate Foreign Relations Committee did Sumner still carry any power. He defeated plans to annex the Dutch West Indies and to buy Samana Bay in the Dominican Republic, prevented the recognition of Cuban rebels as belligerents, and killed the Johnson-Clarendon Convention to settle the *Alabama* Claims (which had been negotiated by Reverdy Johnson during Andrew Johnson's administration). In 1870, Sumner successfully blocked Grant's annexation of the Dominican Republic, which led to maneuvers that resulted in Sumner's removal from the chair of the Foreign Relations Committee. This event, coupled with the administration's lackluster performance in combating corruption and racial violence, drove Sumner into the Liberal Republican camp in 1872. In late 1872, he returned to Europe for health reasons and, while there, declined a nomination for governor of Massachusetts. His health worsening, he returned to the United States to advocate his civil rights bill and, by 1873, women's suffrage. Plagued by angina, seizures, and prostate problems, Sumner turned to morphine injections for relief.

He collapsed from a seizure in his Washington home on March 10, 1874. During a few brief intervals of consciousness Sumner called on those clustered around to save his "bill." He died the following day.

See also: *Alabama* Claims; Alaska, Purchase of; Amnesty Proclamations; Black Suffrage; Chase, Salmon Portland; Congressional Reconstruction; Crittenden-Johnson Resolution; District of Columbia Franchise; Drunkenness; Election of 1864; Election of 1868; Fifteenth Amendment; Foreign Affairs; Fourteenth Amendment; Grant, Ulysses Simpson; Impeachment; Johnson, Reverdy; Lincoln, Abraham; Lincoln, Mary (Ann) Todd; Mexico; Military Governor of Tennessee, Johnson as; Military Reconstruction Acts; National Union Party; Presidential Reconstruction; Republican Party; Ross, Edmund Gibson; Senator, Johnson as; Seward, William Henry; Stanton, Edwin McMasters; Thirteenth Amendment; Vice President, Johnson as; Washington's Birthday Speech; Whig Party.

References: Blue, Frederick J., *Charles Sumner and the Conscience of the North* (1994); Donald, David Herbert, *Charles Sumner and the Coming of the Civil War* (1960); Donald, David Herbert, *Charles Sumner and the Rights of Man* (1970); Sefton, James E., "Charles Sumner for Our Time: An Essay Review," *Maryland Historical Magazine* 66 (1971): 456.

Surratt, Mary (Elizabeth) Eugenia Jenkins (1823–1865)

Mary Elizabeth Jenkins was born in Prince George's County, Maryland. She apparently took the middle name Eugenia, which is more commonly used than Elizabeth, as a confirmation name when she converted to Catholicism in the 1830s while a student at the school run by the Sisters of Charity in Alexandria, Virginia.

In August 1840 she married John H. Surratt and they had three children: Isaac Douglas (1841–1907), Elizabeth Susanna ("Anna") (1843–1904), and John Harrison, Jr. (1844–1916). Mary's husband bought property in Prince George's County in 1852, at the site soon known as Surrattsville, where he built a home and tavern. Unfortunately, he accumulated a sizable debt and began to drink heavily, necessitating the sale of some of his property. The estate was in serious financial trouble when John H. Surratt, Sr., died suddenly on August 26, 1862. Isaac was in the Confederate cavalry and John Jr. was involved in various pro-Confederate activities centered around the tavern. For economic reasons, Mary Surratt finally decided to rent out the tav-

ern to a man named John M. Lloyd and to move to property that the family owned in Washington, D.C., where by November 1864 she had established a boardinghouse.

In early 1865, John Jr. became active in John Wilkes Booth's plot to kidnap Abraham Lincoln. Some of John's friends stayed at his mother's boardinghouse and all of the conspirators met there at various times. Mary Surratt certainly was acquainted with them, and in mid-April she reportedly took guns and field glasses out to Lloyd at her tavern, to be held until someone picked them up. Thus, although Surratt apparently was involved to a small extent in assisting the assassin's escape, there is no real evidence that she was a part of the conspiracy itself.

Arrested on April 17, 1865, Mary Surratt was imprisoned in the Washington Arsenal Penitentiary and tried with seven other alleged conspirators by a military commission (May 9–June 30). She was found guilty largely on the testimony of one of her boarders, Louis J. Weichmann, and the tavern keeper John Lloyd. After Mary was sentenced to be hanged, Anna pled with Joseph Holt, the judge advocate general and the government's prosecuting attorney, and tried to see President Johnson to gain a reprieve for her mother, but without success. Five members of the military commission also signed a clemency plea, but Johnson later claimed that he never saw it, whereas Holt insisted that he had shown the request to Johnson but Johnson signed the death sentence anyway. This dispute was never resolved; the accusation that Johnson was responsible for the murder of Mary Surratt later surfaced periodically, particularly at the time of Johnson's impeachment trial and again in 1873 when Holt published a letter in his own defense.

Hanged on July 7, 1865, Surratt was initially buried with the other conspirators at the Washington Arsenal. However, in February 1869, shortly before Johnson left office, he granted a request from Anna Surratt that her mother's remains be returned to the family for burial in consecrated ground. Mary Surratt was then reburied in Mt. Olivet (Catholic) Cemetery in Washington, D.C.

See also: Ewing, Thomas (Jr. and Sr.); Holt, Joseph; Lincoln Assassination Conspirators; Mudd, Samuel Alexander; Pardons (Individual).
References: Graf, LeRoy P., Haskins, Ralph W., and Bergeron, Paul H., eds., *The Papers of Andrew Johnson* vols. 8–16 (1967–2000); Hanchett, William, *The Lincoln Murder Conspiracies* (1983); Miscellaneous publications of the Surratt Society, Surratt House Museum, Clinton, MD; Turner, Thomas Reed, *Beware the People Weeping: Public Opinion and the Assassination of Abraham Lincoln* (1982).

Swing-around-the-Circle (1866)

During the summer of 1866, Andrew Johnson and his supporters tried to establish a new political party, a coalition of Democrats and conservative Republicans. Although it called itself the National Union Party, as had the coalition party of 1864 that had elected Johnson to the vice presidency, the composition of the two groups was quite different. The 1864 party was heavily Republican, whereas Democrats dominated that of 1866. In Philadelphia in August, the new party held a convention, which met with a good deal of opposition.

When Johnson had experienced opposition in Tennessee he would "stump" the state, traveling all over and giving vigorous speeches. He now saw a way to take his views directly to a wider audience of the American people when he was invited to Chicago to give the main speech at the unveiling of a monument honoring the late Illinois Democratic senator Stephen A. Douglas. Some of Johnson's advisors, including Michigan senator James R. Doolittle, Secretary of the Treasury Hugh McCulloch, and Secretary of the Interior Orville H. Browning, urged him to give nothing but carefully prepared speeches. They knew

how easy it was for Johnson to get carried away by the excitement of impromptu speaking and to say things that, as president of the United States, he should not say. Unfortunately, Johnson ignored this advice.

Johnson left Washington, D.C., on August 28 with a sizable contingent, including cabinet members William H. Seward (who was coordinating the trip) and Gideon Welles, Johnson's daughter Martha Patterson and her husband Senator David T. Patterson, General Ulysses S. Grant, Admiral David G. Farragut, and assorted other generals and political figures. Between August 28 and September 15 the group stopped at Baltimore, Maryland; Philadelphia, Pennsylvania; New York, West Point, Albany, Auburn, Niagara Falls, and Buffalo, New York; Cleveland and Toledo, Ohio; Detroit, Michigan; Chicago, Springfield, and Alton, Illinois; St. Louis, Missouri; Indianapolis, Indiana; Louisville, Kentucky; Cincinnati and Columbus, Ohio; Pittsburgh and Harrisburg, Pennsylvania; and many small towns between these major stops, before finally returning to Washington, D.C.

The president followed his old campaign technique, to prepare one speech and deliver it everywhere. However, what worked well in Tennessee, where newspapers were local in circulation, did not work when Johnson was being followed around by numerous correspondents from all the major dailies who reported his every word and action with varying degrees of accuracy and bias.

The trip began well with enthusiastic crowds in Baltimore, Philadelphia, and New York. In the latter city Johnson spoke at a banquet in his honor at Delmonico's restaurant. Republican officials avoided the festivities at Baltimore and Philadelphia, but their absence was hardly noticeable among the parades, welcoming committees, and enthusiastic speeches. In each place where he spoke, Johnson stressed his opposition to those who were still trying to break up the Union by depriving the Southern states of their congressional representation. He urged the people to take the flag, the Constitution, and the Union into their own hands where they would be "safe."

Cleveland, Ohio, was the first stop where Johnson encountered serious hecklers. True to his nature and against all advice, he responded to their comments, entering into the rough-and-tumble of the stump debate. The *Cleveland Leader,* with partisan exaggeration, called Johnson's speech "the most disgraceful ever delivered by any president of the United States." Although some accused Johnson of drunkenness on the trip, the only member of the party who drank to excess was General Grant, who began to do so at Cleveland.

Although Johnson experienced some opposition in Chicago, his speech and visit there generally went well. But his visit to St. Louis was a disaster. While waiting for a banquet to begin, Johnson reluctantly allowed himself to be persuaded to speak to a crowd gathered outside. Once again he responded to hecklers, insulting certain specific Radical Republicans as he defended himself for being considered a Judas to Radical plans. At Indianapolis Johnson was unable to speak as rowdies loudly shouted "Shut up!" "We don't want to hear you!" and "We want nothing to do with traitors." At Pittsburgh the crowd refused to hear Johnson, shouting loudly for Grant and Farragut instead.

At least Johnson received an enthusiastic greeting when he returned to Washington, D.C., but this could not make up for the serious damage to his cause, resulting from his unpresidential and undignified speechmaking behavior so eagerly detailed in the Radical newspapers. His party lost badly to the Republicans in the fall 1866 elections.

See also: Browning, Orville Hickman; Doolittle, James Rood; Election of 1864; Election of 1866; Grant, Ulysses Simpson; McCulloch, Hugh; National Union Convention and Party; National Union Party; Patterson, David Trotter; Patterson, Martha Johnson; Presidential Reconstruction; Seward, William Henry; Welles, Gideon.

References: Graf, LeRoy P., Haskins, Ralph W., and Bergeron, Paul H., eds., *The Papers of Andrew Johnson* vol. 11 (1967–2000) (for a list of the towns visited by Johnson, see Appendix III of vol. 11 of the Johnson Papers); Milton, George Fort, *The Age of Hate: Andrew Johnson and the Radicals* (1965 [1930]); Trefousse, Hans L., *Andrew Johnson: A Biography* (1989).

T

Taylor, Nathaniel Green (1819–1887)

Born in Happy Valley, Carter County, Tennessee, Nathaniel Green Taylor, a politician and one of Johnson's commissioners of Indian affairs, graduated from Princeton in 1840. Admitted to the bar the next year, he began to practice law in Elizabethton in Carter County. In 1843 Taylor's sister Mary was struck by lightning and killed on the way home from a camp meeting. This family tragedy influenced Taylor to become a Methodist minister, a vocation he combined with his law practice, political office-holding, and management of a large farm. In the early 1840s Taylor married Emma (or Emmaline) Haynes, with whom he had ten children.

In 1849 Taylor, a Whig, was Andrew Johnson's main opponent in Johnson's contest for a fourth congressional term, a contest that Johnson won. Taylor was successful, however, in a March 1854 special election to fill the seat of the deceased Brookins Campbell, who had been elected to Congress when Johnson became governor. Unsuccessful in his reelection attempts in 1855 and 1857, Taylor next achieved a political position as an elector for the John Bell–Edward Everett presidential ticket in 1860.

When the Civil War broke out, Taylor was a Unionist but he remained in East Tennessee until some time in 1863, when he went north as an agent for the Knoxville-based East Tennessee Relief Association. He lectured in Cincinnati, Philadelphia, New York, Boston, and numerous other places in order to raise funds for East Tennessee Unionists who had suffered severely under Confederate persecution. He managed to raise nearly $250,000 for the cause. Taylor asked Johnson's help in procuring transportation for the supplies, and Johnson, as military governor, was able to provide assistance.

After the war, Taylor had personal financial difficulties. He had contracted debts while aiding East Tennessee Unionists and these were now due. He was in danger of losing his property and he had a wife and nine surviving children to support. Although he was elected to Congress in August 1865, like other Southern representatives, he was denied his seat. In June 1866, while waiting in Washington, D.C., for a resolution of the problem, Taylor sent Johnson a plea for a "lucrative appointment," either as naval officer at New York or commissioner of Indian affairs. Before Johnson took any action, Tennessee was readmitted to the Union and Taylor was able to serve as congressman from July 24, 1866, to March 3, 1867.

Johnson's nominee for commissioner of Indian affairs, Lewis V. Bogy, was not confirmed by the Senate, so on March 29,

1867, the president appointed Taylor to the commissionership over a number of candidates who had more experience and better qualifications. Taylor's appointment and confirmation has been attributed to the fact that he was a moderate Republican as well as a minister who could be expected to be honest in a department noted for corruption. Unfortunately, Taylor's cabinet superior, Secretary of the Interior Orville H. Browning, did not think much of Taylor and the two had numerous conflicts over their respective responsibilities for the management of Indian affairs. Taylor served as chairman of the eight-member Indian Peace Commission, which traveled to the west to investigate the Indian situation and in October 1868 issued a report with various recommendations. Taylor served as commissioner until April 1869, when President Ulysses S. Grant replaced him with his own nominee.

Taylor retired to his farm but continued to have financial difficulties. In January 1874 Taylor wrote to Johnson desiring to borrow $17,000 to save his farm from creditors, but Johnson was unable to make the loan because of his own financial difficulties resulting from the failure of the First National Bank in the fall of 1873. Taylor died in Happy Valley on April 1, 1887, and was buried in the family cemetery.

See also: Bell, John; Browning, Orville Hickman; Congressman, Johnson as; Finances, Personal; Indians; Patronage.
References: Graf, LeRoy P., Haskins, Ralph H., and Bergeron, Paul H., eds., *The Papers of Andrew Johnson* vols. 1–3, 6, 10, 12–13, 15–16 (1967–2000); Kvasnicka, Robert M., and Viola, Herman J., eds., *The Commissioners of Indian Affairs, 1824–1977* (1979).

Temple, Oliver Perry (1820–1907)

As a young man, Oliver Perry Temple challenged Andrew Johnson in the congressional race in 1847 and nearly won.

Born near Greeneville, Tennessee, Temple was one of seven children. His father died when Oliver was about two, but the young man was able to attend Greeneville College and Tusculum Academy, both in Greeneville, and Washington College in Washington County, from which he graduated in 1844. He campaigned for the Whig presidential candidate Henry Clay during that same year and then read law, being admitted to the bar in 1846.

Andrew Johnson had been the congressman from the first district of Tennessee since 1843 and he expected to have Landon C. Haynes, a fellow Democrat, as his main opposition in 1847. Therefore, he made a speech critical of President James K. Polk and certain other aristocratic Democratic leaders. When Haynes withdrew from the contest, many of the leading Whigs had either agreed not to enter the race or did not wish to be defeated. Several suggested to Temple that he should run. With little legal business to do and much of the enthusiasm characteristic of young manhood, Temple took the challenge and began campaigning with only about three weeks left before the election. He and Johnson held a number of joint debates. Temple's philosophy was not to attack Johnson so much that other Democrats would rally to Johnson's defense. Instead he reminded listeners of Johnson's inconsistencies, tried to appeal to Johnson's opponents in order to divide the party, and continuously referred to Johnson's speech criticizing members of his own party. Temple's strategy nearly succeeded. Johnson, who usually had majorities of more than 1,000, defeated Temple by only 314 votes. This may have been the peak of Temple's career and certainly made his name known.

In 1848 Temple was offered a law partnership in Knoxville and promptly moved there, in part because he wanted to get out of politics. In 1850–1851 he was part of a commission appointed to visit the Indians in Texas, New Mexico, and Arizona. On his return to Tennessee he married Scotia C.

Hume in September 1851. The couple had one daughter, Mary Boyce Temple, who eventually edited and published her father's last book after his death.

Temple continued his law practice during the 1850s. In 1860 he campaigned for the John Bell–Edward Everett ticket of the Constitutional Union Party. In 1861 he was allied with Andrew Johnson and other Unionists in East Tennessee campaigning against secession. Temple was involved with both the Knoxville and Greeneville conventions, and was credited with strengthening Unionist sentiment in East Tennessee. After Tennessee seceded, Temple apparently remained in East Tennessee serving as a lawyer for local Unionists. At some point, however, he did leave the area and spent some time in Cincinnati. Although some of Johnson's other political opponents eventually became close associates, this was not true of Temple, who disapproved of Johnson's method of trying to reorganize the Tennessee government while he was military governor.

After the war, Temple's lucrative law practice was interrupted when Governor William G. Brownlow appointed him to a vacancy as chancellor (a type of judge) in 1866. Temple was twice reelected to the post, which he held until 1878. He was postmaster of Knoxville (1881–1884), was on the University of Tennessee board of trustees (1854–1907), and was involved with several agricultural organizations. He wrote three books: *The Covenanter, the Cavalier, and the Puritan* (1897), *East Tennessee and the Civil War* (1899), and *Notable Men of Tennessee from 1833 to 1875* (1912), in which he was quite critical of Andrew Johnson.

See also: Bell, John; Brownlow, William Gannaway "Parson"; Congressman, Johnson as; Military Governor of Tennessee, Johnson as; Secession, Johnson's Attitude toward; Secession Referendums; Whig Party.
References: Graf, LeRoy P., Haskins, Ralph W., and Bergeron, Paul H., eds., *The Papers of Andrew Johnson* vols. 4, 6 (1967–2000); Speer, William S., *Sketches of Prominent Tennesseans* (1888).

Tenure of Office Act

The Tenure of Office Act was passed by Congress, along with several other acts, to control President Andrew Johnson and prevent his interference with what Congress regarded as crucial aspects of Reconstruction. Specifically, it would limit Johnson's use of patronage to hinder Reconstruction because it would prevent him from removing Radical Republican officeholders and replacing them with his own conservative supporters. This was a particular concern because Johnson had removed quite a few officials in conjunction with the 1866 congressional election.

On December 3, 1866, George Williams of Oregon introduced a Tenure of Office Bill in the Senate, but it did not come up for discussion until January 10, 1867. The main provision of the bill was that the president could not remove anyone from office who had been appointed with the advice and consent of the Senate without also getting Senate consent for the appointee's removal. This would affect hundreds of officeholders. But the main area of debate in both the Senate and the House was whether or not the bill should also apply to cabinet members. Finally, Senator John Sherman of Ohio proposed a compromise upon which both houses agreed. Cabinet members were to hold office during the term of the president who appointed them plus one month and could be removed only with the consent of the Senate. Although it was widely understood that the bill was intended to protect Radical Republican ally Secretary of War Edwin M. Stanton from removal, no one was certain that the bill actually applied to him because he was appointed by Abraham Lincoln.

Johnson, not surprisingly, vetoed the act and, in fact, he had Stanton's help in preparing the message. Sent to Congress on March 2, 1867, the veto explained why Johnson thought the bill was unconstitutional. He believed that the Constitution gave the president the power to remove officials when necessary, without Senate approval. He also cited a number of historical precedents, some involving the founding fathers and Andrew Jackson, in which the idea of requiring Senate approval was considered but discarded. Congress paid no attention to Johnson's message and repassed the bill on that same day, March 2.

Stanton had disagreed with most of Johnson's policies for months, yet he had refused to resign. Instead, he had been working with the Radical Republicans to foil Johnson's policies, but Johnson had not removed him. Apparently waiting for an appropriate time, Johnson acted in August 1867. Congress had just adjourned, so he would have some months before he had to report the removal to the Senate. Also, two other incidents, which could be blamed on the War Department, occurred, including Johnson's discovery that there had been a clemency petition for Mary Surratt that he had not seen. Johnson asked Stanton for his resignation, and, when Stanton refused, Johnson suspended him on August 12, appointing Ulysses S. Grant interim secretary.

When Congress reassembled in December, Johnson had twenty days to notify the Senate of the reasons for Stanton's suspension. In his letter of December 12, 1867, Johnson explained that the two had no confidence in each other, that Stanton had failed to notify him of problems in New Orleans before the July 1866 riot, and that Johnson was supposed to be the head with his cabinet members as subordinates. Despite the explanation, on January 13, 1868, the Senate voted not to accept Stanton's suspension and restored him to office. Johnson, very angry, decided to oust Stanton anyway, and on February 21 ordered Stanton's removal from office, to be replaced by General Lorenzo Thomas as interim secretary.

This was the action that finally provoked the House of Representatives to impeach Johnson. When they finally drew up the impeachment articles, most pertained to Johnson's alleged violation of the Tenure of Office Act by removing Stanton and appointing Thomas. This act was really a rather weak basis for an impeachment trial because the act was vaguely worded, it was constitutionally questionable because it did limit presidential powers in ways not previously permitted, and it was doubtful whether it even applied to Stanton. Johnson's attorneys were able to make good use of these questions in the president's defense, and Johnson was acquitted.

The Tenure of Office Act, drawn up specifically to restrict Johnson, was not applied to any other president. It was amended, but not repealed, early in Grant's first term. Although Johnson had wished to test the act in the Supreme Court, this was not done. However, the principle was finally considered in the case of *Myers v. United States* (1926) in which the majority of the Court, siding with Johnson, ruled that Woodrow Wilson had had the right to remove a postmaster. But in a 1935 case, *Rathbun v. United States,* the Court ruled that Congress could limit a president's power to remove noncabinet members. No specific Supreme Court ruling ever declared the Tenure of Office Act unconstitutional.

See also: Butler, Benjamin Franklin; Constitution, Johnson's Attitude toward; Election of 1866; Grant, Ulysses Simpson; Holt, Joseph; Impeachment; Impeachment Defense Counsel; Jackson, Andrew; Lincoln, Abraham; Lincoln Assassination Conspirators; New Orleans Riot; Patronage; Stanton, Edwin McMasters; Surratt, Mary (Elizabeth) Eugenia Jenkins; Thomas, Lorenzo; Vetoes.

References: Graf, LeRoy P., Haskins, Ralph W., and Bergeron, Paul H., eds., *The Papers of Andrew Johnson* vols. 12–14 (1967–2000); Hesseltine, William B., *Ulysses S. Grant, Politician* (1935); Patrick, Rembert W., *The Reconstruction of the Nation* (1967); Trefousse, Hans L., *The Impeachment of a President: Andrew Johnson, the Blacks, and Reconstruction* (1975).

Territorial Affairs

When Andrew Johnson became president in 1865 there were nine territories: New Mexico, Utah, Washington, Nebraska, Colorado, Dakota, Arizona, Idaho, and Montana. During the course of his presidency, Nebraska became a state, the territory of Wyoming was created, and Alaska was acquired but did not receive a civil territorial government until 1884. Johnson was primarily concerned with events in the thirty-six states but many territorial issues required his attention. Most of these are summarized here and dealt with in more detail in other entries.

After the Civil War there was increasing settlement in the Plains area in the central part of the nation. Some of this was the result of people taking advantage of the provisions of the Homestead Act, which Johnson had advocated for years and which finally became law in 1862. In addition, the construction of railroads, and particularly the transcontinental railroad, brought workers and camp followers (those who served them or preyed upon them) into some of the territories. Johnson was concerned that the Union Pacific and Central Pacific railroads, constructing the two halves of the transcontinental railroad, finish their tracks properly before they were given the promised government land grants to pay for the construction. There was discussion of these matters in cabinet meetings as the railroad neared completion in May 1869, just after Johnson left office.

The railroad and settlers needed protection from the Indians, who often reacted violently to white invasions of their homelands and hunting grounds. Attempts to force Indians to stay on reservations or permit white settlement led to a number of Indian clashes during Johnson's term, both with settlers and with the military.

Colorado and Nebraska attempted to become states during Johnson's term and he vetoed both attempts, citing undersized populations and other problems. Although he was able to prevent Colorado statehood at this time, Nebraska became the thirty-seventh state in 1867. Johnson favored the purchase of Alaska from Russia and, once the negotiations were completed, sent his friend General Lovell H. Rousseau to receive the territory. Congress created the territory of Wyoming on July 25, 1868, and a number of persons with connections there urged Johnson to appoint territorial officials, but this was not done until after Johnson left office.

Appointment of territorial officials was a part of Johnson's patronage responsibilities. Each territory had an appointed governor, secretary, and three judges, as well as other persons to supervise the land office and Indian affairs. Although many men were appointed and served faithfully, some never even went to the territory when they discovered how far it was from the comforts of home. Some needed to be replaced when their term of service expired, whereas others incurred the wrath of local political opponents who wrote to Johnson asking for removal of these officials. Sometimes Johnson removed them, but many times he did not. As with other appointees in the states, many of Johnson's territorial nominations were obstructed by Congress.

See also: Alaska, Purchase of; Colorado (Admission to Statehood); Homestead Act; Indians; Nebraska (Admission to Statehood); Patronage; Railroads; Rousseau, Lovell Harrison; Vetoes.
References: Berwanger, Eugene H., *The West and Reconstruction* (1981); Graf, LeRoy P., Haskins, Ralph W., and Bergeron, Paul H., eds., *The Papers of Andrew Johnson* vols. 8–15 (1967–2000).

Thirteenth Amendment

The Thirteenth Amendment abolished slavery and indentured servitude in the United States and its territories. Like the other two Reconstruction amendments, the Thirteenth constitutionally validated certain results of the North's victory. Unlike the others, its genesis can be found in the war itself, and its ratification was the culmination of a long and gradual process.

Emancipation and the abolition of slavery were not original war aims for the North, and President Abraham Lincoln was always careful to make this clear. Although he supported eventual abolition, he knew that the wartime coalition, with its slaveholding border states, War Democrats, and racist Northern population, would not accept the freeing of four million blacks.

Some Republicans, who were eventually called Radicals, advocated emancipation early on, but were dismissed as fanatical abolitionists. A few Union generals, David Hunter and John C. Frémont, for instance, freed slaves in their areas of military operations, but Lincoln quickly rescinded their orders.

As the war progressed, slavery came to occupy a bigger part in explaining the war, and, as such, became itself a target. The Northern public and politicians, even those who had no moral objections to slavery, began to see slavery as the underlying difference between North and South, perhaps, in fact, even the cause of the war. As the centrality of slavery to the South became clear, so too did its military applications. Lincoln supported General Benjamin F. Butler's "contraband" policy, which involved the seizure (and subsequent emancipation) of slaves performing labor for the Confederate government. This was formalized in 1862 when Congress passed the Confiscation Acts, which allowed federal officers to liberate blacks who were serving the Confederacy. Congress later abolished slavery in Washington, D.C., and in the territories, and Lincoln freed all slaves in areas under rebellion in his Emancipation Proclamation of January 1, 1863. Although these acts were certainly only chipping away at the edges of a national blight, they demonstrated a momentum and growing unity of purpose.

Some Republicans, Lincoln included, worried that wartime acts held little promise of permanence. Only an amendment could forever abolish slavery, placing it beyond the courts or future Congresses. Securing passage and ratification would not be easy, and emancipation could cost support—and votes in the 1864 election—in the North and in the border states. In addition, amending the Constitution was nearly unprecedented; since the Bill of Rights, only two amendments had been added, and the latest of those was in 1804. So despite growing support, in the spring of 1864 the House of Representatives defeated an emancipation measure passed by the Senate. Lincoln and the Union Party took up the gauntlet, and, despite Democratic charges of radicalism, openly advocated the emancipation amendment. Lincoln followed up his reelection in the fall of 1864 with some clever political deals and arm-twisting, which resulted in the passage of the amendment by the House on January 31, 1865.

Constitutional issues about the status of the seceded states raised serious questions about the fate of the amendment. Any amendment required three-quarters of the states to ratify it for it to become part of the Constitution. By April 1865 it became clear that Southern states were needed for its ratification. With the end of the war and the assassination of Lincoln, new complications arose: Congress was not in session; the war was over, so the new president, Andrew Johnson, could not operate on war powers; and the former Confederate states were in limbo. If they had indeed seceded and were outside the Union—Congress had said as much in the Wade-Davis Bill—then could they ratify an amendment? Andrew Johnson, a conservative Democrat and former slaveholder, agreed that problems existed: should states that were unrepresented in Congress—had no say in the creation of the measure—be forced to vote upon it?

As happened more often than not during

Reconstruction, constitutional misgivings gave way before practical concerns. Republicans, Northerners, and even Andrew Johnson came to the conclusion that the former Confederate states could ratify the amendment. In fact, Presidential Reconstruction, Johnson's program for restoring the Southern states, not only called on states to ratify the amendment, but also required them to write new constitutions that formally abolished slavery—thus eliminating slavery by two authorities, state and federal. An opponent of planters and the "slave power conspiracy," Johnson came to see slavery as a regional blight that made the rich richer, stunted progress and self-motivation, and ultimately led to war. Johnson implemented the Emancipation Proclamation when he was military governor of Tennessee, and now he wanted the rest of the South to follow suit.

Eight of the former Confederate states did ratify the amendment, which was enough to meet the three-quarters requirement. On December 18, 1865, Secretary of State William H. Seward announced that the Thirteenth Amendment had become part of the U.S. Constitution.

Recent historians have questioned whether the amendment actually freed the slaves. Some argue that the Union army was really responsible for slavery's destruction, whereas others contend that the breakdown of authority resulting from the war brought about its demise. Perhaps the most interesting proposals come from historians Louis Gerteis, Ira Berlin, and Leon Litwack, who argue that slaves seized the initiative and were largely responsible for freeing themselves. Nonetheless, countless examples exist of federal soldiers and even Southern planters reading the amendment to their slaves. Moreover, modifying the Constitution abolished the institution itself and guaranteed its extinction in America.

See also: Blacks (Slave and Free), Johnson's Attitude toward; Governors, Provisional; Lincoln, Abraham; Military Governor of Tennessee, Johnson as; "Moses of the Colored Men" Speech; National Union Party; Presidential Reconstruction; Readmission of Southern States; Reconstruction; Seward, William Henry. For complete text of the Thirteenth Amendment, see Appendix I.

References: Berlin, Ira, Fields, Barbara J., Miller, Steven F., Reidy, Joseph P., and Rowland, Leslie, *Slaves No More: Three Essays on Emancipation and the Civil War* (1992); Gerteis, Louis S., *From Contraband to Freedman: Federal Policy toward Southern Blacks, 1861–1865* (1973); Hyman, Harold M., *A More Perfect Union: The Impact of the Civil War and Reconstruction on the Constitution* (1973); Litwack, Leon F., *Been in the Storm So Long: The Aftermath of Slavery* (1979); Long, David E., *The Jewel of Liberty: Abraham Lincoln's Re-election and the End of Slavery* (1994); McPherson, James M., *The Struggle for Equality: Abolitionists and the Negro in the Civil War and Reconstruction* (1964).

Thomas, Lorenzo (1804–1875)

Lorenzo Thomas, a career soldier whom Johnson appointed as interim secretary of war in 1868, was born in Delaware and graduated from West Point in 1823, ranked seventeenth in his class. He served with the 4th Infantry, was a quartermaster during the Seminole War (1836–1837), and was assistant adjutant general of the army (1838–1846, 1848–1853). During the Mexican-American War, he was chief of staff for General William O. Butler and earned the brevet of lieutenant colonel. He eventually became chief of staff (1853–1861) for General Winfield Scott. Thomas, therefore, had a great deal of administrative experience, some of it even in the adjutant general's office, before he became adjutant general himself in 1861.

Thomas was apparently not a very energetic administrator and there was considerable criticism of his department, not all of it warranted. He personally delivered a brigadier general's commission to Andrew Johnson when the latter became military governor of Tennessee. The two also had some correspondence during the Civil War about various troop movements in East Tennessee and the exchange of East Tennessee prisoners of war. Unfortunately for

Thomas, Secretary of War Edwin M. Stanton did not like him and, beginning in 1863, devised a series of projects that would keep Thomas out of Washington, D.C., and permit the office to be run by Assistant Adjutant General Edward D. Townsend, a friend of Stanton's.

Stanton sent Thomas to recruit black troops for Union service, to arrange prisoner-of-war exchanges, and to consolidate depleted regiments. Once the war was over, Thomas served on the military commission that tried Henry Wirz, Confederate commander of the prison camp at Andersonville, Georgia. Thomas also went on an inspection tour of provost marshal offices, followed by an inspection tour of national cemeteries. Gideon Welles suggested to Johnson that Thomas should be recalled to his post, which Johnson did on February 12, 1868.

Johnson then decided to remove Stanton from office, regardless of the Senate's opposition to such an action, and to replace Stanton with Lorenzo Thomas as secretary of war ad interim. Johnson made the change on February 21 and, in fact, had Thomas deliver the removal notice to Stanton. Thomas apparently was rather excited at the prospect of replacing his old nemesis. Prone to excessive talking, Thomas had too much to say (especially after he had had too much to drink at a party on the night of February 21), and threatened to remove Stanton from office by force if the secretary did not vacate peacefully. This threat was in direct contrast to Johnson's expressed desire to have the removal done quietly and peacefully. Early on the morning of February 22, Stanton had Thomas arrested for violation of the Tenure of Office Act (before he even had a chance to eat breakfast, Thomas complained). Thomas was quickly released on bail. Johnson actually hoped that this would be a good opportunity to test the constitutionality of the Tenure of Office Act, but the case was dismissed in less than a week. Stanton also refused to vacate the office.

Johnson's attempt to remove Stanton and replace him with Thomas, in alleged violation of the Tenure of Office Act, was the subject of eight of the eleven impeachment charges against Johnson. Thomas testified during the impeachment trial, but was so naive about the whole matter that it was obvious that there had been no conspiracy between Thomas and Johnson to oust Stanton. Some historians suggest that Thomas's testimony helped gain Johnson's acquittal.

Thomas remained adjutant general until he retired from the army on February 22, 1869. He died in Washington, D.C., on March 2, 1875.

See also: Impeachment; Military Governor of Tennessee, Johnson as; Stanton, Edwin McMasters; Tenure of Office Act; Welles, Gideon; Wirz, Henry.
References: Graf, LeRoy P., Haskins, Ralph W., and Bergeron, Paul H., eds., *The Papers of Andrew Johnson* vols. 5–6, 13 (1967–2000); Trefousse, Hans L., *Impeachment of a President: Andrew Johnson, the Blacks, and Reconstruction* (1975).

Transatlantic Cable

The transatlantic telegraph cable between Ireland and Newfoundland, Canada, was successfully completed in 1866, during Andrew Johnson's presidency. A cable of this sort would speed communication between Europe and North America, aid in resolving delicate diplomatic situations, and assist with trade negotiations. Although several people had had such an idea previously, it was not until 1854, when the wealthy American entrepreneur Cyrus W. Field became interested in the project, that such a cable became a possibility. Field formed several different companies over time, in both England and the United States, to fund the cable.

The effort met with many delays and difficulties. It took two and a half years just to erect a telegraph line across Newfoundland itself and connect it to the mainland by cable. In 1857 British and U.S. ships began to lay the Atlantic cable but it broke and was lost. Several other attempts were equally unsuccessful. But Field persevered, and in August 1858 the 1,950-mile cable was completed. Queen Victoria sent a congratulatory telegram to President James Buchanan. Great celebrations were held in New York. But the cable worked for only three weeks before it failed.

Personal financial problems and the Civil War prevented Field from trying again until the end of the conflict. A cable partially laid in 1865 broke, but connection finally came in July 1866, at which point Field telegraphed President Johnson that the cable had been completed successfully. Johnson congratulated Field, and also exchanged telegrams with Queen Victoria in which both hoped that the cable would strengthen the relationship between England and the United States.

At some point Johnson received a piece of cable, which is on display at the Andrew Johnson National Historic Site in Greeneville, Tennessee.

See also: Foreign Affairs; Greeneville, Tennessee.
References: Graf, LeRoy P., Haskins, Ralph W., and Bergeron, Paul H., eds., *The Papers of Andrew Johnson* vol. 10 (1967–2000).

Truman, Benjamin Cummings (1835–1916)

Born in Providence, Rhode Island, Benjamin Cummings Truman attended both public and Shaker schools and also taught for a year before learning typesetting and becoming a compositor and proofreader for the *New York Times* (1855–1859). He then went to work for John W. Forney, publisher of both the *Philadelphia Press* and the *Sunday Morning Chronicle* of Washington, D.C. In March 1862, Forney sent Truman to Nashville as a special war correspondent with a letter of introduction to Tennessee's military governor, Andrew Johnson.

Apparently the governor and the correspondent got along well because Truman served at least intermittently as private secretary, aide, and messenger for Johnson. In November 1862, Johnson sent Truman to Washington, D.C., with a letter for Abraham Lincoln. With the assistance of Forney, for whom he continued to report, Truman was also able to meet with Secretary of War Edwin M. Stanton and General Henry W. Halleck to plead that Johnson be given the aid he needed to defend the Union-held parts of Tennessee and expand that area.

In May 1863, Truman became founding editor of his own pro-Johnson paper, the *Nashville Press,* but he resigned in July when accused of supplying another paper with controversial information. He returned to Washington, D.C., where he wrote a series of pro-Johnson articles for the *Chronicle.* By early 1864, Truman was back in Nashville as associate editor of the *Times and True Union.* But he still managed to serve as aide to several generals as well as write for several newspapers from such vantage points as William T. Sherman's army outside Atlanta in July 1864.

Truman's wartime association with Johnson proved useful to both after the latter became president. Johnson trusted Truman as an observer, and in the fall of 1865 he sent the reporter south to survey conditions and attitudes. Johnson had received discouraging reports from several Radical Republicans who had traveled in the South, particularly Carl Schurz, and Johnson wanted the opinion of someone whom he trusted. Truman spent nearly eight months visiting Alabama, Georgia, Florida, Tennessee, Arkansas, Mississippi, Louisiana, and Texas, talking with generals and influential Southern whites. He reported his findings to Johnson in a series of letters and to the country at large by another series published in the *New York Times.* He also testified about his observations before the congressional Joint Committee on Reconstruction. He found Southerners to be generally accepting, if not enthusiastic, about being reunited with the North.

In 1866 Johnson appointed Truman as a special agent for the Post Office Department on the Pacific Coast. In this capacity Truman was active in opening new post offices in Southern California, reestablishing some mail routes discontinued during the Civil War, and even visiting China, Japan, and Hawaii. He wrote to Johnson with some regularity about the political scene on the Pacific Coast and occasionally recommended some Johnson supporter for office. He resigned his post on March 4, 1869, the date Ulysses S. Grant assumed the presidency.

On December 8, 1869, Truman married Augusta Mallard of Los Angeles. The couple had two children. Truman continued to be extremely active in newspaper affairs, at various times owning the *Los Angeles Star,* the *Western Graphic,* and the *Capitol,* as well as being involved in other papers that he did not own. He served as special agent of the Post Office Department again, was chief of the literary bureau for the Southern Pacific Railroad (1879–1890), was California commissioner to several world expositions, helped organize the first volunteer fire company in Los Angeles, and wrote at least five books. He died in Los Angeles.

See also: Forney, John Wien; Joint Committee on Reconstruction; Military Governor of Tennessee, Johnson as; Secretaries.
References: Graf, LeRoy P., Haskins, Ralph W., and Bergeron, Paul H., eds., *The Papers of Andrew Johnson* vols. 5–7, 10–16 (1967–2000); Newmark, Harris, *Sixty Years in Southern California, 1853–1913,* 4th ed., ed. by Maurice H. and Marco R. Newmark and W.W. Robinson (1970 [1916]); Simpson, Brooks D., Graf, LeRoy P., and Muldowny, John, eds., *Advice after Appomattox: Letters to Andrew Johnson, 1865–1866* (1987).

Trumbull, Lyman (1813–1896)

Although frequently opposed to Andrew Johnson's presidential policies, Senator Lyman Trumbull ultimately voted for Johnson's acquittal during the impeachment trial. Trumbull was born in Colchester, Connecticut, and attended Bacon Academy there. Because of the tight financial circumstances of his family, Trumbull became a schoolteacher at age eighteen, first in Connecticut, then in New Jersey, and finally in Greenville, Georgia, where he taught for three years (1833–1836) while also reading law. Admitted to the bar, he moved to Belleville, Illinois, where he began to practice law in 1837.

In 1843 Trumbull married Julia Jayne (ca. 1823–1868), a close friend of Mary Todd Lincoln, who served as an attendant at the wedding. They apparently had six children but only three sons survived to adulthood and only one outlived Trumbull. After Julia's death and a period as a widower, Trumbull, then sixty-four, married Mary Ingraham (b. ca. 1845) in November 1877. They had two daughters, both of whom died in childhood.

Trumbull became interested in politics soon after his move to Illinois. At first he was a Democrat and won several elections and appointments. He served in the state house of representatives (1840–1841), as Illinois secretary of state (1841–1843), and as justice of the Illinois supreme court (1848–1853). In 1854 he was elected to the U.S. House of Representatives as an anti-Nebraska (opposed to slavery expansion in the territories) Democrat. But before he could assume his seat, he was elected to the U.S. Senate with the backing of Abraham Lincoln and the Illinois Whigs because of Trumbull's Free Soil sentiments. Trumbull served three Senate terms (1855–1873), most of the time as a Republican, although he joined the Liberal Republicans in the early 1870s, and after that returned to the Democratic Party. During much of his Senate tenure he was chairman of the Senate Judiciary Committee. In this capacity he introduced the First and Second Confiscation Acts and the Thirteenth Amendment during the Civil War.

A strong supporter of Abraham Lincoln, Trumbull expected to support Johnson also when the latter became president. Johnson and Trumbull had known one another in the Senate, although they had been members of opposing parties and usually expressed opposing viewpoints. Trumbull was part of the congressional committee given the formality of notifying Johnson that he had been elected vice president. On April 25, 1865, Trumbull wrote Johnson, newly become president, a letter of support, volunteering to do whatever he could to punish Southern leaders, restore peace to the South generally, and establish new Southern political leadership.

Trumbull and Johnson split over the Freedmen's Bureau and Civil Rights bills, which Trumbull introduced in early 1866 after consultation with the president. No one was more surprised than Trumbull when Johnson vetoed both bills. Trumbull felt deceived and made no further attempt to work with Johnson. In fact, he sided with the Radical Republicans in their attempts to restrain Johnson's participation in Reconstruction. Trumbull was one of the government lawyers in the *Ex parte McCardle* case, which was an attempt to have the Supreme Court rule on the constitutionality of the First Military Reconstruction Act. Trumbull argued that the Supreme Court did not have jurisdiction in the case. In 1868 Trumbull was one of seven moderate Republican senators who joined with their Democratic colleagues to vote that Johnson was not guilty of the impeachment charges.

After his participation in the Liberal Republican Party, Trumbull was not reelected to the Senate. In 1873 he returned to his law practice and never held another political office. He died in Chicago of prostate cancer.

See also: Civil Rights Act; Congressional Reconstruction; Democratic Party; Freedmen's Bureau Bills (and Vetoes); Impeachment; Lincoln, Mary (Ann) Todd; *McCardle, Ex parte;* Military Reconstruction Acts; Thirteenth Amendment; Vetoes.

References: Eubank, Sever L., "The McCardle Case: A Challenge to Radical Reconstruction," *Journal of Mississippi History* 18 (Apr. 1956): 111–127; Graf, LeRoy P., Haskins, Ralph W., and Bergeron, Paul H., eds., *The Papers of Andrew Johnson* vols. 3, 7 (1967–2000); Krug, Mark M., *Lyman Trumbull: Conservative Radical* (1965); Roske, Ralph J., "The Seven Martyrs?" *American Historical Review* 64 (Jan. 1959): 323–330.

Tuberculosis

Tuberculosis was a significant killer of Andrew Johnson's family members. Known in the nineteenth century as "consumption," it is a contagious disease that most commonly affects the lungs, but may locate in other body parts as well. It is usually spread by airborne particles as the sick person coughs, spits, or sneezes. It can also be spread through the unpasteurized milk of diseased cows. In the nineteenth century the disease was most often associated with crowded and unsanitary urban lower-class living and working conditions, but persons of any class could contract the disease and the contagion was quite widespread. In fact, for a time, tuberculosis was seen as a "romantic" disease that afflicted heroes in a number of literary works. A notable example of this trend in the United States was the portrayal of the illness and death of Little Eva in Harriet Beecher Stowe's *Uncle Tom's Cabin* (1852).

For those who had the disease, it was not romantic, however. Although in some cases a tuberculous lesion might heal itself by calcifying over, in many cases the victim underwent a period, often years, of declining health interspersed with remissions as the lungs gradually were destroyed. During the nineteenth century, there was no cure and treatments were limited and not very effective.

In 1882 Edward Koch discovered the responsible germ, the tuberculosis bacilli, with his microscope. Thereafter, treatment improved. A vaccine was developed in

1921, and after World War II the use of antibiotics largely eliminated tuberculosis as a threat to life in the developed world, although it remained a major cause of illness and death in the third world.

Eliza Johnson, wife of Andrew Johnson, had none of these treatments available when she began to suffer from tuberculosis, probably sometime in the early 1850s. Although no one knows where or when she contracted the disease, it is quite probable that she was the source of contagion for many of her family members because she lived with them and lingered with the affliction until January 15, 1876. Eliza's illness prevented her from taking any part as hostess while her husband was president. Her tuberculosis was a major factor in the lives of Andrew Johnson and of his family for four generations.

The first family member to die of tuberculosis was Daniel Stover, the husband of the Johnson's daughter Mary. Eliza is less likely to have been the source of his infection, but it is, nevertheless, possible. Daniel Stover's attending physician claimed that Stover actually contracted consumption from exposure while he was a Union soldier. In any case, his difficult experiences and resulting exposure to inclement weather during the Civil War worsened his condition. He died in Nashville on December 18, 1864.

Andrew Johnson, himself, suffered from a variety of physical ailments, but there is no evidence that he had tuberculosis nor, apparently, did either of his daughters Martha or Mary. The Johnson sons, however, were another matter. Charles is not known to have had tuberculosis, but some sources close to the family have speculated that he had the disease, although this cannot be confirmed. In any case, he died after a fall from a horse. Robert, the second son, most probably had the disease, as he had hemorrhaging from the lungs as early as 1856. His poor health probably contributed to his need for alcohol and opi-

ates, as painkillers or cough suppressants at first, which ultimately led to his death from an overdose of laudanum on April 22, 1869.

Andrew Jr., the third son, known as Frank, suffered from consumption from childhood apparently, which is no surprise since he grew up with a consumptive mother. Attempts to combat the discomforts of the disease may have led to Frank's alcoholism also, although he did die from the tuberculosis itself on March 13, 1879.

In the third generation, all three of Johnson's granddaughters died from tuberculosis. Sarah Drake Stover Bachman, the second Stover daughter, was the first to succumb to the common family illness on March 22, 1886, leaving behind two small sons to be raised by her older sister, Lillie, a divorcée. Lillie herself was unwell, however, and spent her last eleven months at a sanitorium in Knoxville, where she too died of consumption, on November 5, 1892. Although these women could have contracted tuberculosis from their father or someone else, certainly their residence in the White House during Johnson's presidency and the frequency with which their grandmother stayed at the Stover home to be cared for by Mary, do suggest Eliza as a likely source of contagion.

The third granddaughter, Mary Belle Patterson Landstreet, cousin of the Stovers, also died early, on July 8, 1891, at the age of thirty-one. Apparently she also died of tuberculosis, because she suffered from "asthma" in her youth and was in such frail health that her husband took her west in search of healing. She died in California. Neither her brother, Andrew Johnson Patterson, nor her cousin, Andrew Johnson Stover, seem to have contracted the disease.

The final Johnson descendant to die from tuberculosis was Samuel Bernard Bachman, the younger son of Sarah Stover Bachman. He died in Bluff City, Tennessee, on April 3, 1914, at the age of twenty-nine.

See also: Grandchildren; Johnson, Andrew, Jr., "Frank"; Johnson, Charles; Johnson, Eliza McCardle; Johnson, Robert; Patterson, Martha Johnson; Stover, Daniel; Stover (Brown), Mary Johnson.

References: Andrew Johnson National Historic Site, Greeneville, TN: files; Andrew Johnson Project, Knoxville, TN: Patterson and Stover files; *Bristol Herald,* Apr. 4, 1914; Graf, LeRoy P., Haskins, Ralph W., and Bergeron, Paul H., eds., *The Papers of Andrew Johnson* vol. 2 (1967–2000); *Knoxville Chronicle,* Mar. 20, 1879; *Knoxville Daily Journal,* Nov. 6, 1892; McNeill, William H., *Plagues and Peoples* (1993 [1976]); *Nashville Republican Banner,* Apr. 24 and May 1, 1869.

Union Party (1864)

See National Union Party (1864)

University of North Carolina

On June 7, 1866, at its commencement exercises, the "Academic Senate," or faculty of the University of North Carolina, conferred upon President Andrew Johnson the degree of Doctor of Laws. As university president David L. Swain wrote to Johnson, who was not present at the ceremony, the degree was awarded "in consideration of the eminent services rendered to our native State and our common Country . . . under the most trying circumstances." This is the only degree that Johnson is known to have received. It was certainly an honor for someone who had had no formal schooling.

A year later Johnson did attend the university's commencement ceremonies on June 6. He had already accepted an invitation to the dedication of a monument on his father's grave in Raleigh that was to be held on June 4. Consequently he was able to attend the commencement in nearby Chapel Hill as well. Although Johnson did attend commencement exercises at schools in the District of Columbia, this is the only time he is known to have attended such a distant graduation.

See also: Education of Andrew Johnson; Johnson, Jacob; Postpresidential Career; Presidential Travels.

References: Graf, LeRoy P., Haskins, Ralph W., and Bergeron, Paul H., eds., *The Papers of Andrew Johnson* vols. 10, 12 (1967–2000).

Usher, John Palmer (1816–1889)

Born in Brookfield, New York, John Palmer Usher read law with Henry Bennett in New Berlin, New York. Admitted to the bar in 1839, Usher moved to Terre Haute, Indiana, in 1840 to practice his profession. He sometimes argued cases with Abraham Lincoln while riding the legal circuit. In 1844 he married Margaret Patterson and in due time they had four sons.

In 1850–1851 Usher served in the Indiana legislature. Joining the Republican Party as soon as it was organized, he ran for Congress on that ticket in 1856 but was defeated. In November 1861, Usher was appointed attorney general of Indiana but soon resigned when offered the post of assistant secretary of the interior. When Lincoln appointed the secretary, Caleb B. Smith, to a judgeship, the president, in January 1863, appointed Usher as Smith's replacement. In this position Usher oversaw the land office, Indian affairs, and the patent office, among other things. Usher was one of only three cabinet members who went to Gettysburg with Lincoln in November 1863 for the cemetery dedication and the president's address. As Lincoln was planning his cabinet for his second term, Usher resigned on March 8, 1865, to take effect on May 15. Lincoln, never quite satisfied with Usher, was happy to replace him with Senator James Harlan of Iowa, whose daughter Mary would marry Lincoln's oldest son, Robert Todd, in 1868.

Lincoln, however, was assassinated before the change in cabinet personnel actually took place. Certain political friends of Usher's tried to persuade Andrew Johnson to keep him in office, but Johnson was determined to have the cabinet as Lincoln had planned. Consequently, Usher served only a month in Johnson's cabinet.

Usher moved to Lawrence, Kansas, where he practiced law and served as chief counsel for the Union Pacific Railroad. He died in a hospital in Philadelphia, Pennsylvania.

See also: Cabinet Members; Harlan, James; Indians; Lincoln, Abraham.

References: Donald, David Herbert, *Lincoln* (1995); Graf, LeRoy P., Haskins, Ralph W., and Bergeron, Paul H., eds., *The Papers of Andrew Johnson* vol. 13 (1967–2000).

Vetoes

Beginning with the Freedmen's Bureau Bill in 1866, Andrew Johnson vetoed twenty pieces of legislation during his term of office. He usually cited constitutional questions, as he interpreted them, as a large part of his reason for returning the legislation unapproved. Although Congress then passed many of the bills over Johnson's veto and they became law, many Republican members of Congress were angered by Johnson's obstruction of the Congressional Reconstruction program. This anger eventually led to Johnson's impeachment.

Johnson's veto messages are listed below. Those that are most important are discussed in other appropriate topical entries in this volume and are indicated by an asterisk (*).

February 19, 1866	Freedmen's Bureau Bill*
March 27, 1866	Civil Rights Bill*
May 15, 1866	Colorado Statehood Bill*
June 15, 1866	New York and Montana Iron Co. Land Purchase Bill
July 16, 1866	Freedmen's Bureau Bill*
July 28, 1866	Bill Creating Surveying District of Montana Territory
January 5, 1867	District of Columbia Franchise Law*
January 28, 1867	Colorado Statehood Bill*
January 28, 1867	Nebraska Statehood Bill*
March 2, 1867	Tenure of Office Act*
March 2, 1867	First Military Reconstruction Act*
March 23, 1867	Second Military Reconstruction Act*
July 19, 1867	Third Military Reconstruction Act*
March 25, 1868	Judiciary Act Amendment
June 20, 1868	Arkansas Statehood Bill*
June 25, 1868	Admission of Six Southern States*
July 20, 1868	Restrictions on Electoral Votes
July 25, 1868	Freedmen's Bureau Bill*
February 13, 1869	Washington and Georgetown Schools Act
February 22, 1869	Copper Bill

See also: Civil Rights Act; Colorado (Admission to Statehood); Congressional Reconstruction; Constitution, Johnson's Attitude toward; District of Columbia Franchise; Freedmen's Bureau Bills (and Vetoes); Impeachment; Military Reconstruction Acts; Nebraska (Admission to Statehood);

Readmission of Southern States; Tenure of Office Act.

References: Graf, LeRoy P., Haskins, Ralph W., and Bergeron, Paul H., eds., *The Papers of Andrew Johnson* vols. 10–15 (1967–2000); Richardson, James D., comp., *A Compilation of the Messages and Papers of the Presidents* vol. 6 (1896–1899).

Vice President, Johnson as (1865)

Andrew Johnson's vice presidency was the second shortest in U.S. history. Only John Tyler, who served exactly a month before succeeding William Henry Harrison in 1841, held the office for less time than did Johnson.

Originally Johnson wanted to remain in Tennessee until William G. Brownlow was inaugurated as governor, missing his own vice presidential inauguration in Washington, D.C. Abraham Lincoln would not permit this, so Johnson went to Washington, where he resigned his appointment as brigadier general and military governor of Tennessee on March 3, 1865. Unfortunately, Johnson was unwell when he arrived and was not better on the morning of the inauguration, March 4. After drinking three glasses of undiluted whiskey in the vice president's room, Johnson was not sober when he stood up in the Senate chamber to give his inaugural address. The spectacle embarrassed most of the government officials in attendance and provided an opportunity for many comments by the press.

To recover from his illness and embarrassment, Johnson went to the home of his friend Francis P. Blair, Sr., in Silver Spring, Maryland, not far from the capitol. Although he presided over the Senate on March 6, Johnson did not return to the capitol again until March 11, the day the Senate adjourned. Rumors spread that Johnson was on a drunken binge, but the vice president wrote to several people, including Abraham Lincoln, that he was "prostrated" by his illness.

During his brief tenure as vice president, Johnson received many letters from people seeking his aid in gaining patronage, getting payments from the federal government for property the government had used, getting relatives out of prison, and numerous other requests. Some petitioners were old friends of Johnson's, and most others had some Tennessee connection. Several extant documents from mid-April show a request from Johnson that certain prisoners of war be released, which Lincoln granted.

Johnson had planned to leave for Tennessee on March 25 to attend the gubernatorial inauguration of William G. Brownlow on April 5 and also, apparently, to encourage the Tennessee legislature to elect his son-in-law, David T. Patterson, to the Senate. But at the last minute he decided not to go and consequently was in Washington when Richmond fell to the Union forces on April 2. The next evening, in the midst of the wild excitement, Johnson, in front of the Willard Hotel, gave the only public speech of his vice presidency (except for the ill-fated inaugural address). He harshly enunciated the idea that "treason must be made odious and traitors must be punished and impoverished." On April 6 Johnson visited Richmond to see the fallen rebel capitol.

Johnson and Lincoln exchanged several letters during Johnson's vice presidency, but it is not known that they met except on the afternoon of April 14, when Johnson allegedly talked with Lincoln about the importance of punishing leading rebels. That evening Lincoln went to Ford's Theatre to see the play "Our American Cousin" and was fatally shot by the actor John Wilkes Booth. Johnson was actually supposed to be a target as well, but his prospective assassin, George A. Atzerodt, lost his nerve and fled Washington.

Johnson, who had gone to bed early in his room at the Kirkwood House hotel, was awakened about 10:15 P.M. with the news of Lincoln's assassination. Johnson made a brief visit to the dying Lincoln at the Peterson house across the street from Ford's Theatre, but otherwise he spent the night pacing the floor of his hotel room. After Lincoln's death on the morning of April 15, 1865, Johnson was sworn in as president at the Kirkwood House, attended by Chief Justice Salmon P. Chase, the cabinet members, and a few congressmen.

See also: Blair, Francis Preston (Jr. and Sr.); Brownlow, William Gannaway "Parson"; Cabinet Members; Chase, Salmon Portland; Drunkenness; Health of Johnson; Lincoln, Abraham; Lincoln Assassination Conspirators; Patterson, David Trotter.

References: Graf, LeRoy P., Haskins, Ralph W., and Bergeron, Paul H., eds., *The Papers of Andrew Johnson* vol. 7 (1967–2000); Trefousse, Hans L., *Andrew Johnson: A Biography* (1989).

Wade, Benjamin Franklin (1800–1878)

Benjamin Franklin Wade, one of the Radical Republican leaders of the congressional opposition to Andrew Johnson, was born in Feeding Hills near Springfield, Massachusetts. The tenth of the eleven children of James and Mary Upham Wade, he was raised in poverty and educated by his mother, with some attendance at a local school. When he was twenty-one, Wade moved with his parents to Andover, Ohio. After working as a farmer, drover, laborer, and school teacher and studying medicine, Wade began to read law. He was admitted to the bar in 1828 and began to practice law in Jefferson, Ohio, where he became a partner of the noted abolitionist Joshua R. Giddings. Although shy and poor at public speaking, Wade eventually overcame this difficulty. On March 19, 1841, he married Caroline M. Rosecrans, an intelligent, educated woman several years his junior. This happy marriage produced two sons: James F. (b. 1843) and Henry P. (b. 1845).

Even before his marriage, Wade had begun to hold public office. He was prosecuting attorney of Ashtabula County (1835–1837), state senator (1837–1838, 1841–1842), and judge of the third judicial district of Ohio (1847–1851). In 1851 he was elected, as a Whig, to the U.S. Senate and would be elected to two more terms as a Republican, serving March 15, 1851– March 3, 1869. Wade soon became an outspoken leader of the senators who opposed slavery. He was active in opposition to the Kansas-Nebraska Act and to anything that would spread rather than abolish slavery. Andrew Johnson served in the Senate while Wade was there (1857–1862) and the two generally agreed on little. However, Wade was a strong supporter of the Homestead Bill, although his ideas about it differed somewhat from Johnson's. When Johnson made his major "Speech on the Seceding States" on February 5–6, 1861, he resented being labeled as an ally of Wade's because both opposed secession.

In late 1860 and early 1861 Wade was part of the congressional Committee of Thirteen to consider various compromise proposals between the North and the South, rejecting the Crittenden Compromise and others. Despite his antislavery stance, Wade voted for the Crittenden-Johnson Resolution, which specified that the sole purpose of the war was to put down the rebellion and reunite the states. Wade went to watch the battle of First Bull Run (Manassas) and led Senator Zachariah Chandler and several companions in stopping a portion of the Union retreat. At this battle Wade got a bad impression of regular army officers, an impression that he never overcame and that affected his attitude as he headed the Joint Committee on the Conduct of the War. Although Johnson was a member of the committee for a few months, Wade was its leader throughout the war. He was an advocate of swift, decisive, forward movement and had no patience with the slowness of General George B. McClellan nor with other officers, especially Democrats, who did not perform as Wade desired. Wade also criticized Abraham Lincoln and his policies, especially Lincoln's Ten Percent Plan for Reconstruction, which Wade considered too lenient. In 1864, with Congressman Henry Winter Davis, Wade introduced the Wade-Davis Bill, a harsher Reconstruction plan, which Lincoln pocket-vetoed. Wade and Davis angrily published the Wade-Davis Manifesto, which strongly criticized Lincoln for interfering with congressional prerogatives. Wade only reluctantly supported Lincoln's reelection in 1864.

When Johnson succeeded the assassinated Lincoln as president, Wade believed, based on Johnson's past behavior as a Unionist and as military governor of Tennessee, that Johnson would be harsh on the South and was a providential replacement for Lincoln. Wade and other members of the Committee on the Conduct of the War called on Johnson almost immediately, on April 16, 1865, and the new president's statement that "treason must be made infamous" reassured them. Wade also visited Johnson at other times to give advice.

But Wade soon became upset when he saw Johnson pardoning secessionist leaders, failing to enforce his requirements for Restoration when the state conventions refused to abide by them, and failing to object to Black Codes passed by the former Confederate states. Wade still made some allowances for Johnson in the fall of 1865, but the relationship was finally broken irreparably by Johnson's veto of the Freedmen's Bureau Bill in February 1866. Wade was incensed that Johnson told Congress it had no right to pass laws for the South when no Southern states were represented there. Wade believed that Johnson was usurping congressional responsibilities with his own Reconstruction policies. Wade became Johnson's implacable foe and a leader of congressional opposition to Johnson. Because Wade and Johnson were each so single-minded and certain that their own viewpoint was the only correct one, their hostility toward each other was great.

Wade wanted political security for the Republican Party and this was one of the reasons why he opposed Johnson's policies, as well as why he introduced statehood resolutions for Colorado and Nebraska, hopefully future Republican states (only Nebraska achieved statehood in 1867).

Wade was always a strong supporter of black suffrage, regardless of how unpopular the concept was. He was also a supporter of other unpopular causes such as women's suffrage and labor rights, which tended to upset businessmen. Wade's continuing outspoken radicalism had two major results. In 1867 Ohio elected a number of Democrats to the state legislature who would not reelect Wade to the Senate.

The other result pertained to the attempt, which Wade supported, to impeach and convict Johnson. In 1867 Wade had been elected president pro tem of the Senate; this made him Johnson's successor because there was no vice president. As Johnson's trial wore on, some more moderate senators began to rethink the wisdom of removing Johnson, a disliked but known quantity, and replacing him with Wade, an extreme and outspoken Radical. Consequently, Johnson escaped conviction by one vote on each article considered.

After Wade's term in the Senate expired on March 3, 1869, Wade returned to his law practice in Jefferson, Ohio. He never ran for political office again, although he held appointive posts as government director for the Union Pacific Railroad and as commissioner to Santo Domingo (1871). He died at home of typhoid fever in 1878.

See also: Black Codes; Black Suffrage; Colorado (Admission to Statehood); Congressional Reconstruction; Crittenden-Johnson Resolution; Elections of 1867; Freedmen's Bureau Bills (and Vetoes); Homestead Act; Impeachment; Joint Select Committee on the Conduct of the War; Lincoln, Abraham; Military Governor of Tennessee, Johnson as; Nebraska (Admission to Statehood); Pardons (Individual); Presidential Reconstruction; Readmission of Southern States; Republican Party; Secession, Johnson's Attitude toward; Senator, Johnson as; Whig Party.

References: Graf, LeRoy P., Haskins, Ralph W., and Bergeron, Paul H., eds., *The Papers of Andrew Johnson* vols. 4, 7, 10 (1967–2000); Trefousse, Hans L., *Benjamin Franklin Wade: Radical Republican from Ohio* (1963).

Washington's Birthday Speech (1866)

On February 19, 1866, Andrew Johnson angered many members of Congress and other Northerners by vetoing the Freedmen's Bureau Bill. In the midst of the resulting criticism, a group of nonpartisan Unionists met at Grover's Theatre in Washington, D.C., on the afternoon of February 22. They heard speeches and passed resolutions that supported many aspects of Johnson's policy, including his recent veto. A large crowd then went to the White House to serenade Johnson and present him with the resolutions.

Forewarned, several of Johnson's close advisors, well aware of the president's tendency toward a rowdy, impromptu, stump-speaking style, urged Johnson not to make a speech in response to the resolutions. In fact, Johnson agreed not to do so, but the excitement of the moment and the enthusiasm of the crowd led him to break his promise.

Johnson began simply to thank the crowd for endorsing his policy, but he soon went on to discuss George Washington and the yet incomplete monument to him in Washington, D.C. This led on to Andrew Jackson, whose pronouncement, "The Federal Union, it must be preserved," Johnson was trying to fulfill. During the course of the speech Johnson reiterated his stand on the Union and the Constitution numerous times.

Once the Southern states had admitted their mistake and "yielded to the law," renewing their "allegiance to the Constitution," Johnson believed that they should be let back into the Union without exacting vengeance on the masses. Now that the rebellion of the Southern states had ended, Johnson perceived a new rebellion within the federal government, provoked by the congressional Joint Committee on Reconstruction. He complained that the war had proved the point that the states could not go out of the Union, yet now Congress was claiming that the former Confederate states were, in fact, out of the Union and could not come back in until certain laws were passed to allow it. Johnson charged these members of Congress with inconsistency of position.

In the past Johnson had opposed such rebels as Jefferson Davis, Robert Toombs, and John Slidell. "Now when I turn round and at the other end of the line find men— I care not by what name you call them— who still stand opposed to the restoration of the Union of these States, I am free to say to you that I am still in the field. . . . I am still for the preservation of the Union." When someone shouted that he should name three names, Johnson made what many considered to be the biggest blunder of his speech. Because Johnson was speaking to his "friends and fellow-citizens," he felt "free to mention . . . the names of those whom I look upon, as being opposed to the fundamental principles of this government, and who are laboring to destroy it." He then specifically listed Congressman Thaddeus Stevens of Pennsylvania, Senator Charles Sumner of Massachusetts, and Wendell Phillips, also of Massachusetts. Johnson proclaimed that he stood for his country and the Constitution, refused to be overawed or bullied by anyone, and had not usurped any powers.

While he realized that some may say, "You are President, and you must not talk about these things, . . . I intend to talk the truth, and when principle is involved, when the existence of my country is in peril, I hold it to be my duty to speak what I think and what I feel, as I have always done on former occasions."

Johnson defended his various actions in the sequence of offices he had held. Though some peoples' expressions of desire to remove him from the presidency sounded like threats of assassination, he was willing to shed his blood on the altar of the Union if necessary. Johnson again pronounced his determination that "in order to save the Government, we must preserve the Constitution." He would therefore always resist any "encroachment" upon it, that is, any amendments that he felt were unnecessary. After encouraging his audience to stand by the Constitution, Johnson "retired amidst a storm of applause."

Johnson's audience apparently enjoyed his performance, encouraging him with frequent bursts of applause and occasional shouts of "go on!" In the days following the speech, he also received a number of letters lauding his efforts, but the overall response was much more negative. No one would expect the Radical Republicans to like the speech, but even moderate and conservative Republicans, who had previously supported his administration, believed that Johnson had gone too far. His speech was considered to be unacceptable, undignified, and "unworthy of his position and his manhood." In general, his speech was quite self-centered, focusing on his opinions and accomplishments (historian Eric McKitrick has counted 210 uses of first-person pronouns). Some wondered whether Johnson, given his actions at his vice presidential inauguration, might have been drunk, but there is no evidence to suggest that he was. He was merely overexcited by the stump-speaking challenge.

Unquestionably the intemperate nature of Johnson's speech, especially in conjunction with his Freedmen's Bureau Bill veto, damaged his credibility. He would display the same lack of oratorical control in his Swing-around-the-Circle speeches in the fall of 1866.

See also: Congressional Reconstruction; Constitution, Johnson's Attitude toward; Drunkenness; Freedmen's Bureau Bill (and Vetoes); Joint Committee on Reconstruction; Readmission of Southern States; Republican Party; Stevens, Thaddeus; Sumner, Charles; Swing-around-the Circle.

References: Graf, LeRoy P., Haskins, Ralph W., and Bergeron, Paul H., eds., *The Papers of Andrew Johnson* vol. 10 (1967–2000); McKitrick, Eric L., *Andrew Johnson and Reconstruction* (1960); Trefousse, Hans L., *Andrew Johnson: A Biography* (1989).

Welles, Gideon (1802–1878)

*G*ideon Welles, who served as secretary of the navy during the presidencies of Abraham Lincoln and Andrew Johnson, was born in Glastonbury, Connecticut. He was educated at the Episcopal Academy in Cheshire, Connecticut (1819–1821), and the American Literary, Scientific, and Military Academy at Norwich, Vermont (1823–1825). He studied law, but soon became part owner and editor of the *Hartford Times* (1826–1836), a Democratic paper, which supported Andrew Jackson. Welles was a believer in individual rights, strict construction of the Constitution, and states' rights. He had an excellent memory for names and faces and was also an astute judge of character, all useful for a political career. He was a writer, however, rather than an orator.

In July 1835 Welles married his eighteen-year-old cousin Mary Jane Hale. The couple had nine children but only three sons survived to adulthood.

During the 1830s and 1840s Welles held several political posts. He served in the state legislature (1827–1835), as state comptroller of public accounts (1835, 1842, 1843), as postmaster of Hartford (1836–1841), and as chief of the Bureau of Provisions and Clothing of the U.S. Navy (1846–1849). But Welles left the Democratic Party because of its stand on the slavery question, particularly as expressed in the Kansas-Nebraska Act (1854). In 1856 he helped establish a Republican newspaper, the *Hartford Evening Press,* and wrote many political columns for it, as well as for the *New York Evening Post* and the *National Intelligencer* (Washington, D.C.).

Partly because his Democratic antecedents were needed to balance the cabinet, Welles became Abraham Lincoln's choice for secretary of the navy in 1861. With the onset of the Civil War, Welles assumed an enormous task because he needed to produce an effective navy from small beginnings. Despite complaints from persons who did not agree with him, the navy secretary was able to build a navy that was instrumental in the defeat of the Confederacy. He was able to construct or gather enough ships to make the blockade of the South effective, conduct naval business speedily and economically, encourage the construction of ironclad ships before the idea was popular, choose effective advisors, and supervise the various activities of the navy. Welles generally managed to avoid favoritism or political partisanship in appointments and removals, and his efforts to be fair sometimes angered his opponents. Welles's term (1861–1869) was the longest of any navy secretary to that time.

In addition to his naval responsibilities, Welles also contributed to the general policies of both the Lincoln and Johnson administrations, usually espousing moderate to conservative viewpoints. When Johnson succeeded Lincoln, Welles approved of the new president and generally backed his policies. Welles believed with Johnson that suffrage was a matter to be decided by the states, opposed the Civil Rights Bill, backed the formation of the National Union Party in 1866, and traveled with Johnson on the Swing-around-the-Circle tour. Johnson consulted Welles about his prospective removals of General Philip H. Sheridan as commander of the Fifth Military District and Edwin M. Stanton as secretary of war, as well as later questions pertaining to the impeachment. Welles supported Johnson for election as president in 1868, but when he was not nominated, Welles supported Horatio Seymour, although Welles did not take an active part in the campaign. Welles did not have a very high opinion of Ulysses S. Grant.

In March 1869 Welles retired to Hartford, Connecticut, and thereafter wrote a number of historical articles for *The Galaxy.* He had become more of a personal friend of Johnson's than most of the rest of the cabinet members and was the only one with whom Johnson corresponded much after the presidency. In several 1869 letters, Welles discussed things that happened during Johnson's term, particularly related to Edwin M. Stanton, and urged Johnson to write articles about these incidents to justify some of his actions, which had been misinterpreted. Welles also used his extensive diary (1862–1869) to aid Johnson in 1873 when the latter was preparing to respond to Judge Advocate General Joseph Holt's letter about the petition for clemency for Mary Surratt. Johnson sent Welles a draft of his reply and Welles commented on it extensively, using his diary to remind Johnson that the president had been quite ill and so there had been no cabinet meeting during the June 30–July 7, 1865, period. Contrary to Holt's statements, the cabinet as a whole had never discussed the petition. Welles's diary, first published in 1911, has been very useful for historians of Lincoln and Johnson's terms.

Welles died from a streptococcal infection on February 11, 1878.

See also: Civil Rights Act; Democratic Party; Election of 1868; Grant, Ulysses Simpson; Holt, Joseph; Impeachment; Jackson, Andrew; Lincoln, Abraham; National Union Convention and

Party; Postpresidential Career; Seymour, Horatio; Sheridan, Philip Henry; Stanton, Edwin McMasters; Surratt, Mary (Elizabeth) Eugenia Jenkins; Swing-around-the-Circle.

References: Beale, Howard K., ed., *Diary of Gideon Welles* 3 vols. (1960 [1911]); Graf, LeRoy P., Haskins, Ralph W., and Bergeron, Paul H., eds., *The Papers of Andrew Johnson* vols. 11–13, 16 (1967–2000); Niven, John, *Gideon Welles: Lincoln's Secretary of the Navy* (1973); Trefousse, Hans L., *Andrew Johnson: A Biography* (1989).

Whig Party

The Whig Party, whose members were Andrew Johnson's frequent rivals in Tennessee politics, developed in the early 1830s as a coalition of persons opposed to President Andrew Jackson. The period of competition between the Whigs and the Democrats, as Jackson's followers called themselves, is often referred to by historians as the second American party system. (The first was the rivalry between the Federalists and the Jeffersonian Republicans, and the third is between the Democrats and the Republicans.) The main issues dividing the Democrats and the Whigs related to their economic perspectives.

The Whigs' "American System," devised by Henry Clay, called for tariffs to protect and promote goods manufactured in the United States, federal aid to "internal improvements" (railroads, for example), and a national bank to regulate national finances and the money supply. The Whigs wanted to do whatever was necessary to provide a balanced economy of commerce, industry, and agriculture, and favored federal government controls to achieve this. The Democrats, on the other hand, preferred free trade, an agrarian economy, laissez faire, and leaving any government supervision to state and local governments rather than to the federal government. Democrats tended to push for expansion of the United States territory, whereas Whigs sought to improve what the United States already had. Banking became one of the most divisive issues

as Jackson vetoed the new charter for the national bank and the Whigs were not able to resurrect it.

Although both parties were evenly distributed nationally, certain characteristics could make a person more likely to side with one party or the other. Whigs tended to be wealthy planters or business and professional men as well as those at the opposite end of the economic scale who depended on the success of manufacturers for their own jobs. (Even those Northern free blacks who could vote preferred the Whigs to the Democrats.) New England Protestants (especially Presbyterians, Congregationalists, and Unitarians) and immigrants from the British Isles tended to be Whigs. The Democratic Party attracted Dutch and German immigrants as well as Catholics, small farmers, artisans, and merchants.

Elections during this period were quite exciting. More white men than ever before could vote and did so. Campaigning involved plenty of entertainment such as torchlight parades, campaign songs, campaign newspapers, debates, and speeches. (The Whigs' log cabin and hard cider campaign for William Henry Harrison in 1840 was especially notable in this regard.) Both parties did also focus on the issues mentioned above. Although the Whigs won only two of the presidential elections in the period while the Democrats won five, the elections usually tended to be close. The Whigs were also unfortunate in that both their presidents, William Henry Harrison and Zachary Taylor, soon died in office, Harrison after only one month. The Whigs did elect many representatives, senators, and other officials. Among the more famous Whigs were Henry Clay, Daniel Webster, William Henry Seward, and Abraham Lincoln.

The Whig Party was very active at the local level, and Andrew Johnson ran against a number of Whigs in Tennessee. In 1834, as the parties were becoming more distinct, Johnson was not definitely a member of either party. In fact, during his first term in the state house of representatives (1835–1837), Johnson appeared to be an independent with Whig tendencies, although he did honor Jackson. In the election of 1839 Johnson declared himself a Democrat. The following year he put his declaration into action and campaigned in the presidential race for Martin Van Buren against the Whig William Henry Harrison. It was in this campaign that Johnson first clashed with William G. "Parson" Brownlow, editor of the *Jonesboro Whig,* and felt the brunt of the Parson's invective.

In 1841–1842 Johnson, with twelve other state senators, refused to attend any joint session of the legislature, which would permit the slightly Whig-majority body to elect two Whig U.S. senators. Johnson made many speeches criticizing the Whig leaders and Whig program and was considered one of the leaders of the opposition.

When Johnson ran for Congress, he had three particularly vigorous campaigns against Whig challengers: Brownlow in 1845, Oliver P. Temple in 1847, and Nathaniel G. Taylor in 1849. In each case Johnson won. But in 1852 the Whig legislature changed the boundaries of the First Congressional District to make it a majority Whig area. Instead of fighting a losing battle for his seat in 1853, Johnson successfully ran for governor.

The national Whig Party, already in decline, was unable to recover from the defeat of its presidential candidate, General Winfield Scott, in 1852. Northern Whigs, who tended to oppose the expansion of slavery into the territories, mainly joined the Know-Nothing (American) and/or Republican parties, which formed over the next few years. The Whig Party retained local influence in the South until the Civil War. A Whig/Know-Nothing alliance in Tennessee nearly cost Johnson reelection as governor in 1855. Ironically, when Johnson became an outspoken Unionist before the Civil War, he found himself allied with his old Whig enemies, such as Brownlow, who, having a national focus, were more likely than Democrats to oppose secession.

See also: Brownlow, William Gannaway "Parson"; Congressman, Johnson as; Democratic Party; Governor (Civilian), Johnson as; Jackson, Andrew; Lincoln, Abraham; Republican Party; Secession, Johnson's Attitude toward; Seward, William Henry; State Legislator, Johnson as; Taylor, Nathaniel Green; Temple, Oliver Perry.
References: Graf, LeRoy P., Haskins, Ralph W., and Bergeron, Paul H., eds., *The Papers of Andrew Johnson* vols. 1–2 (1967–2000); Holt, Michael F., *The Rise and Fall of the American Whig Party: Jacksonian Politics and the Onset of the Civil War* (1999); Howe, Daniel Walker, *The Political Culture of the American Whigs* (1979); Trefousse, Hans L., *Andrew Johnson: A Biography* (1989).

Wirz, Henry (1823–1865)

Born Heinrich Hartmann Wirz in Zurich, Switzerland, Wirz changed his name when he came to the United States in 1849, probably to avoid some kind of trouble with the law. He apparently worked at various odd jobs in Massachusetts and Louisiana before settling in Kentucky to study medicine in 1854.

In May 1854, after the wife he left behind in Switzerland divorced him for abandonment, Wirz married Elizabeth Savells Wolf, a widow with two young daughters. In 1856 the family moved to Louisiana where Wirz made a meager living as a homeopathic physician.

Although Wirz enlisted as a private in the Confederate army after the firing on Fort Sumter, he was soon functioning as an officer, even before he received his commission as captain, assisting General John H. Winder with prisoners and their records. In 1862 Wirz severely injured his right wrist, but stories conflict as to when and how this happened. In any case, the wound never healed, causing Wirz chronic pain and largely disabling his arm. After commanding prisoners of war in Tuscaloosa, Alabama, and Richmond, Virginia, as well as performing some other duties, Wirz was assigned to command the prisoners at Andersonville, Georgia, where he arrived in early March 1864.

Andersonville suffered from severe supply shortages from the moment construction began until the day the last captive departed. It quickly filled with more prisoners than it was intended to hold and the Confederate authorities continued to send more, despite protests from Wirz and other prison authorities. Prison conditions were truly terrible but, as historians have shown, this was not the result of a deliberate conspiracy by Wirz but of a general failure of supplies in the Confederacy, caused in part by Union raids. In fact, the Confederate guards received the same rations as the prisoners. Records, contemporary diaries, and similar materials show Wirz as a diligent, hard-working officer in an extremely difficult position. Although his temper was volatile (possibly as a result of his chronic pain) and his language profane, he was generally fair and occasionally kind.

Wirz was arrested on May 6, 1865, two days after Andersonville closed, and imprisoned in Washington, D.C., awaiting a trial, which began on August 23. The president of the military court, General Lew Wallace, had already decided that Wirz should be convicted and the trial showed this bias. Much of the prosecution's testimony consisted of exaggerations at best and outright fabrications and purchased testimony at worst. Defense testimony was routinely and unjustly rejected. Media articles had stirred Northern emotions about Andersonville and focused on Wirz as the person who had to be held responsible. He ended up suffering for conditions that had been beyond his control and were, in fact, similar to those in many Union prison camps for Confederates. On October 24, Wirz was sentenced to death.

Louis Schade, Wirz's lawyer, appealed to Andrew Johnson for clemency, citing the numerous injustices of the judicial process, but Johnson signed the death sentence anyway. Hanged on November 10, 1865, Wirz was the only Confederate executed for "war crimes." He was buried at the Washington Arsenal with the Lincoln assassination conspirators. In February 1869, at the same time that Johnson permitted the families of the conspirators to rebury their relatives in cemeteries, he also allowed Schade to claim Wirz's body for burial in Mt. Olivet Cemetery, Washington, D.C. The lawyer was distressed to discover that sections of the body were missing. During Wirz's autopsy, parts of his spine, neck, and right arm had been collected as specimens for the Army Medical Museum, now the National Museum of Health and Medicine in Washington, D.C., which still had two of Wirz's vertebrae in the late 1990s.

See also: Lincoln Assassination Conspirators.
References: Graf, LeRoy P., Haskins, Ralph W., and Bergeron, Paul H., eds., *The Papers of Andrew Johnson* vols. 9, 15 (1967–2000); Marvel, William, *Andersonville: The Last Depot* (1994).

DOCUMENTS

Congressional Acts and Bills

ARMY APPROPRIATIONS ACT (1867)

Passed March 2, 1867, most of the Army Appropriations Act pertained to the usual annual army appropriations. However, section two (the Command of the Army Act) and section six were designed to prevent interference in the Congressional Reconstruction program. These two sections are reproduced below; the entire act (An Act making Appropriations for the Support of the Army for the Year ending June thirtieth, eighteen hundred and sixty-eight, and for Other Purposes) can be found in the Congressional Globe, *39th Congress, 2nd Session, Appendix, pp. 217–218.*

Section 2 And be it further enacted, That the headquarters of the General of the Army of the United States shall be at the city of Washington, and all orders and instructions relating to military operations issued by the President or Secretary of War shall be issued through the General of the Army, and, in case of his inability, through the next in rank. The General of the Army shall not be removed, suspended, or relieved from command, or assigned to duty elsewhere than at said headquarters, except at his own request, without the previous approval of the Senate; and any orders or instructions relating to military operations issued contrary to the requirements of this section shall be null and void; and any officer who shall issue orders or instructions contrary to the provisions of this section shall be deemed guilty of a misdemeanor in office; and any officer of the Army who shall transmit, convey, or obey any orders or instructions so issued contrary to the provisions of this section, knowing that such orders were so issued, shall be liable to imprisonment for not less that two nor more than twenty years, upon conviction thereof in any court of competent jurisdiction.

Section 6 And be it further enacted, That all militia forces now organized or in service in either of the States of Virginia, North Carolina, South Carolina, Georgia, Florida, Alabama, Louisiana, Mississippi, and Texas, be forthwith disbanded, and that the further organization, arming, or calling into service of the said militia forces, or any part thereof, is hereby prohibited under any circumstances whatever, until the same shall be authorized by Congress.

ARTICLES OF IMPEACHMENT

The U.S. House of Representatives impeached President Andrew Johnson on February 24, 1868, for "high crimes and misdemeanors." Formal, more specific charges were drawn up afterward, in the shape of eleven articles of impeachment. They were passed by the House on March 3, 1868, and transmitted to the Senate by the impeachment managers the next day. On March 7 President Johnson received the articles, along with a request for a written reply.

The articles in their entirety can be found in LeRoy P. Graf, Ralph W. Haskins, and Paul H. Bergeron, eds., The Papers of Andrew Johnson *16 vols. (1967–2000) 13:619–628.*

Article I.

That said Andrew Johnson, President of the United States, on the 21st day of February, in the year of our Lord 1868, at Washington, in the District of Columbia, unmindful of the high duties of his office, of his oath of office, and of the requirement of the Constitution that he should take care that the laws be faithfully executed, did unlawfully, and in violation of the Constitution and laws of the United States, issue an order in writing for the removal of Edwin M. Stanton from the office of Secretary for the Department of War, said Edwin M. Stanton having been theretofore duly appointed and commissioned, by and with the advice and consent of the Senate of the United States....

Executive Mansion,
Washington, D.C., February 21, 1868

Sir: By virtue of the power and authority vested in me as President by the Constitution and laws of the United States you are hereby removed from office as Secretary for the Department of War, and your functions as such will terminate upon receipt of this communication.

You will transfer to Brevet Major General Lorenzo Thomas, Adjutant General of the army, who has this day been authorized and empowered to act as Secretary of War *ad interim,* all records, books, papers, and other public property now in your custody and charge.

Respectfully yours,

ANDREW JOHNSON

To the Hon. Edwin M. Stanton,
Washington, D.C.

Which order was unlawfully issued with intent then and there to violate the act entitled "An act regulating the tenure of certain civil offices," passed March second, eighteen hundred and sixty-seven ... whereby said Andrew Johnson, President of the United States, did then and there commit, and was guilty of a high misdemeanor in office.

Article II.

That on said twenty-first day of February, in the year of our Lord one thousand eight hundred and sixty-eight, at Washington, in the District of Columbia, said Andrew Johnson, President of the United States ... [did] issue and deliver to one Lorenzo Thomas a letter of authority in substance as follows, that is to say:

Executive Mansion,
Washington, D.C., February 21, 1868

Sir: The Hon. Edwin M. Stanton having been this day removed from office as Secretary for the Department of War, you are hereby authorized and empowered to act as Secretary of War *ad interim,* and will immediately enter upon the discharge of the duties pertaining to that office....

Respectfully yours,

ANDREW JOHNSON

To Brevet Major General Lorenzo Thomas, Adjutant General U.S. Army, Washington, D.C.

Then and there being no vacancy in said office of Secretary for the Department of War, whereby said Andrew Johnson, President of the United States, did then and there commit, and was guilty of a high misdemeanor in office.

Article III.

That said Andrew Johnson ... did commit and was guilty of a high misdemeanor in office in this, that, without authority of law, while the Senate of the United States was then and there in session ... did appoint one Lorenzo Thomas to be Secretary for the Department of War *ad interim,* without the advice and consent of the Senate....

Article IV.

That said Andrew Johnson ... did unlawfully conspire with one Lorenzo Thomas, and with other persons to the House of Representatives unknown, with intent, by intimidation and threats, unlawfully to hinder and prevent Edwin M. Stanton, then and there the Secretary for the Department of War, duly appointed under the laws of the United States, from holding said office of Secretary for the Department of War, contrary to and in violation of the Constitution of the United States, and of the provisions of an act entitled "An act to define and punish certain conspiracies," approved July thirty-first, eighteen hundred and sixty-one, whereby said Andrew Johnson, President of the United States, did then and there commit and was guilty of a high crime in office.

Article V.

That said Andrew Johnson . . . did unlawfully conspire with one Lorenzo Thomas . . . to prevent and hinder the execution of an act entitled "An act regulating the tenure of certain civil offices" . . . and in pursuance of said conspiracy, did unlawfully attempt to prevent Edwin M. Stanton, then and there being Secretary for the Department of War . . . whereby the said Andrew Johnson, President of the United States, did then and there commit and was guilty of a high misdemeanor in office.

Article VI.

That said Andrew Johnson . . . did unlawfully conspire with one Lorenzo Thomas, by force to seize, take, and possess the property of the United States in the Department of War, and then and there in the custody and charge of Edwin M. Stanton, Secretary for said Department, contrary to the provisions of an act entitled "An act to define and punish certain conspiracies" . . . whereby said Andrew Johnson, President of the United States, did then and there commit a high crime in office.

Article VII.

That said Andrew Johnson . . . did unlawfully conspire with one Lorenzo Thomas with intent unlawfully to seize, take, and possess the property of the United States in the Department of War . . . with intent to violate and disregard the act entitled "An act regulating the tenure of certain civil offices" . . . whereby said Andrew Johnson, President of the United States, did then and there commit a high misdemeanor in office.

Article VIII.

That said Andrew Johnson . . . with intent unlawfully to control the disbursements of the moneys appropriated for the military service and for the Department of War . . . did unlawfully and contrary to the provisions of an act entitled "An act regulating the tenure of certain civil offices" . . . issue and deliver to one Lorenzo Thomas a letter of authority in writing, in substance as follows, that is to say:

Executive Mansion,
Washington, D.C., February 21, 1868

Sir: The Hon. Edwin M. Stanton having been this day removed from office as Secretary for the Department of War, you are hereby authorized and empowered to act as Secretary of War *ad interim,* and will immediately enter upon the discharge of the duties pertaining to that office.

Mr. Stanton has been instructed to transfer to you all the records, books, papers, and other public property now in his custody and charge.

Respectfully yours,

ANDREW JOHNSON

To Brevet Major General Lorenzo Thomas,
Adjutant General U.S. Army, Washington, D.C.

[whereby said Andrew Johnson, President of the United States, did then and there commit and was guilty of a high misdemeanor in office.]

Article IX.

That said Andrew Johnson . . . did bring before himself then and there William H. Emory, a major general by brevet in the army of the United States . . . and did then and there . . . declare to and instruct said Emory that part of a law of the United States, passed March second, eighteen hundred and sixty-seven, entitled "An act making appropriations for the support of the army for the year ending June thirtieth, eighteen hundred and sixty-eight, and for other purposes" . . . was unconstitutional, and in contravention of the commission of said Emory . . . as the said Andrew Johnson then and there well knew, with intent thereby to induce said Emory in his official capacity as commander of the Department of Washington, to violate the provisions of said act, and to take and receive, act upon, and obey such orders as he, the said

Andrew Johnson, might make and give, and which should not be issued through the General of the Army of the United States, according to the provisions of said act . . . whereby said Andrew Johnson, President of the United States, did then and there commit and was guilty of a high misdemeanor in office.

And the House of Representatives, by protestation, saving to themselves the liberty of exhibiting at any time hereafter any further articles or other accusation, do demand that the said Andrew Johnson may be put to answer the high crimes and misdemeanors in office herein charged against him, and that such proceedings, examinations, trials, and judgments may be thereupon had and given as may be agreeable to law and justice.

Article X.

That said Andrew Johnson . . . did attempt to bring into disgrace, ridicule, hatred, contempt and reproach the Congress of the United States, and the several branches thereof, to impair and destroy the regard and respect of all the good people of the United States for the Congress and legislative power thereof . . . and to excite the odium and resentment of all the good people of the United States against Congress and the laws by it duly and constitutionally enacted. . . .

Specification First—In this, that at Washington, in the District of Columbia, in the Executive Mansion, to a committee of citizens . . . said Andrew Johnson . . . did, in a loud voice, declare in substance and effect, among other things, that is to say:

". . . We have witnessed in one department of the government every endeavor to prevent the restoration of peace, harmony, and Union. We have seen hanging upon the verge of the government, as it were, a body called, or which assumes to be, the Congress of the United States, while in fact it is a Congress of only a part of the States. We have seen this Congress pretend to be for the Union, when its every step and act tended to perpetuate disunion and make a disruption of the States inevitable. We have seen Congress gradually encroach step by step upon constitutional rights, and violate, day after day and month after month, fundamental principles of the government. . . ."

Specification Second—In this, that at Cleveland, in the State of Ohio . . . said Andrew Johnson . . . did, in a loud voice, declare in substance and effect among other things, that is to say:

". . . But what had Congress done? Have they done anything to restore the union of these States? No: on the contrary, they had done everything to prevent it; and because he stood now where he did when the rebellion commenced, he had been denounced as a traitor. Who had run greater risks or made greater sacrifices than himself? But Congress, factious and domineering, had undertaken to poison the minds of the American people."

Specification Third—In this, that at St. Louis, in the State of Missouri . . . said Andrew Johnson . . . did, in a loud voice, declare, in substance and effect, among other things, that is to say:

". . . If you will take up the riot at New Orleans and trace it back to the radical Congress, you will find that the riot at New Orleans was substantially planned. . . . You will also find that that convention did assemble in violation of law, and the intention of that convention was to supersede the reorganized authorities in the State government of Louisiana, which had been recognized by the government of the United States; and every man engaged in that rebellion in that convention, with the intention of superseding and upturning the civil government which had been recognized by the government of the United States I say that he was a traitor to the Constitution of the United States, and hence you find that another rebellion was commenced, *having its origin in the radical Congress.*"

". . . And I have been traduced, I have been slandered, I have been maligned, I have been called Judas Iscariot and all that. . . . There was a Judas, and he was one of the twelve apostles. Oh! yes, the twelve apostles had a Christ. . . . If I have played the Judas, who has been my Christ that I have played the Judas with? Was it Thad. Stevens? Was it Wendell Phillips? Was it Charles Sumner? These are the men that stop and compare themselves with the Saviour; and every body that differs with them in opinion, and to try to stay and arrest their diabolical and nefarious policy, is to be denounced as a Judas. . . ."

Which said utterances, declarations, threats, and harangues, highly censurable in any, are peculiarly indecent and unbecoming in the Chief Magistrate of the United States . . . said Andrew

Johnson, President of the United States, did commit, and was then and there guilty of a high misdemeanor in office.

Article XI.
That said Andrew Johnson . . . did . . . by public speech, declare and affirm, in substance, that the thirty-ninth Congress of the United States was not a Congress of the United States authorized by the Constitution to exercise legislative power under the same . . . to wit . . . did, unlawfully, and in disregard of the requirement of the Constitution . . . attempt to prevent the execution of an act entitled "An act regulating the tenure of certain civil offices" . . . and, also, by further unlawfully devising and contriving, and attempting to devise and contrive means, then and there, to prevent the execution of an act entitled "An act making appropriations for the support of the army for the fiscal year ending June thirtieth, eighteen hundred and sixty-eight, and for other purposes" . . . whereby the said Andrew Johnson, President of the United States, did, then, to wit . . . commit, and was guilty of, a high misdemeanor in office.

SCHUYLER COLFAX,
Speaker of the House of Representatives.

Attest:
EDWARD MCPHERSON,
Clerk of the House of Representatives.

CIVIL RIGHTS ACT (1866)

Passed over President Andrew Johnson's veto on April 9, 1866, the Civil Rights Act (An Act to Protect all Persons in the United States in their civil Rights, and furnish the Means of their Vindication) represented a fundamental shift in the understanding of U.S. citizenship and the protection of U.S. citizens' rights. Excerpts taken from the Congressional Globe, *39th Congress, 1st Session, Appendix, pp. 315–317.*

Be it enacted by the Senate and House of Representatives of the United States of America in Congress assembled, That all persons born in the United States and not subject to any foreign Power, excluding Indians not taxed, are hereby declared to be citizens of the United States; and such citizens, of every race and color, without regard to any previous condition of slavery or involuntary servitude, except as a punishment for crime whereof the party shall have been duly convicted, shall have the same right, in every State and Territory in the United States, to make and enforce contracts, to sue, be parties, and give evidence, to inherit, purchase, lease, sell, hold, and convey real and personal property, and to full and equal benefit of all laws and proceedings for the security of person and property, as is enjoyed by white citizens, and shall be subject to like punishment, pains, and penalties, and to none other, any law, statute, ordinance, regulation, or custom, to the contrary notwithstanding.

Section 2 And be it further enacted, That any person who, under color of any law, statute, ordinance, regulation, or custom, shall subject, or cause to be subjected, any inhabitant of any State or Territory to the deprivation of any right secured or protected by this act, or to different punishment, pains, or penalties on account of such person having at any time been held in a condition of slavery or involuntary servitude . . . shall be punished by fine not exceeding one thousand dollars, or imprisonment not exceeding one year, or both, in the discretion of the court.

Section 3 And be it further enacted, That the district courts of the United States, within their respective districts, shall have, exclusively of the courts of the several States, cognizance of all crimes and offenses committed against the provisions of this act, and also, concurrently with the circuit courts of the United States, of all causes, civil and criminal, affecting persons who are denied or cannot enforce in the courts or judicial tribunals of the State or locality where they may be any of the rights secured to them by the first section of this act; and if any suit or prosecution, civil or criminal, has been or shall be commenced in any State court, against any such person, for any cause whatsoever, or against any officer, civil or military, or other person, for any arrest or imprisonment, trespasses, or wrongs done or committed by virtue or under color of authority derived from this act . . . such defendant shall have the right to remove such cause for trial to the proper district court. . . . The jurisdiction in civil and criminal matters hereby conferred on the district and circuit courts of the United States shall be exercised and enforced in conformity with the laws of the United States. . . .

Section 4 And be it further enacted, That the district attorneys, marshals, and deputy marshals of the United States, the commissioners appointed by the circuit and territorial courts of the United States, with powers of arresting, imprisoning, or bailing offenders against the laws of the United States . . . shall be, and are hereby, specially authorized and required, at the expense of the United States, to institute proceedings against all and every person who shall violate the provisions of this act. . . .

Section 5 And be it further enacted, That it shall be the duty of all marshals and deputy marshals to obey and execute all warrants and precepts issued under the provisions of this act. . . . And the better to enable the said commissioners to execute their duties faithfully and efficiently . . . they are hereby empowered, within their counties respectively, to appoint, in writing, under their hands, any one or more suitable persons, from time to time, to execute all such warrants and other process as may be issued by them in the lawful performance of their respective duties; and the persons so appointed to execute any warrant or process as aforesaid shall have authority to summon and call to their aid the bystanders or **posse comitatus** of the proper county, or such portion of the land or naval forces of the United States, or of the militia, as may be necessary to the performance of the duty with which they are charged, and to insure a faithful observance of the clause of the Constitution which prohibits slavery, in conformity with the provisions of this act. . . .

Section 9 And be it further enacted, That it shall be lawful for the President of the United States, or such person as he may empower for that purpose, to employ such part of the land or naval forces of the United States, or of the militia, as shall be necessary to prevent the violation and enforce the due execution of this act.

Section 10 And be it further enacted, That upon all questions of law arising in any case under the provisions of this act a final appeal may be taken to the Supreme Court of the United States.

FIFTEENTH AMENDMENT

Adopted in 1870, the Fifteenth Amendment, the last of the three Reconstruction amendments, limited, but did not eliminate, the methods by which voting could be restricted. The negative phrasing created loopholes that resulted in fraud and abuse because the amendment did not prohibit such voting restrictions as literacy or the payment of poll taxes.

Section 1 The right of citizens of the United States to vote shall not be denied or abridged by the United States or by any State on account of race, color, or previous condition of servitude.

Section 2 The Congress shall have power to enforce this article by appropriate legislation.

FIRST MILITARY RECONSTRUCTION ACT

Passed March 2, 1867, the First Military Reconstruction Act (An Act to Provide for the More Efficient Government of the Rebel States) began Congressional Reconstruction and the accompanying restructuring of the South. Together with its three supplemental acts, this measure divided ten former Confederate states into military districts under U.S. Army supervision and provided the guidelines for their readmission to Congress. The following is taken from the Congressional Globe, *39th Congress, 2nd Session, Appendix, pp. 197–199.*

Whereas no legal State governments or adequate protection for life or property now exists in the rebel States of Virginia, North Carolina, South Carolina, Georgia, Mississippi, Alabama, Louisiana, Florida, Texas, and Arkansas; and whereas it is necessary that peace and good order should be enforced in said States until loyal and republican State governments can be legally established: Therefore,

Be it enacted by the Senate and House of Representatives of the United States of America in Congress assembled, That said rebel States shall be divided into military districts and made subject to the military authority of the United States as hereinafter prescribed, and for that purpose Virginia shall constitute the first district; North Carolina and South Carolina the second district; Georgia, Alabama, and Florida the third district; Mississippi and Arkansas the fourth district; and Louisiana and Texas the fifth district.

Section 2 *And be it further enacted,* That it shall be the duty of the President to assign to the command of each of said districts an officer of the Army, not below the rank of brigadier general, and to detail a sufficient military force to enable such officer to perform his duties and enforce his authority within the district to which he is assigned.

Section 3 *And be it further enacted,* That it shall be the duty of each officer assigned as aforesaid to protect all persons in their rights of person and property, to suppress insurrection, disorder, and violence, and to punish, or cause to be punished, all disturbers of the public peace and criminals; and to this end he may allow local civil tribunals to take jurisdiction of and to try offenders, or, when in his judgment it may be necessary for the trial of offenders, he shall have power to organize military commissions or tribunals for that purpose, and all interference under color of State authority with the exercise of military authority under this act shall be null and void.

Section 4 *And be it further enacted,* That all persons put under military arrest by virtue of this act shall be tried without unnecessary delay, and no cruel or unusual punishment shall be inflicted, and no sentence of any military commission or tribunal hereby authorized, affecting the life or liberty of any person, shall be executed until it is approved by the officer in command of the district, and the laws and regulations for the government of the Army shall not be affected by this act, except in so far as they conflict with its provisions; *Provided,* That no sentence of death under the provisions of this act shall be carried into effect without the approval of the President.

Section 5 *And be it further enacted,* That when the people of any one of said rebel States shall have formed a constitution of government in conformity with the Constitution of the United States in all respects, framed by a convention of delegates elected by the male citizens of said State, twenty-one years old and upward, of whatever race, color, or previous condition, who have been resident in said State for one year previous to the day of such election, except such as may be disfranchised for participation in the rebellion or for felony at common law, and when such constitution shall provide that the elective franchise shall be enjoyed by all such persons as have the qualifications herein stated for electors of delegates, and when such constitution shall be ratified by a majority of the persons voting on the question of ratification who are qualified as elec-

tors for delegates, and when such constitution shall have been submitted to Congress for examination and approval, and Congress shall have approved the same, and when said State, by a vote of its Legislature, elected under said constitution, shall have adopted the amendment to the Constitution of the United States, proposed by the Thirty-Ninth Congress, and known as article fourteen, and when said article shall have become part of the Constitution of the United States, said State shall be declared entitled to representation in Congress, and Senators and Representatives shall be admitted therefrom on their taking the oath prescribed by law, and then and thereafter the preceding sections of this act shall be inoperative in said State: *Provided,* That no person excluded from the privilege of holding office by said proposed amendment to the Constitution of the United States shall be eligible to election as member of the convention to frame a constitution for any of said rebel States, nor shall any such person vote for members of such convention.

Section 6 *And be it further enacted,* That, until the people of said rebel States shall be by law admitted to representation in the Congress of the United States, any civil governments which may exist therein shall be deemed provisional only, and in all respects subject to the paramount authority of the United States at any time to abolish, modify, control, or supersede the same; and in all elections to any office under such provisional governments all persons shall be entitled to vote, and none others, who are entitled to vote, under the provisions of the fifth section of this act; and no person shall be eligible to any office under any such provisional governments who would be disqualified from holding office under the provisions of the third article of said constitutional amendment.

FOURTEENTH AMENDMENT

The second of the Reconstruction amendments, the Fourteenth Amendment conferred U.S. citizenship on black Americans and nationalized civil rights. Adopted in 1868, its scope and intent are still debated to this day.

Section 1 All persons born or naturalized in the United States, and subject to the jurisdiction thereof, are citizens of the United States and of the State wherein they reside. No State shall make or enforce any law which shall abridge the privileges or immunities of citizens of the United States; nor shall any State deprive any person of life, liberty, or property without due process of law; nor deny to any person within its jurisdiction the equal protection of the laws.

Section 2 Representatives shall be appointed among the several States according to their respective numbers, counting the whole number of persons in each State, excluding Indians not taxed. But when the right to vote at any election for the choice of Electors for President and Vice-President of the United States, Representatives in Congress, the executive and judicial officers of a State, of the members of the legislature thereof, is denied to any of the male inhabitants of such State, being twenty-one years of age and citizens of the United States, or in any way abridged, except for participation in rebellion, or other crime, the basis of representation therein shall be reduced in the proportion which the number of such male citizens shall bear to the whole number of male citizens twenty-one years of age in such State.

Section 3 No person shall be a Senator or Representative in Congress, or Elector of President and Vice-President, or hold any office, civil or military, under the United States, or under any State, who, having previously taken an oath, as a member of Congress, or as an officer of the United States, or as a member of any State legislature, or as an executive or judicial officer of any State, to support the Constitution of the United States, shall have engaged in insurrection or rebellion against the same, or given aid or comfort to the enemies thereof. Congress may, by a vote of two-thirds of each house, remove such disability.

Section 4 The validity of the public debt of the United States, authorized by law, including debts incurred for payments of pensions and bounties for services in suppressing insurrection or rebellion, shall not be questioned. But neither the United States nor any State shall assume or pay any debt or obligation incurred in aid of insurrection or rebellion against the United States, or any claim for the loss or emancipation of any slave; but all such debts, obligations, and claims shall be held illegal and void.

Section 5 The Congress shall have power to enforce, by appropriate legislation, the provisions of this article.

THIRTEENTH AMENDMENT

Adopted in 1865, the Thirteenth Amendment was the first of the so-called Reconstruction amendments.

Section 1 Neither slavery nor involuntary servitude, except as punishment for crime whereof the party shall have been duly convicted, shall exist within the United States, or any place subject to their jurisdiction.

Section 2 Congress shall have the power to enforce this article by appropriate legislation.

Speeches, Proclamations, Vetoes, and Letters of Andrew Johnson

AMNESTY PROCLAMATIONS

President Johnson, eager to speed reconciliation and Reconstruction, issued four presidential amnesties (pardons that covered a large group of people) designed to relieve former Confederates of liabilities that their support of the Confederacy had caused. Those persons not included in the amnesties could apply to Johnson directly for an individual pardon. With each successive pardon, however, the number of those excluded dwindled; Johnson's last amnesty—his "Christmas amnesty"—was a general amnesty, pardoning anyone not covered by earlier proclamations.

Johnson's first amnesty is printed in full below. The three successive amnesties have been edited to highlight their differences from one another. They can be found in their entirety in LeRoy P. Graf, Ralph W. Haskins, and Paul H. Bergeron, eds., The Papers of Andrew Johnson *16 vols. (1967–2000) 8:128–131; 13:40–43; 14:317–319; 15:332.*

First Amnesty Proclamation (May 29, 1865).
Whereas the President of the United States, on the 8th day of December, A.D. eighteen hundred and sixty-three, and on the 26th day of March, A.D. eighteen hundred and sixty-four, did, with the object, to suppress the existing rebellion, to

induce all persons to return to their loyalty, and to restore the authority of the United States, issue proclamations offering amnesty and pardon to certain persons who had directly or by implication participated in the said rebellion; and, whereas many persons who had so engaged in said rebellion have, since the issuance of said proclamations, failed or neglected to take the benefits offered thereby; and whereas many persons who have been justly deprived of all claim to amnesty and pardon thereunder, by reason of their participation directly or by implication in said rebellion, and continued hostility to the government of the United States since the date of said proclamation, now desire to apply for and obtain amnesty and pardon:

To the end, therefore, that the authority of the government of the United States may be restored, and that peace, order, and freedom may be established, I, ANDREW JOHNSON, President of the United States, do proclaim and declare that I hereby grant to all persons who have directly or indirectly, participated in the existing rebellion, except as hereinafter excepted, amnesty and pardon, with restoration of all rights of property, except as to slaves, and except in cases where legal proceedings, under the laws of the United States providing for the confiscation of property of persons engaged in rebellion, have been instituted; but upon the condition, nevertheless, that every such person shall take and subscribe the following oath, (or affirmation,) and thenceforward keep and maintain said oath inviolate; and which oath shall be registered for permanent preservation, and shall be of the tenor and effect following, to wit:

I, ———, do solemnly swear (or affirm), in the presence of Almighty God, that I will henceforth faithfully support, protect, and defend the Constitution of the United States, and the union of the States thereunder; and that I will, in like manner, abide by, and faithfully support all laws and proclamations which have been made during the existing rebellion with reference to the emancipation of slaves. So help me God.

The following classes of persons are excepted from the benefits of this proclamation: 1st, all who are or shall have been pretended civil or diplomatic officers or otherwise domestic or foreign agents of the pretended Confederate government; 2nd, all who left judicial stations under the United States to aid the rebellion; 3rd, all who shall have been military or naval officers of said pretended Confederate government above the rank of colonel in the army or lieutenant in the navy; 4th, all who left seats in the Congress of the United States to aid the rebellion; 5th, all who resigned or tendered resignations of their commissions in the army or navy of the United States to evade duty in resisting the rebellion; 6th, all who have engaged in any way in treating otherwise than lawfully as prisoners of war persons found in the United States service, as officers, soldiers, seamen, or in other capacities; 7th, all persons who have been, or are absentees from the United States for the purpose of aiding the rebellion; 8th, all military and naval officers in the rebel service, who were educated by the government in the Military Academy at West Point or the United States Naval Academy; 9th, all persons who held the pretended offices of governors of States in insurrection against the United States; 10th, all persons who left their homes within the jurisdiction and protection of the United States, and passed beyond the Federal military lines into the pretended Confederate States for the purpose of aiding the rebellion; 11th, all persons who have engaged in the destruction of the commerce of the United States upon the high seas, and all persons who have made raids into the United States from Canada, or been engaged in destroying the commerce of the United States upon the lakes and rivers that separate the British Provinces from the United States; 12th, all persons who, at the time when they seek to obtain the benefits hereof by taking the oath herein prescribed, are in military, naval, or civil confinement, or custody, or under bonds of the civil, military, or naval authorities, or agents of the United States as prisoners of war, or persons detained for offenses of any kind, either before or after conviction; 13th, all persons who have voluntarily participated in said rebellion, and the estimated value of whose taxable property is over twenty thousand dollars; 14th, all persons who have taken the oath of amnesty as prescribed in the President's proclamation of December 8th, A.D. 1863, or an oath of allegiance to the government of the United States since the date of said proclamation, and who have not henceforth kept and maintained the same inviolate.

Provided, That special application may be made to the President for pardon by any person belonging to the excepted classes; and such clemency will be liberally extended as may be consistent with the facts of the case and the peace and dignity of the United States.

The Secretary of State will establish rules and regulations for administering and recording the said amnesty oath, so as to insure its benefits to the people, and guard the government against fraud.

In testimony whereof, I have hereunto set my hand, and caused the seal of the United States to be affixed.

Done at the City of Washington, the twenty-ninth day of May, in the year of our Lord one thousand eight hundred and sixty-five, and of the Independence of the United States the eighty-ninth.

ANDREW JOHNSON

Second Amnesty Proclamation (September 7, 1867). Whereas in the month of July, A.D. 1861, the two Houses of Congress, with extraordinary unanimity, solemnly declared that the war then existing was not waged on the part of the Government in any spirit of oppression nor for any purpose of conquest or subjugation, nor purpose of overthrowing or interfering with the rights or established institutions of the States, but to defend and maintain the supremacy of the Constitution and to preserve the Union, with all the dignity, equality, and rights of the several States unimpaired, and that as soon as these objects should be accomplished the war ought to cease. . . .

Whereas there now exists no organized armed resistance of misguided citizens or others to the authority of the United States in the States of Georgia, South Carolina, Virginia, North Carolina, Tennessee, Alabama, Louisiana, Arkansas, Mississippi, Florida, and Texas, and the laws can be sustained and enforced therein by the proper civil authority, State or Federal, and the people of said States are well and loyally disposed, and have conformed, or, if permitted to do so, will conform in their legislation to the condition of affairs growing out of the amendment to the Constitution of the United States

prohibiting slavery within the limits and jurisdiction of the United States. . . .

Whereas a retaliatory or vindictive policy, attended by unnecessary disqualifications, pains, penalties, confiscations, and disfranchisements, now, as always, could only tend to hinder reconciliation among the people and national restoration, while it must seriously embarrass, obstruct, and repress popular energies and national industry and enterprise; and

Whereas for these reasons it is now deemed essential to the public welfare and to the more perfect restoration of constitutional law and order that the said last-mentioned proclamation so as aforesaid issued on the 29th day of May, A.D. 1865, should be modified. . . .

The following persons, and no others, are excluded from the benefits of this proclamation and of the said proclamation of the 29th day of May, 1865, namely:

First. The chief or pretended chief executive officers, including the President, the Vice-President, and all heads of departments of the pretended Confederate or rebel government, and all who were agents thereof in foreign states and countries, and all who held or pretended to hold in the service of the said pretended Confederate government a military rank or title above the grade of brigadier-general or naval rank or title above that of captain, and all who were or pretended to be governors of States while maintaining, aiding, abetting, or submitting to and acquiescing in the rebellion.

Second. All persons who in any way treated otherwise than as lawful prisoners of war persons who in any capacity were employed or engaged in the military or naval service of the United States.

Third. All persons who at the time they may seek to obtain the benefits of this proclamation are actually in civil, military, or naval confinement or custody, or legally held to bail, either before or after conviction, and all persons who were engaged, directly or indirectly, in the assassination of the late President of the United States or in any plot or conspiracy in any manner therewith connected.

In testimony whereof I have signed these presents with my hand . . .

ANDREW JOHNSON

Third Amnesty Proclamation (July 4, 1868).
Whereas in the month of July, A.D. 1861, in accepting the condition of civil war which was brought about by insurrection and rebellion in several of the States which constitute the United States, the two Houses of Congress did solemnly declare that the war was not waged on the part of the Government in any spirit of oppression . . .

Whereas it is believed that amnesty and pardon will tend to secure a complete and universal establishment and prevalence of municipal law and order in conformity with the Constitution of the United States . . .

Now, therefore, be it known that I, Andrew Johnson, President of the United States, do, by virtue of the Constitution and in the name of the people of the United States, hereby proclaim and declare, unconditionally and without reservation, to all and to every person who, directly or indirectly, participated in the late insurrection or rebellion, excepting such person or persons as may be under presentment or indictment in any court of the United States having competent jurisdiction upon a charge of treason or other felony, a full pardon and amnesty for the offense of treason against the United States or of adhering to their enemies during the late civil war, with restoration of all rights of property, except as to slaves, and except also as to any property of which any person may have been legally divested under the laws of the United States.

In testimony whereof I have signed these presents with my hand . . .

ANDREW JOHNSON

Fourth Amnesty Proclamation (December 25, 1868).
Whereas the President of the United States has heretofore set forth several proclamations offering amnesty and pardon to persons who had been or were concerned in the late rebellion against the lawful authority of the Government . . .

Now, therefore, be it known that I, Andrew Johnson, President of the United States . . . do proclaim and declare, unconditionally and without reservation, to all and to every person who, directly or indirectly, participated in the late insurrection or rebellion a full pardon and amnesty for the offense of treason against the

United States or of adhering to their enemies during the late civil war, with restoration of all rights, privileges, and immunities under the Constitution and the laws which have been made in pursuance thereof.

In testimony whereof I have signed these presents with my hand . . .

ANDREW JOHNSON

"HON. D. T. PATTERSON . . ."

In the fall of 1855, while the duties of the governorship kept Andrew Johnson in Nashville, Judge David T. Patterson wrote to him to ask for Martha Johnson's hand in marriage. Johnson, whose somewhat overbearing, truculent nature never seemed to extend to friends and family, provided a reply that appears out of line with his demeanor—and with the general perceptions of nineteenth-century gender and family relations. Martha Johnson married Patterson on December 13, 1855, but her father was unable to attend the wedding.

The letter is housed in the Margaret Johnson Patterson Bartlett Collection at the Andrew Johnson Project. Also see Trefousse, Hans L., Andrew Johnson: A Biography (New York: W. W. Norton, 1989), 101.

Nashville Tenn
Oct. 26th 1855
Hon D. T. Patterson,

Sir,

Your letter of the 20th inst asking me to give you my daughter Martha in marriage was received in due course of mail—If you have obtained Martha's consent to become your companion for life you have mine. This is a question which has been left for her own determination. You have known each other long and well and now that the union has been agreed upon between you and her let it be consumated [*sic*].

It is not necessary for me to State to you the deep interest I feel in regard to the future of my little family and especially my oldest and favorite child—I do most devoutly hope that your union will be attended with all that will make you prosperous and happy.

Yours most Sincerely
Andrew Johnson

"MOSES OF THE COLORED MEN" SPEECH (1864)

Delivered on October 24, 1864, by military governor of Tennessee Andrew Johnson, this speech was made to a crowd of freedpeople who had gathered at the capitol in Nashville. Taken from LeRoy P. Graf, Ralph W. Haskins, and Paul H. Bergeron, eds., The Papers of Andrew Johnson 16 vols. (1967–2000) 7:251–253.

Colored Men of Nashville:

You have all heard of the President's Proclamation, by which he announces to the world that the slaves in a large portion of the seceded States were thenceforth and forever free. For certain reasons, which seemed wise to the President, the benefits of that Proclamation did not extend to you or to your native State. Many of you consequently were left in bondage. The task-master's scourge was not yet broken, and the fetters still galled your limbs. Gradually this iniquity has been passing away; but the hour has come when the last vestiges of it must be removed. Consequently, I, too, without reference to the President or any other person, have a proclamation to make; and, standing here upon the steps of the Capitol, with the past history of the State to witness, the present condition to guide, and its future to encourage me, I, Andrew Johnson, do hereby proclaim freedom, full, broad, and unconditional, to every man in Tennessee.

I invoke the colored people to be orderly and law-abiding, but at the same time let them assert their rights, and if traitors and ruffians attack them, while in the discharge of their duties, let them defend themselves as all men have a right to do.

I am no agrarian. I respect the rights of property acquired by honest labor. But I say, nevertheless, that if the great farm of Mark Cockrill, who gave $25,000 to Jeff. Davis's Confederacy, were divided into small farms and sold to fifteen or twenty honest farmers, society would be improved, Nashville mechanics and tradesmen would be enriched, and the State would have more good citizens, and our city would have a much better market than it now has.

I am no agrarian, but if the princely plantation of Wm. G. Harding, who boasted that he had disbursed over $5,000,000 for the rebel Confederacy, were parcelled out among fifty loyal, industrious farmers, it would be a blessing to our noble Commonwealth. I speak to-night as a citizen of Tennessee. I am here on my own soil, and mean to remain here and fight this great battle of freedom through to the end. Loyal men, from this day forward, are to be the controllers of Tennessee's grand and sublime destiny, and Rebels must be dumb. We will not listen to their counsels. Nashville is no longer the place for them to hold their meetings. Let them gather their treasonable conclaves elsewhere; among their friends in the Confederacy. They shall not hold their conspiracies in Nashville.

The representatives of this corrupt (and if you will permit me almost to swear a little) this damnable aristocracy, taunt us with our desire to see justice done, and charge us with favoring negro equality. Of all living men they should be the last to mouth that phrase; and even when uttered in their hearing, it should cause their cheeks to tinge and burn with shame. Negro equality, indeed! Why pass, any day, along the sidewalks of High street where these aristocrats more particularly dwell—these aristocrats, whose sons are now in the bands of guerrillas and cutthroats who prowl and rob and murder around our city—pass by their dwellings, I say, and you will see as many mulatto as negro children, the former bearing an unmistakable resemblance to their aristocrat owners!

Colored men of Tennessee! This too shall cease! Your wives and daughters shall no longer be dragged into a concubinage, compared to which polygamy is a virtue, to satisfy the brutal lusts of slaveholders and overseer! Henceforth the sanctity of God's holy law of marriage shall be respected in your persons, and the great State of Tennessee shall no more give her sanction to your degradation and shame!

["Thank God! thank God!" came from the lips of a thousand women, who in their own persons had experienced the hellish iniquity of the man-seller's code. "Thank God!" fervently echoed the fathers, husbands, brothers of those women.]

And if the law protects you in the possession of your wives and children, if the law shields those whom you hold dear from the unlawful grasp of lust, will you endeavor to be true to yourselves, and shun, as it were death itself, the path of lewdness, crime and vice?

["We will! we will!" cried the assembled thousands; and joining in a sublime and tearful enthusiasm, another mighty shout went up to heaven.]

"Looking at this vast crowd of colored people," continued the Governor, "and reflecting through what a storm of persecution and obloquy they are compelled to pass, I am almost induced to wish that, as in the days of old, a Moses might arise who should lead them safely to their promised land of freedom and happiness."

["You are our Moses," shouted several voices and the exclamation was caught up and cheered until the Capitol rung again.]

"God," continued the speaker, "no doubt has prepared somewhere an instrument for the great work He designs to perform in behalf of this outraged people, and in due time your leader will come forth; your Moses will be revealed to you."

["We want no Moses but you!" again shouted the crowd.]

"Well, then," replied the speaker, "humble and unworthy as I am, if no other better shall be found, I will indeed be your Moses and lead you through the Red Sea of war and bondage, to a fairer future of liberty and peace. I speak now as one who feels the world his country, and all who love equal rights his friends. I speak, too as a citizen of Tennessee. I am here on my own soil, and here I mean to stay and fight this great battle of truth and justice to a triumphant end. Rebellion and slavery shall, by God's good help, no longer pollute our State. Loyal men, whether white or black, shall alone control her destinies: and when this strife in which we are all engaged is past, I trust, I know, we shall have a better state of things, and shall all rejoice that honest labor reaps the fruit of its own industry, and that every man has a fair chance in the race of life."

"MY DEAR ELIZA . . ."

Only one known letter survives from Andrew Johnson to his wife, Eliza. The letter dates from March 1863, while Andrew Johnson, then military governor of Tennessee, was in Washington consulting with President Abraham Lincoln. At the time, Eliza was in Louisville, Kentucky, with her daughter Mary and son-in-law Daniel Stover.

The letter, which is in the Johnson Papers of the Library of Congress, is printed in LeRoy P. Graf, Ralph W. Haskins, and Paul H. Bergeron, eds., The Papers of Andrew Johnson *16 vols. (1967–2000) 6:195–197.*

Washington City
March 27th 1863—
My dear Eliza,

It is so difficult for me to write I am almost detered [sic] from now trying after having commenced—I desire to know how your health is—I am kept in suspence [sic] all the time in reference to Some one of the family—Col. Stover telegraphed that your health is about the same and that Mary is not well—I have heard nothing from Robert & Charles since I left Nashville—I hope all is right with them— Martha and children I fear I shall never see them again—I feel sometimes like giv[in]g all up in dispare [sic]! but this will not do. we must hold out to the end, this rebellion is wrong and must be put down let cost what it may in the life and treasure—I intend to appropriate the remainder of my life to the redemption of my a[d]opted home East Tennessee and you & Mary must not be weary, it is our fate and we Should be willing to bear it cheerfully—Impatience and dissatisfaction will not better it or shorten the time of our suffering—I expected to have been back some time ago, but have been detained here by the Govmt [sic]—In the event Genls Rosecrans & Burnside fails [sic] to redeem East Tennessee this spring or summer I [am] making arragements [sic] to have a force raised to go there this fall—My matters are now nearly arranged and will leave in day or so for Louisville—Things do not look in Tennessee at this time as [I] would like to see them; but must take them as they are—I would like to see the confederate Army driven back before you and Mary goes [sic] to Nashville, but by the time I reach there we will see ore [sic] about it—You have no doubt seen that there are more troops being sent into Ky and the intention is to send them from there into Tennessee unless they are beaten back by the Rebels which I do not think will be the case—However we must wait and See the result—Washington is about as usual as far as I have seen, nothing more than common—The weather since I left you has been uninterrupted bad—I have scarcely had a well day since reaching the North; aboniable [*sic*] cold, with horseness [*sic*], sore throat and a bad cough—I have been speaking and exposed to some extent which has kept it up—I hope you are gain[in]g strength and some flesh—I trust there is nothing serious the matter with Mary and that she will soon be well again—Tell Mary she must devote much of her time and attention to the instruction and train[in]g of her children and say to them that the're grand father thinks of them evey [*sic*] day and prays for their future happiness—You must tell Andrew that his father's hopes rest upon him now and that he must make a man of himself, he can do it if he will and I expect it of him—If he will only educate himself he has a destiny of no ordinry [*sic*] character—when I get to Louisville I shall expect to find that he has made considerable progress in writing as well as in his books—If he will be a good boy and learn as he can there is nothing that he wants that I can procure for him but what he shall have—Say to Col. Stover that I receiv[e]d his despatch [*sic*] and will try and have it attend to &c—I hope he is filling up his Regiment—

Give my love to all and accept for yourself the best wishes of a devoted husband's heart—

Andrew Johnson

PRESIDENTIAL RECONSTRUCTION

President Andrew Johnson's Reconstruction program began on May 29, 1865, with two proclamations: his first Amnesty Proclamation and his Proclamation Establishing Government for North Carolina. The latter detailed the procedure that the former Confederate state needed to follow to be readmitted to Congress. Over the next two months Johnson delivered similar proclamations for Mississippi, Georgia, Texas, Alabama, South Carolina, and Florida. Taken from LeRoy P. Graf, Ralph W. Haskins, and Paul H. Bergeron, eds., The Papers of Andrew Johnson *16 vols. (1967–2000) 8:136–138.*

Proclamation Establishing Government for North Carolina.

WHEREAS the 4th section of the Constitution of the United States declares that the United States shall guarantee to every State in the Union a re-publican form of government, and shall protect each of them against invasion and domestic violence; and whereas the President of the United States is, by the Constitution, made Commander-in-chief of the army and navy, as well as chief civil executive officer of the United States, and is bound by solemn oath faithfully to execute the office of President of the United States, and to take care that the laws be faithfully executed; and whereas the rebellion, which has been waged by a portion of the people of the United States against the properly constituted authorities of the government thereof, in the most violent and revolting form, but whose organized and armed forces have now been almost entirely overcome, has, in its revolutionary progress, deprived the people of the State of North Carolina of all civil government; and whereas it becomes necessary and proper to carry out and enforce the obligations of the United States to the people of North Carolina, in securing them in the enjoyment of a republican form of government:

Now, therefore, in obedience to the high and solemn duties imposed upon me by the Constitution of the United States, and for the purpose of enabling the loyal people of said State to organize a State government, whereby justice may be established, domestic tranquillity insured, and loyal citizens protected in all their rights of life, liberty, and property, I, ANDREW JOHNSON, President of the United States, and commander-in-chief of the army and navy of the United States, do hereby appoint WILLIAM W. HOLDEN provisional governor of the State of North Carolina, whose duty it shall be, at the earliest practicable period, to prescribe such rules and regulations as may be necessary and proper for convening a convention, composed of delegates to be chosen by that portion of the people of said State who are loyal to the United States, and no other, for the purpose of altering or amending the constitution thereof: and with authority to exercise, within the limits of said State, all the powers necessary and proper to enable such loyal people of the State of North Carolina to restore said State to its constitutional relations to the Federal government, and to present such a republican form of State government as will entitle the State to the guarantee of the United States therefor, and its people to protection by the United States against invasion, insurrection, and domestic violence; *provided* that, in any election that may be hereafter held for choosing delegates to any State convention as aforesaid, no person shall be qualified as an elector, or shall be eligible as a member of such convention, unless he shall have previously taken and subscribed the oath of amnesty, as set forth in the President's proclamation of May 29, A.D. 1865, and is a voter qualified as prescribed by the constitution and laws of the State of North Carolina in force immediately before the 20th day of May, A.D. 1861, the date of the so-called ordinance of secession; and the said convention, when convened, or the legislature that may be thereafter assembled, will prescribe the qualification of electors, and the eligibility of persons to hold office under the constitution and laws of the State, a power the people of the several States composing the Federal Union have rightfully exercised from the origin of the government to the present time.

And I do hereby direct—

First. That the military commander of the department, and all officers and persons in the military and naval service, aid and assist the said Provisional Governor in carrying into effect this proclamation, and they are enjoined to abstain from, in any way, hindering, impeding, or discouraging the loyal people from the organization of a State government as herein authorized.

Second. That the Secretary of State proceed to put in force all laws of the United States, the administration whereof belongs to the State Department, applicable to the geographical limits aforesaid.

Third. That the Secretary of the Treasury proceed to nominate for appointment assessors of taxes, and collectors of customs and internal revenue, and such other officers of the Treasury Department as are authorized by law, and put in execution the revenue laws of the United States within the geographical limits aforesaid. In making appointments, the preference shall be given to qualified loyal persons residing within the districts where their respective duties are to be performed. But if suitable residents of the districts shall not be found, then persons residing in other States or districts shall be appointed.

Fourth. That the Postmaster General proceed to establish post offices and post routes, and put into execution the postal laws of the United States within the said State, giving to loyal residents the preference of appointment; but if suitable residents are not found, then to appoint agents, &c., from other States.

Fifth. That the district judge for the judicial district in which North Carolina is included proceed to hold courts within said State, in accordance with the provisions of the act of Congress. The Attorney General will instruct the proper officers to libel, and bring to judgment, confiscation, and sale, property subject to confiscation, and enforce the administration of justice within said State in all manners within the cognizance and jurisdiction of the Federal courts.

Sixth. That the Secretary of the Navy take possession of all public property belonging to the Navy Department within said geographical limits, and put in operation all acts of Congress in relation to naval affairs having application to the said State.

Seventh. That the Secretary of the Interior put in force the laws relating to the Interior Department applicable to the geographical limits aforesaid.

In testimony whereof, I have hereunto set my hand and caused the seal of the United States to be affixed.

Done at the city of Washington this twenty-ninth day of May, in the year of our Lord one thousand eight hundred and sixty-five, and of the Independence of the United States the eighty-ninth.

ANDREW JOHNSON

PROTEST AGAINST THE ARMY APPROPRIATIONS ACT OF 1867

Because vetoing the Appropriations Act would deny the military necessary expenditures, President Johnson signed the bill on March 2, 1867, but sent this protest to the House of Representatives. Taken from the Congressional Globe, *39th Congress, 2nd Session, Appendix, pp. 217–218.*

To the House of Representatives

The act entitled "An Act making Appropriations for the Support of the Army for the year ending June 30, 1868, and for other purposes" contains provisions to which I must call attention. Those provisions are contained in the second section, which in certain cases virtually deprives the President of his constitutional functions as Commander in Chief of the Army, and in the sixth section, which denies to ten States of this Union their constitutional right to protect themselves in any emergency by means of their own militia. Those provisions are out of place in an appropriations act. I am compelled to defeat these necessary appropriations if I withhold my signature to the act. Pressed by these considerations, I feel constrained to return the bill with my signature, but to accompany it with my protest against the sections which I have indicated.

ANDREW JOHNSON

REPLY TO THE ARTICLES
OF IMPEACHMENT

On March 23, 1868, President Andrew Johnson's five-member defense counsel presented an elaborate response to the Articles of Impeachment passed by the House of Representatives in February. This series of answers to Republican charges served as the basis for the president's defense in his trial before the Senate.

Only selected excerpts are presented here. For a complete version of Johnson's reply see LeRoy P. Graf, Ralph W. Haskins, and Paul H. Bergeron, eds., The Papers of Andrew Johnson 16 vols. (1967–2000) 13:664–689.

Answer to Article I.
For answer to the first article [Andrew Johnson] says: That Edwin M. Stanton was appointed Secretary for the Department of War on the 15th day of January, A.D. 1862, by Abraham Lincoln . . .

. . . And this respondent, further answering, says he succeeded to the office of President of the United States upon, and by reason of, the death of Abraham Lincoln . . . and, not having been removed from the said office by this respondent, the said [Edwin M.] Stanton continued to hold the same under the appointment and commission aforesaid, at the pleasure of the President . . . and this respondent, the President of the United States, responsible for the conduct of the Secretary for the Department of War, and having the constitutional right to resort to and rely upon the person holding that office for advice concerning

the great and difficult public duties enjoined on the President by the Constitution and laws of the United States, became satisfied that he could not allow the said Stanton to continue to hold the office of Secretary for the Department of War without hazard of the public interest . . .

. . . This respondent was also then aware that by the first section of "An act regulating the tenure of certain civil offices," passed March 2, 1867 . . . [it] was understood and intended to be an expression of the opinion of the Congress by which that act was passed, that the power to remove executive officers for cause might, by law, be taken from the President and vested in him and the Senate jointly . . . this respondent considered it to be proper to examine and decide whether the particular case of the said Stanton, on which it was this respondent's duty to act, was within or without the terms of that first section of the act . . . and having, in his capacity of President of the United States, so examined and considered, did form the opinion that the case of the said Stanton and his tenure of office were not affected by the first section of the last-named act.

. . . And to these ends, first, that through the action of the Senate of the United States, the absolute duty of the President to substitute some fit person in place of Mr. Stanton as one of his advisers, and as a principal subordinate officer whose official conduct he was responsible for and had lawful right to control, might, if possible, be accomplished without the necessity of raising any one of the questions aforesaid; and, second, if this duty could not be so performed, then that these questions, or such of them as might necessarily arise, should be judicially determined in manner aforesaid, and for no other end or purpose this respondent, as President of the United States, on the 12th day of August, 1867, seven days after the reception of the letter of the said Stanton of the 5th of August, hereinbefore stated, did issue to the said Stanton the order following, namely:

Executive Mansion,
Washington, August 12, 1867

Sir: By virtue of the power and authority vested in me as President by the Constitution and laws of the United States, you are hereby suspended from office as Secretary of War, and will cease to exercise any and all functions pertaining to the same. . . .

The Hon. Edwin M. Stanton,
Secretary of War.

. . . And this respondent, further answering, says . . . he was compelled to take such steps as might, in the judgment of the President, be lawful and necessary to raise, for a judicial decision, the questions affecting the lawful right of the said Stanton to resume the said office, or the power of the said Stanton to persist in refusing to quit the said office if he should persist in actually refusing to quit the same; and to this end, and to this end only, this respondent did, on the 21st day of February, 1868, issue the order for the removal of the said Stanton, in the said first article mentioned and set forth, and the order authorizing the said Lorenzo F. Thomas to act as Secretary of War *ad interim,* in the said second article set forth.

And this respondent, proceeding to answer specifically each substantial allegation in the said first article, says: He denies that the said Stanton, on the 21st day of February, 1868, was lawfully in possession of the said office of Secretary for [of] the Department of War. He denies that the said Stanton, on the day last mentioned, was lawfully entitled to hold the said office against the will of the President of the United States. He denies that the said order for removal of the said Stanton was unlawfully issued. He denies that the said order was issued with intent to violate the act entitled "An act to regulate the tenure of certain civil offices." He denies that the said order was a violation of the last-mentioned act. He denies that the said order was a violation of the Constitution of the United States, or of any law thereof, or of his oath of office. He denies that the said order was issued with an intent to violate the Constitution of the United States or any law thereof, or this respondent's oath of office; and he respectfully, but earnestly, insists that not only was it issued by him in the performance of what he believed to be an imperative official duty, but in the performance of what this honorable court will consider was, in point of fact, an imperative official duty. And he denies that any and all substantive matters, in the said first article contained, in manner and form as the same are

therein stated and set forth, do, by law, constitute a high misdemeanor in office, within the true intent and meaning of the Constitution of the United States.

Answer to Article II.
And for answer to the second article, this respondent says that he admits he did issue and deliver to said Lorenzo Thomas the said writing set forth in said second article . . . but he denies that he thereby violated the Constitution of the United States, or any law thereof . . . and this respondent maintains and will insist:

1. That at the date and delivery of said writing there was a vacancy existing in the office of Secretary for the Department of War.

2. That, notwithstanding the Senate of the United States was then in session, it was lawful and according to long and well-established usage to empower and authorize the said Thomas to act as Secretary of War *ad interim.*

3. That if the said act regulating the tenure of civil offices be held to be a valid law, no provision of the same was violated by the issuing of said order or by the designation of said Thomas to act as Secretary of War *ad interim.*

Answer to Article III.
And for answer to said third article, this respondent says that he abides by his answer to said first and second articles in so far as the same are responsive to the allegations contained in the said third article . . . that this respondent did appoint the said Thomas to be Secretary for the Department of War *ad interim* . . . [but] denies that there was no vacancy in said office of Secretary for the Department of War existing at the date of said written authority.

Answer to Article IV.
And for answer to said fourth article this respondent denies that on the said 21st day of February, 1868, at Washington aforesaid, or at any other time or place, he did unlawfully conspire with the said Lorenzo Thomas . . . protesting that the said Stanton was not then and there lawfully the Secretary for the Department of War, this respondent states that his sole purpose in authorizing the said Thomas to act as Secre-

tary for the Department of War *ad interim* was, as is fully stated in his answer to the said first article, to bring the question of the right of the said Stanton to hold said office . . . to the test of a final decision by the Supreme Court of the United States in the earliest practicable mode by which the question could be brought before that tribunal.

This respondent did not conspire . . . to use intimidation or threats to hinder or prevent the said Stanton from holding the said office of Secretary for the Department of War . . . the only means in the contemplation or purpose of respondent to be used are set forth fully in the said orders of February 21, the first addressed to Mr. Stanton and the second to the said Thomas. . . .

. . . Respondent gave no instructions to the said Thomas to use intimidation or threats to enforce obedience to these orders . . . [And] Stanton peremptorily refused obedience to the orders so issued. Upon such refusal no force or threat of force was used by the said Thomas . . .

Answer to Article V.
And for answer to the said fifth article this respondent denies that . . . [he] did unlawfully conspire with the said Thomas, or with any other person or persons, to prevent or hinder the execution of the said act entitled "An act regulating the tenure of certain civil offices," or that, in pursuance of said alleged conspiracy, he did unlawfully attempt to prevent the said Edwin M. Stanton from holding said office of Secretary for the Department of War . . . protesting that said Stanton was not then and there Secretary for the Department of War . . .

Answer to Article VI.
And for answer to the said sixth article, this respondent denies that . . . he did unlawfully conspire with the said Thomas by force to seize, take, or possess, the property of the United States in the Department of War, contrary to the provisions of the said acts referred to in the said article . . .

Answer to Article VII.
And for answer to the said seventh article, respondent denies that . . . he did unlawfully con-

spire with the said Thomas with intent unlawfully to seize, take, or possess the property of the United States in the Department of War with intent to violate or disregard the said act in the said seventh article . . .

Answer to Article VIII.
And for answer to the said eighth article this respondent denies that . . . he did issue and deliver to the said Thomas the said letter of authority set forth in the said eighth article, with the intent unlawfully to control the disbursements of the money appropriated for the military service and for the Department of War. . . . On the contrary, this respondent again affirms that his sole intent was to vindicate his authority as President of the United States, and by peaceful means to bring the question of the right of the said Stanton to continue to hold the said office of Secretary of War to a final decision before the Supreme Court of the United States . . .

Answer to Article IX.
And for answer to the said ninth article the respondent states that . . . General [William H.] Emory called at the Executive Mansion according to this request. The object of respondent was to be advised by General Emory, as commander of the department of Washington, what changes had been made in the military affairs of the department. Respondent had been informed that various changes had been made which in nowise had been brought to his notice . . . said Emory had explained in detail the changes which had taken place, said Emory called the attention of respondent to a general order which he referred to . . .

. . . Respondent, after reading the order, observed: "This is not in accordance with the Constitution of the United States, which makes me commander-in-chief of the army and navy, or of the language of the commission which you hold. . . ."

. . . Respondent denies that, in said conversation with said Emory, he had any other intent than to express the opinions then given to the said Emory; nor did he then, or at any time, request or order the said Emory to disobey any law . . . What this respondent then said to General Emory was simply the expression of an opinion which he then fully believed to be sound . . . Respondent doth therefore deny that by the expression of such opinion he did commit or was guilty of a high misdemeanor in office. . . .

Answer to Article X.

And in answer to the tenth article and specifications thereof . . .

. . . this respondent . . . denies that he has ever intended or designed to act aside the rightful authority or powers of Congress, or attempted to bring into disgrace, ridicule, hatred, contempt, or reproach the Congress of the United States . . .

And this respondent, further answering, says that he has, from time to time . . . in the exercise of that freedom of speech which belongs to him as a citizen of the United States, and, in his political relations as President of the United States to the people of the United States, is upon fit occasions a duty of the highest obligation, expressed to his fellow-citizens his views and opinions respecting the measures and proceedings of Congress . . . and whatsoever he has thus communicated to Congress or addressed to his fellow-citizens or any assemblage thereof, this respondent says was and is within and according to his right and privilege as an American citizen and his right and duty as President of the United States.

And this respondent, not waiving or at all disparaging his right of freedom of opinion and of freedom of speech . . . says that the views and opinions expressed by this respondent in his said addresses to the assemblages of his fellow-citizens, as in said article or in this answer thereto mentioned, are not and were not intended to be other or different from those expressed by him in his communications to Congress . . .

. . . And this respondent says that neither the said tenth article nor any specification thereof, nor any allegation therein contained, touches or relates to any official act or doing of this respondent in the office of President of the United States or in the discharge of any of its constitutional or legal duties or responsibilities; but said article and the specifications and allegations thereof, wholly and in every part thereof, question only the discretion or propriety of freedom of opinion or freedom of speech as ex-

ercised by this respondent as a citizen of the United States . . .

Answer to Article XI.

And in answer to the eleventh article, this respondent denies that . . . he did . . . declare or affirm, in substance or at all, that the thirty-ninth Congress of the United States was not a congress of the United States authorized by the Constitution . . . But this respondent, in further answer to, and in respect of, the said allegations of the said eleventh article hereinbefore traversed and denied, claims and insists upon his personal and official right of freedom of opinion and freedom of speech, and his duty in his political relations as President of the United States to the people of the United States in the exercise of such freedom of opinion and freedom of speech . . .

And this respondent further denies that on the 21st day of February, in the year 1868 . . . he did unlawfully, and in disregard of the requirement of the Constitution that he should take care that the laws should be faithfully executed, attempt to prevent the execution of an act entitled "An act regulating the tenure of certain civil offices," passed March 2, 1867 . . .

. . . And this respondent, further answering the said eleventh article, denies that by means or reason of anything in said article alleged, this respondent, as President of the United States, did, on the 21st day of February, 1868, or at any other day or time, commit, or that he was guilty of, a high misdemeanor in office. . . .

ANDREW JOHNSON
Henry Stanbery,
B.R. Curtis,
Thomas A. R. Nelson,
William M. Evarts,
W.S. Groesbeck, of Counsel.

VETO OF THE CIVIL RIGHTS ACT (1866)

Disturbed by the blanket granting of U.S. citizenship to nonwhites and the placing of traditionally state-protected rights under federal jurisdiction, President Johnson vetoed the Civil Rights Act on March 27, 1866. The following excerpts from his veto message are taken from LeRoy P. Graf, Ralph W. Haskins, and Paul H. Bergeron, eds., The Papers of Andrew Johnson *16 vols. (1967–2000) 10:312–320.*

To the Senate of the United States

I regret that the bill, which has passed both Houses of Congress, entitled "An act to protect all persons in the United States in their civil rights and furnish the means of their vindication," contains provisions which I can not approve consistently with my sense of duty to the whole people and my obligations to the Constitution of the United States. I am therefore constrained to return it to the Senate, the House in which it originated, with my objections to its becoming a law.

By the first section of the bill all persons born in the United States and not subject to any foreign power, excluding Indians not taxed, are declared to be citizens of the United States. This provision comprehends the Chinese of the Pacific States, Indians subject to taxation, the people called gypsies, as well as the entire race designated as blacks, people of color, negroes, mulattoes, and persons of African blood. Every individual of these races born in the United States is by the bill made a citizen of the United States. . . .

The right of Federal citizenship thus to be conferred on the several excepted races before mentioned is now for the first time proposed to be given by law. . . . the grave question presents itself whether, when eleven of the thirty-six States are unrepresented in Congress at the present time, it is sound policy to make our entire colored population and all other excepted classes citizens of the United States. Four millions of them have just emerged from slavery into freedom. Can it be reasonably supposed that they possess the requisite qualifications to entitle them to all the privileges and immunities of citizens of the United States? Have the people of the several States expressed such a conviction? . . . Besides, the policy of the Government from its origin to the present time seems to have been that persons who are strangers to and unfamiliar with our institutions and our laws should pass through a certain probation, at the end of which, before attaining the coveted prize, they must give evidence of their fitness to receive and to exercise the rights of citizens as

contemplated by the Constitution of the United States. The bill in effect proposes a discrimination against large numbers of intelligent, worthy, and patriotic foreigners, and in favor of the negro, to whom, after long years of bondage, the avenues to freedom and intelligence have just now been suddenly opened. He must of necessity, from his previous unfortunate condition of servitude, be less informed as to the nature and character of our institutions than he who, coming from abroad, has, to some extent at least, familiarized himself with the principles of a Government to which he voluntarily intrusts "life, liberty, and the pursuit of happiness." Yet it is now proposed, by a single legislative enactment, to confer the rights of citizens upon all persons of African descent born within the extended limits of the United States, while persons of foreign birth who make our land their home must undergo a probation of five years, and can only then become citizens upon proof that they are "of good moral character, attached to the principles of the Constitution of the United States, and well disposed to the good order and happiness of the same." . . .

It is clear that in States which deny to persons whose rights are secured by the first section of the bill any one of those rights all criminal and civil cases affecting them will, by the provisions of the third section, come under the exclusive cognizance of the Federal tribunals. . . . If the offense is provided for and punished by Federal law, that law, and not the State law, is to govern. It is only when the offense does not happen to be within the purview of Federal law that the Federal courts are to try and punish him under any other law. . . . So that over this vast domain of criminal jurisprudence provided by each State for the protection of its own citizens and for the punishment of all persons who violate its criminal laws, Federal law, whenever it can be made to apply, displaces State law. The question here naturally arises, from what source Congress derives the power to transfer to Federal tribunals certain classes of cases embraced in this section. . . . This section of the bill undoubtedly comprehends cases and authorizes the exercise of powers that are not, by the Constitution, within the jurisdiction of the courts of the United States. To transfer them to those courts would be an exercise of authority well calculated to excite distrust and alarm on the part of all the States, for the bill applies alike to all of them—as well to those that have not been engaged in rebellion. . . .

The fifth section empowers the commissioners so to be selected by the courts to appoint in writing, under their hands, one or more suitable persons from time to time to execute warrants and other processes described by the bill. These numerous official agents are made to constitute a sort of police, in addition to the military, and are authorized to summon a **posse comitatus**. . . .

This extraordinary power is to be conferred upon agents irresponsible to the Government and to the people, to whose number the discretion of the commissioners is the only limit, and in whose hands such authority might be made a terrible engine of wrong, oppression, and fraud. . . .

To me the details of the bill seem fraught with evil. The white race and the black race of the South have hitherto lived together under the relations of master and slave—capital owning labor. Now, suddenly, that relation is changed, and as to ownership capital and labor are divorced. They stand now each master of itself. In this new relation, one being necessary to the other, there will be a new adjustment, which both are deeply interested in making harmonious. Each has equal power in settling the terms, and if left to the laws that regulate capital and labor it is confidently believed that they will satisfactorily work out the problem. Capital, it is true, has more intelligence, but labor is never so ignorant as not to understand its own interests, not to know its own value, and not to see that capital must pay that value.

This bill frustrates that adjustment. It intervenes between capital and labor and attempts to settle questions of political economy through the agency of numerous officials whose interest it will be to foment discord between the two races, for as the breach widens their employment will continue, and when it is closed their occupation will terminate.

In all our history, in all our experience as a people living under Federal and State law, no such system as that contemplated by the details of this bill has ever before been proposed or adopted. . . . In fact, the distinction of race and color is by the bill made to operate in favor of the colored against the white race. They interfere with the municipal legislation of the States, with the relations existing exclusively between a State and its citizens, or between inhabitants of the same State—an absorption and assumption of power by the General Government which, if acquiesced in, must sap and destroy our federative system of limited powers and break down the barriers which preserve the rights of the States. . . .

Entertaining these sentiments, it only remains for me to say that I will cheerfully cooperate with Congress in any measure that may be necessary for the protection of the civil rights of the freedmen, as well as those of all other classes of persons throughout the United States, by judicial process, under equal and impartial laws, in conformity with the provisions of the Federal Constitution.

I now return the bill to the Senate, and regret that in considering the bills and joint resolutions—forty-two in number—which have been thus far submitted for my approval I am compelled to withhold my assent from a second measure that has received the sanction of both Houses of Congress.

WASHINGTON'S BIRTHDAY SPEECH (1866)

On February 22, 1866, three days after President Johnson vetoed the Freedmen's Bureau Bill, a crowd gathered at the White House to express their support for Johnson's action. His impromptu address delighted the assembly, but brought sharp criticism from Republicans in and out of Congress. These excerpts are taken from the address as printed in LeRoy P. Graf, Ralph W. Haskins, and Paul H. Bergeron, eds., The Papers of Andrew Johnson 16 vols. (1967–2000) 10:145–157.

Fellow-citizens:

For I presume I have a right to address you as such, I come to tender to you my sincere thanks for the approbation expressed by your Committee in their personal address, and in the resolutions submitted by them, as having been adopted by the meeting which has been held in this city to-day. These resolutions, as I understand them, are complimentary to the policy which had been adopted by the Administration, and which has been steadily pursued since it came into power. . . . That policy is one which is intended to restore all the States to their original relations to the Federal Government of the United States. This seems to be a day peculiarly appropriate for such a manifestation. It is the day that gave birth to that man who, more perhaps, than any other, founded this Government . . .

When rebellion and treason manifested themselves in the South I stood by the Government. I said then that I was for the Union with Slavery—or I was for the Union without Slavery. In either alternate I was for my Government and its Constitution. The Government has stretched forth its strong arm, and with its physical power it has put down treason in the field. . . . But while anxious that leading and intelligent traitors should be punished, should whole communities and States and people be made to submit to the penalty of death? No, no. I have perhaps as much asperity and as much resentment in my nature as men ought to have; but we must reason in great matters of government about man as he is. We must conform our actions and our conduct to the example of Him who founded our holy religion . . . let the leaders, the conscious, intelligent traitors, be punished and subjected to the penalties of the law; but to the great mass, who have been forced into this rebellion, in many instances, and in others have been misled, I say extend leniency, kindness, trust and confidence. My countrymen, when I look back over the history of the rebellion, I trust I am not vain when I ask you if I have not given as much evidence of my devotion to the Union as some who croak a great deal about it. . . . The rebellion has been put down by the strong arm of the Government in the field, but is that the only way in which you can have rebellion? One struggle was against an attempt to dissever the Union; but almost before the smoke of the battle-field has passed away—before our brave men have all returned to their homes, and renewed the ties of affection and love to their wives and their children, we find almost another rebellion inaugurated. We put down the former rebellion in order to prevent the separation of the States, to prevent them from flying off, and thereby changing the character of our Government and weakening its power. But when that struggle on our part has been successful, and that attempt has been put

down, we find now an effort to concentrate all power in the hands of a few at the Federal head, and thereby bring about a consolidation of the Government, which is equally objectionable with a separation. We find that powers are assumed and attempted to be exercised of a most extraordinary character. . . . What is now being proposed? We find that in point of fact nearly all the powers of the Government are assumed by an irresponsible central directory, which does not even consult the legislative or the executive departments of the Government. By resolutions reported from a committee in whom it seems that practically the legislative power of the Government is now vested, that great principle of the Constitution which authorizes and empowers each branch of the legislative department, the Senate and the House of Representatives, to judge for itself of the elections, returns and qualifications of its own members, has been virtually taken away from the two branches of the legislative department of the Government, and conferred upon a joint committee, who must report before either House can act under the Constitution as to accepting the members who are to take their seats as component parts of the respective bodies. . . . You struggled for four years to put down a rebellion. You denied in the beginning of the struggle that any State could go out of the Union. You said that it had neither the right nor the power to do so. The issue was made and it had been settled that the States had neither the right nor the power to go out of the Union. With what consistency, after it has been settled by the military arm of the Government and by the public judgment that the States had no right to go out of the Union, can any one now turn round and assume that they are out, and that they shall not come in? I am free to say to you as your Executive that I am not prepared to take any such position. . . . I fought traitors and treason in the South; I opposed the Davises, the Toombes, the Slidells, and a long list of others, which you can readily fill without my repeating the names. Now, when I turn round and at the other end of the line find men—I care not by what name you call them—who still stand opposed to the restoration of the Union of these States, I am free to say to you that I am still in the field. I am still for the preservation of the Union. I am still in favor of this great Government of ours going on and filling out its destiny.

VOICES—Give us three of these names at the other end.

THE PRESIDENT—I am called upon to name three at the other end of the line. I am talking to my friends and fellow-citizens who are interested with me in this Government, and I presume I am free to mention to you the names of those whom I look upon, as being opposed to the fundamental principles of this Government, and who are laboring to destroy it.

VOICES—Name them—who are they?

THE PRESIDENT—You ask me who they are? I say THADDEUS STEVENS, of Pennsylvania, is one; I say MR. SUMNER, of the Senate, is another, and WENDELL PHILLIPS is another. . . .

Honest conviction is my courage. The Constitution is my guide. I know, my countrymen, that it has been insinuated, it has been said directly in high places, that if such a usurpation of power as I am charged with had been exercised some 200 years ago, in a particular reign, it would have cost an individual his head. Of what usurpation has ANDREW JOHNSON been guilty. None; none. Is it a usurpation to stand between the people and the encroachments of power? . . .

Are those who want to destroy our institutions, and to change the character of the Government, not yet satisfied with the quantity of blood that has been shed? Are they not satisfied with one martyr in this place? Does not the blood of LINCOLN appease their vengeance and their wrath? Is their thirst still unsatisfied? . . . if my blood is to be shed because I vindicate the Union and insist on the preservation of this Government in its original purity, let it be shed out; let an altar to the Union be first erected and then, if necessary, take me and lay me upon it, and the blood that now warms and animates my existence shall be poured out as the last libation as a tribute to the union of the States. . . . I wish there were a vast amphitheatre here capacious enough to sustain the whole thirty millions, and they could witness the great struggle going on to preserve the Constitution of their fathers. They would soon settle the question if they could once see who things are; if they could see the kind of spirit that is manifested in the effort to break up the real principles of free government. . . . The people somehow or other, although their sagacity and good judgment are very frequently underrated and underestimated, generally get to find out and understand who is for them and who is against them. . . . So far, thank God, I can lay my hand upon my bosom, and state with heartfelt satisfaction that in all the positions in which I have been placed—and I have been placed in many that were as trying as any in which mortal man has ever been placed—I have never deserted them, nor do I believe they will desert me. . . .

I thank you for the respect you have manifested to me on this occasion, and if the time shall come during the period of my existence when this country is to be destroyed and its Government overturned, if you will look out you will find the humble individual who stands before you there with you endeavoring to avert its final destruction.

CHRONOLOGY

1778
April 17 Jacob Johnson born

1782
July 17 Mary "Polly" McDonough born

1801
September 9 Jacob Johnson and Mary McDonough marry

1804
October 10 William P. Johnson born

1806
March 14 Elizabeth Johnson born

1808
December 29 Andrew Johnson born

1810
October 10 Eliza McCardle born

1812
January 4 Jacob Johnson dies
May 6 Mary McDonough Johnson and Turner Daughtry marry

1818
November 8 Andrew Johnson apprentices to tailor James J. Selby

1822
February 22 Alternate date for Andrew Johnson's apprenticeship

1824
June Andrew and William Johnson run away from Selby

1824–1826 Andrew lives and works in Carthage, North Carolina; Laurens, South Carolina; Mooresville, Alabama; and Columbia, Tennessee

1826
September Andrew, mother, and stepfather arrive in Greeneville, Tennessee Andrew meets Eliza McCardle
Fall Andrew works in Rutledge, Tennessee

1827
Early Andrew continues to work in Rutledge, Tennessee
March Andrew opens tailor shop in Greeneville
May 17 Andrew Johnson and Eliza McCardle marry

1828
October 25 Daughter Martha born

1829 Elected Greeneville alderman

1830
February 19 Son Charles born
Late in year Reelected alderman

1831
February 21 Purchases house and lot in Greeneville

December	Reelected alderman

1832

May 8	Daughter Mary born
Late in year	Reelected alderman

1833

December 30	Reelected alderman

1834

January 4	Elected mayor of Greeneville by aldermen
February 22	Son Robert born
December	Reelected alderman

1835

	Elected to Tennessee house of representatives
	Reelected alderman

1836

	Reelected alderman

1837

	Elected mayor
	Defeated for reelection to Tennessee house of representatives
	Reelected alderman

1839

	Elected to Tennessee house of representatives

1840

	Runs as elector-at-large for Van Buren

1841

	Elected to state senate

1843

	Elected to U.S. House of Representatives

1845

	Reelected to U.S. House of Representatives

1847

	Reelected to U.S. House of Representatives

1849

	Reelected to U.S. House of Representatives

1851

	Reelected to U.S. House of Representatives
	Buys larger house in Greeneville

1852

April 7	Mary Johnson and Daniel Stover marry
August 5	Son Andrew Jr. (Frank) born

1853

August 4	Elected governor of Tennessee

1855

May 11	Granddaughter Lillie Stover born
August 2	Reelected governor of Tennessee
December 13	Martha Johnson and David T. Patterson marry

1856

February 13	Mary McDonough Johnson Daughtry dies

1857

January 31	Injures arm in train accident near Atlanta
February 25	Grandson Andrew Johnson Patterson born
June 27	Granddaughter Sarah Stover born
October 8	Elected to U.S. Senate
December 22	Introduces Homestead Bill in Senate

1858

May 20	Speech on Homestead Bill

1859

August	Robert Johnson elected to Tennessee legislature
November 11	Granddaughter Mary Belle Patterson born

1860

March 6	Grandson Andrew Johnson Stover born
May 1	Nominated for president at Democratic convention
September– October	Campaigns for Democratic candidates
December 18–19	Speech on secession in Senate

1861

May–June	Campaigns for Union in East Tennessee

June 12	Leaves Greeneville and becomes exile
June 22	Arrives in Washington for congressional session

1862

March 3	Appointed military governor of Tennessee
March 12	Arrives in Nashville
June–July	Controversy with Nashville clergymen
October	Eliza Johnson forced to leave East Tennessee
December 10	Greeneville property sequestered

1863

February 26–March 31	Speeches in Midwest and East
April 4	Son Charles dies

1864

June 8	Nominated for vice president
October 4–14	Campaigns in Indiana
October 24	"Moses of the Colored Men" Speech, Nashville
November 8	Elected vice president

1865

February 25	Leaves for Washington
March 4	Sworn in as vice president, makes undignified speech
April 15	Sworn in as president upon assassination of Lincoln
May 1	Orders military trial of alleged presidential assassins
May 24	Moves into White House
May 29	First Amnesty Proclamation
June 9	Moves into White House residential area
June 19	Some family members arrive in Washington
June–July	Brother William P. Johnson visits in Washington
October 24	William P. Johnson dies in Texas
December 4	First Annual Message to Congress

1866

January 1	New Year's Day reception at White House
February 19	Freedmen's Bureau Bill veto
February 22	Washington's Birthday Address
March 27	Civil Rights Bill veto
April–May	Memphis riot
May 15	Colorado Statehood Bill veto
June 7	Honorary doctorate from University of North Carolina
July 16	Freedmen's Bureau Bill veto
July 30	New Orleans riot
August 14	Reception for Queen Emma of Hawaii
August 20	Proclamation regarding end of insurrection
August 28–September 15	Swing-around-the-Circle
December 3	Second Annual Message to Congress

1867

January 5	District of Columbia Franchise Law veto
January 28	Colorado Statehood Bill veto
January 29	Nebraska Statehood Bill veto
March 2	First Military Reconstruction Act veto
	Tenure of Office Act veto
	Army Appropriations Act approved
March 11	Appoints five military district commanders
March 23	Second Military Reconstruction Act veto
April 9	Senate approves Alaska purchase treaty
June 1–8	Trip to North Carolina, attends ceremony at father's grave
June 21–29	Trip to New England and Northeast
July 29	Third Military Reconstruction Act veto
August 12	Suspends Edwin M. Stanton as secretary of war
August 17	Removes Philip H. Sheridan from command of Fifth District
August 26	Removes Daniel E. Sickles from command of Second District
September 7	Second Amnesty Proclamation
September 17	Speaks at Antietam Battlefield
December 3	Third Annual Message to Congress
December 7	House defeats impeachment resolution

1868

February 21	Removes Stanton as secretary of war
February 24	House votes to impeach Johnson
March 2–3	House adopts impeachment articles
March 23	Formal response to impeachment articles
March 30	Impeachment trial begins in Senate
May 16	Acquitted by Senate on eleventh impeachment article
May 26	Acquitted by Senate on second impeachment article
June 20	Arkansas Statehood Bill veto
June 25	Vetoes admission bill for six Southern states
July 4	Third Amnesty Proclamation
July 9	Democrats nominate Horatio Seymour, not Johnson, for president
July 14	Fourteenth Amendment ratified
July 25	Freedmen's Bureau Bill veto
November 3	Ulysses S. Grant elected president
December 9	Fourth Annual Message to Congress
December 25	Fourth Amnesty Proclamation
December 29	Celebrates sixtieth birthday with children's party at White House

1869

February 25–26	Congress passes Fifteenth Amendment
March 4	Leaves White House, does not attend Grant inauguration, issues Farewell Address
March 11	Attends reception and testimonial dinner in Baltimore
March 18	Leaves Washington for Greeneville, gives speeches en route
March 20	Arrives in Greeneville
Late March	Has severe attack of kidney stones

April 20	Mary Johnson Stover and William R. Brown marry
April 23	Son Robert dies
June–July	Visits Washington, D.C., to get Frank
October 22	Defeated for U.S. Senate

1870

April	Purchases more property in Greeneville

1871

May 27	Speaks at Mechanic's Fair in Knoxville

1872

April	Attends Campbell-Millikin wedding in Cincinnati
Early June	Visits Washington, D.C., to testify before Buell commission
Summer–fall	Campaigns for congressman-at-large seat
November 5	Defeated for congressman-at-large

1873

June–July	Very ill with cholera
August–December	Controversy with Joseph Holt
September	Loses $73,000 in collapse of First National Bank
October 13–27	Visits Washington, D.C., for financial reasons

1874

April	Visits Washington, D.C., for financial reasons
July 4	Speaks in Greeneville
Summer–fall	Campaigns for U.S. Senate seat

1875

January 26	Elected to U.S. Senate
March 5–24	Serves in extra session of Senate
March 22	Makes last Senate speech
July 31	Dies at daughter Mary's home in Carter County

BIBLIOGRAPHY

This bibliography contains only books and journal articles. Specialized information (such as newspapers, censuses, and manuscripts) that pertains to a particular entry is listed in the references to that entry.

Abbott, Richard H. *The First Southern Strategy: The Republican Party and the South, 1855–1877.* Chapel Hill: University of North Carolina Press, 1986.

———. *Ohio's War Governors.* Columbus: Ohio State University Press, 1962.

Abernathy, Thomas Perkins. "Origins of the Whig Party in Tennessee." *Mississippi Valley Historical Review* 12 (no. 4, 1925–1926): 502–522.

Albright, Claude. "Dixon, Doolittle, and Norton: The Forgotten Republican Votes." *Wisconsin Magazine of History* 59 (Winter 1975–1976): 91–100.

Alexander, Roberta Sue. "Presidential Reconstruction: Ideology and Change." In Anderson, Eric, and Moss, Alfred A., Jr., eds., *The Facts of Reconstruction: Essays in Honor of John Hope Franklin.* Baton Rouge: Louisiana State University Press, 1991.

Alexander, Thomas B. *Political Reconstruction in Tennessee.* Nashville: Vanderbilt University Press, 1950.

———. *Thomas A. R. Nelson of East Tennessee.* Nashville: Tennessee Historical Commission, 1956.

American Annual Cyclopaedia. New York: D. Appleton & Co., 1867, 1868.

Anderson, Eric, and Alfred A. Moss, Jr., eds. *The Facts of Reconstruction: Essays in Honor of John Hope Franklin.* Baton Rouge: Louisiana State University Press, 1991.

Baker, Jean H. *Mary Todd Lincoln: A Biography.* New York: W. W. Norton, 1987.

Balch, Thomas W. *The Alabama Arbitration.* Philadelphia: Allen, Lane & Scott, 1900.

Bancroft, Hubert Howe. *History of Alaska, 1730–1885.* San Francisco: A. L. Bancroft & Co., History Company, 1886.

Basler, Roy P., ed. *The Collected Works of Abraham Lincoln* 9 vols. New Brunswick, NJ: Rutgers University Press, 1953–1955.

Baxter, Maurice G. *Orville H. Browning: Lincoln's Friend and Critic.* Bloomington: Indiana University Press, 1957.

Beale, Howard K. *The Critical Year: 1866.* New York: F. Ungar, 1958 (1930).

———, ed. *Diary of Gideon Welles* 3 vols. New York: W. W. Norton, 1960 (1911).

Beauregard, Erving E. *Bingham of the Hills: Politician and Diplomat Extraordinary.* New York: P. Lang, 1989.

Belz, Herman. *Emancipation and Equal Rights: Politics and Constitutionalism in the Civil War Era.* New York: W. W. Norton, 1978.

———. *A New Birth of Freedom: The Republican Party and Freedmen's Rights, 1861–1866.* Westport, CT: Greenwood Press, 1976.

Benedict, Michael Les. *A Compromise of Principle: Congressional Republicans and Reconstruction, 1863–1869.* New York: W. W. Norton, 1974.

———. *The Impeachment and Trial of Andrew Johnson.* New York: W. W. Norton, 1973.

Bentley, George R. *A History of the Freedmen's*

Bureau. Philadelphia: University of Pennsylvania, 1955.

Bentley, Hubert Blair. "Andrew Johnson, Governor of Tennessee, 1853–57." Ph.D. dissertation: University of Tennessee, 1972.

Bergeron, Paul H. *The Presidency of James K. Polk.* Lawrence: University Press of Kansas, 1987.

Bergeron, Paul H., Stephen V. Ash, and Jeanette Keith. *Tennesseans and Their History.* Knoxville: University of Tennessee Press, 1999.

Berlin, Ira, Barbara J. Fields, Steven F. Miller, Joseph P. Reidy, and Leslie Rowland. *Slaves No More: Three Essays on Emancipation and the Civil War.* New York: Cambridge University Press, 1992.

Berlin, Ira, Joseph P. Reidy, and Leslie S. Rowland, eds. *Freedom's Soldiers: The Black Military Experience in the Civil War.* New York: Cambridge University Press, 1998.

Berwanger, Eugene H. "Ross and the Impeachment: A New Look at a Critical Vote." *Kansas History* 1 (Winter 1978): 235–242.

———. *The West and Reconstruction.* Urbana: University of Illinois Press, 1981.

Biographical Directory of the United States Congress. Washington, DC: U.S. Government Printing Office, 1989.

Blue, Frederick J. *Charles Sumner and the Conscience of the North.* Arlington Heights, IL: Harlan Davidson, 1994.

———. *Salmon P. Chase: A Life in Politics.* Kent, OH: Kent State University Press, 1987.

Bowen, David Warren. *Andrew Johnson and the Negro.* Knoxville: University of Tennessee Press, 1989.

Bowers, Claude G. *Making Democracy a Reality: Jefferson, Jackson, and Polk.* Memphis: Memphis State College Press, 1954.

———. *The Tragic Era: The Revolution after Lincoln.* Cambridge, MA: Houghton Mifflin, 1929.

Bradley, Erwin Stanley. *The Triumph of Militant Republicanism: A Study of Pennsylvania and Presidential Politics, 1860–1872.* Philadelphia: University of Pennsylvania Press, 1964.

Brigance, William Norwood. *Jeremiah Sullivan Black: A Defender of the Constitution and the Ten Commandments.* Philadelphia: University of Pennsylvania Press, 1934.

Brodie, Fawn M. *Thaddeus Stevens: Scourge of the South.* New York: W. W. Norton, 1959.

Burgess, John W. *Reconstruction and the Constitution, 1866–1876.* New York: Charles Scribner's Sons, 1902.

Burke's Presidential Families of the United States of America. London: Burke's Peerage, 1975.

Carlson, Oliver. *The Man Who Made News: James Gordon Bennett.* New York: Duell, Sloan & Pearce, 1942.

Carter, Dan T. *When the War Was Over: The Failure of Self-Reconstruction in the South, 1865–1867.* Baton Rouge: Louisiana State University Press, 1985.

Carter, Samuel, III. *The Riddle of Dr. Mudd.* New York: Putnam, 1974.

Caskey, W. M. "First Administration of Governor Andrew Johnson." *East Tennessee Historical Society Publications* 1 (1929): 43–59.

———. "The Second Administration of Governor Andrew Johnson." *East Tennessee Historical Society Publications* 2 (1930): 34–54.

Castel, Albert E. *The Presidency of Andrew Johnson.* Lawrence: University Press of Kansas, 1979.

Clark, John G. "Historians and the Joint Committee on Reconstruction." *Historian* 23 (May 1961): 348–361.

Clark, Patricia P. "A.O.P. Nicholson of Tennessee: Editor, Statesman, and Jurist." M.A. thesis: University of Tennessee, 1965.

Coleman, Charles H. *The Election of 1868: The Democratic Effort to Regain Control.* New York: Columbia University Press, 1933.

Congressional Quarterly's Guide to U.S. Elections Washington, DC: Congressional Quarterly Service, 1975.

Connally, Ernest Allen. "The Andrew Johnson Homestead at Greeneville, Tennessee." *East Tennessee Historical Society Publications* 29 (1957): 118–140.

Cooper, William J., Jr. *The Conservative Regime: South Carolina, 1877–1890.* Baltimore: Johns Hopkins University Press, 1968.

Coulter, E. Merton. *The South during Reconstruction, 1865–1877.* Baton Rouge: Louisiana State University Press, 1947.

———. *William G. Brownlow, Fighting Parson of the Southern Highlands.* Chapel Hill: University of North Carolina Press, 1937.

Cox, John H., and LaWanda Cox. "Andrew Johnson and His Ghost Writers: An Analysis of the Freedmen's Bureau and Civil Rights Veto Messages." *Mississippi Valley Historical Review* 48 (Dec. 1961): 460–479.

Cox, LaWanda F., and John H. Cox. *Politics, Principle, and Prejudice, 1865–1866: Dilemma of Reconstruction America.* New York: Free Press, 1963.

Cox, LaWanda F., and John H. Cox, eds. *Reconstruction, the Negro, and the New South.* Columbia: University of South Carolina Press, 1973.

Cozzens, Peter, and Robert I. Girardi, eds. *The Military Memoirs of General John Pope.* Chapel Hill: University of North Carolina Press, 1998.

Crabb, Alfred Leland. *Nashville: Personality of a City.* Indianapolis: Bobbs-Merrill, 1960.

Crofts, Daniel W. *Reluctant Confederates: Upper South Unionists in the Secession Crisis.* Chapel Hill: University of North Carolina Press, 1989.

Crouthamel, James L. *Bennett's* New York Herald *and the Rise of the Popular Press.* Syracuse, NY: Syracuse University Press, 1989.

Current, Richard N., ed. *Reconstruction, 1865–1877.* Englewood Cliffs, NJ: Prentice-Hall, 1965.

Curry, Richard O. "The Civil War and Reconstruction, 1861–1877: A Critical Overview of Recent Trends and Interpretations." *Civil War History* 20 (Sept. 1974): 215–238.

Curtis, Michael Kent. *No State Shall Abridge: The Fourteenth Amendment and the Bill of Rights.* Durham, NC: Duke University Press, 1986.

Davis, William C. *Jefferson Davis: The Man and His Hour.* New York: HarperCollins, 1991.

Dawson, Joseph G., III. *Army Generals and Reconstruction.* Baton Rouge: Louisiana State University Press, 1982.

———. "General Lovell H. Rousseau and Louisiana Reconstruction." *Louisiana History* 20 (Fall 1979): 373–391.

Dell, Christopher. *Lincoln and the War Democrats: The Grand Erosion of Conservative Tradition.* Rutherford, NJ: Fairleigh Dickinson University Press, 1975.

Denslow, Ray V. *Freemasonry and the Presidency, U.S.A.* Trenton, MO: no pub., 1952.

DeWitt, David Miller. *The Impeachment and Trial of Andrew Johnson, Seventeenth President of the United States: A History.* New York: Macmillan, 1903.

DiNunzio, Mario R. "Lyman Trumbull, the States' Rights Issue, and the Liberal Republican Revolt." *Journal of the Illinois State Historical Society* 66 (Winter 1973): 364–373.

Donald, David Herbert. *Charles Sumner and the Coming of the Civil War.* New York: Alfred A. Knopf, 1960.

———. *Charles Sumner and the Rights of Man.* New York: Alfred A. Knopf, 1970.

———. *Lincoln.* New York: Simon & Schuster, 1995.

———. *The Politics of Reconstruction, 1863–1867.* Baton Rouge: Louisiana State University Press, 1965.

Dorris, Jonathan Truman. *Pardon and Amnesty under Lincoln and Johnson: The Restoration of the Confederates to Their Rights and Privileges, 1861–1898.* Chapel Hill: University of North Carolina Press, 1953.

Doughty, Richard Harrison. *Greeneville: One Hundred Year Portrait, 1775–1875.* Greeneville, TN: Kingsport Press, 1975.

Douglass, Frederick. *Narrative of the Life of Frederick Douglass, an American Slave.* Cambridge, MA: Belknap Press, 1960 (1845).

Du Bois, W. E. B. *The Souls of Black Folk: Essays and Sketches.* Millwood, NY: Kraus-Thomson, 1973 (1903).

Dunning, William. *Reconstruction, Political and Economic.* New York: Harper & Brothers, 1907 (1905).

Durham, Walter T. *Nashville, the Occupied City: The First Seventeen Months, February 16, 1862, to June 30, 1863.* Nashville: Tennessee Historical Society, 1985.

———. *Reluctant Partners: Nashville and the Union, July 1, 1863, to June 30, 1865.* Nashville: Tennessee Historical Society, 1987.

Eisenhower, John S. D. *So Far from God: The U.S. War with Mexico, 1846–1848.* New York: Random House, 1989.

Eubank, Sever L. "The McCardle Case: A Challenge to Radical Reconstruction." *Journal of Mississippi History* 18 (Apr. 1956): 111–127.

Evarts, William Maxwell. *Arguments and*

Speeches of William Maxwell Evarts 3 vols. New York: Macmillan, 1919.

Fairman, Charles. *History of the Supreme Court of the United States, vol. 6: Reconstruction and Reunion, 1864–88.* New York: Macmillan, 1971.

Fehrenbacher, Don E. "The Making of a Myth: Lincoln and the Vice-Presidential Nomination in 1864." *Civil War History* 41 (Dec. 1995): 273–290.

Fleming, Walter L. *The Sequel of Appomattox: A Chronicle of the Reunion of the States.* New York: U.S. Publishers Assoc., 1919.

Foner, Eric. *Reconstruction: America's Unfinished Revolution, 1863–1877.* New York: Harper & Row, 1988.

———. "Reconstruction Revisited," *Reviews in American History* 10 (Dec. 1982): 82–100.

Franklin, John Hope. *Reconstruction: After the Civil War.* Chicago: University of Chicago Press, 1961.

Gambill, Edward L. *Conservative Ordeal: Northern Democrats and Reconstruction, 1865–1868.* Ames: Iowa State University Press, 1981.

Gambone, Joseph G. "*Ex parte Milligan:* The Restoration of Judicial Prestige?" *Civil War History* 16 (Sept. 1970): 246–259.

George, Joseph, Jr. "Subornation of Perjury at the Lincoln Conspiracy Trial? Joseph Holt, Robert Purdy, and the Lon Letter." *Civil War History* 38 (Sept. 1992): 232–241.

Gerteis, Louis S. *From Contraband to Freedman: Federal Policy toward Southern Blacks, 1861–1865.* Westport, CT: Greenwood Press, 1973.

Gienapp, William E. *The Origins of the Republican Party, 1852–1856.* New York: Oxford University Press, 1987.

Gillette, William. *Retreat from Reconstruction, 1869–1879.* Baton Rouge: Louisiana State University Press, 1979.

———. *The Right to Vote: Politics and the Passage of the Fifteenth Amendment.* Baltimore: Johns Hopkins University Press, 1965.

Glatthaar, Joseph T. *Forged in Battle: The Civil War Alliance of Black Soldiers and White Officers.* New York: Free Press, 1990.

Gould, Lewis L. *American First Ladies: Their Lives and Their Legacy.* New York: Garland, 1996.

Graf, LeRoy P. "Andrew Johnson and Learning." *Phi Kappa Phi Journal* (Fall 1962): 3–14.

———. "Andrew Johnson and the Coming of the War." *Tennessee Historical Quarterly* 19 (Sept. 1960): 208–221.

Graf, LeRoy P., Ralph W. Haskins, and Paul H. Bergeron, eds. *The Papers of Andrew Johnson* 16 vols. Knoxville: University of Tennessee Press, 1967–2000.

Grant, Ulysses S. *Personal Memoirs.* New York: Charles L. Webster Co., 1885–1886; numerous later editions.

Gruening, Ernest. *The State of Alaska.* New York: Random House, 1954, 1968.

Hanchett, William. *The Lincoln Murder Conspiracies.* Urbana: University of Illinois Press, 1983.

Handlin, Lilian. *George Bancroft: The Intellectual as Democrat.* New York: Harper & Row, 1984.

Hanna, Alfred Jackson, and Kathryn Abbey Hanna. *Napoleon III and Mexico: American Triumph over Monarchy.* Chapel Hill: University of North Carolina Press, 1971.

Harper, Robert S. *Lincoln and the Press.* New York: McGraw-Hill, 1951.

Harris, William C. *With Charity for All: Lincoln and the Restoration of the Union.* Lexington: University Press of Kentucky, 1997.

Haynes, Sam W. *James K. Polk and the Expansionist Impulse.* New York: Longman, 1987.

Hays, Willard. "Andrew Johnson's Reputation." *East Tennessee Historical Society Publications* 31 (1959): 1–31; 32 (1960): 18–50.

Hendrick, Burton J. *Lincoln's War Cabinet.* Boston: Little, Brown, 1946.

Hennessy, John J. *Return to Bull Run: The Campaign and Battle of Second Manassas.* New York: Simon & Schuster, 1993.

Hesseltine, William B. *Ulysses S. Grant, Politician.* New York: Dodd, Mead & Co., 1935.

Heyman, Max L., Jr. *Prudent Soldier: A Biography of Major General E.R.S. Canby, 1817–1873.* Glendale, CA: Arthur H. Clark, 1959.

Holloway, Laura Carter. *The Ladies of the White House.* New York: United States Publishing, 1870.

Holt, Joseph. "New Facts about Mrs. Surratt." *North American Review* 147 (July 1888): 83–94.

Holt, Michael F. *The Rise and Fall of the American Whig Party: Jacksonian Politics and the Onset of the Civil War.* New York: Oxford University Press, 1999.

Holzman, Robert S. *Stormy Ben Butler.* New York: Macmillan, 1954.

Horn, Stanley F. "Isham G. Harris in the Pre-War Years." *Tennessee Historical Quarterly* (Sept. 1960): 195–207.

Horowitz, Robert F. *The Great Impeacher: A Political Biography of James M. Ashley.* New York: Brooklyn College Press, 1979.

Howe, Daniel Walker. *The Political Culture of the American Whigs.* Chicago: University of Chicago Press, 1979.

Hudson, Frederic. *Journalism in the United States from 1690 to 1872.* New York: Harper & Brothers, 1873.

Hunt, H. Draper. *Hannibal Hamlin of Maine: Lincoln's First Vice-President.* Syracuse, NY: Syracuse University Press, 1969.

Hyman, Harold M. "Johnson, Stanton, and Grant: A Reconsideration of the Army's Role in the Events Leading to Impeachment." *American Historical Review* 66 (Jan. 1960): 85–100.

———. *A More Perfect Union: The Impact of the Civil War and Reconstruction on the Constitution.* New York: Alfred A. Knopf, 1973.

Jenkins, Brian. *Fenians and Anglo-American Relations during Reconstruction.* Ithaca, NY: Cornell University Press, 1969.

Johnson, Allen, and Dumas Malone, eds. *Dictionary of American Biography* 20 vols. New York: Charles Scribner's Sons, 1928–1974.

Johnston, Hugh Buckner. "Andrew McDonough of North Carolina and Tennessee Maternal Grandfather of President Andrew Johnson." *North Carolinian* 2 (year unknown): 209.

Jones, John Paul, ed. *Dr. Mudd and the Lincoln Assassination: The Case Reopened.* Conshohocken, PA: Combined Books, 1995.

Jordan, David M. *Winfield Scott Hancock: A Soldier's Life.* Bloomington: Indiana University Press, 1988.

Kaczorowski, Robert J. *The Nationalization of Civil Rights: Constitutional Theory and Practice in a Racist Society, 1866–1883.* New York: Garland, 1987.

———. *The Politics of Judicial Interpretation: The Federal Courts, Department of Justice and Civil Rights, 1866–1876.* Dobbs Ferry, NY: Oceana Publications, 1985.

Katz, Bernard S., and C. Daniel Vencil, eds. *Biographical Dictionary of the United States Secretaries of the Treasury, 1789–1995.* Westport, CT: Greenwood Press, 1996.

Kendrick, Benjamin B. *The Journal of the Joint Committee of Fifteen on Reconstruction.* New York: Columbia University Press, 1914.

Kent, Frank R. *The Democratic Party: A History.* New York: Century, 1928.

Kincaid, Larry. "Victims of Circumstance: An Interpretation of Changing Attitudes toward Republican Policy Makers and Reconstruction." *Journal of American History* 57 (June 1970): 48–66.

Krauze, Enrique (Hank Heifetz, trans.). *Mexico, Biography of Power: A History of Modern Mexico, 1810–1996.* New York: HarperCollins, 1997.

Krug, Mark M. *Lyman Trumbull: Conservative Radical.* New York: A. S. Barnes, 1965.

Kunhardt, Dorothy Meserve, and Philip B. Kunhardt, Jr. *Twenty Days.* New York: Harper & Row, 1965.

Kvasnicka, Robert M., and Herman J. Viola, eds. *The Commissioners of Indian Affairs, 1824–1977.* Lincoln: University of Nebraska Press, 1979.

Lamar, Howard R. "Edmund G. Ross as Governor of New Mexico Territory: A Reappraisal." *New Mexico Historical Review* 36 (July 1961): 177–209.

Lawing, Hugh. "Andrew Johnson National Monument." *Tennessee Historical Quarterly* 20 (June 1961): 103–119.

Levin, H., ed. *The Lawyers and Lawmakers of Kentucky.* Chicago: Lewis, 1897.

Levstik, Frank R. "A View from Within: Reuben D. Mussey on Andrew Johnson and Reconstruction." *Historical New Hampshire* 27 (Fall 1972): 167–171.

Levy, Leonard W., and Louis Fisher, eds. *Encyclopedia of the American Presidency* 4 vols. New York: Simon & Schuster, 1994.

Litwack, Leon F. *Been in the Storm So Long: The Aftermath of Slavery.* New York: Alfred A. Knopf, 1979.

Long, David E. *The Jewel of Liberty: Abraham*

Lincoln's Re-election and the End of Slavery. Mechanicsburg, PA: Stackpole Books, 1994.

Looney, John Thomas. "Isham G. Harris of Tennessee, Bourbon Senator, 1877–1897." M.A. thesis: University of Tennessee, 1970.

Lovett, Bobby L. "Memphis Riots: White Reaction to Blacks in Memphis, May 1865–July 1866." *Tennessee Historical Quarterly* 38 (Spring 1979): 9–33.

Macaulay, Alexander S., Jr. "Growing Pains: The Immortal Thirteen, the Destructive Twelve, and the Emergence of Two-Party Politics in Antebellum Tennessee." *Journal of East Tennessee History* 70 (1998): 1–33.

Maddex, Jack P., Jr. *The Virginia Conservatives, 1867–1879: A Study in Reconstruction Politics.* Chapel Hill: University of North Carolina Press, 1970.

Maione, Michael, and James O. Hall. "Why Seward? The Attack on the Night of April 14, 1865." *Lincoln Herald* 100 (Spring 1998): 29–34.

Maltz, Earl M. *Civil Rights, the Constitution, and Congress, 1863–1869.* Lawrence: University Press of Kansas, 1990.

Marszalek, John F. *Sherman: A Soldier's Passion for Order.* New York: Free Press, 1993.

Marvel, William. *Andersonville: The Last Depot.* Chapel Hill: University of North Carolina Press, 1994.

Maslowski, Peter. *Treason Must Be Made Odious: Military Occupation and Wartime Reconstruction in Nashville, Tennessee, 1862–65.* Millwood, NY: KTO Press, 1978.

McBride, Robert M., et al., comps. *Biographical Directory of the Tennessee General Assembly* 6 vols. Nashville: Tennessee State Library and Archives, 1975–1991.

McCaslin, Richard B. *Andrew Johnson: A Bibliography.* Westport, CT: Greenwood Press, 1992.

McCulloch, Hugh. *Men and Measures of Half a Century.* New York: Charles Scribner's Sons, 1889.

McDonough, James L. "John Schofield as Military Director of Reconstruction in Virginia." *Civil War History* 15 (Fall 1969): 237–256.

———. *Schofield: Union General in the Civil War and Reconstruction.* Tallahassee: Florida State University Press, 1972.

McDonough, James L., and William T.

Alderson. "Republican Politics and the Impeachment of Andrew Johnson." *Tennessee Historical Quarterly* 26 (Summer 1967): 177–183.

McFeely, William S. *Frederick Douglass.* New York: W. W. Norton, 1991.

McKitrick, Eric L. *Andrew Johnson and Reconstruction.* New York: Oxford University Press, 1960.

McLeary, Ila. "The Life of Isham G. Harris." M.A. thesis: University of Tennessee, 1930.

McNeill, William H. *Plagues and Peoples.* New York: History Book Club, 1993 (1976).

McPherson, Edward. *The Political History of the United States of America during the Great Rebellion* 2nd ed. Washington, DC: Philip & Solomons, 1865.

McPherson, James M. *Ordeal by Fire: The Civil War and Reconstruction.* New York: Alfred A. Knopf, 1982.

———. *The Struggle for Equality: Abolitionists and the Negro in the Civil War and Reconstruction.* Princeton, NJ: Princeton University Press, 1964.

Milton, George Fort. *The Age of Hate: Andrew Johnson and the Radicals.* Hamden, CT: Archon Books, 1965 (Coward-McCann, 1930).

Mitchell, Stewart. *Horatio Seymour of New York.* Cambridge, MA: Harvard University Press, 1938.

Moroney, Rita Lloyd. *Montgomery Blair, Postmaster General.* Washington, DC: U.S. Government Printing Office, 1963.

Morris, Roy, Jr. *Sheridan: The Life and Wars of General Phil Sheridan.* New York: Crown, 1992.

Muir, Andrew Forest. "William P. Johnson, Southern Proletarian and Unionist." *Tennessee Historical Quarterly* 15 (Dec. 1956): 330–338.

Neely, Mark E., ed. *The Abraham Lincoln Encyclopedia.* New York: McGraw-Hill, 1982.

Neidhardt, W. S. *Fenianism in North America.* University Park: Pennsylvania State University Press, 1973.

Newmark, Harris. *Sixty Years in Southern California, 1853–1913,* 4th ed. Los Angeles: Zeitlin & Ver Brugge, 1970 (1916).

Nieman, Donald G. *To Set the Law in Motion: The Freedmen's Bureau and the Legal Rights of*

Blacks, 1865–68. Millwood, NY: KTO Press, 1979.

Niven, John. *Gideon Welles: Lincoln's Secretary of the Navy.* New York: Oxford University Press, 1973.

———. *Salmon P. Chase: A Biography.* New York: Oxford University Press, 1995.

Niven, John, et al., eds. *The Salmon P. Chase Papers* vols. 1–5. Kent, OH: Kent State University Press, 1993–1998.

Notaro, Carmen Anthony. "History of the Biographic Treatment of Andrew Johnson in the Twentieth Century." *Tennessee Historical Quarterly* 24 (Summer 1965): 143–155.

Olsen, James C. *History of Nebraska.* Lincoln: University of Nebraska Press, 1955.

Oubre, Claude F. *Forty Acres and a Mule: The Freedmen's Bureau and Black Land Ownership.* Baton Rouge: Louisiana State University Press, 1978.

Palmer, Beverly Wilson, and Holly Byers Ochoa, eds. *The Selected Papers of Thaddeus Stevens* 2 vols. Pittsburgh: University of Pittsburgh Press, 1997–1998.

Paludan, Phillip Shaw. *The Presidency of Abraham Lincoln.* Lawrence: University Press of Kansas, 1994.

Paolino, Ernest N. *The Foundations of the American Empire: William Henry Seward and U.S. Foreign Policy.* Ithaca, NY: Cornell University Press, 1973.

Parks, Joseph H. *John Bell of Tennessee.* Baton Rouge: Louisiana State University Press, 1950.

Parrish, William E. *Frank Blair: Lincoln's Conservative.* Columbia: University of Missouri Press, 1998.

Patrick, Rembert W. *The Reconstruction of the Nation.* New York: Oxford University Press, 1967.

Patton, James Welch. *Unionism and Reconstruction in Tennessee, 1860–1869.* Chapel Hill: University of North Carolina Press, 1934.

Perman, Michael. *Reunion without Compromise: The South and Reconstruction, 1865–1868.* Cambridge, UK: Cambridge University Press, 1973.

———. "Solving the Riddle of Andrew Johnson." *Journal of East Tennessee History* 62 (1990): 105–114.

Plummer, Mark A. "Profile in Courage? Edmund G. Ross and the Impeachment Trial." *Midwest Quarterly* 27 (Autumn 1985): 30–48.

Polk, James K. *The Diary of James K. Polk during His Presidency, 1845–1849* 4 vols. Milo M. Quaife, ed. Chicago: A. C. McClurg, 1910.

Pollard, Edward A. *The Lost Cause: A New Southern History of the War of the Confederates.* New York: E. B. Treat, 1866.

Potts, James B. "Nebraska Statehood and Reconstruction." *Nebraska History* 69 (Summer 1988): 73–83.

Preston, Dickson J. *Young Frederick Douglass: The Maryland Years.* Baltimore: Johns Hopkins University Press, 1980.

Rable, George. "Memphis: The First Modern Race Riot." *Geoscience and Man* 19 (June 1978): 123–127.

Randall, James G., ed. *The Diary of Orville Hickman Browning* 2 vols. Springfield, IL: Illinois State Historical Library, 1925–1933.

Rehnquist, William H. *All the Laws but One: Civil Liberties in Wartime.* New York: Alfred A. Knopf, 1998.

Remini, Robert V. *Andrew Jackson* 3 vols. New York: Harper & Row, 1977–1984.

Reynolds, Donald E. "The New Orleans Riot of 1866, Reconsidered." *Louisiana History* 5 (Winter 1964): 5–27.

Richardson, James D., comp. *A Compilation of the Messages and Papers of the Presidents, 1789–1897* 10 vols. Washington, DC: Bureau of National Literature, 1896–1899.

Ringwalt, J. L. *Development of Transportation Systems in the United States.* Philadelphia: Railway World Office, 1888.

Roseboom, Eugene. *The Civil War Era, 1850–1873.* Vol. 4 of Carl Wittke, ed., *A History of the State of Ohio* 8 vols. Columbus: Ohio State Archaeological and Historical Society, 1941–1944.

Roske, Ralph J. "The Seven Martyrs?" *American Historical Review* 64 (Jan. 1959): 323–330.

Rothrock, Mary U., ed. *The French Broad-Holston Country: A History of Knox County, Tennessee.* Knoxville: East Tennessee Historical Society, 1946.

Russell, Robert G. "Prelude to the Presidency: The Election of Andrew Johnson to the

Senate." *Tennessee Historical Quarterly* 26 (Summer 1967): 148–176.

Schaefer, James A. "Governor William Dennison and Military Preparations in Ohio, 1861." *Lincoln Herald* 78 (no. 2, 1976): 52–61.

Schell, Herbert S. "Hugh McCulloch and the Treasury Department, 1865–1869." *Mississippi Valley Historical Review* 17 (Dec. 1930): 404–421.

Sefton, James E. *Andrew Johnson and the Uses of Constitutional Power.* Boston: Little, Brown, 1980.

———. "The Impeachment of Andrew Johnson: A Century of Writing." *Civil War History* 14 (June 1968): 120–147.

———. *The United States Army and Reconstruction, 1865–1877.* Baton Rouge: Louisiana State University Press, 1967.

Seitz, Don C. *The James Gordon Bennetts, Father and Son, Proprietors of the* New York Herald. Indianapolis: Bobbs-Merrill, 1928.

Sherman, William T. *Memoirs.* New York: Library of America, 1990 (1875).

Sigler, Jay A., ed. *The Conservative Tradition in American Thought.* New York: Putnam, 1969.

Silber, Nina. *The Romance of Reunion: Northerners and the South, 1865–1900.* Chapel Hill: University of North Carolina Press, 1993.

Silbey, Joel H. *The American Political Nation, 1838–1893.* Stanford, CA: Stanford University Press, 1991.

———. *A Respectable Minority: The Democratic Party in the Civil War Era.* New York: W. W. Norton, 1977.

Simon, John Y., ed. *The Papers of Ulysses S. Grant* 24 vols. to date. Carbondale: Southern Illinois University Press, 1967–.

Simpson, Brooks D. *"Let Us Have Peace": Ulysses S. Grant and the Politics of War and Reconstruction, 1861–1868.* Chapel Hill: University of North Carolina Press, 1991.

———. *The Reconstruction Presidents.* Lawrence: University Press of Kansas, 1998.

Simpson, Brooks D., LeRoy P. Graf, and John Muldowny, eds. *Advice after Appomattox: Letters to Andrew Johnson, 1865–1866.* Knoxville: University of Tennessee Press, 1987.

Sioussat, St. George L. "Notes of Colonel W. G. Moore, Private Secretary to President Johnson, 1866–1868." *American Historical Review* 19 (Oct. 1913): 98–132.

Skaggs, Jimmy M. *The Great Guano Rush: Entrepreneurs and American Overseas Expansion.* New York: St. Martin's Griffin, 1994.

Smith, Elbert B. *Francis Preston Blair.* New York: Free Press, 1980.

———. *The Presidency of James Buchanan.* Lawrence: University Press of Kansas, 1975.

Smith, Gene. *High Crimes and Misdemeanors: The Impeachment and Trial of Andrew Johnson.* New York: William Morrow, 1977.

Smith, William E. *The Francis Preston Blair Family in Politics* 2 vols. New York: Macmillan, 1933.

Speer, William S. *Sketches of Prominent Tennesseans.* Nashville: Albert B. Tavel, 1888.

Sprague, Marshall. *Colorado: A Bicentennial History.* New York: W. W. Norton, 1976.

Stampp, Kenneth M. "The Milligan Case and the Election of 1864 in Indiana." *Mississippi Valley Historical Review* 31 (June 1944): 41–58.

Stebbins, Homer Adolph. *A Political History of the State of New York, 1865–1869.* New York: Columbia University Press, 1913.

Swanberg, W. A. *Sickles the Incredible.* New York: Charles Scribner's Sons, 1956.

Tap, Bruce. *Over Lincoln's Shoulder: The Committee on the Conduct of the War.* Lawrence: University Press of Kansas, 1998.

Taylor, David Gene. "The Business and Political Career of Thomas Ewing, Jr.: A Study of Frustrated Ambition." Ph.D. dissertation: University of Kansas, 1970.

Taylor, Joe Gray. *Louisiana Reconstructed, 1863–1877.* Baton Rouge: Louisiana State University Press, 1974.

Taylor, John M. *William Henry Seward: Lincoln's Right Hand.* New York: HarperCollins, 1991.

Thomas, Benjamin P. *Abraham Lincoln.* New York: Alfred A. Knopf, 1952.

Thomas, Benjamin P., and Harold M. Hyman. *Stanton: The Life and Times of Lincoln's Secretary of War.* New York: Alfred A. Knopf, 1962.

Thomas, Emory M. *Robert E. Lee.* New York: W. W. Norton, 1995.

Tidwell, William A. *April '65: Confederate Covert Action and the American Civil War.* Kent, OH: Kent State University Press, 1995.

Tidwell, William A., James O. Hall, and David Winfred Gaddy. *Come Retribution: The Confederate Secret Service and the Assassination of Lincoln*. Jackson: University of Mississippi Press, 1988.

Trefousse, Hans L. *Andrew Johnson: A Biography*. New York: W. W. Norton, 1989.

———. *Ben Butler: The South Called Him Beast!* New York: Twayne, 1957.

———. *Benjamin Franklin Wade: Radical Republican from Ohio*. New York: Twayne, 1963.

———. *Impeachment of a President: Andrew Johnson, the Blacks, and Reconstruction*. Knoxville: University of Tennessee Press, 1975.

———. *The Radical Republicans: Lincoln's Vanguard for Racial Justice*. New York: Alfred A. Knopf, 1969.

———. *Thaddeus Stevens: Nineteenth Century Egalitarian*. Chapel Hill: University of North Carolina Press, 1997.

Trelease, Allen W. *White Terror: The Ku Klux Klan Conspiracy and Southern Reconstruction*. New York: Harper & Row, 1971.

Trial of Andrew Johnson. 3 vols. Washington, DC: U.S. Government Printing Office, 1868.

Trudeau, Noah Andre. *Like Men of War: Black Troops in the Civil War, 1862–1865*. Boston: Little, Brown, 1998.

Turner, Thomas Reed. *Beware the People Weeping: Public Opinion and the Assassination of Abraham Lincoln*. Baton Rouge: Louisiana State University Press, 1982.

Unger, Irwin. *The Greenback Era: A Social and Political History of American Finance, 1865–1879*. Princeton, NJ: Princeton University Press, 1964.

Van Duesen, Glyndon G. *William Henry Seward*. New York: Oxford University Press, 1967.

Vandal, Gilles. *The New Orleans Riot of 1866: Anatomy of a Tragedy*. Lafayette, LA: Center for Louisiana Studies, University of Southwestern Louisiana, 1983.

Wagstaff, Thomas. "The Arm-in-Arm Convention." *Civil War History* 14 (June 1968): 101–119.

Warner, Ezra J. *Generals in Blue*. Baton Rouge: Louisiana State University Press, 1964.

Waugh, John C. *Reelecting Lincoln: The Battle for the 1864 Presidency*. New York: Crown, 1997.

Weisberger, Bernard A. "The Dark and Bloody Ground of Reconstruction Historiography." *Journal of Southern History* 25 (Nov. 1959): 427–447.

Williams, T. Harry. "Andrew Johnson as a Member of the Committee on the Conduct of the War." *East Tennessee Historical Society Publications* 12 (1940): 70–83.

Wilson, Theodore B. *The Black Codes of the South*. University: University of Alabama Press, 1965.

Winston, Robert W. *Andrew Johnson: Plebeian and Patriot*. New York: Henry Holt, 1928.

Woodward, C. Vann. *Origins of the New South, 1877–1913*. Baton Rouge: Louisiana State University Press, 1951.

———. *Reunion and Reaction: The Compromise of 1877 and the End of Reconstruction*. Boston: Little, Brown, 1966 (1951).

Zalimas, Robert J., Jr. "Black Union Soldiers in the Postwar South, 1865–1866." M.A. thesis: Arizona State University, 1993.

INDEX

Numbers in boldface indicate
    main entries for that subject.

Army of Tennessee (CSA), 251, 266
Army of the Cumberland, 193
Army of the Ohio, 192
Army of the Potomac, 135, 263
Arnold, Benedict, 68
Arnold, Samuel B., 101, 176–178
Arnold's Union Pills, 138–139
Arthur, Chester A., 187
Articles of Impeachment. *See* Impeachment charges
Ashley, Emma J. Smith, 13
Ashley, James Mitchell, 7, **13–14,** 43, 147, 151, 245
Assassination conspirators. *See* Lincoln assassination conspirators
Asthma, 273, 276, 300
Atlanta, GA, 94, 138–139, 251, 266, 297
Attorney general, responsibilities of, 24–25
Atzerodt, George A., 176–178, 306
Augusta College, Augusta, KY, 37, 130
Augusta Constitutionalist, 212
Austria, 188

Bachman, Andrew Johnson, 123
Bachman, Ethel Crockett Irwin, 123
Bachman, Lula May Peterson, 123
Bachman, Samuel Bernard, 123, 300
Bachman, William Bruce, 123–124, 282
Bailey, Frederick Augustus Washington. *See* Douglass, Frederick
Baird, Absalom, 210
Baker, Jean, 180
Baker, Lafayette C., 148, 219
Ball's Bluff, 172
Baltimore, MD, 86, 93, 111, 167, 176, 198, 201, 207, 226, 233–234, 287
  Johnson dinner in, 39, 69, 228, 237
  Masons in, 182, 233
Bancroft, George, 9, 110–111
Bank of Indiana, 185
Bank of Shelbyville, TN, 67
Bank of Tennessee, 120
Bank of the United States. *See* National Bank

Bankers, 67, 185
Banks
  failure of, 217, 230, 265, 290
  opposition to, 277
Banks, Nathaniel P., 46, 209
Baptists, 39, 41
Bartlett, Margaret Johnson Patterson, **15–16,** 124, 129–130
Bartlett, William Thaw, 15
Barton, Clara, 171
Bates, Edward, 38, 144, 271
Beale, Howard K., 142
Beauregard, Pierre G.T., 138
Bell, Jane Erwin Yeatman, 17
Bell, John, **16–18,** 213
  as presidential candidate (1860), 18, 40, 82, 207, 289, 291
Bell, Margaret Edmiston, 16
Bell, Sally Dickinson, 16–17
Bell, Samuel, 16
Belleville, IL, 298
Belmont, August, 79
Benedict, Michael Les, 242
Bennett, Cosmo, 20
Bennett, Henrietta Agnes Crean, 19–20
Bennett, Henry, 303
Bennett, James Gordon, Jr., 18, **20–21**
Bennett, James Gordon, Sr., **18–21**
Bennett, Jeanette, 20
Berlin, Ira, 295
Bermuda Hundred, 42
Bethel Presbyterian Church, Raleigh, NC, 166
Biddle, Nicholas, 162
Big Bethel, 42
Biggs, Elbert, 164
Bill of Rights, 114, 294
Bingham, Amanda, 21
Bingham, John Armor, **21–22,** 145, 153, 157, 171
Bismarck, Otto von, 2
Black, Chauncey, 4
Black Codes, xx, **22–23,** 28, 32–33, 49, 52, 87, 115, 210, 232–233, 245, 279, 310
  reaction to, 23, 231, 310
Black Hawk War, 175
Black, Hugo, 114
Black, Jeremiah Sullivan, 3–4, **24–26,** 101, 111, 155, 184, 198
Black, Mary Forward, 24
Black officeholders, 87

Black Reconstruction (DuBois), 142
Black rights, civil and political, 22–23, 28, 32–33, 49, 52, 82, 113–114, 173, 188, 239, 244–245, 279
Black suffrage, xx–xxi, 8, 13, 20, **26–29,** 32–33, 41, 51, 53, 59–61, 78, 82, 84, 98, 106–107, 113–114, 142, 195, 197, 206, 210–211, 240–241, 244–245, 279, 310
  defeat of in referendums, 84, 98, 106
  in District of Columbia, 28, 84, 106, 151
  Johnson's attitude toward, xx, 10, 20, 27–28, 32–33, 58–60, 84, 87
  for North, 28–29, 106–107, 284
  opposition to, 26–29, 36, 41, 67, 87, 95, 106, 121, 142, 151
  for South, 28–29, 61, 106
  supporters of, 26–28, 47–48, 83, 87, 95, 213, 236, 264, 271
  for territories, 106, 206, 284
Black troops
  accused of bad behavior, 30–31
  attitudes toward, 30–31, 67, 134, 187, 278
  Johnson's attitude toward, 30–32, 193–194
  recruitment of, 67, 87, 193–194, 255, 274, 296
  in the South, **29–31,** 187
  violence against, 30–31, 172, 187
Blacks
  attitudes toward, 187, 195, 266
  Johnson's attitude toward, **32–34,** 87, 142, 232
  in Memphis area, 187
  protection for, xx, 28, 52, 211, 244, 264
  restriction of, 23, 27–28
  violence against, xix–xx, 23, 28–29, 33, 52, 95–97, 187–188, 210–211, 232, 239, 279
Blair, Appoline Alexander, 35
Blair, Carolina Bruckner, 35
Blair, Elizabeth, 34
Blair, Francis Preston, Jr., "Frank," **34–37,** 68, 78, 97, 205
  military career of, 35–36
  as vice presidential candidate, 37, 61, 69, 80, 97, 262

President, direct election of advocated, 10, 65–66, 119, 162, 252

Presidential Reconstruction, xx, 4–8, 10, 19, 27–28, 36, 52, 63–64, 85, 121–122, 126, 141–142, 171, 187, 195, 203, 218–219, **230–233,** 239–240, 244–245, 275, 279, 295, 330–331

support for, 203–204, 266

Presidential succession, 10, 66

Presidential term, six years proposed, 65–66, 162

Presidential travels, 182, 200, **233–234,** 257, 261, 303

Price, Sterling, 101

Princeton, 35, 289

Princeton, USS (ship), 55, 108

Prison Life of Jefferson Davis (Craven), 76

Prisoners of war, 67, 126, 183, 192, 198, 208, 271, 295–296, 306, 315–316

Proclamation of Amnesty and Reconstruction (Lincoln) (1863), 5–6

Profiles in Courage (Kennedy), 247

Promontory Point, UT, 236

Property qualifications, for voting, 29, 60, 107

Public opinion, xx, 7, 20–21

Puerperal fever, 178

Pulitzer, Joseph, 21

Punishment, for former Confederates, 4–6, 22, 27–28, 30–31, 36, 41, 52, 217, 237, 239, 244, 306

Queen Victoria, 111, 297

Quincy, IL, 37–39

Racine, WI, 85–86

Racism, Northern, 141, 294

Radical Democracy, 93

Radical Reconstruction. *See* Congressional Reconstruction

Railroads, xvii, 14, 56, 60, 62, 81, 99, 108, 120, 148, 215, 217, **235–236,** 276, 293, 314

accidents on, 26, 120, 139

transcontinental, 9, 38, 75, 132, 136, 158, 205, 217, 235–236, 279, 293

transcontinental, opposition to, 235, 258

Raleigh, NC, xv–xvi, 11–12, 73, 166–167, 170, 225, 233–234, 268, 303

Raleigh Star, 11, 166, 170

Ramsdell, Hiram J., 212

Randall, Alexander Williams, 38, 45, 59, 84, 203–204, 233–234, 236–237

Randall, Helen M. Thomas, 237

Randall, Mary C. Van Vechten, 236

Randall, Phineas, 236

Rathbun v. United States (1935), 292

Raymond, Henry J., 59

Readmission of Southern states, 52, 54, 189–190, 197, 230–231, **237–238,** 240

Reconstruction, xv, xix, 4–9, 26–28, 36, 46, 50–52, 96, 101, 106, 110, 112–114, 116, 151, 206, 212, **238–242,** 271

Reconstruction: After the Civil War (Franklin), 142

Reconstruction, historical attitudes toward, 140–143, 241–242

Reconstruction, Political and Economic (Dunning), 141

"Redemption" of Southern states, 29, 61

Redfield, Horace V., 212

Reeves, Elbert C., 256, 259

Relief Party, 34

Religion, Johnson's attitude toward, 40, 55, 120, **242–244**

Republican Party, xvii–xxi, 4, 6–8, 12, 21, 26–30, 32, 35–36, 47, 52, 54, 61–65, 78, 81–82, 85, 93–99, 106–107, 111–113, 115–116, 133, 136, 146–147, 151, 171, 175, 193, 195, 205–206, 236, 239, 241, **244–246,** 260, 283–284, 303, 305, 310

convention of (1856), 13, 35, 83

conventions of, 93–94, 97, 99, 127, 134, 154, 278

founding of, 13, 35, 38, 58, 83, 244, 315

in the South, xix, 28, 60–61, 98, 106–107, 239–240

Republicans

conservative, 20, 27, 36, 38, 58–59, 61, 71, 80, 86, 95, 101, 156, 203–204, 287, 312

Liberal (1872), 14, 127, 131, 247, 285, 298

moderate, xix, 21–22, 33, 49, 51–52, 59–60, 64, 86, 99, 106, 115–116, 153, 155, 239–240, 244–245, 290, 299, 312

Radical, xix–xxi, 14, 20–21, 27–28, 33, 35–36, 43, 52, 54, 58–61, 64, 68, 78, 83, 93–96, 98, 107, 110, 112, 114, 126, 134, 137, 140–143, 151–153, 172–173, 184–185, 197, 203–205, 211, 228, 237, 239–240, 244–247, 258, 260, 264, 272, 275, 278–279, 284, 288, 291–292, 294, 297, 299, 309–310, 312

Restoration, xix–xx, 82, 219, 231–233, 237, 239, 310

Revere, Paul, 181

"Revisionist" historians, 142, 242

Revolutionary War, 128, 161

Reynolds, Joseph J., 190

Rhea Academy, Greeneville, TN, 165

Richardson, William A., 38

Richmond, VA, 42, 233–234, 306, 315

Ricks, Augustus J., 212

Riley, Bennet, 45

Rio Grande, 226

Rise and Fall of the Confederate Government (Davis), 76

Rives, John C., 256

Rives, Wright, 256

Robards, Lewis, 161

Rogers, Andrew J., 147–148, 171

Rollins, Edward A., 68, 222

Rome, ancient, 103

Romero, Matias, 189

Roosevelt, Eleanor, 15

Roosevelt, Franklin D., 15, 130, 270

Rosecrans, William S., 169, 189, 193

Ross, Cynthia Rice, 246

Ross, Edmund Gibson, 154, 182, 222, **246–248,** 285

Ross, Fanny M. Lathrop, 246

Ross, Sylvester F., 246

Rossiter, Clinton, 140

Rousseau, George L., 248–249

ABOUT THE AUTHORS

Glenna R. Schroeder-Lein is assistant editor of the Lincoln Legal Papers: A Project of the Historic Preservation Agency, Springfield, Illinois, and was formerly assistant editor for *The Papers of Andrew Johnson*. She holds a Ph.D. in history from the University of Georgia and an M.L.S. from the University of Arizona and is the author of *Confederate Hospitals on the Move: Samuel H. Stout and the Army of Tennessee*.

Richard Zuczek, who received his Ph.D. in history from Ohio State University, teaches U.S. and military history at the U.S. Coast Guard Academy. He previously taught at the University of Tennessee and was assistant editor for *The Papers of Andrew Johnson*. He is the author of *State of Rebellion: Reconstruction in South Carolina*.